T0331851

Solutions for Cyber– Physical Systems Ubiquity

Norbert Druml
Independent Researcher, Austria

Andreas Genser
Independent Researcher, Austria

Armin Krieg
Independent Researcher, Austria

Manuel Menghin
Independent Researcher, Austria

Andrea Hoeller
Independent Researcher, Austria

A volume in the Advances in Systems Analysis,
Software Engineering, and High Performance
Computing (ASASEHPC) Book Series

Published in the United States of America by
    IGI Global
    Engineering Science Reference (an imprint of IGI Global)
    701 E. Chocolate Avenue
    Hershey PA, USA 17033
    Tel: 717-533-8845
    Fax: 717-533-8661
    E-mail: cust@igi-global.com
    Web site: http://www.igi-global.com

Library of Congress Cataloging-in-Publication Data

Names: Druml, Norbert, 1980- editor.
Title: Solutions for cyber-physical systems ubiquity
  / Norbert Druml, Andreas Genser, Armin Krieg, Manuel Menghin, and Andrea
  Hoeller, editors.
Description: Hershey, PA : Engineering Science Reference, [2018] | Includes
  bibliographical references.
Identifiers: LCCN 2017012032| ISBN 9781522528456 (hardcover) | ISBN
  9781522528463 (ebook)
Subjects: LCSH: Cooperating objects (Computer systems)--Handbooks, manuals,
  etc. | Internet of things--Handbooks, manuals, etc. | Automatic
  control--Handbooks, manuals, etc.
Classification: LCC TK5105.8857 .H367 2018 | DDC 004.67/8--dc23 LC record available at https://lccn.loc.
gov/2017012032

This book is published in the IGI Global book series Advances in Systems Analysis, Software Engineering, and High Performance Computing (ASASEHPC) (ISSN: 2327-3453; eISSN: 2327-3461)

British Cataloguing in Publication Data
A Cataloguing in Publication record for this book is available from the British Library.

All work contributed to this book is new, previously-unpublished material. The views expressed in this book are those of the authors, but not necessarily of the publisher.

For electronic access to this publication, please contact: eresources@igi-global.com.

Advances in Systems Analysis, Software Engineering, and High Performance Computing (ASASEHPC) Book Series

Vijayan Sugumaran
Oakland University, USA

ISSN:2327-3453
EISSN:2327-3461

Mission

The theory and practice of computing applications and distributed systems has emerged as one of the key areas of research driving innovations in business, engineering, and science. The fields of software engineering, systems analysis, and high performance computing offer a wide range of applications and solutions in solving computational problems for any modern organization.

The **Advances in Systems Analysis, Software Engineering, and High Performance Computing (ASASEHPC) Book Series** brings together research in the areas of distributed computing, systems and software engineering, high performance computing, and service science. This collection of publications is useful for academics, researchers, and practitioners seeking the latest practices and knowledge in this field.

Coverage

- Computer graphics
- Performance Modelling
- Enterprise information systems
- Computer System Analysis
- Virtual Data Systems
- Engineering Environments
- Storage Systems
- Parallel Architectures
- Human-Computer Interaction
- Computer Networking

IGI Global is currently accepting manuscripts for publication within this series. To submit a proposal for a volume in this series, please contact our Acquisition Editors at Acquisitions@igi-global.com or visit: http://www.igi-global.com/publish/.

The Advances in Systems Analysis, Software Engineering, and High Performance Computing (ASASEHPC) Book Series (ISSN 2327-3453) is published by IGI Global, 701 E. Chocolate Avenue, Hershey, PA 17033-1240, USA, www.igi-global.com. This series is composed of titles available for purchase individually; each title is edited to be contextually exclusive from any other title within the series. For pricing and ordering information please visit http://www.igi-global.com/book-series/advances-systems-analysis-software-engineering/73689. Postmaster: Send all address changes to above address. Copyright © 2018 IGI Global. All rights, including translation in other languages reserved by the publisher. No part of this series may be reproduced or used in any form or by any means – graphics, electronic, or mechanical, including photocopying, recording, taping, or information and retrieval systems – without written permission from the publisher, except for non commercial, educational use, including classroom teaching purposes. The views expressed in this series are those of the authors, but not necessarily of IGI Global.

Titles in this Series

For a list of additional titles in this series, please visit: www.igi-global.com/book-series

Large-Scale Fuzzy Interconnected Control Systems Design and Analysis
Zhixiong Zhong (Xiamen University of Technology, China) and Chih-Min Lin (Yuan Ze University, Taiwan)
Information Science Reference • copyright 2017 • 223pp • H/C (ISBN: 9781522523857) • US $175.00 (our price)

Microcontroller System Design Using PIC18F Processors
Nicolas K. Haddad (University of Balamand, Lebanon)
Information Science Reference • copyright 2017 • 215pp • H/C (ISBN: 9781683180005) • US $195.00 (our price)

Probabilistic Nodes Combination (PNC) for Object Modeling and Contour Reconstruction
Dariusz Jacek Jakóbczak (Technical University of Koszalin, Poland)
Information Science Reference • copyright 2017 • 312pp • H/C (ISBN: 9781522525318) • US $175.00 (our price)

Model-Based Design for Effective Control System Development
Wei Wu (Independent Researcher, USA)
Information Science Reference • copyright 2017 • 299pp • H/C (ISBN: 9781522523031) • US $185.00 (our price)

Comparative Approaches to Using R and Python for Statistical Data Analysis
Rui Sarmento (University of Porto, Portugal) and Vera Costa (University of Porto, Portugal)
Information Science Reference • copyright 2017 • 197pp • H/C (ISBN: 9781683180166) • US $180.00 (our price)

Developing Service-Oriented Applications Using the Windows Communication Foundation (WCF) Framework
Chirag Patel (Charotar University of Science and Technology, India)
Information Science Reference • copyright 2017 • 487pp • H/C (ISBN: 9781522519973) • US $200.00 (our price)

Resource Management and Efficiency in Cloud Computing Environments
Ashok Kumar Turuk (National Institute of Technology Rourkela, India) Bibhudatta Sahoo (National Institute of Technology Rourkela, India) and Sourav Kanti Addya (National Institute of Technology Rourkela, India)
Information Science Reference • copyright 2017 • 352pp • H/C (ISBN: 9781522517214) • US $205.00 (our price)

Handbook of Research on End-to-End Cloud Computing Architecture Design
Jianwen "Wendy" Chen (IBM, Australia) Yan Zhang (Western Sydney University, Australia) and Ron Gottschalk (IBM, Australia)
Information Science Reference • copyright 2017 • 507pp • H/C (ISBN: 9781522507598) • US $325.00 (our price)

701 East Chocolate Avenue, Hershey, PA 17033, USA
Tel: 717-533-8845 x100 • Fax: 717-533-8661
E-Mail: cust@igi-global.com • www.igi-global.com

Table of Contents

Section 1
CPS Applications and Trends

Section 3
Security Concerns in CPS

Detailed Table of Contents

Section 1
CPS Applications and Trends

Chapter 1
    Hannes Plank, Infineon Technologies Austria AG, Austria
    Josef Steinbaeck, Infineon Technologies Austria AG, Austria
    Norbert Druml, Independent Researcher, Austria
    Christian Steger, Graz University of Technology, Austria
    Gerald Holweg, Infineon Technologies Austria AG, Austria

In recent years, consumer electronics became increasingly location and context-aware. Novel applications, such as augmented and virtual reality have high demands in precision, latency and update rate in their tracking solutions. 3D imaging systems have seen a rapid development in the past years. By enabling a manifold of systems to become location and context-aware, 3D imaging has the potential to become a part of everyone's daily life. In this chapter, we discuss 3D imaging technologies and their applications in localization, tracking and 3D context determination. Current technologies and key concepts are depicted and open issues are investigated. The novel concept of location-aware optical communication based on Time-of-Flight depth sensors is introduced. This communication method might close the gap between high performance tracking and localization. The chapter finally provides an outlook on future concepts and work-in progress technologies, which might introduce a new set of paradigms for location-aware cyber-physical systems in the Internet of Things.

Chapter 2
    Laszlo Z. Varga, ELTE, Hungary

Ubiquitous IoT systems open new ground in the automotive domain. With the advent of autonomous vehicles, there will be several actors that adapt to changes in traffic, and decentralized adaptation will be a new type of issue that needs to be studied. This chapter investigates the effects of adaptive route planning when real-time online traffic information is exploited. Simulation results show that if the agents selfishly optimize their actions, then in some situations the ubiquitous IoT system may fluctuate and the agents may be worse off with real-time data than without real-time data. The proposed solution to this problem is to use anticipatory techniques, where the future state of the environment is predicted from the intentions of the agents. This chapter concludes with this conjecture: if simultaneous decision making is prevented, then intention-propagation-based prediction can limit the fluctuation and help the ubiquitous IoT system converge to the Nash equilibrium.

Chapter 3

A cyber-physical system (CPS) is a composition of an embedded computer, a network and a physical process. Usually, the plant, which represents the physical part, is controlled by an embedded system, which consists of computation, communication and control elements, via the global network. This contribution focuses on networked control systems (NCSs) which represents a specific class of CPS. As the problems of CPSs and NCSs are quite similar the goal is to transfer well developed techniques of NCSs to CPSs for analysis purposes. NCSs deal with the analysis of the interaction between the physical system and the cyber system. A main challenge of a control engineer is the development of stable and robust controllers for a NCS. The same goal is present in the design of CPS. To ensure this goal the analysis of such a feedback system has to be performed which is not straight forward and limited by the used modeling approach. This work compares different state-of-the-art modeling approaches for NCSs and stability analysis methods therefore.

Chapter 4

Wireless sensor networks consisting of several sensors deployed in a given area, under an internet of things (IoT) paradigm, are considered. Sensor nodes may or may not be close enough to communicate with each other in order to perform collaborative transmissions. A communication protocol based on random access and orthogonal frequency division multiple access (OFDMA) is proposed in order to allow the sensors to operate autonomously by transmitting their measured data to a central processing system, where it is processed and analyzed. Whenever it has data to transmit, each sensor independently accesses a time-frequency slot in a probabilistic manner to avoid collisions. A controlling entity, e.g., a central base station (BS) covering a certain sensor deployment area receives the sensor transmissions and provides synchronization information by periodically transmitting a pilot signal over the available OFDMA subcarriers. Sensors use this signal for channel quality estimation. Results show that this approach performs well in terms of transmission data rates and collision probability.

Section 2
Safety Concerns in CPS

A Cyber-Physical System (CPS) describes a system or a system-of-systems closely and actively coupled with environment. It comprises the digital intelligence system, a co-dependent physical system (i.e., electrical, mechanical) and the system environment. Since the beginning of modern computer systems integration was ever present challenge, from the huge single room computers to the IoT. Today applications interleave and build larger systems with different system requirements and properties. Implementation of safety critical applications together with non-critical applications within the same platform is almost inevitable in modern industrial systems. This article provides a retrospective overview of the major integration challenges and the current problems in mixed-criticality environments. Finally, it provides an insight in a hardware solution which creates deterministic platform for mixed-criticality applications.

Chapter 8

The electrification of today's vehicles and the high number of new assistance features imply more and more complex systems. New challenges are arising through heterogeneous and distributed systems which interact with each other and have an impact on the physical world, so-called cyber-physical systems. The sensing and controlling of these systems is the work of the highly distributed electronic control units and it is no surprise that more than 100 of these microcontrollers are currently integrated in a modern (electric) car. Technological, organizational and design gaps in today's development flows are not covered by current methods and tools. Therefore, new approaches are essential to support the development process and to reduce costs and time-to-market, especially when systems are safety-critical and demand reliability. Through applying reliability analysis and simulation-based verification methods on the proposed model-based design flow, we are able to reduce the number of tools involved and achieve correctness, completeness and consistency of the entire system.

The advancement and interlinking of cyber-physical systems offer vast new opportunities for industry. The fundamental threat to this progress is the inherent increase of complexity through heterogeneous systems, software, and hardware that leads to fragility and unreliability. Systems cannot only become more unreliable, modern industrial control systems also have to face hostile security attacks that take advantage of unintended vulnerabilities overseen during development and deployment. Self-adaptive software systems offer means of dealing with complexity by observing systems externally. In this chapter the authors present their ongoing research on an approach that applies a self-adaptive software system in order to increase the reliability and security of control devices for hydro-power plant units. The applicability of the approach is demonstrated by two use cases. Further, the chapter gives an introduction to the field of self-adaptive software systems and raises research challenges in the context of cyber-physical systems.

Section 3
Security Concerns in CPS

An increase of distributed denial-of-service (DDoS) attacks launched by botnets such as Mirai has raised public awareness regarding potential security weaknesses in the Internet of Things (IoT). Devices are an attractive target for attackers because of their large number and due to most devices being online 24/7. In addition, many traditional security mechanisms are not applicable for resource constraint IoT devices. The importance of security for cyber-physical systems (CPS) is even higher, as most systems process confidential data or control a physical process that could be harmed by attackers. While industrial IoT is a hot topic in research, not much focus is put on ensuring information security. Therefore, this paper intends to give an overview of current research regarding the security of data in industrial CPS. In contrast to other surveys, this work will provide an overview of the big CPS security picture and not focus on special aspects.

Chapter 11

Nowadays, cyber-physical systems are omnipresent in our daily lives and are increasingly used to process confidential data. While the variety of portable devices we use excessively at home and at work is steadily increasing, their security vulnerabilities are often not noticed by the user. Therefore, portable devices such as wearables are becoming more and more interesting for adversaries. Thus, a robust and secure software design is required for the implementation of cryptographic communication protocols and encryption algorithms. While these topics are well discussed and subject to further research activities, the issue of provisioning the initial device setup is widely uncovered. However, the protection of the initial setup is as important as the protection of the confidential data during the time in use. In this work, the authors will present solutions for a secure initialization of security critical integrated circuits (ICs).

Chapter 12

George Kornaros, Technological Educational Institute of Crete, Greece
Ernest Wozniak, fortiss GmbH, Germany
Oliver Horst, fortiss GmbH, Germany
Nora Koch, fortiss GmbH, Germany
Christian Prehofer, fortiss GmbH, Germany
Alvise Rigo, Virtual Open Systems, France
Marcello Coppola, STMicroelectronics, France

Cyber-physical systems (CPS) are devices with sensors and actuators which link the physical with the virtual world. There is a strong trend towards open systems, which can be extended during operation by instantly adding functionalities on demand. We discuss this trend in the context of automotive, medical and industrial automation systems. The goal of this chapter is to elaborate the research challenges of ensuring security in these new platforms for such open systems. A main problem is that such CPS apps shall be able to access and modify safety critical device internals. Cyber-physical attacks can affect the integrity, availability and confidentiality in CPS. Examples range from deception based attacks such as false-data-injection, sensor and actuator attacks, replay attacks, and also denial-of-service attacks. Hence, new methods are required to develop an end-to-end solution for development and deployment of trusted apps. This chapter presents the architecture approach and its key components, and methods for open CPS apps, including tool chain and development support.

Chapter 13

Andreas Zankl, Fraunhofer AISEC, Germany
Hermann Seuschek, Technical University of Munich, Germany
Gorka Irazoqui, Nagravision, Spain
Berk Gulmezoglu, Worcester Polytechnic Institute, USA

The Internet of Things (IoT) rapidly closes the gap between the virtual and the physical world. As more and more information is processed through this expanding network, the security of IoT devices and backend services is increasingly important. Yet, side-channel attacks pose a significant threat to systems in practice, as the microarchitectures of processors, their power consumption, and electromagnetic emanation reveal sensitive information to adversaries. This chapter provides an extensive overview of previous attack literature. It illustrates that microarchitectural attacks can compromise the entire IoT ecosystem: from devices in the field to servers in the backend. A subsequent discussion illustrates that many of today's security mechanisms integrated in modern processors are in fact vulnerable to the previously outlined attacks. In conclusion to these observations, new countermeasures are needed that effectively defend against both microarchitectural and power/EM based side-channel attacks.

Chapter 14

Tobias Rauter, Graz University of Technology, Austria
Johannes Iber, Graz University of Technology, Austria
Christian Kreiner, Graz University of Technology, Austria

Due to the need of increased cooperation and connectivity, security is getting a vital property of industrial control systems. Besides system hardening, the detection of security breaches in different subsystems has been becoming a research-focus recently. This chapter summarizes the work concerning anomaly detection at different system levels. The, a system that maintains availability and integrity of distributed control systems through automated reconfiguration in case of integrity violations is proposed. We aim to detect such integrity violations through integrity reporting. This is a well-known technology, albeit not widely used in real system because of scalability problems. In this chapter, three different remote attestation methods (binary, privilege and signature-based) are integrated into a remote terminal unit to analyze and discuss the benefits and drawbacks of each method. Depending on the actual RTU architecture and already in-place development and deployment processes, the integration of remote attestation may be feasible for industrial control systems.

Chapter 15

The exciting new features, such as advanced driver assistance systems, fleet management systems, and autonomous driving, drive the need for built-in security solutions and architectural designs to mitigate emerging security threats. Thus, cybersecurity joins reliability and safety as a cornerstone for success in the automotive industry. As vehicle providers gear up for cybersecurity challenges, they can capitalize on experiences from many other domains, but nevertheless must face several unique challenges. Therefore, this article focuses on the enhancement of state-of-the-art development lifecycle for automotive cyber-physical systems toward the integration of security, safety and reliability engineering methods. Especially, four engineering approaches (HARA at concept level, FMEA and FTA at design level and HSI at implementation level) are extended to integrate security considerations into the development lifecycle.

Preface

GENERAL INTRO/MOTIVATION

Around 30 years ago, when the Internet was released to the general public, a minority of people was actively using it and almost none was affected in everyday life. In 2000 when mobile devices started to spread and social networks advanced towards a staggering success, the Internet became mainstream attracting many more active users and adding an integral virtual component to our lives.

Today we are at the beginning of a new Internet era having the potential to disrupt many industries and changing the way we work, the way we live, the way we learn.

What is referred to as the Internet of Things (IoT) will impact on energy infrastructure, health care, agriculture, transportation, the life in future cities or our future education. Governments have established frameworks such as 'Smart Nation', 'Industrie 4.0' or 'The Smart Cities Initiative' to invest in education, research and infrastructure to fully leverage the potential of IoT.

IoT activities soar, easily observable by the increase of scientific publications in recent years and by long-term strategy adaptions towards IoT of major IT-industry players. McKinsey projects the IoT market to grow to $11 trillion by 2025.

Security aspects will play a vital role in the success of IoT. Self-driving vehicles that communicate to each other or energy grids that get interactive require high-security measures in order to guarantee data integrity, prevent fraud and maintain safety.

IoT paves the way for a startup eco-system that will bring many new players in this game. Naturally these players focus on leveraging the potential of the technology to solve societal problems, however until today, arising security and safety threats, they largely neglect.

There is an enormous number of challenges from individual industries that have to be jointly solved in order to pave the way to make IoT become ubiquitous in today's societies. This publication will show applications in the context of IoT, arising challenges and how security, safety and mixed criticality solutions can play a major role in overcoming them.

CPS APPLICATIONS AND TRENDS

Cyber physical systems (CPS) are the key innovation driver for improvements in almost all mechatronic systems. They can be found in automotive, avionics, space, Internet of Things, industrial process control and factory automation (such as Industrie 4.0 and Industrial IoT), healthcare, robotics, energy and smart grids, consumer appliances, civil infrastructure, and many others. Thus, CPS link the digital with the real world with the help of physical, hardware, and software components and employ approaches and solutions from various different disciplines, such as mechatronics, computer science, process control, or cybernetics. Cyber physical systems, as well as embedded systems, presently undergo a disruptive innovation process in every application field. Different kinds of systems are connected to each other, boundaries of application domains are alleviated, and interoperability plays an increasing role. As an inter-system communication enabler, they strongly support today's information society and therefore accelerate the society's currently ongoing digital transformation. This process of digital transformation will be a major game changer coming with new chances but also lots of challenges. In the following, trends, chances, and challenges for the two representative application domains are detailed.

In automotive and transportation we are currently experiencing a major paradigm shift: the introduction of assisted, and most importantly, automated driving vehicles. Fully automated driving will be the enabler for mastering one of the most crucial challenges of humanity: safe, clean, and efficient transportation. This revolution is happening thanks the latest advances in CPS, namely so far unreached quality in environment perception, availability of novel number crunching computing architectures, and advances in intelligent powertrains and actuators. This trend will enable completely new applications for our everyday lives, such as the introduction of transportation as a purchasable service. Apart from huge revenue potentials for the whole automotive value chain, there are two benefits which should be explicitly emphasized:

- According to the European Commission, the total economic damage caused by car accidents in the EU amounts to 229 bn €. If one takes into account that for 76% of all car accidents the human is solely to blame, human car driving errors account for an economic damage of 174 bn €. Therefore, advances in CPS that enable automated driving applications will vastly impact these reparable economic and irreparable human losses in a positive way.
- Traffic jams and congestions cause 40% of the road transportation based CO_2 emissions. These congestions and increased emissions account for additional costs of 100 bn € within the EU. By enabling assisted and automated driving, thanks to the recent advances in CPS, these costs and emissions can be reduced through techniques such as efficient flow management, intelligent traffic balancing, improved path planning, etc.

In order to enable the future automated driving revolution in transportation, fail-operational and high-performing computing platforms are imperative requirements in order to cope with the sheer amounts of sensor data and complex automated driving algorithms. However, today, these in-vehicle computing solutions feature fail-safe or high availability capabilities at most. Only by achieving fail-operational hardware/software architectures, automated driving functions can be continuously provided (with a reduced set of capabilities) even if a fault was detected or environment perception was impaired. In addition, thanks to the forthcoming features of Car-To-Car and Car-To-Infrastructure communication, security becomes an ever-increasing concern. This security topic becomes particularly important when security breaches and security attacks affect the safety of the human driver. Therefore, safety and security co-engineering is one of the most important CPS research and development field in order to enable the future revolution in transportation.

Apart from automotive, we are currently also experiencing a major revolution in industry and production systems – the so-called 4th industrial revolution. This revolution is mainly driven through recent advances in CPS (in particular nanoelectronics and ICT-based systems). The pivotal technologies of this revolution are Industrie 4.0 and Industrial IoT (IIoT) that enable communicating, intelligent, and self-controlled systems through the integration of cyber technologies into the production system. Industrie 4.0 and IIoT not only integrate top-level management systems with shop-floor devices, but also tightly integrate value chain stakeholders across companies. Over the Internet of Things they interact witch each other and humans in real time. Therefore, both horizontal and vertical integration is given. As a result, innovative new services can be offered, such as pay-per-use, lot-size 1, Internet-based diagnostics, or remote maintenance.

The most crucial challenge to be solved by Industrie 4.0 and IIoT is security. Recent security-attacks demonstrated that even industrial control systems (ICSs) that were isolated and thus not connected to the outside world were targeted successfully. Stuxnet, one of the most famous malwares, was discovered in 2010. Its goal was to manipulate the physical production process by loading rouge code onto the controllers of Iranian uranium enrichment plants. Research concluded that most of the controllers and IT hardware currently used in critical production systems don't employ security mechanisms such as digital code signing. We learn from attacks such as Stuxnet and countless further examples that in Industrie 4.0 and IIoT security has not been addressed rigorously enough. Thus, protection against espionage and sabotage are of utmost importance in order to successfully establish smart factories and to continue the currently ongoing 4th industrial revolution.

SAFETY CONCERNS IN CPS

Computer-based systems are penetrating ever more into applications where, until recently, computing technologies played no significant role. Examples include embedded systems that are applied in critical application domains such as medical devices, aerospace systems, transportation vehicles and factory automation. A malfunction of systems that sense and control the physical world could lead to serious consequences such as loss of life, significant property or environmental damage, or large financial losses. Consequently, ensuring that such systems work as intended is of utmost importance. However, since embedded systems have to manage ever more demanding and complex tasks, guaranteeing their correct behavior under any circumstance is more challenging than ever. This challenge of creating dependable systems increases dramatically with the increasing complexity of computing systems. The trend to ever more complex processor-based systems can be demonstrated by the amount of software deployed. Popular examples to express the enormous complexity of embedded software can be found in the avionic and automotive industry. For example, the Boing 787 flight software controlling the fly-by-wire system includes about 14 million lines of code (Lilienthal, 2011) Even a modern car runs about 100 million lines of code (Charette, 2009), and this number is going to grow rapidly with the advent of autonomous driving techniques.

This high level of complexity of the systems itself and the related development processes has never been experienced before. At the same time, developers are facing ever-increasing demands on reducing the time-to-market which results in short development and innovation cycles. Moreover, there is the necessity of mastering essential horizontal topics such as product and lifecycle process quality, reliability, safety, and security. To tackle this challenge, interdisciplinary expertise of engineers and managers is a key factor to success. To create this knowledge appropriate training methods are essential. In this book a course architecture is described to train both, employees in industry and students at universities.

Even if developers of CPS systems do their best to create high quality hardware and software, history shows that the goal to release a system with absolutely no hardware defects or software bugs is virtually impossible to achieve. Unfortunately, it is unavoidable that unexpected environmental factors will not be considered. Even if the system is designed and implemented perfectly, faults are likely to be caused outside the control of the developers. One promising engineering solution to this problem is inspired by nature. In his famous quote "It is not the strongest of the species that survives, nor the most intelligent that survives. It is the one that is most adaptable to change.", Charles Darwin stated that in nature, self-adaption is the key success factor. This is the way living organisms change their structure and/or behavior in order to retain or achieve a better compatibility with their environment. When looking at future CPS systems, there is also the need to adapt themselves for maintaining resilience even if there are changes in the environment or the system itself (e.g. unforeseen faults in the system). For example, self-healing systems autonomously detect and recover from faulty states by changing their configuration.

Finding appropriate methods for CPS to recover from an unhealthy state is still a research challenge. In critical domains, nondeterministic reconfiguration and inadequate safety assurance might result in unacceptable risks. For such domains, functional safety standards are guiding assurance activities that should be executed. These standards typically provide requirements for risk identification and classification and propose how to reduce the risk to an acceptable level. Nowadays, all applied methods to fulfill the safety standards require that the entire CPS system and the environment in which the system will operate are well defined and understood at design time. Currently this is the prerequisite for the subsequent design of necessary analysis and measures that are introduced for creating a sound and comprehensive safety argument. However, the inherent uncertainty of dynamic compositions and reconfigurations of adaptive CPS systems does not allow to fully analyze them before runtime. To this end, current practice requires that the entire system and all system contexts are well defined and understood at design time so that the necessary analysis can be conducted, measures can be introduced and a sound and comprehensive safety argument can be designed. This prerequisite is clearly not fulfilled by adaptive CPS due to the uncertainty of dynamic compositions and reconfigurations, which can hardly be foreseen and analyzed before runtime. So, established safety engineering approaches and standardization can therefore not be readily applied for future CPS systems raising the requirement for new innovative approaches such as those presented in this book.

SECURITY CONCERNS IN CPS

As described in earlier clauses, cyber-physical systems organized in the Internet of Things are deployed to a wide variation of different environments. A result of this deployment is the risk that these systems process sensitive data such as personal, operation critical, or secretive information. One main advantage of the IOT, it's openness, is also one of its major weaknesses, potentially providing adversaries easy access to data they could not access before. To counteract a future catastrophe of data theft, system manipulation and cyber-terrorism, the complete chain of operation needs to be secured. This starts with the deployment of the devices and ends with the (long-term) operation in very diverse fields of operation.

This situation necessitates the industrial and research communities to find solutions in the following coarse engineering disciplines.

When handling a secure communication or storing sensitive information, it always comes down to the secure storage of a secret. Be it the temporary key created during authentication, a master key for cost sensitive mass products or any certificate proving the authenticity of a product. This information must never leave the device and as such its readout must be protected actively and passively, to avoid the leakage via side-channels. While devices specifically designed for secure applications can include significant defenses, this is not true for off the shelf products. As such, techniques to handle sensitive information of general purposes systems are needed.

When storage requirements have been met, it is of upmost importance that every processing of the key does not open it to an adversary. As such an attacker could be a financially powerful organization, even the initialization of the device in a production environment needs to be secured. The same is true for any update process when the device has been deployed. Hence, secure key distribution, initialization and authentication need to be carefully considered during software and system development.

Authentication and data encryption, classical security engineering topics, providing the protected data transfer using well tested open standards, is of high importance. Still, it will only play a small role in this publication which concentrates on the specific requirements of CPS.

Similarly to the problem of proper key storage, secure data processing is a major problem in CPS made of off-the-shelf components. A system that has not been designed to be secure on a hardware-level, requires sophisticated countermeasures on a software and design flow level to close potential side channels. Also, different data groups need to be separated e.g. to avoid data leakage through system internal side channels and to provide damage containment (ARM, 2009).

As discussed, CPS are deployed to an increasing number of fields and as such, some common groups can be identified. Depending on the attack scenarios and the possible implications of a successful assault, the following are the most common targets:

Machine to Machine Communication in Consumer Products

Comfort functions like regular content updates, and the integration of cloud functionality provide also easy access to consumer products for adversaries. The issues range from rather simple theft of private data to manipulation of critical functions, if paths from such convenience functionality to safety related ones exist. A widely known and already targeted environment would be for example automotive systems. In this case there have already been successful attacks on critical parts like breaks through online multimedia technology in the automobile (Woo, Jo, & Lee, 2015).

Sensors and Actors in Private Environments

The increasing spread of home automation systems raises privacy issues with open availability of direct sensor data in private environments. As hacks of simple web cameras showed (Symantec, 2017) hardening of external interfaces is necessary to avoid the risk of espionage or criminal activity like blackmail. Especially critical is the linking of remote home locking mechanisms, which could provide criminal elements with the possibility to sense if home owners are at home and opening the house for potential thieves.

Critical Industrial Infrastructures

Complex supply chains and the introduction of decentral power generation using renewable power sources, made it necessary to provide online control and maintenance functionality. This opens critical infrastructures to possible cyber terrorists, blackmailers and thieves of intellectual property.

Especially when customers are given the possibility to link their consumer products with unforeseen application environments, such as in bring-your-own-device workplaces, catastrophic security issues can evolve.

ORGANIZATION OF THE BOOK

The book is organized into 15 chapters. A brief description of each of the chapters follows:

Chapter 1 describes a CPS application in the domain of 3D imaging. Through 3D imaging the device is aware of its location and can use this information to track objects or even to improve optical communication approaches. This chapter describes the concept of Time-of-Flight sensing and how this can be used for optical communication.

Chapter 2 deals with the challenge of route planning optimization in the automotive sector. The chapter describes the approach to use decentralized ubiquitous IoT technologies to provide navigation systems live information about the traffic status. This chapter describes the concept and also shows simulation results regarding the achieved traveling times.

Chapter 3 outlines the challenges of CPS regarding network performance. This performance evaluation is compared to network controlled systems and the same algorithms are applied and compared in terms of stability and recommendations what to use for CPS. This chapter provides a mathematical analysis and a description of different sampling models.

Chapter 4 focuses on the topic of wireless sensor networks. For this networks an orthogonal frequency division multiple access (OFDMA) communication protocol is analyzed and proposed. This chapter compares the protocol with others in terms of bit rates, collision probability, node outages, etc.

Chapter 5 focuses on the domain of CPS training concepts. It describes how courses should be structured, the certification approach, and how they can be delivered to the participants. This chapter describes the structure in detail and the already established project called AQUA. The courses domain is mainly situated on CPS for automotive.

Chapter 6 describes ConSerts M which is used to evaluate the safety of new system compositions at runtime. Each component provides a certificate/contract about its safety. This chapter provides a description how this system works including a case study.

Chapter 7 examines mixed criticality systems and its challenges. The CPS themselves can perform different applications at once while having to fulfill safety requirements for some applications. This chapter describes multiple concepts and their integration and provides a use case analysis.

Chapter 8 presents a design and verification process for safety-critical systems. This process uses UML to represent the design flow. This flow covers the design, the architecture, and the virtual prototyping of the system. This chapter provides a background description and a description of the steps down to the virtual prototype.

Chapter 9 offers an overview and approach regarding self-adaptive software on CPS. This chapter also describes an approach called Scari, shown in a case study which focuses on adaption on hardware faults and malicious software.

Chapter 10 focuses on security for Internet of Things (IoT). The chapter is split into giving an overview of possible attacks, research trends, and security mechanisms in software and hardware. Also, commonly used layers from application to the physical layer are described including references to get additional information about the single aspects.

Chapter 11 writes about key management for IoT devices. This involves the complete lifecycle of the product and is divided into 6 phases, describing topics like the personalization, authentication methods, ownerships of keys, etc.

Chapter 12 offers a detailed overview of open CPS platforms. Describing how the architecture can be adjusted to maintain security while allowing to update the system and add new software components during runtime. This chapter also proposes a model based toolchain for development.

Chapter 13 writes about side channel attacks on devices in the IoT. The authors describe a trusted execution environment which includes side channel attack resistant processor cores. Also combined attacks are highlighted in this chapter by capturing multiple sources to leak information.

Chapter 14 evaluates wider scaled systems like SCADA systems. The authors present intrusion detection systems based on integrity analysis. Additionally, integrity reporting technologies are evaluated in terms of operational overhead, configuration updates, development process, and secure provisioning.

Chapter 15 concludes the security part of this book in the automotive domain. This chapter describes the challenge to provide both safety and security in one system. The authors provide a solution in form of a cooperative safety and security framework. Additionally, several methods are described to perform a security and safety analysis in parallel. To conclude the chapter a case study is presented.

Norbert Druml
Independent Researcher, Austria

Andreas Genser
Independent Researcher, Austria

Andrea Hoeller
Independent Researcher, Austria

Armin Krieg
Independent Researcher, Austria

Manuel Menghin
Independent Researcher, Austria

REFERENCES

ARM. (n.d.). *Trustzone Security White Paper*. Retrieved from http://infocenter.arm.com/help/topic/com.arm.doc.prd29-genc-009492c/PRD29-GENC-009492C_trustzone_security_whitepaper.pdf

Charette, R. N. (2009). *This Car Runs on Code*. Retrieved from http://spectrum.ieee.org/transportation/systems/this-car-runs-on-code

Lilienthal, D. (2011). Top 4 Fun Boeing 787 Technical Facts. *NYC Aviation*. Retrieved from http://www.nycaviation.com/2011/09/fun-facts-revealed-at-boeings-787-technical-panel

Symantec. (2017). *Internet Security Threat Report 2017*. Retrieved from https://resource.elq.symantec.com/LP=3980?cid=70138000001BjppAAC&mc=202671&ot=wp&tt=sw&inid=symc_threat-report_regular_to_leadgen_form_LP-3980_ISTR22-report-main

Woo, S., Jo, H. J., & Lee, H. L. (2015). A Practical Wireless Attack on the Connected Car and Security Protocol for In-Vehicle CAN. *IEEE Transactions on Intelligent Transportation Systems, 16*(2).

Acknowledgment

We, the editors, would first like to thank all who have been involved in the process of bringing this book to life.

Our acknowledgments go specifically to the reviewers of the submitted chapters. They were a great help in steering book contents and significantly improving quality.

Foremost, our gratitude goes to the authors. The diversity of the field of the Internet-of-Things is reflected greatly by the different angles the authors looked at it. Many important aspects are reflected ranging from security to pedagogical aspects. Only these substantial scientific contributions made this book possible. Thank You.

Norbert Druml
Independent Researcher, Austria

Andreas Genser
Independent Researcher, Austria

Andrea Hoeller
Independent Researcher, Austria

Armin Krieg
Independent Researcher, Austria

Manuel Menghin
Independent Researcher, Austria

Section 1
CPS Applications and Trends

Chapter 1
Localization and Context Determination for Cyber–Physical Systems Based on 3D Imaging

Hannes Plank
Infineon Technologies Austria AG, Austria

Josef Steinbaeck
Infineon Technologies Austria AG, Austria

Norbert Druml
Independent Researcher, Austria

Christian Steger
Graz University of Technology, Austria

Gerald Holweg
Infineon Technologies Austria AG, Austria

ABSTRACT

In recent years, consumer electronics became increasingly location and context-aware. Novel applications, such as augmented and virtual reality have high demands in precision, latency and update rate in their tracking solutions. 3D imaging systems have seen a rapid development in the past years. By enabling a manifold of systems to become location and context-aware, 3D imaging has the potential to become a part of everyone's daily life. In this chapter, we discuss 3D imaging technologies and their applications in localization, tracking and 3D context determination. Current technologies and key concepts are depicted and open issues are investigated. The novel concept of location-aware optical communication based on Time-of-Flight depth sensors is introduced. This communication method might close the gap between high performance tracking and localization. The chapter finally provides an outlook on future concepts and work-in progress technologies, which might introduce a new set of paradigms for location-aware cyber-physical systems in the Internet of Things.

DOI: 10.4018/978-1-5225-2845-6.ch001

INTRODUCTION

3D imaging technologies have seen rapid developments in the past years. The introduction of the Microsoft Kinect depth sensor to the consumer market in 2010 triggered a massive research interest and effort. In 2016, the first mass-produced smartphone appeared, featuring depth sensing based on Time-of-Flight. The availability of such ubiquitous and miniaturized depth sensing solutions can tremendously help any kind of electronic device to sense and understand its environment.

A crucial part of operation for certain devices is localization. While depth sensors provide geometric information about the immediate surrounding, determining location and orientation within a certain co-ordinate system is a challenge of its own. This chapter explores the opportunities depth sensing systems provide to localization. A focus is set on applications in fields such as consumer electronics, internet of things and autonomous robots. Localization and tracking of electronic devices has a long history and has seen the use of a variety of different principles. This work focuses on the fields of high performance localization based on optical and sensor fusion solutions. Localization principles in general can be categorized into passive, guided and cooperative solutions.

A passive system is able to determine its position in a local or global coordinate system without external help. An increasing number of applications also require information about the orientation of the device. A combination of position and rotation sensing is often referred to as pose determination. A pose has of six degrees of freedom (dof) and completely describes the static position and orientation of an entity in 3D space. Each axle in 3D space presents one degree of freedom for the position and one degree for rotation around the axle. Passive 6-dof localization is often used in computer vision based positioning systems, where features are matched with prerecorded databases. Early examples are cruise missiles using terrain contours for navigation.

A well-known example for guided localization is GPS, where devices use the aid of satellites to determine their position. Cooperative localization solutions use a communication channel, which is often used for active identification and position forwarding. Optical tracking, using image sensors and active markers is an example for cooperative tracking. In such system, an external base-station with an image sensor can sense a tracked device equipped with active LED markers, and has the ability to toggle the LEDs for identification. Another example are beacon based systems, where active beacons forward information about their location.

When classifying the location-awareness of cyber-physical systems, it is important to distinguish between localization and tracking. While these terms are sometimes used ambiguously, tracking is commonly used in a relative context, where the registration of movements is important. Tracking the pose of a device does not always lead to the determination of a position within a meaningful coordinate system. However relative position and rotation changes can be detected. For certain applications, this is sufficient and no broader localization is required. Examples for such systems are instruments measuring rotations, such as gyroscopes or compasses, some 3D scanning solutions or human interface devices.

Localization is often associated with position determination without focus on detecting relative pose changes. A combination of tracking and localization is used in a lot of location-aware systems and leads to localization at a high update rate. Tracking and localization are often performed by different sensors, because localization solutions often lack of the desired accuracy to track relative pose changes. While localization can provide the position and orientation within a greater context, tracking sensors provide the accuracy and update-rate required for the application.

A great example of sensor fusion for localization and tracking is Wikitude (2016). This smartphone application provides augmented reality on smartphones. It annotates the video stream of the internal camera with meaningful information about the environment and displays it on the screen. GPS or WIFI is used for positioning. The absolute orientation is determined by the gravity and compass sensors. The gyro sensors are used to track movements to enable a high update rate of the rotation. This enables to robustly attach information to certain landmarks and directions in the smartphone video stream.

Arising technologies such as virtual and augmented reality, autonomous driving and indoor localization demand precise pose determination at very high update rates. These demands are tackled in state-of-the-art systems with a sensor fusion approach, combining optical and inertial sensors. Optical sensors are used in the form of 2D and 3D cameras, LiDAR (light detection and ranging) and optical triangulation.

Data fusion with inertial sensors can compensate the flaws of optical sensors. Most optical positioning sensors require a line of sight connection and sometimes feature a slow update rate and too much latency as well as visual artifacts such as motion blur. Inertial sensors are commonly miniaturized, using MEMS technology and feature high update rates. These sensors are already well-established in mobile devices. Inertial sensors however base their measurements on differential movements and rotations. In order to measure absolute movements and rotation, the measurements need to be integrated. This introduces an integration error which introduces drift (Woodman, 2007). This drift can be compensated by fusing these measurements with non-drifting data, as optical systems can produce.

Using cameras for localization is traditionally accomplished by sophisticated computer vision methods, which are often solely based on 2D images. A common approach is simultaneous localization and mapping (SLAM), where a 3D representation of the environment is created during localization. Depth sensors are capable to improve the performance of such monocular SLAM systems (Steinbrücker, Sturm, & Cremers, 2011). A prominent example is Google Tango, which uses a number of sensors, including a Time-of-Flight depth camera for SLAM based localization on mobile devices.

Depth sensing systems are devices capable to directly gather geometric information about the immediate environment. A measurement typically consists of a coordinate in three dimensions, usually relative to the depth sensor itself. In a depth camera, every pixel produces such measurement. If the shutter of the camera triggers all pixels at the same time, every measurement is captured simultaneously. Since all available depth imaging systems are limited in range and show systematic measurement errors, some systems also attach a confidence measure to each measurement.

One of the reasons that the vast research effort on optical localization systems are based on 2D cameras, is that the field of depth sensors is much younger than 2D sensors and they are not yet part of common vision systems. This might change in the smartphone and tablet domain, since as of 2016 the first smartphone featuring a Time-of-Flight depth camera appeared on the consumer market. Measuring depth based on the Time-of-Flight principle is the most miniaturized solution available and has the flexibility to be used in a manifold of applications.

DEPTH IMAGING FOR 6-DOF LOCALIZATION

This section introduces current depth imaging solutions with focus on Time-of-Flight technology. Depth sensors alone are usually not directly associated with localization, although they provide 3D-context awareness of the immediate surrounding. A sensor fusion approach, incorporating depth sensors however offers advantages in SLAM based systems (Steinbrücker, Sturm, & Cremers, 2011), and can improve tracking precision in general. In this work, we focus on depth sensing based on Time-of-Flight, since it is the most miniaturized solution, and is the only depth sensor, which can be found in mass produced smartphones. We also present a concept in this chapter, where Time-of-Flight sensors are directly used for location-aware optical communication, closing the gap between depth sensing and localization.

THE PRINCIPLE OF TIME-OF-FLIGHT DEPTH SENSING

Time-of-Flight imaging is based on measuring how long light takes to travel from the sensing system to the scene and back to a photosensitive sensor. These systems can be distinguished by their operating principle, as illustrated in Figure 1. Direct Time-of-Flight systems emit short light pulses and measure the time between emission and reception. Each pulse corresponds with one measurement. A prominent example is LiDAR, where bundled light pulses are emitted by a laser and detected by photodiodes. The angle of these pulses is modulated to receive a spatial image of the surroundings. Indirect ToF imaging sensors relay on a continuous wave approach.

The operating principle of this indirect approach is illustrated in Figure 2 and works by emitting pulsed infrared light at a wide radiation angle. An image sensor receives the reflected light and is able to measure the phase-shift between incoming and outgoing signal, which is proportional to the distance.

The emitted light pulses usually have a frequency of up to 100 MHz. They originate from an active illumination unit, which typically consists of an infrared LED or vertical cavity surface emitting laser (VCSEL). The pulses travel to the sensed object and back to the image sensor. The lens projects the light onto a ToF image sensor.

Each pixel of the ToF sensor contains a photonic mixer device, which produces a signal corresponding to the phase-shift between the outgoing and incoming light (Tobias, 2005). The incoming photons generate charge-hole pairs in the silicon, which are moved into either of two charge buckets A and B. This is decided by the logical state of the modulation signal. This signal is generated on the ToF sensor and is also used to emit light pulses. In order to control the PMD devices, the signal is directly supplied to each pixel. The charge difference between bucket A and B is the output of the ToF sensor and is related to the phase-shift of the incoming and outgoing signals. This phase output value however also depends on the amount of incoming light. Reflection properties of the sensed material and as well the

Figure 1. The different principles of Time-of-Flight based depth measuring

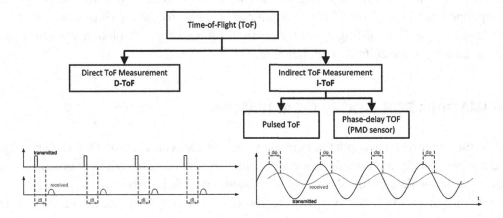

Figure 2. The working principle of continuous wave indirect Time-of-Flight 3D imaging

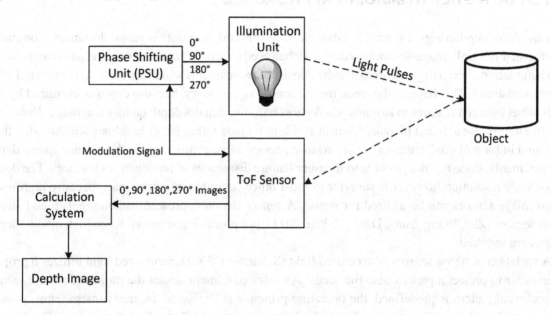

distance influence this value. In order to determine the exact phase-shift, the most common way is to conduct four or more different measurements. In these measurements, the phase-shift offset between the outgoing light and the modulation signal is changed, producing four or more different phase images.

A well-established procedure is to take four measurements I with four equidistant phase offsets (e.g. 0°, 90°, 180°, 270°) and calculate the phase-offset by the following relation:

$$p = \operatorname{atan}\left(\frac{I_0 - I_{180}}{I_{90} - I_{270}}\right)$$

Since p is proportional to the phase-shift of a pulsed light signal, the phase values wrap and start again at zero, if the distance is too long. Time-of-Flight sensors are capable to change their modulation frequency in order to produce another different set of four phase images to unwrap these ambiguous phases. The final measurement for a depth image consists then of eight phase-images, which results in a larger range, while maintaining precision. The tradeoff is a decreased frame-rate and potential motion artifacts. The eight-phase mode is commonly used in SLAM applications, which prefer depth quality over frame-rate.

The drawback of Time-of-Flight sensors is limited resolution of the depth image, since each pixel contains the circuit of the photonic mixer device. The limited photo-sensitive area on the silicon is compensated partly by using micro-lenses directly applied above the silicon to focus light to the photo-sensitive areas of a pixel. Since continuous wave Time-of-Flight sensing is the most miniaturized depth sensing system available, increasing the sensor size to enhance resolution or photosensitivity is often not feasible. Another drawback is the sensitivity to incoming background light. Despite countermeasures such as background illumination suppression (BSI) and infrared filters, very bright light sources such as reflected sunlight can reduce the signal to noise ratio, but do not directly influence the measurement.

ALTERNATIVE DEPTH IMAGING APPROACHES

Each available depth imaging system has its own trade-offs and no system is yet predominant. Compared to Time-of-Flight, all image-sensor based approaches need a certain size to conduct measurements based on triangulation. Stereo depth sensors usually consist of two cameras which are mounted in parallel with a certain distance. This baseline between these cameras is necessary, because depth is measured by the pixel offset between features in two images. A short baseline impairs depth quality and range. However, progression in research and increased sensor resolution made rather small baselines feasible, like they are found in form of dual camera systems in smartphones. Stereo cameras usually produce sparse depth measurements, since it is not possible to measure feature disparities of homogenous surfaces. The depth image's x/y resolution however is superior to most other depth sensing principles, because high resolution image sensors can be utilized for stereo. A sensor fusion approach, combining ToF and stereo depth sensors (Zhu, Wang, Yang, Davis, & Pan, 2011), is a promising solution, when high quality depth images are required.

A variation of stereo sensors is structured light (Scharstein, 2003). Structured light utilizes a projector in order to project a pattern onto the scene. An infrared camera senses the projected pattern. Since the projected pattern is predefined, the operating principle is similar to a stereo camera setup, as both systems are based on extracting the feature disparity caused by the distance to the camera. The famous Microsoft Kinect sensor is based on this technology. Unlike stereo, dense depth images cannot be gathered, as the projected pattern is also reflected on homogenous surfaces. Due to the active illumination principle, structured light based systems can also operate in low light conditions. The drawback of this system is that the active illumination requires more energy, like ToF, and the system is also impaired by ambient light. Unlike ToF, such systems also require a certain distance between projector and camera.

Depth imaging based on LiDAR is most commonly used in automotive applications. Unlike image sensor based approaches, the angular variation of LiDAR measurements does not stem from optical projection onto an imaging sensor, but from mechanical scanning devices. This mitigates multi-path interference, and allows the usage of highly sensitive photo elements, such as single photon avalanche diodes. This increases the effective range at the cost of more complex sensing systems.

DIRECT LOCALIZATION WITH DEPTH SENSORS

Depth imaging sensors currently are not commonly used in the field of localization of electronic devices. One of the reasons is that most of the research on image based localization is focused on the far more established and ubiquitous color cameras. 3D data does not have as much variation and distinctive features as 2D images. Geometry is more generic and repetitive than reflected light. Due to the measurement principles, 3D imaging also suffers from resolution and limited range. Geometry however is more consistent, since it is not influenced by different illumination. With depth sensors, it is possible build dense 3D models of the environment, as demonstrated by Newcombe et al. (2011) in their Kinect Fusion approach. Such 3D models can be used for re-localization and mapping the environment for systems such as autonomous robots. Another application for such high-quality depth maps is augmented reality. Due to the integration of depth data to a dense model, it is possible to embed virtual objects, using the high-quality depth data.

Biswas and Veloso (2012) present an indoor navigation system based on depth information using a plane filtered pointcloud and Monte Carlo localization. Since solely depth sensors are used, the robots can also dynamically avoid obstacles, which are not in the reference map. While these approaches might work in a smaller context, with distinctive geometry, sensor fusion approaches are more favorable for localization. Later in this chapter, we explore the concept of using Time-of-Flight depth sensors in a novel way to establish location-aware optical communication links to embedded devices. If these devices forward positional information, highly accurate cooperative localization is possible by solely using miniaturized depth sensors.

DEPTH AND COLOR SENSOR FUSION

Depth and color cameras can be combined to create a unified RGB-D sensor, capable to capture images containing both depth and color information. When a SLAM or visual localization system is provided with depth information, the system can either build better 3D maps, but also benefit in robustness from the immediately available distance data (Steinbrücker et al., 2011). The process of 3D and 2D data fusion can also improve depth image resolution, if the required processing power is available. This is due to the principle that depth edges often correlate with edges in color and intensity images. Color edges without any depth discontinuity can be simply ignored, when the lower resolution depth image does not show any variation. Since depth imaging systems usually lack high resolution, color edge information can be used to interpolate and upscale depth images in a meaningful way.

Research has produced a large number of image-guided depth upscaling algorithms (Chetverikov, Eichhardt, & Jankó, 2015). The input for most methods is a high resolution color image and sparse depth measurements which are mapped into the color image space. This sparse RGB-D image is produced by 3D measurements which are mapped to the 2D image. The requirement for such mapping is knowledge about the intrinsic camera parameters of both cameras, which include distortion coefficients, focal length and pixel offsets of the optical centers. These parameters are usually derived by checkerboard calibration, which is also possible for Time-of-Flight depth cameras, since they are able to produce a grey-scale intensity image. The extrinsic parameters of a dual camera system are in this case a translation vector T and a rotation matrix R, which describe the transformation from the depth camera's coordinate system to the color camera. These parameters can also be gathered by capturing images of a checkerboard pattern, and using a toolchain, such as Camera Calibration toolbox (Bouguet, 2016). If intrinsic and extrinsic camera parameters are known, depth measurements with depth $d_{i,j}$ and pixel position $x_{i,j}$ can be mapped to 3D space of the color camera, using the pseudoinverse P of the intrinsic depth camera matrix:

$$X_{i,j} = T + R d_{i,j} \frac{P x_{i,j}}{P x_{i,j}}$$

The 3D measurements $X_{i,j}$ can be projected to 2D image space coordinates $v_{i,j}$ by multiplication with the intrinsic matrix I of the color camera.

$$v_{i,j} = I X_{i,j}$$

Methods to interpolate these projected depth images involve various principles, such as energy minimization (Ferstl, Reinbacher, Ranftl, Ruether, & Bischof, 2013), graph based methods (Dai, Zhang, Mei, & Zhang, 2015) or edge aware interpolation (Plank, Holweg, Herndl, & Druml, 2016). Most methods are designed with focus on depth image quality and not for efficiency. In location-aware cyber-physical systems, interactive framerates are desired. When the depth images are used to build 3D maps in a SLAM system, several depth images per second are desired. Methods to create high resolution depth images on restricted hardware are relatively rare. While there are approaches, which emphasize on low computational complexity (Dai et al., 2015), there are not many implementations which can be executed on parallel processing systems such as GPUs. The joint bilateral filter, developed by Kopf et al. (Kopf, Cohen, & Lischinski, 2007) can be executed in parallel and works by weighting image filter kernels on color similarity. This works well with relatively small upscaling factors. If, however, more than just a few pixels between depth values need to be interpolated, depth values influence pixels despite edges between the interpolated pixel and the original depth value. We therefore developed an edge-aware interpolation approach which is optimized for GPUs on mobile devices (Plank, Holweg, Herndl, & Druml, 2016). In this approach, sparse depth values are mapped to high-resolution color images. Each depth value propagates its influence among circular paths to the surrounding pixels. If edges are crossed, the influence drastically decays. If no edges are crossed, the influence is evenly distributed, suppressing sensor noise. Our prototype implementation is capable of producing 13 frames per second, when executed on GPUs on mobile devices. Beside the capability of SLAM systems to create better geometric models of the environment, the availability of high resolution 1-1 mapped depth and color images, enables better context awareness, since combined depth and color data benefits 2D object detection algorithms (Yu & Zhao, 2012).

A rather unexplored issue is synchronization among camera systems. Most academic work assumes that color and depth sensors operate in synchronous mode, since the technical solution to a synchronous camera system seems trivial. In practical applications, however, synchronization is often not feasible as it usually requires tight cooperation across multiple hardware vendors. The vast majority of image sensors are developed to be integrated into monocular systems, not offering any option for hardware synchronization. For RGB-D SLAM systems however, synchronization can be avoided by using additional sensors. Such system is usually in motion while the environment remains static. If color and depth cameras gather information at different times, this can be corrected by using motion tracking data from an inertial sensor. Inertial sensors can operate at a high update-rate. If all measurements, including the depth and color images are accurately timestamped, the actual pose difference between depth image and color image can be calculated by transforming the depth data by the relative pose derived by the motion tracking system. By using physical models of the tracking system, the relative pose can be even more refined.

Ovren et al. (2013) introduce this approach in their attempt to correct the effect of rolling shutter image sensors. A rolling shutter is caused by the pixel readout process, and means, that not all color pixels are captured at the same time. Inertial based depth image alignment is only possible with static scenes, because they are only able to compensate the motion of the camera system.

LOCALIZATION WITH 2D IMAGING SENSORS

Feature Based Localization

Color information alone can be directly used for localization by matching visual input data against databases (Vedaldi & Soatto, 2008). This works by finding features, which are regions or points in input images which are significant and distinctive. Feature descriptors are an abstract representation of these regions with the goal of being able comparable to other features, while being resilient against pose and intensity variations. These feature descriptions can be stored in a visual dictionary, associating these features with localization information. These databases are either generated systematically via 3D scanning systems, or using topologic information. If these features are recognized by a vision system, the pose of the system can be calculated by triangulation. This kind of visual localization can also be used to initialize a visual SLAM system (Lepetit, Arth, Pirchheim, Ventura, & Schmalstieg, 2015). SLAM can provide more accurate localization, by creating a 3D data representation of the sensed environment.

Visible Light Localization

The motivation of visible light localization (VLC) is caused by the increasingly ubiquitous LED lights. Due to the fast switching speed, it is possible to transmit information from repurposed existing illumination systems. With appropriate modulation, it is possible to use lights for communication without perceivable flickering. Visible light based localization has different applications with different demands in precision. Current products, such as Qualcomm Lumicast (Jovicic, 2016), repurpose image sensors for visible light localization. The distinction between vision based methods with active targets and visible light localization is that base-stations transmit information to help with localization. This can be either IDs or positional information of the base station.

Do and Yoo (2016) provide an extensive survey on methods and implementations of visible light based positioning systems. Such systems usually consist of base-stations, which emit encoded light to electronic devices, equipped with photo-detection sensors. The base stations are either re-used light sources, such as traffic lights or lamps, or dedicated infrared beacons. The simplest solution is based on proximity detection. Such systems can be implemented with just a photodiode as receiver. It is however only possible to detect the base-station itself, so only a very coarse localization with an uncertainty of several meters (Campo-Jimenez, Martin Perandones, & Lopez-Hernandez, 2013) is possible.

Finger printing based methods can achieve more precise positioning, but require pre-recorded maps for localization. Time difference of arrival (TDOA) is another method, which works by receiving light signals from multiple base-stations. For 3D localization, at least three base-stations need to be in the direct field of view. The tracked device directly measures the distance to the base-station in this method. This is accomplished by measuring the time it takes the light pulses of each base station to travel to the device. The position is then determined by trilateration. Such localization systems require a good synchronization of the base stations and the localized device. A single photodiode can be used to receive the signals, and a method to separate the received signals of the base-stations has to be employed. This is possible by using time or frequency division multiplexing (Liu, et al., 2014). TDOA localization is not limited to the optical domain. It is possible to also use radio or sound waves; however, multi-path effects need to be considered. Image sensors might be capable to measure time-differences, and also offer light-source separation due to the projection via lenses. The position on the pixel can be used to detect the angles between the base-stations. Due to the pixel readout process, image sensors usually cannot be sampled at the required rates. It either requires dedicated image sensors, featuring customized electronic shutter units or direct pixel readout. Dynamic vision sensors (Censi, Strubel, Brandli, Delbruck, & Scaramuzza, 2013) are a promising development, and might be able to conduct such measurements. An active vision sensor does not produce images, but events which describe local pixel value changes. The difficult synchronization between device and base-stations might deem such image sensor based approaches unfeasible, because it is also possible to determine the position on triangulation alone. Time-of-Flight 3D imaging sensors might be capable to support TDOA based localization, but to our knowledge, this has not yet been investigated and is subject for future research.

Another method to determine the distance between optical receivers and LEDs is to measure the received signal strength (RSS). Calculating the distance to light sources is based on modelling the light source and its propagation path to photo sensors. After calibration, distances can be associated with the output of optical receivers. When receiving the signal from multiple base-stations, the signal differences between the base-stations can be used to calculate the distance. This mitigates the influence of background illumination. RSS based positioning has the potential to be simply implemented and widely adopted, since no synchronization is necessary. The problem however is that the received signal strength depends on the orientation of the photo detector relative to the LEDs as well. The light strength also depends on the orientation of the LEDs, since light is radiated inhomogeneously. It is however possible to combine RSS with angle based localization methods (Mauro Biagi, 2015).

Localization based on triangulation requires systems, which are able to measure the angle of arrival (AOA). This can be either accomplished by an array of photodiodes (Lee & Jung, 2012) or by using image sensors. AOA systems are in general more complicated, but do not require synchronization. With the help of a 3D camera, it is possible to localize the relative positions of the base stations, and combine trilateration and triangulation in order to improve the localization accuracy. It is also possible to avoid determining the positions of the base-stations beforehand. If only relative movements need to be detected, the base stations can be supplied with their relative locations from the 3D camera system via optical communication. In the next section, we present our OptiSec3D approach, which enables these concepts by combining Time-of-Flight depth sensing with optical communication.

LOCATION-AWARE OPTICAL COMMUNICATION BASED ON TIME-OF-FLIGHT SENSORS

The operating principle of Time-of-Flight depth sensors requires an image sensor, capable of demodulating phase differences of pulsed light. In this section, we present our effort to create a novel location-aware optical communication system. We further go into detail, how it might benefit future localization and tracking systems in the fields of IoT and cyber physical systems.

The most significant feature of image sensor based optical communication is the directional awareness of the communication partner. If depth imaging sensors are used for optical communication, it is even possible to track communication partners in 3D. While there exists a manifold of image sensor based optical communication systems, Time-of-Flight sensors have not yet been widely explored for optical communication.

A first attempt was made by Yuan et al. (2014), who establish a one-way communication link between a Time-of-Flight camera and an array of modulated LED lights. The sending device avoids the required synchronization by recovering the Time-of-Flight sensor's modulation signal with a photodiode. The emitting LEDs are supplied with a phase-modulated modulation signal and manipulate depth measurements of the ToF sensor. These depth measurements are analyzed and the received information is extracted. Since the Time-of-Flight sensor is operated in normal depth sensing mode at relatively low frame-rates in this approach, multiple LEDs are used to transmit information in parallel. Such multiple input approaches are limited in range, since the pixel array cannot resolve individual LEDs when a certain distance is exceeded.

If a system however is capable of configuring and controlling Time-of-Flight 3D imaging systems with a direct connection and a real-time system with low level configuration access, optical communication parameters can be changed to increase readout speeds and it is also possible to use just single modulated LEDs to send information. In our OptiSec3D approach, we utilize Time-of-Flight sensors as optical transceivers, which are also capable to incorporate depth measurements into the communication protocol. Our approach has the potential to reach a throughput of several kilobits per second.

Operation Principle of the OptiSec3D Approach

Indirect Time-of-Flight sensing works by emitting pulsed infrared light. The active illumination unit of such system can be used as transmitter, since it is designed to emit pulsed infrared light at different phase-shifts. The pixels of the receiving Time-of-Flight image sensor are capable to demodulate the phase-shifted signal. This allows optical communication based on pulsed light phase-shift keying (PLPSK). The vast advantage of PLPSK is that multiple bits can be encoded in one image. In most image sensor based approaches, simple binary modulation schemes, such as on/off keying (Roberts, 2013) or pulse position keying are used. They support the transmission of one bit per frame at best. PLPSK takes advantage of the photonic mixer device (PMD), located on each pixel of a Time-of-Flight sensor. The PMD decodes phase differences of incoming light pulses, by sorting the incoming charges into charge storage buckets A and B on the pixels. After the readout process, the voltage difference of these buckets is proportional to the phase difference between the own modulation signal and the incoming light pulses. If these light pulses are phase-modulated, the output of the ToF sensor contains the decoded phase offset signal. Since at least four equidistant phases are used during communication, it is possible to decode phase differences by just using one frame, instead of at least four frames used during depth measurement.

Channel Characteristics

Due to the measurement principle of the PMD on each pixel, the sensor is sensitive to pulsed light within a certain frequency range. Non-pulsed background light does not have a direct influence on the measurement. The photons of continuous light arrive during both switching states of the PMD with near equal intensity. This fills both charge buckets equally, leading to increased noise but no measurement bias. Due to this principle, extensive image processing is unnecessary, as it can be assumed, that all detected signals originates from potential communication partners.

Another side-effect of the PMD pixels is that sensors can choose modulation frequencies from a large spectrum to communicate. Stray light from different connections from different systems do not directly influence the measurement, as long the light pulse frequency is just several thousand Hertz apart. There exist no experimental evaluations so far, but a viable spectrum of 16 to 26 MHz can potentially yield to

1000 different channels, with a rather large distance of 10000 Hz. Using fast-switching VCELs, instead of LEDs, the upper boundary of the spectrum can be extended to over 100 MHz.

Image sensor based optical communication usually suffers from the low frame-rates of the sensors. While there exist experimental dedicated communication image sensors (Takai, 2013), the necessary digitization of complete frames has been holding back high speed image sensor based communication links so far.

Time-of-Flight sensors need to capture up to eight phase images in order to create one depth image. Therefore, the readout and analog-digital conversion circuitry is often optimized for fast readout and digitization. In order to demodulate a line-of-sight communication signal, just a very short exposure time is required. These characteristics enable high frame-rates during optical communication. We manage to operate our Time-of-Flight sensor at 500 frames per second with full sensor readout. This however can be massively increased, if the sensor is only read-out partially. By configuring the readout region to a minimum of 16x32 pixels, we are able to reach 7300 frames per second. This can lead to a transmission throughput of 14600 bits per second, when using 4-PLPSK. This high framerate leads to fast light source tracking capabilities, supported by fast adoption of the readout window, to accommodate moving targets.

Sensor Synchronization

A technical challenge throughout many communication systems is synchronization. In Time-of-Flight based communication, it is important that the frequency of the modulation signal of a ToF camera matches the frequency of its communication partner. If the modulation frequency of a ToF sensor is different from the frequency of the incoming light pulses, the measured phase values start to drift. Figure 3 shows sampled phase values, when the sender continuously emits pulsed infrared light without phase-shift. If this signal is measured and digitized, the frequency of this signal is the absolute modulation frequency difference between both communication partners.

Figure 3. The observed phase with corresponding charge bucket contents, if sender and receiver are not synchronized

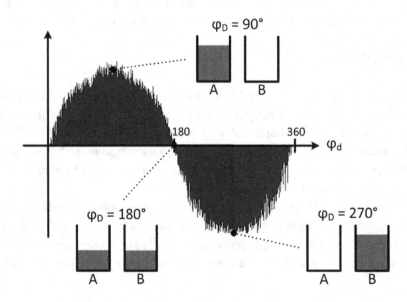

Synchronization can be accomplished by sampling the incoming light pulses, and calculating the frequency difference of the communication partner. The modulation frequency of Time-of-Flight cameras is usually configurable to accommodate different use-cases. In the case of OptiSec3D, the frequency is adapted by configuring a phase locked loop (PLL) on the sensor. Synchronization can be reached, if the PLL is adapted by the measured frequency difference.

Implementation of OptiSec3D

The core of each OptiSec3D communication partner is an Infineon Real3™ 3D imaging sensor, based on Time-of-Flight technology of pmd technologies. The Xilinx Zynq 7000 platform is used in our platform to operate the sensor with software executed on its integrated ARM processors, while the FPGA is used as glue logic and for imaging data transmission. The software uses an I2C bus to configure the ToF imaging sensor. This live-configuration of the sensor allows changing the internal workings of a normal depth sensor in such way, that it is possible to transmit and decode data. This works by limiting the number of digitized pixels per frame to a small area around modulated lightsources. With this configuration, the sensor is able to sample the image of the communication partner at over 7300 frames per second. The received signal directly contains the transmitted decoded information, since ToF pixels are sensitive to phase-shift differences.

Communication Modes

Time-of-Flight cameras could be either used to communicate with each other, or with different electronic devices. While it is not difficult to implement a PLPSK transmitter, receiving PLPSK is not trivial, since a photonic mixer device is required. ToF cameras however are able employ alternative modulation schemes, such as pulse position modulation. A receiver would just need to be able to detect the presence of light within certain time-slots. Time-shifts could be implemented either directly by accessing the illumination unit, by varying the frame-rate, or the number of read-out pixels.

Optical line-of-sight communication is not limited to two communication partners. The aforementioned concepts can be employed to multiplex communication between multiple partners. For synchronization, the adapted frequency for each communication partner can be stored, and the PLL adapted each time, when switching the focus to a different partner. If multiple devices want to communicate with a single node, all other devices could alternatively adjust their frequency to the node. If the focus of an application is on low latency rather than throughput, the sensor can be read-out completely, instead of adapting the readout region to the location of each communication partner.

Localization Principles with Location-Aware Optical Communication

Location-awareness and re-usability are the main motivations for optical communication based on image sensors. While 2D image sensors are only capable to determine the incident angles of a line-of-sight connection, Time-of-Flight sensors can locate communication partners in 3D.

Since Time-of-Flight imaging systems can be used as optical transmitter and receiver, the simplest use case is optical communication between two Time-of-Flight cameras. When both communication partners measure their mutual distance, they can both locate each other in 3D. In the application of e.g. encrypted device authentication, both partners can forward their mutual distance measurement and check for consistency. This effectively defeats relay attacks, where an attacker relays communication without alteration, using two relay boxes. In such relay attack, the distance between sender and relay box A is not consistent to the distance of receiver and relay box B.

Communication between Time-of-Flight cameras could also be employed in localization solutions. In that case, a stationary camera with a light emitter serves as beacon. Electronic devices, equipped with a Time-of-Flight camera can contact one beacon to determine its position and orientation. An example could be an autonomous robot, desiring to navigate around a building.

The beacon's purpose is to forward its own position and the angles relative to the device. When simple LED beacons are used, at least three of them are necessary to determine the camera's position, even when the camera can determine the distance to each beacon. If the beacon however features an image sensor, as depicted in Figure 4, the incidence angle of the line-of-sight can be determined by the beacon and forwarded to the device. This enables 5-dof localization of embedded devices, using a single beacon. The only unknown degree of freedom is the roll angle, since the beacons optical signature is invariant to rotations around this axis. Sensor fusion with a gravity sensor or computer vision methods can effectively help reach full 6-dof localization. In the case of autonomous robots, this angle might already be locked due to the camera mounting method.

While beaconing with Time-of-Flight sensors enables a miniaturized localization system, simpler and cheaper beacons might be desirable. If three or more beacons are visible at the same time, a device using an imaging sensor can reach 6-dof localization by solving the perspective-n-point problem. When using depth sensors, the relative 3D position between camera and each beacon is directly available. This enhances the positioning robustness, since both trilateration and triangulation can be used to determine the position.

When no absolute localization within a predetermined coordinate system is desired, it is sufficient to use beacons which initially do not hold information about their location. A device can determine the relative positions of the beacons by using a 3D camera. With optical communication, it is possible to assign IDs to each of them and re-localize them in the local coordinate system. It is also possible to forward localization information to these beacons, so that simpler devices with 2D cameras can later on use them for navigation. In the last section of this chapter, the idea of forwarding positional information to small IoT devices is further discussed.

Augmented Internet of Things

So far, the main focus of augmented reality (AR) is fusing virtual and real worlds in order to receive an augmented world. The main mechanisms so far are putting virtual objects into a live camera stream (e.g. Google Tango, Qualcomm Vuforia), or embedding them into the viewport of a user (e.g. Microsoft HoloLens). We propose a concept with our OpticSec3D approach, to use 3D location-aware optical communication in order to enable embedded devices to interact with the augmented world. This would enable electronic devices within the viewport of an AR, to transfer information and interaction possibilities to the augmented world. These devices could be any kind of system, requiring human interaction, such as light switches, payment terminals, heating and climate control. They could also serve as virtual signs, or display promotions in supermarkets, or be used for pairing with local WIFI or Bluetooth connections.

A Time-of-Flight depth sensor on such AR system can receive optical signals from such devices and can use distance measurements to determine the 3D position. When the 3D position relative to the AR device is known, it can be embedded into the augmented reality. The concept, of mapping a 3D posi-

Figure 4. Depth sensing, combined with optical communication leads to 5-dof localization with just one base-station. The base-station is equipped with an image sensor, and transmits its position $\vec{L}$ and the direction $\vec{p}$ vector of the localization device. The localization device can calculate its own position $\overrightarrow{L_s}$ and direction $\overrightarrow{d_s}$ by combining the received information with a distance measurement

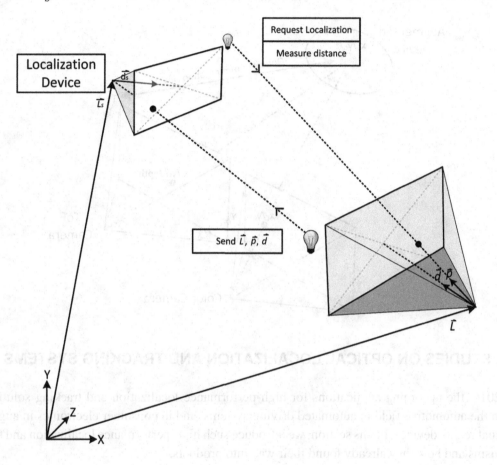

tion into AR space, is shown in Figure 5. Since the pixel position of the depth camera is different to the augmented color image stream, the 3D position needs to be transformed to color camera image space and projected to the 2D image space.

When the 3D position of a stationary device is determined, there are two possibilities. On the one hand, AR device can be equipped with a variety of pose tracking sensors. In this case, the 3D position can be placed into the augmented coordinate system and the pose tracking sensor would keep track of the position at this point. If the AR system does not feature such additional tracking system, the position solely relies on tracking the modulated light source. This requires continuous tracking, which means, that depth measurements need to be incorporated into the communication protocol.

It is however sufficient to conduct these measurements infrequently, since only larger changes in distance create different pixel mappings to the augmented reality stream. For rotations, it is possible to track the incident angle of the modulated light sources during communication with low latency.

Figure 5. With 3D-location-aware optical communication, electronic devices can be embedded into augmented reality. A Time-of-Flight sensor is able to combine depth measurements with pixel coordinates (x_T, y_T) to calculate the 3D coordinates (x_D, y_D, z_D) of the augmented device. Using calibrated camera parameters, it is possible to transform and project the 3D position to the image coordinates (x_C, y_C) of an augmented image stream

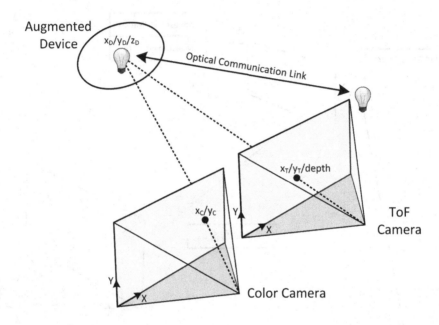

CASE STUDIES ON OPTICAL LOCALIZATION AND TRACKING SYSTEMS

As of 2016, the upcoming applications for high-performance localization and tracking solutions are found in the automotive field in automated driving systems, and in consumer electronics in augmented and virtual reality devices. In this section, we introduce such high-performance localization and tracking mechanisms and how they already found their way into products.

Google Tango

Google started Tango with the goal to provide smartphones and tablets a human-like understanding of the environment. The central ambition is to produce a reference design and software to enable smartphone and tablet vendors to implement Tango's functionality into their devices. A large part of Tango is to support application developers by providing support, tools and development kits. A Tango enabled mobile device is able to record and locate itself in a 3D map of its environment and track its pose at a very high update rate. This enables indoor localization and augmented reality. Google categorizes the aspects of its platform into motion tracking, area learning and depth perception. These main features are mutually dependent from each other and rely on a sophisticated software and hardware implementation.

Motion Tracking

Project Tango devices feature 6-dof motion tracking. While current mobile devices are often capable of orientation tracking, by using gyroscopic magnetic and gravity sensors, Tango adds sophisticated 3D pose tracking. This is realized with a sensor fusion approach, including inertial sensors and a motion tracking camera. The motion tracking camera has a very wide field of view and records black and white images. Tango detects features and uses frame-to-frame feature correspondences to detect camera movements. The data from the inertial sensors complements the data of the motion tracking camera to receive a higher update rate and to increase robustness during strong motions and featureless images. The outcome from motion tracking is continuously available pose information, containing the position and orientation of the device, but neither provides a reference coordinate system or localization in a larger context.

Area Learning

The goal of area learning is to build a 3D model of the environment. This is accomplished by a simultaneous mapping and localization approach. Data from the color, depth and motion tracking sensors are combined to create a 3D presentation of the environment. Image features which are especially unique are saved as landmarks. According to Google, these landmarks are saved about every 50 cm of tracked camera displacement. Landmarks along with the available 3D data enable fast localization within previously recorded datasets. The captured area learning data can be exported and stored into area description files (ADF).

These files enable Tango devices to remember the environment without re-scanning. It is also possible to use externally provided area description files for localization. An example would be indoor navigation system, where the building was initially recorded with Tango. Waypoints for navigation could be placed into such an area description file to directly support navigation.

The area description file along with navigation information is then provided to Google Tango enabled devices, and they are able to precisely locate themselves in the coordinate system of the provided file.

Navigation and location based services are possible, if the ADF is associated to mapping data.

Jeon et al. (2016) enhance this concept, by scanning the indoor environment with a 3D laserscanner, and use their own method to build a database. Google Tango enabled devices can use the database for localization, but also to push new data to the database. This enables to update the database automatically with change to the environments.

Depth Understanding

The latest iteration of Google Tango incorporates a depth sensor based on Time-of-Flight technology. This sensor is important for area learning, but also gives the Tango platform an immediate understanding of the geometric context. Since Time-of-Flight is a dense depth sensing method, it is possible to gather 3D information on texture-less flat surfaces. This helps to create a denser map during area learning, but also enables the augmented reality applications which are one of the most significant selling points of the platform. With depth understanding, it is possible to integrate virtual objects into the augmented world. Besides gaming and other entertainment purposes, depth sensing enables to measure distances without measuring tape, and even preview furniture in its determined surrounding before buying.

Head-Mounted Virtual Reality Devices

Virtual reality is currently the most demanding application for indoor positioning and tracking systems. The demand for operating range of consumer-grade head mounted devices (HMD) is limited, but the precision, update rate and latency are critical. User experience motion sickness, if there is a discrepancy between their motion and visual stimuli. A common term is the motion to photon delay, which is the time from a user's movement to the point, when the displays in the HMD update their images to accommodate the movement.

The main measure to reduce this delay is a high display frame-rate. This is currently 90 frames per second in the current top products such as the Oculus Rift and the HTC Vive. On the other hand, the tracking sensors require an even higher update rate. Since visual output and tracking are usually not synchronized, a higher tracking update rate enables to associate frames with better tracking results.

The common denominator of current VR tracking systems is that they are based on sensor fusion approaches, using MEMS-based inertial sensors for a high update rates in combination with optical sensors for positioning and error correction.

For the optical tracking part, there exist two major paradigms, as illustrated in Figure 6. While the exact definition is debated, the main difference is the position of the optical localization device (Foxlin, 2002). An inside-out tracking system has the localization device mounted on the device, while outside-in systems have a stationary tracking device, facing the tracked object. Fixed reference points are used to localize the device within a given coordinate system. The fixed locations can be either active beacons, or passive visual markers. Even normal visual features might be sufficient in future iterations of HMD tracking systems. In 2016, Oculus invited journalists to demonstrate a prototype, based on Inside-out tracking and just using visual features of a typical living room environment (Orland, 2016).

The advantage of inside-out tracking is that the system is not limited to certain boundaries, as long as enough reference points are within the field of view of the tracking sensors. A problem of practical

Figure 6. The difference between outside-in and inside-out tracking. 2D-projections (x, y) of features or active markers with known relations $\vec{d}$, are used to determine the 6-dof pose of the tracking device. In inside-out tracking, the tracking device observes the static environment. In outside-in tracking systems a stationary base-station observes the device and forwards the pose over a communication link

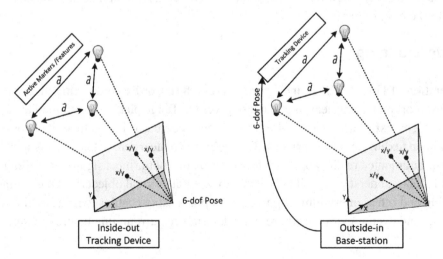

implementations however is that usually with 2D image sensors, only incident angles of the line-of-sight to the reference points can be measured. Since it is not feasible in consumer electronic, to let the user calibrate the positions of the reference points, the points need to be located. This can be achieved by image to image correspondences, but requires view disparity and is subject to inaccuracy. Another reason, why as of 2016, inside-out tracking is not used in virtual reality is that the pose tracking precision of active visual markers depends on the distribution of the markers. At least three markers are required to be in sight at the same time, and they must not be arranged in a straight line.

An outside-in tracking system has one or more localization sensors mounted on a fixed point, while the tracked objects are observed. This currently dominant tracking paradigm can be categorized into the following principles:

Tracking With LED Markers and Image Sensors

This technology is currently used by Oculus Rift, OSVR and PlayStation VR. These outside-in tracking systems are based on 2D infrared cameras, which sense active markers on the HMD. It case of the Oculus Rift, these markers consist of LED lights, which are toggled by the tracking system for identification. Since the positions of these markers on the HMD are fixed and known, finding the pose of the head-mounted device can be mapped to the perspective-n-point problem. This problem describes finding the 6-dof pose of a set of points in 3D space, by analyzing 2D projections on images, gathered by a calibrated camera. While the pose can be determined by sensing three or more points, the robustness and precision are enhanced by additional points. The problem with outside-in tracking is the stationary position of the camera. This limits the usage to viewport of the tracking camera. Due to limited sensor resolution, the precision decreases with distance limiting the tracking solution to medium sized rooms. This can however be counteracted by using multiple tracking cameras.

Tracking With Laser Beacons and Photodiodes

This tracking solution is used by HTC Vive HMD in its Lighthouse tracking system. It is based on photosensitive element instead of image sensors. These elements are distributed among the surface of the device. Two base stations are positioned in front of the user. Each feature two rotating lasers, which scan the X and Y axis of the room at precisely 60 Hz. A synchronization pulse sequence is broadcasted to all sensors. Then each element counts the time until the laser beam reaches its position. With the timing information, it is possible to reconstruct the angle of the laser, when it reached the element. By using two lasers, it is possible to triangulate the position of the element. Using the 3D positions of all elements, it is possible to determine the 6-dof pose of the HMD. The advantages of this system, are that it has an increased range, minimum computation overhead, potentially lower latency, and the possibility to track multiple devices without additional effort in the base stations (Deyle, 2016). The update-rate however is too low for optical tracking alone, and thus sensor fusion with inertial sensors is necessary. Another advantage is that the base-station is independent of the tracked device. The positional information could be calculated on the tracked device itself.

The scanning principle of Lighthouse also permits 3rd parties to use the base stations to develop their own tracking solutions. Since inexpensive microcontrollers and photodiodes can be used, this tracking system has the potential to be widely used for localization and positioning in areas like internet of things or smart-homes. State-of-the-art HMDs are dedicated to electronic entertainment. The devices are localized by the tracking system into a coordinate system, defined by the base stations. This pose is then transformed into the coordinate system of the virtual world. If the pose of the base station within a mapping system of the real world is known, virtual reality tracking systems can provide high fidelity localization.

Another aspect is awareness of the immediate surroundings. Virtual worlds usually do not have boundaries, so the users need to be prevented from stumbling over objects or colliding with walls. An elegant solution would be to detect these obstacles by using a depth camera. The first generation of consumer grade HMDs does not feature such a camera, but let the user manually define virtual boundaries before usage.

VEHICLE LOCALIZATION

This section briefly introduces some special use-cases where different forms of localization and tracking are employed in the very important vehicular context.

Fleet Management

A company owing a number of cars (for example a taxi company or a truck company) can strongly benefit from knowing the current position of all their cars in order to improve the offered service. Since such systems do not require a very precisely measured location they get along with a GPS device. Those systems are inexpensive and are currently widely used for fleet management, since they can be built up using a mobile phone with GPS capability. A famous example is the taxi company Uber, which displays the current position of the closest available vehicles via their smartphone application. Additionally, the GPS in the car replaces the taximeter, since it tracks the actually driven distance and time.

Assisted Driving Functions

Some assisted driving functions require environment data of the direct surroundings, for example the detection of other cars and objects for parking assistance or collision avoidance (Winner, 2015). For that purpose, sensors for object detection are mounted on modern vehicles. Those include radar sensors, LiDAR sensors, ultrasonic sensors and cameras. Since each of those sensors has shortcomings in certain environments, typically more than one sensor technology is implemented and considered by the assisted driving system.

Other assisted driving functions require the vehicle to not only know its direct surroundings, but also know the current position on the map. It can be very beneficial for a collision avoidance system to have information about the current context (for example an urban area or a motorway) (Levinson, 2008). This can easily be acquired using GPS localization.

Then there are also systems which communicate with infrastructure objects (Vehicle-to-infrastructure, V2I) or other cars (Vehicle-to-vehicle, V2V) in order to gain additional knowledge of the surrounding environment. This can be information about dangers on the upcoming road, the timing of the next traffic lights or other relevant information for the vehicle. Today, the information is communicated using the mobile network or a Wi-Fi-like short range network. Yet, the presented novel optical line-of-sight communication techniques may be used in future.

Automated Driving

Although fully autonomous driving is not reality yet, automakers are putting a lot of effort in that topic in order to preserve their position in the market. Localization of a vehicle using only the GPS is considered to be insufficient for the use in (partwise) automated driving systems (Bar, 2014). The current approaches depend on up-to-date HD maps and the exact position of the vehicle within that map. The exact position in addition with the data from multiple environmental perception sensors enables the potential for fully autonomous driving.

The solely use of current GPS systems for localization is not precise and reliable enough for direct mapping into HD maps. Therefore, the issue can be resolved by using the environmental perception sensors (radar, LiDAR, cameras) of the vehicle. For instance, Time-of-Flight based sensors can measure the distance to certain points of interest in the environment and align them with the corresponding points within the HD maps. Using the inertial sensors and odometric data, it is possible to keep tracking the exact position on the map even if the GPS is in a non-functional state (for example in a tunnel).

FUTURE CONCEPTS

Inside-Out Tracking Without Active Markers

Vision based inside-out tracking has is already extensively been used in augmented reality. Google Tango, Microsoft HoloLens and Qualcomm Vuforia are well known examples. In these applications, the required latency and update rate allows feature based tracking and localization. In augmented reality, latency is more tolerable, than in virtual reality, because it does not cause motion sickness. The 2D imaging pipeline of an inside-out tracking system introduces such latency which creates a massive technical hurdle in high fidelity tracking and localization applications such as virtual reality. Despite these circumstances, Oculus presented a working prototype in 2016, using four motion capture cameras in order to provide 6-dof tracking without requiring any peripherals.

Position Forwarding to IoT devices

With an increasing number of 6-dof location-aware devices on the consumer market, it is possible to use image sensors along with optical communication to detect and localize embedded devices of all kind. An example could be a smartphone equipped with a location-aware AR platform such as Google Tango and an optical communication solution. By sensing the presence of embedded IoT devices, it would be possible to localize them and use a communication channel to directly forward them their position. Potential applications involve secure device pairing, location-aware temperature control, geometry-aware audio systems or all kinds of intelligent sensors. If desired, surveillance cameras could be provided their pose in order to be able to reliably track persons throughout buildings.

In professional settings such as fabrication, workshops or warehouses, the location of tools and parts can be determined by using optical communication along with positioning.

Figure 7. A device is aware of its own location $\vec{L}$ and orientation $\vec{p}$ is able to localize embedded IoT devices in 3D. It can forward the localization information via optical communication.

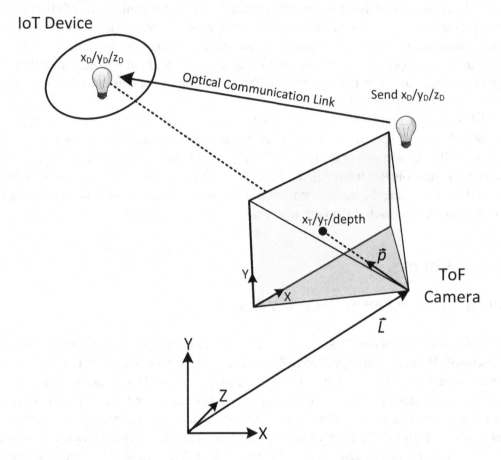

CONCLUSION

This chapter discusses concepts, methods and opportunities for optical localization of cyber-physical systems and future IoT devices. A focus is placed on Time-of-Flight depth imaging systems, and how they can benefit existing and future localization systems. Examples of high-performance localization and tracking systems in existing products are introduced in form of case-studies.

As the field of visible light communication shows, optical communication is a crucial aspect of modern optical localization systems. We introduce our own location-aware optical communication approach, based on Time-of-Flight depth sensors. With this approach, it is going to be possible to localize communication partners in 3D with high accuracy and very low latency. We are also confident that 3D-location aware optical communication will close the gap between augmented reality and IoT, by enabling embedded devices to participate in an augmented world.

REFERENCES

Bar, A. R. (2014). Recent progress in road and lane detection a survey. *Machine Vision and Applications*, 25(3), 727–745.

Biswas, J., & Veloso, M. (2012). Depth Camera based Localization and Navigation for Indoor Mobile Robots. In *Proceedings of IEEE International Conference on Robotics and Automation*. doi:10.1109/ICRA.2012.6224766

Boger, Y. (2016). (OSVR). Retrieved 11 21, 2016, from The VRguy's Blog: http://vrguy.blogspot.de/

Bouguet, J.-Y. (2016, 12 11). Camera Calibration Toolbox for Matlab. Retrieved from https://www.vision.caltech.edu/bouguetj/calib_doc/#start

Campo-Jimenez, G., Martin Perandones, J., & Lopez-Hernandez, F. (2013). A VLC-based beacon location system for mobile applications. In *Proceedings of the International Conference on Localization and GNSS* (pp. 25–27). Turin: IEEE. doi:10.1109/ICL-GNSS.2013.6577276

Censi, A., Strubel, J., Brandli, C., Delbruck, T., & Scaramuzza, D. (2013). Low-latency localization by Active LED Markers tracking using a Dynamic Vision Sensor. In *Proceedings of the IEEE/RSJ International Conference on Intelligent Robots and Systems 2013*. doi:10.1109/IROS.2013.6696456

Chetverikov, D., Eichhardt, I., & Jankó, Z. (2015). *A Brief Survey of Image-Based Depth Upsampling*. KEPAF.

Dai, L., Zhang, F., Mei, X., & Zhang, X. (2015). Fast Minimax Path-Based Joint Depth Interpolation. *IEEE Signal Processing Letters*, 22(5), 623–627. doi:10.1109/LSP.2014.2365527

Deyle, T. (2016, 12 11). Valve's "Lighthouse" Tracking System May Be Big News for Robotics. *Hizook*. Retrieved from http://www.hizook.com/blog/2015/05/17/valves-lighthouse-tracking-system-may-be-big-news-robotics

Dhome, K. M.-B.-A. (2015). Bundle adjustment revisited for SLAM with RGBD sensors. In *Proceedings of the 14th IAPR International Conference on Machine Vision Applications (MVA)*.

Do, T.-H., & Yoo, M. (2016). An in-Depth Survey of Visible Light Communication Based Positioning Systems. *Sensors (Basel, Switzerland)*, 16(5), 678. doi:10.3390/s16050678 PMID:27187395

Ercan, A. T. (2015). Fusing Inertial Sensor Data in an Extended Kalman Filter for 3D Camera Tracking. *IEEE Transactions on Image Processing*, 24(2), 538-548.

Ferstl, D., Reinbacher, C., Ranftl, R., Ruether, M., & Bischof, H. (2013). Image Guided Depth Upsampling Using Anisotropic Total Generalized Variation. In *Proceedings of the IEEE International Conference on Computer Vision*, Sydney (pp. 993-1000).

Foxlin, G. W. (2002). Motion tracking: No silver bullet, but a respectable arsenal. *IEEE Computer Graphics and Applications*, 22(6), 24–38. doi:10.1109/MCG.2002.1046626

Github. (2016, 12 11). *DIY Position Tracking using HTC Vive's Lighthouse*. Retrieved 11 21, 2016, from https://github.com/ashtuchkin/vive-diy-position-sensor

Jeon, C. J., Ji, M., Kim, J., Park, S., & Cho, Y. (2016). Design of positioning DB automatic update method using Google tango tablet for image based localization system. In *Proceedings of the Eighth International Conference on Ubiquitous and Future Networks (ICUFN)*, Vienna (pp. 644-646). doi:10.1109/ICUFN.2016.7537112

Jovicic, A. (2016). *Qualcomm Lumicast: A high accuracy indoor positioning system based on visible light communication*. Qualcomm Flarion Technologies.

Kopf, J., Cohen, M. F., & Lischinski, D. (2007). *Joint Bilateral Upsampling*. SIGGRAPH. doi:10.1145/1275808.1276497

Lee, S., & Jung, S. (2012). Location awareness using Angle-of-arrival based circular-PD-array for visible light. In *Proceedings of the 18th Asia-Pacific Conference on Communications (APCC)*, Jeju Island (pp. 480–485).

Lepetit, V., Arth, C., Pirchheim, C., Ventura, J., & Schmalstieg, D. (2015). Instant Outdoor Localization and SLAM Initialization. In *Proceedings of the International Symposium on Mixed and Augmented Reality*.

Levinson, J. M. (2008). Map-Based Precision Vehicle Localization in Urban Environments. *Robotics: Science and Systems*, *III*, 121–128.

Liu, M., Qiu, K., Che, F., Li, S., Hussain, B., Wu, L., & Yue, C. (2014). Towards indoor localization using visible light. In *Proceedings of the International Conference on Intelligent Robots and Systems (IROS)*, Chicago (pp. 143–148).

Mauro Biagi, S. P. (2015). LAST: A Framework to Localize, Access, Schedule, and Transmit in Indoor VLC Systems. *Journal of Lightwave Technology*, *33*(9), 1872–1887. doi:10.1109/JLT.2015.2405674

Newcombe, R. A., Izadi, S., Hilliges, O., Molyneaux, D., Kim, D., Davison, A. J., & Fitzgibbon, A. et al. (2011). KinectFusion: Real-time 3D Reconstruction and Interaction Using a Moving Depth Camera. In *Proceedings of the 24th Annual ACM Symposium on User Interface Software and Technology*.

Orland, K. (2016). Oculus working on wireless headset with "inside-out tracking". *ars Technica*. Retrieved from http://arstechnica.com/gaming/2016/10/oculus-working-on-wireless-headset-with-inside-out-tracking/

Ovren, H., Forssen, P.-E., & Törnqvist, D. (2013). Why Would I Want a Gyroscope on my RGB-D Sensor? In *Proceedings of the IEEE Workshop on Robot Vision (WORV)*. doi:10.1109/WORV.2013.6521916

Plank, H., Holweg, G., Herndl, T., & Druml, N. (2016). *High performance Time-of-Flight and color sensor fusion with image-guided depth super resolution. In Design, Automation & Test in Europe Conference & Exhibition* (pp. 1213–1218). Dresden: DATE.

Roberts, R. D. (2013). A MIMO protocol for camera communications (CamCom) using undersampled frequency shift ON-OFF keying (UFSOOK) In Proceedings of the Globecom Workshops (pp. 1052–1057). doi:10.1109/GLOCOMW.2013.6825131

Scharstein, D., R. S. (2003). High-accuracy stereo depth maps using structured light. In *Proc. IEEE Computer Society Conference on Computer Vision and Pattern Recognition* (pp. 1–195-1–202). doi:10.1109/CVPR.2003.1211354

Shen, Y. L. (2015). Dense visual-inertial odometry for tracking of aggressive motions. In *Proceedings of the IEEE International Conference on Robotics and Biomimetics (ROBIO)*.

Steinbrücker, F., Sturm, J., & Cremers, D. (2011). Real-time visual odometry from dense RGB-D images. In *Proceedings of the 2011 IEEE International Conference on Computer Vision Workshops (ICCV Workshops)*, Barcelona. doi:10.1109/ICCVW.2011.6130321

Takai, I., Ito, S., Yasutomi, K., Kagawa, K., Andoh, M., & Kawahito, S. (2013). LED and CMOS image sensor based optical wireless communication system for automotive applications. *IEEE Photonics Journal*, 5(5), 6801418. doi:10.1109/JPHOT.2013.2277881

Tobias, M. H. (2005). *Robust 3D Measurement with PMD Sensors*. Zürich: Range Imaging Day.

Törnqvist, H. O. (2013). Why would i want a gyroscope on my RGB-D sensor? In *Proceedings of the 2013 IEEE Workshop on Robot Vision (WORV)*.

Vedaldi, A., & Soatto, S. (2008). Localizing objects with smart dictionaries.

Wikitude. (2016). Wikitude GmbH. Retrieved 12 05, 2016, from http://www.wikitude.com/

Winner, H. H. (2015). *Handbuch Fahrer- assistenzsysteme*.

Woodman, O. J. (2007). An introduction to inertial navigation.

Yu, J., & Zhao, J. (2012). *Segmentation of depth image using graph cut. In Fuzzy Systems and Knowledge Discovery* (pp. 1934–1938). FSKD.

Yuan, W., Howard, R., Dana, K., Raskar, R., Ashok, A., Gruteser, M., & Man-dayam, N. (2014). Phase messaging method for time-of-flight cameras. In *Proceedings of the Conference on Computational Photography (ICCP)*.

Zhu, J., Wang, L., Yang, R., Davis, J. E., & Pan, Z. (2011). Reliability fusion of time-of-flight depth and stereo geometry for high quality depth maps. *IEEE Transactions on Pattern Analysis and Machine Intelligence*, 33(7), 1400–1414. PMID:20820074

KEY TERMS AND DEFINITIONS

Active Markers: A light source which serves as point of orientation for tracking and localization systems. Infrared light is predominately used, since it is invisible to the human eye.

Beacon: An optical beacon is an active light source which transmits its ID or position to the localization device.

Degree of Freedom: The position of an object in 3D space has a degree of freedom for position on each 3D axis. The orientation of an object has also three degrees of freedom which are the rotations around each 3D axle.

Head-Mounted Device: An electronic device, which is mounted on the head of a user. In the current form, either information is blended into the field view user (augmented reality), or the field of view is replaced by displays, simulating a three dimensional space (virtual reality).

Line-of-Sight Communication: Communication partners need to face each other for data exchange.

Pose: Description of the geometric position and orientation of an object. A relative pose can be used to transfer objects to different coordinates systems or to describe movements.

Time-of-Flight: In context of 3D sensing systems, this refers to the time photons need to travel to the measurement point and back to the device. This time is proportional to the measured distance.

Chapter 2
Ubiquitous IoT in the Automotive Domain:
Decentralized Adaptation

Laszlo Z. Varga
ELTE, Hungary

ABSTRACT

Ubiquitous IoT systems open new ground in the automotive domain. With the advent of autonomous vehicles, there will be several actors that adapt to changes in traffic, and decentralized adaptation will be a new type of issue that needs to be studied. This chapter investigates the effects of adaptive route planning when real-time online traffic information is exploited. Simulation results show that if the agents selfishly optimize their actions, then in some situations the ubiquitous IoT system may fluctuate and the agents may be worse off with real-time data than without real-time data. The proposed solution to this problem is to use anticipatory techniques, where the future state of the environment is predicted from the intentions of the agents. This chapter concludes with this conjecture: if simultaneous decision making is prevented, then intention-propagation-based prediction can limit the fluctuation and help the ubiquitous IoT system converge to the Nash equilibrium.

INTRODUCTION

Ubiquity and interconnection are important in information systems, and they are behind many concepts like pervasive computing, ubiquitous computing, ambient intelligence and the internet of things (IoT). IoT is a concept of everyday objects having built-in sensors to gather data across a network and then helping the IoT system and the users to take actions based on that data. Such systems are developed in the hope that we can derive economic benefit from analyzing and utilizing the generated data streams in several application areas. IoT systems open new ground in the automotive domain by introducing entirely new services to the traditional concept of a car. The connected, smart car provides a way to stay in touch with the world during drive time. There is a possibility for new kind of infotainment services and connected car applications to provide better services for drivers and the automotive industry as well, as Table 1

DOI: 10.4018/978-1-5225-2845-6.ch002

Table 1. There are several application scenarios in the automotive domain to exploit IoT capabilities

IoT Sensor Capabilities	IoT Innovative Services
• Vehicle sensors • Real-time car operation tracking • Vehicle location tracking • Fuel consumption tracking • Speed measurement • Real-time vehicle monitoring • Fault detection, testing • Alerts • Seatbelt sensor • Acceleration • Driver attention monitoring	• Vehicle scheduling • Speed control • Vehicle usage analytics • Smart car leasing • Usage-based insurance • Fleet management • Traffic management • Remote diagnostics • Automated maintenance scheduling • Maintenance history analytics • Acceleration control • Anti-sleepiness warning • In-lane positioning • Navigation • Location-based services • Driver-assist applications • News and entertainment • Integration with smart home • Car-on-demand • Car security services • Over-the-air updates

shows a few of them. The novel applications include fleet management based on data collection via embedded software, data management in the cloud, and data analytics. The predictive maintenance can be based on the monitoring of the state of the vehicle, and the analytics can be based on cloud-enabled platforms to provide new services to car manufacturers, maintenance and service companies, insurance companies, and entertainment providers.

Automotive manufacturers and suppliers can utilize these IoT services to diagnose vehicle malfunctions on the road. This direct and immediate information can be used to avoid costly recalls by understanding product quality and rapidly assessing safety issues in order to optimize production. Telecommunication companies can develop new connected applications and services, which may be consumed either in vehicles or remotely through smartphone apps. Better driving experience can be delivered by exploiting information about the location, movement, and status of vehicles by analyzing map context and driver behavior. Non-traditional automotive industry participants may provide many of these novel services.

The novel services mentioned in Table 1 are mainly centralized services, in the sense that there is a single organization that collects data from the IoT sensors, analyses it, and then takes actions. Because there is only one actor that senses the environment and takes actions, this is centralized adaptation. This model suits well the traditional automotive industry.

Ubiquitous IoT helps the development of self-driving cars as well. Autonomous vehicles can detect their environment, using different sensors like radar, LIDAR, GPS, computer vision and shared smart phone data. The planning unit of the autonomous vehicle merges and interprets the sensor information to determine the necessary control actions to navigate the car and avoid obstacles. Autonomous vehicle technology is expected to provide several benefits like those shown in Table 2. In order to achieve these benefits, the autonomous vehicles have to act collectively. Because there are several actors that sense the environment and take actions, this is decentralized adaptation.

With the advent of autonomous vehicles, decentralized adaptation will be a new type of issue and it needs to be investigated. Humans and software agents are working together in such decentralized

Table 2. There are several application scenarios for autonomous vehicles to exploit IoT capabilities

Autonomous Vehicle IoT Capabilities	Benefits of Autonomous Vehicles
• Environment Sensing (Perception) • Radar, Ultrasonic, Video camera, Laser Scanner (LIDAR) • Floating Car Data, Mobile Phones or GPS • Vehicle to Vehicle interactions (V2V) • Vehicle to Infrastructure interaction (V2I) • Vehicle to Environment interactions (V2E)	• The mobility of the elderly and disabled people can be increased • Traffic flow can be more efficient and congestions might be avoided • Finding urban parking places can be faster • Fuel efficiency can be increased • The travel time can be used for other activities

autonomous vehicle environments. The critical challenge (Çolak et al., 2016) is using the generated big amount of real-time data in a way that the overall decentralized adaptive human-agent collective benefits from the instant availability of information. The availability of real-time data changes the behavior of the active entities (agents) of the system as well because they try to adapt to the observed situation. Classical autonomous vehicle research focuses on how to control a single vehicle to get to its destination. The control of a single vehicle needs adaptation to the environment. If there are several active entities in the environment and all of them try to adapt to the observed and predicted changes, then the overall system may demonstrate strange behavior as well. Just imagine two people going in the opposite direction on a corridor, and then they try to avoid a possible collision by trying to bypass in the same direction at the same time. Sometimes there is a hesitation until they finally settle who goes in which direction to avoid the collision. In order to foster the development of practical ubiquitous IoT applications in the automotive domain for decentralized adaptation, researchers have to prove that we are better off with real-time IoT data than without.

This chapter will discuss different models, methods and challenges, which are investigated in a decentralized autonomous vehicle environment where things have embedded intelligence and sensor capabilities. In these environments, autonomous adaptive entities play an important role. The Autonomic Road Transport Support Systems initiative (McCluskey et al., 2016) studied the models and methods applied in autonomous transport systems.

Next section will overview methods and models identified in the Autonomic Road Transport Support Systems initiative. The second next section will discuss decentralized adaptation. The simulation of the game theory model of adaptation will be presented, and the challenge posed by the instant availability of real-time data in ubiquitous IoT systems will be discussed. The third next section will present decentralized adaptation with intention-propagation-based prediction as a solution to the problem presented in the previous section. Finally, future research directions will be projected in the form of a conjecture and the chapter will be concluded.

Autonomic Road Transport Support System Models and Methods

IoT software systems applied in transportation nowadays are getting more and more complex and there is a need for investigating their engineering methods. IoT software systems in transportation have self-managing properties as well. The aim of the Autonomic Road Transport Support Systems initiative (McCluskey et al., 2016) was to bring together technologies and research expertise from several disciplines to support the engineering of self-managing autonomous software systems. In the following selected outcomes of the initiative will be overviewed.

Simulation Testbed

Transportation systems are complex systems, and the creation of a complete formal model is often very difficult. In order to study subtle details, it is often better to create a simulation environment. Simulation systems use different modelling paradigms to deal with the complexity of transportation systems. Agent-based simulations (Uhrmacher et al., 2010) are well-established approaches for analyzing the behavior of complex socio-technical systems because multi-agent technology has already been successfully applied in different application areas (Cockburn et al., 1992; Hajnal et al., 2007; Campana et al., 2008). The agent-based simulation testbed, called Flexible Mobility Services Testbed (Čertický et al., 2016) was designed to help research oriented investigations by providing a universal experimentation in the transportation domain. The users can experiment with several mechanisms and algorithms for the management and control of autonomous transportation systems in order to select the best configurations by assessing the performance in different scenarios. The testbed can be used to implement testbed control algorithms, to define experimentation scenarios, to execute the simulations, to visualize the execution of the simulation, and finally to analyze and interpret the simulation results.

Identification of Undesired Adaptive Behavior

Because transportation systems are complex systems, the designers of classic road transport support systems may not know every possible situation in advance, and they may have difficulties to design a system that can adapt to changes in their environment without human intervention. The goal of autonomous adaptation is to adapt to unpredictable situations in the environment. The performance of the system can be measured with an objective function, and the goal of the adaptive system is to maximize the objective function (Schumann, 2016). The adaptation is undesirable if the value of the objective function decreases during the runtime of the adaptive system. The system would be optimal if the undesirable adaptive behavior was avoided in all of the potential operating environments.

If there is no formal model, then adaptive behavior is empirically investigated in different simulated environments with different simulation settings. It is not known in advance which setting of the simulation parameters will result in undesirable adaptive behavior, therefore a lot of simulation runs have to be executed. (Schumann, 2016) proposes a modified version of the approach of (Lattner et al., 2010) for an automated simulation model modification. The systematic simulation parameter setting starts from a base scenario, which is then evolved. A modifier function transforms a configuration of the simulation model parameters into another configuration. The modifier function creates a neighborhood relation between two configurations of the simulation model parameters by typically modifying one parameter. The neighborhood relations create a graph of possible worlds. Starting from the base scenario, the proposed approach systematically searches this graph by applying different sequences of modifiers to the base scenario.

Organic Control

(Sommer et al., 2016) propose an organic computing approach to resilient traffic management. The self-organized and self-adapting system is based on autonomic computing (Kephart et al., 2003) and organic computing (Müller-Schloer, 2004) principles. The autonomic and organic computing methods were created because the increasing complexity of technical systems can hardly be managed by traditional methods.

The organic computing approach transfers the design time processes to the system's responsibility at runtime, making the decentralized system self-optimizing and self-organized. Organic computing systems are expected to be robust, adaptive and flexible. In traffic management, decentralization means that each traffic object (e.g. traffic lamp, intersection control, etc.) has a self-controlled component, which senses its local environment and takes actions. The self-control of the traffic object means that the control strategy is adapted to the observed changes in the environment. The self-adaptation process is optimized with safety oriented learning mechanisms. Communication and collaboration between neighboring traffic objects ensures that self-adaptation is coordinated and higher-level goals can be achieved. The control strategies can be changed proactively in order to make the system resilient.

Reinforcement Learning Algorithms

Traffic congestion is a major issue that might be solved with ubiquitous IoT devices, which serve as basis for smart cities. A relatively inexpensive way to improve traffic control is to improve the efficiency of the existing road network. The optimization of the usage of the existing road network can be done for example by using adaptive traffic signal controllers. Adaptive traffic signal controllers are needed because setting the optimal traffic light timings is too complex to be solved by humans. The application of reinforcement learning to traffic signal control was proposed by (Mannion et al., 2016) in order to continuously improve the performance of traffic control signals by adaptation to changes in traffic demand.

The traffic control problem is considered by (Mannion et al., 2016) as a multi-agent system, where each agent is responsible for controlling the traffic light sequences of a single junction. It is not feasible to apply an approach where a single agent would control all junctions because that would not scale to large networks. In the multi-agent model, there is multi-agent reinforcement learning. The reinforcement learning model for large-scale transportation networks is a partially observable Markov decision process because agents may not know every detail about the environment.

The major challenge in multi-agent reinforcement learning is the implementation of the co-ordination and information sharing between agents, as observed by for example (El-Tantawy et al., 2013) and (Kuyer et al., 2008). Like in game theory, as discussed later in this chapter, the effect of a single agent's actions on the environment is also influenced by the actions of other agents. Single agents pursue their own goals by maximizing their own reward function. The basic problem of multi-agent system manifests here as well: a control policy learnt by an agent may result in a local optimum, but may have a negative effect on traffic flows in the network as a whole. Therefore, reinforcement learning algorithms must implement co-ordination or information sharing mechanisms in order to be relevant for real applications.

Multilevel Formalization

Multilevel theory approaches problems by decomposing the main problem into sub-problems and solves the lower level problems by mathematical programming. This divide and conquer approach allows the original complex optimization problem to be reduced to a set of low order optimization sub-problems. This way the solution of the complex problem is the sum of the vector of the sub-problem solutions. The higher-level sub-problems influence the lower level sub-problems when the sub-problem solutions are integrated together to create the solution of the global solution of the original problem. Many practical problems are formulated in terms of multilevel optimization models (Stackelberg, 1952). The multilevel optimization problem is hard to be solved as observed by for example (Bard et al., 1998) and (Dempe,

2000). Even in the simplest version of two level optimization, it becomes non-convex and/or non-smooth and belongs to the class of global optimization (Dempe, 2000).

A multilevel hierarchical approach can be applied for the traffic management as proposed by (Stoilov et al., 2016). The multilevel approach is good for autonomous traffic control because it decomposes the global problem and coordinates the different control subsystems. The multilevel optimization makes it possible to order and consciously link a sequence of operations, which results in a hierarchy of self-organizing systems: control, optimization, adaptation, and self-organization (in the order from bottom to top). This hierarchical order can be used as a framework to formalize the operation rules in autonomous systems.

A multilevel hierarchical system may cope with the different aspects of the traffic modelling, control and optimization. It may also integrate different traffic characteristics and control influences as a complex argument of a common optimization problem. With this integration, the traffic control can operate as an autonomous system, the different control influences can be obtained in an automatic way.

Decision Support System

The tool TIMIPLAN was developed by (García et al., 2016) to solve multi-modal transportation problems. The inputs of the tool are the positions of the set of all available resources and a number of services to be performed. The tool generates a plan with actions to be performed: where to load the goods in containers; where to unload the goods; the assignment of resources (trucks, containers, ships, trains, etc.) to goods, and the itinerary of the assigned resources to achieve all goals. The tool can take into account several constraints, like pick-up and delivery times or driving hours, as well as taking into account all related costs. The objective is to minimize the cost of servicing all the daily requests.

The planner of TIMIPLAN combines Operations Research and Automated Planning techniques (García et al., 2013). If constraints and goals that cannot be formalized explicitly, or if the plans contain unexpected failures, then human experts can interact with TIMIPLAN. The system incorporates a simulator that allows the analysis of potential plan alternatives generated by the user.

Validation of Communication with Simulation

A concept of integrated multi-agent simulation platform of cooperative cars is proposed by (Schaefer et al., 2016) for the validation of autonomic car-to-car systems. Cooperative driver models implement the multi-agent simulation of cooperative cars. The system features realistic drive because it integrates a drive simulator. The Human Machine Interface manager between the cooperative system and the driver makes human-in-the-loop simulation testing and validation possible. The system can integrate different drive simulators and different car control strategies. The platform can simulate several scenarios. The lane change maneuver scenario was validated on the system first.

Decentralized adaptation

Ubiquitous IoT, the proliferation of information and communication technologies in everyday life, opens new possibilities in intelligent traffic systems as well. Most of the car drivers have smart phones equipped with mobile internet and GPS, the latest cars have built-in internet access and the road infrastructure is also connected to online information. Information and communication technologies allow that cars and drivers can get up-to-date online traffic related information from the traffic infrastructure and, in addition, share with each other what they experience on the road. Navigation software can be found in many of the cars, and these navigation systems use more and more live information on the current status of the traffic in order to optimize the route of the cars and avoid congestion. Many of the navigation systems use real-time, online and shared traffic information. These navigation systems are called ubiquitous IoT navigation systems because traffic participants share real-time traffic information from different sensors with each other to self-optimize their route. There are navigation systems like Waze (Waze, 2016) and Google Maps, which have ubiquitous IoT navigation features because they have real-time online traffic information generated by traffic participants.

It is known that individually self-optimizing travel routes does not necessarily result in globally optimal traffic and the travel time of each participant may be longer than the optimal. This phenomenon is known as the price of anarchy and its properties were extensively investigated by the 2012 Gödel prize (Gödel Prize, 2012) winners Roughgarden and Tardos, who provided results on the relationship between central control and selfish routing in networked traffic (Roughgarden et al., 2002). They investigated the old conundrum in transportation science known as the Braess paradox (Braess, 1968) (described later in this chapter in the "Problem Scenario" subsection). These investigations revealed important basic properties of traffic networks. However, their algorithmic game theory approach includes assumptions, which do not handle the real-time online information environment of ubiquitous IoT systems. The algorithmic game theoretic approach assumes that

- The throughput characteristic of the network does not change with time, and the drivers can compute or learn this characteristic by repeatedly passing the road network
- The drivers simultaneously and selfishly decide their optimal route
- The outcome travel time for a given driver depends on the choice of the other drivers and the characteristic of the network, but not on the schedule of the trip of the drivers

In the algorithmic game theory model, each flow (controlled by a single agent) continuously occupies its route, and if another flow distribution is considered, then the change is considered to take effect immediately along the full route. However, if each subsequent car of the traffic flow is a separate agent which may select its own route depending on the real-time traffic situation, then the algorithmic game theory model needs to be extended along these assumptions:

- The throughput characteristic of the network may change with time, and the drivers cannot compute or learn this characteristic by repeatedly passing the road network
- Drivers decide their optimal route when they enter the road network, and the decision is based on the real-time situation of the road network
- The outcome travel time for a given driver depends also on the trip schedule of other drivers that entered the network previously or will enter the network later

These differences in the assumptions make IoT navigation different from the algorithmic game theory approach. In order to have better understanding of the traffic network of the near future when traffic routing is planned widely by autonomous IoT navigation systems, we need new experiments, models and theories. If we understand the basic properties of traffic coordinated by autonomous IoT navigation systems, then we can tell how it relates to central control and we will be able to design, develop and apply better autonomous systems for interactive online IoT navigation systems. In the end, this line of research improves how society works by contributing to the reduction of congestion and environmental pollution.

The first step in this direction is a simulation environment, which can be used to experiment with IoT navigation and to compare IoT navigation with central control and the theoretical findings of the algorithmic game theory approach. This will be discussed in the following subsections.

Theoretical Background of Algorithmic Game Theory and IoT Routing Problems

The most important results of the algorithmic game theory approach for the traffic routing problem and its differences from the IoT navigation problem will be summarized in the following. This is needed because later the IoT navigation simulator will be used to investigate if and how the results of the algorithmic game theory approach manifest themselves in real-time IoT navigation systems.

Algorithmic Game Theory Approach

Algorithmic game theory (Nisan et al., 2007) studies networks with source routing, in which end users simultaneously choose a full route to their destination and the traffic is routed in a congestion sensitive manner. The agents control a complete traffic flow and can divide the traffic flow among the different routes to the destination. Two models are used: non-atomic selfish routing and atomic selfish routing. The non-atomic routing model describes the case when there are very many actors, each influencing a very small fraction of the overall traffic flow. The atomic routing model describes the case when each actor influences a considerable amount of traffic flow. The main difference between the two models is that the non-atomic model has continuous functions having unique extreme values, while the atomic model has discrete functions approximating the extreme values at several points.

The algorithmic game theory model of the routing problem is the (G, r, c) triple, where

- G is the road network given by a directed graph $G=(V, E)$ with vertex set V and edge set E;
- r is the total traffic flow given by a vector r of traffic flows with r_i denoting the amount of traffic flow on trip P_i which is from the source vertex s_i of G to the target vertex t_i of G; and
- c is the throughput characteristic of the road network given by a cost function with $c_e: R^+ \to R^+$ for each edge e of G mapping the total traffic on edge e to the total travel time on that edge.

The graph G may contain parallel edges. The cost functions c_e are nonnegative, continuous and non-decreasing. The traffic flow r_i on the trip P_i is routed somehow on the paths leading from s_i to t_i. The cost of a path is the sum of the costs of the edges in the path at a given flow[1]. The cost of a traffic flow r_i on the trip P_i is the sum of the cost of all the paths in P_i. In the case of a non-atomic routing problem, the traffic flow r_i on the trip P_i may be divided arbitrarily among several paths leading from s_i to t_i. In the case of an atomic routing problem the traffic flow r_i on the trip P_i can be sent on one single path leading from s_i to t_i. In the routing problem, each actor is interested in a traffic flow r_i on a trip P_i. The terms "actor", "agent", and "traffic flow r_i" will be used interchangeably.

A flow distribution is optimal if it minimizes the cost of the total traffic flow over all possible flow distributions. A flow distribution is an equilibrium[2] flow distribution if none of the actors can change its traffic flow distribution among its possible paths to decrease its cost. The equilibrium flow distribution is a rational choice for every autonomic actor because deviating from the equilibrium would increase the cost for the actor.

It is proven (Roughgarden, 2007) that every non-atomic routing problem has at least one equilibrium flow distribution and all equilibrium flow distributions have the same total cost. The price of anarchy is the ratio between the cost of an equilibrium flow distribution and the optimal flow distribution. It is proven (Roughgarden, 2007) that if the cost functions are of the form $ax + b$, where x is the traffic flow, then the price of anarchy in any non-atomic routing problem is not more than $4 \div 3$. If the cost functions can be nonlinear, then one can create cost functions to exceed any given bound on the price of anarchy of non-atomic routing problems.

In atomic routing problems, the existence of equilibrium flow distribution is not always guaranteed. Atomic routing problems have equilibrium flow distribution if every traffic flow r_i has the same value, or if the cost functions are of the form $ax + b$ (Roughgarden, 2007). If there are more than one equilibrium flow distributions, then their total costs may be different. If the cost functions of an atomic routing problem are of the form $ax + b$, then the price of anarchy is at most $(3 + \sqrt{5}) \div 2$. If the cost functions of an atomic routing problem are of the form $ax + b$ and in addition every traffic flow r_i has the same value, then the price of anarchy is at most $5 \div 2$ (Roughgarden, 2007).

It is known that if the routing problem has an equilibrium and the actors try to minimize their own cost with regret minimization, then the traffic flow distribution converges to an equilibrium (Blum et al., 2010).

Intelligent transportation systems are an important application area of ubiquitous IoT systems. One of the fundamental issues of intelligent transportation systems is the routing problem, and it can be modelled with the above routing game model. The above highlighted properties of the routing game model are important findings for that case, where the decision is made on the flow level. The routing game model is in accordance with the equilibrium model (Wardrop, 1952) (Beckmann et al., 1956) of traffic engineers who assume that the traffic is always assigned to match the equilibrium. This chapter investigates the open research question whether the availability of real-time online data in IoT environments changes the equilibrium traffic assignment assumption of traffic engineers or not.

Routing in an IoT Environment

The model of the IoT routing problem to be used in the simulation is an extension of the algorithmic game theory model of the routing problem. It is based on the online routing game model, which was developed in (Varga, 2014), and later refined in (Varga, 2015).

The online routing game is the sextuple (t, T, G, r, c, k), where

- $t = \{1, 2, \dots\}$ is a sequence of equal time periods
- T is a natural number with T time periods giving one time unit (e.g. one minute)
- G is the road network given by a directed graph $G = (V, E)$ with vertex set V and edge set E where each $e \in E$ is characterized by a cost function c_e and a time gap gap_e
- r is the total traffic flow given by a vector of traffic flows with r_i denoting the traffic flow (number of cars in T time periods) on the trip P_i which is from the source vertex s_i of G to the target vertex t_i of G. The flow r_i is given by $T \div n_i$ where $n_i \in [1 \dots T]$ is a natural number constant, meaning that the following distance of the agents of the flow r_i are n_i time periods. (Note that T, and the time unit to be modelled by T, have to be selected according to the flow values to be modelled.)

- c is the cost function of the road network with $c_e : R^+ \rightarrow R^+$ for each edge e of G, and it maps the flow[3] $f_e(\tau)$ (that enters the edge e at time τ) to the travel time on the edge. The cost c_e for the agent entering the edge e is never less than the remaining cost of any other agent already utilizing that edge increased with a time gap[4] gap_e, which is specific to edge e. The value of the flow $f_e(\tau)$ is the number of agents that entered the edge e between τ-T (inclusive) and τ (non-inclusive). If two agents enter an edge exactly at the same time τ, then one of them (randomly selected) suffers a delay gap_e, which is part of its cost on edge e, and its remaining cost is determined at the delayed time, so its cost on edge e will be $gap_e + c_e(f_e(\tau + gap_e))$. The cost functions have a constant part which does not depend on the flow on the edge, and a variable part which depends on the flow on the edge.;

- $k = (k^1, k^2, \ldots)$ is a sequence of decision vectors with decision vector $k^t=(k^t_1, k^t_2, \ldots)$ made in time period t. k^t_i is the decision made by the agent of traffic flow r_i in time period t. The decision k^t_i is how the trip P_i is routed on a single path of the paths leading from s_i to t_i. The actual cost of a path is the sum of the actual cost of the edges, and the actual cost of an edge is determined at the time when the agent of the flow enters the edge.

The graph G may contain parallel edges. The cost functions c_e are nonnegative, continuous and non-decreasing, but they are not known to any of the actors of the model, and the actors can learn the actual cost only when a car exits an edge and reports its cost.

The online routing game model is similar to a sequence of atomic routing problems with the difference that the flows are not "continuous" in the sense explained in the following. In the atomic routing problem if r_1 decides to send one unit of flow on a path (e_1, e_2, e_3) and r_2 decides to send one unit of flow on path (e_4, e_2, e_5), then the two flows are "continuous" and surely will influence each other on e_2. In the online routing game model, the flows are not "continuous" and they have "atomic sections". If the above two flows start at the same time period t, then they will influence each other on e_2 only if $c_{e1}(f_{e1}(t)) > c_{e4}(f_{e4}(t))$ and $c_{e1}(f_{e1}(t)) + c_{e2}(f_{e2}(t+c_{e1}(f_{e1}(t)))) - c_{e4}(f_{e4}(t)) < T$ or $c_{e4}(f_{e4}(t)) > c_{e1}(f_{e1}(t))$ and $c_{e4}(f_{e4}(t)) + c_{e2}(f_{e2}(t+c_{e4}(f_{e4}(t)))) - c_{e1}(f_{e1}(t)) < T$.

Because IoT navigation is like a sequence of routing problems, determining the best decision vector k of the model would require an online algorithm (Albers 2006). In practice, typical navigation software in cars use simple shortest path search in the road network, possibly weighed with the online information on the actual traffic delay. The simulation will use this simple non-online algorithm approach, called simple naive decision strategy.

The online routing game model does not say anything whether the cost function c is the same over the sequence of time periods, or it may change from one time period to another (modeling accidents on roads). The model could accommodate such changes because the actors can learn the actual cost at a given time period only from the cost reported by the cars exiting an edge.

Although the online routing game model resembles a sequence of atomic routing problems, the online routing game model is much more complex than the atomic routing problem. This is why the online routing game is investigated with the help of a simulator that uses a small, but still complex instance of the above general online routing game model. The small but complex instance corresponds to the Braess paradox and it is described in the next section.

Problem Scenario

The simulation investigates the IoT routing problem on the Braess paradox (Braess 1968) using the $SN_{Braess} = (t, T, G, r, c, k)$ model corresponding to the online routing game model of the previous section, with the following concrete values:

- $t = \{1, 2, \ldots\}$ is a finite sequence of time periods
- T is 600, modeling one minute
- G is the road network (see *Figure 1.*) given as a four-node directed graph with vertex set $V = (v_0, v_1, v_2, v_3)$ and edge set $E = (e_1, e_2, e_3, e_4, e_5, e_6)$. The edges are $e_1 = v_0 \rightarrow v_1$, $e_2 = v_0 \rightarrow v_2$, $e_3 = v_1 \rightarrow v_2$, $e_4 = v_2 \rightarrow v_1$, $e_5 = v_1 \rightarrow v_3$, and $e_6 = v_2 \rightarrow v_3$
- $r = (r_1)$ is the total traffic flow with only one flow on the trip P_1 from the source vertex $s_1 = v_0$ of G to the target vertex $t_1 = v_3$ of G
- c is the cost function of the road network with $c_{e1} = 1 + x \div 10$, $c_{e2} = 15$, $c_{e3} = 7.5$, $c_{e4} = 7.5$, $c_{e5} = 15$, $c_{e6} = 1 + x \div 10$, [5] where x is the total number of cars entering an edge from time period t-T to time period t. As discussed in the previous section, this cost function is used to compute the travel time on an edge, but the actors learn the actual travel time only when it is reported on the exit of the edge
- $k = (k^1, k^2, \ldots)$ is a sequence of decision vectors with decision vector $k^t = (k^t_1)$ made in period t. The decision is based on the currently reported travel times, and it selects the path on trip P_1 that currently has the minimum reported cost. This is the simple naive decision making mechanism. The trip P_1 has the set of paths $\{p_1, p_2, p_3, p_4\}$, where $p_1 = (e_1, e_5)$, $p_2 = (e_1, e_3, e_6)$, $p_3 = (e_2, e_6)$, $p_4 = (e_2, e_4, e_5)$ and the costs of the paths used for decision making are the sum of the cost of the edges at the time of decision making.

Figure 1. The SN$_{Braess}$ road network

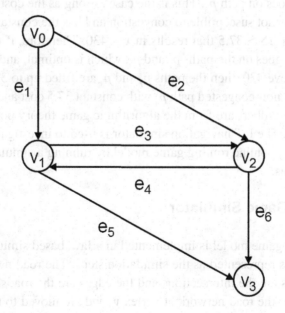

From the algorithmic game theory point of view this network can demonstrate the "paradox" that the equilibrium flow has a price of anarchy with at most $4 \div 3$ ratio (in the given case with the given cost functions it is definitely lower). The "paradox" is that if non-atomic selfish traffic allocation is used, then at some flow values edge e_3 increases the total cost, and without the edge e_3 (seemingly smaller throughput) the cost is smaller (faster travel). The non-atomic model simulates the case when large number of cars continuously enter the network, and make a flow distribution decision knowing the throughput characteristics.

The edges e_1 and e_6 are susceptible to congestion but if the traffic is low, then they are fast roads, therefore at low traffic flow all the traffic goes on path p_2. In this case, this is the optimal traffic distribution and the anarchy has no price. This is the case as long as distributing the traffic equally between path p_1 and path p_3 has higher cost than path p_2. Using the above c cost functions we get the inequality $1 + x \div 20 + 15 > 1 + x \div 10 + 7.5 + 1 + x \div 10$, which results in $130 \div 3 > x$. Therefore, as long as the flow is below the approximate 43.33 value, the network behaves without "paradox" and the anarchy has no price.

At somewhat higher traffic flow, the optimal traffic allocation would send half of the flow on path p_1 and half of the flow on path p_3. As long as the total cost of the edges e_1 and e_3 is less than the cost of edge e_2 (and symmetrically the total cost of edges e_3 and e_6 is less than the cost of edge e_5), the selfish traffic allocation still would use path p_2. This gives the inequality $1 + x \div 10 + 7.5 < 15$, which results in $x < 65$. Therefore, if the flow is above the approximate 43.33 value and below 65, then all the traffic goes on path p_2 and the anarchy has price.

If the total cost of edges e_1 and e_3 is more than the cost of edge e_2, then the traffic flow is distributed among the left-hand path p_1, the central path p_2, and the right hand path p_3. Let us denote the three flows L, C and R accordingly. The cost of all three paths must be the same which gives the following equalities: $15 + 1 + (L + C) \div 10 = 15 + 1 + (R + C) \div 10$; and $15 + 1 + (L + C) \div 10 = 1 + (L + C) \div 10 + 7.5 + 1 + (R + C) \div 10$; and $L + R + C = x$, which results in $C = 130 - x$. So, if the flow is above 65 and below 130, then the traffic is divided among paths p_1, p_2 and p_3, and the anarchy has price.

If x is above 130, then there is no traffic on the central path p_2, and half of the traffic goes on path p_1, and half of the traffic goes on path p_3. This is the case as long as the costs of these paths are below the cost of path p_4, which is not susceptible to congestion and has the constant cost of 37.5. This gives the inequality $1 + x \div 20 + 15 > 37.5$ that results in $x > 430$. Therefore, if the flow is above 130 and below 430, then the traffic goes on the paths p_1 and p_3, which is optimal, and the anarchy has no price.

If the traffic flow is above 430, then the paths p_1 and p_3 are filled up to 37.5 travel time and the remaining traffic goes on the non-congested path p_4 with constant 37.5 cost and the anarchy has no price.

The above traffic flow numbers are from the algorithmic game theory point of view and are shown in the diagram of Figure 2. The IoT navigation simulator is used to investigate how these numbers and limits manifest in the SN_{Braess} online routing game model by running a simulation with different traffic flows from the above ranges.

The Online Routing Game Simulator

The SN_{Braess} online routing game model is implemented in a Java based simulation program. The finite sequence of time periods is represented as the simulation steps. The road network G is represented as a graph, where the vertices are the intersections and the edges are the roads. The traffic flow r is represented as cars. Cars enter the road network at vertex v_0 and are moved to the road as determined by the simple naive navigation strategy. The cars remain on the road for the number of simulation steps

Figure 2. The SN$_{Braess}$ road network

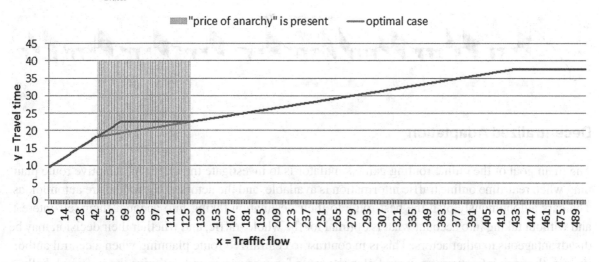

determined by the cost functions c, and after this, they are moved to the intersection at the end of the road. Roads keep track of the number of cars entering the road during the last T number of navigation steps, and this number is used by the cost function c. When cars are moved to the intersection at the end of the road, they report to all actors their actual travel time on the given road. This travel time is used by the simple naive navigation strategy to calculate the shortest path in the road network. When cars arrive at the destination vertex v_3, they report the actual total travel time of their route in the road network.

The implementation has a graphical user interface where the value T and the natural number constant n_1 can be set to change the total traffic flow value $r = (r_1)$. The user interface displays the status of the road network by showing the number of cars on each road and the number of cars entering each road during the last T number of simulation steps as shown in Figure 3. The actual total travel time of the cars in the road network is plotted at each simulation step, and they are shown on a diagram as in Figure 4. The user can start and stop the simulation run with the press of a button.

Figure 3. The status of the SN$_{Braess}$ road network

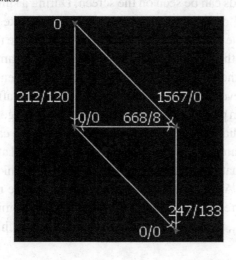

Figure 4. The diagram of the travel time of the cars in the SN_{Braess} road network at incoming traffic flow 120

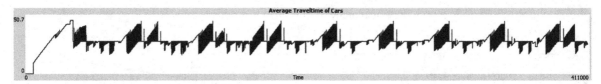

Decentralized Adaptation

The main goal of the online routing game simulator is to investigate the effects of adaptive route planning when real-time online traffic information is available, and the actors of the model are autonomous. The cars autonomously plan the best route to their destination taking into account their self-interest, and without taking into account what is optimal for the whole traffic, and whether their decision may be disadvantageous to other actors. This is in contrast to centralized route planning when a central authority, e.g. the road infrastructure, would plan the route for every actor and optimize the traffic globally.

The current implementation uses the simple naive route planning strategy, which does not include any reasoning on the presence of other actors in the system and their possible decision. The optimal planning strategy would be individually rational, so that all actors would apply it, and would produce traffic that is close to the global optimum.

The online routing game simulator could be extended with an autonomous property of the road infrastructure, where the road infrastructure would enforce some normative agent rules on the network in order to influence the selfish behavior of the cars toward the global optimality. In this case, the actors would still be autonomous and plan their routes selfishly, but because they are forced by the normative rules, their autonomous decisions would be closer to the optimum. One of the goals of the simulator is to enable the experimentation into this direction as well.

Simulation Results

The online routing game simulator can be run on a single PC or laptop. The speed of the simulation run can be changed from very slow, when the changes in every time period can be seen, to very fast, when changes of blocks of time periods can be seen on the screen. During a simulation run, one can modify at any time the amount of traffic flowing into the network and follow (like in Figure 3) how it propagates through the network and how the autonomic route planning cars change their behavior to accommodate to the changing traffic load on the roads of the road network. At the same time, a diagram shows (like in Figure 4) the full history of the travel time of the cars arriving to their destination at node v_3.

The travel time diagrams revealed different patterns at different traffic flow values. At low traffic flow, the IoT navigation problem produces the same travel time as the algorithmic game theory approach. Figure 5 shows the travel time diagram at incoming traffic flow 40. We can see that in the beginning the travel time is 0 because all cars are on the road and none of them arrived at the destination node v_3. When the first car arrives at the destination, the reported travel time is 9.5 which is the shortest travel time of the uncongested road network. As there are more and more cars on the road, all of which take path p_2, the travel time increases until it reaches the value 17.5 from the algorithmic game theory model. Since p_2 is still the fastest path on trip P_1, none of the cars deviates from this path, so this value remains forever.

Figure 5. The diagram of the travel time of the cars in the SN_{Braess} road network at incoming traffic flow 40

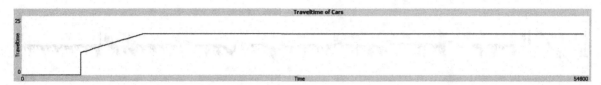

Figure 4 shows the travel time diagram at incoming traffic flow of 120. This diagram also has a starting phase where the travel time is increasing, but later, as the shortest path becomes congested, the drivers deviate to other routes and they keep deviating to other routes, so the travel time does not get to a constant value and, as the figure shows, it does not seem to converge to a constant value. The travel time varies around about 28 with amplitude between 16 and 46.5 values. The overall travel experience of the cars in the network is measured with the average travel time. The average travel time of Figure 4 is 30.73.

Note that the travel time in this road network at incoming traffic flow of 120 is

- 22.0 with optimal central control
- 22.5 in the algorithmic game theory model (with price of anarchy)
- 33.5 if all cars select path p_2 (which is the shortest path if congestion delay is not taken into account in the planning)
- 37.5 if all cars select path p_4 (which is not susceptible to congestion and is the longest path if congestion delay is not taken into account in the planning)

The diagram indicates that IoT navigation using real-time online traffic information and simple naive planning has a fluctuation, the cars often experience fast traffic, but sometimes they experience considerable congestion delay, sometimes even more than the worst case would be without IoT navigation optimization.

Figure 6 shows the travel time diagram at incoming traffic flow of 75. Here the travel time varies between 16 and 36.5 with an average of 24.75. The fluctuations at this incoming flow have a higher frequency with some sudden peaks.

Figure 7 shows the travel time diagram at incoming traffic flow of 150. Here the travel time varies between 16 and 55.8 with an average of 32. The fluctuations seem to be smoother with some disturbance periods.

Too many travel time diagrams cannot be included here, instead the key travel time values at different incoming flows are shown in Table 3. The first column contains the incoming traffic flow computed as T/n, where n is a natural number and $T=600$ from the SN_{Braess} model. The second column contains the corresponding travel time from the algorithmic game theory (AGT) model, with price of anarchy be-

Figure 6. The diagram of the travel time of the cars in the SN_{Braess} road network at incoming traffic flow 75

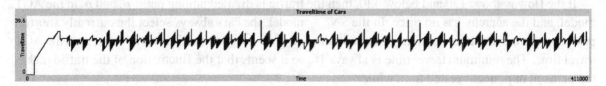

Figure 7. The diagram of the travel time of the cars in the SN_{Braess} road network at incoming traffic flow 150

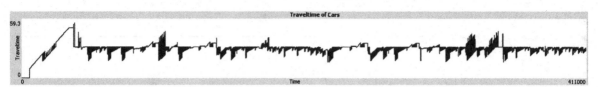

Table 3. Travel times in the SN_{Braess} road network

Traffic Flow	AGT Travel Time	SN_{Braess} Travel Times		
		Minimum	Average	Maximum
0.00	9.50	9.50	9.50	9.50
40.00	17.50	17.50	17.50	17.50
50.00	19.50	19.50	19.50	19.50
66.66	22.50	16.00	22.24	23.50
75.00	22.50	16.00	24.75	36.50
85.71	22.50	16.00	26.03	38.70
100.00	22.50	16.00	28.23	40.30
120.00	22.50	16.00	30.73	46.50
150.00	23.50	16.00	32.00	55.80
200.00	26.00	16.00	35.94	71.30
300.00	31.00	16.00	46.47	102.30
600.00	37.50	25.00	56.36	135.30

tween the incoming traffic flow values 43.33 and 120.00. The remaining columns contain the measured minimum, average and maximum travel times from the SN_{Braess} simulation. The values of Table 3 are shown in graphical form on Figure 8.

We can observe that at low incoming traffic flows the cars do not deviate from the shortest path, so the AGT and the SN_{Braess} travel times are the same.

At the incoming travel flow of 50, there is price of anarchy, but all the traffic goes on path p_2, as in the AGT model. The travel times are the same in the SN_{Braess} model at this traffic flow value.

If the flow is above 65 and below 130, then the traffic is divided among paths p_1, p_2 and p_3 in the AGT model, and the anarchy has price. In the SN_{Braess} model, the cars always select the currently shortest path, and there is some fluctuation. The maximum travel time is longer than the AGT travel time. The measured average travel time is longer than the AGT travel time, except at incoming travel flow of 66.66, when it is somewhat shorter. The minimum travel time is always 16, which is possible through paths p_1 or p_3 if there is no congestion. It seems that the fluctuation of the traffic makes one of the paths p_1 or p_3 uncongested for a while.

If the flow is above 130 and below 430, then the traffic is divided among paths p_1 and p_3 in the AGT model, and the anarchy has no price. In the SN_{Braess} model, the cars always select the currently shortest path, and there is some fluctuation. The maximum and the average travel times are longer than the AGT travel time. The minimum travel time is always 16, so it seems that the fluctuation of the traffic makes the paths p_1 or p_3 uncongested for a while.

Figure 8. Maximum, minimum and average travel times in the SN_{Braess} road network depending on the selected traffic flows and compared to the algorithmic game theory approach

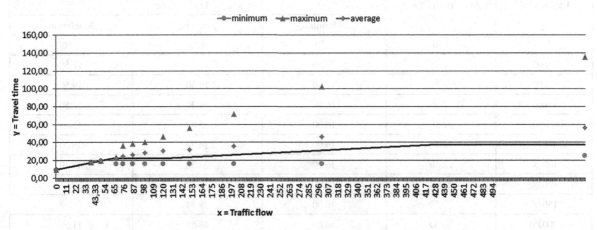

If the flow is above 430, then the traffic goes through path p_4 in the AGT model with constant 37.5 cost, and the anarchy has no price. In the SN_{Braess} model, the cars always select the shortest path, and there is some fluctuation. The maximum and the average travel times are longer than the AGT travel time. The minimum travel time is 25, so during the observed period, the fluctuation of the traffic did not make the paths p_1 and p_3 uncongested.

Dynamic Route Planning

A possible further development of the SN_{Braess} model is to allow the cars to change their route plan during their trip when they discover that a road section on their planned way becomes congested. This dynamic version of the SN_{Braess} model was implemented and simulations were run with the same incoming traffic flows as in Table 3. It was found that this change does not improve travel times because the maximum and average travel times are almost always higher than those of the non-dynamic SN_{Braess} model. The measured values are shown in Table 4.

Summary of the Simulation Investigation of Decentralized Adaptation

This section investigated with simulation an instance of a new model of traffic routing: the Braess scenario of the IoT navigation problem. IoT navigation is modelled with the online routing game model, which extends the algorithmic game theory model by taking into account a) that cars travelling on overlapping congested routes may not influence each other if they pass the congested section at different times, and b) that route planning is based on real-time online observable travel times on each road section. These extensions allow the modeling of the new possibilities of ubiquitous IoT systems. In the simplest implementation, real-time online information is made available by online navigation software running on smart phones. The presented simulations allow us to investigate how the traffic will behave if the majority of the cars are autonomously directed on the roads by navigation software based on data from ubiquitous IoT systems.

Table 4. Travel times in the dynamic SN_{Braess} road network

Traffic Flow	AGT Travel Time	SN_{Braess} Travel Times		
		Minimum	Average	Maximum
0.00	9.50	9.50	9.50	9.50
40.00	17.50	17.50	17.50	17.50
50.00	19.50	19.50	19.50	19.50
66.66	22.50	16.00	22.30	23.50
75.00	22.50	16.00	25.87	46.69
85.71	22.50	16.00	26.52	36.20
100.00	22.50	16.00	29.32	43.30
120.00	22.50	16.00	33.77	52.90
150.00	23.50	16.00	39.34	68.67
200.00	26.00	16.00	46.55	71.30
300.00	31.00	16.00	51.75	99.50
600.00	37.50	16.00	58.59	181.21

DECENTRALIZED ADAPTATION WITH PREDICTION

The agents of a ubiquitous IoT system perceive the current state of their environment and make decisions which action to perform. The actions are both reactive and proactive. The more complex the environment, the more difficult to predict the behavior of the environment, and more difficult for the agents to decide which reactive or proactive action to perform. The simulation results in the previous section have shown that if the agents selfishly optimize their strategy, and they take into account only the real-time data of the current state of the environment, then in some situations the ubiquitous IoT system may start to fluctuate, and sometimes the agents may be worse off with real-time data than without real-time data. This was also observed by traffic engineers in real world and by multi-agent researchers in simulations (Wahle et al., 2000). The problem of fluctuation was formally underpinned recently by theoretical proofs based on the novel online routing game model (Varga, 2014).

In order to be able to investigate formally the effect of real-time data on the routing problem, the online routing game model was developed in (Varga, 2014), and later refined in (Varga, 2015). In order to formally measure the effect of real-time data, the "benefit of online real-time data" concept was defined in (Varga, 2014):

Definition 1: The worst-case benefit of online real-time data at a given flow is the ratio between the cost of the maximum cost of the flow and the cost of the same flow with an oracle using the same decision making strategy and only the fixed part of the cost functions.

Definition 2: The best-case benefit of online real-time data at a given flow is the ratio between the cost of the minimum cost of the flow (after the initial running up) and the cost of the same flow with an oracle using the same decision making strategy and only the fixed part of the cost functions.

Definition 3: The average case benefit of online real-time data at a given flow is the ratio between the cost of the average cost of the flow and the cost of the same flow with an oracle using the same decision making strategy and only the fixed part of the cost functions.

The agents are happy with real-time data, if the benefit value is below 1. If the benefit value is greater than 1, then it is in fact a "price".

The class of simple naive (SN) online routing games (Varga, 2014) is the model of current commercial vehicle navigation systems, which select the possibly multiple objective (Blue et al., 1997) shortest route, with taking into account the real-time information available at decision time.

It is formally proved in (Varga, 2014), that in SN online routing games, equilibrium is not guaranteed, "single flow intensification" is possible, and the worst-case benefit of online real-time data is not guaranteed to be below 1. In practical terms, these mean that if the vehicles use simple naive strategy, and they exploit real-time data, then the traffic may sometimes fluctuate: if there is congestion on some road, then many vehicles try to adapt to the situation, they select other route, and they cause congestion on some other road. Congestion may be created by the "single flow intensification" phenomenon as well because vehicles that enter the road network later may select alternative faster routes, and they may catch up with the vehicles already on the road, and this way they cause congestion. The result of all these is, that sometimes in some networks the traffic may be worse off by exploiting real-time information than without exploiting real-time information. One of the causes of this strange behavior (also demonstrated in the previous subsection) is that vehicles become aware of congestions with delay, only after the congestion is formed and reported by IoT sensors.

Researchers tried to add proactive flavor to the selfish strategy with anticipatory techniques (Rosen 1985), where the future state of the environment is predicted from the intentions of the agents. Anticipation (Rosen 1985) is essential to be able to behave proactively, and adapt to changing situations. Several design patterns were studied (Babaoglu et al., 2006) to help the systematic design of self-organizing emergent systems that show anticipatory behavior. Many of these design patterns are inspired by biological systems, which are well suited to design ubiquitous service ecosystems like crowd steering (Montagna et al., 2013). The anticipatory techniques usually apply bio-inspired design patterns (Babaoglu et al., 2006) to propagate the intentions of the agents. Among the bio-inspired design patterns (Fernandez-Marquez, 2013), the digital pheromone pattern and the evaporation pattern are the two most relevant to implement intention propagation, as it was done in (Claes et al., 2011).

Basically, the application of these anticipatory techniques means, that the agents perceive not only the current state of their environment, but also an aggregation of the mental state of other agents already in their environment, with the assumption that the agents truthfully reveal their intentions. Simulation results in traffic scenarios indicated (Claes et al., 2011), that these anticipatory techniques improve the properties of the ubiquitous IoT system.

The anticipatory vehicle routing simulation system of (Claes et al., 2011) uses delegate multi-agent systems to forecast future traffic conditions, based on the broadcast intention of the agents. The delegate multi-agent system can be implemented by the ubiquitous IoT system of the road infrastructure. The forecast information from the delegate multi-agent system is then used by the agents to make routing decisions. The approach was evaluated in a simulated network of Leuven, using a statistical approach, and the authors concluded that the use of forecast data results in shorter trip durations than the use of real-time data from the commercially available Traffic Management Channel.

In order to formally underpin the above empirical investigations, the class of simple naive intention propagation online routing games was defined in (Varga, 2015):

Definition 4: Simple naive intention propagation online routing games (SNIP online routing games) are online routing games where a) the decision making agents of the flows are the vehicle agents of the anticipatory vehicle routing system, b) the infrastructure of the anticipatory vehicle routing system predicts the travel times for each path of the trip, based on the planned routes[6] of the agents currently in the system, c) and the decision of the agents is to select the path with the shortest travel time among the predicted travel times on the different paths of the trip. The agent tells its selected path to the infrastructure of the anticipatory vehicle routing system, and the infrastructure remembers this selection while the agent is in the road network, and the infrastructure invalidates it when the vehicle agent exits the network.

The first findings of the formal investigations with SNIP online routing games are, that the problem of the fluctuation of the decentralized adaptation in some cases is not fully solved (Varga, 2015). The findings are that SNIP online routing games may also have ''single flow intensification'' (although in a ''lighter'' way), the worst-case benefit of online real-time data may go above 1, and the traffic may fluctuate. One of the causes of this surprising result is that anticipation predicts future traffic conditions, based on the intentions of the agents already on the road, but it does not predict the intentions of the agents simultaneously making decisions.

The state-of-the-art is the following conjecture: if simultaneous decision making is prevented, then intention-propagation-based prediction can limit the fluctuation (Varga, 2016a) and help the ubiquitous IoT system approximate to the Nash equilibrium (Varga, 2016b). This conjecture is proved for the road network of the Braess paradox (Varga, in press), but further investigations are needed to prove that this conjecture is valid in any type of road network.

CONCLUSION

Ubiquitous IoT technologies allow modern navigation systems to use live online information about the status of traffic in order to optimize the route planning of autonomous vehicles. In order to investigate how the traffic would behave if the majority of autonomous vehicles based their route planning on such IoT navigation systems, this chapter presented a formal model of IoT navigation systems as an extension to the classic algorithmic game theory model. This chapter presented an innovative simulator of this IoT navigation model for the Braess scenario using the simple naive planning strategy to experiment with different traffic flows. Several simulations run at different traffic flows were recorded with this IoT navigation demonstrator, and the results were compared with the results of optimal central control and the results of algorithmic game theory model. The simulation results indicate that IoT navigation using real-time online traffic information and simple naive planning sometimes produces some fluctuation. Sometimes the IoT navigation is fast, but sometimes the cars experience considerable congestion delay. The dynamic re-routing version of the IoT navigation model with simple naive planning strategy does not seem to improve travel times.

In order to alleviate the presented problem, researchers propose to add proactive flavor to decentralized ubiquitous IoT systems by using anticipatory techniques, where the future state of the environment is predicted from the intentions of the agents. With such anticipatory techniques, the agents of the decentralized ubiquitous IoT systems can take into account not only the current state of the environment, but also an aggregation of the mental state of other agents.

The conjecture is that if simultaneous decision making is prevented, then intention-propagation-based prediction can limit the fluctuation of the decentralized ubiquitous IoT systems. The online routing game model is used to formally prove properties of the IoT routing problem. Recent research investigated a Simple Naive Intention Propagation online routing game, where there is only one incoming flow, therefore simultaneous decision making is not possible. The investigated network is based on the Braess paradox because the Braess paradox exhibits the basic problem of multi-agent systems[7]. The results are promising because the research formally proved a guaranteed worst-case benefit of online real-time data in this version of the Braess paradox. These results show that intention-propagation-based prediction establishes some kind of coordination among the agents entering this ubiquitous IoT system in a sequence.

REFERENCES

Albers, S. (2006). Online algorithms. In D. Q. Goldin, S. A. Smolka, & P. Wegner (Eds.), *Interactive Computation: The New Paradigm* (pp. 143–164). Springer. doi:10.1007/3-540-34874-3_7

Babaoglu, O., Canright, G., Deutsch, A., Caro, G. A. D., Ducatelle, F., Gambardella, L. M., & Urnes, T. et al. (2006). Design Patterns from Biology for Distributed Computing. *ACM Transactions on Autonomous and Adaptive Systems*, *1*(1), 26–66. doi:10.1145/1152934.1152937

Bard, J., Plummer, J., & Sourie, J. (1998). Determining Tax Credits for Converting Non-food Crops to Biofuels: An Application of Bi-level Programming. In Multilevel Optimization: Algorithms and Applications (pp. 23-50).

Beckmann, M. J., McGuire, C. B., & Winsten, C. B. (1956). *Studies in the economics of transportation*. Cowles Commission for Research in Economics, Yale University Press.

Blue, V. J., Adler, J. L., & List, G. F. (1997). Real-Time Multiple-Objective Path Search for In-Vehicle Route Guidance Systems. *Intelligent Transportation Systems and Artificial Intelligence*, *1588*(3), 10–17.

Blum, A., Even-Dar, E., & Ligett, K. (2010). Routing Without Regret: On Convergence to Nash Equilibria of Regret-Minimizing Algorithms in Routing Games. *Theory of Computing*, *6*, 179–199.

Braess, D. (1968). Über ein Paradoxon aus der Verkehrsplanung. *Unternehmensforschung*, *12*(1), 258–268.

Campana, F., Moreno, A., Riano, D., & Varga, L. (2008). K4Care: knowledge-based homecare e-services for an ageing Europe. In R. Annicchiarico, U. Cortés, & C. Urdiales (Eds.), Agent Technology and E-Health (pp. 95-116). Basel: Birkhäuser Verlag. doi:10.1007/978-3-7643-8547-7_6

Čertický, M., Jakob, M., & Píbil, R. (2016). Simulation Testbed for Autonomic Demand-Responsive Mobility Systems. In T.L. McCluskey, A. Kotsialos, J.P. Müller et al. (Eds.), Autonomic Road Transport Support Systems (pp. 147-164). Birkhäuser Basel.

Claes, R., Holvoet, T., & Weyns, D. (2011). A decentralized approach for anticipatory vehicle routing using delegate multi-agent systems. *IEEE Transactions on Intelligent Transportation Systems*, *12*(2), 364–373. doi:10.1109/TITS.2011.2105867

Cockburn, D., Varga, L. Z., & Jennings, N. R. (1992). Cooperating Intelligent Systems for Electricity Distribution. In M.A. Bramer, & R.W. Milne (Eds.), BCS Expert Systems 92 Conference (Application Track), Churchill College, Cambridge, UK.

Çolak, S., Lima, A., & González, M. C. (2016). Understanding congested travel in urban areas. *Nature Communications*, *7*. doi:10.1038/ncomms10793 PMID:26978719

Dempe, S. (2003). Annotated Bibliography on Bi-level Programming and Mathematical Programs with Equilibrium Constraints. *Journal of Optics*, *52*(3), 333–359.

El-Tantawy, S., Abdulhai, B., & Abdelgawad, H. (2013). Multiagent Reinforcement Learning for Integrated Network of Adaptive Traffic Signal Controllers (MARLIN-ATSC): Methodology and Large-Scale Application on Downtown Toronto. *IEEE Transactions on Intelligent Transportation Systems*, *14*(3), 1140–1150. doi:10.1109/TITS.2013.2255286

Fernandez-Marquez, J. L., Marzo Serugendo, G. D., Montagna, S., Viroli, M., & Arcos, J. L. (2013). Description and Composition of Bio-inspired Design Patterns: A Complete Overview. *Natural Computing*, *12*(1), 43–67. doi:10.1007/s11047-012-9324-y

García, J., Florez, J. E., Torralba, Á., Borrajo, D., López, C. L., García-Olaya, A., & Sáenz, J. (2013). Combining linear programming and automated planning to solve intermodal transportation problems. *European Journal of Operational Research*, *227*(1), 216–226. doi:10.1016/j.ejor.2012.12.018

García, J., Torralba, Á., Florez, J. E., Borrajo, D., López, C. L., & García-Olaya, Á. (2016). TIMIPLAN: A Tool for Transportation Tasks. In T.L. McCluskey, A. Kotsialos, J.P. Müller et al. (Eds.), Autonomic Road Transport Support Systems (Autonomic Systems) (pp. 269-286). Birkhäuser Basel. doi:10.1007/978-3-319-25808-9_16

Gödel Prize. (2012). Retrieved November 28, 2016, from http://www.acm.org/press-room/news-releases/2012/goedel-prize-2012/

Hajnal, Á., Isern, D., Moreno, A., Pedone, G., & Varga, L. (2007). Knowledge Driven Architecture for Home Care. In Burkhard, H-D., Lindemann, G., Verbrugge, R., & Varga, L., (Eds.), *CEEMAS 2007. Multi-agent systems and applications V: 5th International Central and Eastern European Conference on Multi-agent Systems, Lecture Notes in Computer Science, Lecture Notes in Artificial Intelligence (Vol. 4696*, pp. 173-182). Springer Berlin Heidelberg

Kephart, J. O., & Chess, D. M. (2003). The Vision of Autonomic Computing. *IEEE Computer*, *36*(1), 41–50. doi:10.1109/MC.2003.1160055

Kuyer, L., Whiteson, S., Bakker, B., & Vlassis, N. (2008). Multiagent Reinforcement Learning for Urban Traffic Control Using Coordination Graphs. In W. Daelemans, B. Goethals, & K. Morik (Eds.), *Machine Learning and Knowledge Discovery in Databases,* LNCS (Vol. 5211, pp. 656–671). Springer Berlin Heidelberg. doi:10.1007/978-3-540-87479-9_61

Lattner, A. D., Bogon, T., Lorion, Y., & Timm, I. J. (2010, April 12 - 15). A knowledge-based approach to automated simulation model adaptation. In S. Biaz (Ed.), *Proceedings of the 43rd Annual Simulation Symposium (ANSS'10), Spring Simulation Multi-Conference (SpringSim'10)*, Orlando, Florida, USA (pp. 200-207). doi:10.1145/1878537.1878697

Mannion, P., Duggan, J., & Howley, E. (2016). An Experimental Review of Reinforcement Learning Algorithms for Adaptive Traffic Signal Control. In T.L. McCluskey, A. Kotsialos, J.P. Müller et al. (Eds.), Autonomic Road Transport Support Systems (Autonomic Systems) (pp. 47-66). Birkhäuser Basel. doi:10.1007/978-3-319-25808-9_4

McCluskey, T. L., Kotsialos, A., Müller, J. P., Klügl, F., Rana, O., & Schumann, R. (2016). *Autonomic Road Transport Support Systems. (Autonomic Systems)*. Birkhäuser Basel. doi:10.1007/978-3-319-25808-9

Montagna, S., Viroli, M., Fernandez-Marquez, J. L., Serugendo, G. M., & Zambonelli, F. (2013). Injecting Self-Organisation into Pervasive Service Ecosystems. *Mobile Networks and Applications*, *18*(3), 398–412. doi:10.1007/s11036-012-0411-1

Müller-Schloer, C. (2004, September 8-10). Organic Computing: On the feasibility of controlled emergence. In *Proceedings of Second IEEE/ACM/IFIP International Conference on Hardware/Software Codesign and System Synthesis*, Stockholm, Sweden (pp 2-5). ACM Press. doi:10.1145/1016720.1016724

Nisan, N., Roughgarden, T., Tardos, É., & Vazirani, V. V. (2007). *Algorithmic Game Theory*. New York, NY, USA: Cambridge University Press. doi:10.1017/CBO9780511800481

Rosen, R. (1985). *Anticipatory Systems: Philosophical, Mathematical, and Methodological Foundations (IFSR International Series on Systems Science and Engineering)*. Pergamon Press.

Roughgarden, T. (2007). Routing games. In *N. Nisan, T. Roughgarden, É. Tardos et al. (Eds.), Algorithmic Game Theory* (pp. 461–486). New York, NY: Cambridge University Press. doi:10.1017/CBO9780511800481.020

Roughgarden, T., & Tardos, É. (2002). How bad is selfish routing? *Journal of the ACM*, *49*(2), 236–259. doi:10.1145/506147.506153

Schaefer, M., Vokřínek, J., Pinotti, D., & Tango, F. (2016). Multi-Agent Traffic Simulation for Development and Validation of Autonomic Car-to-Car Systems. In T.L. McCluskey, A. Kotsialos, J.P. Müller et al. (Eds.), Autonomic Road Transport Support Systems. (Autonomic Systems) (pp. 165-180). Birkhäuser Basel. doi:10.1007/978-3-319-25808-9_10

Schumann, R. (2016). Performance Maintenance of ARTS Systems. In T.L. McCluskey, A. Kotsialos, J.P. Müller et al. (Eds.), Autonomic Road Transport Support Systems. (Autonomic Systems) (pp. 181-196). Birkhäuser Basel. doi:10.1007/978-3-319-25808-9_11

Sommer, M., Tomforde, S., & Hähner, J. (2016). An Organic Computing Approach to Resilient Traffic Management. In T.L. McCluskey, A. Kotsialos, J.P. Müller et al. (Eds.), Autonomic Road Transport Support Systems (Autonomic Systems) (pp. 113-130). Birkhäuser Basel. doi:10.1007/978-3-319-25808-9_7

Stackelberg, H. (1952). *The Theory of the Market Economy*. Oxford University Press.

Stoilov, T., & Stoilova, K. (2016). A Self-Optimization Traffic Model by Multilevel Formalism. In T.L. McCluskey, A. Kotsialos, J.P. Müller et al. (Eds.), Autonomic Road Transport Support Systems (Autonomic Systems) (pp. 87-112). Birkhäuser Basel. doi:10.1007/978-3-319-25808-9_6

Uhrmacher, A. M., & Weyns, D. (2010). *Multi-Agent systems: Simulation and applications*. CRC Press.

Varga, L. Z. (2014, May 5-6). Online Routing Games and the Benefit of Online Data. In *Proceedings of Eighth International Workshop on Agents in Traffic and Transportation, at 13th Int. Conf. on Autonomous Agents and Multiagent Systems (AAMAS 2014)*, Paris, France (pp. 88-95).

Varga, L. Z. (2015). On Intention-Propagation-Based Prediction in Autonomously Self-adapting Navigation. *Scalable Computing: Practice and Experience*, *16*(3), 221–232.

Varga, L. Z. (2016a, July 18-22). Benefit of Online Real-time Data in the Braess Paradox with Anticipatory Routing. In *Proceedings of 2016 IEEE International Conference on Autonomic Computing*, Würzburg, Germany (pp. 245-250). doi:10.1109/ICAC.2016.68

Varga, L. Z. (2016b, August 29-September 2). How Good is Predictive Routing in the Online Version of the Braess Paradox? In *Proceedings of 22nd European Conference on Artificial Intelligence (ECAI 2016)*, The Hague, The Netherlands, *FIAA* (Vol. 285, pp. 1696-1697).

Varga, L. Z. (in press). Equilibrium with Predictive Routing in the Online Version of the Braess Paradox. *IET Software*.

Wahle, J., Bazzan, A. L. C., Klügl, F., & Schreckenberg, M. (2000). Decision dynamics in a traffic scenario. *Physica A: Statistical Mechanics and its Applications, 287*(3-4), 669-681.

Wardrop, J. G. (1952). Some theoretical aspects of road traffic research. *Proceedings of the Institution of Civil Engineers, Part II, 1*(36), pp. 352-378. doi:10.1680/ipeds.1952.11362

Waze. (2016). Retrieved November 28, 2016, from http://www.waze.com

KEY TERMS AND DEFINITIONS

Benefit of Online Real-Time Data: The benefit of online real-time data is the ratio between the cost of the travel time with exploiting online real-time data in the online routing problem and the cost of the travel time without exploiting online real-time data. The agents are happy with real-time data, if the benefit value is below 1. If the benefit value is above 1, then it is more like a "price".

Braess Paradox: Braess paradox is the phenomenon when adding a road to a congested road traffic network can increase overall journey time, although the additional road seemingly increases the throughput capacity of the road network. It demonstrates the price of anarchy.

Connected Car: The connected, smart car provides a new way to stay in touch with the world during drive time.

Intention-Propagation-Based Prediction: Intention-propagation-based prediction is when the future state of the environment is predicted from the intentions of the agents in the IoT system.

IoT Navigation: Traffic participants of IoT navigation systems share real-time traffic information with each other to self-optimize their route.

Online Routing Game: Online routing game is an extension of the algorithmic game theory model of the routing problem for the online routing problem.

Online Routing Problem: Online routing problem is the routing problem of IoT navigation, where each subsequent car of the traffic flow is a separate agent, which may select different route, depending on the current, real-time traffic situation.

Price of Anarchy: The price of anarchy is the ratio between the cost of an equilibrium flow distribution and the optimal flow distribution.

Routing Game: Routing game is the algorithmic game theory model of the routing problem.

Routing Problem: The routing problem is a problem of networks with source routing, in which end users simultaneously choose a full route to their destination and the traffic is routed in a congestion sensitive manner.

ENDNOTES

[1]   The cost of an edge depends on the total traffic on the given edge.

[2]   Called Nash equilibrium in game theory.

[3]   The flow consists of units, called agents that enter the network in one of the time periods.

[4]   In this model, cars cannot overtake the cars already on the road and there is a time gap, i.e. minimum "following distance".

[5]   The actual cost functions are slightly modified from http://vcp.med.harvard.edu/braess-paradox.html.

[6]   These are the intentions of the agents in the IoT routing problem.

[7]   Autonomous local decisions may not lead to globally optimal solution.

Chapter 3
Influence of Network Constraints on Modeling and Analysis of Cyber–Physical Systems

Stephanie Grubmüller
Virtual Vehicle Research Center, Austria

Georg Stettinger
Virtual Vehicle Research Center, Austria

Martin Benedikt
Virtual Vehicle Research Center, Austria

Daniel Watzenig
Virtual Vehicle Research Center, Austria & Graz University of Technology, Austria

ABSTRACT

A cyber-physical system (CPS) is a composition of an embedded computer, a network and a physical process. Usually, the plant, which represents the physical part, is controlled by an embedded system, which consists of computation, communication and control elements, via the global network. This contribution focuses on networked control systems (NCSs) which represents a specific class of CPS. As the problems of CPSs and NCSs are quite similar the goal is to transfer well developed techniques of NCSs to CPSs for analysis purposes. NCSs deal with the analysis of the interaction between the physical system and the cyber system. A main challenge of a control engineer is the development of stable and robust controllers for a NCS. The same goal is present in the design of CPS. To ensure this goal the analysis of such a feedback system has to be performed which is not straight forward and limited by the used modeling approach. This work compares different state-of-the-art modeling approaches for NCSs and stability analysis methods therefore.

DOI: 10.4018/978-1-5225-2845-6.ch003

INTRODUCTION

Cyber-physical systems (CPS) represent a composition of an embedded computer, a network (cyber system) and a physical process (physical system) (Lee, 2006). Usually, the plant, which represents the physical part, is controlled by an embedded system via the global network (Lunze & Grüne, 2014). In the work of Baheti and Gill (2011) a more common definition of a CPS has been introduced, "The term cyber-physical systems refers to a new generation of systems with integrated computational and physical capabilities that can interact with humans through many new modalities" (p. 161). The physical component, which can be either a physical, biological or engineered system, is usually of large scale. Due to more efficient software, hardware and network systems, embedded systems can be found in all parts of the physical environment. As a result, a tight integration of the cyber and physical component is very important (Antsaklis, et al., 2013). A detailed analysis on the joint dynamics of the computational and physical part are the keys for a stable, robust, efficient and reliable system design (Kim & Kumar, 2013), (Antsaklis, et al., 2013), (Derler, Lee, & Vincentelli, 2012). A CPS design involves knowledge from disciplines like control, software, mechanical and network engineering. For a successful CPS design, it is important to enable a knowledge transfer between the different engineering areas (disciplines). Especially the cooperation between control and embedded systems engineers (Derler, Lee, Tripakis, & Törngren, 2013) supports the complex design process. In that context networked control systems (NCS) are getting more and more important. To optimize the hardware architecture of an embedded system and to reduce wiring as well as weight, shared buses are introduced. This means more than one control loop is closed over the communication network. Other advantages of NCS compared to point-to-point wiring are higher reliability, lower costs, less needed power and simpler installation (Walsh & Ye, 2001). To reduce communication efforts in modern vehicles, a high-speed Controller Area Network (CAN), for e.g. engine control, and a low-speed CAN, for e.g. window control are integrated (Walsh & Ye, 2001).

Apparently, a shared network represents an unreliable communication link. Hence, packet loss may occur during the system's runtime. Such data loss probably degrades the system's performance (Zhang, Branicky, & Phillips, 2001).

In addition, the scheduling of the control tasks within a shared network may influence the feedback system's behavior and performance. Different scheduling algorithms cause different values of time delays which can lead to different stability properties. Thus, the control system closed over the networked, together with a specific scheduling, need to be analyzed (Walsh & Ye, 2001).

Nowadays, cyber-physical systems become very important in the field of engineering. They include devices, vehicles, management processes, web services etc. (Geisberger & Broy, 2012).

During the last century, our society has steadily increased the dependence on engineered systems. Engineered systems are such as vehicles, health systems or smart buildings. CPS are expected to positively influence the way of interaction and operation between human beings and engineered systems. Besides technology, society is a driver for CPS (Kim & Kumar, 2013). For example, to increase the passenger's safety in vehicles driver assistance functions like adaptive cruise control are introduced (Goswami, et al., 2012). Current popular examples of CPS are: Automated traffic control (Antsaklis, et al., 2013), Drive-by-Wire systems (Howser & McMillin, 2013), power grids (Kim & Kumar, 2013) etc.

A representative automotive CPS example is the adaptive cruise control unit interacting with the vehicle itself which represents the plant. The controller is implemented on an ECU (electronic control unit, discrete part) and interacts with a real-world model (continuous part). Additionally, a CPS within a vehicle environment, like adaptive cruise control, consists of spatially distributed controllers, sensors and actuators which interact over a shared communication network (Zhang, Gao, & Kaynak, 2013). In modern vehicles, the standard communication network implemented is the CAN. Usually, the control function is designed without considering network induced imperfections like time delays which is referred to an emulation based approach (Heemels & van de Wouw, 2010). Hence, under the assumption of ideal communication the behavior of the vehicle including the controller is stable and predictable. But under real circumstances the shared communication induces time delays caused by e.g. access limitation. That time delays may lead to a misbehavior of the overall system (Heemels & van de Wouw, 2010). In the case of adaptive cruise control, it can even lead to a safety critical behavior in the worst case. Thus, it is of importance to analyze CPS with well-developed NCS techniques. As a consequence, a NCS model it is able to analyze how a shared communication network and e.g. the induced time delays influence the overall system's closed loop performance and behavior (Heemels & van de Wouw, 2010), (Hespanha, Naghshtabrizi, & Xu, 2007), (Yang, 2006), (Zhang, Gao, & Kaynak, 2013), (Zhang, Branicky, & Phillips, 2001)).

Another CPS example is the unmanned air vehicle (UAV) which also represents a classical NCS problem. The employment of a UAV is constraint due to stealth requirements. This leads to a limitation of the data rates (Hespanha, Naghshtabrizi, & Xu, 2007).

To give a more general example of a CPS wireless computing is introduced which is strongly affected by the network, e.g. power grids, platooning, etc. The communication network is highly unreliable and data losses are common. These systems strongly depend on the physical states of every communication device. Consequently, it is important to analyze how the network affects the performance of the whole system (Fitzgerald, Larsen, & Verhoef, 2014).

The deployment of NCS results in flexible architecture and lower costs in installation as well as maintenance. Traditional control systems are represented by a plant and a controller which are connected via an ideal communication network. A lot of stability proofs are provided therefore. Imperfections induced by a shared communication network may lead to a destabilization of the whole system (Hespanha, Naghshtabrizi, & Xu, 2007).

Applying NCS analysis tools during the CPS development process provides information about destabilizing time delays and sampling periods, influences of quantization errors and packet losses. During the system's implementation phase, the gained information can lead to reduce costs and time caused by design failures. Or in the best case the results of the NCS analysis are considered and incorporated in the controller design.

This contribution focuses on NCSs which represents a specific class of CPS. Additionally, this work gives an overview about networked induction imperfections and their corresponding analysis and design techniques.

Altogether, the BACKGROUND section summaries all important and currently known existing CPS challenges and gives an elementary description about NCS. The section NCS TECHNIQUES FOR HANDLING CPS CHALLENGES gives a detailed overview about the existing challenges in NCS and what are the state-of-the art modelling and analysis tools and methods to handle the existing challenges. Subsequently, the discussed methods are applied to a CPS example and the results are analyzed and discussed in detail. Finally, an outlook on future research topics is given and the topic within that contribution is concluded.

BACKGROUND

During the last years, a lot of research in the field of CPS has been done. There are still a lot of open challenges: Numerous publications address these issues, i.e. (Kim & Kumar, 2013), (Lee, 2008), (Fitzgerald, Larsen, & Verhoef, 2014), (Rajkumar, Lee, Sha, & Stankovic, 2010), (Sha, Gopalakrishnan, Liu, & Wang, 2009), (Shi, Wan, Yan, & Suo, 2011). In conclusion, the following research issues are the most critical ones.

- **Composition:** It is the science of composing subsystems, networks, protocols and different architectures (Rajkumar, Lee, Sha, & Stankovic, 2010). By composing systems, it has to be ensured that Quality of Service (QoS) properties (like stability or schedulability) and functional properties (like functional correctness) are possible to derive from architectural structure, the interaction of the subsystems' protocols and the subsystem's QoS and functional properties. The composition can lead to large CPS with different QoS properties and several protocols. Thus, for analyzing the system distinct methods may be needed. For a successful system composition, the QoS properties as well as the protocol interaction must be addressed (Sha, Gopalakrishnan, Liu, & Wang, 2009).
- **Robustness, Safety and Security:** Typically, a CPS exists of numerous subsystems (sensing, actuation, computation and network) which affect the overall physical system's behavior (Sha, Gopalakrishnan, Liu, & Wang, 2009). Especially for safety-critical systems it is important to ensure stability, even during the appearance of any type of failure (Kim & Kumar, 2013). Recently, security in CPS became very popular due to the increasing deployment of wireless communication media. Thus, a secure system is able to deflect security attacks from outside the system (Sha, Gopalakrishnan, Liu, & Wang, 2009). In conclusion, robustness, safety and security are still major research challenges.
- **Architecture and Abstractions:** The architecture of a CPS represents the communication system design and keeps physical information (Kim & Kumar, 2013). For correct work flows it is mandatory that in large-scale CPS the architectures are consistent. In this context, the term abstractions contains computational abstractions and real-time embedded abstractions. Physical and logical properties shall be captured by computational abstraction. Whereas real-time embedded abstraction deals with resource allocation of distributed systems, optimization of performance, distributed real-time computing methods as well as group communications methods (Rajkumar, Lee, Sha, & Stankovic, 2010).
- **Computing, Sensing and Networking Systems:** When sharing a resource in distributed real-time systems, regardless whether computing unit or network, a real-time schedule algorithm is needed. These algorithms provide temporal predictability of communication systems which is important for the system's stability, performance as well as safety. For various network mediums and inherent protocols the achievement of real-time properties has different level of severity. According to the interference and power issues the integration of wireless communication network systems is more difficult than wired one (Kim & Kumar, 2013).
- **Modelling and Control:** Techniques for analyzing and designing CPS are mandatory to analyze their behavior in detail (Sha, Gopalakrishnan, Liu, & Wang, 2009). Therefore, modelling techniques for CPS play an important role during analysis. The modelling approach must merge discrete-time together and continuous-time elements within a CPS. This leads to the modelling approach of hybrid systems (Kim & Kumar, 2013). Control approaches for CPS must combine

time-based as well as event-based systems in a stable way and must handle asynchronous dynamics (Rajkumar, Lee, Sha, & Stankovic, 2010). Model-based development helps to improve the CPS design process by considering hardware, software and communication (Sha, Gopalakrishnan, Liu, & Wang, 2009). To handle the rising complexity and heterogeneity of CPS, research in the designing and especially detailed modelling is mandatory.

- **Verification, Validation and Certification:** After the development of a CPS testing is very important, especially for safety-critical systems like automotive systems. If the complexity of CPS increases the certification, verification and validation will become difficult and expensive (Kim & Kumar, 2013). In the last years, a lot of research was done in the field of formal verification and is still a field of research.

As the problems of CPSs and NCSs are quite similar the goal is to transfer well developed techniques of NCSs to CPSs for analysis purposes. Before the definition of NCSs can be given, the meaning of feedback control needs to be discussed. The classical closed-loop feedback control system is given in Figure 1a).

Typically, a state controller, either discrete-time or continuous-time, transfers the states of the plant in such a way that the plant's output signal tracks the desired reference. For that an ideal connection between controller and plant is assumed. In contrast see Figure 1b), the NCS is spatially distributed and the feedback loop is closed over a shared network. In detail, the NCS theory deals with the analysis of the interaction between the physical system (plant) and the cyber system (controller). A NCS can be seen as the intersection of communication, computation and control (Lunze & Grüne, 2014). The plant's states are actuated or measured with actuation and sensing technologies, which are connected with the controller via a shared network (Branicky, 2005). A main challenge of a control engineer is the

Figure 1. a) Classical closed-loop feedback control system; b) control loop closed over a shared network

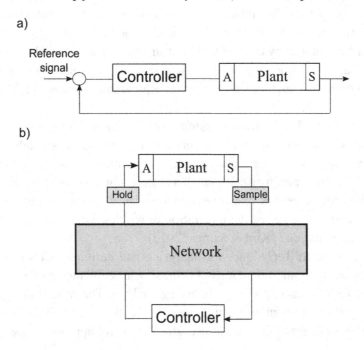

development of stable and robust controllers for a NCS which is not a trivial problem. The same goal is present with respect to robustness, safety and security in the design of CPS. The communication system and the limited computing resources cause time delays within the closed loop control system. In general, time delays restrict the achievable closed-loop dynamics (Skogestad & Postlethwaite, 2007). To ensure system's stability the analysis of such a feedback system has to be performed which is not straight forward and limited by the used modelling approach. As mentioned before, for analyzing the behavior of a CPS a multi-domain modelling approach is required to model the physical components as well as the cyber components of the entire CPS. A NCS itself represents also a hybrid control system (Sanfelice, 2015). There exist different modelling approaches for hybrid system (Lunze & Lamnabhi-Lagarrigue, 2009), which depends on the analyzed property and will be outlined in detail in the following sections. Regarding the security aspect in CPS and NCS, the security challenge is a big research topic by its own and not further discussed in this contribution. More information about security in NCSs can be found in (Cardenas, Amin, & Sastry, 2008) and (Teixeira, Sandberg, & Johansson, 2010).

Numerous survey papers were published in the last years which deal with NCSs analysis methods (e. g. (Heemels & van de Wouw, 2010), (Hespanha, Naghshtabrizi, & Xu, 2007), (Yang, 2006), (Zhang, Gao, & Kaynak, 2013), (Zhang, Branicky, & Phillips, 2001)). This work concentrates on the state-of-the-art NCS synthesis techniques, results and open issues (future topics). NCS modelling approaches and the resulting stability analysis are treated in more detail resulting in a specific pro and cons list for each approach.

NCS TECHNIQUES FOR HANDLING CPS CHALLENGES

In general, time delays restrict the achievable closed-loop bandwidth (dynamics). Due to this important restriction, from a control oriented point of view a detailed analysis of the time delay origins is presented to handle them. Time delays represent the most important networked induced imperfection with the most distinct effect. But also, the other types of networked induction imperfection have to be analyzed due to their destabilizing effects on control systems.

NCS Challenges

In NCSs continuous subsystems and embedded controllers share one communication medium. The computer software interacts via a communication network with the physical system and therefore the information is discretized (Liberzon, 2005). The focus lies on how the stability of the whole system is influenced by the communication media. In Hespanha, Naghshtabrizi and Xu (2007) NCSs are defined as "…spatially distributed systems in which the communication between sensors, actuators and controllers occurs through a shared band-limited digital communication network" (p. 138). Due to the data exchange via the shared communication medium, networked induced time delays and constraints occur. Time-delays have negative effects on the performance of closed loop (continuous) systems due to their band limiting effect (Lunze & Grüne, 2014). Classical control theory deals with ideal conditions like ideal transmission channels, unlimited bandwidth and ideal sampling. The work of Hespanha, Naghshtabrizi and Xu (2007) summarizes four key issues which degrade the system's performance. First one is the limited bandwidth of the transmission channel. Another issue is the sampling and the present dead-time. The system's stability is affected by the limited sampling rate and the present delays. The delays typically originate by the constrained network access, encoding as well as decoding of the signal, computation and the network scheduling. Also, packet dropouts caused by transmission errors have negative effects on the stability properties of the closed-loop system. The last key issue is the quantization of control signals as a result of the applied networked protocol and its packet size. In (Heemels & van de Wouw, 2010) a more detailed investigation of the before defined key issues lead to five categories of networked induced imperfections and constraints: Variable sampling and transmission intervals, variable communication delays, packet dropouts, communication constraints due to a shared network and quantization errors. Hence, these constraints influence the in- and output signals of controller and plant and further the performance of the closed-loop system.

- **Time Delays:** Time delays in NCS are caused by processing units which perform the controller task in real-time and the communication between subsystems. Ben Khaled-El Feki (2014) gives an introduction into real-time computing and the real-time parameters are given. When different tasks share one processor a scheduling algorithm with corresponding real-time parameters is mandatory. Based on (Ben Khaled-El Feki, 2014), the real-time parameters are defined and highlighted in Figure 2a). After the task release at time instant r_k and some Jitter, the task is started at time s_k. To generate correct results, each task must be finished before its deadline d_k. Important is the Worst Case Execution Time (WCET) for each Task, which is the longest possible duration of the task's execution. The WCET can for example be determined via an end-to-end analysis. If embedded control systems are under consideration, the delays caused by sample and hold have also be taken into account. This is discussed in detail in (Derler, Lee, Tripakis, & Törngren, 2013). A system under control represents a periodic control system and is described by specific timing variables. These timing variables are illustrated in Figure 2b). The plant is sampled theoretically every $k \cdot h$ time instant. In practice the sampling is done after some Jitter J_k connected with a sampling period h_k. After sampling, the controller computes a control signal and subsequently sends it to the plant's actuator. The time between sampling and actuation represents the controller's computation time τ_k. In NCS the controller is connected with the plant via a shared network. In the work of Nilsson (1998) general networked delays has been defined, which are highlighted in Figure 2c). Under the assumption that between sensing and sampling is no time delay, the communication delay between sensing and receiving at the controller is represented by $\tau_{k,sc}$. The networked-induced delay between controller and actuator is analog as $\tau_{k,ca}$. The computational delay $\tau_{k,c}$ caused by processing the control task is equal to the response time R_k. Commonly the Jitter between the task release and task start time is neglected (Walsh & Ye, 2001). That means that $\tau_{k,c}$ is equivalent to WCET. In addition, the sum of all delays in a NCS $\tau_{k,sc} + \tau_{k,c} + \tau_{k,ca}$ is equivalent to the sampling-to-actuation time τ_k and is also called control delay. Typically, the computational delays are neglected because the networked-induced delays are significant (Walsh & Ye, 2001). Due to the neglect, in NCS communication delays mainly are analyzed. Nilsson (1998) distinguishes three different models of delays: a constant delay, a time varying delay and a random delay according to a probability distribution. In the work of Zhang, Gao, & Kaynak (2013) a summary of the NCS' time delay characteristics is given. They highlighted three characteristics. One is the difference between constant and time-varying delays. The second is the consideration

Figure 2. a) Real-time parameters based on (Ben Khaled-El Feki, 2014); b) timing parameters of embedded control system based on (Derler, Lee, Tripakis, & Törngren, 2013); c) delays in NCS based on (Nilsson, 1998)

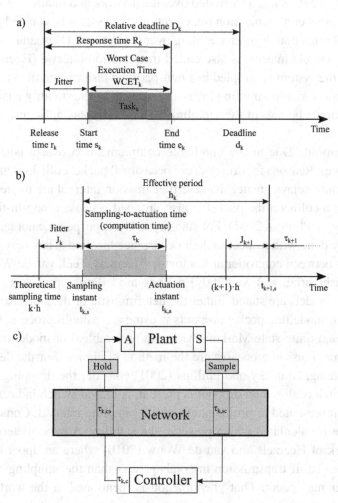

of the delay, either it is deterministic or stochastic. The last one is the difference between the duration of the delays. Small delays are smaller than one sampling interval and long delays are greater. In most stability analysis frameworks, the presence of small delays are assumed. The simplest approach is to assume all time delays to be constant for each transfer interval (Nilsson, 1998). For small delays compared to the sampling time this is typically sufficient. One drawback is that it leads probably to wrong conclusions about stability and performance (Nilsson, 1998). Usually, network delays are time varying which is highlighted in Figure 2b) by the Jitter. The time variance is caused by the waiting time for the network availability and the frame time delay. The frame time delay is the time delay between placing a packet on the network and the propagation delay, which is also known as the packet's traveling time through the network (Lian, Moyne, & Tilbury, 2001). Furthermore, these delays depend on the variable network conditions such as channel quality. The time varying delays can be considered as deterministic or stochastic (Nilsson, 1998). According to the time-variant delays the overall system is time variant as well.

- **Transmission Intervals:** Typically, in NCS a continuous -time system (i.e. the plant) needs to transmit or receive signals over a network. For that the signal is sampled and afterwards encoded into a digital format before it is transmitted over the network and finally decoded at the receiver. In the ideal case without communication imperfections the system is sampled periodically. The signal is transmitted immediately after sampling over the network (Hespanha, Naghshtabrizi, & Xu, 2007). Thus, the sample interval is also called transmission interval (Heemels & van de Wouw, 2010). In reality the system is sampled in a non-periodic fashion and the system is no longer time invariant due to the variable sampling intervals. A result of the stability analysis of these systems is the lower and upper bounds of the sampling interval (Hespanha, Naghshtabrizi, & Xu, 2007).

- **Packet Loss/Dropout:** Due to the unreliable communication over a (shared) network, packet dropouts may occur. Reasons for dropouts are occasional packet collisions and failures of network nodes. In NCS, time delays greater than the transmission interval are treated as packet dropouts. In addition, after a collision the packet is also dropped because a non-in-time-arrival is useless (Zhang, Branicky, & Phillips, 2001). For stability analysis purposes, another classification of data losses is typically done with respect to their occurrence location. They may occur between sensor and controller or between controller and actuator (Heemels, Teel, van de Wouw, & Nesic, 2010). Hespanha, Naghshtabrizi, and Xu (2007) discuss modelling approaches of packet dropouts in detail. Two main models are stated, either the deterministic or the stochastic approach. The simplest approach for modelling packet dropouts is using a Bernoulli process. If correlated dropouts need to be modeled finite-state Markov chains are preferable. For modelling stochastic dropouts in continuous time, Poisson processes are the method of choice. For the deterministic approach, the authors of Zhang, Branicky and Phillips (2001) consider the dropping of a data packet as a switch. If the switch is closed no dropout is present. A closed switch indicate that a dropout happened, which is represented as prolongation of the sampling interval. Consequently, a sampling/transmission rate is calculated which preserve the stability. Another deterministic modelling is given in the work of Heemels and van de Wouw (2010) where an upper bound of consecutive dropouts is presented. If transmission intervals greater than the sampling rate are allowed, then a packet disorder may occur. That phenomenon is mentioned in the work of Zhang, Gao and Kaynak (2013). A packet disorder appears when the packets arrive at the receiver node in another sequence than released by the sender node. In this contribution is only the small delay case considered. Consequently, packets with time delays greater than the sampling/transmission interval are discarded (Zhang, Gao, & Kaynak, 2013).

- **Network Constraints:** In NCS a number of network nodes access to one shared network. These nodes may belong to the same control loop, to other control loops or other data communication tasks (Zhang, Gao, & Kaynak, 2013). Consequently, per transmission only one node is allowed to transmit a packet. Therefore, that shared network causes communication constraints (Heemels & van de Wouw, 2010). To avoid network congestions or packet losses a scheduling policy is mandatory. As a result, each node needs to be equipped with a scheduler. In addition, each node has to determine a packet transmission deadline which is called Maximum Allowable Transmission Interval (MATI) (Zhang, Gao, & Kaynak, 2013). In principle two different scheduling methods are distinguishable: static and dynamic scheduling. If static scheduling is used the network is allocated before runtime. A popular example is Round Robin (RR), which is a token-ring-type scheduling method. An allocation during runtime is called dynamic scheduling, like Try Once

Discard (TOD). TOD is a maximum-error-first scheduling method which means that the node containing the biggest networked induced error is allowed to access the network (Walsh & Ye, 2001). In the work of Walsh, Ye and Bushnell (2002) the modelling of the networked-induced error due to scheduling is analyzed in detail. The error is incorporated into the system's equations and determines the deviation between the value of the most recent sample of a state and the actual value of the state.

- **Quantization:** Data quantization is the phenomenon when an analog signal is converted into a digital signal with finite word length. Consequently, the quantization error caused by the limited resolution can affect the closed-loop stability and performance. The quantization error can be neglected if a sufficient number of bits are transmitted per packet which depends on the network technology (Zhang, Gao, & Kaynak, 2013). Nowadays quantization aspects are of less importance due to fast and accurate analog-digital converters. Therefore, this imperfection is not further discussed in that contribution but listed for completeness.
- **Clock Asynchronization:** Zhang, Gao and Kaynak (2013) analyzed the asynchronization of the clock between the network nodes as a network-induced constraint caused by practical implementation. The work of Zhang, Branicky and Phillips (2001) points out that for exact calculation of the time delay the nodes need to be synchronized. For the synchronization process the round-trip time and clock offset has to be measured. The round-trip time defines the time between a node sending a request and receiving an acknowledgement. In addition, the different ways of clock synchronization (hardware, software and both synchronization methods) are outlined in Zhang, Branicky and Phillips (2001). In general, for the control oriented analysis of NCS the clock synchronization can be neglected (Zhang, Gao, & Kaynak, 2013). For this contribution clock asynchronization is not further considered and just mentioned for completeness.

Modelling of NCS

For analyzing the behavior of a CPS a modelling approach is mandatory including the discussed network induced imperfections and constraints. Often a multi-domain modelling approach is required to model the physical components (dynamic systems) as well as the cyber components of the entire CPS. The dynamic system usually consists of continuous differential equations describing the physical behavior of the system. Sanfelice (2015) split up the modelling of the cyber part is into two parts: first the model of cyber components such as algorithms, computation and the transmission of digital data over a network. The cyber part typically results in a finite state machine or a discrete system. The second part concentrates on the interconnection of the cyber- and physical-part which focuses on the modelling of the sample and hold of the signals. This combination of the physical- and cyber part results in a hybrid system description (Branicky, 2005) and (Sanfelice, 2015). Based on this hybrid system description of the CPS, typical control theory oriented statements about reachability, safety, security, attractivity, temporal logic, timing, stability, etc. can be determined (Sanfelice, 2015). As stated in the contribution of Samad and Annaswamy (2011): "The control engineering research community can play a leading role in the development of cyber-physical systems." (p.163), due to their widely-spread understanding in system theory.

In (Heemels & van de Wouw, 2010) three different NCS modelling approaches are presented:

- **Discrete-Time Approach:** That approach intensively studied by different papers, i.e. (Cloosterman, 2008), (Cloosterman, van de Wouw, Heemels, & Nijmeijer, 2009), (Heemels & van de Wouw, 2010), (van de Wouw, Naghshtabrizi, Cloosterman, & Hespanha, 2010) and (van de Wouw, Naghshtabrizi, Cloosterman, & Hespanha, 2009). For that approach the sampled-data NCS is represented in discrete-time form (see Figure 3). For linear systems, an exact time discretization can be done. Consequently, that approach focuses on linear systems. In the literature, it is mainly focused on time-driven models than on event-driven models (Cloosterman, 2008). After the time discretization, the model contains uncertainties. These uncertainties cover time constant and time varying delays, time varying sampling and consecutive packet loss. For stability analysis, a poly-topic over-approximation of the discrete-time model leads to a finite number of linear matrix inequalities. Finally, the stability of the intersample behavior needs to be analyzed.

- **Sampled-Data Approach:** This approach analyzes the sampled-data NCS model in the contin-uous-time domain. Which means that the sampled-data NCS system is modeled using delay-dif-ferential equations and in recent publications as impulsive delay-differential equations as given in (Fridman, 2014), (Liu, Fridman, & Hetel, 2015) and (Liu, Fridman, & Hetel, 2014). The stability approval is based on a Lyapunov-Krasovskii functional. That approach is not further considered in that contribution.

- **Emulation-Based Approach:** For that approach a system under control is analyzed which was designed without the presence of a shared network. For analysis reasons, the NCS model is con-sidered as continuous-time (sampled-data) with continuous-time controller (Heemels, Teel, van de Wouw, & Nesic, 2010).

The discrete-time and the emulation-based modelling approach are analysed in detail with the help of simple examples to point out their characteristics. Starting with a simple NCS model with constant delays followed by a NCS model with constant sampling and varying delays the prospects of the approaches are presented. Both examples are based on the discrete-time approach. To address the emulation-based approach the least three different imperfections are analysed in detail.

Figure 3. Sampled-data control systems: the block A/D samples the plant's output y(t) every time instant t_k. The digital to analog converter is given by the block D/A and is equal to a ZOH. Continuous-time signals are the reference r(t), the output y(t) and the piecewise constant control input u*(t) after the digital to analog conversion. Digital signals are the sampled output y_k and u_k.

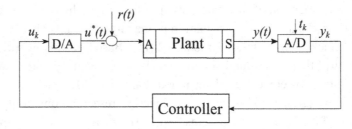

Periodic Sampling with Constant/Varying Delays

The system under consideration is shown in Figure 3. The model consists of a continuous time plant, which is periodically sampled at time instants $t_k = kh$, and a discrete time controller as described by the authors of Zhang, Branicky and Phillips (2001), Heemels and van de Wouw (2010) and Cloosterman, van de Wouw, Heemels and Nijmeijer (2009). The model of the plant without time delays is represented by

$$
\begin{aligned}
&\dot{x}(t) = Ax(t) + Bu^*(t) \\
&y(t) = Cx(t) \\
&u^*(t) = u_k, \text{ for } t \in \left[t_k, t_{k+1} \right)
\end{aligned}
\tag{1}
$$

Where the state x, the control input u and the output y are defined as $x \in \mathbb{R}^n$, $u \in \mathbb{R}^m$ and $y \in \mathbb{R}^l$. The matrices A, B and C have compatible dimensions. The Zero-Order-Hold (ZOH) block holds the value of the control input u_k constant for one sample. Thus, u^* is a piecewise constant signal which changes at each sampling time instant. The control law is given in equation (2) which represents a static state feedback controller:

$$
u_k = -Kx_k, \text{ with } K \in \mathbb{R}^m \times \mathbb{R}^n
\tag{2}
$$

To model a system with constant time delays, typically a input-delay system is considered in the work of Zhang, Gao and Kaynak (2013). One representation is outlined i.e. by Cloosterman (2008) and given in equation (3).

$$
\begin{aligned}
&\dot{x}(t) = Ax(t) + Bu^*(t) \\
&y(t) = Cx(t) \\
&u^*(t) = u_k, \text{ for } t \in \left[t_k + \tau_k, t_{k+1} + \tau_k \right)
\end{aligned}
\tag{3}
$$

For time-invariant controllers, like the static state feedback controller, the constant or time-variant delays τ_{sc} and τ_{ca} are lumped together (see equation (4)) (Zhang, Branicky, & Phillips, 2001).

$$
\tau_k = \tau_{sc} + \tau_{ca}
\tag{4}
$$

For further considerations a number of assumptions based on (Zhang, Branicky, & Phillips, 2001) and (Heemels & van de Wouw, 2010) are made: i) the sensor is time-driven, ii) actuator and controller are event-driven, which guarantees an immediate reaction when a sample arrives, iii) all states of system (1) are measured, iv) the sampling period h is constant, v) the hold functionality is done by a ZOH interpolation, vi) the output is sampled $y_k := y(t_k)$ and fully measured, vii) the control input u_k is based on the output sample y_k and viii) small delays are considered $\tau_k < h$.

To analyze sampled-data systems as given in equations (1) – (3) a discrete-time representation is needed. As mentioned by Heemels and van de Wouw (2010) for linear systems the discretization at sampling instant t_k can be done exactly. The differential equation for the discrete-time system of the plant is shown in equation (5) (see also i.e. in (Cloosterman, 2008)).

$$x_{k+1} = e^{Ah}x_k + \int_0^{h-\tau_k} e^{As}Bu_k ds + \int_{h-\tau_k}^h e^{As}Bu_{k-1}ds$$

$$y_k = Cx_k$$

(5)

The discrete-time closed-loop state-space model is given by (6), which represents the NCS model.

$$z_{k+1} = \underbrace{\begin{pmatrix} e^{Ah} - \int_0^{h-\tau_k} e^{As}BK ds & \int_{h-\tau_k}^h e^{As}B ds \\ -K & 0 \end{pmatrix}}_{\Phi(h,\tau_k)} z_k$$

(6)

The augmented state vector z_k is defined by $z_k = \left[x_k^T, u_{k-1}^T\right]$.

Non-Periodic Sampling and Varying Delays

In NCS time-varying transmission intervals and delays are very popular problems as mentioned before. A lot of research regarding this topic was done the last years. Important publications were contributed to that topic by Hetel, Daffouz and Iung (2008), van de Wouw, Naghshtabrizi, Cloosterman, and Hespanha (2009), Cloosterman (2008), van de Wouw, Naghshtabrizi, Cloosterman and Hespanha (2010) and Hespanha, Naghshtabrizi and Xu (2007). Here the discrete-time approach presented by Cloosterman (2008) is outlined in detail. This approach is based on the model in (3) with additional time-varying sample intervals $h_k \in \left[h_{\min}, h_{MATI}\right]$ and delays $\tau_k \in \left[\tau_{\min}, \tau_{MAD}\right]$. The approach is extensible for long delays as described in the work of Heemels and van de Wouw (2010) and Cloosterman (2008). Due to time-varying delays the overall system is time-variant as well.

Non-Periodic Sampling, Varying Delays and Network Scheduling

The former modelling approaches do not incorporate communication constraints. The emulation-based approach as defined by the authors Heemels, Teel, van de Wouw, and Nesic (2010), Heemels and van de Wouw (2010), Nesic and Teel (2004a) and Nesic and Teel (2004b) considers that NCS challenge including time-varying sampling and delays, as well as packet dropouts and quantization. The mentioned approach provides the basis to analyze a system which was designed without a network. Therefore, it considers a continuous time plant and controller. The state-space models of plant and controller are given by equation (7).

$$\dot{x}_p = f_p\left(x_p, \hat{u}\right), \ y = g_p\left(x_p\right)$$
$$\dot{x}_c = f_c\left(x_c, \hat{y}\right), \ u = g_c\left(x_c\right) \quad t \in \left[t_k, t_{k+1}\right]$$

(7)

The state of the plant is defined by $x_p \in \mathbb{R}^{N_p}$, the plant's output is given by $y \in \mathbb{R}^{N_y}$ and the most recent (sampled) input is expressed as $\hat{u} \in \mathbb{R}^{N_u}$. The controller state is defined by $x_c \in \mathbb{R}^{N_c}$, the continuous-time control input is given by $u \in \mathbb{R}^{N_u}$ and the sampled plant's output is given as $\hat{y} \in \mathbb{R}^{N_y}$. Parts of the input u and output y are sampled and immediately transmitted over the network. For the digital to analog signal conversion a ZOH interpolation is applied. In addition, the restrictions defined before hold: $h_k \in \left[h_{\min}, h_{MATI}\right]$ with $h_{\min} > 0$, as well as the increasing transmission times and $\tau_k \in \left[\tau_{\min}, \tau_{MAD}\right]$. The framework includes statements about stability and performance of the system when a shared network is included and small delays are considered. At transmission time the protocol selects which network node gets network access and sends its data. Two popular scheduling policies are mentioned above RR and TOD. The values $\hat{u}$ and $\hat{y}$ for each network note are updated by $y(t_k)$ and $u(t_k)$ at time instants $t_k + \tau_k$ related to the relevant scheduling update function h_u and h_y (see equation (8))

$$
\begin{aligned}
\hat{y}\left(t_k^{+}\right) &= y\left(t_k\right) + h_y\left(k, e\left(t_k\right)\right) \\
\hat{u}\left(t_k^{+}\right) &= u\left(t_k\right) + h_u\left(k, e\left(t_k\right)\right)
\end{aligned}
\tag{8}
$$

The scheduling policy for two nodes and RR is defined in equation (9), and for TOD in equation (10).

$$
h(k,e) =
\begin{cases}
\begin{pmatrix} 0 \\ e_2 \end{pmatrix}, & \text{if } k = 0, 2, 4, \ldots \\[2ex]
\begin{pmatrix} e_1 \\ 0 \end{pmatrix}, & \text{if } k = 1, 3, 5, \ldots
\end{cases}
\tag{9}
$$

$$
h(k,e) =
\begin{cases}
\begin{pmatrix} 0 \\ e_2 \end{pmatrix}, & \text{if } |e_1| \geq |e_2| \\[2ex]
\begin{pmatrix} e_1 \\ 0 \end{pmatrix}, & \text{if } |e_2| > |e_1|
\end{cases}
\tag{10}
$$

A network node can be either a subsystem's input or output or both. The network induced error is denoted by the vector $\left(e_y, e_u\right) = \left(\hat{y} - y, \hat{u} - u\right)$. For each node, a networked induced error vector e_j exists, hence for the whole system the vector e is denoted by $e = \left(e_1, e_2, \ldots\right)$. As shown i.e. shown in the work of Heemels and van de Wouw (2010), this leads to the reset conditions $e\left(t_k^{+}\right) = h\left(k, e\left(t_k\right)\right)$ at arrival times $t_k + \tau_k$. For analysis purposes the system given in (7) is reformulated to a closed-loop system with jumps. Detailed information regarding this procedure is outlined in work of the authors Heemels, Teel, van de Wouw and Nesic (2010), Heemels and van de Wouw (2010), Nesic and Teel

(2004a) and Nesic and Teel (2004b). As a result a hybrid system framework is available for stability analysis. The flow equations of the hybrid model are given by equation (11a).

$$
\left.\begin{array}{l}
\dot{x} = f(x,e) \\
\dot{e} = g(x,e) \\
\dot{s} = 0 \\
\dot{\kappa} = 0 \\
\dot{\tau} = 1 \\
\dot{l} = 0
\end{array}\right\}
\left(l = 0 \wedge \tau \in \left[0, h_{MATI}\right]\right) \vee \left(l = 1 \wedge \tau \in \left[0, \tau_{MAD}\right]\right) \text{(11.a)}
$$

Here $x = \left[x_p, x_c\right]^T$ denotes the state of the closed-loop feedback system without the network, e is the network induced error, s is an auxiliary variable which stores the update values for e at time instant $t_k + \tau_k$, κ counts the number of transmissions, τ is the timer and l provides information if the next event will be either a transmission $\left(l = 0\right)$ or an update $\left(l = 1\right)$. Hence, the model needs two reset equations. When $l = 0$ and $\tau = t_k$ the transmission reset is active like in equation (12).

$$
\left(x^+, e^+, s^+, \tau^+, \kappa^+, l^+\right) = \left(x, e, h\left(\kappa, e\right) - e, 0, \kappa + 1, 1\right) \tag{12}
$$

When $l = 1$ and $\tau = t_k + \tau_k$ the reset update in (13) is active:

$$
\left(x^+, e^+, s^+, \tau^+, \kappa^+, l^+\right) = \left(x, s + e, -s - e, \tau, \kappa, 0\right) \tag{13}
$$

The hybrid system in equation (11a) considers the force-free or disturbance free case. If a disturbance input w influences the system, the flow equations are extended to $\dot{x} = f(x,e,w)$ and $\dot{e} = g(x,e,w)$. Consequently, the extended hybrid system is given in equation (11.b) as proposed by Heemels, Teel, van de Wouw and Nesic (2010).

$$
\left.\begin{array}{l}
\dot{x} = f(x,e,w) \\
\dot{e} = g(x,e,w) \\
\dot{s} = 0 \\
\dot{\kappa} = 0 \\
\dot{\tau} = 1 \\
\dot{l} = 0
\end{array}\right\}
\left(l = 0 \wedge \tau \in \left[0, h_{MATI}\right]\right) \vee \left(l = 1 \wedge \tau \in \left[0, \tau_{MAD}\right]\right) \text{(11.b)}
$$
$$
z = q(x,w) = C_z x + D_z w
$$

The variable z as the output of the whole systems includes the information how the disturbance input w affects the output as well.

Stability of NCS

The stability analysis is based on the specific system model including the network induced imperfections.

Periodic/Non-Periodic Sampling and Constant/Varying Delays

The first two models defined in the previous section, modelling in NCS, are analyzable by the same mathematical tools. To analyze the delayed sampled-data system as in equation (3), the lifted closed loop model given by (6) is employed. For constant delays the stability analysis is relatively simple. The system is exponentially stable if $\Phi(h, \tau_k)$ is Schur (Hespanha, Naghshtabrizi, & Xu, 2007). For the linear time invariant case, all eigenvalues need to be located within the unity circle. If the time-varying time delay case is under consideration, the analysis is not straight forward because the eigenvalues are not representative to make stability statements. Hence, the lifted system in (6) becomes linear parameter-varying, so the parameters appear in a nonlinear manner, like the exponential form in system (6) (Heemels & van de Wouw, 2010). A sufficient condition for global asymptotic stability is to find a Lyapunov function $V(z)$ for the time-discrete system given in (6). One approach is to find a quadratic Lyapunov function of the form $V(z) = z^T P z$. The stability is given if a symmetric matrix P exists and the conditions (14) are fulfilled (Boyd, El Ghaoui, Feron, & Balakrishnan, 1994).

$$P \succ 0$$
$$P = P^T \tag{14}$$
$$\Phi\left(h_k, \tau_k\right)^T P \Phi\left(h_k, \tau_k\right) - P \prec 0, \forall \tau_k \in \left[\tau_{min}, \tau_{MAD}\right] \wedge \forall h_k \in \left[h_{min}, h_{MATI}\right]$$

For varying h_k and τ_k these conditions lead to an infinite number of Linear Matrix Inequalities (LMIs) (Hespanha, Naghshtabrizi, & Xu, 2007). A reformulation of (6) and a polytopic overapproximation of uncertainty terms lead to a finite number of LMIs which is described in (Heemels & van de Wouw, 2010). For that, the uncertainty matrix set $\Phi\left(h_k, \tau_k\right)$ is embedded into a polytopic matrix set with vertices $\Phi_1, ..., \Phi_N$ of the convex hull, see equation (15).

$$\begin{aligned} &\left\{\Phi\left(h_k, \tau_k\right), h_k \in \left[h_{min}, h_{MATI}\right], \tau \in \left[\tau_{min}, \tau_{MAD}\right]\right\} \subseteq \text{convex hull}\left\{\Phi_1, ..., \Phi_N\right\} \\ &= \left\{\sum_{i=1}^{N} \beta_i H_i, \text{with } \beta_i \geq 0 \text{ and } \sum_{i=1}^{N} \beta_i = 1\right\} \end{aligned} \tag{15}$$

To embed $\Phi(h_k, \tau_k)$ into a polytopic matrix set, first vertices $\Phi_1, ..., \Phi_N$ need to be chosen and second the boundaries of the uncertainties have to be added as norm-bounded uncertainties. Thus, the polytopic system can be stated as:

$$z_{k+1} = \left(F_0 + \sum_{i=1}^{N} \beta_i^k F_i\right) z_k + \left(G_0 + \sum_{i=1}^{N} \beta_i^k G_i\right) u_k \tag{16}$$

Various overapproximation methods exist: Real Jordan form, interval matrices, Taylor series, Cayley-Hamilton theorem and gridding with or without interpolation. In this work the real Jordan form is outlined in detail (Cloosterman, 2008). Basically, the dynamic matrix of a system is decomposable by $A = TJT^{-1}$. Hence T is the transformation matrix and J is the real Jordan which consists of Jordan block matrices. The real Jordan form lead to a generic model of form given by equation (17).

$$z_{k+1} = \left(F_0 + \sum_{i=1}^{N} \alpha_i \left(h_k, \tau_k \right) F_i \right) z_k + \left(G_0 + \sum_{i=1}^{N} \alpha_i \left(h_k, \tau_k \right) G_i \right) u_k \tag{17}$$

Here N is the number of time-varying uncertainty functions $\alpha_i(h_k, \tau_k)$. It is assumed that all eigenvalues λ of A are real then $\alpha_i \left(h_k, \tau_k \right) = \left(h_k - \tau_k \right) e^{\lambda(h_k - \tau_k)}$. The boundaries of the uncertainty parameters can be expressed on boundaries of α_i and are given by $\bar{\alpha}_i$ and $\underline{\alpha}_i$. That leads to the finite set of matrix pairs in the system given in equation (18):

$$z_{k+1} = \left(F_0 + \sum_{i=1}^{N} \alpha_i F_i \right) z_k + \left(G_0 + \sum_{i=1}^{N} \alpha_i G_i \right) u_k, \text{ with } \alpha_i \in \left\{ \bar{\alpha}_i, \underline{\alpha}_i \right\} \tag{18}$$

The convex hull of (18) is then given by the polytopic system in (16). For stability analysis the closed loop system, which is shown in equation (19), is reformulated by the real Jordan form as well as the norm-bounded uncertainties are added and finally the convex hull is given by system in (20).

$$z_{k+1} = \left(A\left(h_k, \tau_k \right) - B\left(h_k, \tau_k \right) K \right) z_k \tag{19}$$

$$z_{k+1} = \left(\left(F_0 - G_0 K \right) + \sum_{i=1}^{N} \alpha_i \left(F_i - G_i K \right) \right) z_k \tag{20}$$

That results in a finite number of LMIs formulated by equation (21):

$$P \succ 0$$
$$P = P^T \tag{21}$$
$$\left(\left(F_0 - G_0 K \right) + \sum_{i=1}^{N} \alpha_i \left(F_i - G_i K \right) \right)^T P \left(\left(F_0 - G_0 K \right) + \sum_{i=1}^{N} \alpha_i \left(F_i - G_i K \right) \right) - P \prec 0$$

In addition, to ensure asymptotic stability of the system also the intersampling behavior needs to be asymptotically stable as well. Cloosterman (2008) proves that if the system given in (3) satisfies the LMIs in (21), the behavior between samples is asymptotically stable.

Non-Periodic Sampling, Varying Delays, and Network Scheduling

The stability analysis of the disturbance-free hybrid model (11.a)-(13) is provided in Heemels and van de Wouw (2010). The analysis is based on a Lyapunov function $U(\vartheta)$ which is constructed for the flowing part and reset conditions. Therefore, $U(\vartheta)$ fulfills the condition $U(\vartheta)^+ \leq U(\vartheta)$ at reset time instants and the condition $\dot{U}(\vartheta) < 0$ during the flow part is active. As a result, conditions for the reset part, which are defined by the protocol h, and for the flow part can be concluded. First the condition on the protocol part is discussed. For stability, the protocol h needs to be uniformly globally exponential stable (UGES). It is assumed that there exists a function $W : \mathbb{Z} \times \mathbb{R}^{n_e} \to \mathbb{R}_{\geq 0}$ which is Lipschitz continuous in the second argument and the following conditions in (22)-(26) are fulfilled:

$$\underline{\alpha}_W \left|e\right| \leq W\left(\kappa, e\right) \leq \bar{\alpha}_W \left|e\right| \tag{22}$$

$$W\left(\kappa + 1, h(\kappa, e)\right) \leq \lambda W(\kappa, e) \tag{23}$$

$$0 < \underline{\alpha}_W \leq \bar{\alpha}_W, 0 < \lambda < 1 \tag{24}$$

$$W\left(\kappa + 1, e\right) \leq \lambda_W W(\kappa, e), \lambda_W \geq 1, \forall e \in \mathbb{R}^{n_e}, \forall k \in \mathbb{Z} \tag{25}$$

$$\left|\frac{\partial W}{\partial e}\left(\kappa, e\right)\right| \leq M_1, M_1 > 0 \tag{26}$$

Most of the deterministic network protocols are UGES (Tabbara & Nesic, 2008). The constant values $\lambda_W, \underline{\alpha}_W, \bar{\alpha}_W, \lambda, M_1$ for RR and TOD are calculated in the literature i.e. (Nesic & Teel, 2004a) and (Heemels, Teel, van de Wouw, & Nesic, 2010). Furthermore the conditions on the flow part (27)-(33) are stated. In equations (27) and (28) the growing conditions of the differential equations are given.

$$\left|g\left(x, e\right)\right| \leq m_x\left(x\right) + M_e \left|e\right| \tag{27}$$

$$m_x : \mathbb{R}^{n_x} \to \mathbb{R}_{\geq 0}, M_e \geq 0 \tag{28}$$

Additionally, a local continuous Lipschitz function $V(x)$ exists which fulfills the conditions given in equation (29)-(33):

$$V : \mathbb{R}^{n_x} \to \mathbb{R}_{\geq 0} \tag{29}$$

$$\underline{\alpha}_V \left(\|x\| \right) \leq V(x) \leq \bar{\alpha}_V \left(\|x\| \right), \text{with} \tag{30}$$

$$\alpha : \mathbb{R}_+ \to \mathbb{R}_+, \text{continuously, strictly increasing with } \alpha(0) = 0 (\alpha \in K_\infty) \tag{31}$$

$$\left\langle \nabla V(x), f(x,e) \right\rangle \leq -m_x^2(x) - \rho(\|x\|) + (\gamma^2 - \varepsilon) W^2(\kappa, e) \tag{32.a}$$

$$x \in \mathbb{R}^{n_x}, e \in \mathbb{R}^{n_e}, \rho \in K_\infty, \gamma > 0, 0 < \varepsilon < \max\left\{ \gamma^2, 1 \right\} \tag{33}$$

These conditions are related to Lyapunov-stability analysis techniques for the system $\dot{x} = f(x,e)$ given in equation (11.a). They guarantee a L_2 gain from $W^2(\kappa, e)$ to $m_x^2(x)$ that is strictly smaller than γ together with the globally asymptotic stability of the equilibrium $e = 0$. To get a strictly decreasing solution of the differential equations in (34) and (35), the parameters L_0, L_1, γ_0 and γ_1 are derived by conditions (22)-(33).

$$\dot{\varphi}_0 = -2L_0 \varphi_0 - \gamma_0 \left(\varphi_0^2 + 1 \right) \tag{34}$$

$$\dot{\varphi}_1 = -2L_1 \varphi_1 - \gamma_0 \left(\varphi_1^2 + \frac{\gamma_1^2}{\gamma_0^2} \right) \tag{35}$$

Conditions (36)-(38) for MAD and MATI are derived from equations (34) and (35) to guarantee global symptotic stability for system (11.a) and for $x = e = s = 0$ and $0 \leq \tau_{MAD} \leq \tau_{MATI}$ and:

$$\varphi_0(\tau) \geq \lambda^2 \varphi_1(0), \forall \tau \in \mathbb{R}_0 : 0 \leq \tau \leq \tau_{MATI} \tag{36}$$

$$\varphi_1(\tau) \geq \varphi_0(\tau), \forall \tau \in \mathbb{R}_0 : 0 \leq \tau \leq \tau_{MAD} \tag{37}$$

$$\varphi_1(0) \geq \varphi_0(0) \geq \lambda^2 \varphi_1(0) \geq 0, \varphi_0(\tau_{MATI}) > 0 \tag{38}$$

For different start values the solutions of (34) and (35) are derived. As a result, trade-off curves between MAD and MATI are generated. In the work of Heemels and van de Wouw (2010) an algorithm for generating these trade-off curves is presented: First the Lyapunov function W needs to be constructed by $\lambda_W, \underline{\alpha}_W, \overline{\alpha}_W, \lambda, M_1$. Afterwards m_x and M_e are calculated. Then the L_2 gain from $W^2(\kappa, e)$ to $m_x^2(x)$ is computed by using $V(x)$. Further, L_0, L_1, γ_0 and γ_1 are determined. In the last step the maximal values for τ_{MAD} and τ_{MATI} out of the solutions φ_0 and φ_1 for different start values $\varphi_0(0)$, $\varphi_1(0)$ have to be calculated. The value of τ_{MAD} results out of the intersection of φ_0 and φ_1 while, the value of τ_{MATI} results out of the intersection of φ_0 and $\lambda^2 \varphi_1(0)$. That step has to be repeated for different start values to generate the trade-off curves.

Equations (22) – (38) determine the stability of the free-force or disturbance free hybrid system (11.a). In the case of present disturbance inputs, the L_p-stability of system (11.b) needs to be analyzed. The L_p gain points out how to reduce the influence of the disturbance input w on the controlled output z (or parts of z) (Heemels, Teel, van de Wouw & Nesic, 2010). For that, equation (32.a) is extended to equation (32.b).

$$\langle \nabla V(x), f(x, e, w) \rangle \leq -m^2(x, w) + \gamma^2 W^2(\kappa, e) + \mu \left(\theta^p |w|^p - |q(x, w)|^p \right) \quad (32.b)$$

In (32.b) $p \in \mathbb{Z} \geq 1$ indicates the norm, $\theta \geq 0$ defines the bound of the L_p gain between the disturbance input w and the controlled output z.

SOLUTIONS AND RECOMMENDATIONS

An example based on the contribution of Cloosterman (2008) is used to show the differences between the three presented stability analysis approaches in CPS example 1)-3). CPS example 1) and 2) deal with the general discrete-time modelling approach. CPS example 1) shows the analysis of the NCS and constant time delays. CPS example 2) handles time-varying delays. In CPS example 3) the emulation-based modeling approach is applied to the test system and the stability investigated. The plant is given as:

$$\begin{pmatrix} \dot{x}_1 \\ \dot{x}_2 \end{pmatrix} = \underbrace{\begin{bmatrix} 0 & 1 \\ 0 & 0 \end{bmatrix}}_{A} \begin{pmatrix} x_1 \\ x_2 \end{pmatrix} + \underbrace{\begin{bmatrix} 0 \\ b \end{bmatrix}}_{B} u, \text{ with } b = \frac{qr_R}{J_M + q^2 J_R} = 1267 \frac{1}{kgm}$$

$$\begin{pmatrix} y_1 \\ y_2 \end{pmatrix} = \underbrace{\begin{bmatrix} 1 & 0 \\ 0 & 1 \end{bmatrix}}_{C} \begin{pmatrix} x_1 \\ x_2 \end{pmatrix}. \quad (39)$$

The plant is interconnected with a state feedback controller of the form $K = \begin{bmatrix} 10 & 1 \end{bmatrix}$. The control system has the same form as that one shown in Figure 3. If for the reference signal a unity step function is applied, the system is supposed to change its position from the start location to the end position of $x_1 = 0.1m$.

CPS Example: Periodic Sampling and Time Constant Delay

First an exact discretization is needed, as described in the modelling section above. The sampling time is set to $h = 1ms$. That leads to the following closed-loop time-discrete model with augmented state vector as defined in (6):

$$\begin{pmatrix} x_{1,k+1} \\ x_{2,k+1} \\ u_k \end{pmatrix} = \underbrace{\begin{bmatrix} e^{Ah} - \int_0^{1ms-\tau_k} e^{As}BKds & \int_{1ms-\tau_k}^{1ms} e^{As}Bds \\ -K & 0 \end{bmatrix}}_{\Phi(1ms,\tau)} \begin{pmatrix} x_{1,k} \\ x_{2,k} \\ u_{k-1} \end{pmatrix} \tag{40}$$

For different values of τ the matrix Φ is Schur and the maximum time delay for which the system is barely stable is given by $\tau = 0.78ms$. For that the system equation results in:

$$\begin{pmatrix} x_{1,k+1} \\ x_{2,k+1} \\ u_k \end{pmatrix} = \begin{bmatrix} 0.9997 & 0.0009721 & 0.0006055 \\ -2.661 & 0.7339 & 1.001 \\ -10 & -1 & 0 \end{bmatrix} \begin{pmatrix} x_{1,k} \\ x_{2,k} \\ u_{k-1} \end{pmatrix} \tag{41}$$

For $\tau = 0.78ms$ the absolute value of the discrete eigenvalues of system (41) is $z_1 = 0.99$ and $z_{2/3} = 0.9972$ and obviously within the unity circle. The resulting behavior for a unity step reference function using start values $x_1 = x_2 = 0$ is shown in Figure 4. After the transient oscillation of state x_2 which is the acceleration and depicted as the red curve in Figure 4, the trajectory converges to zero. For that specific given delay of $\tau = 0.78ms$ the states x_1, which is depicted by the blue curve, and x_2 have equilibriums of $x_1 = 0.1m$ and $x_2 = 0\frac{m}{s^2}$ which leads to a stable behavior of the systems.

CPS Example: Periodic Sampling and Time Varying Delay

Here the same example is used, but the time delay is assumed to be time-varying and just the sampling period is periodic and $\bar{K} = \begin{bmatrix} 10 & 1 & 0 \end{bmatrix}$ for the augmented state which is defined as $z_k = [x_k^T, u_{k-1}^T]$. Consequently, the third entry of $\bar{K}$ is chosen to be zero to analyze the same system as given above. After exact discretization and applied Jordan from transformation the closed loop system like in (20) is given by:

Figure 4. MATLAB simulation results for a time constant delay of 0.78ms

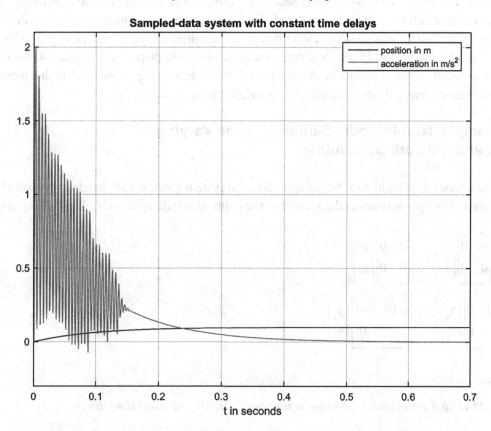

$$z_{k+1} = \left(\left(F_0 - G_0 K \right) + \sum_{i=1}^{N} \alpha_i \left(F_i - G_i K \right) \right) z_k$$

$$= \left(\begin{bmatrix} 1 & h & \dfrac{b}{2}h^2 \\ 0 & 1 & bh \\ -\bar{K}(1) & -\bar{K}(2) & -\bar{K}(3) \end{bmatrix} + \alpha_1(\tau_k) \begin{bmatrix} 0 & 0 & 0 \\ -b\bar{K}(1) & -b\bar{K}(2) & b(1-\bar{K}(3)) \\ 0 & 0 & 0 \end{bmatrix} \right.$$

$$\left. + \alpha_2(\tau_k) \begin{bmatrix} -\dfrac{b}{2}\bar{K}(1) & -\dfrac{b}{2}\bar{K}(2) & \dfrac{b}{2}(1-\bar{K}(3)) \\ 0 & 0 & 0 \\ 0 & 0 & 0 \end{bmatrix} \right) z_k. \tag{42}$$

The functions $\alpha_1(\tau_k)$ and $\alpha_2(\tau_k)$ stated in (42) are defined by $\alpha_1 = (h - \tau_k)$ and $\alpha_2 = (h - \tau_k)^2$. For the over-approximation of system (42) four vertices defines the convex hull. That is the number of all combinations for the lower and upper boundaries of the uncertainty functions $\alpha_1 \in \{\bar{\alpha}_1, \underline{\alpha}_1\}$ and $\alpha_2 \in \{\bar{\alpha}_2, \underline{\alpha}_2\}$ in system (42). In this case only the time delay τ_k appears as an uncertainty. The boundaries of τ_k for small delays are defined as $\tau_k \in [0, h]$. Consequently, the LMIs for stability analysis presented in equation (21) can be implemented in MATLAB. The LMIs are solved by the Yalmip Toolbox (Lofberg, 2004) and the solver named Sedumi (Sturm, 1999). For this example and small delays a symmetric positive definite matrix P was found. Thus, the system is asymptotic stable for time-varying small delays. The system was simulated with random distributed delays between 0 and h seconds. The simulation result is shown in Figure 5. Compared to the solution displayed in Figure 4, for the same system the constant delays result in smaller values than the time-varying approach. But the over-approximation and consequently the convex hull highly influence the solution.

CPS Example: Non-Periodic Sampling, Time Varying Delays, and Network Scheduling

For the disturbance-free emulation-based approach, the system given in (39) needs to be extended. The plant's system description remains the same, but the controller state space model has changed to:

$$
\begin{aligned}
\begin{pmatrix} \dot{x}_{C1} \\ \dot{x}_{C2} \end{pmatrix} &= \underbrace{\begin{bmatrix} 0 & 0 \\ 0 & 0 \end{bmatrix}}_{A_C} \begin{pmatrix} x_{C1} \\ x_{C2} \end{pmatrix} + \underbrace{\begin{bmatrix} 0 & 0 \\ 0 & 0 \end{bmatrix}}_{B_C} \begin{pmatrix} y_1 \\ y_2 \end{pmatrix} \\
\begin{pmatrix} u_1 \\ u_2 \end{pmatrix} &= \underbrace{\begin{bmatrix} 0 & 0 \\ 0 & 0 \end{bmatrix}}_{C_C} \begin{pmatrix} x_{C1} \\ x_{C2} \end{pmatrix} \cdot + \underbrace{\begin{bmatrix} -10 & -1 \\ 0 & 0 \end{bmatrix}}_{D_C} \begin{pmatrix} y_1 \\ y_2 \end{pmatrix}.
\end{aligned}
\tag{43}
$$

Figure 5. MATLAB simulation results for a randomly distributed small time delays

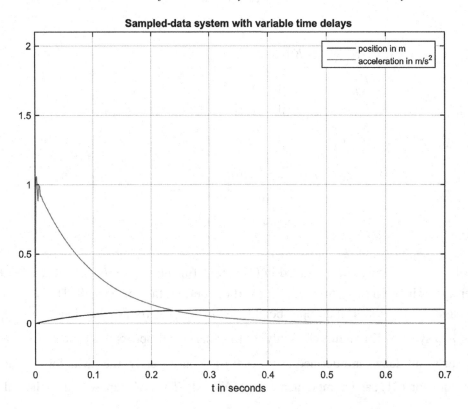

74

According to the work of Walsh, Ye and Bushnell (2002), the closed loop and disturbance free system, which represents the flow part in the hybrid system (11.a), is given by:

$$
\begin{pmatrix} \dot{x} \\ \dot{x}_C \\ \dot{e}_u \\ \dot{e}_y \end{pmatrix} = \begin{bmatrix} A_{11} & A_{12} \\ A_{21} & A_{22} \end{bmatrix} \begin{pmatrix} x \\ x_C \\ e_u \\ e_y \end{pmatrix}
\tag{44}
$$

In (44) the states are defined as $x^T = (x_1, x_2)$, $x_C^T = (x_{C1}, x_{C2})$, $e_u^T = (e_{u1}, e_{u2})$ and $e_y^T = (e_{y1}, e_{y2})$. In the work of Walsh, Ye and Bushnell (2002) definitions for the matrices A_{11}, A_{12}, A_{21} and A_{22} are given. These equations applied to our example leads to:

$$
A_{11} = \begin{bmatrix} 0 & 1 & 0 & 0 \\ -12670 & -1267 & 0 & 0 \\ 0 & 0 & 0 & 0 \\ 0 & 0 & 0 & 0 \end{bmatrix}
$$

$$
A_{12} = \begin{bmatrix} 0 & 0 \\ -12670 & -1267 \\ 0 & 0 \\ 0 & 0 \end{bmatrix}
\tag{45}
$$

$$
A_{21} = \begin{bmatrix} 0 & -1 & 0 & 0 \\ 12670 & 1267 & 0 & 0 \end{bmatrix}
$$

$$
A_{22} = \begin{bmatrix} 0 & 0 \\ 12670 & 1267 \end{bmatrix}
$$

The number of network nodes is $N = 4$. By solving the LMIs in (29)-(33) (LMIs are solved by the Yalmip Toolbox (Lofberg, 2004) and solver Sedumi (Sturm, 1999)) for RR and TOD, as well as for a quadratic Lyapunov function of form $V(z) = z^T P z$ with $z^T = \left(x^T, x_C^T, e_u^T, e_y^T\right)$ and the conditions (22)-(28) leads to the resulting parameters L_0, L_1, γ_0 and γ_1 used in equations (34) and (35). By solving (34) and (35) with different starting values for φ_0 and φ_1 leads to the trade-off curves for RR and TOD in Figure 6. This approach considers the network scheduling, non-periodic transmission times and time-varying time delays. The incorporation of these additional imperfections leads to more conservative results than before, compare CPS examples 1) and 2) with CPS example 3). For instance, when the RR is chosen with maximum transmission interval $h_{MATI} = 5.65 \cdot 10^{-6}$ for stability reasons no delay is allowed. Additionally, Figure 6 shows that dynamic protocols like TOD produce less conservative results.

For I/O Stability the system under consideration is given in equation (46).

Figure 6. Trade-off curves for h_{MATI} and τ_{MAD} for the free system and different protocols

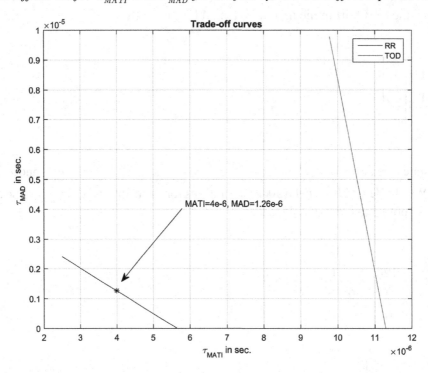

$$
\begin{pmatrix} \dot{x} \\ \dot{x}_C \\ \dot{e}_u \\ \dot{e}_y \end{pmatrix} = \begin{bmatrix} A_{11} & A_{12} & A_{13} \\ A_{21} & A_{22} & A_{23} \end{bmatrix} \begin{pmatrix} x \\ x_C \\ e_u \\ e_y \\ w \end{pmatrix}
$$

$$
z = q(x,w) = C_z x + D_z w = \begin{bmatrix} 1 & 0 & 0 & 0 \\ 0 & 1 & 0 & 0 \end{bmatrix} \begin{pmatrix} x \\ x_C \end{pmatrix} + \begin{bmatrix} 0 & 0 \\ 0 & 0 \end{bmatrix} w
$$

(46)

Here A_{13} and A_{13} are defined in equation (47).

$$
A_{13} = \begin{bmatrix} 0 & 0 \\ 1267 & 0 \\ 0 & 0 \\ 0 & 0 \end{bmatrix}
$$

$$
A_{23} = \begin{bmatrix} 0 & 0 \\ 0 & 0 \\ 0 & 0 \\ 0 & 0 \end{bmatrix}
$$

(47)

The input, which is defined as disturbance w, affects the second state of the plant x. Solving the LMIs (29)-(33) while considering equations (11.b) and (32.b), which are given in (Heemels, Teel, van de Wouw & Nesic, 2010) lead to another trade-off curves. For completeness, values for MATI and MAD under consideration of RR are given. For the same MAD of $\tau_{MAD} = 1.26 \cdot 10^{-6}$ the MATI which preserves I/O stability results in around $h_{MATI} = 1 \cdot 10^{-6}$.

To compare the result of the emulation-based approach with the results of the former approaches the values $h_{MATI} = 4 \cdot 10^{-6}$ and $\tau_{MAD} = 1.26 \cdot 10^{-6}$ for the RR protocol and disturbance free case are chosen. The simulation result for a specific schedule is depicted in Figure 7. Obviously, the system is stable for the varying sampling interval and delay.

CPS Examples: Summary

According to the demonstrated examples the properties of the specific approaches are compared:

Approach 1 represents the stability analysis of the sampled-date system (39) with constant delays. The simulation result for a specific time delay is depicted in Figure 4. It is the simplest NCS approach which is able to deal with linear time-invariant systems with constant delays. Due to its simplicity, the gained results are quite conservative but the stability evaluation is straight forward.

In general, approach 2 is designed to cope with variable time delays, non-periodic sampling and packet-losses. Due to the simultaneous consideration of more challenges, the procedure is much more

Figure 7. Simulation result of the test control systems and all four signals transmitted over a shared network with chosen values $h_{MATI} = 4 \cdot 10^{-6}s$ and $\tau_{MAD} = 1.26 \cdot 10^{-6}s$ for RR protocol.

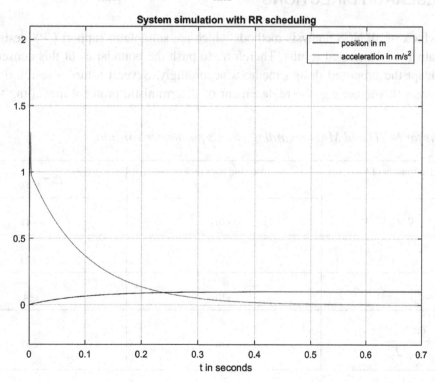

complicated. In detail the discretization of nonlinear systems is not straight forward and the number of considered LMI has to be overestimated robust stability analysis purposes. Regarding the given example in (39), approach 2 considers the stability of a sampled-data system with time-varying delays. The result is given in Figure 5.

Approach 3 is the most general one due to the underlying hybrid system representation. In Figure 6 the trade-off curves for different protocols and the example (39) is shown. In addition, in Figure 7 the step response of the control system including the RR scheduling algorithm is highlighted. In this case all networked induced imperfections mentioned in this work can be considered simultaneously by the presented framework. One restriction is that the network protocol used needs to be UGES. Due to the complex optimization procedure, which is needed to cope with all imperfections typically conservative results are expected. Furthermore, the approach is limited to continuous-time controllers. The hybrid system description allows extensions concerning nonlinear systems and consideration of multiple network nodes. Additionally, an analysis was done how variation on the plant's parameter b in (39) affects the values of MAD and MATI. The result for the value $h_{MATI} = 4 \cdot 10^{-6}\,s$ is given in Table 1. The change of the vector b directly affects MAD and MATI. The denominator most affects the stability which is expressed in the variation of the values of MAD and MATI. The smallest influence shows the parameter J_R, which is scaled by q. Obviously, if varying the parameters about +10% or -10% will lead to the same change rate.

For the reason of completeness, the value of MATI was varied. For $h_{MATI} = 2.3 \cdot 10^{-3}\,s$ the system is no longer stable.

FUTURE RESEARCH DIRECTIONS

The main drawback of all NCS analysis methods which are suitable to support CPS design problems is the conservatism of the gained results. Therefore, to push the boundaries of this conservatism it is important to adapt the proposed design methods accordingly. Several future research directions are possible to address this issue: e.g. the replacement of deterministic protocol modelling to stochastic

Table 1. Results for MATI and MAD regarding plant's parameter variations

Varying Parameters of b	Varying Rate in %	$\Delta \tau_{MAD}$ in %
$(J_M + q^2 J_R)$	±10	~±44
J_M	±10	~±30
J_R	±10	~±4
$\dfrac{qr_R}{J_M + q^2 J_R}$	±10	~±35

nature should lead to less conservative results of MAD and MATI (Tabbara & Nesic, 2008), alternatively discrete-time approaches deal with this issue in a significantly less conservative way compared to the general-purpose continuous-time approaches (Donkers, Heemels, van de Wouw, & Hetel, 2011), furthermore impulsive delayed system approach (Liu, Fridman, & Hetel, 2015) are under consideration to improve the same issue .

Beside the conservatism also the extension of the proposed frameworks to nonlinear system is a topic of interest (e.g. (Tolic & Hirche, 2016)). The nonlinear system characteristics have to be included in the different design procedures to the rid of the linear system constraint. Another system theoretical extension is the extension of the approaches to large scale systems independent of their linear or nonlinear character (Borgers, Geiselhart, & Heemels, 2016). Both system theoretical extensions are of huge interest in the CPS domain.

Concerning the NCS challenges the packet drop out problem is an important topic of future research. The main focus in the field lies on relaxing the tight conditions which have to be met in the current approaches (e.g. (Antunes & Heemels, 2016)).

To enhance the discussed NCS approaches for dealing with CPS challenges the conservatism and the inclusion of nonlinear and large-scale systems represent the most important future challenges.

CONCLUSION

As outlined in the chapter the challenges of CPS and NCS are quite similar in the design process. The considered NCS challenges such as time delays, sampling, data-losses, quantization and scheduling are present nearly in every CPS set-up and have to be handled adequately. Also, the interactions between them are important.

So a knowledge transfer between NCS design approaches to CPS problem statements is meaningful as many well-established NCS methods for dealing with such challenges exist. Typically, NCS approaches are designed to cope with a specific or more challenges with respect to some constraints which have to be met during the design process. Time delays, which are the most important networked induced imperfections, are analyzed in every detail in the control theory as their system's performance degradation effect is of large interest. The more challenges are considered simultaneous the more conservative the results are. Furthermore, the number of NCS approaches dealing with nearly all listed challenges is rare because they are not fully developed. The simultaneous consideration of all challenges is important because the interactions between them are of significant interest.

ACKNOWLEDGMENT

The work reported in this paper was partially funded by the Austrian Research Promotion Agency and the Austrian Federal Ministry for Transport, Innovation and Technology within the Talente nützen: Chancengleichheit Dissertationen im Thema Mobilität der Zukunft project DistrTempDESIGN, by the COMET K2 - Competence Centres for Excellent Technologies Programme of the Austrian Federal Ministry for Transport, Innovation and Technology (bmvit), the Austrian Federal Ministry of Science, Research and Economy (bmwfw), the Austrian Research Promotion Agency (FFG), the Province of Styria and the Styrian Business Promotion Agency (SFG).

REFERENCES

Antsaklis, P. J., Goodwine, B., Gupta, V., McCourt, M. J., Wang, Y., Wu, P., . . . Zhu, F. (2013). Control of cyberphysical systems using passivity and dissipativity based methods. *European Journal of Control*, *19*(5), 379-388.

Antunes, D., & Heemels, W. (2016, August). Frequency-Domain Analysis of Control Loops With Intermittent Data Losses. *IEEE Transactions on Automatic Control*, *61*(8), 2295–2300. doi:10.1109/TAC.2015.2492199

Baheti, R., & Gill, H. (2011). Cyber-physical systems. *The impact of control technology, 12*, 161-166.

Ben Khaled-El Feki, A. (2014). *Distributed real-time simulation of numerical models: application to power-train* [Doctoral dissertation].

Benvenuti, L., Balluchi, A., Bemporad, A., Di Cairano, S., Johansson, B., Johansson, R., & Tunestal, P. (2009). Automotive control. In *J. Lunze, & F. Lamnabhi-Lagarrigue (Eds.), Handbook of hybrid systems control: Theory, tools, applications* (pp. 439–470). New York: Cambridge University Press. doi:10.1017/CBO9780511807930.016

Borgers, D., Geiselhart, R., & Heemels, W. (2016). *Tradeoffs between quality-of-control and quality-of-service in large-scale nonlinear networked control systems.* doi:10.1016/j.nahs.2016.10.001

Boyd, S., El Ghaoui, L., Feron, E., & Balakrishnan, V. (1994). Linear matrix inequalities in system and control theory (15th ed.). Philadelphia: Society for industrial and applied mathematics.

Branicky, M. S. (2005). Introduction to hybrid systems. In *D. Hristu-Varsakelis, & W. S. Levine (Eds.), Handbook of networked and embedded control systems* (pp. 91–116). Boston: Birkhäuser. doi:10.1007/0-8176-4404-0_5

Cardenas, A. A., Amin, S., & Sastry, S. (2008). Secure control: Towards survivable cyber-physical systems. In *Proceedings of the International Conference on Distributed Computing Systems* (pp. 495-500). Beijing.

Cloosterman, M. (2008). *Control over communication networks: modelling, analysis and synthesis* [Doctoral dissertation]. Technische Universiteit Eindhoven. Retrieved from (https://pure.tue.nl/ws/files/3251237/200810902.pdf)

Cloosterman, M., van de Wouw, N., Heemels, W., & Nijmeijer, H. (2009, July). Stability of networked control systems with uncertain time-varying delays. *IEEE Transactions on Automatic Control*, *54*(7), 1575–1580. doi:10.1109/TAC.2009.2015543

Derler, P., Lee, E. A., Tripakis, S., & Törngren, M. (2013). Cyber-physical system design contracts. *IC-CPS '13 Proceedings of the ACM/IEEE 4th International Conference on Cyber-Physical Systems* (pp. 109-118). New York: ACM.

Derler, P., Lee, E. A., & Vincentelli, A. S. (2012, January). Modelling cyber-physical systems. *Proceedings of the IEEE*, *100*(1), 13–28. doi:10.1109/JPROC.2011.2160929

Donkers, T., Heemels, W., van de Wouw, N., & Hetel, L. (2011). Stability analysis of networked control systems using a switched linear systems approach. *IEEE Transactions on Automatic Control. Institute of Electrical and Electronics Engineers*, *56*(9), 2101–2115.

Fitzgerald, J., Larsen, P. G., & Verhoef, M. (2014). From embedded to cyber-physical systems: Challenges and future directions. In J. Fitzgerald, P. G. Larsen, & M. Verhoef (Eds.), *Collaborative design for embedded systems: Co-modelling and Co-simulation* (pp. 293–303). Berlin, Heidelberg: Springer. doi:10.1007/978-3-642-54118-6_14

Fridman, E. (2014). *Introduction to time-delay systems*. Basel, Switzerland: Springer International Publishing. doi:10.1007/978-3-319-09393-2

Geisberger, E., & Broy, M. (2012). agendaCPS: Integrierte Forschungsangende Cyber-Physical Systems. Berlin Heidelberg: Springer Verlag.

Goswami, D., Schneider, R., Masrur, A., Lukasiewycz, M., Chakraborty, S., Voit, H., & Annaswamy, A. (2012). Challenges in automotive cyber-physical systems design. In *Proceedings of the 2012 International Conference Embedded Computer Systems (SAMOS)* (pp. 346-354). Samos: IEEE. doi:10.1109/SAMOS.2012.6404199

Heemels, W., Teel, A., van de Wouw, N., & Nesic, D. (2010, August). Networked control systems with communication constraints: Tradeoffs between transmission intervals, delays and performance. *IEEE Transactions on Automatic Control*, *55*(8), 1781–1796. doi:10.1109/TAC.2010.2042352

Heemels, W. P., & van de Wouw, N. (2010). Stability and Stabilization of Networked Control Systems. In A. Bemporad, W. P. Heemels, & M. Johansson (Eds.), *Networked Control Systems* (pp. 203–253). Berlin, Heidelberg: Springer-Verlag. doi:10.1007/978-0-85729-033-5_7

Hespanha, J., Naghshtabrizi, P., & Xu, Y. (2007, January 1). A survey of recent results in networked control systems. *Proceedings of the IEEE*, *95*(1), 138–162. doi:10.1109/JPROC.2006.887288

Hetel, L., Daffouz, J., & Iung, C. (2008). Analysis and control of LTI and switched systems in digital loops via an event-based modelling. *International Journal of Control*, *81*(7), 1125–1138. doi:10.1080/00207170701670442

Howser, G., & McMillin, B. (2013). A multiple security domain model of a drive-by-wire system. In *Proceedings of the 2013 IEEE 37th Annual Computer Software and Applications Conference (COMPSAC)* (pp. 369-374). Kyoto: IEEE. doi:10.1109/COMPSAC.2013.62

Kim, K.-D., & Kumar, P. (2013, July 18). An Overview and Some Challenges in Cyber-Physical Systems. *Journal of the Indian Institute of Science: A Multidisciplinary Review Journal*, *93*(3), pp. 341-351.

Lee, E. (2006). Cyber-physical systems - Are computing foundations adequate? *Paper presented at the NSF Workshop On Cyber-Physical Systems: Research Motivation, Techniques and Roadmap*, Austin, TX.

Lee, E. (2008). *Cyber physical systems: Design challenges. University of California at Berkeley, Electrical Engineering and Computer Sciences*. Berkeley: University of California at Berkeley.

Lian, F.-L., Moyne, J., & Tilbury, D. (2001, February). Performance evaluation of control networks: Ethernet, ControlNet, and DeviceNet. *IEEE Control Systems*, *21*(1), 66–83. doi:10.1109/37.898793

Liberzon, D. (2005). Switched systems. In *D. Hristu-Varsakelis, & W. S. Levine (Eds.), Handbook of networked and embedded control systems* (pp. 559–574). Boston: Birkhäuser. doi:10.1007/0-8176-4404-0_24

Liu, K., Fridman, E., & Hetel, L. (2014). Networked control systems: A time-delay approach. In *Proceedings of the 2014 European Control Conference* (pp. 1434-1439). Strasbourg, France: IEEE.

Liu, K., Fridman, E., & Hetel, L. (2015). Networked control systems in the presence of scheduling protocols and communication delays. *SIAM Journal on Control and Optimization*, *53*(4), 1768–1788. doi:10.1137/140980570

Lofberg, J. (2004). YALMIP: A Toolbox for modelling and optimization in MATLAB. In *Proceedings of the 2004 IEEE International Conference on Robotics and Automation (IEEE Cat. No.04CH37508)* (pp. 284-289). Taipei: IEEE. doi:10.1109/CACSD.2004.1393890

Lunze, J., & Grüne, L. (2014). Introduction to networked control systems. In J. Lunze (Ed.), *Control theory of digitally networked dynamic systems* (pp. 1–30). Switzerland: Springer International Publishing. doi:10.1007/978-3-319-01131-8_1

Lunze, J., & Lamnabhi-Lagarrigue, F. (2009). *Handbook of hybrid systems control: Theory, tools, applications*. New York: Cambridge University Press. doi:10.1017/CBO9780511807930

Nesic, D., & Teel, A. (2004a, October). Input-output stability properties of networked control systems. *IEEE Transactions on Automatic Control*, *49*(10), 1650–1667. doi:10.1109/TAC.2004.835360

Nesic, D., & Teel, A. (2004b, September 11). Input-to-state stability of networked control systems. *Automatica*, (40): 2121–2128.

Nilsson, J. (1998). *Real-time control systems with delays* [Doctoral dissertation]. Lund university. Retrieved from http://lup.lub.lu.se/record/18692

Rajkumar, R., Lee, I., Sha, L., & Stankovic, J. (2010). Cyber-physical systems: The next computing revolution. In *Proceedings of the 47th Design Automation Conference* (pp. 731-736). Anaheim, California: ACM.

Samad, T., & Annaswamy, A. (2011). *The impact of control technology: Overview, success stories and research challenges*. IEEE Control Systems Society.

Sanfelice, R. G. (2015). Analysis and design of cyber-physical systems: A hybrid control systems approach. In D. B. Rawat, J. Rodrigues, & I. Stojmenovic (Eds.), Cyber-physical systems: From theory to practice (pp. 3-33). Boca Reton: CRC Press. doi:10.1201/b19290-3

Sha, L., Gopalakrishnan, S., Liu, X., & Wang, Q. (2009). Cyber-physical systems: A new frontier. In J. J. Tsai, & P. S. Yu (Eds.), Machine Learning in Cyber Trust (pp. 3-13). Springer US. doi:10.1007/978-0-387-88735-7_1

Shi, J., Wan, J., Yan, H., & Suo, H. (2011). A survey of cyber-physical systems. In *Proceedings of the 2011 International Conference on Wireless Communications and Signal Processing (WCSP)*, Nanjing, China (pp. 1-6). IEEE.

Skogestad, S., & Postlethwaite, I. (2007). Multivariable feedback control (2. ed.). West Sussex, England: Jon Wiley & Sons Ltd.

Sturm, J. (1999). Using SeDuMi 1.02, a MATLAB toolbox for optimization over symmetric cones. *Optimization methods and software, 11*(1-4), 625-653.

Tabbara, M., & Nesic, D. (2008, June). Input-Output Stability of Networked Control Systems with Stochastic Protocols and Channels. *IEEE Transactions on Automatic Control, 53*(5), 1160–1175. doi:10.1109/TAC.2008.923691

Teixeira, A., Sandberg, H., & Johansson, K. H. (2010). Networked control systems under cyber attacks with applications to power networks. In *Proceedings of the 2010 American Control Conference* (pp. 3690-3696). Marriott Waterfront, Baltimore, MD, USA: IEEE. doi:10.1109/ACC.2010.5530638

Tolic, D., & Hirche, S. (2016, April). *Stabilizing transmission intervals for nonlinear delayed networked control systems [Extended Version]*. Retrieved December 5, 2016, from http://adsabs.harvard.edu/abs/2016arXiv160404421T

van de Wouw, N., Naghshtabrizi, P., Cloosterman, M., & Hespanha, J. (2009). Tracking control for sampled-data systems with uncertain time-varying sampling intervals and delays. *International Journal on Robust Nonlinear Control, 20*(4), 387–411.

van de Wouw, N., Naghshtabrizi, P., Cloosterman, M., & Hespanha, J. (2010). Tracking control for sampled-data systems with uncertain sampling intervals and delays. *International Journal Robust and Nonlinear Control, 20*(4), 387–411.

van de Wouw, N., Nesic, D., & Heemels, W. (2012, March 30). A discrete-time framework for stability analysis of nonlinear networked control systems. *Automatica, 48*(6), 1144–1153. doi:10.1016/j.automatica.2012.03.005

Walsh, G., Ye, H., & Bushnell, L. (2002, May). Stability analysis of networked control systems. *IEEE Transactions on Control Systems Technology, 10*(3), 438–446. doi:10.1109/87.998034

Walsh, G. C., & Ye, H. (2001, February). Scheduling of networked control systems. *IEEE Control Systems, 21*(1), 57–65. doi:10.1109/37.898792

Yang, T. C. (2006, July 4). Networked control system: A brief survey. *IEEE Proceedings- Control Theory and Applications, 153*(4), 403-412.

Zhang, L., Gao, H., & Kaynak, O. (2013, February). Network-induced constraints in networked control systems - A survey. *IEEE Transactions on industrial informatics, 9*(1), 403-416.

Zhang, W., Branicky, M. S., & Phillips, S. M. (2001, February). Stability of networked control systems. *IEEE Control Systems Magazine, 21*(1), 84–99. doi:10.1109/37.898794

KEY TERMS AND DEFINITIONS

Closed-Loop System: A system consisting of a plant equipped with actuators as well as sensor and a controller which stabilizes the plant based on control input generated by the controller and the plant's output.

Hybrid System: A modelling approach for systems with a continuous-time part and switching signals.

Lyapunov Function: A function which is used to prove the equilibrium's stability of a system of differential equations.

Network Node: A system consisting of either an input or output or both which is has access to the network.

Networked Control System: A closed-loop feedback system that consists of a plant, a controller and a network. In sends information between plant and controller over a shared network.

Packet: A specific amount of information sent together over a network.

Round Trip Time: It defines the time between a node sending a request and receiving an acknowledgement.

Scheduling: An access policy for all participants of a shared resource.

Chapter 4
An Efficient Channel–Aware Aloha–Like OFDMA–Based Wireless Communication Protocol for IoT Communications in Wireless Sensor Networks

Elias Yaacoub
Arab Open University, Lebanon

ABSTRACT

Wireless sensor networks consisting of several sensors deployed in a given area, under an internet of things (IoT) paradigm, are considered. Sensor nodes may or may not be close enough to communicate with each other in order to perform collaborative transmissions. A communication protocol based on random access and orthogonal frequency division multiple access (OFDMA) is proposed in order to allow the sensors to operate autonomously by transmitting their measured data to a central processing system, where it is processed and analyzed. Whenever it has data to transmit, each sensor independently accesses a time-frequency slot in a probabilistic manner to avoid collisions. A controlling entity, e.g., a central base station (BS) covering a certain sensor deployment area receives the sensor transmissions and provides synchronization information by periodically transmitting a pilot signal over the available OFDMA subcarriers. Sensors use this signal for channel quality estimation. Results show that this approach performs well in terms of transmission data rates and collision probability.

1. INTRODUCTION

The Internet of Things (IoT) is expected to be a key enabler for smart cities, where sensor and actuator devices will be ubiquitous and will monitor every aspect of our lives (Ejaz et al., 2017). With the billions of devices expected to be deployed under the IoT paradigm, next generation cellular networks are

DOI: 10.4018/978-1-5225-2845-6.ch004

expected to face enormous challenges (Chen, 2012). In fact, they need to be able to support this large number of devices through the use of machine-to-machine (M2M) communications. The quality of service (QoS) requirements of IoT devices are expected to be varying and different, depending on the purpose for which each device was designed. Thus, these devices will affect the network in different ways since they will have different behaviors. For certain devices, the network will need to be accessed in a frequent and periodic manner for the sake of transmitting small amounts of measurement data. This would be the case in advanced metering infrastructure (AMI) where smart meters deployed in a smart grid setup would be sending their data (Yaacoub & Kadri, 2015). In other scenarios, it could be possible for devices to temporarily store their measured data and then transmit the stored data in bulk later on. A typical example would be the case of sensor networks deployed for monitoring the environment (Lloret et al., 2015). Indeed, the IoT will significantly consist of wireless sensor networks (WSNs) comprising a number of sensor nodes (SNs) that capture certain information and then transmit it wirelessly over the network (Mainetti et al., 2011). WSNs have a broad spectrum of applications. They can be used in intelligent transportation systems for road safety purposes, in military applications for border control and surveillance, and in environmental applications for the sake of air pollution monitoring, detection of water pollution, smart agriculture, etc. (Vieira et al., 2003).

An SN is, in most cases, an autonomous device that comprises: a sensing unit to measure the required data, a processing unit to process and (temporarily) store the measured information, a communication unit to transmit the data over the network, and a power unit to provide power for the device. Generally, the most important limiting factor for the operation of an SN is power consumption, since it is expected to operate for extended periods in areas where power infrastructure could be absent. Consequently, SNs should have the capability to perform their intended tasks with very low power consumption. Certain SNs can be powered by batteries that benefit from energy harvesting from the environment and thus, for example, can use solar power to replenish their energy, which allows them to operate autonomously for a longer time. Energy saving can also occur via the wireless communication unit. In fact, short range ad-hoc communication between SNs in a WSN via multihop communications can prove to be more energy efficient than a single hop long distance transmission to a base station (BS) or access point (AP) (Vieira et al., 2003).

In this Chapter, a wireless communication protocol for WSNs is presented and analyzed. It is an extension of the protocol presented in (Yaacoub et al., 2011) in order to apply it in various WSN scenarios. The presented protocol deals with the communication between SNs and APs or BSs. It is however applicable to scenarios where multihop communications take place in WSNs. In such scenarios, SNs communicate with each other over multihop links using a pre-defined communication protocol, and the SN at the last hop communicates with the BS by relaying the aggregated multihop data using the approach discussed in this Chapter. The presented protocol enables SNs to communicate efficiently with an AP by operating autonomously in different parts of the cell area covered by the BS or AP. It is a channel aware extension of slotted reservation Aloha to orthogonal frequency division multiple access (OFDMA) systems.

The chapter is organized as follows. Section 2 presents the relevant background/literature review. The proposed approach is presented in Section 3. Simulation results are presented and analyzed in Section 4. Finally, in Section 5, conclusions are drawn and future research challenges are outlined.

2. LITERATURE REVIEW

In IoT systems, with excessively large deployments of SNs, centralized resource allocation becomes extremely challenging due to high computational complexity and increased overhead. Thus, a distributed resource allocation approach might be more convenient. Game theory is generally a good tool in such scenarios. However, conventional game models still suffer slow convergence and excessive overhead in in such large-scale systems (Semasinghe et al., 2017). A modification of Bluetooth presenting a low power alternative called Bluetooth Low Energy (BLE), results in high collision rates and wasted energy when applied in an IoT scenario (Harris et al., 2016). To alleviate this problem, opportunistic listening was proposed in (Harris et al., 2016). To provide sufficient spectrum for the large expected traffic demand in IoT/Cyber-Physical systems, a shared spectrum access model in Radar bands is proposed in (Khan et al., 2017).

Thus, distributed scheduling methods along with dynamic spectrum random access seem to be recognized as the most efficient methods for IoT, with several challenges still to be overcome. This chapter proposes an enhancement of the Aloha method to address these challenges.

In fact, Aloha can be considered as one of the first random access algorithms (Roberts, 1973). In general, it is investigated under the assumption that there is a single channel assumption, and users contend to transmit over that channel. An enhancement was made with slotted Aloha, where users cannot transmit at any time, but rather can send their packets during time slots of fixed length. Collision would occur whenever more than one user attempt to transmit simultaneously in the same time slot (Shen & Li, 2002). Reservation Aloha is another variant that was proposed in order to reduce collisions (Roberts, 1973). In this scheme, reservation slots of short duration precede the actual transmission slots of fixed length (similarly to slotted Aloha). Transmission requests are sent in the small reservation slots during a reservation phase, using the slotted Aloha random access technique, in order to reserve the actual transmission slots. This allows collisions to occur in the reservation phase before actual transmission, thus preventing more serious collisions during the transmission phase.

Reservation Aloha is used in several applications, including satellite networks (Lepaja & Benji, 2001), wireless local area networks (WLANs) (Tasaka et al., 1995), and vehicle-to-vehicle communication (Alsbou et al., 2010). The implementation of classical Aloha (without reservation) was even studied for communication in underwater acoustic sensor networks (Xiao et al., 2009). With the adoption of OFDMA as the accessing scheme in state-of-the-art cellular systems like the long-term evolution (LTE) and LTE-Advanced (LTE-A), in addition to WiMAX, extensions of Aloha and its variants to OFDMA-based networks were investigated in the literature (Shen & Li, 2002; Choi et al., 2006; Han et al., 2006; Ganesan & Li, 2007; Wang et al., 2009; Yumei & Su, 2009). OFDMA consists of a set of orthogonal subcarriers. In general, a fixed number of consecutive subcarriers are grouped to form a subchannel, and thus they can be allocated together to a user for transmission (Shen & Li, 2002; Lunttila et al., 2007).

In (Shen & Li, 2002), slotted Aloha over OFDM was studied. In (Choi et al., 2006), the authors presented a backoff scheme for multichannel slotted Aloha. In the approach of (Choi et al., 2006) backoff is performed on different subchannels instead of performing backoff on a different time slot on a single subchannel. In (Han et al., 2006), a class of multichannel MAC schemes based on Aloha contention resolution and on the RTS/CTS (Ready-To-Send/Clear-To-Send) dialogue is investigated. In the approach of (Han et al., 2006), a single subchannel called the control subchannel is used to transmit the RTS/

CTS dialogues, whereas the other subchannels are dedicated for data transmissions. The RTS packets contend on the right to use one of the data subchannels. The winner in a contention can then use one of the data subchannels for transmission without facing the risk of collisions. This method was shown in (Han et al., 2006) to reduce collisions for a fixed total bandwidth scenario. However, the sum-rate of the multichannel MAC schemes was shown to be less than that of the corresponding single channel MAC scheme that sends the RTS/CTS and data packets on a single shared channel. Channel sensing was used in (Kwon et al., 2009) to deal with this problem. Thus, in (Kwon et al., 2009), carrier sense multiple access with collision avoidance (CSMA/CA) over OFDMA is proposed, and a backoff mechanism is investigated without resorting to slotted reservation.

In (Wang et al., 2009), an OFDMA-based reservation Aloha scheme is proposed. Users compete for subcarriers in the contention period, and the winner transmits over the reserved subcarrier until the next contention period. Furthermore, channel state information (CSI) is assumed to be known by the users when they access the channel. Capture effects are not investigated in (Wang et al., 2009). With capture effects, even if some collisions occur during the contention period, the BS could still succeed in detecting one of the contending users and allow this user to transmit over the corresponding slot. In (Zhang et al., 2006), CSI awareness is not assumed, but collisions are resolved through the use of the capture effect: users with better channels succeed in accessing the channel through this effect and thus this exploitation of multiuser diversity allows reaching enhancements in reservation Aloha. In (Ganesan & Li, 2007), a scheme for reservation Aloha with CSI is proposed, where capture effect is used for collision resolution and a user reserves the OFDMA subchannel for the whole transmission time of a frame. In (Yumei & Su, 2009), slotted Aloha is investigated and a Markov model of the wireless channel is adopted: In this model, slotted Aloha is implemented by users to transmit on a subchannel in "good" state, whereas no transmission occurs on a subchannel if it is in the "bad" state.

In this Chapter, reservation Aloha over OFDMA is investigated. The proposed approach uses a frequency-time grid for reservations, in contrast to classical reservation Aloha where the reservation of time slots occurs over the whole bandwidth (Roberts, 1973; Alsbou et al., 2010), and as opposed to the OFDMA extensions of reservation Aloha (Han et al., 2006; Ganesan & Li, 2007; Wang et al., 2009), where an OFDMA subchannel can be reserved for the whole transmission period of the frame. A WSN scenario is considered, where a group of SNs are assumed to communicate with a single receiver, such as an AP or BS. With the proposed approach, the transmission frame is subdivided into several time-frequency slots. SNs contend for a particular transmission slot over a certain subchannel such that, in a given Aloha frame, several SNs could be transmitting on the same subchannel but at different time slots, and several SNs could be transmitting at the same time but over different subchannels. The presented scheme is compared to other schemes and is shown to lead to significant improvements.

3. CHANNEL-AWARE OFDMA-BASED ALOHA PROTOCOL FOR WIRELESS SENSOR NETWORKS

In this section, the proposed protocol is presented. The proposed approach uses a frequency-time grid for reservations, in contrast to classical reservation Aloha where the reservation of time slots occurs over the whole bandwidth (Roberts, 1973), and as opposed to subchannel reservation (Ganesan & Li, 2007; Wang et al., 2009), where an OFDMA subchannel can be reserved for the whole transmission period of the frame.

In fact, reservation in slotted reservation Aloha is performed over transmission slots in the time domain in an approach similar to time division multiple access (TDMA). All the bandwidth is used for transmission, e.g., (Roberts, 1973; Thomopoulos, 1988). In this Chapter, an extension of slotted reservation Aloha to OFDMA is considered in order to perform a fair comparison with the presented approach. It will be referred to as the TDMA approach and it is shown in Figure 1. Thus, if an SN reserves a certain time slot, it will transmit over all the subcarriers for the duration of that slot. The extension of Figure 1, in addition to using OFDMA in the reserved transmission slots, makes use of channel knowledge in the reservation phase. Consequently, similarly to the proposed approach, the OFDMA reservation Aloha scheme shown in Figure 1 contains a channel estimation phase that permits to SNs to estimate the data rate that they can achieve over a reserved slot.

With the wide adoption of OFDMA in wireless communications systems, several random-access schemes based on OFDMA were presented in the literature (Wang et al., 2009; Yumei & Su, 2009). A common aspect for all these schemes is that reservations are made over subchannels. Then, a single user is allowed to transmit over a reserved subchannel. Transmission lasts until the next frame where a new reservation is performed. In this Chapter, these schemes are extended in order to take into account pilot measurement and channel state information (CSI) estimation so that SNs can benefit from channel knowledge while making their reservations during the reservation phase. This subchannel reservation scheme, shown in Figure 2, will be referred to as the FDMA approach in this Chapter.

3.1 Details of the Proposed Approach

The proposed method allows performing distributed resource allocation for SNs over OFDMA. In this approach, SNs can compete over transmission slots, or transmission time intervals (TTIs), over all the available subchannels. It is illustrated in Figure 3. Each frame of duration N_{TTI} is subdivided into three phases: a pilot transmission and channel estimation phase of duration 1 TTI, a reservation phase of duration 1 TTI, and a transmission phase of duration N_{TTI} - 2, with each TTI having a duration T. The proposed method can be described as follows:

Figure 1. TDMA approach

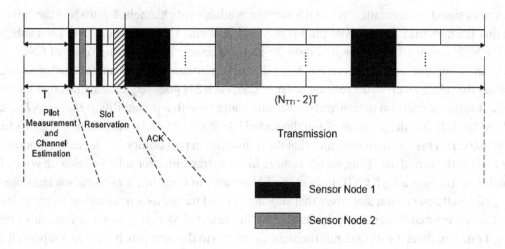

Figure 2. FDMA approach

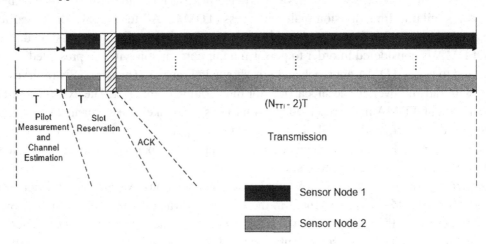

Figure 3. Proposed OFDMA-based Aloha-like approach

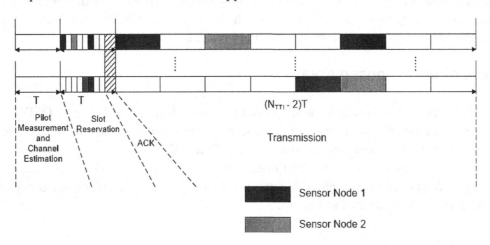

Step 1: A pilot signal is transmitted by the BS over the available subchannels. Each SN in the cell covered by that BS measures the received pilot power and performs CSI estimation over each subchannel.

Step 2: Each SN performs a sorting operation for its subchannels in decreasing order of CSI.

Step 3: In the reservation phase, there are N_{TTI} - 2 small reservation slots over each subchannel. After sorting the subchannels in decreasing order of CSI, each SN goes sequentially through its subchannels. It makes a decision to transmit over a subchannel i with a probability $p_T(k, i) = f(Rank(k, i))$, where $Rank(k, i)$ is the position of i in the sorted list of subchannels and $f(Rank(k, i))$ is a function of $Rank(k, i)$. This equation indicates that the transmission probability is selected as function of the rank of i in the sorted list. Thus, an SN is more likely to transmit over subcarriers with good channel conditions (having a high CSI). In case the SN decides to transmit, it randomly selects one of the N_{TTI} - 2 small reservation slots over that subchannel and transmits a reservation signal in that slot.

Step 4: The SN estimates its achieved data rate on the selected slot. If it is not sufficient to reach its target rate mandated by its QoS requirements, it moves to the next subchannel and repeats the same operation. In case it goes over all subchannels without achieving the target rate, the SN returns to the first subchannel and repeats the process. This iterative approach continues until the SN achieves its target rate or until a pre-defined maximum number of slots are reserved.

Step 5: Once the reservation phase is complete, the BS transmits an ACK message containing $N_{sub}(N_{TTI}$ - 2) bits, with N_{sub} representing the number of subchannels. These bits correspond to the reservation slots over all the subchannels. If a reservation was successfully made on a given TTI over a certain subchannel, the corresponding bit is set to 1. However, in case a collision has occurred during the reservation phase, or even when no reservation was made, the bit is set to 0. Consequently, an SN that attempted to reserve a slot and found a 1 in the corresponding bit in the ACK message knows that the slot was successfully reserved. In case it encounters a 0, it knows that a collision has occurred and thus refrains from transmitting on that slot.

This proposed approach has the benefit of allowing collisions to occur only in the reservation phase, but not in the transmission phase. Thus, it avoids unnecessary transmissions and wasted power, which is a scarce resource in WSNs. Furthermore, collision detection is done at the BS. Consequently, there is no need for SNs to perform channel sensing in order to detect the transmissions of other SNs, as in the 802.11 standard for example. This allows avoiding the hidden terminal problem and leads to more efficient collision detection. Hence, once a collision is detected at a given slot, no transmission occurs in that slot. It should be noted that the pilot signal transmitted by the BS at the beginning of each frame has an important role in the proposed approach: It allows the SNs to keep their synchronization with the BS, while also being used by the SNs for CSI estimation.

3.2 Data Rate Calculations

A single cell uplink orthogonal frequency division multiple access (OFDMA) system is considered. It is assumed that there are K sensor nodes (SNs) and N subcarriers to be allocated. For each SN k and subcarrier i, the transmit power, channel gain, and total noise power are respectively denoted by $P_{k,i}$, $H_{k,i}$, and $\sigma^2_{k,i}$. The signal-to-noise ratio (SNR) is given by:

$$\gamma_{k,i} = \frac{P_{k,i}H_{k,i}}{\sigma^2_{k,i}} \quad k = 1,...,K; \ i = 1,...,N; \tag{1}$$

Each SN k operates under a peak power constraint given by:

$$\sum_{i=1}^{N} P_{k,i} \leq P_{k,\max} \quad k = 1,...,K; \tag{2}$$

This constraint indicates that the power spent by the SN over all its allocated subcarriers cannot exceed its maximum transmission power $P_{k,\max}$.

The total data rate achieved by SN k is given by:

$$R_k = \sum_{i=1}^{N} R^d_{k,i}\left(\gamma_{k,i}\right) \tag{3}$$

where $R^d_{k,i}$ is the discrete rate of SN k over subcarrier i. Conversely to continuous rates, which can take any non-negative real value according to the Shannon capacity formula $\log_2(1 + \gamma_{k,i})$, discrete rates represent the quantized bit rates achievable in a practical system as follows:

$$R^d_{k,i}(\gamma_{k,i}) = \begin{cases} r_0, & \eta_0 \leq \gamma_{k,i} < \eta_1 \\ r_1, & \eta_1 \leq \gamma_{k,i} < \eta_2 \\ r_2, & \eta_2 \leq \gamma_{k,i} < \eta_3 \\ \vdots \\ r_{L-1}, & \eta_{L-1} \leq \gamma_{k,i} < \eta_L \end{cases} \tag{4}$$

In (4), η_l corresponds to the target SNR required to achieve the rate r_l with a predefined bit error rate (BER). It should be noted that in the limit, $r_0 = 0$, $\eta_0 = 0$, and $\eta_L = \infty$. Thus, the sum-rate of the system can be expressed as:

$$R_{tot} = \sum_{k=1}^{K} \sum_{i=1}^{N} R^d_{k,i}(\gamma_{k,i}) \tag{5}$$

The channel gain of SN k over subcarrier i is given by:

$$H_{k,i,dB} = \left(-\kappa - \lambda \log_{10} d_k \right) - \xi_{k,i} + 10 \log_{10} F_{k,i} \tag{6}$$

In (6), the first factor captures propagation loss, with κ the pathloss constant, d_k the distance in km from SN k to the BS, and λ the path loss exponent. The second factor, $\xi_{k,i}$, represents log-normal shadowing, assumed to have a zero-mean and a standard deviation σ_ξ, and the last factor, $F_{k,i}$, corresponds to Rayleigh fading with a Rayleigh parameter a such that $E[a^2] = 1$, with $E[]$ being the expectation operator.

3.3 Reservation Policy to Achieve the Target Data Rates

A single cell scenario is considered, with SNs competing for resources to communicate with a BS by using the presented communication protocol. SNs are assumed to perform continuous monitoring of an environmental parameter. For example, a measurement is taken every few seconds or minutes. The measured data can be transmitted immediately or several measurements can be aggregated before transmission, which leads to different target transmission rates needed, depending on the scenario. Thus, SNs always have data to transmit, and each SN has to meet a target average data rate R_T. If an SN fails to achieve this data rate after a certain number of frames N_{frames}, the SN can be considered to be in outage. SNs regulate their transmissions in order to achieve R_T after N_{frames}. The procedure they follow is described next. The number of bits that should be transmitted in order to achieve R_T after N_{frames} is given by:

$$N_{b,T} = R_T \cdot N_{frames} \cdot N_{TTI} \cdot T \tag{7}$$

Denoting by n_F the number of the current frame in a window of length N_{frames}, and by $N_{b,nf}$ the number of bits transmitted in frame n_f, the number of previously transmitted bits is expressed as:

$$N_{b,n_F}^{(p)} = \sum_{n_f=1}^{n_F-1} N_{b,n_f} \tag{8}$$

Consequently, an SN makes enough reservations in frame n_f in order to transmit $N_{b,nf}$ bits with:

$$N_{b,n_F} = \frac{N_{b,T} - N_{b,n_F}^{(p)}}{N_{frames} - (n_F - 1)} \tag{9}$$

Hence, an SN attempts to subdivide the remaining $(N_{b,T} - N^{(p)}{}_{b,nF})$ bits equally over the remaining $[N_{frames} - (n_F - 1)]$ frames.

3.4 Setting the Transmission Probabilities in the Proposed Approach

This section is dedicated to describing the selection of the values of the transmit probabilities $p_T(k, i)$ = $f(Rank(k, i))$. The function $f(Rank(k, i))$ is chosen as a decreasing function with respect to $Rank(k, i)$, whereas $p_T(k, i)$ has to take values in the interval $[0\ 1]$ since it is a probability measure. Consequently, SN k has a higher transmission probability on subchannels having good channel conditions. Thus, a better channel state information (CSI) for SN k on a given subchannel means this subchannel has higher chances of being selected for transmission.

A simple approach would be to select:

$$p_T(k, i) = p_T \tag{10}$$

i.e., use constant probabilities for all SNs and subchannels. This would favor subchannels having better channel conditions through by the sorting process only, not through the transmission probabilities. On the other hand, we can set:

$$f(Rank(k, i)) = p_{T0} / Rank(k, i) \tag{11}$$

where p_{T0} is a constant. In (11), a simple straightforward approach is presented in order to make the transmission probability of SN k over subchannel i vary with its CSI level: a high CSI leads to a lower $Rank(k, i)$, and thus to a higher transmission probability. The constant p_{T0} should ideally be set to a value close to 1, e.g. 0.9, in order to increase the transmission probability on subchannels that are positioned higher in the sorted list. Thus, the transmission probability on the first subchannel in the list will be 0.9; whereas the transmission probabilities on the second and third subchannels will be 0.9/2 = 0.45 and 0.9/3 = 0.3, respectively, and so on.

A more aggressive reservation strategy could use, for example, a function of the form:

$$f(Rank(k, i)) = p_{T0} / [c_1 log_b(c_2 Rank(k, i) + c_3)] \qquad (12)$$

With b the base of the logarithm and c_1, c_2, and c_3 are constants selected such that the value of the transmission probabilities remains in the interval *[0 1]*. The selection of a logarithmic variation for the probabilities allows a slow decrease with the rank of the subchannel in the sorted list; consequently, even when the CSI decreases, the transmission probabilities would generally be higher than the case represented by Eq. (11).

On the other hand, a more restrictive approach can use functions of the form:

$$f(Rank(k, i)) = p_{T0} / [c_1 exp(c_2 Rank(k, i) + c_3)] \qquad (13)$$

The selection of an exponential variation for the probabilities in Eq. (13) allows a fast decrease with the rank of the subchannel in the sorted list; therefore, when the CSI decreases, the transmission probabilities would generally be lower than the case of Eq. (11). Consequently, each SN will concentrate its transmissions on its subchannels having the best channel conditions.

3.5 Possible Implementation in a Practical LTE System

This section describes a possible implementation of the proposed IoT communication approach in a practical cellular system, e.g. LTE/LTE-A. In fact, with 3GPP LTE, OFDMA is used in the downlink (DL) direction. In the uplink (UL) direction, a modified form of OFDMA called single carrier frequency division multiple access (SCFDMA) is used. The LTE spectrum is subdivided into resource blocks (RB) where each RB consists of 12 adjacent subcarriers. The shortest allocation time of a single RB is 1 ms, known as the duration of one transmission time interval (TTI), or the duration of two 0.5 ms slots in LTE (3GPP TS 36.211; 3GPP TS 36.213). With the expected large numbers of SN devices in a typical IoT deployment, congestion would be natural to occur whenever the SNs use the cellular network for their communications. However, the amount of data to be sent by each sensor is generally limited; which contrasts with the much larger data rates that can be supported by the smallest LTE allocation unit. This problem is solved by the proposed method that subdivides the LTE RBs into their corresponding smaller subchannels of pre-defined size. Then, it allows the devices to compete dynamically by contending over the subchannels of the RBs that are not scheduled by the BS at a given instant. Thus, the proposed approach is channel-aware, energy efficient, OFDMA based, and can use subsets of the LTE RBs for transmission. Consequently, it allows the spectrum to be used efficiently without interfering with the traffic dedicated to LTE mobile users.

In fact, the proposed approach could make use of a device acting as access point AP/controller/coordinator, covering a geographical area and deployed in a strategic location, preferably co-located with a cellular BS covering the same area. It is referred to as AP in the sequel. The AP communicates with IoT devices that could be either SNs communicating directly with the AP, or aggregators collecting information from SNs and relaying it to the AP. The AP informs the devices in the network of the free wireless channels available for transmission, and handles communication with these devices. The AP receives the data from the devices and routes it over a backbone network to the servers of the utility provider. The devices should be enabled with OFDMA wireless transmission capability in order to communicate with the AP according to the proposed method. The details of the practical implementation of the proposed approach in an LTE system are summarized in Figure 4, and can be described as follows:

- The AP uses the cellular bandwidth that is subdivided into subchannels of fixed size.
- The AP communicates with the radio resource management (RRM) module of the cellular BS in a periodic fashion, in order to get a list of the channels that will be free for an estimated time pe-

Figure 4. Flowchart describing the operation of the proposed method with collaboration from LTE BSs

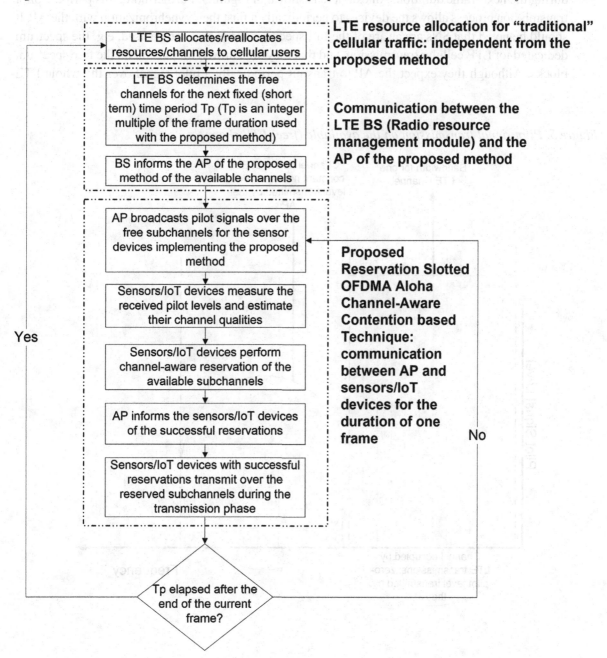

riod, specified by the RRM module. Typically, this time period could be from the order of tens of milliseconds. It should be relatively small so that the proposed method does not impact the RRM process of cellular users, since the free channels can be used later by the BS. Nevertheless, this does not prevent the time period from being longer whenever the BS channel assignments are less frequent in case the LTE cellular network dynamics are varying slowly.

- The AP sends periodic pilot signals to the SNs over the available cellular spectrum as indicated by the BS. The signal is non-zero only over the free subchannels, and it is zero over the ones occupied by the cellular system. Thus, devices know which subchannels are available for transmission during the next frame duration. An example is shown in Figure 5. Furthermore, this periodic pilot transmission process allows the devices to periodically adjust their synchronization with the AP. It should be noted that SNs are aware of the full spectrum range that can be used, e.g. the spectrum dedicated for LTE cellular transmission, and that they are allowed to transmit on the free spectrum blocks. Although they expect the AP to transmit periodically a pilot signal over the whole LTE

Figure 5. Pilot signal transmission on the available (free) LTE channels

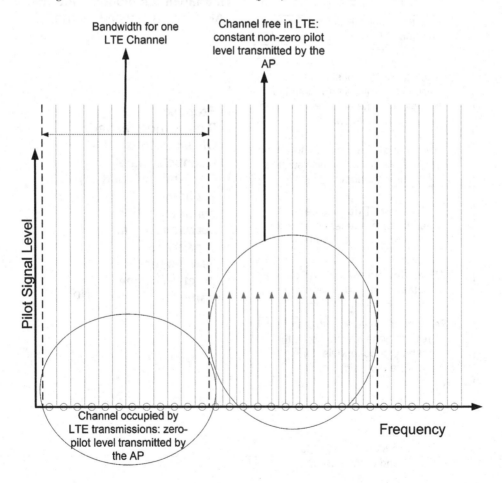

spectrum, they know that a particular channel is not available if the pilot signal level received over that channel is zero. If the pilot level higher, they implement the proposed channel-aware approach by ranking the channel according to its received signal strength as described in the previous sections. In the example of Figure 5, for illustration purposes, one LTE channel is subdivided into four subchannels that can be used with the proposed method.

- SNs measure their channel quality on the subchannels and make channel-aware decisions during a reservation slot, by contending over the subchannels needed for their data transmission. The intelligent channel aware decision making process can be imbedded in the devices processing units, where it makes use of probabilistic decision making: The probability of a device contending for a subchannel increases with the quality of the wireless link between the SN and AP over that subchannel, as described previously.
- The AP informs the devices of the successful reservations
- In the transmission phase, the transmissions take place only on the time/frequency slots where successful reservations were made. Hence, significant energy savings can be achieved since collisions might occur only in the reservation phase, but not in the transmission phase.

3.6 Simulation Parameters

The proposed approach was presented in the previous sections. The following section presents detailed simulation results along with the relevant performance analysis and comparison to other methods. Whenever possible, the values for the parameters used in the simulation are set in compliance with the LTE standard. Nevertheless, it is worth mentioning that the proposed method is an Aloha based approach and can be implemented with any system using OFDMA. The selection of parameters in-line with the LTE/LTE-A standards is to complement the discussion of the previous section, where a possible implementation of the proposed method in an LTE/LTE-A system, in order to support the anticipated IoT/Cyber-Physical systems traffic, is presented.

Thus, in this section, the simulation parameters used throughout the Chapter are described. These parameters are common to all the investigated scenarios. Parameters that are specific to a particular scenario are described in the relevant section.

Each frame is assumed to comprise $N_{TTI} = 10$ transmission time intervals (TTIs), i.e., eight of these TTIs are dedicated for transmission. Each SN would attempt to achieve its target rate as described previously, and it is considered be in outage if it does not succeed to reach the target rate after $N_{frames} = 100$ frames. The duration of a TTI is set to 1 msec, sufficient to transmit 12 symbols over each subcarrier (3GPP TS 36.211). Results are averaged over 50 iterations, each corresponding to 100 frames. The bandwidth considered is set to $B = 5$ MHz. The maximum SN transmit power is considered to be 125 mW. All SNs are assumed to transmit at the maximum power, and the power is subdivided equally among all subcarriers allocated to the SN.

In Eq. (6), κ is set to 128.1 dB, and λ is set to a value of 3.76. For log-normal shadowing, $\sigma_\xi = 8$ dB is used. The SNR thresholds of the various modulation and coding schemes are shown in Table 1 (Yaacoub et al., 2011).

Table 1. Discrete rates and SNR thresholds with 14 modulation and coding schemes

MCS	r_i (bits)	η_i (dB)
No Transmission	0	$-\infty$
QPSK, R = 1/8	0.25	-5.5
QPSK, R = 1/5	0.4	-3.5
QPSK, R = 1/4	0.5	-2.2
QPSK, R = 1/3	0.6667	-1.0
QPSK, R = 1/2	1.0	1.3
QPSK, R = 2/3	1.333	3.4
QPSK, R = 4/5	1.6	5.2
16-QAM, R = 1/2	2.0	7.0
16-QAM, R = 2/3	2.667	10.5
16-QAM, R = 4/5	3.2	11.5
64-QAM, R = 2/3	4.0	14.0
64-QAM, R = 3/4	4.5	16.0
64-QAM, R = 4/5	4.8	17.0
64-QAM, R = 1 (uncoded)	6.0	26.8

4. SIMULATION AND RESULTS: SCENARIO OF A SENSOR NETWORK FOR AIR POLLUTION MONITORING

The communication protocol presented in this Chapter can be implemented in various WSN scenarios. In this section, an implementation scenario related to WSNs for air pollution monitoring is studied as an illustrative example. The same approach can be applied for other scenarios such as: water pollution monitoring, home automation (a multitude of sensors sending measurement data to an AP installed inside a home), etc.

In fact, monitoring of environmental parameters is an important application of WSNs, especially with the technology advancements leading to the production of small, lightweight, low power sensors that can monitor environmental parameters with increasing accuracy. These advancements facilitate the deployment of WSNs for the continuous monitoring of air quality. The concentration of pollutants in the atmosphere can be measured and reported by the SNs, and the measurements can be shared with the concerned public through websites, mobile applications, etc. Furthermore, the measurements sent by the SNs can be stored on a server for advanced processing. This can be performed by expert environmental scientists who analyze and assess pollution information and can accordingly send recommendations to the relevant authorities in order to take appropriate action.

4.1 Description of the Sensor Network Setup for Detecting Air Pollution

In this section, a high-level overview of the system architecture is presented. Furthermore, the role of the SNs is described. The investigated system is shown in Figure 6, where the architecture consists of three tiers:

Figure 6. Implementation scenario for air pollution monitoring

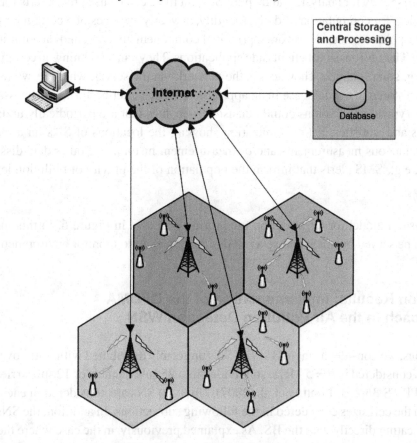

1. **The Sensor Nodes (SNs):** They include the sensors that measure the level of pollutants in the atmosphere. Typical monitored pollutants include: carbon monoxide (CO), nitrogen oxides (NOx), Ozone, and Particulate Matter (PM). Other environmental parameters can also be monitored, e.g., relative humidity and temperature. Generally, one or more sensors can be accommodated within the same SN enclosure, with each sensor measuring one of the mentioned parameters. The SNs transmit the measured data to the BS using the presented communication protocol. SNs can communicate directly with the BS. Another scenario is to communicate with a nearby relay node (RN) using limited power, and the RN would relay the data to the BS wirelessly, or to the data center containing the database server using the wired network. The most challenging scenario is in the case of collaboration between the nodes (in case of very high density of small SNs), where the nodes can form cooperative clusters, and relay the data in a multihop fashion ensuring energy efficiency. The presented protocol is applicable to these scenarios. However, in scenarios with RNs or multihop communications, the protocol is applicable at the last hop for communication with the BS.

2. **The Database Server:** The monitoring data received at the BS is sent to a database server. There, it can be in a common format which would facilitate data extraction and analysis. The measurement data could contain missing, noisy, or erroneous values. Appropriate data processing techniques and integrity checks are generally performed before storing the data for subsequent use. Afterwards, the

data becomes ready for analysis and display. Several tools can be used by experts for data analysis, e.g., statistics (for computation of daily, monthly, or yearly averages of a certain air pollutant), advanced interpolation, neural networks, principal component analysis, and data mining techniques.

3.   **The Client Tier:** It consists of client-side applications. They can be running on computers or mobile devices, e.g. smart phones. They access the network via the server, which forwards the pollution information stored in the database in an appropriate format after performing necessary processing if needed. Typical applications could consist of web sites that are periodically updated with data summaries and statistics, data visualization showing the locations of SNs on a map along with their instantaneous measurements and/or measurement history, and other data dissemination applications, e.g., SMS alerts that inform the population of the gravity of pollution levels in certain areas.

A typical system model for air pollution monitoring is shown in Figure 6. In this model, a cell of certain area can be served by a BS, and several SNs are deployed to monitor environmental parameters in each cell.

4.2 Simulation Results: Implementation of the OFDMA Aloha Approach in the Air Pollution Detection WSN

In the simulations, we consider a single BS with SNs uniformly distributed within its coverage area. The total bandwidth considered is $B = 5$ MHz, subdivided into 25 subchannels of 12 subcarriers each (3GPP TS 36.211; 3GPP TS 36.213; Lunttila et al., 2007). Up to 30 SNs are considered in each cell, which is reasonable with the cell sizes considered in the following subsections. In addition, the SNs represent the nodes communicating directly with the BS. As explained previously, in the case where they are relaying other SNs data via multihop, the actual number of SNs in the cell would be larger.

4.2.1 Results with Different Transmission Probabilities

In this section, a cell radius of 500 m is considered and a target rate of 128 kbps is assumed for SNs. The impact of varying the transmission probability is studied. The case of constant transmission probabilities $p_T(k, i) = p_T$, while setting $p_T = 0.2$, $p_T = 0.5$, and $p_T = 0.7$, is compared to the case of dynamic transmission probability according to Eq. (11). In the dynamic scenario, $p_{T0} = 0.9$ is used in order to increase the probability of selecting the subchannels having the best channel gain for transmission.

The collision probability results are displayed in Figure 7. It can be noted that for fixed p_T, reservations become more aggressive as p_T increases. This leads to a slight increase in collision probability, but the results remain comparable for the three values considered in the fixed p_T scenario. However, the performance of the dynamic scheme is significantly better, since this scheme intelligently exploits the frequency diversity.

Figure 8 shows the outage results. In all the investigated scenarios, when the number of SNs is 25 or lower, the percentage of SNs in outage can be considered to be negligible. An increase of the number of SNs to 30 SNs in the cell leads to unstable results with the cases having $p_T = 0.2$, $p_T = 0.5$, and $p_T = 0.7$, since they lead to 96.13, 91.53, and 99.33% of SNs in outage, respectively. The dynamic approach has a remarkable performance with 0% of SNs in outage for all the simulated values. The sum-rate results, presented in Figure 9, show a comparable performance for all the studied cases when the number of

Figure 7. Collision probability of the proposed scheme for a target rate of 128 kbps, a cell radius of 500 m and different values of the transmission probability

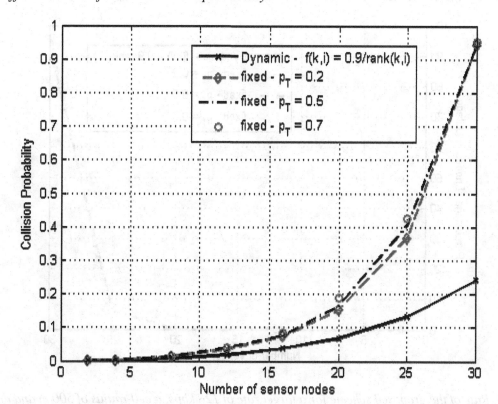

SNs is less than 25. When this number exceeds 25 SNs, the superiority of the dynamic scheme becomes evident, since it has no SNs in outage. In fact, with the dynamic scheme, all SNs achieve their target rate (0% outage), which leads to a sum-rate of 3.93 Mbps, compared to 2.16 Mbps for the case $p_T = 0.5$, where a high outage rate is achieved.

The change in performance at the threshold of 25 SNs can actually be explained by the fact that the simulation parameters assume the existence of 25 subchannels. Thus, with the fixed probability schemes, when the number of SNs exceeds the available number of subchannels, it becomes difficult to achieve the target rates for all SNs. However, with the dynamic approach, SNs can successfully transmit their data even when their number exceeds the number of available subchannels, due to the intelligent use of the channel state information by the dynamic scheme.

4.2.2 Results with Different Target Rates

Simulation results for a cell radius of 500 meters and three different target rates: 64 kbps, 128 kbps, and 256 kbps are presented in this section. A constant $p_T = 0.5$ is used. The sum-rate results, the percentage of SNs in outage, and the collision probability results are shown in Figs. 10-12, respectively. When the number of SNs is small (up to four SNs), the investigated schemes perform comparably. In addition, all SNs achieve their target data rate. However, as soon as the number of SNs increases, the TDMA approach

Figure 8. Percentage of SNs in outage of the proposed scheme for a target rate of 128 kbps, a cell radius of 500 m and different values of the transmission probability

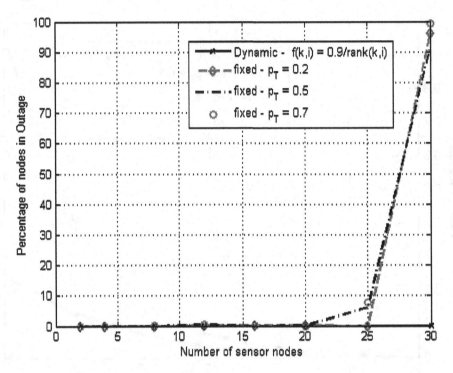

Figure 9. Rate of the proposed scheme for a target rate of 128 kbps, a cell radius of 500 m and different values of the transmission probability

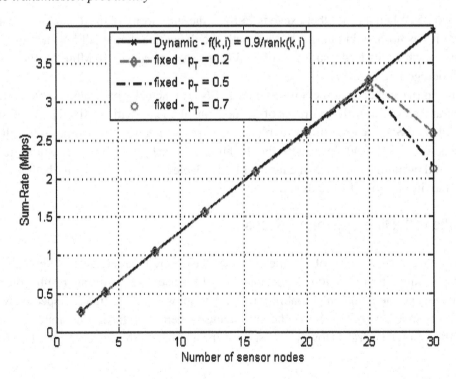

and the FDMA approach degrade significantly, whereas the proposed scheme shows better performance when the number of SNs increases.

Using the proposed scheme with $R_T = 64$ kbps, all the SNs are successfully transmit their data even when the number of SNs reaches 30. With $R_T = 128$ kbps, performance degrades when the number of SNs exceeds 25. With $R_T = 256$ kbps, the degradation is noted when the number of SNs exceeds 20. Indeed, an increasing number of SNs and/or target data rate increases imply that more packets should be transmitted at the same time in order to achieve the target data rate for all SNs. Consequently, this is expected to lead to an increase in collision probability during the reservation phase, as shown in Figure 12. Thus, fewer transmissions occur during the transmission phase, hence reducing the sum-rate, as shown in Figure 10. A straightforward consequence is the increase of the number of SNs in outage, as shown in Figure 11.

4.2.3 Results with Different Cell Radii

This section presents simulation results for a target rate of 128 kbps and three different values for the cell radius: 250 m, 500 m, and 1000 m. A constant $p_T = 0.5$ is used in this section. Figs. 13-15 show the sum-rate results, the percentage of SNs in outage, and the collision probability results, respectively. Naturally, an increase in the distance leads to a significant reduction in the SNR received at the BS, which reduces the achievable rate within a reserved time slot. However, the proposed scheme outperforms the other schemes and achieves the target rate when the distance increases, for a relatively small number of SNs. In fact, in this case, enough time slots are available with the proposed scheme to compensate the

Figure 10. Sum-rate of the compared methods for a cell radius of 500 m and different target rates

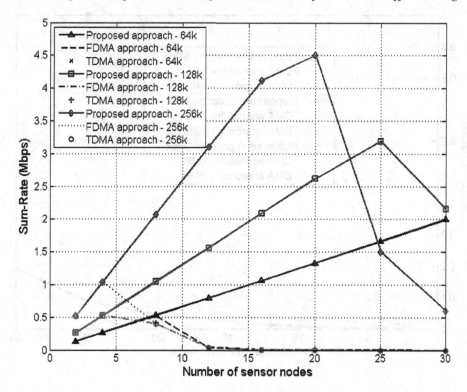

Figure 11. Percentage of SNs in outage for a cell radius of 500 m and different target rates

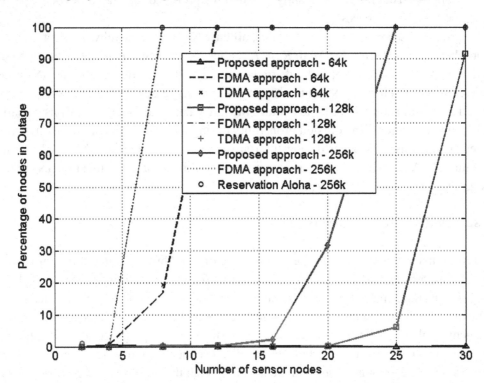

Figure 12. Collision probability of the different schemes for a cell radius of 500 m and different target rates

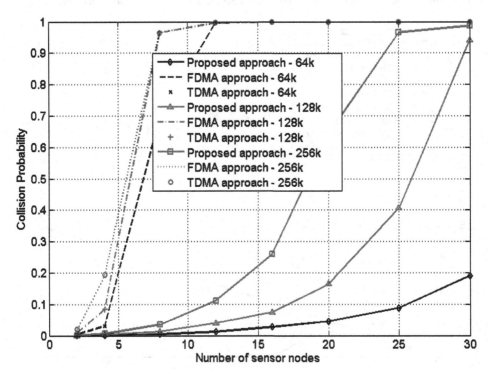

increase in the distance, although each SN would require a higher number of time slots to compensate the increased distance. When the number of SNs increases, more collisions will occur in the reservation phase, as shown in Figure 15, which leads to fewer transmissions in the transmission phase, thus reducing the achieved rate, as shown in Figure 13, and increasing the number of SNs in outage, as shown in Figure 14.

4.3 Implementation Challenges

Despite its superior performance, there are some implementation issues and tradeoffs that should be taken into account while implementing the proposed approach.

An important challenge is to maintain accurate synchronization. Although this is largely facilitated by periodically transmitting a pilot sequence by the BS, the SNs still have to be able to determine the boundaries of the small reservation slots over all available subcarriers. In addition, although the number of available subcarriers might be limited at a given time due to being used for more "traditional" cellular traffic, SNs still have to be able to "listen" to all subcarriers, since the set of subcarriers that are "free" for SN transmission will naturally vary with time. Another challenge is to appropriately determine the

Figure 13. Sum-rate of the different schemes for a target rate of 128 kbps and different values of the cell radius

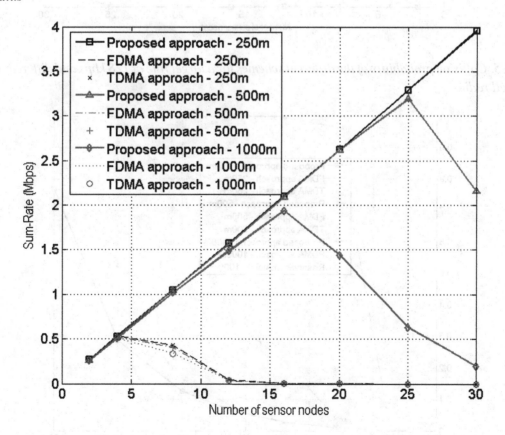

Figure 14. Percentage of SNs in outage for a target rate of 128 kbps and different values of the cell radius

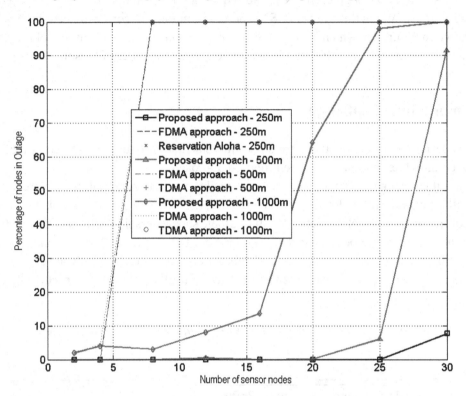

Figure 15. Collision probability of the different schemes for a target rate of 128 kbps and different values of the cell radius

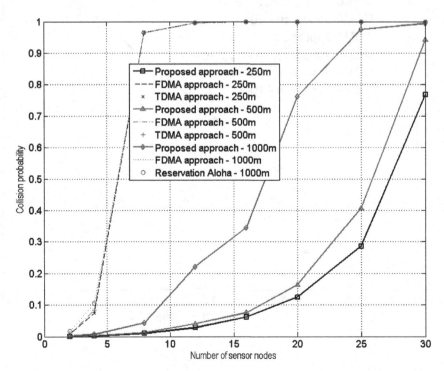

transmission probabilities in an optimized way that allows serving the largest possible number of SNs. Finally, the "possible" implementation in an LTE system proposed in this chapter is not possible without successful standardization, and then successful implementation by equipment manufacturers.

5. CONCLUSION AND FUTURE WORK

A communication protocol for WSNs was presented and analyzed. It is based on OFDMA, and allows the SNs to estimate the CSI on the various subchannels. Thus, they can perform independent subchannel reservation based on random access. The presented approach was investigated in the context of WSNs for air pollution monitoring. It was shown to lead to increased data rates and reduced collisions. Furthermore, collisions occur during the reservation phase, but not during the transmission phase, which avoids unnecessary wasted power due to colliding transmissions, thus leading to energy savings much needed in WSNs.

Although current communication techniques like GPRS and HSPA can be used with WSNs, the network is expected to be quickly congested in an IoT scenario when the number of SNs transmitting over the cellular system increases. On the other hand, the presented approach is based on OFDMA, and thus could be implemented in conjunction with state-of-the-art wireless communication systems, e.g., LTE/LTE-Advanced. For example, the APs of the presented protocol could be co-located with cellular BSs (e.g. LTE BSs), which could inform the WSN AP of the occupied subchannels within its cell, and the AP would transmit pilot signals only on the available (free) subchannels. Then, SNs would apply the presented approach to dynamically share these free subchannels, without impacting the primary cellular traffic in the network.

Future work consists of studying the feasibility of incorporating the proposed method in standardization releases relevant to IoT/Cyber-Physical systems. Furthermore, it would be interesting to study variations of the proposed approach that might be more suitable to specific IoT scenarios. For example, in the scenario of (near) real-time smart meter reading, or in the studied scenario of air pollution monitoring with periodic transmission of sensor data, the locations of IoT devices, and the time of their scheduled transmissions, are generally known in advance. Pre-scheduling or preliminary resource allocation can be performed in conjunction with the proposed approach to avoid collisions even in the reservation phase. For general scenarios, or for unscheduled transmissions, e.g., a pollution monitoring sensor raising an alarm before its periodic transmission time, the proposed approach remains applicable as is. Another important area for future study is the implementation of security and privacy techniques in conjunction with the proposed approach. Last but not least, an interesting research area would be to benefit from the large antenna arrays in massive MIMO systems in order to combine spatial diversity and/or beamforming (at the BS) with the proposed approach in order to successfully accommodate the largest possible number of SNs while avoiding to increase the feedback overhead on these SNs.

REFERENCES

Alsbou, N., Henry, D., & Refai, H. (2010). R-ALOHA with Priority (PRALOHA) in Non Ideal Channel with Capture Effects. In *Proceedings of the International Conference on Telecommunications (ICT 2010)*. doi:10.1109/ICTEL.2010.5478849

Chen, Y.-K. (2012). Challenges and opportunities of internet of things. In *Proc. of the Asia and South Pacific Design Automation Conference (ASP-DAC)*, Sydney, Australia (pp. 383–388). doi:10.1109/ASPDAC.2012.6164978

Choi, Y. J., Park, S., & Bahk, S. (2006). Multichannel Random Access in OFDMA Wireless Networks. *IEEE Journal on Selected Areas in Communications*, 24(3), 603–613. doi:10.1109/JSAC.2005.862422

Ejaz, W., Naeem, M., Shahid, A., Anpalagan, A., & Jo, M. (2017). Efficient Energy Management for the Internet of Things in Smart Cities. *IEEE Communications Magazine*, 55(1), 84–91. doi:10.1109/MCOM.2017.1600218CM

Ganesan, G., & Li, Y. (2007). A Simple Reservation Scheme for Multicarrier Channel Aware Aloha. In *Proceedings of the IEEE Global Communications Conference (GLOBECOM 2007)* (pp. 1451-1455). doi:10.1109/GLOCOM.2007.279

Han, Y. S., Deng, J., & Haas, Z. J. (2006). Analyzing Multi-Channel Medium Access Control Schemes with ALOHA Reservation. *IEEE Transactions on Wireless Communications*, 5(8), 2143–2152. doi:10.1109/TWC.2006.1687730

Harris, A. F. III, Khanna, V., Tuncay, G., Want, R., & Kravets, R. (2016). Bluetooth Low Energy in Dense IoT Environments. *IEEE Communications Magazine*, 54(12), 30–36. doi:10.1109/MCOM.2016.1600546CM

Khan, Z., Lehtomäki, J. J., Iellamo, S., Vuohtoniemi, R., Hossain, E., & Han, Z. (2017). IoT Connectivity in Radar Bands: A Shared Access Model Based on Spectrum Measurements. *IEEE Communications Magazine*, 55(2), 88–96. doi:10.1109/MCOM.2017.1600444CM

Kwon, H., Seo, H., Kim, S., & Lee, B. G. (2009). Generalized CSMA/CA for OFDMA Systems: Protocol Design, Throughput Analysis, and Implementation Issues. *IEEE Transactions on Wireless Communications*, 8(8), 4176–4187. doi:10.1109/TWC.2009.080816

Lepaja, S., & Bengi, K. (2001). A Random-Reservation Medium Access Protocol For Satellite Networks To Accommodate Real-Time Traffic. In *Proceedings of the IEEE Vehicular Technology Conference-Spring* (pp. 861–865). doi:10.1109/VETECS.2001.944501

Lloret, J., Canovas, A., Sendra, S., & Parra, L. (2015). A Smart Communication Architecture for Ambient Assisted Living. *IEEE Communications Magazine*, 53(1), 26–33. doi:10.1109/MCOM.2015.7010512

Lunttila, T., Lindholm, J., Pajukoski, K., Tiirola, E., & Toskala, A. (2007). EUTRAN Uplink Performance. In *Proceedings of the International Symposium on Wireless Pervasive Computing (ISWPC)*.

Mainetti, L., Patrono, L., & Vilei, A. (2011). Evolution of wireless sensor networks towards the internet of things: A survey. In *Proc. of the International Conference on Software, Telecommunications and Computer Networks (SoftCOM)*, Split, Croatia.

3.   rd Generation Partnership Project (3GPP). (2016). 3GPP TS 36.211 3GPP TSG RAN Evolved Universal Terrestrial Radio Access (E-UTRA) Physical Channels and Modulation, version 13.1.0, Release 13, March 2016.

3.   rd Generation Partnership Project (3GPP). (2016). 3GPP TS 36.213 3GPP TSG RAN Evolved Universal Terrestrial Radio Access (E-UTRA) Physical layer procedures, version 13.1.1, Release 13, March 2016.

Roberts, L. G. (1973). Dynamic Allocation of Satellite Capacity through Packet Reservation. In *Proceedings of the AFIPS Conference, National Computer Conference and Exposition* (Vol. 42, pp. 711-716). doi:10.1145/1499586.1499753

Semasinghe, P., Maghsudi, S., & Hossain, E. (2017). Game Theoretic Mechanisms for Resource Management in Massive Wireless IoT Systems. *IEEE Communications Magazine, 55*(2), 121–127. doi:10.1109/MCOM.2017.1600568CM

Shen, D., & Li, V. O. K. (2002). Stabilized Multi-Channel ALOHA for Wireless OFDM Networks. In *Proceedings of the IEEE Global Communications Conference (GLOBECOM 2002)* (pp. 701–705). doi:10.1109/GLOCOM.2002.1188169

Tasaka, S., Hayashi, K., & Ishibashi, Y. (1995). Integrated Video and Data Transmission in the TDD ALOHA-Reservation Wireless LAN. In *Proceedings of the IEEE International Conference on Communications (ICC 1995)* (pp. 1387–1393). doi:10.1109/ICC.1995.524431

Thomopoulos, S. (1988). Simple and Versatile Decentralized Control for Slotted ALOHA, Reservation ALOHA, and Local Area Networks. *IEEE Transactions on Communications, 36*(6), 662–674. doi:10.1109/26.2786

Vieira, M. A. M., Coelho, C. N. Jr, da Silva, D. C. Jr, & da Mata, J. M. (2003). Survey on Wireless Sensor Network Devices. In *Proceedings of the IEEE Conference on Emerging Technologies and Factory Automation* (Vol. 1, pp. 537-544). doi:10.1109/ETFA.2003.1247753

Wang, D., Minn, H., & Al-Dhahir, N. (2009). A Distributed Opportunistic Access Scheme and its Application to OFDMA Systems. *IEEE Transactions on Communications, 57*(3), 738–746. doi:10.1109/TCOMM.2009.03.070084

Xiao, Y., Zhang, Y., Gibson, J. H., & Xie, G. G. (2009). Performance Analysis of p-persistent Aloha for Multi-hop Underwater Acoustic Sensor Networks. In *Proceedings of the International Conference on Embedded Software and Systems* (pp. 305–311). doi:10.1109/ICESS.2009.61

Yaacoub, E., & Kadri, A. (2015). LTE Radio Resource Management for Real-Time Smart Meter Reading in the Smart Grid. *Proceedings of the IEEE ICC '15.*

Yaacoub, E., Kadri, A., & Abu-Dayya, A. (2011). An OFDMA Communication Protocol for Wireless Sensor Networks used for Leakage Detection in Underground Water Infrastructures. In *Proceedings of the IEEE International Wireless Communications and Mobile Computing Conference (IWCMC 2011)*. doi:10.1109/IWCMC.2011.5982823

Yumei, Z., & Yu, S. (2009). Analysis of Channel-aware Multichannel ALOHA in OFDMA Wireless Networks. *Information and Communications Technologies*, *3*(2), 56–61.

Zhang, N., Vojcic, B., Souryal, M. R., & Larsson, E. G. (2006). Exploiting Multiuser Diversity in Reservation Random Access. *IEEE Transactions on Wireless Communications*, *5*(9), 2548–2554. doi:10.1109/TWC.2006.1687778

Chapter 5
Effective Approaches to Training CPS Knowledge and Skills

Christian Kreiner
Graz University of Technology, Austria

Richard Messnarz
ISCN GmbH, Austria & University of Applied Sciences Joanneum, Austria

ABSTRACT

Training of skills for engineering CPS systems requires to convey deeper understanding of complex and multidisciplinary processes and products. Companies are facing complex challenges and encounter demands for specialized skills and interdisciplinary collaboration to achieve dependable mass products for end customers. Furthermore, industry demands flexibility, effectiveness, and efficiency in qualifying trainees. Usually they ask for: deliver yesterday, no time committed to training, and perfectly qualified trainees as outcome. The modular matrix course architecture is described for those in need to devise a complex training for industry. It is complemented by best practice recommendations for course development, delivery, and certification. The training and certification toolbox of the AQUA Knowledge Alliance for Automotive has fully implemented the described approach, and serves as a case study.

INTRODUCTION

Nowadays electronics and software control take over functionality at a tremendous rate - we are heading for software-defined anything. This leads to a level of complexity that has never been experienced before - both of the (connected!) CPS itself, and the related development processes. There is a strong common agreement that interdisciplinary expertise is indispensable. It is a fundamental basis for being able to tackle this complexity under the heavy pressure of shorter development and innovation cycles. Moreover, this demand is reinforced by the necessity of mastering essential horizontal topics such as product and lifecycle process quality, reliability/resilience, functional safety, security.

DOI: 10.4018/978-1-5225-2845-6.ch005

Looking at the example of the automotive industry, e.g. international standards on development quality like Automotive SPICE, ISO/ IEC 15504 (The SPICE User Group, 2015), functional safety according to ISO 26262 (ISO, 2011), and Design for Six Sigma methods (ISO, 2011) for production and process quality have to be mastered. Only together, they ensure both the successful integration of all parts and subsystems, and smooth cooperation in the modern automotive supply chains. These quality aspects need to be implemented in an integrated way because of their holistic nature as such, but also due to shorter and shorter product development cycles that pushes development steps to overlap each other.

This leads to a strong need for qualified specialists and even more for interdisciplinary allrounders. Such people are sometimes referred to as T-shaped people, able to drill deep in one (or more) of their specialized areas, and having a broad "integration T roof" to understand and effectively integrate the expertise and skills of specialists from other areas in the overall CPS development team.

The modular matrix approach for a course architecture is described for those in need to devise a complex training for industry, and universities in turn. In particular, this often requires to convey deeper understanding of complex processes and products. Companies are facing complex challenges and encounter demands for specialized skills and interdisciplinary collaboration to effect a dependable mass product for end customers. Furthermore, industry demands flexibility, effectiveness, and efficiency in qualifying trainees. Usually they ask for: deliver yesterday, no time committed to training, and perfectly qualified trainees as outcome.

Methodically, the approaches described support and incorporate many well-known pedagogical patterns in both course architecture, and use cases of training delivery.

Among others, the presented course architecture has been implemented in the course of the European Commission supported Sector Skills Alliance project AQUA for the Automotive domain (Kreiner, et al., 2013). A training toolbox like AQUA allows to be reconfigured according to the needs of in-house company trainings and university courses. This leads to effective and quick proliferation of "young" state of the art knowledge and skills across universities and industry. Throughout the chapter AQUA will serve as reference implementation and example.

CONTEXT AND CHALLENGES OF TRAINING CPS SKILLS

Mastering a whole bunch international standards in addition to state of the art technologies is key for being able to place a competitive product on the market. In Automotive system development, standards like Automotive SPICE (The SPICE User Group, 2015) for development process quality, ISO 26262 for functional safety (ISO, 2011), and Design for Six Sigma for production and process quality (ISO, 2011) have to be implemented in one integrated, multi-disciplinary, seriously complex product development lifecycle. See Figure 1 for a typical high-level view of an Automotive development process – based on the well-known "V" model covering all development phases, augmented with quality gates as mandated by IATF 16949:2016 (Automotive Industry Action Group (AIAG), 2016), mandatory safety activities, and best-practice method selection for Design for Six Sigma. Each method is complex by itself to understand and implement. Successful Automotive product development requires all, in an integrated way. While specialized courses are available, training leading-edge integration is a major challenge – because of an ever-moving target of state-of the art knowledge, and the sheer organizational complexity of integration.

Figure 2 illustrates the cognitive complexity as encountered by an engineering team during product design. It just schematically focuses on the intricate relationship of tasks and methods to be executed.

*Figure 1. Typical Automotive product "V" development model, integrating methods of Automotive SPICE,
Functional Safety, and Design for Six Sigma*
From: AQUA training material (Kreiner, et al., 2013).

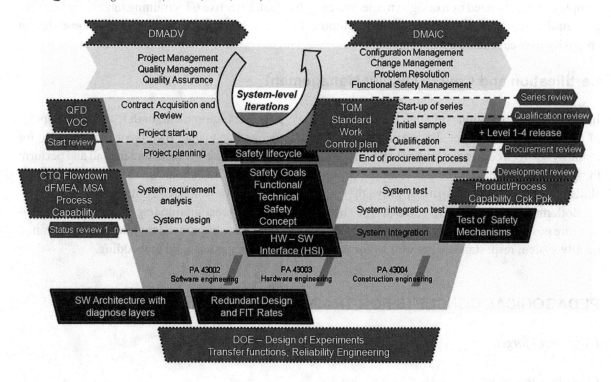

Figure 2. Cognitive complexity experienced during CPS engineering: conceptual elements and engineering tasks for safety relevant Automotive CPS (selection)
Adapted from Christian Kreiner (2015).

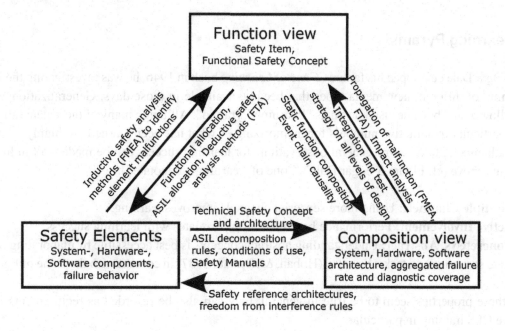

Numerous iterations around the design triangle function – elements – composition are necessary to finally arrive at a consistent design honoring all requirements and standards. This again is an overwhelming complexity experienced by a design engineer as an individual. Effective CPS training must therefore also give guidance to professionally execute development processes, and at the same time not loose design creativity in such situations.

Certification and Course Quality Management

Independent certification with high recognition value is a further requirement, both from the viewpoint of a trainee and companies. Important aspects for a trainee include his/her own labor market value for mobility between companies and/or locations, besides the personal motivation to understand and perform things better. Companies' human resource departments need to formally manage the company internal skills resources, and even formally prove their employees' skills for standards compliance.

Both market recognition (e.g. ECQA, see below) and authority recognition (e.g. university certification) are possible strategies for certification. Both require following an approved training and certification quality system resp. standard, as well as formal curriculum management and embedding.

PEDAGOGICAL CONCEPTS FOR TRAINING CPS DEVELOPMENT SKILLS

I hear and I forget.

I see and I remember.

I do and I understand.

Confucius

The Learning Pyramid

When Edgar Dale developed his famous *Cone of Learning* back in 1946, he was investigating the impact to learning of different new media types that became available in those days. Generalizations of that cone followed and became also known as "Learning Pyramid". Although many of these generalizations and in particular quantitative numbers for memorizing of what has been learned are highly controversial (Thalheimer, 2006), some general observations for learning success can be made – all in line with Confucius above (cf. Figure 3 Edgar Dale's Cone of Learning – annotated):

- **Multiple Channels:** Using more sensorial channels improves learning.
- **Active Involvement:** Performance based learning correlates with learning success.
- **Concrete vs. Abstract:** Understanding abstract concepts is best accessible by elaborating on concrete scenarios and tasks. See also (Hoban, & Zisman, 1937) in context with the Cone of Learning.

As these properties seem to be true in general, they can also be regarded as requirements for any effective CPS training in particular.

Figure 3. Edgar Dale's Cone of Learning: annotated

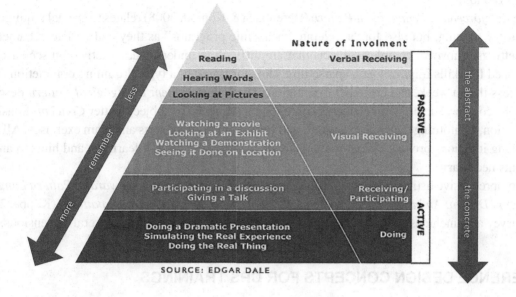

Pedagogical Patterns

Many patterns useful for training development and delivery have been collected in the *Pedagogical Patterns Project* (Bergin et al., 2012). Most notably, the *Seminars pedagogical pattern language* (Fricke & Völter, 2000) forms a large core of it. For the described approach, mostly patterns from the "Teaching" category is relevant and being followed resp. supported. Patterns from this collection referenced in the following:

- *General Concepts*
- *One concept - several implementations*
- *Relevant Examples*
- *Digestible Packets*
- *Expand the known world*
- *Let them decide*
- *Spiral*
- *Seminar Plan*
- *Let The Plan Go*

In particular in the context of industry trainings some of Rick Rodin's *Meta patterns for Developing a Minimalist Training Manual* (Rodin, 2012) are relevant in the context of effective CPS training design. These patterns boil down to a consequent practice-grounded and student-driven *Guided Exploration*, that in turn heavily evolves during delivery. *Guided Exploration* has been successfully applied in a university setting as core paradigm for an inductive teaching approach and was systematically evaluated in a case study (Köppe & Rodin, 2013). Results proved it effective and showed evolving diversity of exploration paths in different teams during the experiment. The approach described further down follows some of these minimalist principles, but tends to have primary pathways trough the course while still maintaining high flexibility.

The *Reinforcement Pedagogical Pattern* (Berenbach & Konrad, 2008) relates to special requirements for industry training, but also for "accelerated academic programs" as they call it. They characterize these settings to involve complex subjects that are difficult to understand, a motivation scenario by a strong need for skills improvement, sparse time slots for training, a typical training completion timespan of less than a week, and customer orientation. The *Reinforcement Pedagogical Pattern* describes a modular course structure with elements containing a sequence of subject matter *Concepts* consisting of definition, reinforcing concrete examples, and further reinforcing class and team exercises. All these reinforcing iterations provide almost immediate feedback on the pace of learning, and hints to any adjustments necessary.

A comprehensive listing of known pedagogical patterns can be found in *Towards a Pattern Language for Lecture Design: An inventory and categorization of existing lecture-relevant patterns* (Köppe, 2013). This survey also includes short descriptions and categorizes the patterns into several dimensions.

REFERENCE DESIGN CONCEPTS FOR CPS TRAININGS

Building on requirements and aggregated pedagogical pattern knowledge referenced above, the approach described here defines a strictly modular course architecture together with rules for content. Where applicable, references are pointed out to pedagogical patterns implemented, as well as to such supported at delivery of the course.

The Module Matrix: A Course Content Architecture

In particular the *Reinforcement Pedagogical Pattern* already addresses a number of typical requirements and constraints relevant for CPS training: industrial settings and their special requirements, flexible modular structure, *Concepts* as cognitive backbone(s), examples and exercises aligned to the participants' domains.

The *Module Matrix* approach described here uses the term concept both in the subject-specific streams, and in a more abstract sense as well, using common cross-discipline concepts to link more together more than one subject matter. To address the multidisciplinary nature of knowledge and skills in CPS training, the proposed course content architecture follows a strictly modular principle in (at least) two dimensions (Figure 4). These dimensions are denoted as *Common Concepts*, that must be implemented, and specialized *Subject matter* dimensions.

Validating experience for the *Module Matrix* mainly comes from currently implemented courses in the Automotive and Automation domains, the AQUA course being one of these. These courses share certain characteristics like group sizes of 10-18 trainees for in-house classroom trainings, resp. 2-6 persons when delivered as on-line training. The on-line variant also includes web-based interactive exercise discussion sessions for the entire group.

Context: Setting the Stage

The *Module Matrix* is well suited to teach specialized, interconnected multi-disciplinary knowledge and skills. While primarily designed for industry – they have the more challenging requirements – it can be successfully incorporated to university curricula as well.

What Is the Challenge?

Industry needs skills built up effectively and efficiently for expert subjects in interdisciplinary development, production, maintenance, and decommissioning processes. Of course, all this has to consider the business domain and the needs of the organization to be trained. Given this real-world complexity and constraints, it can be hard to design and structure an appropriate course.

While in-depth specialized training programs often exist, these often cannot be used directly for an integrated, joint interdisciplinary training course by just plugging the subjects together. This is also because almost every industry training de facto has to fit within a few days less than a week (Berenbach & Konrad, 2008), and real-world interdisciplinary complexity would not be addressed adequately. Furthermore, many participants have a background as a specialist in one or the other area, bringing in pre-existing skills that must be honored in commercial courses. To summarize the requirements briefly, industry has demand for courses that

1. Effectively qualify staff for tasks needed in development projects and/or production. In particular, it must honor pre-existing knowledge and skills.
2. Address practical, complex, domain specific problems and skills needed.
3. Compile expertise of several disciplines in an interdisciplinary, integrated way, reflecting the real-world nature and complexity of development/production processes.
4. Are compact and do interfere as little as possible with daily work schedule.
5. Exhibit flexibility and modularity that allow for scoping of content and schedule the teaching.
6. Can be delivered in both classroom and online settings. Online delivery provides completely individual learning schedules, while classroom settings provide possibly more interaction and activity.
7. Are appropriate for participants whose primary occupation is industry work, who are not used to everyday learning like full-time students on the other hand.

Module Matrix: A Proven Solution Pattern for CPS Training Structure

As the name indicates, *Module Matrix* uses a matrix organization of course content. This allows a participant or group of participants to take steps in either matrix dimension in order to explore complex topics and relations within the material. In the two-dimensional structure explained below, one can broaden knowledge within a subject exploring concept by concept, or explore the interdisciplinary relation of a common concept between two or more subjects. There are only little restrictions to selecting a concrete path of exploration. In this way, participants are not only passengers to the course, their pre-existing skills as well as individual goals can be honored, as participant can start at different points, and can skip known concepts. Practical examples and exercises during the course give opportunities and guidance to a self-assessment in this respect.

The principal architecture of *Module Matrix* is shown in Figure 4. It is structured in two dimensions:

- **Subject Matter:** Subject matter lines in the course architecture contain specialized single-subject matter training material (see Figure 4). As a whole, each of these subject matter lines forms a compact, maybe even minimal, role-oriented body of knowledge and skills. Subject matter lines essentially resemble what is described in the *Reinforcement Pedagogical Pattern* as a sequence of concept bricks. They should also contain real-world examples from the participant's domain, illustrating the topic and grounding it to real world. This is very much in line with the *Relevant Examples* and *Expand the known world* pedagogical patterns. For industry courses, concept bricks must be very compact, if not to say minimal, because they are economically forced to work efficiently, especially in terms of time resources. Care must be taken not to lose training efficiency thereby. This idea references the *Digestible Packets* pattern. In the AQUA example, the subject matter lines are Automotive SPICE, Functional Safety, and Six Sigma. The individual concept bricks are compact slide sets of approx. 10-15 slides including examples.
- **Common Concepts:** Common, integrating concepts form the column views in Figure 4. Each common concept has anchors in many or all subject matters, and describes a significant relation between them. These concepts are the integration cores welding together subject specific concept bricks in an interdisciplinary way. Pedagogical patterns followed here are *General Concepts* and *One concept - several implementations*. Integration can take on many facets, e.g. there can be analog structures in the specialized subjects that can be mapped, or complementing topics that are aggregated to form a larger, integrated concept by its own. Integration of concepts is the most

Figure 4. Two-dimensional modular course content architecture
Source: Kreiner, Module matrix: a pattern for interdisciplinary industry training design, 2014.

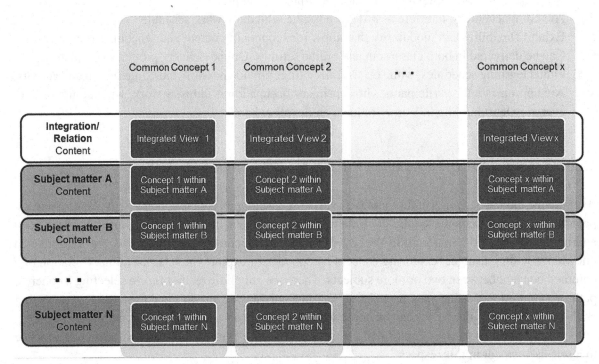

challenging part in terms of complexity in this kind of trainings. Learning and understanding such kinds of integration mainly happens during active and concrete exercising. An additional integrative content element for each vertical *Common Concept* is helpful to explain explicitly how special subject concept topics get integrated in practice and theory. Together with according exercises, each of these elements gives deeper insights into complexity encountered in real-world engineering and production processes. Very often, this can take on the following characteristics. In the simple case, for some concepts, the integration element can simply take on a translation role between the subject matter terms and topics. This leads to better mutual understanding between experts of different areas that have to work together. For other concepts, the integration element can also show a complex dependency of engineering tasks and artifacts across all expert fields. Naming just two examples to illustrate the shared concepts in the AQUA example below, let us look at the lifecycle (mapping), and capability (complementing):

- **Mapping of Lifecycle Understanding:** All three, Automotive SPICE, Functional Safety, and Six Sigma know the concept of a lifecycle. All three are executed together in an overall complex Automotive product lifecycle. Lifecycle phases can be mapped onto a common development process where the quality gates serve as synchronization points (see also Figure 1).
- **Complementing:** Different concepts of "capability" can be found in the specific expert domains. These are oriented towards development process maturity (Automotive SPICE), product integrity for safety in case of component failures (Functional Safety), and mass production process accuracy and repeatability (Six Sigma). Each and every expert subject must contribute to yield a high quality and trustworthy (mass) product for the end customer.

Expected Benefits and Risks

Using *Module Matrix* for organizing CPS course contents allows high flexibility for consuming the course, or only parts of it:

- Compact elements allow to learn in small chunks. This is well suited to organize training in parallel to daily work (*Digestible Packets*). Especially on-line course settings can benefit greatly from packaging course materials into small chunks.
- A compact elements structure allows to honor pre-existing knowledge easily and in a fine-granular way. This holds true for sufficiently homogeneous training groups as well as for individuals. The first case applies to most in-house training courses for single companies. Individual skills can be best taken into account in self-study or guided exploration settings, in particular also when delivered as on-line course.
- In principle, every learning path through the maze of training elements is allowed (c.f. *Reading in any order*), so the concrete approach taken can be decided upon by the student or student group (*Let them decide*). The following use cases are the primary ones how to use a *Module Matrix*:
  - A subject matter expert wants to broaden skills starting from his pre-existing knowledge that allows him to recognize possible entry points. He would learn by exploring along the integration concept columns to the other subjects and get a deeper insight in the integration element (*Expand the known world*).

- ○ When starting with the integration modules, concepts are trained in an interdisciplinary way, showing and giving deeper insight into interdependencies and real-world complexity (similar to *Spiral*).
  - ○ The modules belonging to a single subject matter can be used as a compact introductory training course for that subject.
  - ○ Individual curiosity can be met by a zig-zag course through the course element matrix (*Reading in any order*).
- However, the inherent flexibility can easily lead to confusion of the students, as possible routes are overwhelming. It is a necessary to have a *Seminar Plan* and offer a navigation aid *Reference the Plan* throughout the course. Of course, in case the group feels secure enough the trainer can *Let The Plan Go*, put the group into the driver's seat, and use the full potential of the matrix architecture.
- Depending on the domain, it is not always be possible to fully populate the subject matter vs. common concept matrix. However, industry demand for a multidisciplinary course can be considered a strong indicator for being able to substantially fill the matrix. The rationale is that industry articulates no demand without having an issue in practice. Further, if there were no common concepts and interdisciplinary entangling, industry would rather go for less complex single-subject courses.

Course Development and Delivery Considerations

When starting to design such an integrated, multidisciplinary course, special subject course material most probably is already available, yet not integrated. The creative part here is to search for subject specific concepts that have some meaningful relation: touchpoints, mappings, process or other dependencies, a common generalization, complementary properties, etc. The criteria for "meaningful" have to be derived from the real-world complexity of the domain. The common concept relation must be valuable for the participants, i.e. relevant in reality and/or provide deeper (non-trivial) insight to real-world complexity. Due to the minimalism to be applied in industry courses, such a clearly perceptible added value is key.

It is absolutely essential to have a *Seminar Plan* and offer continuous guidance when training topics of overwhelming complexity like in integrated engineering of CPS. As a best practice recommendation, such guidance should follow a powerful concept experienced in practice. When teaching about engineering of CPS, an integrated product lifecycle can often serve as rough conceptual guidance for a learning path, if applicable.

Due to the multidisciplinary complexity of CPS knowledge, and hints given by the learning pyramid, interweaving of concepts is best learned during a hands-on exercise learning experience. Trying to perform the integrated skills – especially in small group settings – involves multiple sensorial channels, and lets the participants "feel" what integrating concepts or methods from more than one discipline means in practice. Dedicated presentation and discussion phases with peer groups and trainers lead to deep insights for both the presenting and the reviewing roles.

For industrial courses, exercise assignments should be based on the participants' daily work - not just mimicking an abstract scenario, but taking a concrete problem from their current work. In this way, the participant's motivation is high because of his awareness to the problem. As well, the exercise results might be even directly reusable in his daily work, a benefit for the company as well. Still, this poses also some challenges for the trainer(s), as there is normally no prepared model solution. Instead, the trainer(s) must be capable to moderate the exercise process towards a reviewed solution proposal. However, this is anyway the way of working experienced in practice, and after some help-seeking moments, this approach is normally highly valued by the trainees.

Providing an online training platform greatly helps to distribute the latest versions of course material, provide multimedia lectures for on-demand study, virtual discussion forums, supplementary material, management of trainee registration, and more.

INDUSTRY TRAINING CASE STUDY: AQUA: KNOWLEDGE ALLIANCE FOR TRAINING, QUALITY, AND EXCELLENCE IN AUTOMOTIVE

By learning you will teach,

by teaching you will learn.

Latin proverb

Electronics and software control a major share of a modern car's functions, with rising tendency. In future, cars will not only be largely self-driving, but also provide a software-defined user experience. This lead to a stunning level of complexity both of the CPS "car" and the related development processes – and this level is still rising.

There is a strong common agreement in the Automotive sector that interdisciplinary expertise and competencies are a fundamental basis for being able to tackle this complexity under the heavy pressure of ever shorter development and innovation cycles. Moreover, this demand is reinforced by the necessity of mastering essential horizontal topics such as product and process quality, reliability, and functional safety.

International standards on development quality Automotive SPICE (The SPICE User Group, 2015), Functional Safety ((ISO, 2011), (ISO, 2009), and Design for Six Sigma (production and process quality) (ISO, 2011) form the backbone of the modern automotive and supplier industry. These standards contribute to the smooth coupling of the different companies along the supply chain, and enable the successful integration of all parts and subsystems. In order to be eligible as supplier in this industry, you have to implement and master all relevant standards for your scope. This applies for all – large, medium, and small companies. The holistic nature of these quality requirements and the ever increasing need for shortening development cycles imply that the topics linked to quality aspects have to be addressed in an integrated way. This strong need, however, is confronted with a lack of qualified specialists and even more so of interdisciplinary allrounders.

AQUA is a certified job role at European Certification and Qualification Association[1] (ECQA). ECQA imposes a quality framework compliant to ISO 17024, provides training portals, examination services, and issues person certification.

AQUA is just one of many ECQA professions. A similar approach to that described below has been successfully implemented in the ECQA Functional Safety Manager/Engineer course[2] (Riel, et al., 2012) (Messnarz, et al., 2013). There, the linked subjects are safe function, system design, software design, hardware design, management, production. The integrating concepts follow the lifecycle activities including specialized (holistic) safety analysis methods. However, in that implementation the course material is not modularized as cleanly as in the AQUA case.

AQUA Knowledge Alliance and Stakeholder Involvement

The AQUA Knowledge Alliance project (Kreiner, et al., 2013) was one of four pilot projects for a Sector Skills Alliance pilot projects funded by the European Commission, DG EAC under their Lifelong Learning Programme. It mainly targeted at the Automotive industry sector. The AQUA project has a number of successors. One of these is the Automotive Quality Universities (AQU) project, an ERASMUS+ project adapting and rolling out the AQUA skills in several European Technical Universities (Jakub Stolfa, 2016).

AQUA aims at integrating the essence of the above mentioned topics Automotive SPICE, Functional Safety, and Design for Six Sigma in a compact and modular certified training program. Common cross-domain concepts like requirements, assessments, etc. are used for linking corresponding aspects of disciplines. The resulting matrix of small course modules helps prospective students to hook up with their individual skills and extend them in an interdisciplinary way.

AQUA and AQU involve relevant stakeholders and base on several networks, effectively forming an alliance to promote the program:

- Relevant Automotive industry companies greatly helped to assure relevance and effectiveness of the course contents and modes of delivery. They contributed requirements (role-based training, certification), relevant knowledge to be incorporated to the curriculum, and received (free) trial trainings in order to collect feedback. Beyond others, the one of the most active industry stakeholder group came from the SoQrates Quality Initative (Initiative, 2015) with companies cooperating like Continental AG, Elektrobit GmbH, Schäffler AG, MAGNA, SIEMENS, ZF Friedrichshafen AG, HELLA AG, EPCOS & TDK AG, KTM Motorcycles, and more. Some incorporated AQUA courses into their company-internal academies in turn.
- Automotive Clusters in several countries (AT, CZ, SI, NL, EU) promote AQUA, and offer AQUA courses in their course programs.
- Universities participating in the alliance incorporated teaching of AQUA skills into their study programs. The AQU project partners are Graz University of Technology, AT; UAS FH Joanneum, AT; INP Grenoble, FR; Technical University Ostrava, CZ; University of Maribor, SI; UAS FH Düsseldorf, DE. More universities already decided to participate.
- EuroSPI (European Systems and Software Process Improvement and Innovation) organises an international conference series since 1994. AQUA/AQU has been positioned there with an international workshop, papers, and exhibition. This created a target group on a world-wide basis.

The AQUA Modular Course Architecture: An Application of Module Matrix

The current content of the AQUA integrated course architecture is illustrated in Table 1. A base layer of core modules was established that provide an integrated and complementary view about the three approaches, including Automotive SPICE, Functional Safety, and selected topics of Lean and Design for Six Sigma.

Table 1. AQUA course structure: vehicular knowledge items arranged in the form of a skills set module matrix

Learning Elements	Integration	ASPICE	Functional Safety	Design for Six Sigma
UNIT 1: Introduction				
U1.E1 Standards, Norms, and Guidelines	Model comparison, purpose of norms, benefits of integration Background, IATF 16949, etc.	ISO 15504 and 33000 series, VDA 6.1, Automotive SPICE	ISO 26262, IEC 61508	ISO 13053
U1.E2 Organisational Readiness	Multifunctional teams, Quality managers, quality planning, control, assurance	Quality managers, independent quality assurance	Safety engineer and manager, presumes quality management	Champions, Green & Black Belts, TQM
UNIT 2: Product Development				
U2.E1 Lifecycle	V-model integration PEP, APQP, QSFD, PPAP, VDA Product life-cycle	V-model	W-model, safety life-cycle, DIA, safety plan	DMAIC, DMADV/IDOV
U2.E2 Requirements	V-model integration Functional requirements, QFD	Customer, system, SW, HW, mechani-cal requirements	Functional and technical safety requirements	VOC, CTQ
U2.E3 Design	V-model integration Scope of system architecture, performance	System and SW architecture, CPU load, memory consumption	System-, HW-, SW-, reference architectures, PFD, PFH	Transfer functions, DoE, Yield, DPMO, CpK
U2.E4 Integration and Testing	V-model integration Test, verification, validation, design reviews	System, SW unit test, traceability to requirements, test coverage	Release levels, fault injection, equivalence class tests	Reliability, preliminary capability, DoE tests
UNIT 3: Quality and Safety Management				
U3.E1 Capability	Holistic notion of capability (development, manufacturing) Definition of capability from different views and for various goals	Capability Levels, Maturity Levels, Rating Scale Profile	Safety Integrity Levels SIL and ASIL, HW reliability, SW diagnostic coverage	Process Capability (CpK), Process Performance (PpK)
U3.E2 Hazard & Risk Management	Holistic risk management framework, Risk management, FMEA	Re-use and risk management	SIL and ASIL, FMEDA, Hazard & Risk Analysis	Design FMEA
U3.E3 Assessment and Audit	Integrated Assessment Auditing, Process Audit VDA 6.3	Process Management	Safety Audit	Internal and external audits
UNIT 4: Measure				
U4.E1 Measurements	Aggregated dashboard, experience values, Consolidated table of KPIs	Requirements-, test coverage, trend analysis	Requirements, diagnostic, test coverage, resource usage	Measurement system analysis, internal CTQs
U4.E2 Reliability	Deriving reliability requirements from hazards and risks, Define reliability from different viewpoints and goals	ASIL classification and diagnostic measures	QM = ASPICE level 2; level 4 requires quantitative methods, i.e. reliability	Hazard, life distribution function, failure in time, MTTF, accelerated life testing, failure rate curve

Fields of Expertise United in AQUA

Automotive SPICE (The SPICE User Group, 2015) is used to perform assessments of the system and software development process capability of automotive suppliers in accordance with the requirements of ISO/IEC 15504 and now 33000 series (ISO/IEC, 2015). The Automotive SPICE Process Assessment Model has been developed under the Automotive SPICE initiative by consensus of the car manufacturers within the Automotive Special Interest Group (SIG), a joint special interest group of the Procurement Forum and the SPICE User Group. Members of the Automotive SIG include AUDI AG, BMW Group, Daimler AG, Fiat Auto S.p.A., Ford Werke GmbH, Jaguar, Land Rover, Dr.-Ing. h.c. F. Porsche AG, Volkswagen AG and Volvo Car Corporation.

Functional safety is an integral part of each critical product development phase, ranging from the specification, to design, implementation, integration, verification, validation, and production release. It aims to mitigate possible hazards caused by the malfunctioning electronic and electrical systems. The ISO 26262 (ISO, 2011) is an adaptation of the generic Functional Safety standard IEC 61508 (ISO, 2009) for Automotive electric/electronic systems. ISO 26262 defines functional safety for automotive equipment applicable throughout the lifecycle of all automotive electronic and electrical safety-related systems. It provides requirements for validation and confirmation measures to ensure a sufficient and acceptable level of safety is being achieved.

The application of Lean Six Sigma allows quality and efficiency improvements to be effectively realized. Lean Six Sigma combines Lean Manufacturing (originally developed by Toyota) and Six Sigma (originally developed by Motorola). It results in first the elimination of the eight kinds of wastes (Muda): over-production, waiting, transport, over-processing, inventory, movement, defects, and unused expertise), and secondly, high-quality provisioning of goods and service at a rate of 3.4 defects per million opportunities (DPMO) or better.

AQUA Course Content Architecture

The innovative integrated approach taken by the AQUA alliance extracts and teaches "the essence" - common concepts and principles - from the base layer subject matter modules. The AQUA integrated view layer expresses the mapping or translation to Automotive SPICE, Functional Safety, and Lean Six Sigma (see Table 1). In this way, the complexity of learning and mastering all three standards can be significantly reduced.

The interdisciplinary AQUA course also points forward to specialized, single-subject courses to dive deep into the respective subject, always being able to subordinate the in-depth knowledge into the overall, integrated picture.

Table 1 shows the complete list of common concept course elements[3]. Each covers all four bricks: an integration view, an Automotive SPICE view, a Functional Safety view, and a Design for Six Sigma view.

Integration of Concepts by Mapping: On the Example of Course Unit "Lifecycle"

AQUA uses a best-practice integrated V-Model development lifecycle to create a mapping of activities in all three disciplines Design for Six Sigma, Functional Safety, and Automotive SPICE as shown in Figure 1. Such an integrated view also helps to improve planning of lifecycle activities.

Integration of Concepts by Dependency: A Design Process Example

A typical example of an interaction/dependency link between Design for Six Sigma (DfSS), Functional safety, and Automotive SPICE engineering cycles can be observed as follows:

1. The Failure Modes and Effects Analysis (FMEA) is a DfSS tool. It analyzes components for possible failures and the resulting effects on the overall system.
2. Consequently, in Functional Safety, FMEA results are often taken as input to drive the design of sophisticated counter measures for avoiding hazards due to failures. (By the way, the ISO26262 safety standard imposes mandatory methodical safety analysis, explicitly mentioning FMEA)
3. These newly designed safety mechanisms are formulated as requirements that are being traced in ASPICE towards complete and correct implementation.
4. Testing and experimental use might lead to new unknown failures being incorporated into the FMEA database in turn.
5. Iterate to Step 1.

As a conclusion, in projects developing a hardware/ software/ mechanics products, it is required to integrate methods from all three domains to assure that

- All functions are complete, tracked, and finally implemented (Automotive SPICE),
- All functions and design measures to avoid hazards are in place and effective (Functional safety), and
- That the dependency of design parameters is understood to assure life-time reliability and mass production repeatability of product as well (Six Sigma).

Organizational and Tactical Aspects of Training Development and Delivery

AQUA is a certified job role at *European Certification and Qualification Association* (ECQA). ECQA certified job roles must adhere to the ECQA quality framework.

ECQA: Role-Based Qualification, Certification, and Quality Framework

The *European Certification and Qualification Association* (ECQA) is a result of the *European Qualification Network* EQN project (Messnarz, 2006; Messnarz, Ekert, Reiner, & O'Suilleabhain, 2006; Messnarz, Reiner, & Ekert, 2012). EQN was a strategic network project in education in which industry and educational institutions from 13 countries networked to propose a solution to this demographic problem. It was also expected to deliver an initiative of innovation in education (Messnarz & Ekert, 2007). Key outcomes - and now key features of ECQA are:

- **Job Role Based Qualification Strategies:** While the universities teach for a domain (e.g. electrical engineer), job role based qualifications base on short courses which re-qualify people in industry during 2-3 weeks (access from the workplace). The goal is to sustain their value for the company and remain employed. Job roles are described as skills sets similar to the skill cards in the Department of Trade and Industry in the UK. Skills sets are mapped onto training, exercises and exams. Given someone studies for an informatics engineering degree this takes approx. 5 years at a university. Starting from a basis like that, a job role qualification might then be to upgrade to a safety architect, software process improvement manager, etc. A job role committee (JRC) is an international working group that signed the standard ECQA JRC agreement and annually maintains the skills card and exam questions pool. ECQA certifies training bodies who train assessors in this new assessment model.

- **Modular Certification:** Typically, people in industry at the work place are under time pressure and cannot take the entire training at once. They might want to do a part in year 1 and the rest in the next year. In the light of the European mobility strategy, they could also do the first part from one country, and the rest from work place in another country. Thus, the skills sets are structured into smaller skill elements where each skill element has so called performance criteria agreed by the JRC. Each certificate lists elements and a full certificate is achieved if all elements are passed.

- **European Mobility Strategy:** If, for instance, in the economic situation would force Spanish workers to move to Germany for employment, later maybe move on to another country, and finally back to Spain, all collected certifications are valid and accepted across all countries. This led to the concept of a so called lifelong learning accounts for people. An individual person can register at the ECQA system for a lifelong learning account (like an international bank account but for education). Using that account, he/she can do self-assessments, achieve skills profiles, and receive training. The account sustains and is a central service countries worldwide.

- **Europe/World-Wide Standardized Approach:** To be able to roll out this strategy in all countries the design of standard guidelines is important. The ECQA has established a set of ISO 17024 (ISO, 2012) compliant standard quality guidelines. These were also translated into all major European languages. ECQA has guidelines for:
  - Certification of new job roles.
  - Certification of training bodies.
  - Certification of trainers.
  - Certification of people.

Training Platform for Course Delivery

As an ECQA certified job role, AQUA can use ECQA online training and certification platforms. These web platforms allow people to attend online skills portals, receive training, do exams, and receive a certification directly from the work place (Messnarz, 2006; Messnarz, Reiner, & Ekert, 2012). With their personal account, attendees can register for any of the offered ECQA job roles. After registering for a job role, they can browse the skills card, do a self-assessment, and access the training portal. The learning process (see Figure 5) incorporates the following steps:

1. **Self-Study:** Course attendees have access to skills and learning portals where multimedia lectures, student's notes, slides, and supplementary materials are available. Attendees can study according to their individual schedule and very own pace. Further, they have the possibility to explore the AQUA module matrix in any direction.

Figure 5. The ECQA learning process, employed in AQUA as well
Source: Michael Reiner, 2014.

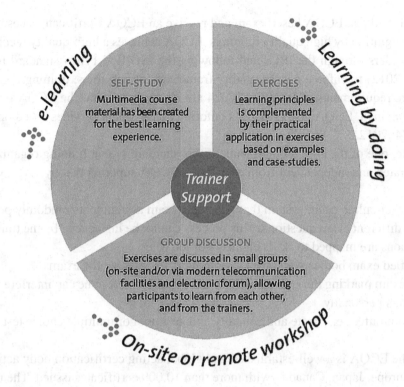

2.   **Exercises:** Attendees meet trainers online who assign them a "learning by doing" exercise. They elaborate on this exercise offline and upload their results to a group discussion forum that is part of the learning platform.

3.   **Group Discussion and Review:** The results are reviewed by the trainers. Upon feedback from trainers and peer, trainees improve and refine their exercise work products. A common discussion session of the entire training group (e.g. in a videoconference) is very helpful to produce intensive learning experience, and often lead to surprising insights that emerge during discussion. Usually, these exercises base on examples of the attendees' own organization so that results of the course can be directly implemented and useful for the participating organization.

Experience shows that this type of training is highly successful because:

- Attendees can use their own examples and elaborate them in the course.
- Attendees are part of an interactive learning environment where the whole team reviews each other's work and the reviewed results have a direct practical value.
- Online course multimedia lectures can be attended asynchronously (when the attendees have time) and only the group meetings need to be coordinated.
- The uploaded results can be used as learning evidences for the certificates to be issued.

Certification and Recognition

Attendees of courses do an ECQA based exam and receive an ECQA Certificate. These achieve a high valued market recognition by high quality trainings. ECQA achieves a high-quality record by involving necessary stakeholders through the JRCs and following the ISO/IEC 17024 standard for certification of persons (ISO, 2012) to enforce a strict quality framework on job roles, training organizations, and certification. Core requirements of ISO/IEC 17024 are incorporated into the ECQA guidelines which are regularly maintained. ECQA also provides conformity assessment services based on the principles of ISO/IEC 17024: 2012.

As an example, one of the core requirements of this standard is that training organizations and examiners are separated and independent from each other. ECQA supports that by:

1.   Establishing an online exam system that generates exam assignments randomly per person. Each person gets different exam questions. This process cannot be influenced by the training body. The exam questions are mapped to skills elements of job roles.
2.   Using certified exam bodies who provide examiners to organize the exams.
3.   Automatic exam marking through the ECQA test system so that none can interfere with the exams and the results personally.
4.   Job Role Committees elaborate and annually update a pool of multiple choice test questions.

Meanwhile, the ECQA is a well-established and global acting certification body actively providing certification in Europe, Japan, Canada - with more than 10.000 certificates issued. The ultimate goal is to provide standardized quality services world-wide and stay a reliable brand. The vision of ECQA is that each person might have an educational skills profile in form of an online skills profile which a person can maintain in a private lifelong learning account. A skills profile is a representation of the coverage of competencies of a person in different skills elements.

Extensibility and Evolution

Keeping Up-to-Date: Integrating New Subjects

The AQUA course architecture is extensible by its *Module Matrix* design. As new challenges unfold, new concept "lines" and new expert pillars can be cleanly added to the AQUA course. At the time of writing, cybersecurity is a more than hot topic throughout the Automotive industry (Cercone & Ernst, 2012). New standards like SAE J3061 (SAE Vehicle Electrical System Security Committee, 2016) arrive, new integrated best practice approaches emerge (Messnarz, Kreiner, & Riel2016), all pushing a strong need for training that topic in an integrated design approach.

Improving Industry: University Permeability

The Automotive Quality Universities (AQU) project a is an ERASMUS+ follow-up project to the AQUA project (Jakub Stolfa, 2016). As a strategic partnership for higher education, it launches AQUA education at several European universities, with agreed ECTS points (European Credit Transfer System). Its motivation is to close an observed knowledge gap between universities typically teaching in-depth courses on well-established specialized subjects, and the industry's need for integrated hands-on skills in highly complex and leading edge product and process development environments (Figure 6).

The project partner universities implement AQUA in different ways, however always with agreed ECTS credits that have universal European recognition (see Table 2). In this way, both integration into course offerings can be managed, and the requirements of the European Qualification Framework (EQF) can be met. Further, a mapping between ECTS and ECVET is achieved that de facto also includes ECQA certificates – a certification with market recognition - in the circle of mutual recognition of universities.

Figure 6. Motivation of the AQU project: knowledge gap between university graduates and industry needs regarding Integrated engineering skills as taught in AQUA
Source: Jakub Stolfa, 2016

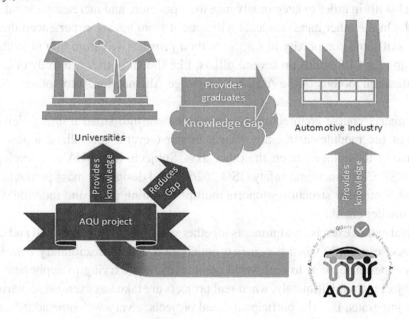

Table 2. Individual ways of implementing AQUA education in participating universities

University	EQF Level 6 Bachelor	EQF Level 7 Master	EQF Level 8 Doctorate
Technical University of Ostrava, CZ	Intro parts in quality course	2 advanced courses, project	
Graz University of Technology, AT		Regular 1 week block course, project	
	VET: Life Long Learning university course, Project and seminal work		
UAS Joanneum, Graz, AT	Parts in quality basics courses	Advanced course, project	n/a
University of Maribor EE + CS, SLO	Concepts incorporated into existing course	Distribute into 2 advanced courses, project & lab	
Grenoble INP Grenoble, FR		Thematic distribution into 4 courses, project	
HSD Hochschule Düsseldorf, DE (UAS)		Regular block course, project	

CONCLUSION

Effective training of skills for CPS engineering poses a number of challenges. By their nature, engineering a CPS is a multidisciplinary endeavor. In addition, also driven by the criticality of many CPS, it is de facto mandatory to be compliant to complex engineering, process, and quality standards. All this must be accomplished in a competitive business environment with tremendously accelerating product development cycles. Both engineers as individuals and companies as an engineering organization are facing an overwhelming complexity in this respect. Highly experienced engineers with interdisciplinary understanding and integrative skills are strongly needed, but rare.

Effective training approaches have to step in here to ease the situation by both re-qualifying industry people, and qualifying university students. Re-qualifying engineers helps them to stay up to date with their technological skills in order to keep or advance their position, and increase their value on the labor market in general. On the other hand, students will benefit from having experienced the challenges of multidisciplinary skills and complexity in respect to their prospective future role in industry.

Effective training for CPS builds on several pillars, like shown in the case study of this chapter, the training and certification toolbox of the AQUA Knowledge Alliance for Automotive:

- A modular matrix course architecture structures content into small training elements. The two dimensions of the module matrix are subject matter (several specialized topics) and common concepts linking those together on the other axis. Subjects in AQUA are development quality (Automotive SPICE), functional safety (ISO 26262), and design for mass production quality (Six Sigma). Such a modular structure supports multiple learning paths and individual scheduling of learning in smaller chunks.

- Hands-on, real-world exercise assignments together with peer discussion yield and effective learning experience, especially when it comes to integration of interdisciplinary concepts and skills. Participants experience close to real-world complexity while trying to apply new skills in more than one subject matter. Ultimately, when real projects are taken as exercise scenario, the elaborations can be integrated into the participants' real projects, a very welcome added value.

- Certification with high recognition value is a key feature for CPS training in industry context, as companies have to be able to prove their employees' competences, and course participants want to have personal formal evidence of successful training. AQUA is a certified job role of the ECQA (European Certification and Qualification Association) and thus follows the ECQA quality rules that conform to ISO/IEC 17024. The course has been developed involving relevant stakeholders such as major companies, Automotive clusters, and experts in the field. A growing number of universities incorporates AQUA courses in their curriculum in the AQU project. In this way, AQUA/AQU also builds a bridge of mutual recognition between the worlds of university education (ECTS) and vocational training (ECVET).

ACKNOWLEDGMENT

The "AQU" project is financially supported by the European Commission in the Erasmus+ Programme under the project number 2015-1-CZ01-KA203-013986. This publication and the project's publications reflect the views only of the authors, and the Commission cannot be held responsible for any use which may be made of the information contained therein.

Erasmus+

REFERENCES

Automotive Industry Action Group (AIAG). (2016).

Avizienis, A., Laprie, J.-C., & Randell, B. (2004). Dependability and its Threats - A Taxonomy. In *Proceedings of the IFIP Congress Topical Sessions*, 91-120.

Avizienis, A., Laprie, J.-C., Randell, B., & Landwehr, C. (2004). Basic Concepts and Taxonomy of Dependable and Secure Computing. *IEEE Transactions on Dependable and Secure Computing, 1*(1), 11–33. doi:10.1109/TDSC.2004.2

Berenbach, B., & Konrad, S. (2008). The Reinforcement Pedagogical Pattern for Industrial Training. In *REET '08 Proceedings of the 2008 Requirements Engineering Education and Training*. IEEE. doi:10.1109/REET.2008.7

Bergin, J., Eckstein, J., Völter, M., Sipos, M., Wallingford, E., & Marquardt, K. (Eds.). (2012). Pedagogical Patterns: Advice for Educators. Joseph Bergin Software Tools.

Cercone, M., & Ernst, T. (2012). *An EU Cybercrime Center to fight online criminals and protect e-consumers.*

Despotou, G., & Kelly, T. (2004). Extending the safety case concept to address dependability. In *Proceedings of the 22nd International System Safety Conference*.

EUROCONTROL - European Organisation for the safety of air navigation. (2006). *Safety Case Development Manual Edition 2.2*. DAP/SSH/091.

Fricke, A., & Völter, M. (2000). SEMINARS: A Pedagogical Pattern Language about teaching seminars effectively. In Proceedings of the EuroPLoP 2000.

Gallina, B., Kashiyarandi, S., Martin, H., & Bramberger, R. (2014). Modeling a Safety- and Automotive-oriented Process Line to Enable Reuse and Flexible Process Derivation. In *Proceedings of the 8th IEEE International Workshop on Quality-Oriented Reuse of Software (QUORS)*.

Goal Structuring Notation Working Group. (2011). *GSN Community Standard version 1*. Retrieved from http://www.goalstructuringnotation.info/documents/GSN_Standard.pdf

Hawkings, R., Habli, I., Kelly, T., & Mc Dermid, J. (2013). *Assurance cases and prescriptive software safety certification: a comparative study.*

Hoban, C.F., & Zisman, S.B. (1937). Visualizing the Curriculum.

Soqrates Initiative. (2015). *SOQRATES Initiative.* Retrieved 31. March 2016 from http://www.soqrates.de

International Electrotechnical Commission. (2011). *ISO/IEC 15026-2: Systems and Software Engineering – Systems and Software Assurance – Part 2: Assurance case.*

International Electrotechnical Commission. (2015). *IEC EN 62741 – Guide to the Demonstration of Dependability Requirements –.*

ISO. (2009). *IEC 61508 Functional safety of electrical/ electronic / programmable electronic safety-related systems.*

ISO. (2011). *ISO 13053 Quantitative methods in process improvement – Six Sigma – Part 1–2.*

ISO. (2011). ISO 26262 Road vehicles Functional Safety Part 1-10. ISO - International Organization for Standardization.

ISO. (2012). *ISO/IEC 17024:2012 Conformity assessment - General requirements for bodies operating certification of persons.* ISO.

ISO/IEC. (2015). *ISO/IEC 33000 series.*

Jakub Stolfa, S. S. (2016). Automotive Quality Universities - AQUA Alliance Extension to Higher Education. In *EuroSPI 2016 Proceedings: 23rd European Conference on Systems, Software and Services Process Improvement* (pp. 176-187). Springer.

Kelly, T., Bate, I., Mc Dermid, J., & Burns, A. (1997). Building a preliminary safety case: an example from aerospace. In *Proceedings of the Australian Workshop of Industrial Experience with Safety Critical Systems*, Sydney, Australia.

Köppe, C. (2013). Towards a Pattern Language for Lecture Design: An inventory and categorization of existing lecture-relevant patterns. In Proceedings of the EuroPLoP 2013. ACM.

Köppe, C., & Rodin, R. (2013). Guided Exploration: an Inductive Minimalist Approach for Teaching Tool-related Concepts and Techniques. In *CSERC 13: Proceedings of the 3rd Computer Science Education Research Conference on Computer Science Education Research.* ACM.

Kreiner, C. (2014). Module matrix: a pattern for interdisciplinary industry training design. In *Euro-PLoP 14: Proceedings of the 19th European Conference on Pattern Languages of Programs.* ACM. doi:10.1145/2721956.2721983

Kreiner, C., Messnarz, R., Riel, A., Ekert, D., Michael Langgner, D. T., & Reiner, M. (2013). Automotive Knowledge Alliance AQUA – Integrating Automotive SPICE, Six Sigma, and Functional Safety. In *EuroSPI 2013: 20th European Conference Systems, Software and Services Process Improvement, Dundalk, Ireland.* Springer. doi:10.1007/978-3-642-39179-8_30

Kreiner, C. (2015). Trident architectural views: a pattern for dependable systems design. *EuroPLoP '15 Proceedings of the 20th European Conference on Pattern Languages of Programs.* ACM.

Macher, G., Armengaud, E., Brenner, E., & Kreiner, C. (2016). A Review of Threat Analysis and Risk Assessment Methods in the Automotive Context. In *Proceedings of the International Conference on Computer Safety, Reliability, and Security (SafeComp 2016).* doi:10.1007/978-3-319-45477-1_11

Macher, G., Hoeller, A., Sporer, H., Armengaud, E., & Kreiner, C. (2015). A Comprehensive Safety, Security, and Serviceability Assessment Method. In *Proceedings of the 34th International Conference on Computer Safety, Reliability, and Security - SAFECOMP '15,* Delft, The Netherlands. doi:10.1007/978-3-319-24255-2_30

Macher, G., Hoeller, A., Sporer, H., Armengaud, E., & Kreiner, C. (2015). Service Deterioration Analysis (SDA): An Early Development Phase Reliability Analysis Method. In *Review at 45th Annual International Conference on Dependable Systems andNetworks (DSN) - RADIANCE Workshop.*

Macher, G., Sporer, H., Berlach, R., Armengaud, E., & Kreiner, C. (2015). SAHARA: A security-aware hazard and risk analysis method. In Design, Automation Test in Europe Conference Exhibition (DATE 2015) (pp. 621-624).

Macher, G., Sporer, H., Brenner, E., & Kreiner, C. (2016). Supporting Cyber-security based on Hardware-Software Interface Definition. In *Proceedings of the 23nd European Conference on Systems, Software and Services Process Improvement - EuroSPI '16,* Graz, Austria. doi:10.1007/978-3-319-44817-6_12

Martin, H., Krammer, M., Bramberger, R., & Armengaud, E. (2016). *Process-and Product-based Lines of Argument for Automotive Safety Cases.*

Messnarz, R. (2006). From process improvement to learning organisations. *SPIP Journal, 11*(3).

Messnarz, R., & Ekert, D. (2007). Assessment-based learning systems - learning from best projects. SPIP (Software Process: Improvement and Practice), 12(6).

Messnarz, R., Ekert, D., Reiner, M., & O'Suilleabhain, G. (2006). Human resources based improvement strategies - the learning factor. (Wiley, Ed.) SPIP (Software Process Improvement in Practice), 13(3).

Messnarz, R., Kreiner, C., Bachmann, O., Riel, A., Dussa-Zieger, K., Nevalainen, R., & Tichkiewitch, S. (2013, June 25-27). Implementing Functional Safety Standards - Experiences from the Trials about Required Knowledge and Competencies (SafEUr). In *EuroSPI 2013: 20th European Conference Systems, Software and Services Process Improvement,* Dundalk, Ireland (pp. 323-332). Springer. doi:10.1007/978-3-642-39179-8_29

Messnarz, R., Kreiner, C., & Riel, A. (2016, Sept.). Integrating Automotive SPICE, Functional Safety, and Cybersecurity Concepts: A Cybersecurity Layer Model. *Software Quality Professional, 18*(4).

Messnarz, R., Reiner, M., & Ekert, D. (2012). Europe wide industry certification using standard procedures based on ISO 17024. In *Technologies Applied to Electronics Teaching (TAEE).* IEEE Computer Society. doi:10.1109/TAEE.2012.6235462

Michael Reiner, G. S. (2014). European Certification and Qualification. In EuroSPI 2014, Industrial Proceedings. Delta.

Microsoft. (2016). *Microsoft Threat Modeling Tool.* Retrieved from https://www.microsoft.com/en-us/download/details.aspx?id=49168

Microsoft Corporation. (2005). The stride threat model. Retrieved from http://msdn.microsoft.com/en-us/library/ee823878/%28v=cs.20/%29.aspx

Miller, C., & Valasek, C. (2013). Adventures in Automotive Networks and Control Units. In *Proceedings of the DEF CON 21 Hacking Conference*, Las Vegas, NV.

Miller, C., & Valasek, C. (2015). *Remote Exploitation of an Unaltered Passenger Vehicle.* Retrieved from http://illmatics.com/Remote%20Car%20Hacking.pdf

Office for Nuclear Regulation. (2013). *The purpose, scope, and content of safety cases, NS-TAST-GD-051 Revision 3.* Retrieved from http://www.onr.org.uk/operational/tech_asst_guides/ns-tast-gd-051.pdf

Riel, A., Bachmann, V. O., Dussa-Zieger, K., Kreiner, C., Messnarz, R., Nevalainen, R., . . . Tichkiewitch, S. (2012, June 25-27). EU Project SafEUr – Competence Requirements for Functional Safety Managers. In *EruoSPI 2012: 19th European Conference Systems, Software and Services Process Improvement*, Vienna, Austria. Springer. doi:10.1007/978-3-642-31199-4_22

Rodin, R. (2012). Meta Patterns for Developing a Minimalist Training Manual. In *Proceedings of the 19th Conference on Pattern Languages of Programs PLoP 2012*. ACM.

SAE Vehicle Electrical System Security Committee. (2016). *SAE J3061- Cybersecurity Guidebook for Cyber-Physical Automotive Systems.* SAE - Society of Automotive Engineers.

Schmittner, C., Gruber, T., Puschner, P., & Schoitsch, E. (2014). Security application of failure mode and effect analysis (FMEA). In *Proceedings of the International Conference on Computer Safety, Reliability, and Seucirty (SafeComp 2014)*. doi:10.1007/978-3-319-10506-2_21

Shostack, A. (2008). *Experiences threat modeling at Microsoft.* Dept. of Computing, Lancaster University UK, Modeling Security Workshop.

Shostack, A. (2014). *Threat modeling: Designing for security*. Wiley & Sons.

Sporer, H., Macher, G., Kreiner, C., & Brenner, E. (2016). Resilient Interface Design for Safety-Critical Embedded Automotive Software. In *Proceedings of the Sixth International Conference on Computer Science and Information Technology, Academy & Industry Research Collaboration Center (AIRCC)*. doi:10.5121/csit.2016.60117

Szijj, A., Buttyan, L., & Szalay, Z. (2015). *Hacking cars in the style of Stuxnet.* Retrieved from http://www.hit.bme.hu/~buttyan/publications/carhacking-Hacktivity-2015.pdf

Thalheimer, W. (2006). *People remember 10%, 20%...Oh Really?* Retrieved from http://www.willatworklearning.com/2006/05/people_remember.html

The Common Criteria Recognition Agreement Members. (2014). *Common Criteria for Information Technology Security Evaluation.*

The SPICE User Group. (2015). *Automotive SPICE Process Assessment / Reference Model V3.0.*

UK Ministry of Defence. (1997). *Defence Standard 00-55, Requirements for safety related software in defence equipment.*

ENDNOTES

[1] http://ecqa.org

[2] http://safeur.eu

[3] http://automotive-knowledge-alliance.eu/index.php/skill-set

Section 2
Safety Concerns in CPS

Chapter 6
Runtime Safety Assurance for Adaptive Cyber–Physical Systems:
ConSerts M and Ontology–Based Runtime Reconfiguration Applied to an Automotive Case Study

Tiago Amorim
Fraunhofer IESE, Germany

Daniel Schneider
Fraunhofer IESE, Germany

Denise Ratasich
Vienna University of Technology, Austria

Mario Driussi
Kompetenzzentrum - Das virtuelle Fahrzeug Forschungsgesellschaft mbH, Austria

Georg Macher
AVL List GmbH, Austria

Radu Grosu
Vienna University of Technology, Austria

Alejandra Ruiz
Tecnalia, Spain

ABSTRACT

Cyber-Physical Systems (CPS) provide their functionality by the interaction of various subsystems. CPS usually operate in uncertain environments and are often safety-critical. The constituent systems are developed by different stakeholders, who – in most cases – cannot fully know the composing parts at development time. Furthermore, a CPS may reconfigure itself during runtime, for instance in order to adapt to current needs or to handle failures. The information needed for safety assurance is only available at composition or reconfiguration time. To tackle this assurance issue, the authors propose a set of contracts to describe components' safety attributes. The contracts are used to verify the safety robustness of the parts and build a safety case at runtime. The approach is applied to a use case in the automotive domain to illustrate the concepts. In particular, the authors demonstrate safety assurance at upgrade and reconfiguration on the example of ontology-based runtime reconfiguration (ORR). ORR substitutes a failed service by exploiting the implicit redundancy of a system.

DOI: 10.4018/978-1-5225-2845-6.ch006

INTRODUCTION

For over 20 years, the trend towards more collaboration has been prevalent for rather closed systems, such as communicating ECUs within a vehicle. But roughly since the 2000s, it has been extended towards open systems such as dynamic compositions of different vehicles, traffic infrastructure, and Internet-based services. New computing paradigms have been coined along the way, most notably pervasive computing, ubiquitous computing, ambient intelligence, and cyber-physical systems. At the heart of these paradigms, different types of computer-based systems, from different application domains (of information systems as well as of embedded systems), and from different manufacturers, collaborate with each other to render higher-level services that a single system would be unable to provide. The systems are integrated - more often dynamically, that is during runtime - into so-called Systems of Systems (SoS), which consist of different collaborating systems (i.e., entities encompassing both hardware and software) that might in turn be built upon multi-core technology and host several applications. Moreover, dynamic application updates, reconfigurations or adaptations are most probably a key feature of many future systems to gain in resilience and flexibility. Technologically, this is driven by ever more closely interconnected distributed embedded systems of systems running under the umbrella terms of cyber-physical systems (CPS) and Internet of Things (IoT).

However, whereas CPS offer tremendous potential for new applications, they also impose significant challenges regarding the assurance of safety. In critical domains, nondeterministic reconfiguration and inadequate safety assurance might result in unacceptable system-inherent risks related to (per typical "safety" definition) physical harm to people, but also to financial loss or damage to the environment.

In most critical domains, assurance activities are guided by functional safety standards. Such standards typically provide means for risk identification and classification and, based thereon, give guidance as to how the risk shall be reduced to an acceptable level and how this shall be documented. To this end, current practice requires that the entire system and all system contexts are well defined and understood at design time so that the necessary analyses can be conducted, measures can be introduced and a sound and comprehensive safety argument can be designed. This prerequisite is clearly not fulfilled by *adaptive* CPS due to the uncertainty of dynamic compositions and reconfigurations, which can hardly be foreseen and analyzed before runtime. Thus, for future CPS contexts, established safety engineering approaches and standardization can therefore not be readily applied.

In typical CPS domains, e.g., automotive or railway, there is often no easy way to bring the system into a safe state. This is because we often demand from a CPS to be fail-operational, i.e., the system should preserve a degraded functionality or limited operation in case of failures rather than just switching to a safe mode (fail-safe). This is especially crucial, e.g., when dealing with autonomous vehicles where the driver is no longer the actor who will take control of the system in case of a failure. The system shall make decisions to ensure the safety of its passengers. A fail-operational functionality makes the system go through different states where a failure is detected, the hazard is avoided, and finally the system provides a solution to maintain its functionality without any interruption. While self-adaptation or runtime reconfiguration is already being applied in several domains (e.g., in the Worldwide Web where clients, servers, and gateways continuously change) and with different objectives (e.g., fault tolerance or resource management), the approach is hardly used in CPSs. The reason is mostly because of the aforementioned complexity issues and the fact, that CPSs typically have to provide a temporally correct behavior and need to be predictable to ensure safe operation.

In safety-critical systems, it is especially relevant to ensure standard compliance. Established certification processes require all assurance artifacts related to the software (i.e., its system's context) to be available for inspection by the authorities in their final completed form before a system enters production. The operational behavior of adaptive systems is not fully determined at the time of certification design, so the system's behavior can change during its operation. This causes problems when facing classical safety engineering practices. As Rushby states in (Rushby, 2009), it is especially challenging to certify those safety-critical functions that operate adaptively, so an adaptation mode will be employed only when conventional controls are unable to improve performance when a malfunction is detected. Certification approaches are deterministic in that developers should anticipate possible configurations whereas current practice lack a systematic approach for verifying and assuring the safety of adaptive SoS dynamically composed at runtime

One potential solution to the lack of adequate safety assurance approaches for open and adaptive CPS is to shift parts of the safety assurance and certification activities to runtime, where the necessary information can be obtained and uncertainty can be truly resolved - what would not be possible at development time already. Modern development practices often postpone the determination of the final system configuration from design time to integration time, load time, or even runtime (Rushby, 2008).

This chapter proposes an approach created to tackle the aforementioned issues. This is the idea behind *Multidirectional Conditional Safety Certificates* (ConSerts M) (Amorim, Ruiz, Dropmann, & Schneider, 2015), a safety certification solution for safety-critical, open, and adaptive multi-core systems. ConSerts M consists of safety contracts created at development time as part of a sound and mostly traditional safety argumentation, but they are designed to be evaluated at runtime by the systems themselves. The approach hence shifts certain checks to lifecycle phases when the actual system constituents are known, thus solving the problem of the immense combinatorial complexity of CPS (i.e. instead of capturing and analyzing the whole variability space at development time, the actual variant can be considered specifically based on the contracts). This ensures safety through the system lifecycle, even if parts are replaced or updated as part of maintenance or upgrades. We further present Ontology-based runtime reconfiguration (ORR) (Höftberger & Obermaisser, 2013), a mechanism enabling structural adaptation for CPS. ORR adds or removes services or changes the interaction between services, e.g., to tolerate failures. ORR is temporally predictable and can be implemented as an anytime-algorithm to meet deadlines.

The combination of ORR and ConSerts M enables safe self-adaptive CPS which assess their own safety operational conditions automatically and autonomously during runtime. In particular, our novel contributions are as follows:

- **To Bring Vertical Interface Assessment to Runtime:** contracts addressing vertical interfaces are used at integration and deployment time. This is very useful for modular certification and reuse, saving lots of effort. The next step is to bring the contract assessment to runtime and have it done automatically by the system themselves.
- **To Enhance the Granularity of the Horizontal Interfaces to the Level of Applications:** The current state-of-the-art addresses runtime contracts to the system level. This is enough when thinking about complete systems, however those systems might be built of parts from different manufacturers and updated/upgraded within their lifetime.

- **To Create a Machine Readable Language Unifying Both Vertical and Horizontal Interfaces:** A language was created to unify both interfaces with meaningful relations, binding together functional and technical safety requirements in contracts that can be evaluated at runtime by the composing parts enabling dynamic safe integration of systems of systems.
- **To Apply ORR With Safety Contracts:** The case study presents how to combine ORR, initially developed for real-time systems, with the proposed safety contracts.

This chapter presents ConSerts M and is organized as follows. The section "Safety-Certification in Adaptive Cyber-Physical Systems" contains background information and definitions. Subsequently, ConSerts M are introduced and explained. The section "Case Study" shows how to integrate ConSerts M into an adaptive automotive CPS and how it can be applied during system upgrade and reconfiguration. To this end, ORR is briefly introduced, which is a reconfiguration mechanism for CPS. Finally, the chapter concludes by summarizing ConSerts M and outlining future work.

SAFETY-CERTIFICATION IN ADAPTIVE CYBER-PHYSICAL SYSTEMS

This section introduces terms and concepts, the system model used and background to self-adaptation.

System Model

A system is "…an entity capable of interacting with its environment and may be sensitive to the progression of time…" (AMADEOS, 2015). To cope with the complexity of a system, system designers usually structure the system into several subsystems, e.g., a motor controller, a sensor, or a communication network. Subsystems, whose internal structure is of no interest, are called components and include hardware and/or software parts. We distinguish between platform and application components. RTCA DO-297 (RTCA/DO-297, 2005) defines a platform as a combination of software and hardware to "…provide computational, communication, and interface capabilities for hosting at least one application. […] Platforms by themselves do not provide any […] functionality…" Platforms are composed not only of hardware parts but also of operating systems, drivers, or more generally, of platform software or middleware. Applications are function-specific software. They require a platform to run and are designed with some usage in mind. The functionality of a system is implemented by application components enabled and supported by the platform. The service-oriented view of the system abstracts away the hierarchical structure of the system to focus on the behavior or functionality of the system. A service is the intended behavior of a system (AMADEOS, 2015). Services may rely on services of other components, i.e., services can be consumed or provided. A summary and an example of the system model used is depicted in Figure 1.

Often, several independent and operable systems (usually provided by different stakeholders) are networked together to achieve a certain goal, known as a *System of Systems* (SoS) (AMADEOS, 2015). "A system consisting of a computer system (cyber-part), a controlled object (a physical system) and possibly of interacting humans forms a cyber-physical system (CPS)…" (AMADEOS, 2015). CPSs often have more or less strict requirements on timeliness, safety and security compared to general-purpose computing. For example, in a *safety-critical* system a failure can cause severe consequences like accidents.

Figure 1. Architecture of a safe self-adaptive system

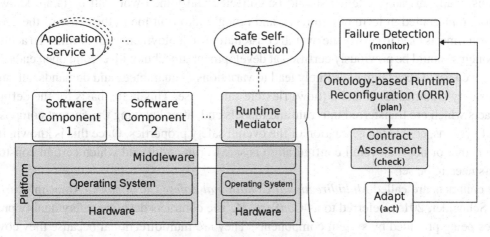

Self-Adaptation

More and more CPSs are desired to be adaptive, in order to react to unforeseen behavior of the system or environment (e.g., failures). In general, adaptation or reconfiguration repeatedly changes the components and their interactions (AMADEOS, 2015). In particular, structural adaptation adds, removes or rearranges components during runtime, while parametric adaptation changes the behavior of a component itself (Cheng, Lemos, Giese, & Inverardi, 2009). When runtime adaptation is used to mitigate unforeseen failures, it is also called self-healing (Ghosh, Sharman, Raghav Rao, & Upadhyaya, 2007). Typically, self-healing is associated with graceful degradation, i.e., the system is reconfigured, however, losing capabilities or accuracy to ensure functionality (cf. fail-operational) (Heckemann, et al., 2011). This chapter includes a case study performing self-healing through structural adaptation with a mechanism called ontology-based runtime reconfiguration (ORR) (Höftberger & Obermaisser, 2013), introduced in the equally named section.

Self-adaptation in general includes several steps (Cheng, Lemos, Giese, & Inverardi, 2009): i) collect and analyze information, ii) plan the adaptation and finally iii) act. However, an adaptation invalidates the safety certification obtained during/after design. Hence, before every adaptation the safety of the planned reconfiguration has to be reevaluated. The component performing such safe self-adaptation is denoted as runtime mediator (cf. Figure 1). This chapter proposes to assess each reconfiguration plan by checking the consistency of safety contracts between components to ensure safety.

MULTIDIRECTIONAL CONDITIONAL SAFETY CERTIFICATES

In order to tackle the safety assurance of (open adaptive) CPS, the authors propose an approach which still complies with the idea that the assurance of the whole composition is necessary and that a diligent analyses and a sound and thorough safety argument needs to be conducted by qualified persons at development time. However, instead of having the evaluation completely done at development time, the final parts of the evaluation are shifted to deployment time and runtime, more precisely at the moment of the integration of the systems. In a nutshell, the safety critical information of the components (i.e.

applications, platforms and systems) should be collected and joined when all parts are known. This information, represented in form of contracts, and brought into runtime in the sense of the concept of models at runtime, is used to certify the overall constellation at deployment and runtime. To achieve this, the components should be previously certified at development time, but with certain open ends that cannot be resolved yet. These open ends likely lead to variations in guarantees and demands, all supported by sound safety argumentation and a (now) flexible safety case. This is the basis for the definition of the contracts which are transferred into runtime models and, after knowing the current composition of systems of systems, enable the evaluation of the overall safety properties. Once this is known, it can be decided whether or not the overall configuration is safe to run and if and which certain constraints or parameters need to be set.

These contracts are called *Multidirectional Conditional Safety Certificates* (Amorim, Ruiz, Dropmann, & Schneider, 2015), referred to as *ConSerts M*. The contracts describe safety quality properties of services being provided by system components. They are multidirectional because they cover both horizontal interfaces (between applications and/or systems) and vertical interfaces (between platform and application). They are conditional because they typically have open ends (demands) that need to be fulfilled by the environment to determine the currently valid guarantees. To fulfill their purpose, the contracts are required to be modular and composable. They can be defined from the granularity of platforms and applications to the size of systems of systems, and can encompass functional and technical safety. Figure 2 depicts contracts related to services and their respective demands and guarantees as well as their relation to other contract's services.

If a component has adaptive properties, it will have more than one configuration or operation mode and a respective contract (cf. Figure 3). Each safety-critical service can be provided with certain guarantees and related to it are its respective demands. This information is described within a contract (cf. Figure 2).

The contracts have open ends that need to be fulfilled by the environment before providing services with the stated assurance level. They are composed of two parts, a Guarantee part, which is always

Figure 2. Notation of guarantees and demands of services

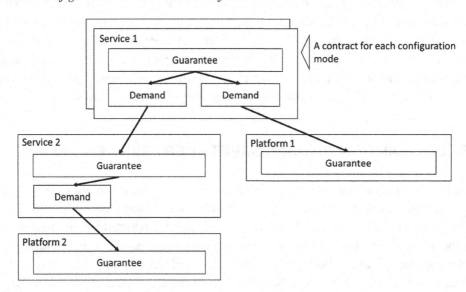

Figure 3. Entity-relationship diagram of contracts

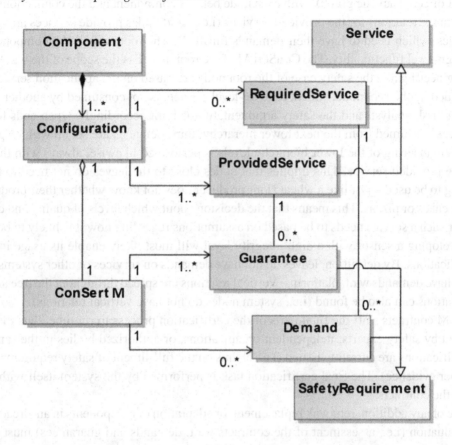

present, and a Demand part, which may only be present in some types of contracts. The Guarantee part describes the quality properties of a service. These properties might be bound to the fulfillment of certain conditions by the environment, which are called demands. A demand is typically bound to services provided by other applications, a platform or other systems that are consumed in order to render more complex functionalities.

The Demands and Guarantees are safety requirements by nature (i.e., a safety requirement is either requested to be fulfilled by somebody else (Demand) or is guaranteed to be fulfilled for somebody else (Guarantee)). They always consist of a statement (i.e., what is guaranteed or demanded) together with a level of confidence w.r.t. to the actual fulfillment of that statement. For this purpose, integrity levels are used (e.g., SIL, ASIL or DAL) as means to express the associated level of confidence. The statements can be specified based on the potential failure modes of a service (further denoted as safety properties), thus stating that a certain failure must not/will not occur with a certain level of confidence. Just like the functional aspects of the services, the failure modes need to be defined for a whole domain to ensure that all participants have the same understanding.

Most safety-critical functionalities from an SoS are composed from services of several other components. A Service Supply Chain (SSC) is the set of all services and their respective components needed to render a functionality. Just like a product supply chain, an SSC is built on the work of several stakeholders, which are the components needed to provide the service. The SSC can be modeled as a tree (i.e., a type of directed acyclic graph), with each node being a component and the connections being the demand-guarantee relations for the provided services (i.e., child nodes provide services and guarantees to parent nodes, which need to have their demands fulfilled). The root node is the component able to realize the high-level functionality. The ConSert M of the root node has the scope of the whole tree, i.e., the safety engineering and the safety case of the root node are based on the application service (i.e., the service provided by the root node, which, as a top-level service, is not consumed by another system) in the hazard and risk analysis and the safety argumentation is built accordingly. Open ends for the root are the services consumed from the next lower hierarchy; thus, demands are set up with respect to that level. Safety engineering of the lower hierarchy levels is performed likewise, always with the scope of the respective provided service. This implies that nodes close to the leaves do not need to know how they are going to be used – just like a wheat flour producer does not know whether their product will be used to make cakes or pizzas. This means that the decision about which levels of quality and confidence to provide for such a service needs to be based on assumptions regarding how it is likely to be used. For example, developing a sensor with a high integrity level will most likely enable its usage in a broader range of applications. By definition, leaves do not have demands on services of other systems, although they can still have demands w.r.t. platforms. Vertical relations are spread throughout the tree at the nodes where applications can also be found (i.e., system nodes do not have vertical relations).

ConSerts M contracts shift the final parts of the certification process to runtime, thus the contracts are still issued by safety experts, independent organizations, or authorized bodies in the same fashion as safety certifications are currently issued (i.e., claims on the fulfillment of safety requirements proved through proper evidence). The final certification task is performed by the system itself with the information from the contracts.

In the case of any addition, removal, replacement, or adaptation of components in an already certified SoS, a re-evaluation (i.e., assessment of the contracts w.r.t. demands and guarantees) must be carried out and the new composition certificate must be updated. If a subsystem adapts, the contracts of its services change. In this case, a re-evaluation shall also be carried out at an individual certificate level. If the new configuration cannot achieve the safety requirements of the top-level service, a reconfiguration of the SoS is required to regain sufficient trust guarantees (e.g., by graceful degradation, consequently causing a loss of application features). Another driver of change might be physical phenomena in the environment to the extent they are factored in and subject to runtime evidences. Such phenomena could be observed wear and tear or even bad weather. On the one hand, factoring in such aspects could lead to a much more optimized "trade-off" between performance and safety. That is, safety is always warranted, but performance is managed so that it is always as high as possible (in contrast to the status quo, where worst-case assumptions are made and performance is sacrificed). On the other hand, such aspects would clearly result in additional engineering complexity.

Multidirectional Interfaces

The multidirectional nature of the ConSerts M contracts is due to an abstraction of how the contracts are described and which kinds of components participate in the interaction. The authors identify two types of interfaces: vertical interfaces, which occur between applications and platforms, and horizontal interfaces, which occur among applications, systems, or both (cf. Figure 4). Platforms never have horizontal relations since they do not provide function specific services, although they might communicate with

Figure 4. Vertical and horizontal interfaces

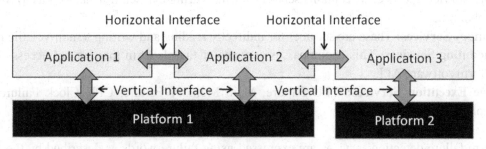

other platforms through the horizontal interfaces running on those platforms (i.e., the platforms realize the horizontal relations of the applications).

Vertical Interfaces

The goal of ConSerts M vertical interfaces is to assess, at deployment time, if the platform and its running applications are able to deliver their functionalities with the expected level of safety confidence. Vertical interfaces describe safety-relevant relations between applications and platform services. Platform services are typically developed for reuse, e.g., libraries, communication protocols, or operating systems. Platform developers cannot know all future systems that a platform service will be a part of, and they do not know in which way the service will be part of the application functionality.

The vertical interface demands describe the safety-related behavior of the platform as required for the safe execution of the application. Consequently, a demand is associated with a specific application. The guarantees, on the other hand, are linked to a specific platform and define the actual safety-related capabilities of the platform. Systems are not a part of vertical relations because the internals (including the platform) are abstracted away.

On the technical level, the vertical interfaces are not clearly separated into software and hardware relations. The hardware is a resource used by the software, therefore the vertical interfaces do not focus on hardware-specific aspects such as manufacturing technology or special-purpose hardware components. Examples of platforms from the software point of view are AUTOSAR (AUTOSAR, 2016) and the ARINC 653 (ARINC, 2005) Integrated Modular Avionics standard.

The vertical interfaces can be separated into four different classes:

Platform failure detection services are services used for the detection or avoidance of platform failures (e.g., a service signal with a value failure larger than a specified threshold must be detected within a specific timeframe). The language covers failures from the following services:

- **Synchronization Services:** This includes services for synchronization, such as barriers or events, services for realizing critical regions, such as spin-locks or binary semaphores, and mechanisms for exchanging data, such as buffers.
- **Communication Services:** This service class covers all mechanisms for data exchange.
- **Input/Output Services:** These are services for reading and writing from/to sensors/actuators (e.g., A/D converters, PWM channels, or digital input/output channels).

- **Time Services:** This class contains services for measuring elapsed time as well as for retrieving a global time.
- **Memory Services:** These are services for indirectly reading and writing to non-volatile memory.
- **Scheduling Services:** This encompasses services of the platform that are not accessed via the platform software API.
- **Basic Execution Services:** CPU Failure, Main Memory Failure, CPU Clock Failure, Power Supply Failure, CPU Failure.

Platform failure detection services are expressed using failure words as described by the HAZOP technique (Fenelon & Hebbron, 1994), e.g., Commission, Omission, Late, Early, Value Coarse, Value Subtle.

- **Health Monitoring Services:** Are services used to trap and encapsulate application and execution failures, e.g., the platform has to detect and arbitrate an execution time overrun.
- **Service Diversity Services:** Are a group of services that aim at reducing the likelihood of common-cause systematic failures in redundant components (i.e., double comparable input signal). Service diversity focuses on the independence of input services, communication links, and output services.
- **Resource Protection Services:** Focus on protection from interferences between applications due to shared resources that potentially violate safety requirements. Interferences can also propagate through applications via commonly used resources. The goal of this service is to avoid these.

Horizontal Interfaces

Horizontal interfaces describe safety-relevant relations among applications or systems that enable emergent functionalities that these elements would not be able to perform on their own, such as Platooning of Autonomous Vehicles (Fernandes & Nunes, 2010) and Tractor Implement Automation (Hoyningen-Huene & Baldinger, 2010). In horizontal relations, there exist the roles of service consumer (which establishes demands to be fulfilled by the consuming services) and service provider (which states guarantees for the provided services). A component can play both roles, being the consumer of horizontal interface services while being the provider of services for others. Platforms are never a part of horizontal relations.

The demands and guarantees are derived from the *Functional Safety Requirements* of the *Safety Analysis*. They describe safety properties of services, the level of scrutiny to which they were developed and tested, and the operational situations in which these characteristics hold.

The guarantees and demands among applications are associated with services required and provided by applications. However, different applications (and thus systems/devices) are typically combined to jointly render higher-level services that could not be rendered by a single system alone. Conceptually, dynamic composition hierarchies are created in this process.

In summary, if the guarantees are fulfilled by the demands, the applications can function in the way they were designed; otherwise, the available system safety level will be below the specified level.

Horizontal interfaces occur only among applications and/or systems. Vertical interfaces might be a component's internal demands of horizontal guarantees. All contracts have at least one horizontal guarantee, except for platform contracts. A functionality being provided to the end user is also a horizontal guarantee.

Contract Types

Based on the components' characteristics, the following types of contracts can be defined:

- **Platform Contracts:** Describe the guarantees provided by the platform to the applications deployed to it. Platform contracts do not have any demands, only guarantees. Platform service guarantees are always related to technical safety properties demanded by the applications. A platform contract encompasses only vertical interfaces.
- **Application Contracts:** Describe services provided by applications. These services are consumed by other applications to build more complex services (e.g., a signal from a radar controller is used to create an adaptive cruise control functionality) or delivered directly to the end user as a functionality (e.g., acceleration of the car by the driver). The application contract describes the safety service properties that are directly linked to one or more configuration modes. Different configuration modes can have different safety properties for a service, or the service might be provided only in some configuration modes. This means a service might require a different contract for each configuration mode of the component to which it belongs. The service's safety properties can depend on the fulfillment of associated demands. These demands are fulfilled by application, platform, or system guarantees. Also, within a specific configuration mode, a service can have more than one contract, each providing different guarantees and requiring different demands, which allows systems to be used in a variety of critical contexts. Application contracts can have horizontal and vertical interfaces.
- **System Contracts:** Describe systems that are composed of several other contracts (e.g., a vehicle contract composed of the applications, platforms, and systems integrated to make up the vehicle itself), or highly coupled systems, where it makes no sense to differentiate between applications and platform (e.g., the gas pedal of a vehicle). System contracts include guarantees and might have demands on other systems or applications, but never on platforms (i.e. a system encompasses both application and platform meaning that the vertical interfaces are already considered within the system). They might also have no demands at all.

Contract Language Description

In the next paragraphs ConSerts M contract language is described using BNF notation. The language is used to specify ConSerts M contracts. It has a well-structured grammar, which, on the one hand, reduces the ambiguity of the demands and guarantees specification and, on the other hand, supports runtime validation. The specification presented in this chapter is designed to be used with ISO 26262 risk levels, but it can be adapted to address any safety standard. The language, based on an extension of XML, ties together vertical and horizontal interfaces and facilitates the automated evaluation process. In the BNF specification, we use the conventions: {def}* to denote 0 or more repetitions of def, and {def}+ to denote 1 or more repetitions of def. Also we assume infinite sets of names. Blocks' names are represented in bold. 'n', 'm' will serve as typical representatives for the Natural numbers, 'd' for double numbers. String values are put within single quotes, e.g., 'avoided'.

```
<ConsertM>
<ComponentName> ComponentName </ComponentName>
(Horizontal_Guarantee | Vertical_Guarantee)*
</ConsertM>
 ConsertM: indicates the start and end of the contract
ComponentName: a text including A-Z, a-z, 0-9. The name cannot start with a
number.
 Horizontal Guarantee
<Horizontal_Guarantee>
    <ConfigurationName> ConfigurationName </ConfigurationName>`
    <IntegrityLevel> IntegrityLevel </IntegrityLevel>`
    (<SafetyProperty> Property+=SafetyProperty
    </SafetyProperty>)*
    (ANDDemandSet | ORDemandSet | DemandSet)*
</Horizontal_Guarantee>
```

- **Horizontal_Guarantee:** Denotes that the specification between these tags refers to an horizontal interface guarantee.
- *ConfigurationName*: A unique name of the service, is specified by text including A-Z, a-z, 0-9. The name cannot start with a number
- *IntegrityLevel*: Could be any of these values: 'A','B','C','D','QM'
- **SafetyProperty:** Indicates that the specification between these tags refers to a properties characteristic associated with the service indicated in the *ConfigurationName*

```
Property
    (<Commission> IntegrityLevel </Commission>)*
    (<Omission> IntegrityLevel </Ommission>)*
(<Early> TimeProperty </Early>)*
    (<Late> TimeProperty </Late>)*
    (<ValueTooLow> IntegrityLevel </ValueTooLow>)*
  (<ValueTooHigh> IntegrityLevel </ValueTooHigh>)*
```

The properties were defined based on HAZOP guidewords (Fenelon & Hebbron, 1994). They describe which types of failures were taken into consideration when the service was designed and the associated integrity level states how critical the failure was cared for. There are six different properties:

- **Commission:** The integrity level provided in case the value is provided even though it has never been requested.
- **Omission:** The integrity level provided in case the value is never provided even though it has been requested.
- **Early:** Between these tags we shall include information about the time. It indicates the maximum time in advance a service can be provided

- **Late:** Between these tags we shall include information about the time. It indicates the maximum delay time a service can be provided
- **ValueTooLow:** The integrity level provided in case the value is lower than expected.
- **ValueTooHigh:** The integrity level provided in case the value is higher than expected

```
ANDDemandSet
     <AND>
             DemandSet
     </AND>
ORDemandSet
     <OR>
             DemandSet
     </OR>
DemandSet
     <DemmandSet>
             (Demand) *
     </DemmandSet>
Demand
             Horizontal_Demand | Vertical_Demand
 Horizontal_Demand
<Horizontal_Demand>
     <ConfigurationName> ConfigurationName </ConfigurationName>
     <IntegrityLevel> IntegrityLevel </IntegrityLevel>'
     (<SafetyProperty> Property+=SafetyProperty
     </SafetyProperty>)*
</Horizontal_Demand>
```

It has the same structure as a horizontal guarantee. See **Horizontal_Guarantee** block for details.

```
TimeProperty
<IntegrityLevel> IntegrityLevel </IntegrityLevel>
<SPSpec> n time_unit </SPSpec>
<Situation> situation </Situation>
time_unit: It could be either 'ms' or 'us'
situation: a text indicating the context environment
Vertical_Guarantee
<Vertical_Guarantee>
(PlatformService | ServiceDiversity | HealthMonitoring | ResourceProtection)
</Vertical_Guarantee>
Vertical_Guarantee: Between the tags, we shall specify the guarantee about the
services provided by the platform.
Vertical_Demand
<Vertical_Demand>
```

```
(PlatformService | ServiceDiversity | HealthMonitoring | ResourceProtection)
</Vertical_Demand>
```

It has the same structure as a vertical guarantee. See **Vertical_Guarantee** block for details.

```
PlatformService
      <Platform_Service>
            <Failure>
(inFMX | outFMX | comFMX | synchFMX | schedFMX | basExFMX | timeFMX | memFMX)
            </Failure>
            <Reaction> ('avoided'|'detected') </Reaction>
            <IntegrityLevel> IntegrityLevel </IntegrityLevel>
             (Latency | Error)*
      </Platform_Service>
<Failure>: a text indicating the type of malfunction anticipated in the plat-
form service
<Reaction>: indicates whether the platform is able to avoid the failure when
it is detected or to just detect the failure and provide a warning
```

Latency:

```
      <Latency>
('less than'|'more than') n time_unit ('+ -' n time_unit)*</Latency>
```

Error:

```
      <Error>
 d ('ms')|('us')|('%')
</Error>
```

HealthMonitoring:

```
      <HealthMonitoring> appFailure|failureReaction
            <IntegrityLevel> IntegrityLevel </IntegrityLevel>
      </HealthMonitoring>

appFailure
      <Failure>
            <Application> 'appFMX' </Application>
            <ApplicationResourceName> 'resourcename' </ApplicationResourceName>
 'lr=(Latency|Error)*'
   </Failure>
failureReaction
```

```
      <Reaction>
<Failure>
(inFMX | outFMX | comFMX | synchFMX | schedFMX | basExFMX | timeFMX | memFMX)
</Failure>
             <Action> appFRX </Action>
             <Value> d time_unit (AdditionalConditionOrInfo)* </Value>
      </Reaction>
```

AdditionalConditionOrInfo: a text including A-Z, a-z, 0-9, which cannot start with a number, which provides more information about the time unit.

ServiceDiversity:

```
      <ServiceDiversity>
         <Channel> 'analog'|'digital' </Channel>
         <Operation> 'read'|'write'|'execute' ArrayOfChannelSignalName </Operation>
         <CommonCauseType>
(inFMX| outFMX | comFMX | synchFMX | schedFMX | basExFMX | timeFMX | memFMX)
</CommonCauseType>
            <IntegrityLevel> IntegrityLevel </IntegrityLevel>
      </ServiceDiversity>
```

ArrayOfChannelSignalName: a text including A-Z, a-z, 0-9, which cannot start with a number which indicates the name of channel for the signal

ResourceProtection:

```
<ResourceProtection>
      <PlatformResource> ('cpu'|'memory'|'platform-service') </PlatformResource>
      <InterferenceType>
'interferences'|'temporal interferences'|'spatial interferences'|'behavioral
interferences'
</InterferenceType>
      <SharingType>
('private/ not shared'|'the resource is spatial partitioned'|'shared, but not
at the same time'|'shared dynamically')
</SharingType>
      <IntegrityLevel> IntegrityLevel </IntegrityLevel>
</ResourceProtection>
```

- *comFMX:* Indicates possible malfunction of the communication. It could be any of the following texts: 'Message Corruption', 'Message Insertion', 'Message Loss', 'Incorrect Message Sequence', 'Late Transmission', 'Early Transmission';

- **synchFMX:** Indicates possible malfunction of the synchronization. It could be any of the following texts: 'Mutex Access Commission' | 'Mutex Access Omission' | 'Mutex Release Commission' | 'Mutex Release Omission' | 'Mutex Timeout Failure' | 'Event Signal Commission' | 'Event Signal Omission' | 'Event Timeout Failure';
- **schedFMX:** Indicates possible malfunction of the scheduling It could be any of the following texts: 'Scheduling Jitter Failure', 'Scheduling Deadline Failure', 'Interrupt Handler Latency Failure'
- **inFMX:** Indicates possible malfunction of the input signals. It could be able of the following texts: 'Digital Input Omission', 'Digital Input Late Read', 'Digital Input Early Read', 'Digital Input Late Return', 'Digital Input Early Return', 'Digital Input False Positive', 'Digital Input False Negative', 'Analog Input Omission', 'Analog Input Commission', 'Analog Input Late Sampling', 'Analog Input Early Sampling', 'Analog Input Sampling Jitter', 'Analog Input Late Return', 'Analog Input Early Return', 'Analog Input Value Failure'
- **basExFMX:** Indicates possible malfunction of the basic execution. It could be any of the following texts: 'CPU Failure', 'Main Memory Failure', 'CPU Clock Failure', 'Power Supply Failure'
- **outFMX:** Indicates possible malfunction of the output signals. It could be any of the following texts: 'Digital Output Late', 'Digital Output Early', 'Digital Output False Positive', 'Digital Output False Negative', 'Analog Output Late', 'Analog Output Early', 'Analog Output Value Failure';
- **timeFMX:** Indicates possible malfunction in the timing service of the platform. It could be any of the following texts: 'Global Time Failure', 'Relative Time Failure', 'Wait Time Failure';
- **memFMX:** Indicates possible malfunction of the memory. It could be any of the following texts: 'Memory Late Read via', 'Memory Read Access Denial via', 'Memory Read Data Failure via', 'Memory Late Write via', 'Memory Write Access Denial via', 'Memory Write Data Failure via'
- **appFMX:** Indicates possible malfunction of an application. It could be any of the following texts:
- 'Arrival Rate Failure' | 'Inter Arrival Time Failure' | 'Execution Time Deviation' | 'Logical Sequence Failure' | 'Application Runtime Failure'
- **appFRX:** Indicates possible action of an application when a failure is detected. It could be any of the following texts: 'Restart' | 'Shut Down' | 'Send of the Default Signal' | 'Send of the Default Message' | 'Indication of an Error' | 'Handler Execution'

Runtime Mediator

The application responsible for managing contracts, applications, and systems in a SSC is called Runtime Mediator (RM). In a nutshell, this application is responsible for adapting a system and ensuring the safety of the SSC. RM can accumulate many functionalities such as:

Monitoring or auditing communication in a SSC. The RM should collect and analyze information about components, e.g., via exchanged messages. The monitor has to reason about when to reconfigure the system, e.g., when a failure is detected. The RM may further store the information being shared among the systems in an airplane black-box fashion. This is required in case an accident happens and investigations need to be carried out. This functionality is limited to some types of systems and to some granularity of composition. This functionality should not compromise the performance of the systems, thus affecting safety properties.

Graceful degradation or self-healing of SSC allows avoiding hazards in case of failure of some of the SSC components. A failure in a component can trigger some graceful degradation behavior (e.g., ontology-based runtime reconfiguration). Self-adaptation in general, e.g., to optimize the efficiency of the system, can be part of a runtime mediator. However, in an SoS context, such behavior might unfold in different types of hazards. Managing how the components undergo graceful degradation and the possible impacts on other components can minimize the creation of new hazards. The reconfiguration mechanism or an adapted component has to update the system's or component's safety contracts, respectively. For instance, the contract of a generated component has to be created (e.g., from a template) and added to the collection of system contracts. Finally, the new set of contracts can be reevaluated.

Contract assessment verifies whether the SSC composition is qualified to deliver a functionality with the desired assurance level. This is performed when the components are put together and before they cooperate with each other. A contract assessment also needs to be performed whenever the SSC under control of the RM changes. A change to the SSC is characterized by the addition, removal, or update of any of its constituents, or by an adaptation. On the vertical level, the contracts are assessed the latest at deployment time, that is, before deploying an application to a platform, their contracts need to be assessed so the application will provide its functions safely. In the case of horizontal interfaces, the contract evaluation can be realized at runtime, when the systems are providing services to each other.

The ConSerts M contracts are located in the applications and systems themselves, or can be fetched from contract databases that are accessible through networks. When downloading an update of an application, the Runtime Mediator should also fetch its contract and verify with the other contracts if the state after the update will uphold the required level of safety confidence.

Reconfiguration has to be finally performed by the RM, e.g., components have to be created and attached to the system (structural adaptation like ORR) or parameters of components have to be changed.

We take graceful degradation with ORR as an example to show how ConSerts M can avoid hazards possibly emerging due to adaptation. The next section introduces ORR for the case study.

ONTOLOGY-BASED RUNTIME RECONFIGURATION

Ontology-based runtime reconfiguration (ORR) is a fault-tolerance mechanism for service-oriented cyber-physical systems (CPS). ORR substitutes a failed service by exploiting the implicit redundancy of a system.

CPSs are often composed of several subsystems, each providing specific services. A service usually consumes other services to provide its own functionality. Due to the interdependency among services, a failed service may break the overall system's functionality. A traditional method for tolerating failed services is to provide explicit redundancy to the system, i.e., critical components are replicated. In case a component fails – which is determined by voting on the results of the replicated services – the substitute can take over the failed component's functionality. However, explicit redundancy increases power consumption and the costs of the system.

A CPS usually performs a feedback loop of observation and control. In particular, it observes and estimates the state of its environment and sets control signals to bring the environment into a desired state. For example, a thermostat measures the temperature and controls the valve of the radiators to reach a desired room temperature. So, a CPS typically contains various services exchanging measurable or quantifiable states about the system or measurements, which are referred to as properties. Properties may be static (e.g., wheel radius) or dynamic (e.g., wheel speed). For example, a service estimating the state-of-charge (SoC) of a battery relies on the samples provided by an amperemeter measuring the current consumption (I) of an electric vehicle. The relations of such properties (e.g., SoC, I) of a CPS can be modeled in a knowledge base, e.g., an ontology that describes entities and their relations to each other. ORR uses such an ontology to derive a property that was provided by a now failed service from other related properties (cf. Figure 5: property *a* can be derived by service *A'* from related properties *b* and *c* provided by services *B* and *C* respectively).

A larger ontology usually leads to extra implicit redundancy and, as a further consequence, more failures can be tolerated. Especially when CPSs are assembled from several subsystems of different manufacturers, the advantage of ORR is apparent: Redundancy that cannot be considered during the design time of a constituent system becomes available at runtime and can be used to tolerate failures. Furthermore, ORR can automatically consider added or removed services in adaptive CPSs.

The ontology can also be used to generate state estimators (e.g., Kalman filters) to provide properties with better accuracy by incorporating related properties. However, here we use the ontology to reconfigure the system in the case of failures; in particular, we add substitution nodes and do not change the behavior of existing components.

Ontology

An ontology is a description of properties and their relations to each other. We depict each property as an ellipse and each relation – or so-called transfer function – by rectangles (see Figure 6). In most cases, a transfer function can be rearranged to relate several input properties to one output property. For example, the state-of-charge (SoC) of a battery (the output property in this case) can be estimated given the battery current or voltage (the input properties in this case) and its relations (the transfer functions).

Besides measured and derived properties, constants (such as the efficiency factor of a motor or a wheel radius) can also be part of the ontology as (constant) properties.

Figure 5. Explicit (left) and implicit redundancy (right)

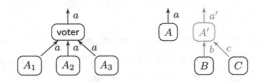

Figure 6. Example ontology

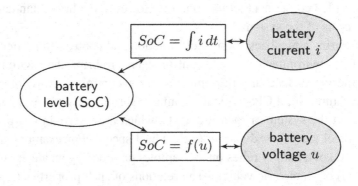

We here omit further features of our knowledge base (e.g., structuring of properties), which are not relevant to the case study of ConSerts M. The interested reader is referred to (Höftberger & Obermaisser, 2013).

Ontology to Service Mapping

Typically, the ontology of a system is static, i.e., properties and relations do not change during runtime (although the ontology may be extended when new subsystems are connected). However, in adaptive systems, services may be added, changed, or removed, i.e., the provision of properties can indeed change. Shaded ellipses present properties that are provided by some service, e.g., the battery current and voltage is measured by a sensor (Figure 6). Hence, besides the ontology, a property-to-service map has to be kept up to date by the reconfiguration component. It can be compared to the service registry and discovery of an SoA, where all provided services including their descriptions are maintained.

There may be different services providing the same property, e.g., via redundant sensors, or properties that may be fused to provide (probably derived) properties with better accuracy. For example, the SoC of a battery may be estimated by integrating the battery current or by mapping the battery voltage to the SoC via a function assessed a priori. These methods can be combined to achieve a better SoC estimate in terms of accuracy and precision. However, in this chapter our interests lie in determining whether a property is provided or not.

Runtime Reconfiguration

Assuming that each service is needed, i.e., consumed by other services, a failed service has to be substituted to maintain the system's functionality (otherwise we could just remove the failed service). A monitor shall therefore notify the reconfiguration component in case a service is malfunctioning, e.g., the output property is wrong or missing. The reconfiguration component will traverse the ontology in a breadth-first search starting from the now failed property (provided by the failed service). Basically, we recursively substitute missing properties.

1. The transfer functions connected to the failed or missing property are investigated. Let's consider, without loss of generality, that the output property of the associated transfer function is the missing property. Regarding the input properties to the transfer function, we can distinguish two cases:

    a. All input properties are provided, i.e., the transfer function can be used to estimate the missing property using the provided input properties. For the sake of simplicity, let the search stop here. However, the ontology may be searched for the best substitute in terms of, e.g., accuracy or number of inputs.
    b. Not all input properties are provided, i.e., the ontology has to be searched further. To this end, the missing input property is treated like the failed property, i.e., back to step 1.

The result of the search is a tree of transfer functions and provided properties that are used to generate a substitute component. An example can be found in the following case study.

CASE STUDY

Development of embedded automotive systems faces many challenges. The complexity and connectivity of embedded systems in these domains have grown significantly in the recent years. This trend is also strongly supported by the ongoing introduction of advanced driving assistance systems and automated driving functionalities leading to cars as software-intensive systems (SIS). The higher amount of software in combination with short development cycles raise new engineering challenges. In particular, the need for more agile engineering processes that better leverage legacy assets, and more systematic and automated variability management processes. Current dependability development methods and processes hardly cope with modern automotive ad-hoc system of systems (SoS) and their dependability validation during operation. This dynamic compositions and reconfigurations (due to web-based functionalities and update-over-the-air functions) of these systems, hamper the use of established engineering approaches, which cannot be applied without further ado.

As a result, a shift of parts of the safety certification activities to runtime, where the complete information can be obtained and uncertainty can be truly resolved, is also required. Contract-based design is a promising paradigm for filling or narrowing this gap. Feasible implementation of contract evaluation at runtime must be able to be implemented in resource-limited environments and to deal with limited processing power.

This setup and the following sections, will demonstrate ConSerts M and ORR in the automotive domain. ConSerts M will demonstrate the functionality of Contract Assessment, and ORR will demonstrate graceful degradation of SSC during runtime. The ConSerts M approach will be demonstrated via runtime reconfiguration of the system and of some of its parts. In particular, this will be depicted in a graceful degradation scenario of the certified safety-critical system by replacing software functions in a dynamic reconfiguration performed by ORR. ORR aims to enhance the resilience of the system against failures, but nevertheless safety-related constraints are ensured by ConSerts M. Both features will be required for future (autonomous driving) vehicles.

Initial System

To demonstrate ConSerts M we define illustrative contracts for the drivetrain components of an electric vehicle. The granularity here perceived is of applications (some) running on the same platform (here a multi-core device) and sharing resources (e.g., access to the communication network). Other applications may provide services from a closed constituent system. The drive-by-wire system has three main building blocks: i) The acceleration pedal is controlled by the driver to increase the speed of the vehicle. ii) The controller "E-Gas" reads the pedal position and transforms it to a torque set point for the motor controller. It further uses the actual e-motor speed to optimize the torque set point. iii) The motor control is the actuator node of the functionality, controlling the torque of the electric engine. The acceleration pedal is assumed to be a black-box, i.e., a closed constituent system of our SoS, that provides the desired acceleration. The same goes for the e-motor speed sensor. Figure 7 depicts the structure of the initial system, including exemplary demands and guarantees. For example, E-Gas demands health monitoring from the platform and the acceleration information from the pedal. Furthermore, E-Gas guarantees the requested torque.

Figure 7. Initial system of our use case

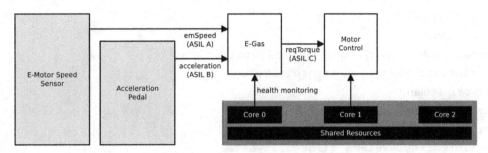

The acceleration pedal has a system contract type (i.e., the contract has no associated demands). The safety information below is based on (Work group EGAS, 2015).

```
<ConSertsM>
<ComponentName> AccelerationPedal </ComponentName>
<Horizontal_Guarantee>
        <ConfigurationName> acceleration </ConfigurationName>
        <IntegrityLevel> B </IntegrityLevel>
</Horizontal_Guarantee>
</ConSertsM>
```

The components E-Gas and Motor Control have horizontal and vertical demands and guarantees. The E-Gas component provides the torque set point – a horizontal guarantee – for the motor control with integrity level C. To determine the torque set point, E-Gas requires acceleration and motor speed, which are horizontal demands. The platform has to provide means to detect failures of input values, to do health monitoring, and to ensure resource protection for the application. These are the vertical demands of E-Gas. For example, the underlying platform of E-Gas shall be able to detect an analog input value failure higher than 3% with an integrity level C. The listing below shows the contracts of the E-Gas component.

```
<ConSertsM>
<ComponentName> EGas </ComponentName>
<Horizontal_Guarantee>
<ConfigurationName> setTorquePoint </ConfigurationName>
<IntegrityLevel> C </IntegrityLevel>
        <SafetyProperty>
                <Commission> D </Commission>
        </SafetyProperty>
<DemandSet>
<Horizontal_Demand>
<ConfigurationName> acceleration </ConfigurationName>
<IntegrityLevel> B </IntegrityLevel>
<SafetyProperty>
                <Late> C </Late>
```

```
                </SafetyProperty>
</Horizontal_Demand>
<Horizontal_Demand>
<ConfigurationName> reqTorque </ConfigurationName>
        <IntegrityLevel> C </IntegrityLevel>
</Horizontal_Demand>
<Horizontal_Demand>
<ConfigurationName> emSpeed </ConfigurationName>
        <IntegrityLevel> A </IntegrityLevel>
</Horizontal_Demand>
<Vertical_Demand>
        <Platform_Service>
        <Failure> Analog Input Value Failure </Failure>
        <Reaction> detected </Reaction>
        <IntegrityLevel> C </IntegrityLevel>
        <Error> 3% </Error>
        </Platform_Service>
</Vertical_Demand>
<Vertical_Demand>
        <HealthMonitoring>
        <Failure>
        <Application> Application Runtime Failure </Application>
        <ApplicationResourceName> EGas </ApplicationResourceName>
        <Latency> more than 10 ms </Latency>
        </Failure>
        <IntegrityLevel> C </IntegrityLevel>
        </HealthMonitoring>
</Vertical_Demand>
<Vertical_Demand>
        <ResourceProtection>
        <PlatformResource> cpu </PlatformResource>
<InterferenceType> spatial interferences </InterferenceType>
        <SharingType> private/ not shared </SharingType>
        <IntegrityLevel> B </IntegrityLevel>
        </ResourceProtection>
</Vertical_Demand>
</Horizontal_Guarantee>
</ConSertsM>
```

The contracts of all those components belonging to the SSC of the functionality setTorquePoint need to be assessed to verify if the desired trust can be achieved. The first step performed by the Runtime Mediator is checking if the vertical demands of the applications can be fulfilled by the platform guarantees. In this example, the demands of the applications E-Gas and Motor Control against the guarantees

Figure 8. Ontology of our application (only the relevant part is depicted)

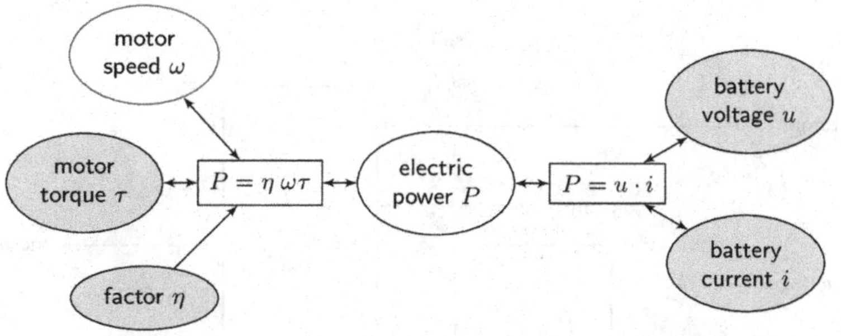

of the multi-core platform are checked. The acceleration pedal has a system type contract, being only relevant for the horizontal interfaces.

The next step is to verify the horizontal interfaces. In the previous step, the Runtime Mediator could identify which horizontal guarantees can be not considered due to not-strong-enough guarantees provided by the platform. In this example, the platform is able to provide enough confidence and the vertical demands linked to horizontal interfaces are fully supported. The horizontal demands and guarantees are compared. E-Gas contract requires the service acceleration to be delivered with ASIL B of assurance against failures. The acceleration pedal contract tells us that it is able to deliver the service acceleration with ASIL B, fulfilling the demand of the E-Gas contract. Also, the demands towards the Motor Control (reqTorque)need to be verified as well as the E-motor Speed Sensor (emSpeed). The contracts guarantee of both components, although not described here due to space constraints, mirrors the demands of the E-Gas contract. The setting is successfully assessed and can cooperate to deliver the setTorquePoint functionality with the desired trust. E-Gas has another version of the contract that requires not-so strong-guarantees as the contract presented above (see next section).

Reconfiguration

In this example, ORR provides fault-tolerance to the motor speed. In case the sensor measuring the motor speed fails, the system is reconfigured. The monitor detects this failure and triggers ORR. The ORR algorithm searches the ontology of the system (see Figure 8) and generates a substitute, estimating motor speed ω from torque and battery voltage and current.

The search starts at the failed property ω and investigates the connected transfer function ($P=\eta$ $\omega\tau$). In order to estimate ω using this transfer function, the input properties motor torque, a constant factor, and the electric power P are needed. Unfortunately, the electric power is not provided directly, hence the search continues with the missing property set to electric power. P can be estimated by the transfer function P=u·i where both input properties (voltage and current) are provided. Hence, all missing properties are substituted and the search stops. Finally, the reconfiguration unit collects the transfer functions and constructs the substitute, as depicted in Figure 9.

Subsequently, ORR requests an evaluation of the new configuration. As stated before, E-Gas has a second contract version which is able to function with lower guarantees. Part of this contract is shown in the next lines.

Figure 9. Substitute in detail

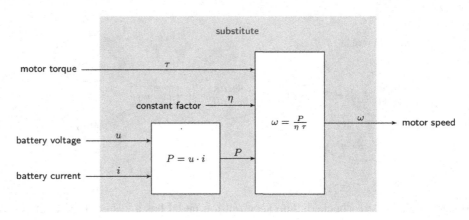

```
<ConSertsM>
<ComponentName> EGas </ComponentName>
<Horizontal_Guarantee>
<ConfigurationName> setTorquePoint </ConfigurationName>
<IntegrityLevel> B </IntegrityLevel>
        <SafetyProperty>
                  <Commission> C </Commission>
        </SafetyProperty>
<DemandSet>
<Horizontal_Demand>
<ConfigurationName> acceleration </ConfigurationName>
<IntegrityLevel> A </IntegrityLevel>
<SafetyProperty>
                  <Late> B </Late>
        </SafetyProperty>
</Horizontal_Demand>
<Horizontal_Demand>
<ConfigurationName> reqTorque </ConfigurationName>
        <IntegrityLevel> B </IntegrityLevel>
</Horizontal_Demand>
<Horizontal_Demand>
<ConfigurationName> emSpeed </ConfigurationName>
        <IntegrityLevel> QM </IntegrityLevel>
</Horizontal_Demand>
```

This contract delivers the functionality setTorquePoint with lower integrity level, compared to the first one (ASIL B). It also requires less strong demands from the services (emSpeed ASIL QM, acceleration ASIL A). The contracts of the new constituent system (the substitute, see contract outline below) are communicated to the ConSerts M evaluator.

```
<ConSertsM>
<ComponentName> Substitute </ComponentName>
<Horizontal_Guarantee>
        <ConfigurationName> emSpeed </ConfigurationName>
        <IntegrityLevel> QM </IntegrityLevel>
        <DemandSet>
                // functional requirements:
                // actual motor torque, battery voltage and current
        </DemandSet>
</Horizontal_Guarantee>
</ConSertsM>
```

When the contracts evaluation is successful, the substitute is connected to the system (see Figure 10). The lines above show the outline of the substitutes contract. The new system can still drive, but with lower integrity level (ASIL B). That, for instance, could impact the maximum speed that the vehicle can reach, but still being able to reach a workshop and fix the problem (i.e., the damaged sensor).

This example can also be applied with other reconfiguration mechanisms performing structural adaptation. It remains to the runtime mediator to create and update the ConSerts M contracts accordingly, e.g., add a new contract, move demands and guarantees as the new component is connected.

The current ORR prototype (Ratasich, Höftberger, Isakovic, Shafique, & Grosu, 2017) is implemented upon the Robot Operating System (ROS, 2017) and a Linux system, which does not provide real-time capabilities. However, ORR may run in real-time environments with additional facilities, e.g., an interpreter and a schedulability test for substitutes. The contract check is currently implemented in a Java tool. The presented tools work on deterministic and predefined data (cf. ontology, contracts), hence can be used in real-time systems with appropriate extensions.

RELATED WORK

The term adaptation itself is quite often used ambiguously, although its specific definition plays a central role when trying to apply functional safety standards to adaptive systems. (Whittle, Sawyer, Bencomo, Cheng, & Bruel, 2009) argues that adaptation is a general feature when dealing with availability rather

Figure 10. Reconfigured system of our use case

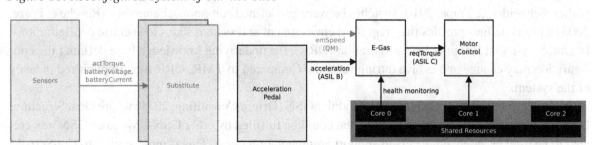

than with safety. In contrast, in (Güdermann, Ortmeier, & Reif, 2006) adaptability is presented as a way to make the function of a system available again.

We can identify three main classes of adaptive systems: static reconfigurable systems, self-adaptive systems, and fully self-adaptive systems. Static configurable systems can work on different configurations which imply different functions working on different hardware. Such functions are defined before the system starts running. On step further, dynamic configurable systems are those with a predefined list of acceptable configurations which can be modified at run-time (Ruiz, Juez, Schleiss, & Weiss, 2015). The last evolutions are the adaptive systems which are defined as systems which do not have a predefined list of configurations but rather define the boundaries of acceptable configurations that could run and can be modified at operational time.

The other two groups refer to those systems that have the capability to autonomously modify their behavior at runtime in response to changes of their environment. They need to adapt to situations that the designer was not able to foresee at design time. Today, this is also denoted as model@runtime to support dynamic adaptation (Morin, Barais, Jezequel, Fleury, & Arnor, 2009). Self-adaptive systems are known to have a predefined list of acceptable configurations that can be modified at runtime. Conversely, the latest evolution is heading towards fully self-adaptive systems approaches, which are defined as systems with no predefined list of configurations but which rather define the boundaries of acceptable configurations that could run and which can be modified at runtime.

From a safety point of view, self-adaptation can generally be both, a blessing and a curse. On the one hand, it can significantly increase a system's complexity, detriment its analyzability and thus induce unwanted uncertainty. On the other hand, it can be one method of reacting to unforeseen undesired behavior such as a failure. An example of this is described in (Ruiz, Juez, Schleiss, & Weiss, 2015) where a generic adaptation mechanism is designed to handle failures and provide a fail-operational behaviour.

Runtime adaptive systems have been used in different domains for many years already. Service-oriented Architecture (SOA) (MacKenzie, et al., 2006) is known as one popular method for creating dynamically changing, distributed applications. It basically consists of encapsulating all functionalities into so-called services that can be reached via a well-defined interface from anywhere in the network. Each service holds a contract that describes the ways of accessing this functionality, and the different services are composed by an orchestration algorithm to build an application. (Höfig, Armbruster, & Schmid, 2014) implemented an agent-oriented paradigm to self-adapt industrial automation systems. The DySCAS project (Anthony, et al., 2007) goes through a novel approach that includes middleware allowing self-configuration in automotive systems without considering safety implications.

Traditionally in safety-critical critical systems, redundant components (so-called replicas) are used to tolerate failures. For instance, triple modular redundancy (TMR) votes over the result of three redundant components to identify and ignore a failed component (Kopetz, 2011). Related mechanisms to Reconfiguration mechanisms typically adapt a CPS by switching between predefined modes. For example, (Adler, Schneider, & Trapp, 2010) switches between predefined component behaviors. (Rasche & Polze, 2005) a priori defines profiles that map from environment and system states to specific configurations. In Ontology-based Runtime Reconfiguration (ORR), the underlying knowledge base defining the configuration may change and evolve during runtime. Compared to TMR, ORR uses implicit redundancy of the system.

Modular safety case was explored by Modular GSN (Origin Consulting, 2011) where Goal Structural Notation was used with incomplete parts that could be fulfilled by other GSNs. Modular GSN was created to be used by safety engineers to support argumentation reuse. This is quite similar to ConSerts M approach which is realized by the demand/guarantee relation between systems.

The SafeAdapt project (www.safeadapt.eu/), investigates the applicability of a functional safety standard such as ISO 26262 in adaptive systems, and concludes with some recommendations for the standard interpretation (Deliverable D3.3).

Contract-based design is an enabling technology of the presented approach. Beugnard (Beugnard, Jezequel, Plouzeau, & Watkins, 1999) presents an overview of design by contract in the context of embedded systems, component architecture and SOA. Later on, he published a survey on the state-of-the-art of contract-based design (Beugnard, Jézéquel, & Plouzeau, 2010). Also, relevant in this area is the work of Kaiser (Kaiser, et al., 2014) on nominal behavior and safety in contracts. Very related to what we want to address is the work Sangiovanni-Vincentelli (Sangiovanni-Vincentelli, Damm, & Passerone, 2012) with the focus on contracts for CPS. Other than that, the research projects SafeCer (SafeCer, 2017) used failure guide words and association with integrity levels in their tool called SafetyADD (Warg, Vedder, Skoglund, & Soderberg, 2014), and DECOS (DECOS) which goal was to facilitate the systematic design and deployment of integrated systems, both having similarities to ConSerst M horizontal and vertical relations.

A related principle to ConSerts M is known as assume-guarantee reasoning (Henzinger, Minea, & Prabhu, 2001). It is a method to verify a system's composition. The system is modeled by discrete or continuous components that may be hierarchically structured. Similar to ConSerts M, each component has assumptions (cf. demands) and guarantees, concerning the interface (inputs and outputs) and behavior of components. However, safety properties or certification are not considered.

VerSaI (Vertical Safety Interfaces) (Zimmer, Bürklen, Knoop, Höfflinger, & Trapp, 2011) is a contract-based approach created to assist the integrator of an integrated architecture (e.g. AUTOSAR) in checking whether the application software components are able to run safely on the execution platforms of the system, and if so, provide assistance in generating appropriate evidence. VerSaI checks the safety compatibility between the application and the platform through demands and guarantees. Demands are used to express all the properties an application needs the platform to have in order to be executed safely. Guarantees represent the safety-related properties the platform possesses. They are modeled using a language that consists of a number of elements, each representing a certain type of demand or guarantee exchanged by an application and a platform. The VerSaI language is formal and each language element has a representation in natural language. This allows humans to read and evaluate the specification of demands and guarantees as well as the final argument generated after integration, which is required for reviews and assessments. The language was derived from the description of platform services in the standardized software architecture for automotive control units called AUTOSAR (AUTOSAR, 2016) and a similar standard for avionics called IMA (RTCA/DO-297, 2005). VerSaI allows integrating formalized safety cases into model-driven development artifacts. It is a product-oriented approach for efficient vertical modularization. Openness and adaptivity are not in the focus of this approach, however. VerSaI was the starting point of ConSerts M Vertical Interfaces. The original human readable language used to describe VerSaI contracts was adapted to XML, enabling; machine runtime evaluation of demands and guarantees, and intertwined usage with Horizontal Interfaces.

ConSerts (Conditional Safety Certificates) were introduced by Schneider in (Schneider & Trapp, 2013). In ConSerts, contracts are defined on the level of functional safety requirements, which are refined using safety properties encapsulating failure modes and operation modes. These contracts are post-certification artifacts developed using traditional safety engineering methods. They operate in the horizontal interfaces, i.e., describe safety attributes of services. The contracts are called conditional because they are equipped with certain variation points bound to formalized external dependencies (demands) that cannot be resolved at development time but at runtime. The conditional nature of the contracts enables the flexibility required for a sufficiently wide range of concrete integration scenarios. The contracts shall be issued at development time and supported by evidence or argumentation. ConSerts has a machine-readable language to describe safety properties, however, the approach was designed for system of (self-contained) systems only.

FUTURE RESEARCH DIRECTIONS

- **Adding Deployment Information to the Contracts:** Adding performance attributes (e.g., processing time and memory size required, resource consumption) and verifying them with the capability of the platform is the next step. Applications running on the same platform and sharing resources would need to have their performance needs compared against the platform capacity.

- **Encompass Security Properties in Contracts:** Security concerns are very prevalent in CPS settings due to the high number of communication links, open interfaces and heterogeneous levels of integrity between the participating systems. Without proper safety and security assurance we face the problem that we might not be able to unlock the full economic potential behind CPS. As starting point, the results of the European project EVITA (EVITA, 2016) which focused on security within the network of ECU of commercial vehicles could be used.

- **Integrate Runtime Evidences to the RM:** A special case of a Demand is a so-called runtime evidence (i.e., any safety-relevant information attainable by the system through a dedicated runtime evidence mechanism, e.g., quality of the communication channel), which is the conceptual hook to factor in arbitrary safety-relevant information that cannot be linked directly to a service. Such information might be the actual independence (in the sense of valid redundancy) between services, or something completely different, such as physical phenomena (e.g., weather situation, driver fitness, etc.).

- **Extension of ORR Knowledge Base with Additional Properties:** The knowledge base (ontology) currently only considers the relationships between the CPS properties. When implementing ORR in a CPS further specifications of the services' properties have to be available, e.g., sample rate of a CPS property. In the current implementation, such values are statically defined. To find the right reconfiguration plan, additional information shall be incorporated. Furthermore, the contracts may also be used to search for the safest reconfiguration.

CONCLUSION

ConSerts M addresses the uncertainty issue in SoS by modularizing safety information and using it to evaluate the safety of newly arising system compositions at runtime. This is achieved by formalizing guarantees and demands of a CPS unit of composition and specifying the logic in between in the form of a ConSerts M (i.e. a contract with embedded variants). Very complex functionalities are built from several services, of several components, each of them having their own ConSerts M. Due to the embedded variability, ConSerts M enable different modes of operation and different levels of assurance which might be switched dynamically. An additional benefit in that is that the number of "worst case assumptions" in safety engineering could be reduced, because the systems are now aware w.r.t. the relevant conditions in the environment and can thus operate at an optimal performance level without jeopardizing safety.

The massive adoption of ConSerts M, or a similar modular conditional safety certificate approach, among manufacturers would enable a system-of-systems ecosystem, pushing decentralized development of functionalities. Such a trend would allow technologies to be fast-forwarded through increasing division of responsibilities on the component level. The benefits of using ConSerts M are manifold:

- Straightforward reuse of established platforms and applications in new systems through the use of contracts and precertification.
- Possibility to upgrade execution platforms, therefore fighting hardware obsolescence
- Addition of novel applications to expand or modify system functionalities.
- Possibility for components (hardware and software) from different producers to be safely integrated at runtime.

This chapter also shows how to apply ConSerts M on the example of graceful degradation with ontology-based runtime reconfiguration (ORR) in an electric vehicle. ORR enables fault-tolerance to services of a CPS by exploiting implicit redundancy in the system. The reconfiguration mechanism uses an ontology that relates properties of a CPS (e.g., state variables or measurements), provided by services, to each other. The knowledge base is used to search for and construct a semantically equivalent service – a substitute – for a failed service.

The case study depicted a not-so-distant scenario where ConSerts M and ORR can be applied. Further application of the ideas presented become clearer as technology evolves. Security and improvements in functionalities will surely become strong drivers for software updates in CPS.

ACKNOWLEDGMENT

The research leading to these results has received funding from the ARTEMIS Joint Undertaking within the project EMC^2, under grant agreement no. 621429.

REFERENCES

Adler, R., Schneider, D., & Trapp, M. (2010). Engineering Dynamic Adaptation for Achieving Cost-Efficient Resilience in Software-Intensive Embedded Systems. In *Proceedings of the IEEE International Conference on Engineering of Complex Computer Systems*. (pp. 21-30). Los Alamitos, California: IEEE Computer Society Press. doi:10.1109/ICECCS.2010.22

AMADEOS. (2015). *AMADEOS Conceptual Model. Deliverable 2.2*. Retrieved from http://amadeos-project.eu/wp-content/uploads/2015/07/AMADEOS_D2.2_v2.6-final.pdf

Amorim, T., Ruiz, A., Dropmann, C., & Schneider, D. (2015). Multidirectional Modular Conditional Safety Certificates. In *Proceedings of the 4th International Workshop on Next Generation of System Assurance Approaches for Safety-Critical Systems - SAFECOMP*, Delft.

Anthony, R., Rettberg, A., Chen, D., Jahnich, I., de Boer, G., & Ekelin, C. (2007). *Towards a Dynamically Reconfigurable Automotive Control System Architecture. In Embedded System Design: Topics, Techniques and Trends* (pp. 71–84). Springer.

ARINC. (2005). *Arinc 653, avionic application software standard interface, part 1.*

AUTOSAR. (2016, 12 12). *Website of the autosar standard.* Retrieved 07 27, 2015, from http://www.autosar.org/

Beugnard, A., Jézéquel, J., & Plouzeau, N. (2010). Contract Aware Components, 10 years after. In Proceedings of the Component and Service Interoperability (WCSI10) (pp. 1-11).

Beugnard, A., Jezequel, J., Plouzeau, N., & Watkins, W. (1999, June). Making components contract aware. *Computer*, *32*(7), 38–45. doi:10.1109/2.774917

DECOS. (2007). Dependable Embedded Components and Systems .

DO-297. (2005). *Integrated Modular Avionics (IMA).* Development Guidance.

EVITA. (2016, 12 12). *EVITA.* Retrieved 08 03, 2016, from http://www.evita-project.org/

Fenelon, P., & Hebbron, B. (1994). Applying HAZOP to Software Engineering Models. *Risk Management And Critical Protective Systems: Proceedings of SARSS*, (pp. 1/1–1/16). Altrinchan.

Fernandes, P., & Nunes, U. (2010). Platooning of Autonomous Vehicles with Intervehicle Communications in SUMO Traffic Simulator. In *Proceedings of the International IEEE Conference on Intelligent Transportation Systems (ITSC).* doi:10.1109/ITSC.2010.5625277

Güdermann, M., Ortmeier, F., & Reif, W. (2006). Safety and dependability analysis of self-adaptive systems. In *Proceedings of the Second International Symposium in Leveraging Applications of Formal Methods, Verification and Validation.* Paphos: IEEE. doi:10.1109/ISoLA.2006.38

Henzinger, T. A., Minea, M., & Prabhu, V. (2001). Assume-Guarantee Reasoning for Hierarchical Hybrid Systems. In *Proceedings of the 4th International Workshop on Hybrid Systems: Computation and Control (HSCC 2001)* (pp. 275-290). Rome: Springer.

Höfig, K., Armbruster, M., & Schmid, R. (2014). A vehicle control platform as safety element out of context. HiPEAC Computing Systems Week. Barcelona.

Höftberger, O., & Obermaisser, R. (2013, June). Ontology-based runtime reconfiguration of distributed embedded real-time systems. In *Proceedings of the 2013 IEEE 16th International Symposium on Object/Component/Service-Oriented Real-Time Distributed Computing (ISORC).*

Höftberger, O., & Obermaisser, R. (2013). Ontology-based Runtime Reconfiguration of Distributed Embedded Real-Time Systems. In *Proceedings of the 16th IEEE International Symposium on Object/Component/Service-Oriented Real-Time Distributed Computing (ISORC 2013).* Paderborn: IEEE. doi:10.1109/ISORC.2013.6913205

Hoyningen-Huene, M., & Baldinger, M. (2010). Tractor-Implement-Automation and its application to a tractor-loader wagon combination. In *Proceedings of the 2nd International Conference on Machine Control & Guidance.* University of Bonn, Germany.

Kaiser, B., Weber, R., Oertel, M., Böde, E., Nejad, B. M., & Zander, J. (2014). *Contract-Based Design of Embedded Systems Integrating Nominal Behavior and Safety. Complex Systems Informatics and Modeling Quarterly.*

Kopetz, H. (2011). *Real-Time Systems: Design Principles for Distributed Embedded Applications.* New York: Springer. doi:10.1007/978-1-4419-8237-7

MacKenzie, C. M., Laskey, K., McCabe, F., Brown, P. F., Metz, R., & Hamilton, B. A. (2006). *OASIS standard.* Retrieved from https://www.oasis-open.org/standards/#soa-rmv1.0

Morin, B., Barais, O., Jezequel, J.-M., Fleury, F., & Arnor, S. (2009). *Models at Runtime to Support Dynamic Adaptation.* Los Alamitos: IEEE.

Origin Consulting. (2011). GSN Community Standard Version 1.

Rasche, A., & Polze, A. (2005). Dynamic reconfiguration of component-based real-time software. In *Proceedings of the 10th IEEE International Workshop on Object-Oriented Real-Time Dependable Systems (WORDS 2005)*, Sedona (pp. 347-354). doi:10.1109/WORDS.2005.31

Ratasich, D., Höftberger, O., Isakovic, H., Shafique, M., & Grosu, R. (2017). A Self-Healing Framework for Building Resilient Cyber-Physical Systems. In *Proceedings of the 20th IEEE International Symposium on Object/Component/Service-Oriented Real-Time Distributed Computing Conference (ISORC 2017)*, Toronto.

ROS. (2017, 03 17). *Open Source Robotics Foundation.* Retrieved from Robot Operating System: http://www.ros.org/ RTCA/DO-297.

Ruiz, A., Juez, G., Schleiss, P., & Weiss, G. (2015). *A safe generic adaptation mechanism for smart cars. In Proceedings of the 2015 IEEE 26th International Symposium on Software Reliability Engineering (ISSRE)* (pp. 161–171). ISSRE. doi:10.1109/ISSRE.2015.7381810

Rushby, J. (2008). Runtime certification. In *Proceedings of the Eighth Workshop on Runtime Certification,* Budapest, Hungary (pp. 21-35). Springer-Verlag. doi:10.1007/978-3-540-89247-2_2

Rushby, J. (2009). A safety-case approach for certifying adaptive systems. In *Proceedings of the AIAA Infotech @ Aerospace Conference.*

SafeCer. (2017, 03 17). *Safety Certification of Software-Intensive Systems with Reusable Components.* Retrieved from http://www.safecer.eu/

Sangiovanni-Vincentelli, A., Damm, W., & Passerone, R. (2012). Taming Dr. Frankenstein: Contract-Based Design for Cyber-Physical Systems. *European Journal of Control, 18*(3), 217-238.

Schneider, D., & Trapp, M. (2013). Conditional Safety Certification of Open Adaptive Systems. *ACM Trans. Auton. Adapt. Syst., 8*(2), 8.

Warg, F., Vedder, B., Skoglund, M., & Soderberg, A. (2014). SafetyADD: A Tool for Safety-Contract Based Design. In *Proceedings of the IEEE International Symposium on Software Reliability Engineering Workshops WoSoCer Workshop.* Naples, Italy.

Whittle, J., Sawyer, P., Bencomo, N., Cheng, B. H., & Bruel, J.-M. (2009). Relax: Incorporating uncertainty into the specification of self-adaptive systems. In *Proceedings of the 17th IEEE International Requirements Engineering Conference* (pp. 79-88). Atlanta: IEEE. doi:10.1109/RE.2009.36

Work group EGAS. (2015). *Standardized E-Gas Monitoring Concept for Gasoline and Diesel Engine Control Units, Version 6.0.*

Zimmer, B., Bürklen, S., Knoop, M. I., Höfflinger, J., & Trapp, M. (2011). Vertical Safety Interfaces - Improving the Efficiency of Modular Certification. In Proceedings of the SAFECOMP 2011 (pp. 29–42). Naples: Springer.

KEY TERMS AND DEFINITIONS

Component: A subsystem of the system which internals are of no interest.

Cyber-Physical System: A networked computer system interacting with its environment.

Interface: The point of interaction between (sub-)systems.

Ontology: An explicit description of domain knowledge.

Reconfiguration: The change of a system during runtime. Reconfiguration in software is often referred to as adaptation.

Runtime: Lifecycle phase of a software system when it is in use.

Safety Assurance: Set of activities designed to gain confidence on the safety characteristics of a system.

Safety Contracts: Models used to describe safety properties of components.

Safety-Critical Systems: A system where a failure can lead to catastrophes (e.g., a car accident).

Service: The intended behavior or functionality of a component.

Chapter 7

A Mixed–Criticality Integration in Cyber–Physical Systems:
A Heterogeneous Time–Triggered Architecture on a Hybrid SoC Platform

Haris Isakovic
Vienna University of Technology, Austria

Radu Grosu
Vienna University of Technology, Austria

ABSTRACT

A Cyber-Physical System (CPS) describes a system or a system-of-systems closely and actively coupled with environment. It comprises the digital intelligence system, a co-dependent physical system (i.e., electrical, mechanical) and the system environment. Since the beginning of modern computer systems integration was ever present challenge, from the huge single room computers to the IoT. Today applications interleave and build larger systems with different system requirements and properties. Implementation of safety critical applications together with non-critical applications within the same platform is almost inevitable in modern industrial systems. This article provides a retrospective overview of the major integration challenges and the current problems in mixed-criticality environments. Finally, it provides an insight in a hardware solution which creates deterministic platform for mixed-criticality applications.

1. INTRODUCTION

The topic of cyber-physical systems (CPS) is an interdisciplinary subject that connects computer engineering and computer science with other disciplines like electrical, mechanical, chemical and bio-engineering. In essence, it provides a shell for the system design which binds digital and physical world in a compact methodological form. It provides a better understanding of the system from various perspectives, it increases time to market and overall efficiency of the product. This concept was crafted

DOI: 10.4018/978-1-5225-2845-6.ch007

as a response to the increasingly complex structure of modern systems. The advantages of computer driven physical systems were recognized in the early stages of the computer development timeline. The physical systems controlled by a computer would reach their physical limits much rapidly, they were getting upgraded more frequently and in conclusion getting more complex. The initial approach of the system design was highly segregated in means of engineering disciplines. For the most part physical components of a system would be designed according to the techniques and methods used in a specific discipline, and then interfaced with a specific computer system. This approach provided a relatively clean design methodology, but as the systems got more complex it was more difficult to ensure that the functional properties of the system conform to the system specifications and regulatory guidelines. The work presented in this chapter reflects on the challenges present in the domain of mixed-criticality systems and the overcoming need for seamless integration. It also offers a viable solution based on a time-triggered architecture implemented on a hybrid system-on-a-chip platform. This novel approach to create a modular configurable deterministic hardware architecture combats core problems of industrial computer systems, where safety critical applications interact and operate under same conditions as non-critical applications. This closely coupled relation is extremely complicated on a commercial off the shelf (COTS) hardware. It is also highly expensive in terms power consumption, performance and utilization. The presented architecture enables clear separation between different tasks in space and time without performance loss. The extended plans foresee a tool chain integration to increase the ability to build an application directly from hardware level up.

1.1 Chapter Outline

This chapter provides a short reflection on mixed-criticality integration in cyber-physical systems. It explores the challenges and basic properties for the seamless integration not only user applications, but also underlying platform components, hardware, software and the physical environment. Section 1 gives a short introduction in cyber-physical systems and mixed-criticality integration, in particular Section 1.1 gives a short historical summary of the cyber-physical systems and turning points that lead to the modern state of CPS. Also, Section 1.3 gives an overview of the major challenges or objectives for mixed-criticality integration. Further, Section 2 gives a brief introduction in the background knowledge on the relevant topics. First, Section 2.1 describes spatial and temporal isolation as vital properties in the design of systems for mixed-critical integration. Section 2.2 introduces an innovative computer architecture that combines a hard-coded computer processing units with an FPGA device on a single chip, it is a synergy of different approaches and a product of merging knowledge from two different directions. Further, Section 2.3 describes an architecture built for mixed-criticality integration based on time-triggered communication and FPGA technology. Section 3 provides a description of the architecture that merges technologies described in Sections 2.2 and 2.3. Section 4 offers a brief overlook on the presented architecture and its ability to meet the challenges described in Section 1.3. The ability of the architecture to resolve practical issues has been shortly visited in Section 4.1. Finally, Sections 5 and 6 provide future work potentials and closing thoughts.

1.2 A Historical Overview

- **The Origins:** The name cyber-physical system was derived from the term "cybernetics", which is used to describe systems that used closed-loop feedback control. The term was introduced by an extraordinary 18th century physicist and mathematician A.M. Ampere (Ampère, 1838), and later revived by a 20th century mathematician and pioneer of modern control theory Norbert Wiener (Wiener, 1961). However, use of the term cyber-physical system was adopted as recently as 2006, it is used as an umbrella for all computer controlled systems that in one or the other way interacted with the physical world around it.
- **The Computer:** The first computers were originally created with a purpose of performing complex calculations, they were big machines installed in large rooms with highly complex structure and handling. As the computers became more accessible and affordable their services were adopted in other disciplines i.e., manufacturing, space, robotics, and consumer appliances.

In the 1950s computers were first applied in a control of industrial equipment, in the process called computer assisted manufacturing (CAM) using Automatically Programmed Tools (APT) language, it was a system designed to control a milling machine with a help of a computer (Ross, 1978). These machines were forerunners for the modern computer numerical control (CNC) machines and computer aided manufacturing. However, 1960s is the time when the age of computers really began, more and more fields in civil and military domains started using computers for various purposes. In 1961 a first mass-produced industrial robot UNIMATE was integrated in the production lines at General Motors (Nof, 1999). Around the same time, NASA included first digital computers in space programs Gemini and Apollo (NASA, 2016). This was followed by an introduction of the first commercial minicomputer DEC's PDP-8 (DEC, 1967). In the 1970s the development of computerized systems was highly accelerated and commercialized, new actors in computer technology development (i.e., Intel, Microsoft, HP, etc.) emerged and set the course for the next few decades.

- **The Microprocessor:** With the development of micro processing a huge spotlight was set computer architectures for personal computing, bringing computer aided development in completely new areas and disciplines. The micro processing found its way in other applications like control of fuel injection in cars or handheld calculators. The whole surge of new application was followed by a massive change in software as well, new computer languages like Pascal or C were introduced. (Wirth, 1971) (Kernighan & Ritchie, 1978). There was also a strong breakthrough of mass networking systems with Teletext information system and research-oriented network ARPAnet (BBC, 2012) (O'Regan, 2012).
- **The Embedded World:** The development of micro-controllers in 1980s enabled mass utilization of embedded computer systems in new applications, from industrial machines and communication devices to consumer electronics, and entertainment systems. In 1981 a first prototype for the direct drive arm was proposed, it shared the same basic principles used in industrial robots today (Asada & Kanade, 1983). An introduction of small-sized computers and networking breakthroughs influenced put high accent on communication disciplines. In 1983 Bell Labs introduced a first mobile

phone communication standard called Analogue Mobile Phone System (AMPS). It was embodied in a first commercial mobile phone Motorola DynaTAC 8000X (O'Regan, 2012). At the same time, multi-annual research efforts to build more flexible hardware resulted in the development of first Field-Programmable Gate Arrays (FPGAs). In 1985 Xilinx released their first FPGA device (Trimberger, 2012). It is a programmable logic device that can be customized for a specific application by a user. It combines logic blocks with programmable interconnects and multiplexed sets of IOs. The FPGAs changed the view on product development, allowed high integration capabilities and faster time-to-market (Carter, 1994). The development of FPGAs remained one of the most vibrant fields in computer science and electronics.

- **The Network:** The development of mobile phones was followed by networking revolution and introduction of OSI model, and consequently the invention of World Wide Web by Tim Berners-Lee. The interaction between systems and distributed computing became critical topics in industrial and scientific circles. The distributed computing was a significant change to the legacy systems that operated completely in isolation. At this point computers were already on multiple levels: large mainframe and server computers, personal office or home computers, and embedded or small-scale integrated computers. The high level of interaction between individual units had been already available for the first two groups, however, it was still relatively new in the scope of embedded systems. The distributed embedded systems yielded the term "Feldbus", it symbolizes a network of local field level devices with a focus on reliability, availability and safety of the system. They provided the ability to control processes efficiently and in real-time (Kopetz, et al. 1989). Throughout 1990s trends of miniaturizing chips and increasing connectivity among system continued. The personal computers became a common tool in both business and private sector (see Figure 1). The number of networked and distributed embedded systems increased immensely, for example a number of mobile phone subscriptions had an average growth of 36% of new subscribers per year over the period between 1984 and 2003 (see Figure 2).

- **The Model:** The initial computer controlled systems were built to explore the capabilities of this new technology and with focus on basic functions. In most cases, they represented ad-hoc solutions with a low dependability level. A major challenge at the time was to ensure reliability of the systems even for the applications that required strict safety insurance levels. The challenge of simply creating efficient computer system and applying it was not the largest problem anymore. How to make it safe and reliable for all applications was a question more difficult to answer (Bowen & Stavridou, 1993). At the same time, there was a strong shift towards knowledge based or model based design of systems in computer engineering. A model based design reduces building efforts, system testing and maintenance efforts of complex systems (Studer, Benjamins, & Fensel, 1998). A first version of Common Object Request Broker Architecture and Specifications (CORBA) was released in 1991, and up to these dates it represents a state-of-the-art framework for integration of heterogeneous systems (Vinoski, 1993). The networking increased efficiency of the system in a number of ways, but it created a huge space for other obstacles in system design and operation i.e., synchronization and coordination, security and integration. A guideline of security standards and principles by NIST in 1995 identifies integration as one of the basic elements in the design of secure systems (NIST, 1995). The integration understands connecting systems and subsystems using hardware, software or physical interfaces such that they operate as a single functional unit, providing emerging functionalities that are impossible to implement using individual components.

Figure 1. Number of mobile cellular subscribers in United States per 100 people: 1984-2003
The World Bank Group, 2016.

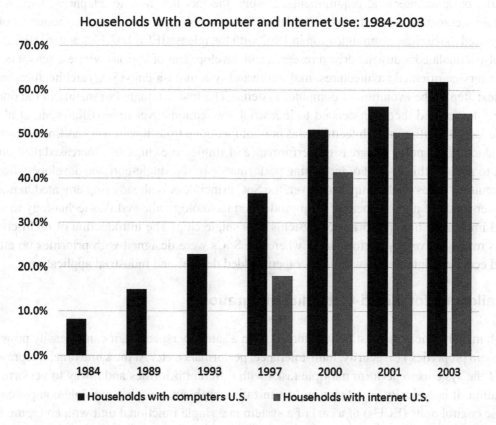

Figure 2. Number of mobile cellular subscribers in United States per 100 people: 1984-2003
The World Bank Group, 2016.

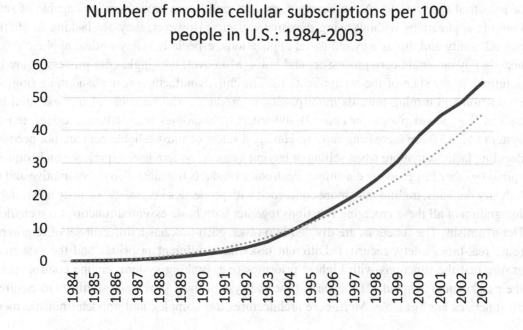

- **The Integration:** The technologies that followed were designed with seamless integration as one of the basic architectural requirements. Despite the fact that mobile telephony, used means of wireless communication since 1980s, the traditional cable operated computer networks officially migrated to wireless communication in 1997 with the release IEEE 802.11 standard (IEEE, 2016). It also stimulated industrial driven research and development of various wireless sensor networks. The service-oriented architectures, multi-core and system-on-a-chip (SoC) architectures represent a next step in the evolution of computer systems. The first originated in mainly in the domain of the Internet, and then transcended to industrial applications over time (Blomstedt, et al. 2014). The idea of multi-core architectures was present for a long time, however it was limited by the chip production technology. Increasing performance of single-core chips also increased their complexity, to manage this instead of increasing performance of the single-core the developers find a way to multiply cores on the chip. Moreover, the SoC principle was already implemented in microcontrollers and the improvement of chip production technology allowed this technology to scale up and implement high performance systems on a single chip. The introduction of multi-core chips was mainly driven by performance, where the SoCs were designed with priorities on efficiency and economic integration with focus on embedded devices and industrial applications.

1.3 Challenges for Mixed-Criticality Integration

Although mixed-criticality question was forced from a safety perspective, it can be easily projected on other system properties i.e. security, fault-tolerance, performance etc. At the same time, it represents the ability of the systems to perform multiple tasks with different priorities and a way to perform system optimization. It is basically an integration/optimization problem, merging multiple components (e.g., electronic control units (ECUs) of a car) of a system in a single functional unit with emerging benefits in the likes of cost, performance or power consumption.

- **Performance:** When it comes to performance the computer systems surpass current demands of industrial applications. As an example, modern multi-core processors are capable of serving multiple applications without using maximal capacity. However, they are lacking in efficiency and reliability and this is why industrial applications, especially safety critical applications, still heavily rely on single-core processors and SoCs. Moreover, the single-core processors are being outgrown by the state-of-the-art applications. The chip manufacturers are abandoning single-core production and turning towards more profitable products. The numbers of non-essential applications (e.g., smart phone car control) and smart technologies (e.g., advance driver assistance system (ADAS)) are increasing rapidly. Having a safest or most reliable cars are not necessarily deciding factors anymore when selling or buying a car. A modern user experience and comfort inspired by other fast growing consumer electronics products translate also in automotive and other industry domains, traditionally more concerned with properties i.e., safety, security and reliability. Integration of all these emerging functions together with basic essential functions is a challenge.
- **Determinism**: The functions are divided into tasks, each task has a different set of requirements (e.g., real-time, safety, security). Different tasks have different priorities and the system must ensure that the functions with highest priorities (e.g. braking system, engine control) perform their tasks uninterrupted. At the same time the system must provide best efforts to ensure that all functions are available. Multi-core architectures use complex and nondeterministic memory

hierarchies and inter-core communication, and highly improbable to provide sufficient guarantees that a high priority task will finish its execution on time and not get interrupted by any other action. Single-core platforms are slowly being retired, as they are becoming obsolete in terms of performance and efficiency. However, they are still the best option for a deterministic hardware architecture. A big question is how to ensure needed performance and ensure the necessary level of deterministic behavior for different applications or sets of applications?

- **Optimization:** A way to deal with the above-mentioned issues, is to increase the number of computer units in a system and provide complete hardware and software isolation of different functions. This would enable an increase of system functions and maintained the classic approach on cross-critical integration. On the other side, it would increase the complexity of the system and reduced overall efficiency. A good example is the automotive industry. The number of electronic control units (ECUs) in an average personal vehicle almost doubled in the last ten years and it currently ranges between 50 and 100 ECUs, depending on the size and class of the car (Johnson, Gannamaraju, & Fischmeister, 2015). Alone weight and power consumption of those ECUs and the wires that connect them are significant factors in the fuel economy of a car. The efforts required to ensure error-free operation from design to testing is also a significant factor in the overall economics of a vehicle. It is clear that merging individual ECUs in "larger" mixed-functionality units could result in reduced overall weight, power consumption, complexity, and space. An additional aspect is the development process these systems. Figure 3 provides an illustration of a development process in CPSs, although it provides just a portion of an actual development procedure it demonstrates the complexity level of the task. It usually includes several often-incompatible tools for collecting and verification of requirements, for design and configuration of hardware, system software, communication, applications, and for analysis, testing and certification of the system. The optimization of systems is equally challenging and important as optimization of the design and development process of these systems.

- **COTS:** Designing a hardware platform specifically for an individual application or a set of functions is must be economically justified. The number of manufactured and sold units must justify the amount of efforts to build such a system. Such platform provides the exact intended functionality, but it enables very little flexibility and it requires significant costs compared to COTS solutions. On the other hand, COTS solutions are generic and they are designed for multiple purposes, which means that they are rather limited when it comes to specific niche applications. One of the major challenges is how to build a system platform flexible enough to integrate multiple domain applications and combine functions with different levels of criticality using generic COTS platforms?

- **Taxonomy:** The classification of systems according to stakeholder requirements and system properties is another large issue. The spectrum of system requirements depending on the domain and application type can be vast. System properties i.e. Reliability, safety, security is complementary, however, one doesn't necessarily guarantee the other. The reliable system doesn't always represent a safe system, and unreliable system can be safe (Rushby, 1994). Similar conjunctions can be established with other properties, so it is important that a system is correctly classified from the start. Different properties have different levels of criticality, they also have different domains of implementation. Some properties are implemented in hardware, where others are provided by a software program or realized using mechanical or electrical mechanisms. If the system is defined

Figure 3. An abstract illustration of a design and development process in CPSs

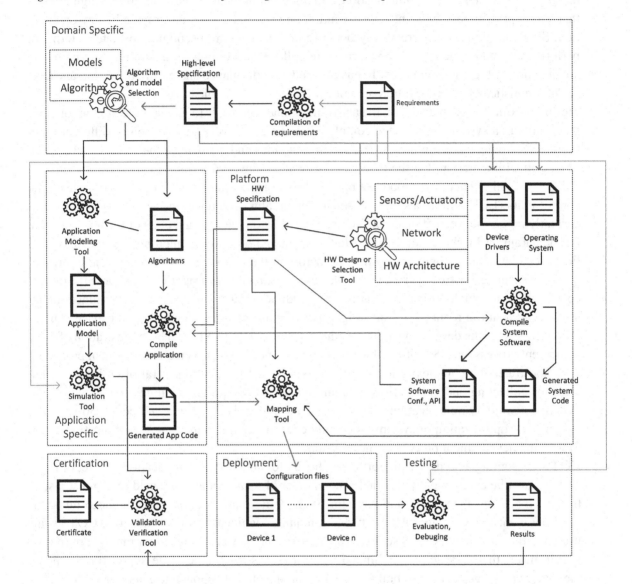

appropriately in all domains, unnecessary redundancies could be avoided, thus saving efforts and reducing cost.

- **Modeling**: A CPS is a set of systems co-dependently operating in different domains. On one side, there is an analog domain, described using continuous mathematics, it represents the physical world in CPS. On the other side, there is a digital domain. It uses discrete mathematics and it represents the computer realm. Models are used on both sides to describe the system and to provide designers with a chance to evaluate its basic properties before they actually start building it. A number of modeling tools and languages used on both sides is enormous. To ensure interoperability, traceability and verification between different models is a task that needs to be undertaken at multiple levels of in the CPS design process. It is one of the crucial requirements for mixed-critical integration in CPS.

2. BACKGROUND

A single hardware platform to host multiple functions using software based separation solutions could be an optimal solution for cross application and cross domain integration. This needs to be supported throughout the design process of a system, from the models of the physical part to computer hardware and software. The SoC platforms have emerged as a bridging solution for this problem. They are able to integrate multiple processors with different performance characteristics, together with other components (e.g., memories, peripherals) which can be tailored for a specific domain, specific application or a specific set of functions. Moreover, a new generation of SoC that integrates a hardcoded processor with flexible FPGA devices are being utilized to create platforms for development of CPSs. They ensure a sufficient level of dynamicity where at the same time are able to provide enough performance to host state-of-the-art industrial and consumer oriented applications.

2.1 Spatial and Temporal Isolation

Mixed-criticality integration relies on a group of basic system properties. Most of all, separation or isolation of individual tasks or functions must be guaranteed. Each task must be ensured that during its operation all required resources are available. A given task can be a simple software computing routine which requires only computing resources i.e., processor and corresponding memory infrastructure. Depending on constraints of the given task the extent of the resource's availability and readiness level it's determined. If the task is hard real-time, the result of the tasks must be delivered in an only in a given timeframe. If the task were isolated, implemented alone on a single processor, with almost private memory, it would be easy to reserve a time and a place for it to perform its duties. However, real systems and the corresponding tasks are generally more complex. They control functions that rely on a complex chain of codependent tasks, a series of peripheral devices for input/output purposes and communication, and sensors and actuators for interacting with the environment. To ensure causality of events and accuracy of values of different variables all components need to be separated and integrated at the same time. System resources need to be shared between the individual tasks and functions, and these need to be isolated in the system both in space and time. A spatial isolation guarantees that a task or a function can occupy a system resource or set of resources (e.g., memory, processor, communication channel) without interferences of any other activities in the system. A temporal isolation guarantees that the execution of any task cannot influence the temporal behavior of any other task or function, and that the execution time of the task cannot be influenced by the execution of any other task or function.

Most frequent problem for the spatial isolation is memory management. In the modern systems, the size of the memory and number of memory accesses is extremely large what makes the duty of managing them highly complex. It takes a series of hardware components and specialized software routines to manage memory during the execution. The memory is a storage device organized in cells and each cell is marked with an address, this address also called a physical address. The memory can be accessed by a CPU directly via physical address, but there is usually an intermediate component between CPU and memory called memory management unit (MMU). It is a specialized component that arranges physical memory in a set of pages, addressed by a set of virtual addresses which are then provided to the CPU for memory operations. It makes the memory access substantially faster and more efficient. It also provides the ability for a system to assign a specific process with section of memory and to control it, such that sections from different processes do not interleave. The functionality of the MMU is controlled by a system software, it can be part of an operating system or a dedicated task for this purpose. The MMU is a first step towards spatial isolation in modern computer systems. A memory protection unit (MPU) is component that ensures no unauthorized memory access is allowed during execution. System software provides additional level of isolation, it controls hardware to provide higher levels of software, namely application software, required functionality. An operating system is a set of system functions that provide the ability for multiple applications to share the same hardware platform. A standard operating system ensures that hardware can be used by several applications simultaneously. Each application is divided tasks which are then organized in processes, the isolation performs on a process level. More specific solutions like microkernel based operating systems or hypervisors provide fully isolated partitions which could host whole partitions and even operating systems themselves. In general, even most complex architectures provide the ability to host multiple applications and provide spatial isolation. The advances in the system software technology (e.g., virtualization) enabled highly advanced control over hardware mechanisms and ensured properties like spatial isolation.

The temporal isolation is a multilayer problem which spreads from hardware architecture to design and execution of both system and application software. The development of hardware architectures was driven by an ever-growing hunger for ability to perform more tasks in less time. As the frequency of processors grew faster and memories grew bigger it was essential that data latency between these two are reduced to a minimum. This is why a number of mechanisms were introduced to accelerate date transfer between CPU and memory. A typical example is the cache memory. It is a high-speed memory built in between the CPU and memory intended as an intermediate storage for a date or instructions that might be used more frequently. Some parts of a program execute more than others and there are mechanisms that predict these repetitions and preloaded them in the cache memory thus allowing the CPU to access it faster. The same technique makes it highly difficult to predict the timing constraints for a specific task as they are implemented on the instruction level. The execution of instructions in a CPU is measurable and the execution time of each task in the CPU can be calculated. The memory access latency can also be determined a priory. The caching mechanisms on the other hand, are based on a series of proprietary algorithms with little or no reference to timing behavior. Thus, making the system unpredictable. In order to ensure temporal isolation tasks or processes need to be evaluated at execution time. This process is called static analysis, and its goal is to determine a worst-case execution time (WCET) of each task. It represents a maximum time that a task can take to execute. With this value a scheduling algorithm determines an execution sequence based on specific constraints, such that any interferences between tasks are avoided. Non-deterministic components (i.e., cache) significantly reduce the ability to calculate WCET for any task. A partial solution for this problem is an overcompensation, by providing more time for execution of a task than initially predicted. However, if the architecture scales up from a single-core architecture to a multi-core architecture the ability to provide temporal guarantees drops even lower. The multi-core architectures use virtual threads across cores to ensure maximal performance. They are also implemented with multi-level cache memories, with each core heaving an exclusive L1 cache, while the L2 cache memory is shared among processors. This increases the level of non-determinism immensely. This is perfectly understandable as the multi-core architectures were not built for the purpose of temporal isolation of mixed-criticality applications.

2.2 Hybrid System-on-a-Chip

FPGAs and hybrid SoC provide an ability to design a domain and application independent architectures which can be configured according to the needs of a specific use case. The process can be integrated within the design process of the whole system, thus having application specific integration already included in the architecture by design (El Salloum, Elshuber, Höftberger, Isakovic, & Wasicek, 2013). Originally FPGAs were used as a prototyping platform where the designers would test hardware components before going for a more permanent ASIC solution. As the technology advanced the FPGAs became more reliable and are more frequently used in different applications, especially where hardware reconfiguration is a system requirement. It ensures longevity of the platform and flexibility if additional applications or functions are necessary. It is an economical approach that which allows designers to define certain properties of the system already in hardware, which increases overall efficiency of the system. In the last decade, FPGAs improved immensely by means of energy efficiency, capacity and pricing. They reached the point where they can be used as a viable replacement for standardized, generic components in hardware platform design. They are heavily utilized in applications that require hardware flexibility and dynamicity (e.g., deep neural learning, satellite on-board computers). Figure 4 illustrates a surge in the progress of FPGA technology in recent years.

Some of the most relevant innovations surrounding FPGAs that have been commercialized in recent years are hybrid SoC architectures, dynamic partial reconfiguration of FPGA fabric and high-level synthesis (HLS). Although all three concepts are not a novelty as such, they came under focus as of recent as the necessary technology became more accessible. All three concepts could be highly important for mixed-critical integration and integration as properties in CPSs in general. The high-level synthesis is a digital design method that creates digital hardware based on abstract behavioral description (McFarland, Parker, & Camposano, 1990). A system described using abstract programming language (i.e., C++) is automatically translated into functional hardware components that perform the same task. Having a

Figure 4. The advancement of FPGA technology in terms of fundamental logic blocks
Altera, 2016; Xilinx, 2016.

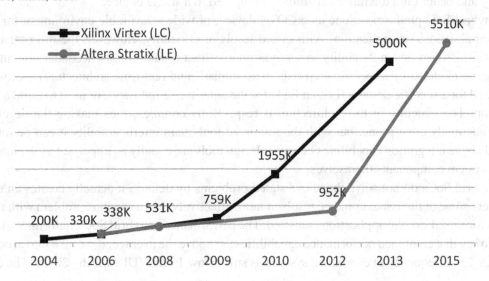

hardware implementation of a function can be manifold beneficial (e.g., performance, energy consumption) and having an automated way to implement it is a great advantage.

The dynamic partial reconfiguration of FPGAs allows the system to change the functionality while the system is still operational. A standard way of configuring or programming FPGAs is considered a full re-configuration. The idea behind the concept of partial reconfiguration is analogue to the use of dynamically linked libraries (DLLs) in software applications, a component or a function is added or removed on the fly (Horta, Lockwood, Taylor, & Parlour, 2002). The use partial reconfiguration is suitable for the applications built from multiple configurations which are not active at the same time. It is the way to optimize the resource management of the FPGA. It can be used to increase the fault tolerance of a system in general, by allowing the system to reconfigure certain parts in case of a fault or an error.

The hybrid SoC is a combination of two different hardware design approaches, a multi-core general purpose computing architecture and an FPGA device on a single chip. It represents a synergy of two concepts that operate on different sides of the application spectrum. The general purpose multi-core architectures were designed with the primary goal of increasing performance in general purpose applications (e.g., personal computers, server computers, multimedia devices). The FPGAs traditionally utilized as prototyping devices or used in particular applications where reconfigurable custom hardware design enhances overall system performance, ensures flexibility and ability to adapt the system if necessary (e.g., network routers and switches). The hybrid SoC ensures both by intelligently connecting both architectures in a single device. It allows both devices to operate in isolation while at the same time it is possible to extend one with the other.

The forerunners in hybrid SoCs technology are Xilinx with Zynq 7000 series devices (Xilinx, 2016), Altera (as of recent Intel) with Cyclone and Arria devices (Altera, 2016), and MicroSemi with SmartFusion2 devices (Microsemi, 2016). The devices share the same basic concept and all use ARM architectures, the differences are mainly in the FPGA devices and design tools. The hard-coded processor units are based on ARM Cortex series devices (i.e., A9, M3).

The interface between ARM cores and FPGAs is established over AXI bus bridges that provide full integration of devices in a single system, or partial integration as resources dedicated to each device can be channeled directly to the other. They also allow mutual control between the devices, the FPGA can be re-configured using the HPS and HPS can be initialized from the FPGA side. This allows more flexibility and better fault tolerance capabilities compared to a single device.

The hybrid SoC platforms, alone as a COTS device, provide a favorable environment for hosting multiple applications or applications with mixed levels of criticality. However, the full potential of a hybrid SoC platform lies in its ability to serve as an excellent foundation for secondary architectures. These can be modeled by a specific goal (e.g., deterministic and real-time architecture), or they could be designed for a specific domain (i.e., an ECU for the automotive industry), or used to build a specific application. The structure of the architecture is respectfully complex, thus making the development process potentially error prone, but with the improved tool chain interoperability it can be mitigated. As stated above integration capabilities between design tools are equally as important as the integration between system components themselves.

The hybrid SoCs do not solve the above stated problems by default, it actually creates an environment where some of the issues could be resolved more effectively. It is a sandbox problem with the basic premises for mixed-critical applications satisfied. The performance of hybrid SoC platforms varies, but it it's safe to say that combined performance capabilities are above the average, if we take into account that an average CPU frequency in embedded systems is still below 1 GHz (UBM tech., 2013). The capacity of FPGAs has been increased by multiple factors in the last five years (see Figure 4), this allows more functions to be hosted on FPGAs. There are a few basic approaches for implementing applications on hybrid SoC platforms:

- A software application hosted exclusively on the hard processing subsystem (e.g., ARM dual-core). It provides good performance characteristics, but it basically has the same characteristics of standard multi-core platforms.
- An application hosted on the hard processing subsystem, with parts of the application implemented on FPGA fabric as a type of an accelerator. This approach is application dependent and could only benefit specific cases. However, it might give a significant performance boost.
- An application implemented in hardware with support of the hard processing system. It is a typical use of FPGA, and it is favorable only in certain cases.
- Use of heterogeneous approach with both HPS and FPGA active. The FPGAs could host multiple generic soft-core based components, dedicated to a specific task or application. It provides multiple layers of separation:
  - **Platform Level:** HPS and FPGA
  - **Core Level:** Multiple cores on HPS, or FPGA, and
  - **Process or Task Level:** Multiple tasks on a single core.

This approach provides multiple benefits with the ability to separate applications physically as well as virtually. It enables multiple instances of the same application, thus providing fault-tolerance. The soft-cores could be heterogeneous depending on a type of the function they are implementing (e.g., for signal processing a digital signal processor is a more effective mechanism then a standard CPU). Although, the soft-cores offer lower performance capabilities with the higher FPGA capacity this could be compensated with high number of components. The components could be individual or connected via on-chip interconnect in a network-on-chip or a bus topography.

This article provides an overview of the approach an overlaying architecture on top of a hybrid SoC platform designed to withhold specific standards and ensure the properties necessary for the mixed-critical integration. A similar approach is described in the next sections of this article. Section 3 describes an architecture that integrates both devices in a reliable and deterministic fashion. It shows how the hybrid SoCs can respond to the challenges of cross-application and cross-domain integration.

2.3 A Time-Triggered Many-Core Architecture

Two main requirements for mixed-critical integration are spatial and temporal isolation. A way to separate applications based on resources and ensure the temporal integrity between them. The commercial solutions are driven with performance capabilities, not intended for safety critical applications or applications with mixed criticality. A time-triggered many-core architecture ACROSS MPSoC was proposed to overcome limitations of the commercial off the shelf solutions (El Salloum, et. al., 2013). It uses time-triggered communication technology and FPGA programmable logic to implement a many-core architecture capable of executing multiple applications, with different criticality levels and with different domain of operation. It is using a service oriented approach with trilateral service hierarchy: core services, optional services and application specific services.

The ACROSS MPSoC is a many-core system with eight soft-coded cores organized in self sustainable components. Each component was a fully functional computer system. The components were assigned particular roles to accommodate service oriented approach. Four components were reserved for core services and optional system services, and the remaining four as application components. Application components can be interfaced with peripheral devices directly or through system components. The backbone of the SoC is a time-trigger network-on-a-chip (TTNoC). A message based communication system controlled by a notion of time. Each component was connected to the TTNoC via the generic interface called trusted interface sub-system (TISS). A property of time-triggered communication is that all members of a network share the same notion of time, called global time. The messages are transmitted between members using a fixed time schedule and it is possible to determine full causality of events between components. This enables system to behave in a fully deterministic fashion. The architecture implements both spatial and temporal isolation, the properties needed for the mixed-critical integration.

A component includes a single-core Nios 2 processor, tied with a physically independent memory unit. The only connection with the rest of the system was trough the deterministic NoC. Thus, each component operated fully independent if not otherwise configured. Each component is defined by a specific set of IO connections, depending on a component's function within the system.

The service oriented approach allows use of the architecture for multiple types of applications and multiple industrial domains. The core services provide basic properties which ensure that the system can be used from a safety critical to a non-critical application. The additional two levels of services, mold the architecture towards a specific domain or application, as additional services can be introduced and integrated into the hierarchy as they are sitting on top of the cores which are ensuring the integrity of the basic properties. The core services would be: configuration, TTNoC communication, execution control, global time, and diagnostics. The optional services are services that provide system level functions, but they are not necessary for the operation of the MPSoC (i.e., operating system, security, IO communication, monitoring, etc.) Application specific services allow the end user to integrate application specific functions into the system. Examples would be: a video service or human interaction interface (HMI) service. A service management layer is missing from the original design. Full service oriented architectures provide a service management services such that users can subscribe or unsubscribe from a specific service. In this case a static configuration of services is necessary. The whole architecture is based on the concept of static configuration at this instance. A dynamic configuration or reconfiguration is extremely difficult to certify for safety applications. One of the goals of this architecture in addition to the feasibility study for mixed criticality integration was evaluation of certifiability of such architecture for safety critical applications.

3. A HETEROGENOUS TIME-TRIGGERED ARCHITECTURE ON A HYBRID SOC PLATFORM

The ACROSS MPSoC provided a concrete solution for the problem of mixed-integration. Some of the ideas were not explored, although they seemed fully reachable. The platform offers the ability to increase or decrease the number of components as the TTNoC infrastructure is fully flexible it was able to connect up to 250 components in the current implementation. The TTNoC allows use of heterogeneous components, however, this hasn't been applied due to limitations of the underlying platform. Also, the ability to scale up and implement higher powered components. The hybrid SoC architectures allow more space for these experiments. In the following section a heterogeneous time-triggered architecture implemented on hybrid SoC (HTTSoC) is described (Isakovic & Grosu, 2016). It is based on the ACROSS architecture with an extension to accommodate a hard-coded ARM processor component. This approach also slightly deviates from the original static service-oriented approach, and explores the possibility of modular architecture with generic component templates. The architecture is organized in three parts: the TTNoC, a cluster soft-core components, and a single hard-coded component. The tunic has the same core from the ACROSS MPSoC, with a different topology and an additional TISS interface to connect the hard-coded component. A component is a fully functional computing device similar to a microcontroller, it is a system within a system, and they were marked as µComponent. The fundamental elements of the communication infrastructure the TTNoC, TISS and a component called trusted resource manager (TRM) are essential for the structure and organization of the architecture.

The implementation uses Altera Arria V SoC as an underlying platform. Figure 5 depicts a block diagram of Arria V SoC. It contains an ARM Cortex A9 dual-core processor described as a hard proces-

Figure 5. A block diagram of Arria V SoC

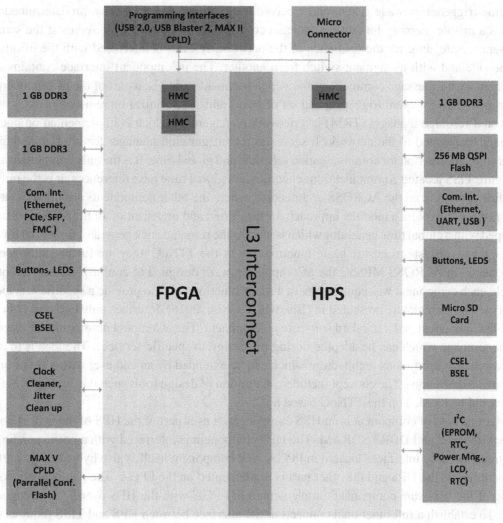

sor system (HPS) and an Arria V FPGA device. Each processor core runs with a frequency of up to 1 GHz, 32 KB L1 cache memory, and 512 KB of L2 cache memory. In addition, the SoC is equipped with three blocks of 1 GB DDR3 memory and a number of other peripheral memories and IO interfaces that can be used by both devices. The SoC uses AMBA Network Interconnect (NIC-301), marked as an L3 Interconnect, as an on-chip communication backbone between FPGA and HPS.

A core of the communication infrastructure is the TTNoC, a mesh of an arbitrary number of multidirectional switches, called fragment switches interconnected in a specific topology. A fragment switch is a module with four bi-directional channels that relay data either to another fragment switch or to a µComponent interface. Topology of the TTNOC can vary, it is not necessary that each channel is occupied, but the most effective layout is of course a mesh where each channel is closed. It increases routing capabilities and increases maximum throughput and efficiency of the network. The size of the network is bounded by clock distribution limitations of an underlying platform. Essentially, there are two types of data transmitted over TTNoC, time-triggered messages and signals for event-triggering and maintenance of global time.

A next essential element in the communication infrastructure of the architecture is a trusted interface subsystem (TISS). It is trusted interface between TTNoC and components. It is an information gateway where time-triggered message is sent and received transparently according to a predetermined schedule. It has a private memory for storing data and configuration. This is why it serves at the same time it represents a safeguard for the resilience of the network. A TISS is interfaced with the µComponent from one side and with a fragment switch from another. The µComponent interface contains a dual-ported memory for message communication, which is considered to be a part of the µComponent, a set of interrupt signals for event triggering and set of status and synchronization registers.

A trusted-resource manager (TRM) is a network management which is implemented on one of the components connected to the network. It serves as a configuration manager for all TISSs, delivering configuration information for communication schedule and global time. It is the only component allowed to configure TISS located communication schedules and global time base references. It is the only component fully ported from the ACROSS architecture, where the other components are implemented in a generic fashion to explore a modular approach for the design and organization of the MPSoC. The TRM is equipped with a global time generator which is used as the reference tick generator for global time base.

These three subsystems ensure basic functionality of the TTNoC, they are further interfaced with µComponents. In ACROSS MPSoC the µComponents were designed to conform the service-oriented approach, each component was equipped with a set of functionalities to provide a specific service or set of services. The architecture presented in (Isakovic & Grosu, 2016) describes only two types of components HPS Component and a standard soft-core µComponent. The µComponents are implemented using a generic template which can be adapted during the design to specific services. The idea is to create a stable base which or sandbox architecture which can be extended by an end user with a set of premade or custom designed apps. The concept includes integration of design tools such that a custom high-level design would be molded on the TTNoC based SoC.

The second type of component is an HPS component. It uses part of the HPS of the hybrid SoC with a single ARM core and DDR3 SDRAM. The HPS component is interfaced with a corresponding TISS and required memory interfaces located in FPGA. The component itself is also hybrid as the part of the component lies on the HPS and the other part is implemented on the FPGA. The platform allows direct coupling of the hardware components implemented in FPGA with the HPS over L3 interconnect bus bridges. To establish a full functional connection the interface between HPS and TISS requires two L3

Figure 6. ACROSS MPSoC architecture

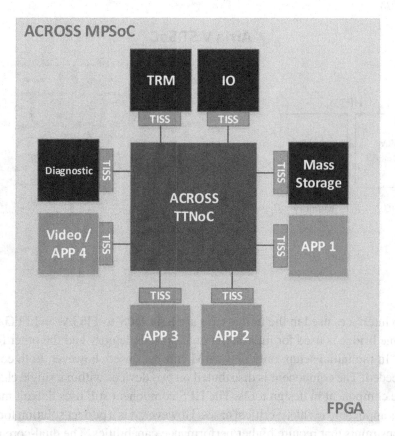

Figure 7. Service hierarchy in ACROSS MPSoC

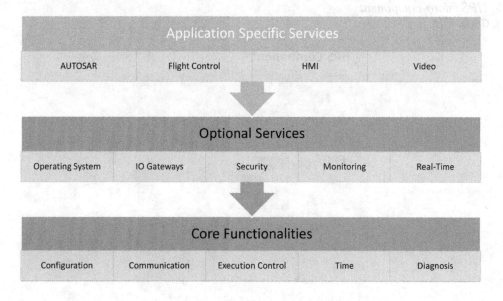

Figure 8. Heterogeneous time-triggered architecture on a hybrid SoC platform
Isakovic & Grosu, 2016.

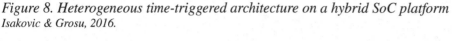
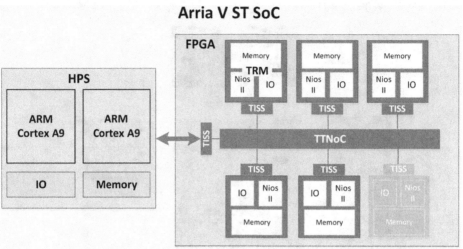

bus bridges. Two interfaces used in the in this case are light HPS-to-FPGA, and FPGA-to-HPS bridge (see Figure 9). One bridge is used for interfacing dual-ported memory and the other for the routing of interrupt signals. In the initial setup, only one ARM core was used, however, both cores could access the interface if needed. The component is distributed on two devices within a single chip, but it is represented as a single component in design tools. The HPS component still uses default memory hierarchy what makes it less applicable in safety-critical cases. However, it is a perfect solution for the applications without safety constraints that require higher performance capabilities. The dual-core processor can be

Figure 9. HPS micro-component
Isakovic & Grosu, 2016.

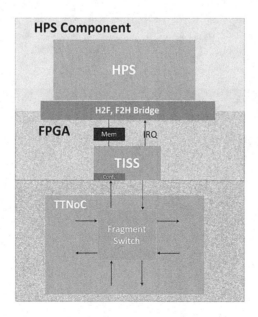

run in a symmetric multiprocessing mode or in an asymmetric multiprocessing mode. This provides additional width in the design of applications where on core can be used as a work core and the other as a diagnostic or monitoring unit. The HPS component confirms the ability of TTNoC to integrate heterogeneous components. This means that FPGA can host use case specific accelerators which can be integrated in the architecture instead or alongside Nios 2 components. This way application can utilize modular approach to build a application specific architecture from a generic set of building blocks.

The presented architecture represents a corner stone for the idea of a modular hardware architecture which can be molded on a specific application using a set of high level tools. This way utilization of system resources, power consumption, performance is optimized during the design phase. The required set of tools for this objective is not included in the original platform set of tools. The lack of tool integration presents a major challenge and requires significant amount of efforts to fit the given application on the platform. The goal is to create a configuration tool which maps application requirements on to hardware architecture. This would increase usability and scalability of the presented architecture. The tools would cover hardware requirements, system software requirements and system properties (e.g., safety or security). The original architecture was created with a set of basic tools for configuration of the architecture. To explore full potential of the platform a more powerful set of tools is required which can bridge the manual tasks in the design process, from hardware to an application.

In the case of ACROSS MPSoC each component is considered fault containment unit and the MPSoC as a whole an error containment unit. The global time and synchronization mechanism of TTNoC provide an excellent foundation for component replication. The heterogeneous approach adds another layer of fault and error containment. Although the HPS system is integrated into the TTNoC architecture, it is still a fully independent unit, and the faults in FPGA cannot resonate to the HPS and vice versa. However, the system provides a set of interfaces that enable bidirectional reprogram or reconfiguration. Both devices can be used to monitor and replicate the functionality of the other. The component and the chip represent two levels of fault tolerance in the solution with only FPGA device. In case of hybrid SoC platform there is an additional level between two devices. The above-mentioned tools would be able to integrate a fined grained fault tolerance mechanisms based on this basis.

Tested architecture implementation has four µComponents with a rudimentary design, and a HPS component. A huge factor in the selection hardware platform during application design process is the cost. One of the goals is to explore usability of the presented architecture on a larger scale. The absence of tools that bridge the gaps between hardware design, architecture configuration and application design was mentioned as one of the major challenges. However, it is not the only one in this case as the presented hybrid SoC is still relatively expensive. The modular approach examines the minimal set of components necessary for this architecture to operate. The current design uses about 12% of the FPGA logic elements, 22% of block memory bits and 12% of pins. This platform is capable of hosting a much larger architecture. Also, the modular approach allows us to implement this platform even on the low scale platform, making it more accessible. This also means that the architecture can be scaled down on for low power and low cost applications (e.g., industrial IoT). Deterministic computing in IoT is a major challenge and the time-triggered nature of the presented architecture provides a perfect basis for integration with time-sensitive networks (TSN).

The modular approach in a design process of HTTSoC is a way to explore the optimal design process in CPS where an application can be modeled from the physical environment and computer hardware, system software and application software. The goal of mixed-critical integration is optimal performance, energy consumption and functionality. The FPGA was created with the purpose of having customized hardware for specific applications, however design process is more challenging than the process of writing software for a generic off-the-shelf computer architecture. The described architecture aspires towards this objective of hardware that can be programmed using established programming techniques and still be able to optimize performance and other system properties according to the requirements of a specific application.

The tool integration is still behind this objective and interoperability needs to be improved in order to allow the integration seamless hardware, software and user tasks and functions.

4. DISCUSSION

This article reflects on the problem of mixed-criticality integration in the CPS, the challenges that are met upon the development of each part of a CPS. From the historical overview of the computer systems and cyber-physical systems in Section 1.2 can be concluded that the integration question dominated throughout all stages of development. Integration is the act or process or an instance of integrating as incorporation as equals into society or an organization of individuals of different groups (as races) (Merriam-Webster, 2016). In the scope of CPS the integration depending on the segment where it is applied e.g., integration between physical system and computer system, integration between hardware and software, or integration between different tasks of an application, an integration of all these segments together. The mixed-criticality integration refers to the incorporation of functional units with different priority levels in relation to a specific system property (e.g., safety, security, real-time). A safety critical system must ensure that all parts of the system are safety proficient, what can be a major overcompensation and extremely inefficient (El Salloum, et. al., 2013). The consumer electronics value user experience as a top priority and this is why the focus is strongly oriented on performance and usability. An average personal computer really reaches the maximum of its abilities; however, it is evaluated on these extremes. The idea of mixed-critical integration also involves partial validation or certification of the system, meaning that only individual components need to be verified for a specific property and their level of criticality.

The performance is a challenge that arises from the current switch in processor technology, in particular single-core processors era is ending and manufacturers are slowly abandoning the production of single-core processors in favor of multi-core CPUs. However, multi-core processors provide insufficient support for safety critical or mixed-critical applications. A TTNoC architecture implemented on a hybrid SoC platform combines hard-coded CPU with a cluster of μComponents based on soft-core CPUs located on an FPGA device in a deterministic fashion without major loss in performance. Moreover, it creates more space for optimization as better utilization of resources. New generations of FPGA devices provide are able to implement extremely fast custom hardware solutions, but also soft-coded micro-controllers more than capable of sustaining state-of-the-art applications. If considered that the processor frequency of embedded architectures which are mostly a subset of cyber-physical systems are averaging around 500 MHz (UBM tech., 2013), it is evident that current hybrid SoC are capable of providing the same service. The next generation of hybrid devices are increasing their performance between 50%-100% (Altera, 2016), it can be concluded that the future platforms would be more than capable of leading mixed-criticality migration.

A system optimization considers multiple measures to create more efficient and stable system. In the concept of the HTTSoC optimization is considered in multiple steps:

- Considering a modular approach as a way to offer sandbox architecture which can be molded on a specific application starting from hardware.
- An integration of design tools, such that mixed-criticality is supported by default and designs optimized transparently.
- Each component can be adapted or replaced with a more effective hardware solution. As the TTNoC generic interfaces can be easily coupled with heterogeneous components.

Having a fully deterministic hardware architecture is currently unreachable, but their numbers of ways to ensure that applications perform deterministically. The communication infrastructure can be deterministic and the TTNoC used in HTTSoC is an excellent example. This means that each information that enters the interface of TTNoC is transmitted in a deterministic fashion, even if the component behind is not. The absence of information is also an information in deterministic networks and can be used to detect faults. As am overcompensation is the main method to achieve determinism on a CPU level, having number of smaller but independent units can achieve the same and even better effect.

The classification of systems is a problem beyond hardware and must be addressed on a larger scale. It is a crucial part of an overall system optimization and a seamless tool interoperability. Having a distributed network of computers with low latency communication on a single platform enables easier segregation of applications according their corresponding sets of functional properties. It is a process that starts with collecting requirements and stretches throughout the design process of each system.

Having an accurate image of a system, *a model*, is pivotal in the design process of CPS. There are examples like the architecture described in (Schuster, Meyer, Buchty, Fossati, & Berekovic, 2014) where a hardware architecture can be modeled in a virtual environment and almost fully evaluated. Such architecture is portable to FPGA design and can be implemented on hybrid SoC platforms. Although, it was not explored the idea of creating a virtual model of HTTSoC has been considered as a part of the tool chain. It would serve as a prototyping platform, the task that was exclusively reserved for early FPGA devices.

The HTTSoC architecture, together with ACROSS MPSoC, fully support the concept of mixed-criticality integration and explores other properties which would improve the design and implementation process of CPS in general. It strongly enforces spatial and temporal isolation which represent a cornerstone for mixed-criticality integration and safety applications.

4.1 Use Case Analysis

The following section provides a short analysis of applications where architecture i.e., HTTSoC might be an advantage. The analysis is concentrating on automotive domain as a one of the largest groups of CPSs. The automotive industry is an industrial with the highest number of manufactured units annually, approximately 90 million units in 2015 (OICA, 2015). The number of ECUs in a car averages between 50 and 100 ECUs depending on the size and a class of the car (Johnson, Gannamaraju, & Fischmeister, 2015). The trends show that a number of functions in a car increases with every generation. The applications like ADAS, car-2-car communication or car-2-OEM communication are becoming a part of the standard car package. The complexity of these new function requires a significant increase in computing power and increase in a number of ECUs. Without merging functionalities, the costs in energy, weight, and fuel economics would surpass benefits. The architectures like HTTSoC and ACROSS MPSoC provide a solution for integrating multiple function new functions and optimize existing functions in a vehicle. The approach not only provides a platform for integration of mixed-critical integration and implementation of safety-critical application, but also offers a way to reduce power consumption and weight of a car. This could significantly improve fuel economy in a car. A number of communication channels and cables in a car puts significant overhead on the energy consumption and weight. Use of HTTSoC or ACROSS MPSoC enables virtualization of communication channels, like CAN lines that reduces the number of physical devices in the car (Wasicek, Höftberger, Elshuber, Isakovic, & Fleck, 2014).

Another major challenge in a car industry is security, the performance of a car and other safety related aspects are tightly connected with other non-essential systems in a vehicle. Also, it is crucial that only verified replacement parts can be installed in a car. Use of TTNoC reduces number of physical connections of the system, this a significant feature as even non-essential channels can be source of security vulnerabilities. *Security* as a property is supported by design in HTTSoC and ACROSS and with few additional features can be transformed in a secure platform, fully transparent to the end user (Isakovic & Wasicek, 2013).

5. FUTURE DIRECTIONS

As stated earlier in the text implementation of hardware without support of software and design tools leaves more space for design faults. Full tool interoperability that captures a design process of a CPS from a requirement phase to deployment is a future objective. The tool chain for the development of hardware and software in the described architectures is a rather complex structure. This could be simplified with a couple of bridges in the configuration scheme.

Another goal is to fully use heterogeneous design capabilities and integrate other types of cores, a typical example is Leon 3 SPARC processor from Geisler (Geisler, 2016). It has a fault-tolerant configuration and it is highly utilized in the space domain. Integrating this process would open the door for the architecture in space related applications.

To increase the spectrum of applications the architecture needs to be expanded on different hybrid SoC platforms, e.g., Xilinx Zynq. It is a more common platform, with the capability of high level synthesis, which can be used to integrate the design process better and to implement software functions as TTNoC components.

The next generation of hybrid SoCs provides ability to perform a partial dynamic reconfiguration of FPGA fabric. This can be used as a tool to increase resilience of a system, or to enhance the system during runtime. The goal is to explore these capabilities within the presented architecture and provide tool integration for the application development process.

6. CONCLUSION

The number of functions in modern CPS (e.g., motor vehicles) is increasing with each new generation and the way to accommodate the necessary increase in computing power is to merge multiple applications on a single power and reduce the physical footprint of computer hardware in a system. To accomplish this objective a number of obstacles need to be overcome. The performance of the hardware architecture needs to match the requirements of the increasing number of applications and the complexity of applications. The hardware ensures deterministic behavior in order to ensure spatial and temporal isolations of individual applications. The shift from single-core to multi-core architectures created a vacuum in for safety critical systems, as COTS multi-core architectures provide insufficient guarantees for safety critical applications. The safety regulations impose the rule that a system must ensure the safety integrity level of the application with highest safety integrity level. For multi-core architectures with symmetric multiprocessing this increases problem of mixed-criticality integration even further. The qualification and classification of applications according to their functional requirements is necessary to avoid over-compensations during design and implementation process.

The HTTSoC and ACROSS MPSoC provide a viable solution for mixed-criticality integration and a number of ways to face the above stated challenges head on. The introduction of hybrid SoC platforms provided a sandbox environment for the design of hardware architectures that match COTS hardware in terms of performance and outran them in terms of efficiency. It solves some fundamental problems, however there are still more detailed challenges, like tool integration and modular design process that would ensure the full sandbox experience for users and still preserve fundamental properties necessary for mixed-critical and safety-critical applications.

ACKNOWLEDGMENT

The research presented in the article is a product of two major research initiatives from the ARTEMIS Joint Undertaking (JU), in particular projects ACROSS (N° 2009-1-100208) and EMC2 (N° 621429). Also, this work has been supported by the company TTTech a long-term partner of Vienna University of Technology.

REFERENCES

Ampère, A. M. (1838). *Essai sur la philosophie des sciences*. Paris: Bachelier.

Asada, H., Kanade, T., & Takeyama, I. (1983). Control of a Direct-Drive Arm. *Journal of Dynamic Systems, Measurement, and Control, 105*(3), 136–142. doi:10.1115/1.3140645

BBC. (24. 10 2012). *BBC Ceefax, the world's first teletext service, has completed its final broadcast after 38 years on air*. Retrieved from http://www.bbc.com/news/uk-20032882

Blomstedt, F. (2014). The arrowhead approach for SOA application development and documentation. In *Proceedings of the IECON 2014 - 40th Annual Conference of the IEEE Industrial Electronics Society*, Dallas (pp. 2631-2637). IEEE.

Bowen, J., & Stavridou, V. (1993). Safety-critical systems, formal methods and standards. *Software Engineering Journal, 8*(4), 189–209. doi:10.1049/sej.1993.0025

Carter, W. S. (1994). The future of programmable logic and its impact on digital system design. In *Proceedings of the IEEE International Conference on Computer Design: VLSI in Computers and Processors* (pp. 10-16). Cambridge: IEEE. doi:10.1109/ICCD.1994.331842

DEC. (1967). *The digital small computer handbook.* Digital equipment corp.

El Salloum, C., Elshuber, M., Höftberger, O., Isakovic, H., & Wasicek, A. (2013). The ACROSS MPSoC - A new generation of multi-core processors designed for safety-critical embedded systems. *Microprocess. Microsyst., 37*, 0141-9331.

Geisler. (2016). *Leon 3 SPARC.* Von Geisler: http://www.gaisler.com/index.php/products/processors/leon3?task=view&id=13

Grimwood, J. M. B. C. (1969). Project Gemini; Technology and Operations. Washington, D.C.: G.P.O.

Horta, E. L., Lockwood, J. W., Taylor, D. E., & Parlour, D. (2002). Dynamic hardware plugins in an FPGA with partial run-time reconfiguration. In *Proceedings of the Design Automation Conference* (pp. 343-348). IEEE.

IEEE. (20. 11 2016). *Official timeline of 802.11 development.* Retrieved from http://grouper.ieee.org/groups/802/11/Reports/802.11_Timelines.htm

Isakovic, H., & Grosu, R. (2016). A heterogeneous time-triggered architecture on a hybrid system-on-a-chip platform. In *Proceedings of the 25th International Symposium on Industrial Electronics (ISIE), Santa Clara* (pp. 244-253). IEEE. doi:10.1109/ISIE.2016.7744897

Isakovic, H., & Wasicek, A. (2013). Secure channels in an integrated MPSoC architecture. In *Proceedings of the 39th Annual Conference of the IEEE Industrial Electronics Society, Vienna* (pp. 4488-4493). IEEE. doi:10.1109/IECON.2013.6699858

Johnson, T. T., Gannamaraju, R., & Fischmeister, S. (2015). A Survey of Electrical and Electronic (E/E) Notifications for Motor Vehicles. In *Proceedings of the 24th International Technical Conference on the Enhanced Safety of Vehicles (ESV), Gothenburg* (pp. 1-15).

Johnson, T. T., Gannamaraju, R., & Fischmeister, S. (2015). A SURVEY OF ELECTRICAL AND ELECTRONIC (E/E) NOTIFICATIONS FOR MOTOR VEHICLES. *24th International Technical Conference on the Enhanced Safety of Vehicles (ESV), Gothenburg* (pp. 1-15).

Kernighan, B., & Ritchie, D. (1978). *The C Programming Language* (1st ed.). Prentice-Hall.

Kopetz, H., Damm, A., Koza, C., Mulazzani, M., Schwabl, W., Senft, C., & Zainlinger, R. (1989). Distributed fault-tolerant real-time systems: The Mars approach. *IEEE Micro, 9*(1), 25–40. doi:10.1109/40.16792

McFarland, M. C., Parker, A. C., & Camposano, R. (1990). The high-level synthesis of digital systems. In *Proceedings of the IEEE* (pp. 301-318). IEEE.

Merriam-Webster. (2016). *Merriam-Webster Dictionary.* Von Merriam-Webster: https://www.merriam-webster.com/ abgerufen

NASA. (2016). *Computers in Spaceflight: The NASA Experience.* Retrieved from http://history.nasa.gov/computers/contents.html

NIST. (1995). *An Introduction to Computer Security: The NIST Handbook.*

Nof, S. Y. (1999). *Handbook of Industrial Robotics* (Vol. 1). John Wiley & Sons. doi:10.1002/9780470172506

O'Regan, G. (2012). *A Brief History of Computing*. London: Springer Science & Business Media. doi:10.1007/978-1-4471-2359-0

OICA. (2015). *Production Statistics for Motor Vehicels*. Retrieved from http://www.oica.net/category/production-statistics/2014-statistics/

Ross, D. T. (1978). Origins of the APT language for automatically programmed tools. In R. L. Wexelblat (Ed.), *In History of programming languages I* (pp. 279–338). New York: ACM. doi:10.1145/960118.808374

Rushby, J. (1994). Critical System Properties:Survey and Taxonomy. *Reliability Engineering & System Safety*, *43*(2), 189–219. doi:10.1016/0951-8320(94)90065-5

Schuster, T., Meyer, R., Buchty, R., Fossati, L., & Berekovic, M. (2014). SoCRocket - A virtual platform for the European Space Agency's SoC development. In *Proceedings of the 9th International Symposium on Reconfigurable and Communication-Centric Systems-on-Chip (ReCoSoC)*, Montpellier (pp. 1-7). IEEE. doi:10.1109/ReCoSoC.2014.6860690

Studer, R., Benjamins, R. V., & Fensel, D. (1998). Knowledge engineering: Principles and methods. *Data & Knowledge Engineering*, *25*(1-2), 161–197. doi:10.1016/S0169-023X(97)00056-6

The World Bank Group. (2016). *Mobile cellular subscriptions (per 100 people)*. Retrieved from http://data.worldbank.org/indicator/IT.CEL.SETS.P2?end=2003&start=1984&view=chart

Trimberger, S. (2012). *Field-Programmable Gate Array Technology*. Springer, US.

UBM tech. (2013). *Embedded Market Survey*. UBM.

US Census Bureau. (02 2010). *Computer and Internet Use in the United States: 1984 to 2009*. Retrieved from http://www.census.gov/data/tables/time-series/demo/computer-internet/computer-use-1984-2009.html

Vinoski, S. (1993). *Distributed Object Computing with Corba 1.0 Introduction*.

Wasicek, A., Höftberger, O., Elshuber, M., Isakovic, H., & Fleck, A. (2014). Virtual CAN Lines in an Integrated MPSoC Architecture. In *Proceedings of the 17th International Symposium on Object/Component/Service-Oriented Real-Time Distributed Computing*, Reno (S. 158-165). IEEE. doi:10.1109/ISORC.2014.34

Wiener, N. (1961). *Cybernetics Or Control and Communication in the Animal and the Machine*. MIT Press. doi:10.1037/13140-000

Wirth, N. (1971). The programming language pascal. *Acta Informatica*, *1*(1), 35–63. doi:10.1007/BF00264291

KEY TERMS AND DEFINITIONS

ASIC: Application specific integrated circuit.
ECU: Electronic Control Unit.
HTTSoC: Heterogeneous Time-Triggered SoC.
Mixed-Criticality: A system with multiple tasks of different property requirements.
MPSoC: Multiple processor System-on-a-chip.
SoC: System-on-a-chip.
TRM: Trusted Resource Manager.
TTNoC: Time-triggered network-on-a-chip.

Chapter 8
Generation and Verification of a Safety–Aware Virtual Prototype in the Automotive Domain

Ralph Weissnegger
CISC Semiconductor GmbH, Austria

Martin Schachner
Graz University of Technology, Austria

Markus Pistauer
CISC Semiconductor GmbH, Austria

Christian Kreiner
Graz University of Technology, Austria

Kay Römer
Graz University of Technology, Austria

Christian Steger
Graz University of Technology, Austria

ABSTRACT

The electrification of today's vehicles and the high number of new assistance features imply more and more complex systems. New challenges are arising through heterogeneous and distributed systems which interact with each other and have an impact on the physical world, so-called cyber-physical systems. The sensing and controlling of these systems is the work of the highly distributed electronic control units and it is no surprise that more than 100 of these microcontrollers are currently integrated in a modern (electric) car. Technological, organizational and design gaps in today's development flows are not covered by current methods and tools. Therefore, new approaches are essential to support the development process and to reduce costs and time-to-market, especially when systems are safety-critical and demand reliability. Through applying reliability analysis and simulation-based verification methods on the proposed model-based design flow, we are able to reduce the number of tools involved and achieve correctness, completeness and consistency of the entire system.

DOI: 10.4018/978-1-5225-2845-6.ch008

INTRODUCTION

In the world of today, the number of embedded electrical/electronic (E/E) systems used in many different domains is increasing greatly. When we review the complexity issue over the past years, it is plain that new applications have now emerged in which systems not only interact with each other but also have impact on the physical world. These systems are known as cyber-physical systems. Depending on their application, they must fulfill different requirements such as timing constraints, performance behavior, low power consumption and cope with thermal or even different environmental conditions. The point at issue here is, we live in a world where cyber physical systems are ubiquitous, they have a direct impact on our daily life and it is imperative that we must assure the dependability of these systems.

This is nowhere more clearly apparent than in the automotive domain. We are witnessing a shift to towards fully E/E systems resulting from the trend to electric vehicles. In fact, a car has now become more or less a smartphone on wheels. The sensing and controlling is the work of the highly distributed electronic control units (ECU) and it is no surprise that all these new features mean more than 100 microcontrollers (Charette, 2009) are currently integrated in a modern car and can require up to 150 million lines of code (FORD GT - Lines of code, 2016). The communication between these systems has now extended far across the internal borders of a car. When complex assistance features are in use, cars now need to communicate with each other (Car2Car) and the infrastructure must also be involved in the computation (Car2X). The goal in the development of a car has remained the same as ever: to develop better, more reliable and safer products to reduce the number of deadly accidents. But the industry is facing new problems through the emergence of many new (assistance) features that are also influencing each other. This in turn raises the complexity level in the design, development and verification of complex systems and imposes a task of enormous dimensions on the engineers who develop the applications.

In terms of safety, these systems must fulfill standards such as the ISO26262 (functional safety for road vehicles), (ISO, Road vehicles - Functional safety, 2011). Since this standard is now treated as state of the art in court, OEMs and their suppliers are required to develop and test their systems directed specifically to the recommended measures and methods. Moreover, it is no longer sufficient to test single hardware or software components, the functionality of the entire system must be given.

Whenever the design of a system is in discussion, one modeling language always comes to mind, the Unified Modeling Language (UML), (Group, 2015). Having the routes in the software domain, UML paved the way and established model-based thinking in various engineering domains and far across the borders of conventional software design. Engineers from different domains can use the full potential of an object-oriented approach here, since UML comes with several extensions such as MARTE (The UML Profile for MARTE: Modeling and Analysis of Real-Time and Embedded Systems, 2015), SysML (Omg, 2015) or EAST-ADL (EAST-ADL Association, 2014). MARTE was introduced to overcome the enormous complexity issues in the design of real-time and embedded systems. It provides capabilities to model hardware, software and also system design and provides the representation of timing, resource and performance behavior. Furthermore, UML/MARTE is already in use for several reliability analysis techniques. In addition, many semiconductor companies and suppliers are relying on this modeling language and it is used by several European projects such as the OpenES (Catrene, 2016). OpenES is a European initiative to fill the gaps in today's design flows and to develop common solutions to stay competitive on the global market.

Since a modern car o today no longer exists in one single version, but rather in several hundreds of variants all with different features, each of them must be exhaustively tested to fulfill the standards. Millions of test kilometers must be driven (Maurer, Gerdes, Lenz, & Winner, 2015) to ensure the reliability of a car and it is not economic or safe to test them in a real environment. Simulation plays an ever increasing and more important role in the verification of the modern car, because of its advantage to easily vary the virtual environment and also to represent the car in different variations and it is also economical. These tests can be monitored and reproduced every time. Another advantage of simulation is that it can be run not only day and night, but also massively in parallel. A specification and simulation language, which shares the same philosophy as the UML/MARTE approach, is SystemC (SystemC- Accellera Systems Initiative, 2016). Like UML, it shares the MDA (Model Driven Architecture) approach, starting from a computational independent system design, down to hardware and software design.

The overall structure of this chapter is presented in Figure 1. It shows an industrial V-model with safety extensions as it is specified in the functional safety standard ISO26262. The contributions to this chapter are listed as numbers in this V-model. Contribution 1 to 4 handle the existing process from an early system specification down to the hardware evaluation regarding safety constraints. Contribution to 5 build on these contributions, to generate a first virtual prototype of a safety-critical hardware. Furthermore, we discuss state of the art approaches of development processes in the automotive domain.

The Contribution to number 1 will handle the entire design flow for safety-critical systems, based on the modeling language UML/MARTE. Furthermore, it will show how different analysis techniques can be applied on these models. Number 2 will focus on the seamless integration of simulation-based verification with UML/MARTE models within the design flow. An automatic testbench will verify the functional specification, based on automatic generated testbenches from safety requirements in contribution number 3. Contribution 4 will give insights into the evaluation of the hardware platform and how to perform tests to evaluate the reliability of the design. After the platform is correctly designed and

Figure 1. Industrial V-model including the listed contributions of this chapter
Adapted from (Weissnegger et al., 2016).

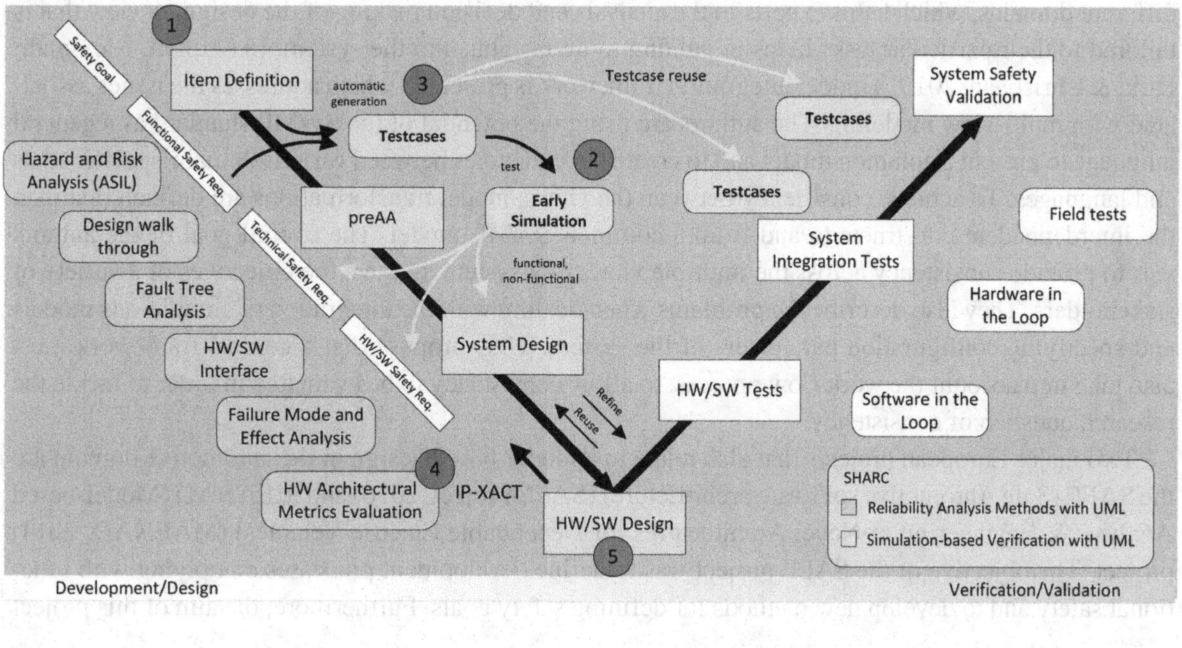

evaluated by the recommended ISO26262 methods, this specification is used to automatically generate a first virtual prototype (Contribution 5), which is reapplied to the functional specification to guarantee consistency, correctness and completeness with the overall system design and specified functionality.

RELATED WORK

The effort and the costs involved in today's development of cyber-physical systems are enormous. This not only includes the engineering effort, but also the tools involved in the whole process. In the automotive domain of today, there is no single approach that unites the design and verification tools in one single environment and which can also be used throughout the whole development process. In current development processes several different tools are used such as Matlab Simulink (MathWorks, 2017) for the functional specification, Rational Doors (IBM, 2017) for requirements specification, document-centric approaches such as Excel for failure mode and effect analysis (FMEA), hardware architectural metrics, hardware software interface or even the entire design, furthermore Maggilem (Magillem, 2017) for traceability and Mentor (Mentor, 2017) /Candence (Candence, 2017) for hardware simulation, to name only a few. For each of these steps, data from the design must be exhaustively exported to other tools and vice versa. System-wide and even cross-domain constraints, such as safety features must be exchanged between tools manually, which results in redundancy and inconsistency. Today's approaches lack proper design flow, a modeling language to communicate between different engineering and management teams and furthermore traceability between requirements, design, tests and results.

The MDE vision emphasizes to increase the abstraction level and automation through modeling. Thus, bringing advantages in reduced development costs, increased quality and reduction of maintenance costs (Alajrami, Gallina, & Romanovsky, 2016). Machine-executable models are essential in today's design flows, since companies are seeking for increased automation. Increased automation also means faster development and lower costs. Multi-view modeling is one approach to deal with complex embedded systems in the development process. There are often many different experts and tools involved, also from different domains, which helps experts in the analysis and decision making of the design. A view that is tailored to their particular tasks helps in gaining more insights into the system. In (Aditya, Alexsandr, Dirk, & Christiaan, 2010) a model integration framework is presented which addresses the issues associated with multi-view modeling. The authors are using the potential of the SysML standard as a general language to present a common model and to create dependencies between various domain-specific tools and languages. To achieve consistency between the views, model transformations are defined that map the interdependent constructs to and from a common SysML model. The overall goal of the authors was to provide consistency across the multiple views of a system, to meet the objectives of a variety of stakeholders. They also describe the problems when dealing with the integration of simulations models and specifying configuration parameters of the system. They propose that a general framework must also take into account the work flow process, to allow consistency to be evaluated in order to tackle the research question of consistency.

Two major European projects that also relate to a model-based design in the automotive domain are the SAFE (Safe Automotive soFtware architEcture) (SAFE Project, 2016) and MEANAD (Model-based Analysis & Engineering of Novel Architectures for Dependable Electric Vehicles) (MAENAD, 2014) project. The objective of the SAFE project was to define development processes complying with functional safety and to develop new methods for defining safety goals. Furthermore, the aim of this project was to improve dependability from vehicle to component and the early evaluation of safety architecture. In the course of the project, this has been achieved by defining a meta-model for a model-based safety analysis, which is based on existing technologies (ReqIF, EAST-ADL and AUTOSAR). Furthermore, they defined a toolset to capture requirements, modeling, safety analysis based on formal models and to support automated safety analysis to reduce the manual effort. Within the scope of the Fully Electric Vehicle (FEV) and to bring the engineering of FEV to a next level, the MAENAD project extended the EAST-ADL2 standard with advanced capabilities to facilitate development of dependable, efficient and affordable products. The three goals of this projects were to support the ISO26262 safety standard and to support automatic allocation of safety requirements to components of an evolving architecture. An effective model-based prediction of quality attributes of FEV (dependability, performance). Moreover, automated exploration of huge design spaces to achieve an optimal trade-off between dependability, performance and costs. By using a common modeling language in the project, they achieved a shared understanding of engineering information across different departments and companies, the exchange of engineering models between different organizations and joint progress on tools and methodologies for modeling, analysis and synthesis. In addition, the MAENAD project proposes to use an overall design methodology for FEV development.

In (Murillo, Mura, & Prevostini, 2009), the authors build on the work of (Murillo, Mura, & Prevostini, 2010) Gaspard2 and presented a semi-automated design flow where HW/SW Codesign and the MDE methodologies are merged and exploited to enable a fast design process. The aim of the authors was to help and design complex real-time embedded systems, by allocation and binding within design space exploration, schedulability analysis, HW/SW portioning and estimation techniques. To achieve these goals they agreed on using UML profiles such was SysML and MARTE. By using the Computational Independent Model (CIM), Platform Independent Model (PIM), Platform Specific Model (PSM) approach and model to model transformation, they described their system at different levels of abstraction, until sufficient details had been added. At the end of the design process, including structural and behavioral models, they generated the corresponding SystemC executable models for simulation and verification. Nevertheless, none of these approaches is taking safety into account in their design processes.

How to develop hardware according to functional safety and the ISO 26262 is described in (Seo-Hyun, Jin-Hee, Yangjae, Sachoun, & Tae-Man, 2011) and (Yung-chang, Li-ren, Hsing-chuang, Chih-jen, & Ching-te, 2014). In this papers, the quantitative hardware architecture of an automotive safety microprocessor is evaluated. The data for the diagnostic coverage of the hardware components comes from a commercial EDA environment and no evidence is given about correctness. Neither of the two approaches takes modeling approaches into account nor do they recommend safety mechanisms to improve their use cases. Furthermore, they do not use tools to support their methodology.

BACKGROUND

Functional Safety

The ISO 26262 is the functional safety standard for safety-critical systems in road vehicles. The standard addresses possible hazards caused by malfunctioning behavior of safety-related systems. It also provides an automotive safety life cycle that covers safety aspects throughout the whole design and development process of modern products and systems. In the first phase, the concept phase (Part 3), the item is defined. The item definition describes the boundaries and interfaces as well as assumptions about systems or array of systems, to which functional safety is applied. After performing a hazard and risk analysis on the item to identify and categorize the hazards, the safety goals are derived and the corresponding Automotive Safety Integrity Levels (ASIL) are determined. The ASIL levels (Table 1) specify the item's essential safety requirements to avoid unreasonable risk due to malfunction. The ASIL is determined by 3 impact factors: severity (S0-S3), probability (E0-E4) and controllability (C0-C3). This results in four ASIL levels (A to D), where ASIL A is the lowest and ASIL D the highest level. The class quality management (QM) denotes no safety requirements to comply with ISO 26262.

After determination, the product is developed using the recommended methods and measures according to its ASIL. The derived functional safety concept contains safety measures, including the safety mechanisms to be implemented in the item's architectural elements and are specified in the functional safety requirements. After defining the functional safety requirements, the technical requirements, including hardware and software requirements, are derived. This in turn results in a safety case, to show that the system is acceptably safe. The safety case is used to collect and present evidence, to support safety claims and arguments.

Functional Coverage

Functional coverage is defined as a metric which is used to determine the completeness and verification progress of a design. It emphasizes design verification where the focus, besides functional verification, is also on non-functional aspects such as safety, timing or power. Functional coverage tells us about the quality of a testbench and what portion of the design has been activated and tested during the simulation run (controllability). On the other hand, observability shows the ability to observe effects of the simulation (white-box vs. black-box testing). Thus, this metric allows us to answer the crucial question in the verification process "Are we done, yet?". Through coverage metrics we are able to adjust our tests

Table 1. ASIL classification according to ISO26262

Severity Class	Probability Class	Controllability Class		
		C1	C2	C3
S1	E1	QM	QM	QM
	E2	QM	QM	QM
	E3	QM	QM	ASIL A
	E4	QM	ASIL A	ASIL B
S2	E1	QM	QM	QM
	E2	QM	QM	ASIL A
	E3	QM	ASIL A	ASIL B
	E4	ASIL A	ASIL B	ASIL C
S3	E1	QM	QM	ASIL A
	E2	QM	ASIL A	ASIL B
	E3	ASIL A	ASIL B	ASIL C
	E4	ASIL B	ASIL C	ASIL D

and stimuli to optimize the verification. Moreover, it helps us to reduce debug time and to increase the correlation between specification, design and verification. Were all design features and requirements identified in the tests? Have there been any lines of code or structures in the design that have never been exercised? We can classify coverage (Academy, 2012) by the method of creation (implicit vs. explicit) and their origin of source (specification vs. implementation). Line coverage and expression coverage are two examples of an implicit coverage metric and can be automatically derived from the code, whereas functional coverage (explicit coverage metric) must be defined and implemented by the engineer, derived from the various requirements and the specification document. None of these metrics is sufficient to make a statement about the completeness of the system. As an example, we might achieve a 100% code coverage during our simulation runs, but still do not know if we verified 100% of our functionality. This is because coder coverage, does not measure the interaction and behavior between the systems, nor the temporal sequences of functional events. On the other hand, we might achieve 100% functional coverage but only 90% code coverage, because of an important feature missing in the testplan or specification, which never reaches the specific part of the code. A complete functional coverage can only be achieved if there are tests for all the features, which are indicated in the specification and which the engineer has thought of. Functional coverage distinguishes between two simulation methodologies, direct testing and constrained random verification, whereas the later one is able to achieve a higher distribution over the huge space of the available input stimuli. This mechanism increases the coverage and the ability to find corner cases in the design, by creating random tests, which not have been found by direct testing. The coverage space classified by an implicit specification (also known as intelligent verification) is a current academic research area, where the coverage metrics are automatically extracted by a tool and are derived from the design specification. These higher-level functional behaviors cannot be automatically derived from the implementation alone and also need the information from the specification.

EXAMPLE CASE STUDY: BATTERY MANAGEMENT SYSTEM

Throughout this chapter, we will demonstrate our methodologies on a relevant problem in today's automotive domain, a battery management system for Li-ion powered electrical vehicles. This industrial use case was provided by CISC Semiconductor GmbH (CISC Semiconductor GmbH, 2017), based in Austria and the United States. This use case will help to more fully illustrate the innovative capabilities and benefits of our approach. As more and more vehicles are now powered by Li-ion batteries, the challenge for engineers to ensure reliability and fault tolerance is also greatly increasing. Crucial for ensuring safe operating conditions is to have the battery management systems (BMS) measure voltage, temperature and current of the battery very precisely. This information must be forwarded to a vehicle-wide controller network to ensure a reliable and fully utilized system. Problems with overheating or even explosions have been frequent in the past. The main cause of these problems was an excessively high energy intake from regenerative braking or harsh environmental conditions. Management systems and mechanisms are thus essential to assure that persons are not put at risk and that no damage is caused.

The overall system of the eVehicle is depicted in Figure 2. For reasons of simplification, we only consider the major components of the electric vehicle, for the analysis of the battery and the BMS. This includes the battery pack on Li-ion technology, the BMS which measures voltage and temperature of the battery, an inverter ECU to switch between 240V high-voltage and 12V peripheral power supply, a controller and the electric motor model. Two main factors influence the behavior of the eVehicle. The

Figure 2. Overall system level description of the electric vehicle use case

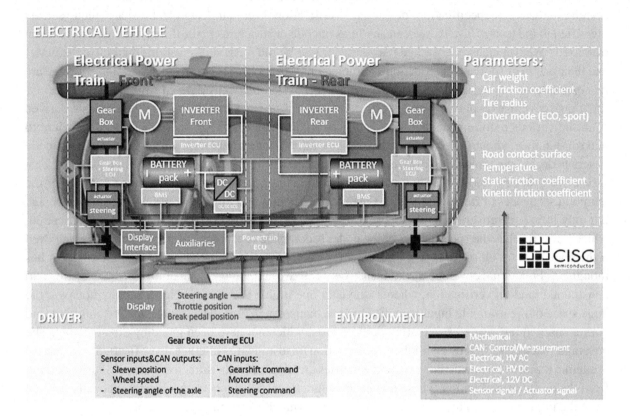

driver provides the desired speed (rounds per minutes) and on the other hand, the load of the motor shaft. These stimuli can be set according to standardized maneuvers such as the New European Drive Cycle (NEDC) or the newer standard called worldwide harmonized light-duty vehicles test procedure (WLTP), which will be introduced in 2017. The controller is a model for a PI state-space controller and maintains a constant speed based on the information about the state variables, motor armature current and motor-speed. The inverter model implements an inverter function for a PM-DC motor driving stage. It compares the actual battery voltage and the requested controller voltage to maintain the PM-DC motor terminal voltage. The battery model simulates the behavior of a Li-ion battery pack composed of a defined set of single cell Li-ion batteries. The appropriate number of single cells is connected in parallel and series to obtain the necessary capacity, maximum current and terminal voltage. The battery pack's terminal voltage is calculated based on the defined parameter and the battery current. A BMS is connected to the battery to measure voltage, current and temperature of the cells/modules. The BMS computes the state of charge (SOC), State-Of-Health (SOH) and is responsible for cell balancing, cell protection and demand management of the battery. These computed values are processed via a CAN controller as digital values to the power train controller. In addition, the external load environmental conditions such as temperature can be changed during the simulation.

The battery model is a central component of the electric vehicle. It's a detailed model of a Li-ion battery pack and a BMS, which computes internally the new state of charge based on the last one for each timestep. Changes in temperature are also calculated. The temperature can subsequently be used to calculate the module voltage, taking the current state of charge into account. Battery' reliability is of crucial importance in a vehicle and avoids harmful effects for the occupants in case of a failure. In order to guarantee safety, BMS are used, to control and monitor the behavior of the battery throughout the entire life cycle of a battery.

UML/MARTE DESIGN FLOW: FROM SYSTEM TO HARDWARE AND SOFTWARE DESIGN

Model-based design is playing an ever-increasing role in development today in dealing with complex embedded systems. The organization of specialized people in projects of a certain size requires of the input of great effort. It is thus becoming increasingly important to ensure that stakeholders from different domains, e.g. hardware software, system design but also safety and security engineers can work efficiently and effectively together. Particularly in the verification of safety-critical systems, safety managers and specialists need an entire view of the system that includes all the domains involved. A model-based approach thus helps safety managers to understand problems from the engineering perspective and that for their part the design and verification engineers can understand problems in the context of functional safety. In addition, it also helps to cope with the huge volume of requirements that must now be dealt with.

UML is a model-based language which has its roots in the software domain. It is a modeling standard of the OMG (Object Management Group) (Object Management Group (OMG), 2015) and is a graphical representation for specification and documentation of software and other systems. It delivers a complete view of the system, its individual components and the interaction between them. UML has different types of structural (e.g. Class, Component, Composite Structure) and behavioral (e.g. Activity, UseCase, State Machine) diagrams. Since the source of UML is software engineering, it implements an object-oriented approach, which also helps the process of thinking about virtual objects which corresponds to concrete ones in the real world. Although this language is well suited for developing software, it provides no capabilities to design hardware and non-functional properties.

An additional extension to UML is SysML (Omg, 2015) as domain-specific modeling language. It uses a subset of UML2 and provides additional extensions to describe complex systems in system engineering. SysML supports UML2 by two additional diagrams (requirements, parametric) for requirements-engineering and performance-analysis. It provides a good mechanism for allocating requirements to components or behavioral diagrams, but is inaccurate in modeling hardware and resources.

To overcome the shortcoming of defining hardware platforms in UML and SysML, an extension to UML2 was defined, which provides capabilities to model hardware and software, as well as timing, resource and performance behavior of real-time and embedded systems. This modeling language is called MARTE (The UML Profile for MARTE: Modeling and Analysis of Real-Time and Embedded Systems, 2015), (Selić & Gérard, 2014) which follows the philosophy of cyber-physical systems for dealing with entire systems rather a set of specialized parts. Furthermore, it has established itself in the embedded system domain.

MARTE is defined as a profile in UML2 and provides additional mechanisms for modeling real-time systems, which are missing in UML. Thanks to the UML extension mechanism, the software resource model (SRM) and hardware resource model (HRM) profiles extend UML2 with concepts for software and hardware. The purpose of the SRM packages is to design software of real-time and embedded applications. It consists of the SW_ResourceCore which provides the basic software resource concept. The

HRM is an extension to UML and serves as a description for existing and the conception of new hardware platforms. These descriptions can be made at different levels of granularity. HRM groups most hardware concepts under a hierarchical taxonomy. It is composed of a logical view (HwLogical) that classifies hardware resources depending on their functional behavior and a physical view (HwPhysical) that focus on their physical nature. The HWLogical model provides a classification for different hardware entities such as computing, storage or communication. This includes stereotypes like HwASIC, HwProcessor, HwBus, HwDevice or HwMemory. All the stereotypes defined in the HRM package are organized under a tree of inheritances from more generic stereotypes. This has the advantage, that if no stereotype matches a used hardware component, a more generic stereotype may fit instead. As an example, a HwSensor inherits the properties from HwI/O, and is furthermore a specialization of Hw_Device. In contrast, the HWPhysical package contains stereotypes as physical components. They describe their shape, size, and position within the platform, power consumption or other physical properties.

In addition to these concepts it is possible to allocate software applications to hardware resources with the help of the MARTE allocation mechanism. This is particularly important for schedulability analysis and real-time applications but also multi-core applications. For the modeling of systems on a higher level of abstraction (system level), MARTE provides capabilities with the general resource models (GRM). These models can be used for components, where no early assumptions about implementation in hardware or software can be made. The stereotypes offer concepts to model general platforms for executing real-time embedded applications. This includes the modeling of both hardware and software. With this package, it is possible to model complete systems on a very high abstraction-level. This helps us to model systems very early in the design process, when design choices are still undecided. These models can then be refined in a later step of the design process. The GRM package includes different resource types, representing a physically or logically persistent entity e.g. ComputingResource or StorageResource. These Resources offer services to perform the expected tasks.

A stereotype which helps to simplify the modeling in a component-based approach is GCM (General Component Models). It brings the advantage of describing parts with information about incoming (in), outgoing (out) or bidirectional (inout) communication of the different subsystems. These FlowPorts have been introduced in MARTE to enable a flow-oriented communication paradigm between components.

In addition, UML, has the benefit that this standard is supported by various commercial and open-source tools. We emphasize this implementation using the UML Eclipse editor, "Papyrus" (Eclipse, 2015). This tool already provides the designer with UML extensions such as MARTE, SysML or EAST-ADL. Another advantage of Eclipse is the plugin mechanism, which eases the development of extension for the UML editor.

Modeling languages such as MARTE help to describe the properties of real-time systems and this is especially important in the automotive domain where timing and performance are crucial. To cover also important properties from the functional safety aspect, the authors of (Weissnegger, Kreiner, Pistauer, Römer, & Steger, 2015) showed how to design safety-critical system throughout the design phase of the functional safety standard ISO26262 based on UML/MARTE. In this work, they showed how to map the model driven architecture approach (MDA) of UML to the design phases of the functional safety standard. For this, a refined MDA was defined to extend the standard by an additional level, since they were not adequately specified and lacked a formal definition. These four levels of detail called computation independent model (CIM), platform independent model (PIM), refined PIM and platform specific model (PSM) represent all major design phases of the functional safety standard such as item definition (Figure 3), preliminary architectural assumptions, system design, down to hardware and software design.

Figure 3. Definition of the item on CIM level, with functional models in the UML standard
Adapted from (Weissnegger, Kreiner, Pistauer, Römer, & Steger, 2015).

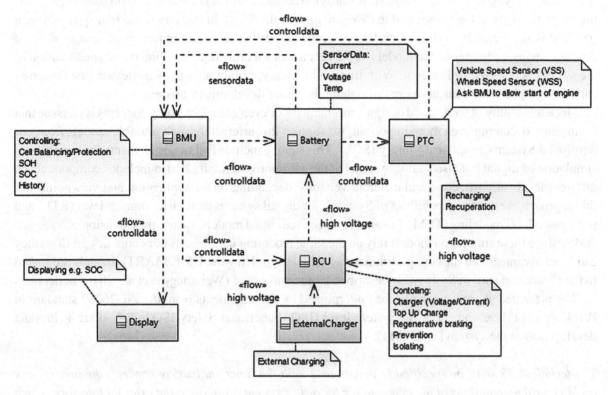

Through applying this approach to an industrial use case, they demonstrated how a safety-critical system can be designed and specified, but also how existing verification methods such as fault tree analysis (FTA), failure mode and effect analysis (FMEA), hardware software interface (HIS) can be applied on these structural and behavioral models. Furthermore, SysML was used in addition to MARTE to define safety requirements and to handle the issues with traceability. Using the link to MARTE components and behavioral diagrams they achieved a horizontal and vertical traceability as required by the ISO26262 standard.

EVALUATION OF THE DESIGN

Simulation-Based Verification

What makes the functional standard ISO26262 "functional", is the aspect that we analyze the function which shall be implemented on the whole system (in this case the item). This starts with a situation analysis and hazard and risk analysis with the help of the item definition. This requires the development of a system definition, including components, hardware (-parts) and software (-units). Based on the resulting ASIL level of the hazard and risk analysis, the safety goals lead to the functional safety concept, which includes the definition of the functional safety requirements with respect with to preliminary architectural assumption (preAA).

Since the step from the first definition of the system and their boundaries (item definition), to the functional safety concept is a cornerstone towards the development of hardware and software, we support this with the methodology described in (Weissnegger et al., 2016). In this paper, the first system design (preAA) is supported by a simulation-based approach. Further technical requirements can be derived through having early executable models of the functional specification. The functional specification of the system is depicted in Figure 4. With this methodology, we are able to evaluate our first design in early design phases and furthermore throughout the entire development process.

Since reusability of well-tested designs, mechanisms or even complete safety concepts is an issue that is currently becoming even more important, we support this artefact through reusable models from our developed System Component Library (SCL). This library includes all major elements for a high-level simulation of digital but also analog systems in the automotive domain. It also includes components on different levels of abstraction and different versions, depending on its application and viewpoint. For this approach, we use the capabilities of SystemC for digital systems on register transfer level (RTL) and transaction level modeling (TLM). For analog and mixed signal models, we use the extension of SystemC AMS. Since these simulation models rely on the same modeling language as our entire design flow, they can be easily integrated into our preliminary system design. How the UML/MARTE models are linked to the simulation core in SystemC is described by the authors of (Weissnegger et al., 2016) in detail.

The presented approach can also be underpinned by the statements from the ISO26262 standard in Part4: Product development at the system level (ISO, Functional Safety ISO26262 - Part 4: Product development at the system level, 2011):

The technical SR shall be specified in accordance with the functional safety concept, the preliminary architectural assumptions of the item and the following system properties: the external interfaces, such as communication and user interface; the constraints, e.g. environmental conditions or functional constraints; and the system configuration requirements. The ability to reconfigure a system for alternative applications is a strategy to reuse existing systems.

Figure 4. Functional specification of the preliminary architectural design
Adapted from (Weissnegger et al., 2016).

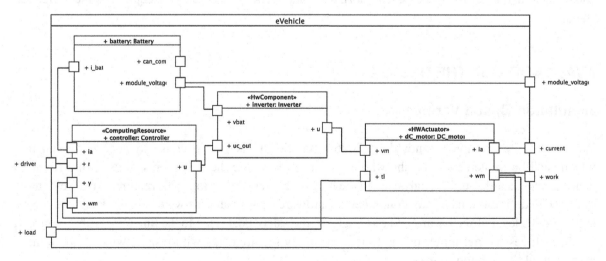

The system design shall be verified for compliance and completeness with regard to the technical safety concept using the verification methods e.g. Simulation for ASIL level higher than B.

As already described in the previous chapter, we made an extension to the requirements of the SysML standard to define also safety requirements (SR). The resulting requirements definition, depicted in Figure 5, helps to define all different requirements from different sources and stakeholders and to keep trace with models, verification tests and results. This becomes even more obvious if we look at the definition of the safety standard Part 8: Supporting Processes, where it is recommended to use semi-formal notations for requirements specifications for ASIL higher than B. Each functional SR in this approach thus has several defined constraints for functional and non-functional properties. These constraints are defined in the MARTE value specification language (VSL) and specify the boundaries for fail-safe operations of the system but also environmental conditions and operation modes. These constraints precisely capture the original requirement and also open up, through computer readable formalism, the possibility for subsequent computer-aided analysis of the design characteristics. The MARTE nfpConstraint is defined by arithmetic, logical or time expressions formed by combining operators such as ('<', '≤', '='. '≠', '≥', '>') but also 'AND', 'OR' and 'XOR'. The syntax used for these constraints follows the pattern:

$$Contraint = Signal, Pin, Port, \langle \leq, =, \neq, \geq, \rangle Value, Signal$$

Multiple constraints can be connected via simple Boolean statements such as:

$$NOT\left(Temp > 100°C \ AND \ Current < 10A\right)$$

Figure 5. Specification of requirements and safety requirements on different abstraction level
Adapted from (Weissnegger et al., 2016).

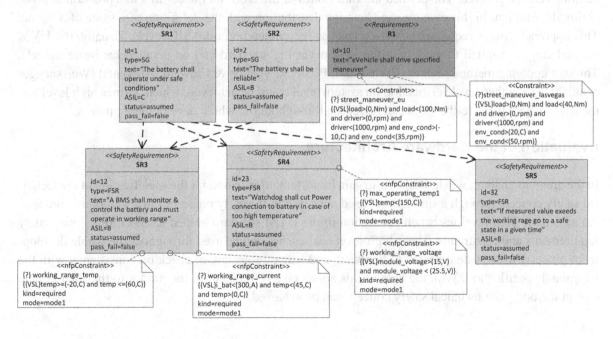

The current shall not exceed 10A if the battery temperature is above 100°C.

In order to support the specification of the technical SR and furthermore enable the verification in compliance with the technical safety concept, we defined a novel methodology to derive further requirements and inputs from the functional SR in coherence with the early system design (preAA). Using the syntax for safety requirements we are able to generate UVM verification components and whole testbenches from the definition of the functional SR and their constraints. For each constraint of the functional SR, a new UVM validator is added on the ports or one end of the signal. A validator consists of a configurable comparator with the pin/port/signal attached to one input and a reference signal or constant value attached to the second input. The outputs of the comparator can be either 1 (true) or 0 (zero) and are connected via arithmetic or algebraic function blocks to create the boolean operations. In addition, we use non-safety requirements in the SysML specification to provide stimuli blocks for relevant operating modes and driving maneuvers. Depending on the non-safety requirements and constraints and if the pin/port/signal is an unused input of a block, the testbench generator creates a stimulus block and attaches it. This block generates either values that are within the specifications in order to validate proper operation or to generate invalid stimuli to verify safety mechanisms within the model. More details on this generation are given in (Weissnegger et al., 2016).

To vary the parameters and stimuli of our system and to cover up corner cases we use the benefits of Coverage-Driven Verification (CDV), with its aim of achieving detachment from direct - user dependent - testing (Accellera, 2015). This methodology provides the definition of so-called verification goals, which can be verified by smart test scenarios. The intelligence is mainly achieved by creating simulation configurations (stimuli), with respect to some predefined constraints. This concept is widely known as Constraint Random Verification (CRV). CRV and consists so called of two core concepts, which are on one hand the usage of Markov-chain Monte Carlo to guarantee coverage through probability and on the other hand the processing of constraints with SAT solvers.

As described above, it is important to vary parameters in such a way that many different input combinations can be covered. The defined internal values of the DUT vary according to a predefined probability distribution. In this case we use Gaussian distribution with the definition of a value of 3 sigma. This approach covers requirements-based tests as recommend on all ASIL levels. Usually, the UVM methodology is applied to models in the SystemVerilog standard and on detailed hardware models. Through applying method such as (Barnasconi, Pêcheux, Vörtler, & Einwich, 2014) and (Weissnegger et al., 2016) a higher-level verification on system level could be achieved, which defines high level testbenches, where these testbenches can be reused throughout the whole development process.

Evaluation of the Hardware Architecture

In the previous chapter, we showed how to gain important information for the specification of the technical safety concept through a simulation-based approach in the early phase of the development process. An automatic high-level testbench generation in the UVM standard helped to check functional safety requirements and constraints. These high-level testbenches can be used throughout the whole development process, from system design to hardware and software design, to check on consistency with the functional specification. With the help of this approach a refinement of the preAA to the final system design including the technical safety concept can be achieved.

Figure 6. Automatic generated UVM testbench from safety requirements
Adapted from (Weissnegger et al., 2016).

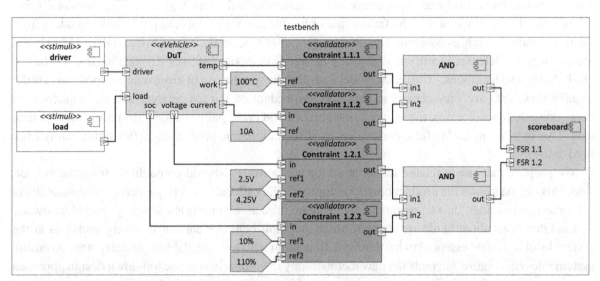

From the information that has been gathered, we are now able to make a start on the safety aware hardware design of our platform. This is an important step in the development process and takes a major effort input into account, since many different methods and measures have to be applied to the platform to guarantee a reliable product in the end.

Part 5 of the ISO26262 standard (26262, 2011) handles the product development at the hardware level, which includes the evaluation of the hardware architectural metrics. It evaluates the hardware architecture of the item against the requirements for fault handling. This part includes guidance on avoiding systematic and random hardware failures by means of appropriate safety mechanisms. Each safety-related hardware element is analyzed in the context of safe, single point (SPFM), residual and multiple point faults (LFM). It also describes the effectiveness of the hardware architecture in coping with random hardware failures (PMHF). Each hardware part is to be protected by means of safety-mechanisms. The diagnostic coverage gives evidence of the effectiveness of these mechanisms. Whether the item (system or array of systems according to ISO26262) passes or fails a given ASIL is also a result of the hardware architectural metrics evaluation. In order to achieve a specific ASIL, the values from Table 2 must be met. It is also important to point out that only safety-related hardware elements that have the potential to contribute significantly to the violation of the safety goal are addressed in this metric. This must be considered in the evaluation of the whole item.

Table 2. Metrics to be achieved by the architectural evaluation, according to ISO26262

	ASIL B	ASIL C	ASIL D
SPFM	$\geq 90\%$	$\geq 97\%$	$\geq 99\%$
LFM	$\geq 60\%$	$\geq 80\%$	$\geq 90\%$
PMHF	$< 10^{-7} \mathrm{h}^{-1}$	$< 10^{-7} \mathrm{h}^{-1}$	$< 10^{-8} \mathrm{h}^{-1}$

The drawback of this mandatory step is, that it is done at a very late phase in the overall development process, where late introduced changes are time-consuming and cause high costs. Furthermore, these safety-related properties such as the failure rate of hardware components are published and taken from various standards such as Siemens Handbook SN 29500 (Siemens, 2004), MIL HDBK 338 (United States. Dept. of Defense: Electronic Reliability Design Handbook, 1988) or IEC 62380 (IEC TR 62380 - Reliability data handbook - Universal model for reliability prediction of electronic components, 2005). Usually these data are very general in character, dependent on the temperature and not applicable to every domain. In some cases, the source is unspecified and principally obtained from field or statistical data. This in turn can lead to false consequences, if the failure rate predictions differ significantly from field data.

We propose that safety-related information for hardware-IPs should come direct from the vendor, since this person knows the product best. Our approach thus allocates safety-properties to vendor IPs in a standardized manner, thus ensuring that there are no false assumptions about safety-critical hardware.

Late decisions about hardware characteristics and fault-behavior can cause wrong decisions at the system level. It is thus essential to have information about hardware available at an early stage to ensure system integrity. Figure 7 depicts the new methodology in comparison to the top-down design approach as executed in ISO26262. The left side shows the different abstraction levels of the design phase and their derivations, from item definition to detailed hardware and software design. It also shows recommended verification methodologies, which are to be used on each abstraction level. The arrow shows the chronology of these methodologies in the verification process. The right side depicts our approach by providing safety properties in the IP-XACT standard, to speed up the verification and design process of safety-critical systems. This so-called meet-in-the-middle approach makes it possible to evaluate the hardware design round $\triangle$t earlier than it is handled in the traditional approach. The time needed for evaluation is reduced through seamless integration of tools in the design process, a hardware IP library and provided design space exploration. Furthermore, the system design layer benefits from our approach, which allows an earlier verification through methods such as FTA and FMEA. The safety properties

Figure 7. Meet-in-the-middle approach: design and verification speedup through failure modes provided by hardware description

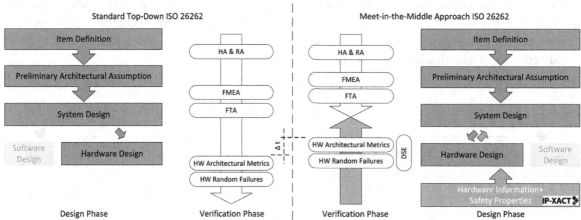

provided are defined in a standardized format, which can be used by many verification engineers and provides important inputs to additional stakeholders.

Using the methodology described, we are able to provide inputs for various evaluation techniques. In this part of the chapter we will focus on the evaluation of the hardware architectural metrics. To evaluate the hardware according to Clause 6, Clause 7, Clause 8 and Clause 9 in ISO26262, the following equations must be tackled and solved to achieve a given ASIL level. This task must be completed separately for each safety goal and requires seamlessly integrated tools to support this evaluation-process:

Single Point Fault Metric (SPFM)

The SPFM reflects the robustness of the item when coping with single point and residual faults. This can either be handled by design or proper safety mechanisms. The higher the value of SPFM, the more robust our applied safety mechanism will be. The following equation is used to determine the SPFM:

$$SPFM = 1 - \frac{\sum_{SafetyRelatedHW} \left(\lambda_{SPF} + \lambda_{RF,est} \right)}{\sum_{SafetyRelatedHW} \lambda}$$

$$\lambda_{RF,est} = \lambda \times \left(1 - \frac{K_{DC,RF}}{100} \right)$$

where Kdc,rf is the diagnostic coverage with respect to residual faults and lambda,rf is the estimated failure rate with respect to residual faults.

Latent Fault Metric (LFM)

The LFM reflects the robustness of the item when coping with latent faults. This can either be handled by coverage of faults through proper safety mechanisms or by the driver, recognizing that the fault exists before the violation of the safety goal. The higher the value of LFM, the more robust our applied safety mechanism will be. The following equation is used to determine the LFM:

$$LFM = 1 - \frac{\sum_{SafetyRelatedHW} \left(\lambda_{MPF,L,est} \right)}{\sum_{SafetyRelatedHW} \left(\lambda - \lambda_{SPF} - \lambda_{RF} \right)}$$

$$\lambda_{MPF,L,est} = \lambda \times \left(1 - \frac{K_{DC,MPF,L}}{100} \right)$$

where Kdc,mpf,l is the diagnostic coverage with respect to multiple point latent faults and lambda is the estimated failure rate with respect to multiple point latent faults.

Probabilistic Metric for Random Hardware Failures (PMHF)

The PMHF evaluates the residual risk of violating a safety goal due to single point faults, residual faults, and plausible dual point faults. It defines the quantitative target values for the maximum probability of the violation. The following equation estimates the failure rate for the failure modes of each hardware part that would cause a single point, residual or dual point fault (ISO 61508).

$$PMHF = \sum \lambda_{SPF} + \sum \lambda_{RF} + \sum \lambda_{MPF, latent}$$

Trawling through datasheets to determine failure rates for hardware components is a cumbersome task. The information about hardware safety properties mostly comes from the vendors themselves. Currently, there is no standardized way to provide information about safety in IPs to tool vendors (EDA) or system-integrators. To do this and furthermore achieve interoperability and reusability with other tools, we propose an extension to a well-known format in industry: IP-XACT (SPIRIT, 2013). IP-XACT is a standard (IEEE 1685) driven by Accellera and its format is used for documenting IPs using meta-data. The data are used for configuring, integrating and verifying IPs in advanced SoC design and interfacing tools. The specifications are derived from the requirements of the industry to enable an efficient design of electronic systems. The 1.4 release of the IP-XACT format also includes implementation models on RTL and TLM level. Furthermore, this format supports the data exchange through a common structured data management. IP-XACT is used today by many different major tool-vendors in the embedded system domain, and several European research projects are working on extensions and standardization, such as OpeneES (Catrene, 2016), the SAFE (SAFE Project, 2016) or the COMPLEX project (COMPLEX | ECSI, 2016).

An IP-XACT model can consist of different files in relation to the IP, such as design files, behavioral models, simulation files and results. It also consists of detailed information about the hardware such as parameters, ports, memory or configuration. The aim of the standard is to support a component-based design of hardware and to enable the reuse and assembly of hardware components such as cores (processors, co-processors, DSPs), peripherals (memories, DMA controllers, timers, UARTs) and buses (simple buses, multi-layer buses, cross bars, network on chip).

Additionally, the IP-XACT format also provides vendor extensions to support user-defined features. Vendor specific IP meta-data can be stored in a vendorExtension element. These extensions can be applied to several elements in the hierarchical manner of the IP-XACT format (components, bus interfaces, registers, etc.). We use the capabilities of IP-XACT to add safety properties to the different elements of the IP. The vendor extensions are composed in a hierarchical manner. The root container can contain one or several vendor extensions. For our purpose, we add following properties to the elements:

- **Failure Rate (FR):** Is usually known by the vendor of the component. It is a result of field return and statistical data, where expert judgment can also be considered. Since IP-XACT is a technology independent specification of an IP, we are providing a "budget" of the failure rate.
- **Failure Modes (FM):** Describes the different modes where a failure can occur. The failure modes depend on the application in which the element is used.
- **Safety Mechanism (SM):** Implemented mechanism to detect and control faults. It prevents faults from violating the safety goal. If a fault is detected, a safe state is initiated.

- **Diagnostic coverage (DC):** Is the effectiveness of the internal safety mechanism implemented to cover single point, residual or latent faults.

The properties for the IP can be defined either at top-level or on a very detailed level (sub-system level) of the different components. The level on which the failure modes and safety mechanisms are described depends on two factors:

- If a failure mode is comprehensive across several components and cannot be assigned to a dedicated unit, it must be described on a higher level.
- Safety-related data is very sensitive information and needs years of research and field tests. For this reason, it must be carefully protected for proprietary reasons. Depending on the use case and how much information I want to relinquish, very detailed information or only top-level information is used to describe the safety of an IP.

In common with the majority of the approaches in this domain, we describe our safety properties not on hardware detailed level but rather on architectural level. The benefit here is that we achieve a much higher level of abstraction, which is closer to the system design. It also leads to a faster evaluation of the hardware design and brings import inputs for potential faults in system and software design. More information about this approach can be found in (Weissnegger, Pistauer, Kreiner, Römer, & Steger, 2015).

GENERATION AND VERIFICATION OF THE SAFETY AWARE VIRTUAL PROTOTYPE

Virtual Prototyping

In the previous chapter, we described how to design our system in the UML standardized modeling language and extensions such as MARTE and SysML. Furthermore, we showed how to derive technical requirements from a first functional specification in simulation, which brings important inputs for our final system design. Following on from the design of our hardware platform, we are also aiming to have a first architectural evaluation including design space exploration regarding the requirements for functional safety. With the help of our extensions for safety-properties such as failure modes and FIT rates in the IP-XACT standard, we are able to execute mandatory methods such as hardware architectural evaluation, FTA or FMEA on hardware level. All these methods are helping us to strengthen the reliability of our system and furthermore to bring us evidence for the technical correctness of the hardware design, which is also a stringent safety case requirement.

Further to the before mentioned verification methodologies, the functional safety standard also recommends using design walk through and design inspection for the platform but more importantly, hardware prototyping and simulation for higher ASIL levels. This virtual prototype can then be used for further hardware verification such as fault injection test, which is at present the key for testing the reliability of the hardware. Several research institutes are currently working on executing fault injection and this also on a higher level (TLM). This has the advantage of the capability for applying this method on faster simulation models without losing information from the more detailed models (RTL).

Virtual prototyping entails the benefit that embedded software can be tested much at a much earlier phase and before a first real hardware prototype is available. In addition, the hardware software interface can be tested for consistency. Changes on a virtual hardware design are much faster than changes on the real platform, which take weeks or months for redesign and production, which in turn has a negative impact on time to market. With intensive simulation, corner cases and also long-term reliability errors can be encountered, which also prevents costly product recalls. Environmental impacts on the virtual prototype can be simulated and reproduced, where real testbeds are not capable of this kind of verification. Instead of building several physical prototypes, different design alternatives of the hardware can be easily explored through virtual prototyping. At the end of the development phases, the final prototype can be tested in terms of consistency, correctness and completeness with the functional specification.

The drawback, however, is that a complex virtual prototype (VP) cannot be developed overnight. It takes a great effort input on the part of experienced designers and engineers to build a so-called digital twin of the actual hardware. The VP should have a modular architecture and be flexible in creating the platform. Depending on the test application, it should also provide different levels of abstraction to distinguish between several levels of detail, since simulation on a detailed level can require immense computing power and is very time consuming work. Furthermore, it should also ease the way to verifying the hardware platform and the embedded software and not require months of work in building the virtual prototype for testing.

Seen in this context there are clearly many benefits to be gained in reusing models for virtual hardware prototyping from open library sources such as Open Virtual Platform (OVP), (Open Virtual Platform, 2016). OVP comes with a growing model library, which offers processor cores, memory and various peripherals. The idea is a modular design with the combination of components in a so-called virtual platform. The generated platform can be simulated with the OVPsim API. OVP was generally founded by Imperas, its commercial brother, and can be used freely for non-commercial/academic use.

One of the goals outlined in this work is to develop and test embedded software within the development phases, on a realistic hardware prototype of the target system, before the actual platform is available. Embedded software is often written in a desktop environment, on a general-purpose operating system of the host system. This approach often differs significantly from the target platform and parts of the written software need to be adjusted. One way to deal with this problem is to use an instruction set simulator (ISS) and hardware visualization. Due to the broad variety of vendor components within SoC design, the simulation can be a very challenging and difficult task. Hardware emulators are very popular for dealing with this issue, but they require the detailed RTL description of the developed system, which is in contradiction to the outlined goal of a homogeneous development environment. OVP makes it possible to create virtual platform models, with SystemC TLM 2.0 support. OVP models can be executed much faster than their counterparts developed in RTL, since their level of abstraction is higher, but still appropriate for modeling purposes.

The instruction set simulator OVPsim is released for 32 bit Windows and Linux and is a just-in-time Code morphing simulator engine, which means that the target instructions are translated to x86 host instructions. This results in a significant speed-up, since the simulation can subsequently be greatly optimized.

The OVP model Generator iGen was written to build simulation models through a TCL (Tool Control Language) script, which contains used platform components and their connection. TCL files can be compared with IP-XACT hardware description, which relies mainly on the VLNV principle, a standardization of the Spirit consortium. VLNV establishes a unique identification for models, by providing the parameters Vendor, Library, Name and Version. The directory structure of the Imperas model library was designed in a similar way, such that the iGen converter, retrieves the necessary information for the instantiated models of the platform and generates a SystemC description.

The use case of a BMS is to be implemented on a micro-controller, which meets high safety requirements in its implementation. The OVP library comes with different peripheral models, from different vendors. These models implement communication interfaces, such as UARTs, I2C, Ethernet or CAN, which is of special interest in the automotive area. Those interfaces work, are purely digital such that message exchange can be established to other control units.

The task of the BMS is to monitor battery temperature and voltage which are analog values in SystemC AMS and to compute the state of charge and state of health. Therefore, the usage of an Analog Digital Converter (ADC) is necessary, to build an accurate system description.

Configuration of the Virtual Prototype

Since OVP consists more or less of a set of SystemC files including a TCL script, one goal of this work is to include the complete generation of the virtual prototype into our design flow for safety critical systems. Furthermore, the design and configuration of the VP on a graphical modeling standard, in this case UML/MARTE. This approach brings the advantage of evaluating and analyzing the configuration of the hardware design before the actual prototype is generated from UML models. OVP itself does not support verification in the safety context, nor has OVP been embedded in a seamless design flow to date.

As mentioned in our design chapter, UML/MARTE provides several levels of detail for the specification of the hardware platform. The hardware resource model (HRM) package provides several models to describe subsystems such as HwProcessor, HwBus, HwDevice or HwMemory in a logical and physical manner. Although, UML/MARTE provides a rich set of different stereotypes to describe the hardware platform, it does not provide the level of detail for the hardware configuration that is expected in the OVP methodology. Several mandatory properties such as the BusInterface or Memory mapped or the VLNV principle are by now not supported in the MARTE standard.

To overcome these issues, we decided to rely on the specification of the IP-XACT standard, which helps us to define our platform in a sufficient high degree of details for the generation of the virtual prototype. Both, IP-XACT and OVP rely on the VLNV principle for structuring the models. We thus built on approaches such as (André, Mallet, Khan, & de Simone, 2008) to extend the MARTE standard by properties in IP-XACT for hardware description.

Figure 8 depicts the composed structural architecture model of the platform consisting of a processor, bus, memory, CAN and two ADC. For the sake of simplification, we only show the major components of the design of the battery management system. The designer can easily compose his system by using the standard models from the MARTE library such as HwProcessor for the CPU, HwI_O or HwComponent for peripherals, HwRam for memory or HwBus for the internal bus or CAN bus. Depending on the nature of the component, the designer is able to extend the component with specific hardware properties in the IP-XACT standard such as MemoryMaps and BusInterface. The properties from the IP-XACT standard are than shown in the description of the MARTE model. Further extensions for IP-XACT such as VLNV can also be added to the hardware components.

Through applying this approach, the designer is able to configure the entire hardware platform, for instance "instructions per seconds" of the processor, which affects the simulation time directly. The designer uses the standard MARTE models from the library and adds additional IP-XACT properties

Figure 8. Hardware platform of SaVeSoC including IP-XACT extensions for MARTE

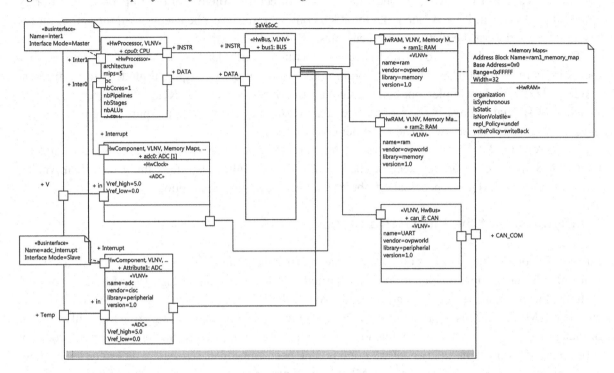

to his models. After the evaluation of the design regarding safety, the description of the platform is converted to a TCL description in the OVP standard. The OVP iGen converter takes the information from the TCL script and generates a full SystemC platform using the modular components of the OVP library. The resulting virtual prototype can then be used for further hardware simulations, such as fault-injections on TLM level.

A small application is now running on the platform for demonstration purpose, which computes state of charge and state of health and checks on plausibility of the incoming measurements. This application is written in c-language and also defined through the allocation mechanism in MARTE. The provided processor is also capable of executing embedded operating systems such as embedded Linux.

Testing the Virtual Prototype

Since the methodology in its entirety relies on the same modeling language and furthermore the same hardware description language respectively system-modeling language, we are easily able to reapply our safety aware virtual prototype into the functional specification of the system design. The whole process is depicted in Figure 9. The hardware description of the SaVeSoC platform with the whole interface specification is added to the component library and can be reapplied to the system design including the generated simulation files in SystemC. This saves time in terms of integration effort, when testing the virtual prototype on the functionality of the whole system. Testbenches can also be reused for the verification of the system including the VP.

Figure 9. Process of SaVeSoC integration into functional specification

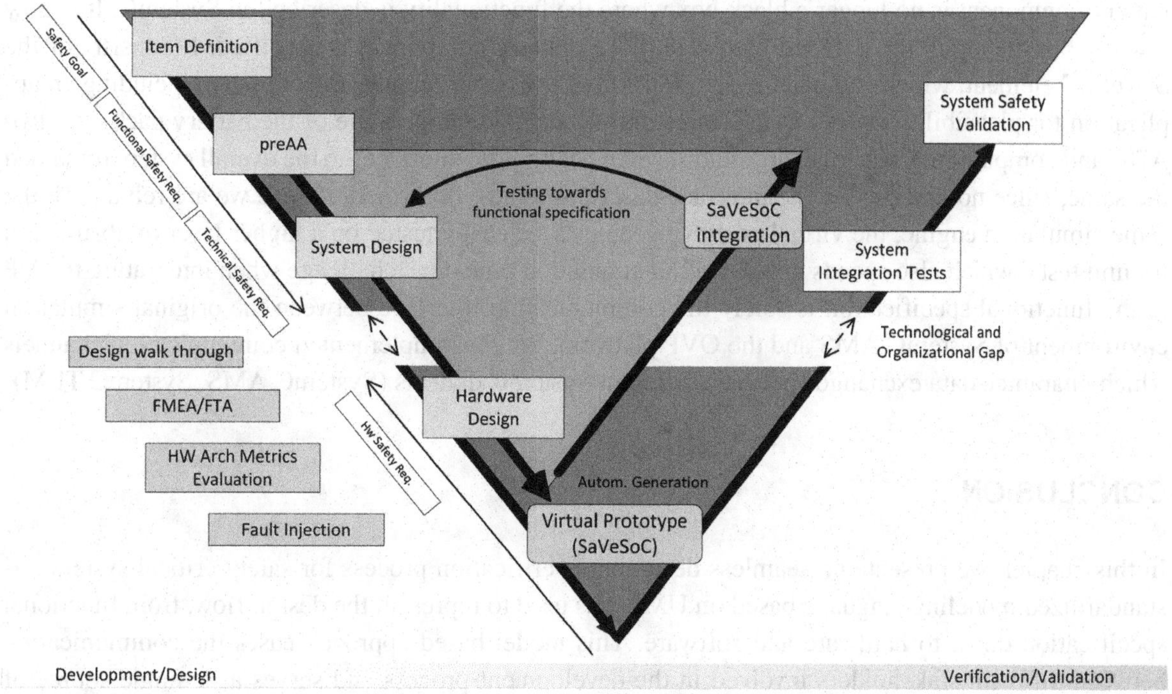

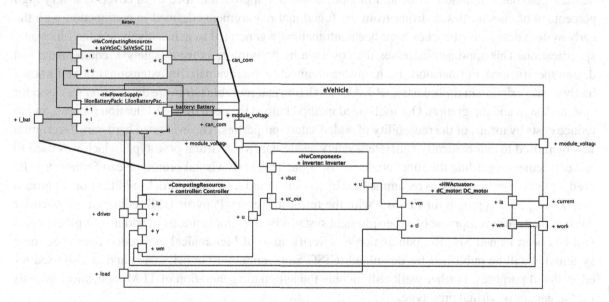

Figure 10. Virtual prototype integration into the functional specification of the system design to verify the functionality

Figure 10 depicts the resulting system level description including the new battery hardware. The battery component is no longer a black box where the functionality is described in SystemC. It is now a white box in which the detailed hardware of the battery component is specified. It consists of the SaVeSoC element, which is the hardware platform of the battery management system including an application for plausibility checks. It measures the voltage and temperature of the battery pack over two ADC and computes the state of charge and stage of health. The interfaces to the overall system remained the same, since no changes on the interface description have been made. Since we are relying on the same simulation engine, the virtual prototype can now be easily tested on a higher layer of abstraction for unit tests, which also speeds up the overall simulation time. One challenge when integrating the VP to the functional specification is solely the communication interface between the original simulation environment of SystemC AMS and the OVP platform. We thus implemented communication channels which guarantee data exchanges between different SystemC dialects (SystemC AMS, SystemC TLM).

CONCLUSION

In this chapter, we presented a seamless design and verification process for safety-critical systems. A standardized modeling language based on UML was used to represent the design flow, from functional specification down to hardware and software. This model-based approach eases the communication between different stakeholders involved in the development process and serves as a single-source of information. Through tight integration of recommended safety analysis methods such as FTA, FMEA, hardware architectural metrics and simulation-based verification, we achieved consistency, correctness and completeness throughout the development process. Since millions of test kilometers now need to be managed, our simulation-based and random constraint approach helped us in covering a very high percentage of possibilities. Starting from the functional requirements defined in conjunction with the early system design, testbenches have been automatically generated to exhaustively test the functional specification. This approach increases the coverage by deriving tests from (safety-) requirements and design specification. Furthermore, the hardware architecture was evaluated by extensions to a well-known hardware description in the industry, IP-XACT. Existing and reusable hardware description was used for system design and integration. Our tool-aided method helped to speed up the evaluation process, and to reduce costs by means of the reusability of added safety-properties. The evaluated hardware description was then used to automatically generate a safety aware hardware virtual prototype, which was used to test correctness regarding the functional specification. This early virtual prototype can furthermore be used for fault-injection tests, as recommended by the functional safety standard. In addition, our approach was developed as a plugin for Eclipse, with the result that every Papyrus UML editor can be used for the safety aware development of cyber-physical systems by the simple means of adding our plugin. This tool has been named SHARC (simulation and verification of hierarchical embedded microelectronic systems) it will be published for download (CISC Semiconductor GmbH, 2017) and is also used for educational purposes. Further work will include the automatic generation of TLM fault-injection tests for the generated virtual prototype.

ACKNOWLEDGMENT

A part of the work has been performed in the project eRamp (Grant Agreement N621270), co-funded by grants from Austria, Germany, Slovakia and the ENIAC Joint Undertaking. Some parts have also been experimented in the OpenES CATRENE Project: CA703 - 2013 research program supported by the FFG (Austrian Research Promotion Agency), project-number 843380 in tight cooperation with CISC Semiconductor.

REFERENCES

Accellera. (2015, May). *Universal Verification Methodology (UVM) 1.2 User's Guide* (Tech. rep.).

Aditya, S., Alexsandr, A. K., Dirk, A. S., & Christiaan, P. (2010). Multi-View Modeling to Support Embedded Systems Engineering in SysML. In Graph transformations and model-driven engineering (pp. 580-601).

Adler, R., Domis, D., Höfig, K., Kemmann, S., Kuhn, T., Schwinn, J. P., & Trapp, M. (2011). Integration of component fault trees into the UML. In International Conference on Model Driven Engineering Languages and Systems (pp. 312-327). doi:10.1007/978-3-642-21210-9_30

Alajrami, S., Gallina, B., & Romanovsky, A. (2016). EXE-SPEM: To- wards Cloud-Based Executable Software Process Models. In *Proceedings of the 4th International Conference on Model-Driven Engineering and Software Development.*

André, C., Mallet, F., Khan, A. M., & de Simone, R. (2008). Modeling SPIRIT IP-XACT with UML MARTE. In *Proc. DATE Workshop on Modeling and Analysis of Real-Time and Embedded Systems with the MARTE UML profile.*

Barnasconi, M., Pêcheux, F., Vörtler, T., & Einwich, K. (2014). Advancing System Level Verification Using UVM in SystemC. In Proceedings of the DVCON 2014, San Jose, California, USA.

Candence. (2017). Retrieved from https://www.cadence.com

Catrene. (2016). OpenES CATRENE Project: CA703. Retrieved from http://www.ecsi.org/openes

Charette, R. N. (2009). This Car Runs on Code - IEEE Spectrum. Retrieved from http://spectrum.ieee.org/transportation/systems/this-car-runs-on-code

CISC Semiconductor GmbH. (2017). Retrieved from https://www.cisc.at/

COMPLEX | ECSI. (2016). Retrieved from http://ecsi.org/complex

David, P., Idasiak, V., & Kratz, F. (2009). Towards a better interaction between design and dependability analysis: FMEA derived from UML/SysML models. In *Proceedings of the Joint ESREL and SRA-Europe Conference* (Vol. 3, pp. 2259-2266). Retrieved from http://www.scopus.com/inward/record.url?eid=2-s2.0-78751589362&partnerID=40&md5=1e1684e4af48e5906773f66766c37201

EAST-ADL Association. (2014). Retrieved from http://www.east-adl.info/

Eclipse. (2015). Papyrus. Retrieved from https://www.eclipse.org/papyrus/

FORD GT - Lines of code. (2016). Retrieved from https://www.eitdigital.eu/news-events/blog/article/guess-what-requires-150-million-lines-of-code/

Group, O. M. (2015). OMG Unified Modeling Language TM (OMG UML), Superstructure v.2.5. *InformatikSpektrum, 21*, 758. doi:10.1007/s002870050092

Gvero, I. (2013, August). Computers As Components 3rd Edition: Principles of Embedded Computing System Design by Marilyn Wolf. *SIGSOFT Softw. Eng. Notes, 38*, 67-68. doi:10.1145/2507288.2507292

IBM. (2017). *Rational Doors*. Retrieved from http://www-03.ibm.com/software/products/de/ratidoor

IEC TR 62380 - Reliability data handbook - Universal model for reliability prediction of electronic components. (2005).

ISO26262. (2011). *Road vehicles-functional safety-Part 5: Product development at the hardware level.*

ISO. (2011). Functional Safety ISO26262 - Part 4: Product development at the system level. *2011*, 1-35.

ISO. (2011). *Road vehicles - Functional safety*. Geneva, Switzerland: ISO.

Macher, G., Stolz, M., Armengaud, E., & Kreiner, C. (2015). Filling the gap between automotive systems, safety, and software engineering. *Elektrotechnik und Informationstechnik, 132*, 142-148. doi:10.1007/s00502-015-0301-x

MAENAD. (2014). *maenad.eu*. Retrieved 2017 from http://www.maenad.eu/

Magillem. (2017). Retrieved from http://www.magillem.com

Marinescu, R., Kaijser, H., Mikucionis, M., David, A., Seceleanu, C., & Henrik, L. (2014). Analyzing Idustrial Architectural Models by Simulation and Model-Checking. *Formal Techniques for Safety-Critical Systems, 419*, 189–205. doi:10.1007/978-3-319-05416-2

MathWorks. (2017). *Matlab Simulink*. Retrieved from https://de.mathworks.com/products/matlab.html

Maurer, M., Gerdes, J. C., Lenz, B., & Winner, H. (2015). *Autonomes Fahren: Technische, rechtliche und gesellschaftliche Aspekte*. Springer Berlin Heidelberg. doi:10.1007/978-3-662-45854-9

Mentor. (2017). Retrieved from https://www.mentor.com

Murillo, L., Mura, M., & Prevostini, M. (2009). Semi-automated Hw/Sw Co-design for embedded systems: from MARTE models to SystemC simulators. In *Proceedings of the Forum on Specification & Design Languages (FDL).*

Murillo, L. G., Mura, M., & Prevostini, M. (2010). *MDE Support for HW/SW Codesign: A UML-based Design Flow*. In *Advances in Design Methods from Modeling Languages for Embedded Systems and SoC's* (pp. 19–37).

Object Management Group (OMG). (2015). Retrieved from http://www.omg.org/

Omg. (2015). OMG Systems Modeling Language (OMG SysML ™) v.1.4. *Source*, 260. Von http://www.omg.org/spec/SysML/1.2/PDF/

Open Virtual Platform. (2016). Retrieved from http://www.ovpworld.org

SAFE Project. (2016). Retrieved from http://www.safe-project.eu/

Selić, B., & Gérard, S. (2014). *Modeling and analysis of real-time and embedded systems with UML and MARTE*. doi:10.1016/B978-0-12-416619-6.00008-0

Seo-Hyun, J., Jin-Hee, C., Yangjae, J., Sachoun, P., & Tae-Man, H. (2011). Automotive hardware development according to ISO 26262. In *Proceedings of the 13th International Conference on Advanced Communication Technology (ICACT2011)* (pp. 588-592).

Siemens. (2004). *SN 29500-1 Expected values, general.*

SPIRIT. (2013). IEEE SA - 1685-2009 - IEEE Standard for IP-XACT, Standard Structure for Packaging, Integrating, and Reusing IP within Tool Flows. Retrieved from http://standards.ieee.org/findstds/standard/1685-2009.html

Sporer, H., Macher, G., Armengaud, E., & Kreiner, C. (2015). Incorporation of Model-Based System and Software Development Environments. *Proceedings of the 41st Euromicro Conference on Software Engineering and Advanced Applications, SEAA 2015* (pp. 177-180). doi:10.1109/SEAA.2015.65

Accellera.org. (2016). SystemC- Accellera Systems Initiative. Retrieved from http://www.accellera.org/downloads/standards/systemc/

The UML Profile for MARTE: Modeling and Analysis of Real-Time and Embedded Systems. (2015). Retrieved from http://www.omgmarte.org/

United States. Dept. of Defense. (1988). Electronic Reliability Design Handbook.

Verification Academy. (2012). *Coverage Cookbook*. Retrieved from https://verificationacademy.com/cookbook/coverage

Weissnegger, R., Kreiner, C., Pistauer, M., Römer, K., & Steger, C. (2015). A Novel Design Method for Automotive Safety-Critical Systems based on UML/MARTE. In *Proceedings of the 2015 Forum on specification {\&} Design Languages*, Barcelona (pp. 177-184).

Weissnegger, R., Pistauer, M., Kreiner, C., Römer, K., & Steger, C. (2015). A novel method to speed-up the evaluation of cyber-physical systems (ISO 26262). In *Proceedings of the 2015 12th International Workshop on Intelligent Solutions in Embedded Systems (WISES)* (pp. 109-114).

Weissnegger, R., Pistauer, M., Kreiner, C., Schuß, M., Römer, K., & Steger, C. (2016, July 25-27). Automatic Testbench Generation for Simulation-based Verification of Safety-critical Systems in UML. In A. Ahrens, & C. Benavente-Peces (Eds.), *Proceedings of the 6th International Joint Conference on Pervasive and Embedded Computing and Communication Systems*, Lisbon, Portugal (pp. 70-75). SciTe-Press. doi:10.5220/0005997700700075

Weissnegger, R., Schuß, M., Kreiner, C., Pistauer, M., Kay, R., & Steger, C. (2016). *Bringing UML / MARTE to life: Simulation-based Verification of Safety-Critical Systems. In Proceedings of the 2016 Forum on Specification and Design Languages.* FDL.

Weissnegger, R., Schuß, M., Kreiner, C., Pistauer, M., Römer, K., & Steger, C. (2016). Seamless Integrated Simulation in Design and Verification Flow for Safety-Critical Systems. In A. Skavhaug, J. Guiochet, E. Schoitsch, & F. Bitsch (Eds.), *Computer Safety, Reliability, and Security: SAFECOMP 2016 Workshops, ASSURE, DECSoS, SASSUR, and TIPS, Trondheim, Norway, September 20, 2016, Proceedings* (pp. 359–370). Cham: Springer International Publishing; doi:10.1007/978-3-319-45480-1_29

Weissnegger, R., Schuß, M., Schachner, M., Pistauer, M., Römer, K., & Steger, C. (2016). A Novel Simulation-based Verification Pattern for Parallel Executions in the Cloud. In *Proceedings of the 21st European Conference on Pattern Languages of Programs Proceedings*. doi:10.1145/3011784.3011806

Yung-chang, C., Li-ren, H., Hsing-chuang, L., Chih-jen, Y., & Ching-te, C. (2014). Assessing Automotive Functional Safety Microprocessor with ISO 26262 Hardware Requirements. In *Technical Papers of 2014 International Symposium on VLSI Design, Automation and Test* (pp. 3-6).

Chapter 9
A Self–Adaptive Software System for Increasing the Reliability and Security of Cyber–Physical Systems

Johannes Iber
Graz University of Technology, Austria

Tobias Rauter
Graz University of Technology, Austria

Christian Kreiner
Graz University of Technology, Austria

ABSTRACT

The advancement and interlinking of cyber-physical systems offer vast new opportunities for industry. The fundamental threat to this progress is the inherent increase of complexity through heterogeneous systems, software, and hardware that leads to fragility and unreliability. Systems cannot only become more unreliable, modern industrial control systems also have to face hostile security attacks that take advantage of unintended vulnerabilities overseen during development and deployment. Self-adaptive software systems offer means of dealing with complexity by observing systems externally. In this chapter the authors present their ongoing research on an approach that applies a self-adaptive software system in order to increase the reliability and security of control devices for hydro-power plant units. The applicability of the approach is demonstrated by two use cases. Further, the chapter gives an introduction to the field of self-adaptive software systems and raises research challenges in the context of cyber-physical systems.

INTRODUCTION

Cyber-physical systems (CPS) are the next-generation of systems that integrate computational and physical components. In contrary to the embedded devices of the last decades, they offer high performance, are interconnected and, with a good chance, somehow connected with the internet. Following

DOI: 10.4018/978-1-5225-2845-6.ch009

this trend, control devices typically found in industry are going to manage more and more functionality with the help of sophisticated software. According to a National Institute of Standards and Technology workshop report (NIST, 2013) the key challenges of CPS development include what is needed to cost-effectively and rapidly build in and assure the safety, reliability, availability, security and performance of next-generation CPS. Industry is using more and more commercial off-the-shelf hardware platforms, which are inexpensive and offer a high performance. The downside of these platforms is that they typically only sparsely offer safety and fault tolerance features (Alhakeem et al., 2015). Further, industrial cyber-physical systems are becoming increasingly targets of security attacks (Miller & Rowe, 2012).

The inherent problem of CPS is complexity. This issue is going to escalate as CPS become large-scale distributed systems. They have to deal with uncertainty, change during operation, be scalable and tolerant to threats (Muccini, Sharaf, & Weyns, 2016). Self-adaptive software systems are systems that target to deal with complexity. Typically, self-adaptive software systems externally observe their managed systems, detect problems and adapt the managed systems in order to repair or circumvent inconsistencies. In the case of security, a self-adaptive software system can detect security attacks and isolate the infected devices or block the attackers. In the case of hardware faults, a self-adaptive software system can detect permanent hardware faults and move the application logic running on a managed system to an alternative hardware. Such problems would be complicated for a managed system itself to circumvent, but through an external overlooking system this becomes possible and the lurking complexity of CPS may become manageable.

Because of the increased performance and connectivity of modern and future hardware, self-adaptive software systems can be deployed to former restricted devices found in industry. In this chapter, ongoing research of an approach is presented that provides a novel application of a self-adaptive software system in an industrial setting, namely control devices for hydro-power plant units which is also the context of our research project. The goal of the presented approach is to increase the reliability and security of systems through anomaly detection and adaption. Simply put, we want to extend the time of control systems as long as possible so that they can carry out undisturbed their intended purposes.

The following Sections are structured as follows: First we give a detailed overview of the underlying principles of self-adaptive software systems. After that we extensive present our approach named Scari (**Se**cure **a**nd **r**eliable **i**nfrastructure); including an overview of our industrial setting (hydro-power plants), the vision of Scari, the detailed approach and two use cases. In the subsequent Section, we present a number of research challenges that we derive from our self-adaptive software system. Last, we conclude this Chapter.

BACKGROUND

Self-adaptive software modifies its own behavior in response to changes in its operating environment. By operating environment, we mean anything observable by the software system, such as end-user input, external hardware devices and sensors, or program instrumentation. (Oreizy et al., 1999)

Historically, the intention of building self-adaptive software systems has been around some time. Though not being the first talking and writing about self-adaptive software systems but making significant investments, IBM introduced in 2001 the Autonomic Computing Initiative in response to their observation that *the main obstacle to further progress in the IT industry is a looming software complexity crisis* (Kephart

& Chess, 2003). They argued that systems become too interconnected, too diverse and complex for even the most skilled system integrators to install, configure, optimize, maintain, and merge. Back then, *IBM researchers predicted that by the end of the decade the IT industry would need up to 200 million workers, equivalent to the entire US labor force, to manage a billion people and millions of businesses using a trillion devices connected via the Internet* (Dobson, Sterritt, Nixon, & Hinchey, 2010). Based on this idea of the future, they envisioned the need to develop computer systems that can manage themselves given high-level objectives. Since then, the term autonomic computing has emerged into a broader context related with organic computing, bio-inspired computing, self-organizing systems, ultrastable computing, and adaptive systems, to name a few (Dobson et al., 2010). As pointed out by Salehie & Tahvildari (2009), the term self-adaptive software system is focused on the domain of software systems. In the following we only use this term instead of autonomic computing or others as it narrows the scope. The fundamental reason for applying self-adaptive software systems is the increasing cost of handling the complexity of software systems to achieve their goals (Laddaga, 2001; Salehie & Tahvildari, 2009).

Typically, self-adaptive software systems follow an external (architecture) approach (Salehie & Tahvildari, 2009). An internal approach interweaves application and adaption logic based on programming language features like exceptions, conditions, and parametrization. The issue with an internal self-adaptive software system is that sensors, actuators, parallel adaption processes and actual purpose of an application are complicated to engineer within one software design. This further leads to notable drawbacks, e.g. with respect to scalability, testability and maintainability. In an external approach, as illustrated in Figure 1, the domain-specific application logic named *Managed Subsystem* is monitored by a *Managing Subsystem*. The *Managing Subsystem* is where the actual adaption logic resides. It additionally monitors the Environment that may consist of other software, hardware, network, or of the physical context (including humans). Based on monitored data and analyzed problems the *Managing Subsystem* decides whether and what to adapt inside the *Managed Subsystem*.

In order to show what a self-adaptive system actually means and what such a system desires we discuss in the next Subsection a hierarchy of self-properties. For the process of collecting data about the environment and *Managed Subsystem*, and finally adapting the *Managed Subsystem*, usually closed-loop

Figure 1. Parts of a self-adaptive software system
Based on Weyns et al., 2013.

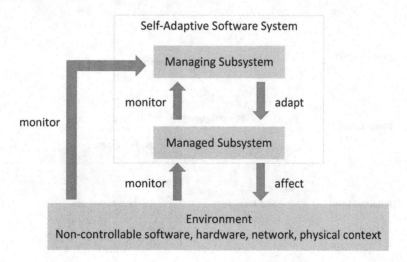

mechanisms are implemented inside the *Managing Subsystem*. We present three so-called adaption loops after the self-properties. These adaption loops represent the essence of architectures that aim to fulfill one or several of the presented self-properties. In the last part of this Section, we present the concept of utilizing models based on the Model-Driven Engineering principles in order to support self-adaptive software systems. This concept is named by its community Models@Run.time.

Hierarchy of Self-Properties

Self-Adaptiveness is a very broad term and represents the sum of several self-properties. Salehie & Tahvildari (2009) discuss these properties in detail and represent them in the hierarchy illustrated in Figure 2.

The top level named *General Level* contains global properties of self-adaptive systems. Terms, found in literature, which are basically a subset of self-adaptiveness are *self-managing, self-governing, self-maintenance, self-control, self-evaluating, and self-organizing*.

The *Major Level* terms are coined by the IBM Autonomic Computing Initiative and serve as the defacto standard in self-adaptive systems (Salehie & Tahvildari, 2009). The following four properties are generally also known as self-CHOP (M. Hinchey & Sterritt, 2006):

- **Self-Configuring:** A system reconfigures itself automatically in response to changes following high-level policies.
- **Self-Healing:** A system automatically detects, diagnoses, and reacts to software and hardware failures by healing itself.
- **Self-Optimizing:** A system continually seeks opportunities to improve its own performance and resource allocation.
- **Self-Protecting:** This property has two aspects. One is that a system automatically defends itself against malicious attacks or cascading failures. The other one is that it mitigates the effects of attacks.

Figure 2. Hierarchy of self-properties
Based on Salehie & Tahvildari, 2009.

The *Primitive Level* represents the base of the *Major Level* and consists of two properties. Without them a self-adaptive system would not be able to realize the properties from the *Major Level*:

- **Self-Awareness:** A system is aware of its own states and behaviors.
- **Context-Awareness:** A system is aware of its operational environment.

All these properties above are defining what self-adaptive systems are targeting to achive. In our approach, we are aiming for all *Primitive Level* and *Major Level* properties except self-optimization. The vision of the proposed system is to autonomously configure, heal, and protect itself based on its own state and the operational environment.

Adaption Loops

There exist different variants of how a self-adaptive software system can be organized. Muccini et al. (2016) reveal in a systematic literature review that concerning CPS, the so-called MAPE-K loop (later explained in detail) is by far the dominant adaptive mechanism with a share of 60%. It is followed by multi-agent and self-organization based technologies (both have 29% - some studies combine technologies). Multi-agent systems are large-scale open decentralized systems that consist of autonomous components or systems (Müller & Fischer, 2014) that work together for achieving a common goal. Self-organization techniques are inspired by nature where behavior emerges e.g. from cells (Jelasity et al., 2006). Multi-agent systems and self-organization techniques are out-of-scope of this work as they do not fit our industrial setting.

In the following we present three adaption loops that try to grasp the necessary steps and activities of a self-adaptive software system. After that, we shortly discuss the commonalities between them and highlight five patterns of how several loops can be organized.

MAPE-K

Figure 3 illustrates the MAPE-K adaptive loop, introduced by Kephart & Chess (2003) defining IBMs autonomic computing vision. It consists of the steps *Monitor, Analyze, Plan, and Execute*, and a shared part representing *Knowledge*. The target of MAPE-K is the *Managed Element* which is monitored with sensors and changed with actuators. The *Monitor* step gathers information about the *Managed Element* that is usually related to the current performance and load of the system (Brun et al., 2013). The *Analyze* step reasons about the data, identifies problems and attempts to find the source or cause of them. The *Plan* step reacts to the results of the *Analyze* step and creates a set of actions to remedy a problem. The last step, named *Execute*, implements these actions and changes the *Managed Element* through actuators. *Knowledge* is the central point where all the information within a MAPE-K loop comes together. The *Monitor* stores its observed data at this point. The *Analyze* step uses it to find anomalies. The *Plan* step leverages it to create actions and gathers its policies and goals from there. Finally, the *Execute* step stores its record of executed actions in it.

As we can see on Figure 3 there is an *Autonomic Manager* around the loop. That is basically an interface for controlling and monitoring the adaptive system. Kephart & Chess (2003) foresaw a plethora of *Autonomic Manager* each managing for instance a hardware resource (e.g. CPU, printer, storage) or software resource (e.g. database, service, legacy system).

Figure 3. MAPE-K
Based on Kephart & Chess, 2003.

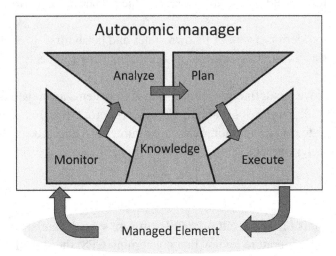

OODA

Colonel John Boyd was a United States Air Force fighter pilot and Pentagon consultant who developed the first version of his OODA-loop for explaining how to achieve success in air-to-air combat in the 1950's. Later he expanded his groundbreaking work and hypothesized that it is the essence of winning and losing of organizations and people (Boyd, 1996). As pointed out by other authors it lends itself well to self-adaptive system (Chandra, Lewis, Glette, & Stilkerich, 2016; Grenander, Simpson, & Sindiy, 2009). In the OODA-loop, *Observe* means to gather, monitor, and filter data. Figure 4 illustrates the type of data that can be observed; implicit guidance and control refers to the significant influence of the *Orientation* step. In the *Orient* step a list of options is derived through analysis and synthesis, previous experience,

Figure 4. OODA-loop
Source: Wikimedia Commons, 2014.

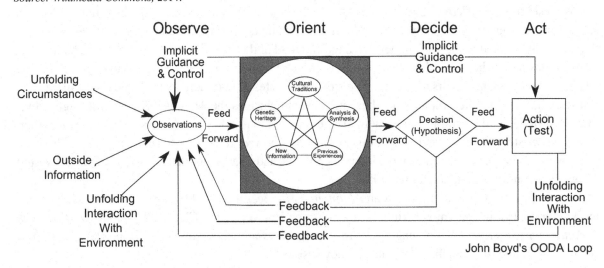

Figure 5. CADA-loop
Based on Dobson et al. (2006).

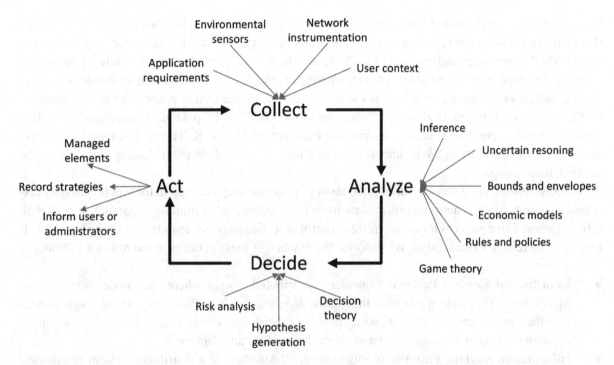

new information, and of course as the loop is intended for humans, genetic and cultural heritage. The derived list of options is then feed forwarded to the *Decide* step where the best hypothesis is selected via a ranking. In the last step, the selected option is acted out and in a way tested in the environment. As pointed out by John Boyd, *orientation shapes observation, shapes decision, shapes action, and in turn is shaped by the feedback and other phenomena* (Boyd, 1996). He demonstrated, that in the direct combat it is crucial to go through this loop faster and better than an opponent. Further, he noted that the entire loop (not just orientation) is an ongoing many-sided implicit cross-referencing process of projection, empathy, correlation, and rejection. We illustrate in our approach how we transfer the OODA-loop to our variant of an adaption loop.

CADA

Dobson et al. (2006) describe the generic *Collect - Analyze - Decide - Act* loop for autonomic communication systems. The field of autonomic communication targets to improve the ability of networks and services to cope with unpredicted changes like topology, load, task and so on. As we can see in Figure 5 it is similar to MAPE-K and the OODA-loop, but way more generic. In the *Collect* activity data is gathered from several sources, in the *Analyze* activity analyzed, then a *Decision* is made, and finally acted out in the *Act* activity. The loop is annotated with several techniques and approaches which can be applied for implementing the single activities. As mentioned by Cheng et al. (2009), reasoning in self-adaptive systems typically involve these four activities.

Discussion of the Adaption Loops

Essentially the three presented loops are variants of the same idea, which is to have a chain of activities that lead to an appropriate response to a problem of the managed system. However, the loops vary concerning the different steps and feedback. MAPE-K introduces the *Knowledge* part as common information source for each activity taking place. OODA emphasizes that the different steps give feedback to what is observed and that the adaptive loop is essentially driven by the *Orient* phase. The *Orient* phase of OODA corresponds to the *Analyze* and *Plan* steps of the MAPE-K loop. OODA introduces an explicit separate *Decide* phase that is embedded into the *Plan* step of MAPE-K. The CADA-loop is a generic version of an adaptive loop. We include it because it highlights the different technologies which can be applied in each step.

Usually, self-adaptive software does not consist of only one adaptive loop in the whole, possibly distributed, system. Such systems incorporate multiple loops connected or running in parallel. Weyns et al. (2013) gathered five patterns for decentralized control in self-adaptive systems that describe how MAPE loops can be related to each other. We describe the essence of these patterns in the following shortly:

- **Coordinated Control Pattern:** Consider a distributed system where each node owns an own MAPE loop. This pattern proposes that all the *Monitor, Analyze, Plan*, and *Execute* steps coordinate their operation with corresponding peers of other loops. For instance, *Analyze* entities interact with each other to make a decision about the need for an adaption.
- **Information Sharing Pattern:** In this pattern, all *Monitors* in a distributed system are sharing their observed states with each other, while *Analyze, Plan* and *Execute* entities are acting independently from their counterparts on other nodes.
- **Master/Slave Pattern:** There exists a central master component that is responsible for the *Analyze* and *Plan* step of adaptions. The other nodes in such a system are responsible for monitoring states and executing actions.
- **Regional Planning Pattern:** Such a distributed system is partitioned into regions where in each region a central component performs the *Plan* step. The *Monitor, Analyze,* and *Execute* steps are deployed on other nodes. The central *Plan* components can be connected with each other.
- **Hierarchical Control Pattern:** This pattern organizes MAPE loops in hierarchies. For instance, a loop is in control of a node. If it cannot adapt, a situation can be escalated to a higher loop that possesses a broader control of the target distributed system.

Another important design decision concerning self-adaptive systems is whether a control loop is realized event-driven or time-driven.

Models@Run.time

Models@Run.time is a term for describing the research field of utilizing software models, specified according to the Model-Driven Software Engineering (MDSE) principles, for self-adaptive software systems (Blair, Bencomo, & France, 2009). The runtime refers to the novelty opposed to the fact that traditional MDSE has been applied for describing the architecture of software and systems at design time. One of the most prominent examples of such a design time technology is the Unified Modeling Language (UML) standardized by the Object Management Group.

Figure 6 illustrates the core principle of MDSE (Brambilla, Cabot, & Wimmer, 2012). Note that a meta-model, also known as modeling language, is in fact a model.

M3: This layer is the basis of the MDSE architecture. Its purpose is to provide a modeling language for defining modeling languages. Usually a meta-meta-model is defined reflexively, that means it can define itself. In practice, it does not make any sense to define further meta layers, (Brambilla et al., 2012). In Figure 6 this behavior is described by a conformsTo relationship.

M2: The purpose of this layer is to describe modeling languages which are used on the next layer for specifying the actual model. It has to conform to the meta-meta-model at layer M3, like a programming language has to conform to its grammar. For instance, UML itself resides on this level.

M1: Models at this layer represent and abstract modeled systems. They have to conform to the corresponding meta-model. An example would be an UML model describing classes of a software.

M0: This layer is not part of the modeling world and part of the real world. It consists of real systems, which are abstracted and represented by M1 models.

Figure 6. Four-layer metamodeling architecture typically used in model-driven engineering
Based on Bézivin (2004).

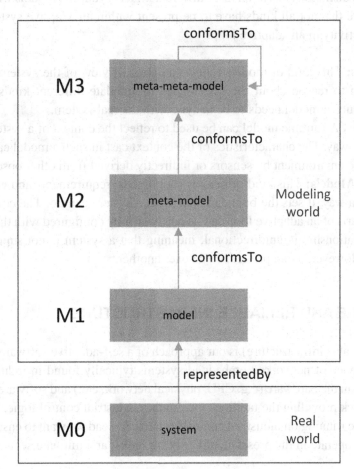

Now, a runtime model is essentially a software model that represents at runtime parts of a real system and is causally connected to it (e.g. a system change leads to a change in the model). Such software model possesses several properties that are in our opinion beneficial for self-adaptive software systems:

- Design time models are in many domains already available and can be transformed to living specifications at runtime.
- A model can be queried in order to find resources and to learn something about a system.
- Software models are based on modeling languages (M2) and adhere to semantics. Simply put, a mechanism cannot easily construct a model randomly and arbitrary.
- Validation is an important aspect of software models and constraints can be provided for ensuring that a runtime model is correct.
- An adaption mechanism can explore if a change would be correct by forking a model and trying out different configurations.
- Transformation is an essential part of MDSE. Manipulating and transforming models to executable artifacts offers systems an opportunity to self-modify. Further a changed runtime model could be transformed to input formats for a variety of simulation and verification software.
- Runtime models which change over time can be transformed back to design models.

Giese et al. (2014) distinguish between three different kinds of runtime models within a self-adaptive software system. Note that not all kinds have to be present within an adaptive system, but all of them are useful for each activity in an adaptive loop:

- **System Models:** This kind of models reflects an abstract view of the system itself. It allows an adaptive system to reason about the system and to simulate different kinds of configurations. Consequently, such a model needs to be in sync with the real system.
- **Context Models:** A runtime model can be used to reflect the context of a system and to specify it in a processable way. The characteristics of the context cast in such a model can either be derived directly from the environment by sensors or indirectly derived from other observations.
- **Requirements Models:** This kind of models captures the requirements and goals of a self-adaptive system. In a way, it sets the boundaries of what a system can do. The collect, analyze, plan/decide, or act parts of an adaptive loop can be partly or fully configured with these kinds of model. Usually this relationship is unidirectional, meaning that a system is not supposed to change its requirements. However, it can prioritize one over another.

SCARI: A SECURE AND RELIABLE INFRASTRUCTURE

Scari (**S**ecure **a**nd **r**eliable **i**nfrastructure) is our approach of a self-adaptive software system that targets to increase the resilience of networked embedded systems typically found in industry. With the term infrastructure, we mean the hardware (e.g. CPU, physical network, etc.) and software (operating system, applications, etc.) stack providing the facilities for running industrial control logic. We do not target to adapt the control logic running on industrial control systems. Instead we want to ensure that devices and networks last longer, operate in the presence of hardware faults, and mitigate security attacks. Further, we target to make control devices smarter in order to recognize anomalies in the data they receive from their environment.

In the following, we start by explaining our specific industrial setting from the hydro-power domain. Then we move on to a detailed specification of the vision of Scari. After that we present thoroughly our approach. Last, we discuss two simplified use cases, one handling a hardware fault, the other illustrates a security attack.

Industrial Setting

The context of this work are distributed control devices that operate hydro-power plant units. The reason why we choose this context is that such systems are also the context of our research project within the presented approach is developed. Figure 7 illustrates a simplified overview of the Supervisory Control And Data Acquisition (SCADA) system we are aiming to make more reliable by applying an adaptive software system.

On network level, control devices are connected via ethernet and operated by a supervisory system. These supervisory computers are mainly responsible for two things. One responsibility is to observe the state of physical processes. The other one is to adjust parameters of control devices in order to control

Figure 7. Overview of the target SCADA system

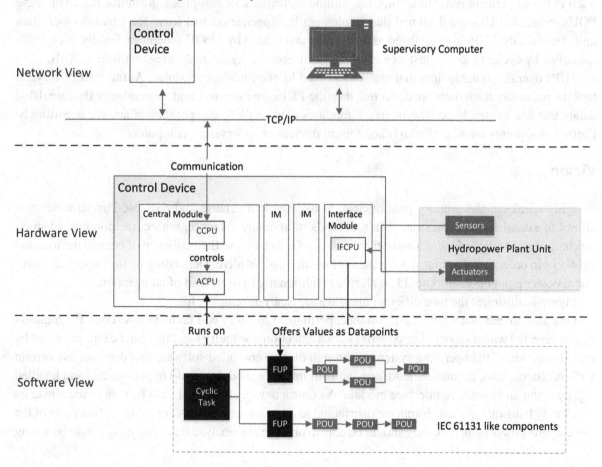

the energy conversions. The observation and adjustment actions are done by using so-called datapoints which are variables with a certain basic data type like integer or Boolean.

The control devices are connected to hydropower plant units. Their functional responsibility is to operate these units through one of the four different phases namely excitation, synchronization, protection and turbine control.

Technically, these devices have a programmable logic controller (PLC) architecture. Concerning the hardware design, a control device is build out of central modules and interface modules. A central module consists of a communication CPU (CCPU) and an application CPU (ACPU). The CCPU is responsible for network connections and controlling/monitoring the ACPU. It runs a customized Linux distribution and can be accessed by various protocols like SSH and Modbus. From the security point of view, it protects the ACPU and verifies incoming commands. The ACPU is a multi-core processor and executes the actual control logic. It runs a real-time operating system in order to ensure guaranteed cycle times. The interface modules are connecting the control device with sensors and actuators of the hydropower plant unit. Central modules and interface modules are connected via Ethernet.

The control logic software executed by the ACPU of a central module is component-based and heavily influenced by the IEC 61131 standard for programmable logic controllers (John & Tiegelkamp, 2010). Basically, the control logic is hierarchically build out of components, compositions and tasks. Components are called Program Organization Units (POU) and compositions are named Function Plans (FUP). POUs are coded with the C-programming language and stored as binaries on the devices. Such POUs implement basic functions, e.g. simple logic gates, or complex algorithms. Based on these POUs, reusable FUPs are designed that implement the specific control logic for a hydropower plant unit. Technically, FUPs are serialized as XML files and loaded by a POU scheduler. Finally, such FUPs are called by cyclic tasks, for instance every 10 milliseconds. Again, tasks are serialized as XML files.

FUPs operate on datapoints that are set and read by the interface modules. At the start of a cyclic task the necessary datapoints are collected, then the FUPs are executed, and subsequently the calculated datapoints are written back. The interface modules receive these datapoints and actuate accordingly. Further, datapoints are shared with other control devices or supervisory computers.

Vision

Roughly speaking, the primary goal of Scari is to provide a generic and reusable infrastructure that allows to establish and orchestrate different kinds of anomaly detection with corresponding adaption mechanisms. The aim of these adaption mechanisms is to increase the resilience of control devices and networks in order to keep control processes as long as possible alive. Depending on the impact of a situation, power plant operators should be alarmed additionally to or instead of an adaption.

Figure 8 illustrates the four different areas we are Scari developing for.

One area are hardware faults. For instance, permanent memory cell faults in RAM or CPU registers can be detected with memory checks. After such a detection, the faulty locations can be circumvented by reconfiguration of the operating system or through diverse compiled software that does not use certain CPU registers. Also, permanent hardware faults in interface modules could be recognized and handled e.g. by using an alternative interface module. A control device should not only be able to recognize its own faulty hardware. As datapoints are distributed to other control devices controlling other parts of the same hydro-power plant unit, they should be able to observe and analyze that something might be wrong

Figure 8. Problem areas we are targeting to detect and adapt to

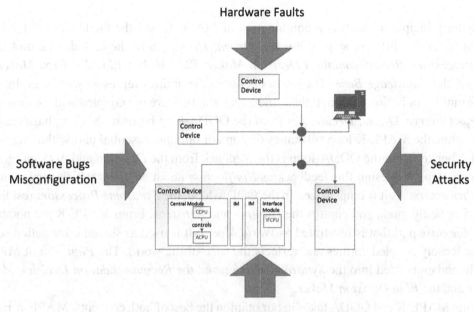

with the hardware of other control devices or networking devices. Ultimately, the control logic running on one device could be migrated to alternative ACPUs, central modules, or devices.

The second area are security attacks. Each control device knows in principal from whom it receives or sends data to. This information could be used for detecting network attacks or attacker that behave like a control device. Further, infected devices can be detected if the datapoints they are distributing are suddenly or over time odd and do not reflect the real environment. Additionally, the behavior of real devices which are unexpectedly trying to access control devices they are not supposed to, can be a hint for a security incident. Revealed attacks can be handled by blocking and isolating infected devices or network resources. Other kinds of attacks are for instance software that tries to access resources it is not allowed to or sensors that are physically manipulated.

The third area is the environment the control devices are interacting with. The control devices are not directly connected with a water turbine. There are sensors and actuators in between that can break or drift over time. Detecting such anomalies and reacting to them would again make a system more reliable.

The last area are software bugs or misconfigurations of the control devices and networking devices. An adaptive software system can detect high CPU loads, memory consumptions or frequent real-time violations.

An adaptive software system dealing with all of these four areas has the potential of increasing the life-time, reliability, and security of industrial systems. As we can imagine of the examples, not only the analyzed datapoints can often be the same, also adaption mechanisms (e.g. migration) can be reused for handling different faults. Therefore, we believe that one generic architecture orchestrating different anomaly detection mechanisms and adaption strategies is needed. Further, a representation of the context, the requirements and the system itself through models has a significant potential of boosting detection, decision, and adaption mechanisms.

Approach

The underlying principle of Scari is a combination of MAPE-K and the OODA-loop of John Boyd. Figure 9 illustrates the different steps (*Observe, Orient, Decide, Act*), the included entities (*Monitor, Syndrome Processors, Recommendation Decision Maker, Plan Maker, Plan Decision Maker, Action Handler*), and the *Knowledge Base*. The arrows between the entities represent messages. Information between the entities only flows through these messages and they are not coupled with other means. We take the steps *Observe, Orient, Decide, Act* from the OODA-loop because they emphasize an explicit *Decide* step while the MAPE-K loop subsumes this, in our opinion, essential part within the step *Plan*. What we also borrow from the OODA-loop is the feedback from the *Decision* and *Act* steps going back to the *Observe* step. We design this feedback as *Notification* about an *Event* which triggers interested *Syndrome Processors*. As it is emphasized in the OODA-loop, the *Syndrome Processors* residing in the *Orient* step implicitly guide and control the *Observe* and *Act* steps. From MAPE-K we notably adopt the *Knowledge Base* part that is illustrated as *World Model*. It is used as shared information source for the different loosely coupled entities and reflects the state of the world. The *Plan* step of MAPE-K is actually split and embedded into the *Syndrome Processors*, the *Recommendation Decision Maker*, the *Plan Maker* and the *Plan Decision Maker*.

Combining MAPE-K and OODA takes in our opinion the best of both concepts. MAPE-K introduces the *Knowledge Base* as a common information source for the different steps. OODA adds an explicit *Decide* part which is useful for the coordination concerning which kind of mechanism is performed. As explained above, the *Plan* step of MAPE-K is distributed over several loosely coupled entities. What we also take from OODA is that each step gives feedback to *Monitors* and *Syndrome Processors*. This is allowing them to take into consideration what happened with their notifications and recommendations.

In detail the adaptive loop illustrated in Figure 9 works as follows: In the first step, named *Orient*, a *Monitor* recognizes an *Event*. This could be for instance an unexpected datapoint value monitored by a simple voter that compares two runs of the same task (we elaborate this example in one of the following

Figure 9. Adaptive loop of Scari

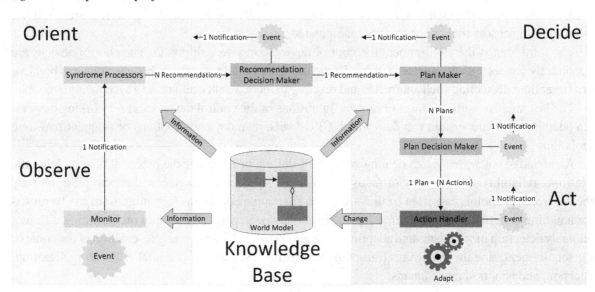

use cases). The voter is the *Monitor* and the unexpected datapoint represents the *Event*. The adaptive loop itself can only be triggered by an *Event*. In principle, the Scari loop is event-driven and not time-driven.

In the next step, the collected data about the Event is distributed by the *Monitor* as *Notification* message to an arbitrary number of interested *Syndrome Processors*. *Syndrome Processors* are part of the *Orient* step and specialized on recognizing specific syndromes e.g. a security attack based on the received *Notifications* (in MAPE-K *Notifications* are called symptoms). The used techniques for analyzing *Events* and to detect anomalies can technically vary. For some cases a classification approach from the machine-learning domain can be beneficial while for others one receive of a specific Event is enough for instantly diagnosing a syndrome. The *Syndrome Processors* do not have to react every time they receive a *Notification*. They can collect several *Notifications* about different *Events* over time in order to diagnose a syndrome. After a *Syndrome Processor* is sure about an anomaly or wants to find out more about a situation it fires a so-called *Recommendation*. A *Recommendation* consists of a *Plan* type and a collection of *Notifications* that are significant for the *Recommendation*. There exist two general classes of *Plan* types. One kind of types is targeting to find out more about a situation, e.g. a memory test. The other kind changes a system and adapts the software. We treat both classes in the same way because they cost time and can delay other computations. Further, it would make adaption mechanisms very fragile if costly analyzing mechanisms are carried out at the same time on the same CPU or device. Therefore, it is important that only one plan mechanism is executed on a system at one point in time.

The *Recommendation Decision Maker* plays a key role in the orchestration of different *Recommendations* that may be received from different *Syndrome Processors* within a short configurable period of time. Based on a simple definable prioritization, first of the covered *Events* and then of the chosen *Plan* types, it decides which *Recommendation* gets selected. Of course, if the world is locked because a *Plan* is currently executed, the *Recommendation Decision Maker* rejects to decide and distributes an *Event* as *Notification* that it currently cannot decide. It is up to the *Syndrome Processors* to evaluate such a situation. If a *Recommendation* is successfully selected, then the *Recommendation Decision Maker* distributes an *Event* and retransmits the final *Recommendation* marked as selected.

In the next phase, part of the same step *Decide*, the selected *Recommendation* is processed by a *Plan Maker* that can create variants of a chosen *Plan* type based on the information from the *World Model*. A *Plan* consists of a collection of *Actions*. An *Action* is an atomic activity carried out on the target system. The potentially more than one *Plans* are again distributed and a corresponding *Event* is thrown.

After that, the *Plans* are processed by a *Plan Decision Maker* which chooses the *Plan* with the least affected systems/resources and the least amount of used Actions.

In the last step, named *Act*, the selected *Plan* is taken by an *Action Handler*. This entity executes the single *Actions* contained within a *Plan* and changes the *World Model* accordingly. Note that this is the only entity in the adaptive loop that can actively change a system.

As mentioned above, the *World Model* is the central knowledge base for all parts of the adaptive loop in Figure 9. It consists of various models describing parts of the architecture of a system at runtime. Examples of such parts are control logic (Tasks, FUPs, POUs), installed software applications, hardware (RAM, CPU, etc.), network connections and so on. We engineer these architecture runtime models according to the model-driven engineering principles (Brambilla et al., 2012). So, we have metamodels defining domain-specific languages and one meta-metamodel serving as a common technical base for the metamodels. One reason for applying model-driven engineering techniques is that we can precisely describe a part of a system with a specialized language that only the interested entities need to understand. A generalized schema for representing data would make it more difficult to grasp the semantics and less effective to support the *Observe*, *Orient*, and *Decide* steps. Another reason is that models are manageable reflections that abstract from unnecessary details of the system (Aßmann, Götz, Jézéquel, Morin, & Trapp, 2014). In addition to the *World Model*, the *Knowledge Base* incorporates a log of the distributed messages (*Notification, Recommendation, Plan, Action*) and a revision hash that changes if the *World Model* changes. The revision hash is used by the *Recommendation* and *Plan* messages in order to ensure that they refer to the current state of the *World Model*. If a message is not referring to the current state it is simply ignored by the *Decide* and *Act* entities because it comes from a former state of the world. Crucial for the adaptive loop is that the *World Model* can only be changed with an *Action* executed by *the Action Handler* while others can just access the *World Model* for deriving information.

Note that all entities within the four steps *Observe, Orient, Decide and Act* are executed in parallel in separate processes. The *Recommendation Decision Maker* may be blocked because the *Action Handler* is adapting but it is always running for denying or allowing *Recommendations*.

So far, we have only explained the entities and steps of the adaptive loop used by Scari but not how and where we want to deploy them. Figure 10 illustrates that we foresee multiple loops on different adaption layers. The lowest layer resides on the ACPU while the parent layer of that loop is located on the CCPU. On top of that are adaptive loops grouping control devices according to their logical structure.

We organize these loops in a directed acyclic graph. That means a loop can have one to several parent loops where it can escalate to if it cannot handle an anomaly. In literature, organizing adaptive loops in the presented way is known as *Hierarchical Control* pattern (Weyns et al., 2013).

There are two reasons for us organizing the Scari adaption loops in a hierarchical way.

The first reason is that *Knowledge Bases* only need to know their subgraphs. If a *World Model* on a node changes, information is only propagated up to the parent nodes. A *Knowledge Base* may be configured

Figure 10. Multi-layer Scari

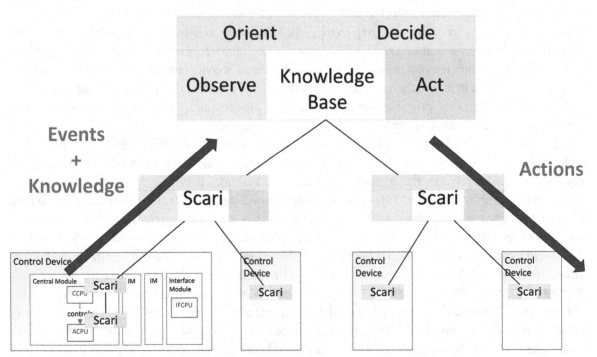

to prune lower node data if it is not needed on the higher levels. Further it is more efficient regarding memory consumption if information is only present on nodes or until certain layers, where it is actually needed. Distributing all information on all nodes would additionally lead to more network traffic.

The second reason for a hierarchical organization is that an adaptive loop only needs to handle its subgraph. A loop does not need to manage other parts of the overall graph which also eases the configuration of Scari. If it is not possible to adapt to an *Event* happening on a node, it can be escalated to a parent node that has more knowledge, more and different resources under control and can therefore leverage mightier adaption mechanisms. In our hydro-power setting, it is imaginable that these adaption layers are even laid over different hydro-power plants (then of course acting on bigger time scales).

As shown in Figure 10 the information that flows a graph up are *Events* and *Knowledge*, while the information going down are *Actions* adjusting lower nodes. It is important to note that an adaptive loop residing on a higher layer needs to lock all *Action Handlers* of the lower loops. Otherwise, one lower adaptive loop could be faster with an own *Plan* and the result of two interfering *Actions* would be unpredictable. Even if a lower node is not in the scope of a higher layer *Plan* it could lead to uncertainty if such a node is allowed to change its behavior.

Another aspect that needs to be taken in consideration are the different time scales residing on the different layers. An adaptive loop on the ACPU can react much quicker than an adaptive loop overlooking several control devices. Also, the communication between the layers can take a notably amount of time. Further, the control logic operating a hydro-power plant unit should not be disrupted by observing *Monitors*.

Last a few words on the technical implementation of Scari. In general, we implement the different entities with the C++ programming language together with the Qt framework. The *messages Notification, Recommendation, Plan and Action* within one adaptive loop are distributed over DBus which is a software bus (the developers call it a smart socket) enabling a loose coupling between *Monitors, Syndrome Processors,* and so on. The communication between the layers is implemented with encrypted websockets. The self-adaptive infrastructure itself has to be secured, otherwise it would represent a huge attack surface. The *Plan Maker* and the *Action Handler* entities are offering a plugin architecture in order to create *Plans* for a specific plan type or to implement the actual *Action*. Concerning the *World Models* we are using an own C++ modeling framework inspired by the Eclipse Modeling Framework. Scari itself with the different adaptive layers is supposed to be statically configured beforehand.

Exemplary Use Cases

In the following we present two examples that demonstrate the potential of Scari. The first one is about a permanent hardware fault located inside the RAM. The second one demonstrates a case where a control device is infected by malicious software.

Hardware Fault Example

Figure 11 shows an overview of a hardware fault case. In this scenario one calculation is running redundant on core 1 and core 3. Both calculations are observed by a voter (*Monitor*). Now, if a data mismatch is happening then the voter notifies a minimalistic syndrome processor that instantly recommends to check the used memory areas and the used CPUs. This *Recommendation* is processed by a *Recommendation Decision Maker* and forwarded to the *Plan Maker*. The *Plan Maker* selects suitable time slots

Figure 11. Overview of the hardware fault example

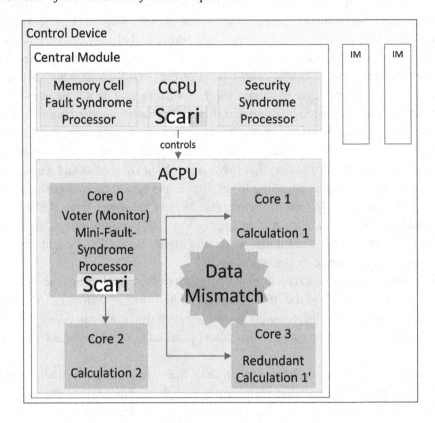

for the checks. This is possible because the actual task execution time is lower than the specified cycle time. Such time windows open the possibility to perform memory checks seeking permanent hardware faults. After the plan is created, we omit the *Plan Decision Maker*. We scale down the Scari loop on the ACPU for performance reasons. We want to react on the ACPU within a short time period because the control loop is directly affected. Therefore, we omit the *Plan Decision Maker* and also drop the *Knowledge Base* as it costs memory and processing power. After the memory checks are performed, we have a result, which is again processed by the minimalistic syndrome processor. If one memory area in the RAM is affected, then the syndrome processor recommends to just use the results of the working calculation and to ignore the other one. This *Recommendation* goes through the reduced adaptive loop and finally an *Event* is thrown by the *Action Handler* that the reconfiguration finished. Again, the minimalistic syndrome processor reacts on such an Event and notifies the higher-layer about the situation on the ACPU. The higher-layer is located on the CCPU where we have more time on analyzing situations. A security syndrome processor may use this as evidence that something suspicious is going on. A memory fault syndrome processor may recommend to start a redundant calculation on another module part of the device. Or it recommends that the memory area of the affected task gets remapped to circumvent the faulty memory cell and to restart the redundant calculation. Hoeller, Spitzer, Rauter, Iber, & Kreiner (2016) show that diverse compilation of software has the potential of circumventing faulty hardware locations. It is imaginable that such an approach is applicable for us to heal the hardware with recompiled software to a certain degree.

What we learn from this example is that the adaptive loops have different temporal properties. A Scari loop on the ACPU has to react faster than the higher loop on the CCPU. On the ACPU, we are also restricted on the use of parallel processes as we usually only have one core available for adaption purposes. Therefore, we omit a *Knowledge Base* and a *Plan Decision Maker*. The *Plan Maker* is configured to only create one *Plan*. If an ACPU does not execute several tasks the Scari loop may be dynamically configured to load functionality in order to diagnose more syndromes.

In the presented example, we are in fact dealing with cross-cutting concerns. The faulty memory location may also be caused by a security-related attack. Orchestrating different detection and adaption mechanisms is one of the main benefits of applying a self-adaptive software system like Scari. Another benefit is that recommendations and actions can be reused by different syndrome processors.

Security Example

Figure 12 illustrates an overview of a security-related example. Let's suppose that control device X has been infected with a malicious software. This hostile software may target to slowly destroy a hydro-power plant unit, similar to the intention of the famous Stuxnet computer worm (Falliere, Murchu, & Chien, 2011; Langner, 2011). Syndrome processors, located on the CCPU of control devices, connected to the same hydro-power plant unit, have the means to detect the slow but harmful drift of datapoints. They can react for instance by notifying a higher-layer adaption loop that the data they are observing, drifts. The notified layer has more insights into the situation and is able to react with mightier mechanisms for instance by isolating a device and migrating the application logic.

Further, if an infected device tries to spread the malicious software to other devices, those devices can detect such an intrusion. They obey structural information of what connections are allowed and can therefore come to the conclusion that an unexpected connection attempt from a device is in fact a hostile

Figure 12. Overview of the security example

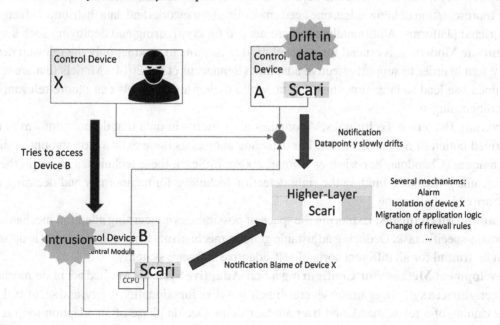

attack. Based on this diagnosed syndrome, devices could react by blaming the infected device and the higher layer could again isolate and migrate to stand-by devices.

In the presented example, we know beforehand that it is a security-related situation. Syndrome processors have to analyze notifications by running algorithms that detect such patterns. It might also be that there are syndrome processors which are dedicated to diagnose hardware faults and interpret the situation differently. This is another benefit of Scari as it provides a common infrastructure for communication. It allows to compete syndrome processors about the best recommendation. Essentially, this is the reason why it is important to prioritize events and plan types in order to make a decision. For instance, we generally suggest that security-related events have a higher priority than hardware-related. However, it depends on the domain and the available means how events and plan types are prioritized.

RESEARCH CHALLENGES

Although, there is a high potential for the proposed self-adaptive software infrastructure, it possesses many research challenges. We derived following challenges based on our experience with Scari.

1. **Determinism:** Applications usually found in industrial settings have to fulfill real-time requirements. Monitor and especially adapt mechanisms introduce time delays that are complicated to predict. In addition, an adaption mechanism needs to be sure that timing constraints are intact after a system change.
2. **Resource Overhead:** The impact of all entities part of the self-adaptive software system on the resource requirements (e.g. performance, memory, network traffic) should be kept low simply because they are deployed on embedded devices.
3. **Tools and Frameworks:** Implementing a self-adaptive software system is not a trivial task. One has to build several tools and frameworks with well-defined interfaces. The software part of the adaption loop has to be generic and adjustable to the specific domain and adaption layer. Concerning the representation of knowledge, one needs modeling frameworks and data distribution facilities for restricted platforms. Additionally, tools are needed for configuring and deploying such a system.
4. **Runtime Models:** It is crucial for a model used at runtime to abstract only the relevant details of a system in order to support effective adaption (Bennaceur et al., 2014). Models that are too fine-grained can lead to large amounts of data, while higher-level models can ignore relevant details for diagnosing syndromes.
5. **Anomaly Detection Techniques:** Anomalies are patterns in data that do not conform to a well-defined notion of normal behavior. For detecting anomalies there exist a vast amount of different techniques (Chandola, Banerjee, & Kumar, 2009). In Scari, these techniques reside in the single syndrome processors. Finding the right detection technique for an anomaly and deciding what is abnormal is challenging.
6. **Adaption Mechanisms:** Exploring the space of possibilities concerning adaption mechanisms is a domain-specific task. Deducing adjustable generic mechanisms from domain-specific approaches can be fruitful for all different sorts of self-adaptive software systems.
7. **Development Methods for Configuring a Self-Adaptive System:** Applied adaption mechanisms directly affect a system regarding several dimensions like functionality, safety, and security. Further, the valuing of a recommendation over another in the Decide phase of an adaption loop is in fact

a design decision made by system architects. Therefore, we advocate that these aspects actively have to be taken into consideration at design time of a system, for instance during a hazard and risk analysis.

8. **Testing and Assurance:** There need to be means in order to verify that a system is still working as expected after an adaption. In Scari we currently assume that an adaption mechanism is behaving as intended. As pointed out by Salehie & Tahvildari (2009) *testing and assurance are probably the least focused phases in engineering self-adaptive software, and there are only a few research efforts addressing this topic.*

9. **Self-Optimization:** Observing a system and adapting it to become better regarding performance and memory consumption may yield significant improvements. There is of course the risk that one causes unintentionally the opposite effect solely by performing costly optimization observations and adaptions.

10. **Interference of the Managed System Through Human Operators:** Industrial control systems have to be adjustable by operators at runtime. An adaptive system has to be aware of such an intentional manipulation and should not counteract by adaption. As far as we know, little has been mentioned about this potential problem in literature.

11. **Interoperability:** As we are facing systems of systems, it can become crucial for self-adaptive software systems to work together. For this issue, there is a need for well-defined standardized protocols and formats.

FUTURE RESEARCH DIRECTIONS

At the time of this writing, we are in the stage of implementing and trying out different detection and adaption mechanisms. This relates to the two challenges *Anomaly Detection Techniques* and *Adaption Mechanisms*. In the near future, we plan to investigate methods for configuring a self-adaptive system and ways of dealing with interferences through human operators. *Testing and Assurance* is another challenge which we want to tackle by conducting research whether the potential of model-driven engineering can be leveraged for increasing the confidence in performing adaptions.

CONCLUSION

In this chapter, we outlined a novel application of an adaptive software system within a CPS setting. Increasing the resilience of current and future CPS system is one of the key challenges in order to relieve the ever increase of complexity and unpredictability. Self-adaptive software systems are a promising approach of dealing with these key challenges as they observe, diagnose problems, and apply mechanisms in order to adapt and enhance a system. With Scari we presented a concept of a self-adaptive system currently targeting hydro-power plants. We are confident that other industrial or Internet of Things domains can learn from our ongoing approach and that many aspects are reusable. We demonstrate the applicability of this system on two uses cases, one handling a hardware fault, while the other identifies a security attack. We outlined several research challenges derived from Scari and are going to investigate several of them in the future.

REFERENCES

Alhakeem, M. S., Munk, P., Lisicki, R., Parzyjegla, H., Parzyjegla, H., & Muehl, G. (2015). A Framework for Adaptive Software-Based Reliability in COTS Many-Core Processors. In *Proceedings the 28th international conference on architecture of computing systems ARCS '15* (pp. 1–4).

Aßmann, U., Götz, S., Jézéquel, J.-M., Morin, B., & Trapp, M. (2014). A Reference Architecture and Roadmap for Models@run.time Systems. In *Models@run.time: Foundations, applications, and roadmaps* (pp. 1–18). doi:10.1007/978-3-319-08915-7_1

Bennaceur, A., France, R., Tamburrelli, G., Vogel, T., Mosterman, P. J., & Cazzola, W. ... Redlich, D. (2014). Mechanisms for leveraging models at runtime in self-adaptive software. In N. Bencomo, R. France, B.H.C. Cheng et al. (Eds.), *Models@run.time: Foundations, applications, and roadmaps* (pp. 19–46). Cham: Springer International Publishing. doi:10.1007/978-3-319-08915-7_2

Bézivin, J. (2004). In search of a basic principle for model driven engineering. *Novatica Journal, Special Issue, 5*(2), 21–24.

Blair, G., Bencomo, N., & France, R. B. (2009). Models@run.time. *Computer, 42*(10), 22–27. doi:10.1109/MC.2009.326

Boyd, J. R. (1996). The Essence of Winning and Losing. Retrieved from http://dnipogo.org/john-r-boyd/

Brambilla, M., Cabot, J., & Wimmer, M. (2012). Model-Driven Software Engineering in Practice. *Synthesis Lectures on Software Engineering, 1*(1), 1–182. doi:10.2200/S00441ED1V01Y201208SWE001

Brun, Y., Desmarais, R., Geihs, K., Litoiu, M., Lopes, A., Shaw, M., & Smit, M. (2013). A Design Space for Self-Adaptive Systems. In R. de Lemos, H. Giese, H. A. Müller, & M. Shaw (Eds.), *Software engineering for self-adaptive systems ii* (pp. 33–50). Berlin, Heidelberg: Springer Berlin Heidelberg. doi:10.1007/978-3-642-35813-5_2

Chandola, V., Banerjee, A., & Kumar, V. (2009). Anomaly Detection: A Survey. *ACM Computing Surveys, 41*(3), 1–58. doi:10.1145/1541880.1541882

Chandra, A., Lewis, P. R., Glette, K., & Stilkerich, S. C. (2016). Reference Architecture for Self-aware and Self-expressive Computing Systems. In P. R. Lewis, M. Platzner, B. Rinner, J. Tørresen, & X. Yao (Eds.), *Self-aware computing systems: An engineering approach* (pp. 37–49). Cham: Springer International Publishing. doi:10.1007/978-3-319-39675-0_4

Cheng, B. H. C., de Lemos, R., Giese, H., Inverardi, P., Magee, J., & Andersson, J. ... Whittle, J. (2009). Software Engineering for Self-Adaptive Systems: A Research Roadmap. In B.H.C. Cheng, R. de Lemos, H. Giese et al. (Eds.), *Software engineering for self-adaptive systems* (pp. 1–26). Berlin, Heidelberg: Springer. doi:10.1007/978-3-642-02161-9_1

Dobson, S., Sterritt, R., Nixon, P., & Hinchey, M. (2010). Fulfilling the Vision of Autonomic Computing. *Computer, 43*(1), 35–41. doi:10.1109/MC.2010.14

Dobson, S., Zambonelli, F., Denazis, S., Fernández, A., Gaïti, D., & Gelenbe, E. … Schmidt, N. (2006). A survey of autonomic communications. *ACM Transactions on Autonomous and Adaptive Systems, 1*(2), 223–259. doi:10.1145/1186778.1186782

Falliere, N., Murchu, L. O., & Chien, E. (2011). W32. stuxnet dossier. *White Paper, Symantec Corp., Security Response, 5*(6).

Giese, H., Bencomo, N., Pasquale, L., Ramirez, A. J., Inverardi, P., Wätzoldt, S., & Clarke, S. (2014). Living with Uncertainty in the Age of Runtime Models. In N. Bencomo, R. France, B. H. C. Cheng, & U. Aßmann (Eds.), *Models@run.time: Foundations, applications, and roadmaps* (pp. 47–100). Cham: Springer International Publishing. doi:10.1007/978-3-319-08915-7_3

Grenander, S., Simpson, K., & Sindiy, O. (2009). The Autonomy System Architecture. In *Proceedings of the AIAA infotech@Aerospace conference*. Reston, Virigina: American Institute of Aeronautics; Astronautics. doi:10.2514/6.2009-1884

Hinchey, M., & Sterritt, R. (2006). Self-Managing Software. *Computer, 39*(2), 107–109. doi:10.1109/MC.2006.69

Hoeller, A., Spitzer, B., Rauter, T., Iber, J., & Kreiner, C. (2016). *Diverse Compiling for Software-Based Recovery of Permanent Faults in COTS Processors. In 2016 46th annual ieee/ifip international conference on dependable systems and networks workshop (dsn-w)* (pp. 143–148). IEEE; doi:10.1109/DSN-W.2016.34

Jelasity, M., Babaoglu, O., Laddaga, R., Nagpal, R., Zambonelli, F., & Sirer, E. … Smirnov, M. (2006). Interdisciplinary Research: Roles for Self-Organization. *IEEE Intelligent Systems, 21*(2), 50–58. doi:10.1109/MIS.2006.30

John, K. H., & Tiegelkamp, M. (2010). *IEC 61131-3: Programming Industrial Automation Systems*. Berlin, Heidelberg: Springer Berlin Heidelberg. doi:10.1007/978-3-642-12015-2

Kephart, J., & Chess, D. (2003). The vision of autonomic computing. *Computer, 36*(1), 41–50. doi:10.1109/MC.2003.1160055

Laddaga, R. (2001). Active Software. In P. Robertson, H. Shrobe, & R. Laddaga (Eds.), *Self-adaptive software: First international workshop, IWSAS 2000* (pp. 11–26). Berlin, Heidelberg: Springer Berlin Heidelberg. doi:10.1007/3-540-44584-6_2

Langner, R. (2011). Stuxnet: Dissecting a Cyberwarfare Weapon. *IEEE Security & Privacy Magazine, 9*(3), 49–51. doi:10.1109/MSP.2011.67

Miller, B., & Rowe, D. (2012). A survey SCADA of and critical infrastructure incidents. In *Proceedings of the 1st annual conference on research in information technology - riit '12* (p. 51). New York, New York, USA: ACM Press. doi:10.1145/2380790.2380805

Muccini, H., Sharaf, M., & Weyns, D. (2016). Self-adaptation for Cyber-physical Systems: A Systematic Literature Review. In *Proceedings of the 11th international workshop on software engineering for adaptive and self-managing systems - seams '16* (pp. 75–81). New York, New York, USA: ACM Press. doi:10.1145/2897053.2897069

Müller, J. P., & Fischer, K. (2014). Application Impact of Multi-agent Systems and Technologies: A Survey. In *Agent-oriented software engineering* (pp. 27–53). Berlin, Heidelberg: Springer Berlin Heidelberg. doi:10.1007/978-3-642-54432-3_3

NIST. (2013). *Foundations for Innovation in Cyber-Physical Systems.*

Oreizy, P., Gorlick, M., Taylor, R., Heimhigner, D., Johnson, G., & Medvidovic, N. ... Wolf, A. (1999). An architecture-based approach to self-adaptive software. *IEEE Intelligent Systems, 14*(3), 54–62. doi:10.1109/5254.769885

Salehie, M., & Tahvildari, L. (2009). Self-adaptive software: Landscape and research challenges. *ACM Transactions on Autonomous and Adaptive Systems, 4*(2), 1–42. doi:10.1145/1516533.1516538

Weyns, D., Schmerl, B., Grassi, V., Malek, S., Mirandola, R., & Prehofer, C. ... Göschka, K. M. (2013). On Patterns for Decentralized Control in Self-Adaptive Systems. In *Software engineering for self-adaptive systems ii* (pp. 76–107). doi:10.1007/978-3-642-35813-5_4

Wikimedia Commons. (2014). OODA loop. Retrieved from https://commons.wikimedia.org/wiki/File:OODA.Boyd.svg

KEY TERMS AND DEFINITIONS

Anomaly: An anomaly is a pattern in data that does not conform to a well-defined notion of normal behavior.

Model: A model is an abstraction of a system allowing predictions or inferences to be made.

Model-Driven Engineering: In this method models are the key artifacts of all development related activities and tasks.

Models@Run.time: A model@run.time is a causally connected model of the associated system that emphasizes the structure, behavior, or goals of the system.

Reliability: Reliability is the ability of a system to continue its correct service for a specified period of time.

Resilience: Resilience refers to the robustness of a system to adapt itself so as to absorb and tolerate the consequences of failures, attacks or changes.

Self-Adaptive Software System: A Self-adaptive software system is a system that modifies its own behavior in response to changes in its operating environment.

Section 3
Security Concerns in CPS

Chapter 10
Cyber–Physical System and Internet of Things Security:
An Overview

Thomas Ulz
Graz University of Technology, Austria

Sarah Haas
Infineon Austria AG, Austria

Christian Steger
Graz University of Technology, Austria

ABSTRACT

An increase of distributed denial-of-service (DDoS) attacks launched by botnets such as Mirai has raised public awareness regarding potential security weaknesses in the Internet of Things (IoT). Devices are an attractive target for attackers because of their large number and due to most devices being online 24/7. In addition, many traditional security mechanisms are not applicable for resource constraint IoT devices. The importance of security for cyber-physical systems (CPS) is even higher, as most systems process confidential data or control a physical process that could be harmed by attackers. While industrial IoT is a hot topic in research, not much focus is put on ensuring information security. Therefore, this paper intends to give an overview of current research regarding the security of data in industrial CPS. In contrast to other surveys, this work will provide an overview of the big CPS security picture and not focus on special aspects.

INTRODUCTION

In recent years, customers' demands for personalized products increased rapidly (Adomavicius & Tuzhilin, 2005). To account for these customer requests, traditional mass production facilities need to be altered such that personalized products can be manufactured in a cost-effective way. One possible

DOI: 10.4018/978-1-5225-2845-6.ch010

way to achieve this goal is to make factories smart by enabling the interconnection of all devices involved in the manufacturing process. The term Smart Factory was introduced by Zuelke (2010) when he described his vision of a factory-of-things. According to Zuelke, in such a factory-of-things, smart objects could interact with each other using Internet of Things (IoT) and cyber-physical systems (CPSs) concepts (Weiser, 1991) (Mattern & Floerkemeier, 2010), (Lee, 2008). Recent high-tech initiatives such as Germany's Industry 4.0 further extend the vision of smart factories beyond providing cost effective personalized products. In these initiatives, smart factories utilize self-organizing multi-agent systems that operate without human assistance. In addition, also big data analysis will play a major role in future smart factories in order to optimize production processes.

To account for the envisioned functionalities of a smart factory, devices ranging from battery operated sensors up to big data servers need to be interconnected. Due to the diversity of devices which might be resource constraint, standard web protocols such as HTTP often cannot be applied, thus making Web of Things (WoT) concepts infeasible. Instead, lightweight protocols and concepts from the IoT can be applied. IoT concepts in industrial contexts offer advantages but also critical disadvantages. One advantage is the possibility to control and reconfigure machines such that personalized products can be manufactured (Gibson, Rosen, Stucker et al., 2010). However, connecting production machinery to the Internet also results in issues that do not arise in traditional production facilities. Machinery that is accessible through the Internet implicates security and safety issues; security breaches in industrial contexts may lead to the loss of highly confidential data or may even threaten employees' lives (Cheng, Zhang, & Chen, 2016).

Security, however, is often not considered in industrial IoT research as current main topics in research are enabling technologies and production strategies. Therefore, the intention of this work is to present an overview of current security related research on industrial IoT and CPSs. In contrast to other works, the authors intend to give a broad overview of security aspects, not focusing on single special topics. This broad overview, however, is given in a compact form to present the big picture of IoT and CPS security. An overview of all topics discussed in this work is presented in the big picture shown in Figure 1.

This work is structured as follows. As background information, attack taxonomies are given and different types of attacks are discerned in Section Attack Taxonomies. Also in this Section, challenges of CPS security and differences compared to traditional IT systems are discussed. This section also lists current research trends regarding CPS security. To highlight the importance of IoT and CPS security, recent attacks targeting IoT devices and CPSs are presented in Section Attacks. The subsequent sections discuss security enhancing technologies on different layers as shown in Figure 1. Section Network Security lists network related security problems and solutions. Issues and fixes related to device security are discussed in Section Device Security where hardware and software related topics are discussed. This work is then concluded with Section Conclusion where also current hot research topics are briefly discussed.

ATTACK TAXONOMIES

Attacks in information security often are associated with the resulting "CIA" (Confidentiality, Integrity, Availability) triad security attributes that are broken by the respective attack. The three security attributes, as defined in principle by Saltzer and Schroeder (1975), are:

Figure 1. Big picture of IoT and CPS related security measures as discussed in this work
Source: Big Picture.

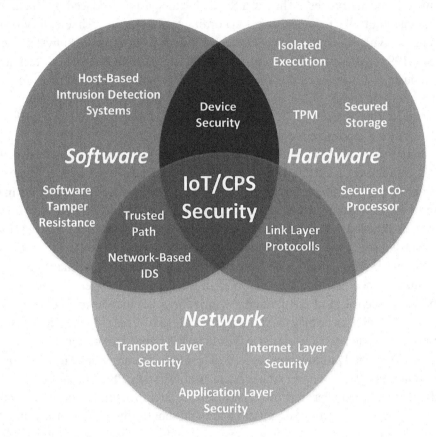

- **Confidentiality:** The property of information that is protected from unauthorized persons, entities or processes.
- **Integrity:** The property of information that is protected from being modified in an authorized, undetected manner during its entire life-cycle.
- **Availability:** Describes the property of information being available when it is needed such that the information system can serve its purpose.

Besides these three most commonly referred to security attributes, there are also many other attributes such authenticity, possession, or non-repudiation.

Attacks on cyber-physical systems can be further divided into two categories (Ravi, Raghunathan, Kocher, & Hattangady, 2004). Attacks corresponding to the first category, logical attacks can be conducted using existing communication interfaces. Logical attacks typically target software weaknesses and can be done remotely. The second category of attacks, physical and side-channel attacks, usually requires an attacker to have physical access to the hardware. An attacker that is able to physically access the targeted hardware is then able to attack both, the software and hardware weaknesses of a system.

Logical Attacks

Logical attacks can target either a single device or a whole network. Hansman and Hunt (2005) give a categorization of possible attacks on network and computer systems. Most of these attacks can also occur in CPSs or IoT systems.

- **Viruses and Worms:** Malicious software components executed at the targeted system. The malicious code is often spread and even updated via a network. Viruses and worms might compromise data confidentiality and integrity as well as the availability of systems.
- **Exploits:** By using weaknesses in a software or hardware implementation, attackers are able to perform various operations such as injecting malicious code or revealing secret data. Exploits include, for example, buffer overflows or various code injections (e.g. SQL-injection, cross site scripting). These attacks also target the confidentiality, integrity and availability of a system.
- **Denial of Service (DoS):** In DoS attacks, the aim is to make the service provided by the targeted system unavailable. This can be achieved in various ways such as flooding a server with a high amount of requests. This kind of attack targets the availability of a system.
- **Network Attacks:** In this type of attack, network related vulnerabilities are used to attack a system. The goal is often to redirect traffic to a malicious system. Examples of attacks include man-in-the-middle attacks or DNS spoofing. The targeted CIA attributes are confidentiality, integrity and availability.
- **Password Attacks:** Attackers try to reveal users' password in order to gain unauthorized access to a system. THIS can be done, for example, via brute force attacks or dictionary attacks. All three CIA attributes might be compromised by such attacks.

The above listed attacks are general attacks on network and computer systems. Pasqualetti et al. (2013) discuss logical attacks that are mainly relevant for CPSs. In contrast to the previously mentioned attacks, these attacks often target information regarding the physical process attached to a CPS.

- **Deception Attacks:** In deception attacks, wrong data (such as sensor data or control data) is injected into the CPS. On the one hand, an attacker might inject data that is false and unrelated to the system; however, such attacks might easily be detected. On the other hand, an attacker might first try to learn a system's behavior and then inject data based on the learned standard behavior (stealthy deception attack) which is harder to detect. This type of attack targets the integrity and as a possible consequence also the availability of a CPS.
- **Replay Attacks:** In replay attacks, an attacker first captures data produced by a CPS which also can be encrypted. After capturing that data, the attacker then injects this data into the system at a later point in time. In contrast to deception attacks, an attacker does not necessarily need to have any knowledge about the sent data. This type of attack also targets the integrity and availability of a CPS.

Physical and Side-Channel Attacks

Physical and side-channel attacks always compromise the confidentiality, integrity, and availability of CPSs due to the information revealed by them. These attacks can be categorized by two criteria: an attacker's behavior and the attack's degree of invasiveness. First, an attacker's behavior can be used to distinguish attacks (Kocher, Lee, McGraw, Raghunathan, & Moderator-Ravi, 2004):

- **Active Attack:** An attacker actively tries to induce faults into the hardware, for example, by injecting power spikes. In unprotected devices, this may lead to failures in the executed software which then might reveal keys or weaknesses of the implementation.
- **Passive Attack:** An attacker passively observes physical properties of the hardware, for example, a CPU's power consumption. These physical properties might reveal details about the implementation or even confidential data such as keys.

The second type of categorization can be done depending on an attack's degree of invasiveness (Kocher, Lee, McGraw, Raghunathan, & Moderator-Ravi, 2004):

- **Invasive Attack:** In invasive attacks, there is no limit regarding the actions an attacker might take. Possible actions include removing the packaging, probing internal bus lines or even permanent changes to the circuits of a hardware element.
- **Semi-Invasive Attack:** In semi-invasive attacks the attacker does not change the attacked hardware. Although semi-invasive attacks often include the de-packaging of hardware, no physical contact with the internal components is made. Desired faults are injected by, for example, using radiation or light to attack the hardware.
- **Non-Invasive Attack:** In non-invasive attacks the attacker observes properties of the hardware without damaging or changing it. Such properties include side-channels (Le, Canovas, & Clédiere, 2008) such as the power consumption or the timing of a certain part of software.

An overview of potential attacks, categorized by these two criteria can be seen in Table 1. All of these attacks can be applied to CPSs.

CPSs are, by definition, seen as an embedded system or controller that is attached to a physical process. The physical process can be monitored using sensors or actively influenced by a CPS using actuators. A wide range of systems can be classified as CPS, such as smart grids, process control systems, (autonomous) robotic systems, (autonomous) car systems, medical devices, and many more. Such systems provide various potential points of attack inside a CPS as depicted in Figure 2. There, *y* is seen as the

Table 1. Physical attacks categorized according to Section Attack Taxonomies

	Active	Passive
Invasive	Circuit Changes, Forcing, …	Probing, …
Semi-Invasive	Light Attacks, Radiation Attacks, …	Inspecting the Hardware, EM Attacks, …
Non-Invasive	Spike Attacks, Low Voltages, …	Side-Channel Attacks (Power, Timing, …)

Attacks extracted from (Weingart, 2000) and (Anderson, Bond, Clulow, & Skorobogatov, 2006).

Figure 2. Potential points of attacks inside a CPS
Adapted from (Cardenas, Amin, & Sastry, Secure Control: Towards Survivable Cyber-Physical Systems, 2008). Source: Attack Points.

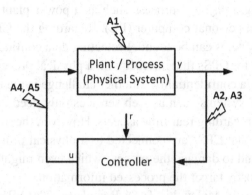

output of a process, for example, sensor measurements and u are the control commands sent to the physical process. The potential attacks on such CPSs and their implications can be categorized into five groups (adapted from Cardenas, Amin, & Sastry, Secure Control: Towards Survivable Cyber-Physical Systems, 2008). A1 are attacks targeted directly at the physical process itself. The aim of such attacks could be actuators or even a physical attack against the plant. A2 are so called deception attacks. In these kinds of attacks the adversary induces false information $\tilde{y} \neq y$ by attacking, for instance, a sensor. Possible information that can be forged includes measurements or the time associated to measurements. A3 represent DoS attacks where an attacker prevents the controller from receiving the physical process' output. A4 represent attacks where an adversary attacks the controller and induces false control commands $\tilde{u} \neq u$. These manipulated control commands could harm and destroy the physical process. A5 is similar to A3; an adversary attacks the data transportation from the controller to the physical process. Because of its nature, this attack is also a DoS attack.

Challenges and Research Trends

The challenges regarding IoT security are manifold (Jing, Vasilakos, Wan, Lu, & Qiu, 2014); therefore, the authors identify four major challenges. (i) A high number of insecure devices is supposed to be already connected to the Internet. Many devices were shown to be vulnerable to simple intrusion attacks by a large scale study (Cui & Stolfo, 2010). The study results show that about 13 percent of all discovered devices are configured with factory default passwords; the carna botnet revealed 1.2 million devices with weak passwords or no password set at all (Le Malécot & Inoue, 2014). (ii) There is believe that current security measures such as public-key infrastructures will not scale to the large number of IoT devices (Roman, Najera, & Lopez, 2011). (iii) As most IoT devices are highly constraint devices, finding a single weak link to attack could be an easy task for attackers. Therefore, efficient security algorithms need to be developed to mitigate attacks. (iv) Being in control of a single device could already lead to failures of many services. Thus, each involved component needs to be secured.

In the context of CPSs, even more security challenges arise compared to traditional ICT systems (Cardenas et al., 2009). For example, a challenge could arise through the necessity for security related software updates that often require reboots of the updated system or additional redundant systems to prevent reboots. Reboots are critical as the physical process also needs to be stopped in order to avoid potential problems. Restarting a physical process such as a power plant will take magnitudes longer than restarting, for example, a personal computer (PC). Regarding the CIA attributes a shift in priorities between CPSs and ICT systems can be found. Protecting data confidentiality is crucial for systems processing private data while for CPSs that interact with a physical process their availability is in most cases more important than data confidentiality. Another challenge is the need for real-time availability of CPSs. Many traditional IT systems such as web services only need to provide availability of their service with no requirements regarding real-time aspects. However, the major difference between CPSs and traditional IT systems is that CPSs are connected to a physical process. Attacks might target the physical process itself or intend to damage the process which even might threaten human lives. In traditional it systems, attacks mostly target the processed information.

Lun et al. (Lun, D'Innocenzo, Malavolta, & Di Benedetto, 2016) describe current trends and hot topics in research related to CPS security. We expand this list by current research trends regarding the challenges mentioned by us:

- Countermeasures against special attacks targeting CPSs (deception, false data injection, etc.) (Kim & Poor, 2011; Lo & Ansari, 2013)
- Prevention, detection and mitigation of attacks (Chaojun, Jirutitijaroen, & Motani, 2015), (Huang, Li, Campbell, & Han, 2011)
- Ensuring integrity of data in case of attacks (Kwon, Liu, & Hwang, 2014), (Vuković & Dán, 2014)
- Security measures for resource constraint devices such as sensors (Mishra, Shoukry, Karamchandani, Diggavi, & Tabuada, 2015; Mo, Weerakkody, & Sinopoli, 2015; Höller, Druml, Kreiner, Steger, & Felicijan, 2014)
- Security concepts for specific CPS application fields (e.g. Power Grid, Autonomous Vehicles, etc.) (Xue, Wang, & Roy, 2014; Zhu & Basar, 2015)
- Security measures for controllers (Dadras, Gerdes, & Sharma, 2015; Urbina et al., 2016)

Lun et al. also state that focus regarding CPS application is almost entirely on power grids. The research interest in the field of communication aspects is very low which is surprising as communication is an essential topic for all networks. This work shows that many topics are addressed currently but many more need to be approached to provide solutions for real world applications of CPSs.

ATTACKS

Cyber-attacks targeting CPSs became the focus of public attention in recent years. The probably best known cyber-attack that focused on physically destroying a target was Stuxnet. Stuxnet's only goal, contrary to traditional worms, was to harm a target instead of stealing, manipulating or erasing information. However, Stuxnet was not the first attack that harmed a physical process. Some other and earlier attacks are listed in Table 2 (collected and adapted from Miller & Rowe, 2012).

Table 2. Attacks

Attack	Reported Description and Sources
Siberian Pipeline Explosion (1982)	The first known cyber-attack targeting critical infrastructure. A trojan planted in a control system caused the explosion of a Siberian pipeline (Daniela, 2011).
Chevron Emergency Alert System (1992)	Chevron's alert system was disabled by a fired employee. The undetected attack threatened people in 22 states in the USA and parts of Canada (Denning, Cyberterrorism: The Logic Bomb versus the Truck Bomb, 2000).
Worcester, MA Airport (1997)	An attacker successfully disabled a telephone computer that serviced Worcester Airport. The outage affected services such as the aviation control tower, the airport fire department or the airport security and thus threatened human lives (Denning, Cyberterrorism: The Logic Bomb versus the Truck Bomb, 2000).
Gazprom (1999)	Attackers supported by a disgruntled employee gained access to the central switchboard that controls the gas flow in pipelines. The attackers reportedly used a trojan horse to gain access (Denning, Cyberterrorism: Testimony Before the Special Oversight Panel on Terrorism Committee on Armed Services US House of Representatives, 2000).
Davis-Besse Nuclear Power Plant (2003)	The Davis-Besse nuclear power plant in Ohio, USA was infected by a worm that disabled the plant's safety parameter display system and the plant process computer for several hours (Beggs, 2006).
CSX Corporation (2003)	Train signaling systems in Florida, USA were shut down by a fast spreading worm. There are no major incidents caused by this attack; however still many lives were threatened by it (Nicholson, Webber, Dyer, Patel, & Janicke, 2012).
Stuxnet (2010)	Stuxnet attacked Iranian nuclear facilities exploiting zero-day vulnerabilities. The worm tried to destroy centrifuges by frequently switching between high and low speeds which ultimately led to the failure of these centrifuges (Langner, 2011).
Night Dragon (2011)	Five global energy and oil companies were attacked by a combination of social engineering, trojans and using Windows exploits. The attacks are said to have been ongoing for about two years. Although no damage has been detected, data such as operational blueprints were stolen (Nicholson, Webber, Dyer, Patel, & Janicke, 2012).
Flame (2012)	Flame, a piece of malware was found on computers operating in Iran, Lebanon, Syria, Sudan and other places in the Middle East and North Africa. The malware was used to extract documents but also opened a backdoor that allowed adding any new functionality that could be used to harm the systems under attack (Lee D., 2012).
HAVEX (2014)	The HAVEX malware primarily targeted the energy sector, collecting data from attacked systems and leaving backdoors to control systems. Through these backdoors, the connected physical process could be controlled in a malicious way and therefore could also be manipulated or destroyed by attackers (Hentunen & Tikkanen, 2014).
Black Energy (2015)	Initially known as a botnet (Lee, Jeong, Park, Kim, & Noh, 2008), Black Energy changed its purpose in 2015. Ukrainian power plants infected were infected with a trojan through a backdoor opened by Black Energy. The trojan then tries to destroy the system by deleting certain files relevant for booting the system (ICS-CERT, 2016).

Mainly collected and adapted from (Miller & Rowe, 2012).

New Attack Dimension

All attacks listed in Table 2 reportedly successfully manipulated or destroyed a physical process. Recently, attacks have not tried to harm a physical process or device, but have tried to capture devices in order to use them in botnets (Dagon, Gu, Lee, & Lee, 2007). Because of their large number, IoT devices are a favored target to be used in botnets (Pa, et al., 2015). In addition, IoT devices are online 24/7, which makes them even better suited to be used in botnets. In 2014 both, Sony's and Microsoft's gaming platforms were attacked by a large number of infected IoT devices (Somani, Gaur, & Sanghi, 2015). The number of infected devices is rising since, culminating in a recent attack that reached traffic peaks of 620 gigabits per second (Gallagher, 2016). In this attack, an IoT botnet called Mirai was involved in attacking DNS services. The Mirai botnet comprises of devices such as WiFi routers and IP cameras.

According to a study, the number of DDoS attacks in 2016 increased by 71 percent when compared to 2015 (Daws, 2016). The attacks originated from countries shown in Figure 3. As the number of IoT devices will continue to grow, also the number of associated attacks will increase.

NETWORK SECURITY

In the context of initiatives such as Industry 4.0 (Referat, 2013), more CPSs are going to be connected to the Internet. These CPSs process confidential data and control production relevant processes. Therefore, securing the data transfer between these devices is of high importance. According to the Internet protocol suite, there are four layers: Link Layer, Internet Layer, Transport Layer and Application Layer (see Figure 4). All four of these layers are capable of providing different security measures that are going to be discussed in this section. In most cases, security measures on multiple levels are needed as sufficient security cannot be provided by one layer due to information not being available. For instance, information such as IP addresses that might be required to detect certain kinds of attacks are not available at the link layer.

Link Layer

On the link layer, there are a couple of protocols that are used in the IoT. The protocols that are of most interest when discussing security are wireless protocols, as this type of communication offers by far more weaknesses than wired communication. For example, eavesdropping in a wireless network can be as easy as positioning a malicious device in the communication range of the attacked devices. However,

Figure 3. Top origins of DDoS attacks
(Daws, 2016). Source: DDoS Origins.

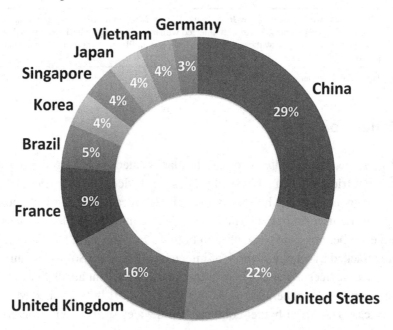

Figure 4. TCP/IP protocol architecture layers with protocols discussed in this work
Source: TCP.

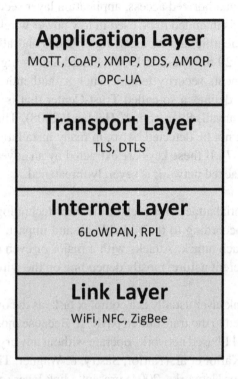

also wired communication technologies can be attacked if communication is not properly secured. The technologies that are seen as most promising (Zorzi, Gluhak, Lange, & Bassi, 2010) for the IoT are Wireless LAN, Near Field Communication and 802.15.4 based technologies such ZigBee. Therefore, these three technologies are analyzed regarding their security vulnerabilities in industrial usage (Plósz, et al., 2014).

- **Wireless LAN (Wi-Fi):** Wi-Fi is a wireless communication technology that has its origin in personal computers. Wi-Fi operates in frequency bands of 2.4 GHz or 5 GHz with a communication range of approximately 100 meters. This rather high range allows adversaries to attack Wi-Fi networks without being, for instance, in the same building. Wi-Fi standards include authentication and encryption mechanisms such as WEP and WPA. The security of Wi-Fi communication therefore relies on the confidentiality of these keys. If, for instance, an adversary is in possession of a Wi-Fi network's WPA key, ongoing communication can be read by the adversary. Therefore, key cracking key cracking by eavesdropping Wi-Fi communication is one of the biggest threats against this technology.
- **Near Field Communication (NFC):** NFC is a wireless communication technology that is based on RFID standards. NFC has a typical communication range of 10 cm and operates at a radio frequency of 13.56 MHz. Because of NFC's limited communication range, attacks need to be conducted in close proximity to the NFC devices. Although communication is limited to a couple centimeters, eavesdropping might be possible in a range of up to 10 m (Haselsteiner & Breitfuß, 2006). Currently there is no dedicated NFC standard for authentication and access control.

Therefore, unauthorized access to NFC devices is seen as the most critical issue with NFC. To mitigate the problem of unauthorized access, application layer security must be implemented.

- **802.15.4/ZigBee:** Zigbee is intended to be used in low power wireless networks. ZigBee operates in the ISM (industrial, scientific and medical) radio bands and allows for communication up to a range of approximately 20 m. The 802.15.4 standard allows higher layers to provide security; therefore, ZigBee implements security features such as authentication, encryption, and key establishment. ZigBee also defines a so-called Trust-Center that is a special node responsible for storing network keys (Lennvall, Svensson, & Hekland, 2008). The biggest weakness of ZigBee is rogue nodes that might not be detected. Also, in many installations master keys are factory installed (Baronti et al., 2007). If these keys are extracted by an adversary with physical access to a device, security of the attacked network is severely threatened.

Plósz et al. (2014) list potential attacks for each of the three technologies, Wi-Fi, NFC, and ZigBee. All attacks are then assessed according to their likelihood and impact. This assessment yields a final rank highlighting the risk of each attack. Attacks with a major or even critical risk are listed in Table 3. The threats listed are of different nature, mostly depending on the wireless technology's architecture and communication range.

Improving security at the link layer usually is a complex task, as the overhead imposed by security at this layer is significant compared to the transmitted payload. Because most CPSs are resource constraint devices, a large number of 802.11 based networks operate without any cryptographic protection (Hurley, 2003). To mitigate this issue, Karlof et al. (Karlof, Sastry, & Wagner, TinySec: A Link Layer Security Architecture for Wireless Sensor Networks, 2004) present a link layer security architecture tailored for resource constraint devices. The authors have chosen to implement security measures at the link layer,

Table 3. Link Layer protocols and possible attacks with major or critical risks

	Threat	Highest Risk
Wi-Fi	WEP Shared Key Cracking	Confidentiality
	WPA-PSK Cracking	Confidentiality
	Application Login Theft	Confidentiality, Authenticity
	Intercepting TCP, SSH, SSL	Confidentiality, Integrity, Authenticity
	Evil Twin Access Point	Confidentiality, Availability, Integrity, Authenticity
	Device Cloning	Confidentiality, Integrity, Authenticity
NFC	Clone or Modify Portable Reader Device	Confidentiality, Authenticity
	Wormhole / Relay Attack	Authenticity
	Rogue Node	Confidentiality, Availability, Integrity, Authenticity
	Unauthorized Access to Node	Confidentiality, Authenticity
ZigBee	Rogue Node	Confidentiality, Integrity, Authenticity
	Device Cloning / Firmware Replacement	Confidentiality, Integrity, Authenticity
	Security Parameter Extraction by Physical Access	Confidentiality, Authenticity
	Plaintext Key Capture	Confidentiality, Integrity, Authenticity

Plósz et al., 2014.

because CPSs often communicate in a many-to-one pattern. In this pattern, many sensors and actuators communicate their data to a central base station, which makes traditional end-to-end security such as SSH, TLS or IPSec infeasible. The approach uses authenticated encryption to secure the transported payload at the link layer.

Internet Layer

Security measures implemented at the Internet layer increased in popularity when the Internet Engineering Task Force (IETF) started the IP Security Working Group. The goal of this working group was to design cryptographic security for IPv6 that could also be ported to IPv4 (Oppliger, 1998). The result, IPSec, is widely known and supported nowadays as it is capable of providing data confidentiality and integrity by mitigating network attacks. IPSec is very popular and integrated in IPv6; therefore, the focus for the rest of this section will be on approaches that are capable to detect attacks at the Internet layer.

IETF introduced IPv6 for Low power Wireless Personal Area Networks (6LoWPAN) for resource constraint IoT devices. 6LoWPAN enables these devices to be connected to the Internet by compressing standard IPv6 headers. Kasinathan et al. (2013) present an approach that includes an Intrusion Detection System (IDS) and DoS detection into 6LoWPAN. A network based IDS analyzes the 6LoWPAN traffic to detect intrusion attempts and to raise alerts in case of detected attacks. The IDS approach helps to detect and mitigate network and DoS attacks and thus, increases confidentiality, integrity and availability of a CPS. The presented network based approach requires the inclusion of IDS Probe nodes that are allowed to analyze all packets, irrelevant of the actual recipient. In case of an attack, the IDS then alerts the DoS protection manager that then further collects data to verify the potentially ongoing DoS attack. The authors claim that their distributed hybrid approach is capable of detecting DoS attacks reliably.

The Routing Protocol for Low-Power and Lossy Networks (RPL) is a standardized routing protocol for IoT devices that use 6LoWPAN. Attacks against routing protocols were successfully applied against wireless sensor networks (WSNs) as well (Karlof & Wagner, 2003). Wallgren et al. (Wallgren, Raza, & Voigt, 2013) propose to place IoT IDSs at the root nodes of RPL routing trees, thus, giving the IDS a global view. This allows the routing protocol, for instance, to exclude malicious nodes from the routing tree in order to prevent network attacks. By excluding malicious nodes, confidentiality, integrity, and availability of a CPS can be increased. In their approach, ICMPv6 messages protected by IPSec with ESP are used to detect anomalies in the network. Wallgren et al. also show that the inclusion of an IDS introduces only a small overhead in power consumption of about 10 percent.

Transport Layer

Transport Layer Security (TLS) is considered to be of utmost importance in IoT applications (Garcia-Morchon, Kumar, Struik, Keoh, & Hummen, 2013). Although considered by some as an application layer protocol, the authors put TLS into the transport layer as its name suggests. Similar to the Internet layer, conventional protocols of the transport layer cannot directly be applied to IoT devices because of resource limitations. Especially in low-power lossy networks, protocols such as conventional TLS cannot be applied. TLS is a stream oriented protocol building on TCP that suffers from frequent packet loss in the form of delays. As an alternative to TLS, the Datagram Transport Layer Security (DTLS) protocol that is using UDP was introduced. DTLS provides the same protection mechanisms as TLS and does not influence the underlying packet transport. Thus, DTLS is able to provide confidentiality and integrity of transferred data by mitigating network attacks. A gateway from the Internet (TLS) to a lossy IoT network (DTLS) is proposed by Brachmann et al. (2012) in order to be able to provide end-to-end security between networks. The DTLS protocol is often used to implement IoT related security mechanisms such as a two-way authentication (Kothmayr, Schmitt, Hu, Brünig, & Carle, 2013) that uses X.509 certificates and an Elliptic Curve Diffie Hellman (EC-DH) key agreement process. By using this approach, both communication partners are authenticated and an encrypted communication is enabled. Kothmayr et al. (2013) show that securing a connection using DTLS imposes minimal overhead for the involved devices and also conclude that the usage of dedicated security hardware such as Trusted Platform Modules (TPM) will further decrease the overhead in power consumption and delay. TPMs and other security related hardware concepts will be discussed in Section Device Security.

Application Layer

Application layer protocols are an essential part when discussing communication in the context of IoT. There is a wide range of protocols that also might be suitable for an industrial context. IoT application layer protocols such as MQTT, CoAP, or DDS typically provide a very low protocol overhead that enables these protocols to efficiently transport the huge amount of data created by IoT devices. To meet the security requirements of industrial IoT applications, these existing protocols need to be adapted. Therefore, existing IoT application layer protocols will be evaluated regarding their built-in security features and the available security extensions for the protocols.

- **MQTT:** MQTT is based on the publish/subscribe principle and uses a client-server architecture (Standard, 2014). Clients publish messages to a specific topic or subscribe to a topic using a so-called broker. The broker is a server which manages the distribution of messages in the network. MQTT Messages are sent using TCP to enable reliable message delivery. Before clients can send and receive messages, they have to connect to the broker. The CONNECT message, sent by the client, contains optional fields for username and password that can be used for authentication. These fields are the only built-in security features MQTT provides. Due to these scarce security mechanisms, OASIS highly recommends the use of TLS (Dierks, 2008) to secure messages from attackers. Unfortunately, TLS suffers from attacks such as BEAST or CRIME (Sarkar & Fitzgerald, 2013). To overcome the issues with TLS and to provide reliable security for MQTT, Singh et al. (Singh, Rajan, Shivraj, & Balamuralidhar, 2015) propose the use of Key/Cipher text Policy-Attribute Based Encryption (KP/CP-ABE) that relies on lightweight Elliptic Curve Cryptography (ECC). ABE using lightweight ECC supports broadcast encryption. Encrypting a broadcast message enables many clients to decrypt a message. ABE are of the types Ciphertext Policy based ABE (CP-ABE) and Key Policy based ABE (KP-ABE). CP-ABE provides private key generation over a set of attributes and uses an access tree to encrypt the data. KP-ABE generates a user's private keys based on an access tree depending on the user's privileges. In KP-ABE the data is encrypted over a set of attributes. The combination of CP/KP-ABE provides data confidentiality and also provides access control. Another approach to secure MQTT was made by Niruntasukrat et al. (Niruntasukrat, et al., 2016) who proposed an authorization mechanism based on the OAuth 1.0 authentication algorithm. With this algorithm, a device can generate an access token to be allowed to subscribe to a specific resource. This authorization only approach is designed for highly constraint devices which cannot carry TLS or perform cryptographic functions.

- **CoAP:** CoAP relies on the request/response principle between endpoints using a client/server architecture (Shelby, Hartke, & Bormann, 2014). Clients can request specific resources using URIs with HTTP media types such as GET. Requests and responses are sent using UDP to keep the protocols footprint small. Although CoAP uses UDP for transport it also offers modes for guaranteed message delivery. CoAP itself does not provide any security features. To secure the sent messages anyway, the RFC 7252 requires the implementation of DTLS (Modadugu & Rescorla, 2004) but allows the NoSec mode to be used where DTLS can be disabled. DTLS, similar to TLS, results in a huge overhead compared to CoAP's overhead. Therefore, Raza et al. (2013) propose Lithe, a lightweight DTLS integration for CoAP. The integration is, among others, done by using the principle of 6LoWPAN header compression mechanisms (Hui & Thubert, 2011). The header compression for DTLS reduces the overhead for the complete handshake headers by about 33%. There are also other approaches such as proposed by Capossele et al. (2015) or Ukil et al. (2014) that try to secure CoAP by manipulating DTLS to reduce the packet overhead and number of messages.
- **XMPP:** XMPP is based on a client/server architecture (Saint-Andre, Smith, Tronçon, & Troncon, 2009) and uses XML to structure the data sent between clients and servers. All clients in a specific domain are connected to one server. Servers can connect to other servers to enable inter domain communication. The communication between client and server can be secured using TLS; the communication between servers however does not necessarily need to be secured. Therefore, the RFC 6120 (Saint-Andre, 2011) recommends end-to-end encryption between clients in different networks to provide data security. One approach to secure XMPP was done by Celesti et al. (2013), who proposed SE Clever. SE Clever is the secure extension of an existing middleware for cloud computing. The security extensions enable XMPP to (i) sign the sent XML files with private key of the sender, (ii) attach content encrypted with receiver's public key to the message body, (iii) attach a session key for symmetric encryption, and (iv) attach signed timestamps. These extensions enable a secure XMPP middleware without establishing TLS connections.
- **DDS:** DDS is a protocol for real-time, high-performance data exchange between clients (Pardo-Castellote, 2003) that relies on the publish/subscribe principle but does not require a broker to distribute messages. DDS clients simply publish data to topics and other clients subscribe to the topics. DDS' architecture is similar to the one of bus systems where every client is connected to the bus. Data is transported using TCP, UDP or any other transport specification. DDS does not provide any security features; therefore, TLS or DTLS should be used to protect the data from manipulation or theft.
- **AMQP:** AMQP is a message-oriented protocol based on publish/subscribe and point-to-point communication (Vinoski, 2006). AMQP uses a broker to distribute messages. The broker provides an exchange service and a message queue service. The exchange service is used to send data to a specific receiver where the data is stored in a queue the receiver can read from. The exchange service uses point-to-point communication with the broker as a forwarding device. The message queue service copies the same message to each client that has subscribed to the message topic. The message queue service uses the publish/subscribe principle for data distribution; the messages are sent using TCP but AMQP can be extended to also use UDP. AMQP does not provide any security features; therefore, Vinoski (2006) recommends the use of TLS to provide data security. Besides TLS no other security extensions for AMQP were proposed yet.
- **OPC-UA:** OPC-UA is based on a client/server architecture using the request/response principle (Mahnke, Leitner, & Damm, 2009). Each client needs an OPC-UA client implementation that

uses the OPC-UA communication stack to create request messages. The client's communication stack communicates with the server's communication stack by sending the request messages. The server's communication stack forwards the request to the server implementation. The server implementation provides the response which is sent to the client by using the server's and client's communication stacks. Furthermore, subscriptions and notifications can be sent between client and server using a publish/subscribe principle (Cavalieri, Cutuli, & Monteleone, 2010). OPC-UA provides two different communication modes for message exchange. The first mode, UA Web Services, uses web services secured with HTTPS to communicate. The second mode is named UA Native and sends data in plain text using TCP. Besides HTTPS, OPC-UA provides a huge amount of built-in security features. The security features include:

- **Session Encryption:** Transmitted messages are encrypted with 128 bit or 256 bit keys.
- **Message Signing:** Messages are signed to prevent data manipulation.
- **Sequenced Packets:** Sequencing eliminates the possibility of replay attacks.
- **Authentication:** OpenSSL certificates are used to authenticate systems or applications.
- **User Control:** Login credentials must be provided by users to access applications.

Because OPC-UA already provides extended security features, no proposed security extensions exist for this protocol. Due to these security features, OPC-UA generates a huge overhead compared to other protocols.

DEVICE SECURITY

When connecting CPSs to the Internet, securing the device itself is as important as securing the communication between devices. Communicating over an unsecured channel might threaten the confidentiality and integrity of transferred data. Leaving weaknesses at a device itself, however, might lead to bigger issues such as the device being overtaken. Such an overtaken device could then forward confidential data to adversaries' servers, use the device in botnet related attacks or even manipulate the device's intended

Table 4. Security analysis of existing IoT application protocols

	Built-In Security	**Extended Security**	**Provides**
MQTT	User/Password Authentication	TLS, KP/CP-ABE (Singh, Rajan, Shivraj, & Balamuralidhar, 2015), Authorization (Niruntasukrat, et al., 2016)	Confidentiality, Integrity
CoAP	None	DTLS, Lithe (Raza, Shafagh, Hewage, Hummen, & Voigt, 2013)	Confidentiality, Integrity
XMPP	None	TLS/SASL, SE Clever (Celesti, Fazio, & Villari, 2013)	Confidentiality, Integrity
DDS	None	TLS/DTLS	Confidentiality, Integrity
AMQP	None	TLS	Confidentiality, Integrity
OPC-UA	Sequencing, Encryption, Authentication, Signing, User Control	None	Confidentiality, Integrity

behavior. The security of a whole network is threatened if an adversary possesses a single device belonging to it. The adversary might apply any type of physical attack to reveal confidential data or even keys stored on the device under attack. These keys could then be used to connect malicious devices to the network without anyone noticing. To counteract all kinds of attacks at the device level, so-called tamper resistance needs to be achieved in software as well as in hardware. A system's tamper resistance can be split into four different steps (Ravi, Raghunathan, & Chakradhar, 2004):

- **Attack Prevention:** Attack Prevention techniques should complicate attacks that target CPSs and thus make the attacks infeasible. Possible techniques include packaging, special hardware design, and software design.
- **Attack Detection:** Attack Detection should detect potential attacks as soon as possible to minimize the effect of them. Possible techniques include, for example, a run-time detection of malicious memory accesses.
- **Attack Recovery:** Attack Recovery is essential in the case of a detected attack to take appropriate countermeasures and to check that the system returns to a normal operation state. Possible techniques include, for example, locking the system or rebooting the system.
- **Tamper Evidence:** Tamper Evidence is responsible for keeping track of past attacks that can be used for inspection later. Tamper evidence be protected from being reversed. Thus, techniques such as seals or wires that have to be cut can be used.

Software

Tamper resistance is a security feature that often is associated with hardware components. However, also software measures can and need to be taken to provide tamper resistance of executed code (Lie, et al., 2000). Horne et al. (Horne, Matheson, Sheehan, & Tarjan, 2001) propose a self-checking code mechanism that can be integrated into existing code segments to provide tamper resistance. Aucsmith et al. (1996) present an approach for tamper resistant software that uses so-called Integrity Verification Kernels to check if software is operating as intended. Integrity verification kernels are self-modifying, self-decrypting, self-checking and installation unique code segments that communicate with other kernels to create an interlocking trust model. Software tamper resistance is able to mitigate physical and side-channel attacks that passively inspect a device and try to reveal data from information such as timings. Thus, these approaches are able to provide data confidentiality. The authors also list design principles for tamper resistant software (Aucsmith, 1996):

- **Secret Dispersion:** Secret Dispersion is used to evenly spread confidential information throughout the whole system. For instance, if a key is distributed in the whole memory instead of being stored in a single location, an attacker is hindered from revealing the whole secret by randomly guessing and observing the correct position in memory.
- **Obfuscating and Interleaving:** This principle converts a program into a state that is harder to understand for humans without changing the functionality of the obfuscated code. Obfuscated code is used to hide its logic and purpose to prevent tampering and reverse engineering.
- **Installation of Unique Code:** Installation of unique code is used to mitigate class attacks (Ouyang, Le, Liu, Ford, & Makedon, 2008) by checking that each code has a unique component. Uniqueness can be added to software by different unique code sequences or encryption keys.

- **Interlocking Trust:** This is the principle of code components relying on other code segments to effectively perform their tasks. Not only are code segments responsible for their own functionality, but also for maintaining and verifying the integrity of other components. Thus, each software component is monitored by another component of the system which forms an interlocking trust relationship between components.

Although software tamper resistance can increase a system's security, it has two major drawbacks compared to tamper resistant hardware. First, most CPSs are constrained in their processing capabilities which limits the feasibility of adding security features in software. Second, software tamper resistance has been shown to be prone to many attacks (Oorschot, Somayaji, & Wurster, 2005), (Wurster, van Oorschot and Paul, & Somayaji, 2005). Therefore, software tamper resistance cannot be relied on to provide a device's security without other security measures.

IDSs are another measure to increase CPS security by potentially detecting viruses, worms, DoS attacks, network attacks, or password attacks. Thus, increasing the confidentiality, integrity, and availability of CPSs. Mitchell and Chen (2014) state the importance of IDSs for CPSs as an unnoticed adversary could set up an attack that is more harmful than attacks that are immediately recognized. The authors further categorize CPS IDSs by their detection technique and the used audit material. The detection technique defines how such IDSs need to be trained and how misbehaving code is detected.

- **Knowledge Based Approach:** These approaches identify runtime features based on specific patterns of misbehavior (Whitman & Mattord, 2011). Because knowledge based approaches only react to known bad code segments, the false positive rate of such approaches is usually low.
- **Behavior Based Approach:** These IDSs approaches identify runtime features that differ from the ordinary (Whitman & Mattord, 2011). Depending on what is defined as ordinary, these IDSs need to be trained live or on supervised data. The advantage of such approaches is that they do not need to previously see the exact code they need to detect. However, the machine learning aspect increases the false positive rate.

In the context of CPSs, there are two possible ways to collect data for analysis.

- **Host Based IDS:** Host based IDSs analyze logs recorded on a single node. The advantage of host based approaches is their independence of other nodes and the corresponding ease of detecting host-level misbehavior (Mitchell & Chen, 2014).
- **Network Based IDS:** These approaches analyze network activity to find compromised nodes (Kasinathan, Pastrone, Spirito, & Vinkovits, 2013). The advantage of this approach is that other, dedicated, and non-compromised nodes are used to identify misbehaving nodes in a network. Dedicated nodes could be equipped with external power sources and more computational power (Wallgren, Raza, & Voigt, 2013).

However, in the context of CPSs, also other indicators such as the physical process itself could be used for intrusion detection. Cardenas et al. (2009) state that traditional IDSs only analyze device or network logs while control systems could be used to monitor the physical process. Anomalies in the physical process could be an indicator for an ongoing attack that might not be detected by traditional IDSs.

Hardware

Secure hardware components need to provide a number of security properties in order to increase the overall security of a system (Vasudevan, Owusu, Zhou, Newsome, & McCune, 2012). The properties considered most important are the following three:

- **Isolated Execution:** A fundamental concept in hardware security is the so-called security by isolation concept (Vasudevan, Owusu, Zhou, Newsome, & McCune, 2012). In this concept, an execution environment is split into two worlds, the normal world and the secure world. The normal world is then used as general-purpose execution environments (GPEE) while the secure world servers as a secure execution environment (SEE). The security by isolation principle can be realized using different hardware elements (Anderson, Bond, Clulow, & Skorobogatov, 2006), on a single CPU (ARM TrustZone (Winter, 2008), Intel Trusted Execution Technology (TXT), AMD SVM), or in software (Madnick & Donovan, 1973). Isolated execution allows software developers to run certain parts of their software in complete isolation from other code that is executed at the same device. Current operating systems (OS) provide isolation at a process level. Security by isolation helps to mitigate the impact of viruses and worms as well as exploits. Also, passive physical and side-channel attacks can be mitigated and thus, confidentiality, and integrity of CPSs is increased. The drawback with this approach is that, if the OS itself is compromised, also the isolation mechanisms are circumvented. Also, Bond and Anderson (2001) highlight that secured execution environments can be targeted by so-called API attacks. The simplest form of such an attack is to issue valid API commands in an unexpected sequence. To account for this type of attack, measures such as security analysis (for example Common Criteria Certification (Mellado, Fernandez-Medina, & Piattini, 2007)) needs to be conducted.
- **Secured Storage:** The need to store confidential data such as key material on a CPS highlights the importance of secured storage. A secured storage therefore should be capable of guaranteeing data integrity and secrecy for any kind of data. Storage secured by software measures is considered to be insecure, as any physical attack can be applied to storage media that is extracted from its coating (Vasudevan, Owusu, Zhou, Newsome, & McCune, 2012). A (now already outdated but simple) possible approach to mitigate physical attacks is to seal the storage by embedding it inside a protective coating that makes the hardware resistant against invasive attacks (Tuyls, et al., 2006). Such protective coatings enable read-proof hardware by being sprayed on traditional hardware. The coating is doped with several random dielectric particles that help to (i) absorb light and UV-light, (ii) make the coating very hard, (iii) provide a certain capacitance of the coating that can be measured by sensors inside of it. These properties not only mitigate physical attacks but also help to identify an ongoing attack by sensing the coating's capacity.
- **Trusted Path:** To provide confidentiality, authenticity and availability for a connection between software and a peripheral such as a sensor, a trusted path needs to be used (Zhou, Gligor, Newsome, & McCune, 2012). Trusted Path are essential to mitigate the problem of malicious applications that try to manipulate data such that a CPS or the associated physical process could be damaged.

Besides these three mentioned properties, Vasudevan et al. (2012) list two additional important properties. Remote Attestation is used to verify the origin of messages from software modules, for example, a remote server could verify the correctness of a client's OS kernel and application. Remote attestation therefore provides data integrity. Secure Provisioning allows data to be sent to a specific software part running on a specific hardware module. For example, data could only be sent to services that were previously verified using remote attestation. Secure provisioning therefore also provides data integrity. Stankovic (2014) notes that in order to meet the security requirements defined for CPSs, hardware support is needed in addition to software mechanisms. He further states that so-called tamper resistant hardware modules will be essential in providing encryption, authentication, attestation, and secured storage.

- **Security Co-Processors:** These are one example of such tamper resistant hardware components (Smith & Weingart, 1999). The security principle used by security co-processors to increase security is isolated execution. Security co-processors are used as trusted devices that execute critical software parts in a tamper resistant environment. The software components that are most frequently executed on security co-processors are cryptographic algorithms such as encryption, decryption, signing and verification (Mclvor, McLoone, & McCanny, 2003). The execution of cryptographic algorithms is especially vulnerable to physical attacks as so-called side-channel attacks can be used to reveal key material or other confidential data (Standaert, Malkin, & Yung, 2009), (Mangard, Oswald, & Popp, 2008). Because side-channel weaknesses might make other security measures such as secured storage useless, the focus in cryptographic co-processor design is often in eliminating all side-channels (Tiri, et al., 2005). In addition to cryptographic operations, there are also other use-case scenarios for security co-processors such as intrusion detection. Zhang et al. (2002) propose to run IDS software on a tamper resistant co-processor instead of a host processor for increased security. This approach has four advantages according to the authors: (i) the intrusion detection is independent from other software components, (ii) the interface between the security- and host processor is very simple, so it is hard to exploit, (iii) the security co-processor can boot the device into a well-known state, (iv) statements made by the software running on a security co-processor can be fully trusted. Security co-processors will be especially useful in the context of cyber-physical systems (Feller, 2014) where, for instance, controller software could be executed in a secure manner. If CPSs are used in industrial processes, many new scenarios such as smart maintenance (Lesjak, et al., 2015) need to be considered for which security co-processors provide confidentiality, integrity, and availability.
- **Trusted Platform Modules (TPM):** TPM are standardized hardware components often associated with personal computers because of their size and power requirements. TPMs typically comprise of several components such as a cryptographic co-processor and secured storage. The CIA attributes provided by a TPM are therefore a combination of the attributes provided by these components. TPMs are capable of providing confidentiality, integrity, and availability for CPSs. Because of the size requirements, CPSs often emulate a TPM's functionality in software (Aaraj, Raghunathan, & Jha, 2008), (Strasser & Stamer, 2008), which poses security risks as well as problems regarding the power consumption of CPU-intensive cryptographic operations. TPMs are decreasing in size, so they nowadays are also included into CPSs (Kinney, 2006) and even smartcards (Akram, Markantonakis, & Mayes, 2014).
- TPM can be used to increase security in CPSs in various other ways too. Hutter and Toegl (2010) present a TPM that is extended by NFC functionality to provide a trusted channel between two devices. The TPM chip is further used for remote attestation that provides trust that the device is

not modified in a malicious way. Kothmayr et al. introduce a two-way authentication (Kothmayr, Schmitt, Hu, Brünig, & Carle, 2013) and end-to-end encryption (Kothmayr, Schmitt, Hu, Brünig, & Carle, 2012) that relies on TPMs in both devices to generate and store RSA keys, and to perform cryptographic operations. Because many IoT devices are resource constraint, the authors argue that TPMs not only need to be included for tamper resistance but also to handle the overhead imposed by using cryptographic security measures. According to Hu et al. (Hu, Tan, Corke, Shih, & Jha, 2010), including TPM into CPSs increases the system's overall price by an average of only 5 percent.

Another possible security feature when using TPM is the so-called authenticated boot as specified by the Trusted Computing Group (TCG). Authenticated boot is a passive method that stores integrity measures such as hashes of software components on the TPM. When booting a device, the integrity measure is applied again and compared against the stored value before loading and executing the software. This security mechanism, however, can only be used to protect a software's integrity at boot time; malicious code that is loaded at run time cannot be detected by such a TPM assisted system. A simple solution to that problem would be to reboot a potentially compromised system to restore a secured system state (Hendricks & Van Doorn, 2004). Raciti and Nadjm-Tehrani (2012) address the problem of many CPSs such as smart meters: the unsecured connection between sensor and controller. They argue that although TPM are included in many solutions nowadays, vulnerabilities persist that still allow CPSs to be attacked. To mitigate some problems, Raciti and Nadjm-Tehrani suggest to include an anomaly detection system in addition to a TPM chip in order to detect potential attacks targeting the communication between sensor and controller.

Tamper resistant hardware is shown to increase security by mitigating various types of physical and also logical attacks. However, as prices for such hardware devices are decreasing, also low cost attacks targeting tamper resistant hardware are possible (Anderson & Kuhn, 1997), (Bao et al., 1997). Anderson and Kuhn (Anderson & Kuhn, Tamper Resistance - a Cautionary Note, 1996) state that trusting a system because of its tamper resistant components is problematic as such systems are broken frequently.

CONCLUSION

The number of IoT devices is rapidly rising and forecasted to reach 50 billion devices by 2020 (Evans, 2011). Initiatives such as Industry 4.0 and Smart Manufacturing will further boost this trend, as they envision connecting production machinery to the Internet. These so-called cyber-physical production systems are attractive targets for adversaries for a number of reasons.

- The number of connected devices is still rapidly increasing while most devices are online 24/7.
- A large number of currently connected devices has no proper security mechanisms implemented or is using default credentials.
- Most of the CPSs are resource constraint which does not allow to implemented traditional security measures.
- Many CPSs process confidential data. Attacks can therefore be used for industrial espionage.
- Attacks might aim at damaging the physical process which could threaten human lives.

Trends in emerging CPS threats (Marinos, Belmonte, & Rekleitis, 2015) show that the number of all top 10 attacks such as DoS attacks, cyber espionage and physically damaging attacks are increasing compared to last year's report. This further highlights the importance of CPS security.

Due to these reasons, an overview of CPS security is given in this work. To be able to categorize attacks as well as the applied countermeasures, the authors have given attack taxonomies for logical as well as for physical attacks. The authors also have shown recent major attacks that increased the public attention regarding IoT security. After that, security measures are discussed for two major aspects of CPSs: on a network level and on the device level. On the network level, all TCP/IP layers and their protocols have been evaluated regarding potential security measures. On device level, software measures and potential security increasing hardware components have been presented. Simply combining some of the presented security measures however might harm a system more than it improves its security (Krawczyk, 2001). Also, a tradeoff between security and other parameters such as overhead needs to be made. Therefore, this publication tends to present an overview of current security related topics rather than suggest to apply certain solutions.

REFERENCES

Aaraj, N., Raghunathan, A., & Jha, N. K. (2008). Analysis and Design of a Hardware/Software Trusted Platform Module for Embedded Systems. *ACM Transactions on Embedded Computing Systems*, 8.

Adomavicius, G., & Tuzhilin, A. (2005). Personalization Technologies: A Process-Oriented Perspective. *Communications of the ACM*, *48*(10), 83–90. doi:10.1145/1089107.1089109

Akram, R. N., Markantonakis, K., & Mayes, K. (2014). Trusted Platform Module for Smart Cards. In *Proceedings of the 2014 6th International Conference on New Technologies, Mobility and Security (NTMS)* (pp. 1-5).

Anderson, R., Bond, M., Clulow, J., & Skorobogatov, S. (2006). Cryptographic Processors - A Survey. *Proceedings of the IEEE*, *94*(2), 357–369. doi:10.1109/JPROC.2005.862423

Anderson, R., & Kuhn, M. (1996). Tamper Resistance - a Cautionary Note. In *Proceedings of the second Usenix workshop on electronic commerce*, 2, pp. 1-11.

Anderson, R., & Kuhn, M. (1997). Low Cost Attacks on Tamper Resistant Devices. In *Proceedings of the International Workshop on Security Protocols* (pp. 125-136).

Aucsmith, D. (1996). Tamper Resistant Software: An Implementation. In *Proceedings of the International Workshop on Information Hiding*, (pp. 317-333).

Bao, F., Deng, R. H., Han, Y., Jeng, A., Narasimhalu, A. D., & Ngair, T. (1997). Breaking Public Key Cryptosystems on Tamper Resistant Devices in the Presence of Transient Faults. In *Proceedings of the International Workshop on Security Protocols* (pp. 115-124).

Baronti, P., Pillai, P., Chook, V. W., Chessa, S., Gotta, A., & Hu, Y. F. (2007). Wireless sensor networks: A survey on the state of the art and the 802.15. 4 and ZigBee standards. *Computer Communications*, *30*(7), 1655–1695. doi:10.1016/j.comcom.2006.12.020

Beggs, C. (2006). Proposed Risk Minimization Measures for Cyber-Terrorism and SCADA Networks in Australia. In *Proceedings of the 5th European conference on information warfare and security (ECIW 2006, Helsinki). Academic Publishing, Reading, UK*, (pp. 9-18).

Bond, M., & Anderson, R. (2001). API-Level Attacks on Embedded Systems. *Computer*, *34*(10), 67–75. doi:10.1109/2.955101

Brachmann, M., Keoh, S. L., Morchon, O. G., & Kumar, S. S. (2012, July). End-to-End Transport Security in the IP-Based Internet of Things. In *Proceedings of the 2012 21st International Conference on Computer Communications and Networks (ICCCN)* (pp. 1-5). IEEE.

Capossele, A., Cervo, V., De Cicco, G., & Petrioli, C. (2015). Security as a CoAP resource: an optimized DTLS implementation for the IoT. In *Proceedings of the 2015 IEEE International Conference on Communications (ICC)* (pp. 549-554). doi:10.1109/ICC.2015.7248379

Cardenas, A. A., Amin, S., & Sastry, S. (2008). Secure Control: Towards Survivable Cyber-Physical Systems. In *Proceedings of the 28th International Conference on, Distributed Computing Systems Workshops ICDCS'08* (pp. 495-500).

Cardenas, A. A., Amin, S., Sinopoli, B., Giani, A., Perrig, A., & Sastry, S. (2009). Challenges for Securing Cyber Physical Systems. In *Proceedings of the Workshop on future directions in cyber-physical systems security*, (p. 5).

Cavalieri, S., Cutuli, G., & Monteleone, S. (2010, May). Evaluating Impact of Security on OPC UA Performance. In *Proceedings of the 3rd International Conference on Human System Interaction*, (pp. 687-694). doi:10.1109/HSI.2010.5514495

Celesti, A., Fazio, M., & Villari, M. (2013). SE CLEVER: A secure message oriented Middleware for Cloud federation. In *Proceedings of the 2013 IEEE Symposium on Computers and Communications (ISCC)*, (pp. 35-40). doi:10.1109/ISCC.2013.6754919

Chaojun, G., Jirutitijaroen, P., & Motani, M. (2015). Detecting False Data Injection Attacks in AC State Estimation. *IEEE Transactions on Smart Grid*, *6*(5), 2476–2483. doi:10.1109/TSG.2015.2388545

Cheng, P., Zhang, H., & Chen, J. (2016). *Cyber Security for Industrial Control Systems: From the Viewpoint of Close-Loop*. CRC Press. doi:10.1201/b19629

Cui, A., & Stolfo, S. J. (2010). A Quantitative Analysis of the Insecurity of Embedded Network Devices: Results of a Wide-Area Scan. In *Proceedings of the 26th Annual Computer Security Applications Conference* (pp. 97-106). doi:10.1145/1920261.1920276

Dadras, S., Gerdes, R. M., & Sharma, R. (2015). Vehicular Platooning in an Adversarial Environment. In *Proceedings of the 10th ACM Symposium on Information, Computer and Communications Security* (pp. 167-178).

Dagon, D., Gu, G., Lee, C. P., & Lee, W. (2007). A Taxonomy of Botnet Structures. In *Proceedings of the Computer Security Applications Conference, 2007. ACSAC 2007. Twenty-Third Annual* (pp. 325-339).

Daniela, T. (2011). Communication Security in SCADA Pipeline Monitoring Systems. In *Proceedings of the 2011 RoEduNet International Conference 10th Edition: Networking in Education and Research* (pp. 1-5).

Daws, R. (2016, 11). Akamai: IoT botnet set a record in a year when DDoS attacks increased 71 percent. IoT Tech News.

Denning, D. E. (2000). Cyberterrorism: Testimony Before the Special Oversight Panel on Terrorism Committee on Armed Services US House of Representatives. *Focus on Terrorism, 9.*

Denning, D. E. (2000). Cyberterrorism: The Logic Bomb versus the Truck Bomb. *Global Dialogue, 2.*

Dierks, T. (2008). *The Transport Layer Security (TLS) Protocol Version 1.2.* IETF. doi:10.17487/rfc5246

Evans, D. (2011). The Internet of Things. *How the Next Evolution of the Internet is Changing Everything* (Whitepaper). *Cisco Internet Business Solutions Group, 1,* 1–12.

Feller, T. (2014). Towards Trustworthy Cyber-Physical Systems. In *Trustworthy Reconfigurable Systems* (pp. 85–136). Springer.

Gallagher, S. (2016, 10). Double-dip Internet-of-Things botnet attack felt across the Internet. *Ars Technica.*

Garcia-Morchon, O., Kumar, S., Struik, R., Keoh, S., & Hummen, R. (2013). *Security Considerations in the IP-based Internet of Things.* IETF.

Gibson, I., Rosen, D. W., & Stucker, B. et al. (2010). *Additive Manufacturing Technologies* (Vol. 238). Springer. doi:10.1007/978-1-4419-1120-9

Hansman, S., & Hunt, R. (2005). A taxonomy of network and computer attacks. *Computers & Security, 24,* 31-43.

Haselsteiner, E., & Breitfuß, K. (2006). Security in Near Field Communication (NFC). In *Proceedings of the Workshop on RFID security.*

Hendricks, J., & Van Doorn, L. (2004). Secure Bootstrap Is Not Enough: Shoring up the Trusted Computing Base. In *Proceedings of the 11th workshop on ACM SIGOPS European workshop.* doi:10.1145/1133572.1133600

Hentunen, D., & Tikkanen, A. (2014). *Havex Hunts For ICS/SCADA Systems.* F-Secure.

Höller, A., Druml, N., Kreiner, C., Steger, C., & Felicijan, T. (2014). Hardware/Software Co-Design of Elliptic-Curve Cryptography for Resource-Constraint Applications. In *Proceedings of the 51st Annual Design Automation Conference.* ACM. doi:10.1145/2593069.2593148

Horne, B., Matheson, L., Sheehan, C., & Tarjan, R. E. (2001). Dynamic Self-Checking Techniques for Improved Tamper Resistance. In *Proceedings of the ACM Workshop on Digital Rights Management*, (pp. 141-159).

Hu, W., Tan, H., Corke, P., Shih, W. C., & Jha, S. (2010). Toward Trusted Wireless Sensor Networks. *ACM Transactions on Sensor Networks*, 7(1).

Huang, Y., Li, H., Campbell, K. A., & Han, Z. (2011). Defending False Data Injection Attack on Smart Grid Network Using Adaptive CUSUM Test. In *Proceedings of the 2011 45th Annual Conference on Information Sciences and Systems (CISS)* (pp. 1-6).

Hui, J., & Thubert, P. (2011). *Compression format for IPv6 datagrams over IEEE 802.15. 4-based networks*. IETF.

Hurley, C. (2003). *The worldwide wardrive: The myths, the misconceptions, the truth, the future*. Defcon.

Hutter, M., & Toegl, R. (2010). A Trusted Platform Module for Near Field Communication. In *Proceedings of the 2010 Fifth International Conference on Systems and Networks Communications* (pp. 136-141). doi:10.1109/ICSNC.2010.27

ICS-CERT. (2016). *Cyber-Attack Against Ukrainian Critical Infrastructure*.

Jing, Q., Vasilakos, A. V., Wan, J., Lu, J., & Qiu, D. (2014). Security of the Internet of Things: Perspectives and challenges. *Wireless Networks*, 20(8), 2481–2501. doi:10.1007/s11276-014-0761-7

Karlof, C., Sastry, N., & Wagner, D. (2004). TinySec: A Link Layer Security Architecture for Wireless Sensor Networks. In *Proceedings of the 2nd international conference on Embedded networked sensor systems* (pp. 162-175). doi:10.1145/1031495.1031515

Karlof, C., & Wagner, D. (2003). Secure routing in wireless sensor networks: Attacks and countermeasures. *Ad Hoc Networks*, 1(2-3), 293–315. doi:10.1016/S1570-8705(03)00008-8

Kasinathan, P., Pastrone, C., Spirito, M. A., & Vinkovits, M. (2013). *Denial-of-Service detection in 6LoWPAN based Internet of Things. In WiMob* (pp. 600–607). doi:10.1109/WiMOB.2013.6673419

Kim, T. T., & Poor, H. V. (2011). Strategic Protection Against Data Injection Attacks on Power Grids. *IEEE Transactions on Smart Grid*, 2(2), 326–333. doi:10.1109/TSG.2011.2119336

Kinney, S. L. (2006). *Trusted Platform Module Basics: Using TPM in Embedded Systems*. Newnes.

Kocher, P., Lee, R., McGraw, G., Raghunathan, A., & Moderator-Ravi, S. (2004). Security as a New Dimension in Embedded System Design. In *Proceedings of the 41st annual Design Automation Conference*,(pp. 753-760).

Kothmayr, T., Schmitt, C., Hu, W., Brünig, M., & Carle, G. (2012). A DTLS Based End-To-End Security Architecture for the Internet of Things with Two-Way Authentication. In *Proceedings of the 2012 IEEE 37th Conference on*, *Local Computer Networks Workshops (LCN Workshops)* (pp. 956-963).

Kothmayr, T., Schmitt, C., Hu, W., Brünig, M., & Carle, G. (2013). DTLS based security and two-way authentication for the Internet of Things. *Ad Hoc Networks*, *11*(8), 2710–2723. doi:10.1016/j.adhoc.2013.05.003

Krawczyk, H. (2001). The Order of Encryption and Authentication for Protecting Communications (or: How Secure Is SSL?). In *Proceedings of the Annual International Cryptology Conference* (pp. 310-331). doi:10.1007/3-540-44647-8_19

Kwon, C., Liu, W., & Hwang, I. (2014). Analysis and Design of Stealthy Cyber Attacks on Unmanned Aerial Systems. *Journal of Aerospace Information Systems*, *11*(8), 525–539. doi:10.2514/1.I010201

Langner, R. (2011). Stuxnet: Dissecting a Cyberwarfare Weapon. *IEEE Security \& Privacy, 9*, 49-51.

Le, T.-H., Canovas, C., & Clédiere, J. (2008). An Overview of Side Channel Analysis Attacks. In *Proceedings of the 2008 ACM symposium on Information, computer and communications security* (pp. 33-43). doi:10.1145/1368310.1368319

Le Malécot, E., & Inoue, D. (2014). The Carna Botnet Through the Lens of a Network Telescope. In *Foundations and Practice of Security* (pp. 426–441). Springer. doi:10.1007/978-3-319-05302-8_26

Lee, D. (2012, May). Flame: Massive cyber-attack discovered, researchers say. *BBC News*.

Lee, E. A. (2008). Cyber Physical Systems: Design Challenges. In *Proceedings of the 2008 11th IEEE International Symposium on Object and Component-Oriented Real-Time Distributed Computing (ISORC)* (pp. 363-369).

Lee, J.-S., Jeong, H., Park, J.-H., Kim, M., & Noh, B.-N. (2008). The Activity Analysis of Malicious HTTP-Based Botnets Using Degree of Periodic Repeatability. In *Proceedings of the International Conference on Security Technology SECTECH'08* (pp. 83-86).

Lennvall, T., Svensson, S., & Hekland, F. (2008). A Comparison of WirelessHART and ZigBee for Industrial Applications. In *Proceedings of the IEEE International Workshop on Factory Communication Systems* (pp. 85-88). doi:10.1109/WFCS.2008.4638746

Lesjak, C., Hein, D., Hofmann, M., Maritsch, M., Aldrian, A., Priller, P., . . . Pregartner, G. (2015). Securing Smart Maintenance Services: Hardware-Security and TLS for MQTT. In *Proceedings of the 2015 IEEE 13th International Conference on Industrial Informatics (INDIN)* (pp. 1243-1250).

Lie, D., Thekkath, C., Mitchell, M., Lincoln, P., Boneh, D., Mitchell, J., & Horowitz, M. (2000). Architectural Support for Copy and Tamper Resistant Software. *ACM SIGPLAN Notices*, *35*(11), 168–177. doi:10.1145/356989.357005

Lo, C.-H., & Ansari, N. (2013). CONSUMER: A Novel Hybrid Intrusion Detection System for Distribution Networks in Smart Grid. *IEEE Transactions on Emerging Topics in Computing*, *1*(1), 33–44. doi:10.1109/TETC.2013.2274043

Lun, Y., D'Innocenzo, A., Malavolta, I., & Di Benedetto, M. (2016). Cyber-Physical Systems Security: a Systematic Mapping Study.

Madnick, S. E., & Donovan, J. J. (1973). Application and Analysis of the Virtual Machine Approach to Information System Security and Isolation. In *Proceedings of the workshop on virtual computer systems* (pp. 210-224). doi:10.1145/800122.803961

Mahnke, W., Leitner, S.-H., & Damm, M. (2009). *OPC Unified Architecture*. Springer Science & Business Media. doi:10.1007/978-3-540-68899-0

Mangard, S., Oswald, E., & Popp, T. (2008). *Power Analysis Attacks: Revealing the Secrets of Smart Cards* (Vol. 31). Springer Science & Business Media.

Marinos, L., Belmonte, A., & Rekleitis, E. (2015). *Enisa Threat Landscape (Technical report)*. ENISA.

Mattern, F., & Floerkemeier, C. (2010). From the Internet of Computers to the Internet of Things. In *From active data management to event-based systems and more* (pp. 242–259). Springer. doi:10.1007/978-3-642-17226-7_15

Mclvor, C., McLoone, M., & McCanny, J. V. (2003). Fast Montgomery Modular Multiplication and RSA Cryptographic Processor Architectures. In *Conference Record of the Thirty-Seventh Asilomar Conference on* Signals, Systems and Computers (Vol. 1, pp. 379-384).

Mellado, D., Fernandez-Medina, E., & Piattini, M. (2007). A common criteria based security requirements engineering process. *Computer Standards & Interfaces*, 29(2), 244–253. doi:10.1016/j.csi.2006.04.002

Miller, B., & Rowe, D. (2012). A Survey of SCADA and Critical Infrastructure Incidents. In *Proceedings of the 1st Annual conference on Research in information technology* (pp. 51-56). doi:10.1145/2380790.2380805

Mishra, S., Shoukry, Y., Karamchandani, N., Diggavi, S., & Tabuada, P. (2015). Secure State Estimation: Optimal Guarantees Against Sensor Attacks in the Presence of Noise. In *Proceedings of the 2015 IEEE International Symposium on Information Theory (ISIT)* (pp. 2929-2933).

Mitchell, R., & Chen, I.-R. (2014). A Survey of Intrusion Detection Techniques for Cyber-Physical Systems. [CSUR]. *ACM Computing Surveys*, 46(4), 55. doi:10.1145/2542049

Mo, Y., Weerakkody, S., & Sinopoli, B. (2015). Physical Authentication of Control Systems: Designing Watermarked Control Inputs to Detect Counterfeit Sensor Outputs. *IEEE Control Systems*, 35(1), 93–109. doi:10.1109/MCS.2014.2364724

Modadugu, N., & Rescorla, E. (2004). *The Design and Implementation of Datagram TLS*. NDSS.

Nicholson, A., Webber, S., Dyer, S., Patel, T., & Janicke, H. (2012). SCADA security in the light of Cyber-Warfare. *Computers & Security, 31*, 418-436.

Niruntasukrat, A., Issariyapat, C., Pongpaibool, P., Meesublak, K., Aiumsupucgul, P., & Panya, A. (2016). Authorization Mechanism for MQTT-based Internet of Things. In *Proceedings of the 2016 IEEE International Conference on Communications Workshops (ICC)* (pp. 290-295).

Oorschot, V., Somayaji, A., & Wurster, G. (2005). Hardware-Assisted Circumvention of Self-Hashing Software Tamper Resistance. *IEEE Transactions on Dependable and Secure Computing*, 2(2), 82–92. doi:10.1109/TDSC.2005.24

Oppliger, R. (1998). Security at the Internet Layer. *Computer*, *31*(9), 43–47. doi:10.1109/2.708449

Ouyang, Y., Le, Z., Liu, D., Ford, J., & Makedon, F. (2008). Source Location Privacy against Laptop-Class Attacks in Sensor Networks. In *Proceedings of the 4th international conference on Security and privacy in communication networks* (p. 5). doi:10.1145/1460877.1460884

Pa, Y. M., Suzuki, S., Yoshioka, K., Matsumoto, T., Kasama, T., & Rossow, C. (2015). IoTPOT: Analysing the Rise of IoT Compromises. In *Proceedings of the 9th USENIX Workshop on Offensive Technologies (WOOT 15)*.

Pardo-Castellote, G. (2003). OMG Data-Distribution Service: Architectural Overview. *Proceedings of the 23rd International Conference on Distributed Computing Systems Workshops* (pp. 200-206).

Pasqualetti, F., Dörfler, F., & Bullo, F. (2013). Attack Detection and Identification in Cyber-Physical Systems. *IEEE Transactions on Automatic Control*, *58*(11), 2715–2729. doi:10.1109/TAC.2013.2266831

Plósz, S., Farshad, A., Tauber, M., Lesjak, C., Ruprechter, T., & Pereira, N. (2014). Security Vulner-abilities and Risks in Industrial Usage of Wireless Communication. In *Proceedings of the 2014 IEEE Emerging Technology and Factory Automation (ETFA)*, (pp. 1-8). doi:10.1109/ETFA.2014.7005129

Raciti, M., & Nadjm-Tehrani, S. (2012). Embedded Cyber-Physical Anomaly Detection in Smart Meters. In *Proceedings of the International Workshop on Critical Information Infrastructures Security*, (pp. 34-45).

Ravi, S., Raghunathan, A., & Chakradhar, S. (2004). Tamper Resistance Mechanisms for Secure Embedded Systems. In *Proceedings of the 17th International Conference on VLSI Design* (pp. 605-611).

Ravi, S., Raghunathan, A., Kocher, P., & Hattangady, S. (2004). Security in Embedded Systems: Design Challenges. *ACM Transactions on Embedded Computing Systems*, *3*(3), 461–491. doi:10.1145/1015047.1015049

Raza, S., Shafagh, H., Hewage, K., Hummen, R., & Voigt, T. (2013). Lithe: Lightweight Secure CoAP for the Internet of Things. *IEEE Sensors Journal*, *13*(10), 3711–3720. doi:10.1109/JSEN.2013.2277656

Referat, B. f. (2013). *Zukunftsbild Industrie 4.0*. Bundesministerium fuer Bildung und Forschung Referat.

Roman, R., Najera, P., & Lopez, J. (2011). Securing the Internet of Things. *Computer*, *44*(9), 51–58. doi:10.1109/MC.2011.291

Saint-Andre, P. (2011). *Extensible Messaging and Presence Protocol (XMPP): Core*. IETF. doi:10.17487/rfc6122

Saint-Andre, P., Smith, K., Tronçon, R., & Troncon, R. (2009). *XMPP: The Definitive Guide*. O'Reilly Media, Inc.

Saltzer, J. H., & Schroeder, M. D. (1975). The Protection of Information in Computer Systems. *Proceedings of the IEEE*, *63*(9), 1278–1308. doi:10.1109/PROC.1975.9939

Sarkar, P. G., & Fitzgerald, S. (2013). Attacks on SSL: A Comprehensive Study of Beast, Crime, Time, Breach, Lucky 13 & RC4 Biases.

Shelby, Z., Hartke, K., & Bormann, C. (2014). *The Constrained Application Protocol (CoAP). Tech. rep.* IETF.

Singh, M., Rajan, M. A., Shivraj, V. L., & Balamuralidhar, P. (2015). Secure MQTT for Internet of Things (IoT). In *Proceedings of the 2015 Fifth International Conference on Communication Systems and Network Technologies (CSNT)* (pp. 746-751).

Smith, S. W., & Weingart, S. (1999). Building a high-performance, programmable secure coprocessor. *Computer Networks, 31*(8), 831–860. doi:10.1016/S1389-1286(98)00019-X

Somani, G., Gaur, M. S., & Sanghi, D. (2015). DDoS/EDoS attack in Cloud: Affecting everyone out there! In *Proceedings of the 8th International Conference on Security of Information and Networks* (pp. 169-176). doi:10.1145/2799979.2800005

Standaert, F.-X., Malkin, T. G., & Yung, M. (2009). A Unified Framework for the Analysis of Side-Channel Key Recovery Attacks. In *Proceedings of the Annual International Conference on the Theory and Applications of Cryptographic Techniques* (pp. 443-461). doi:10.1007/978-3-642-01001-9_26

Standard, O. A. (2014). *MQTT Version 3.1*. OASIS.

Stankovic, J. A. (2014). Research Directions for the Internet of Things. *IEEE Internet of Things Journal, 1*(1), 3–9. doi:10.1109/JIOT.2014.2312291

Strasser, M., & Stamer, H. (2008). A Software-Based Trusted Platform Module Emulator. In *Proceedings of the International Conference on Trusted Computing* (pp. 33-47).

Tiri, K., Hwang, D., Hodjat, A., Lai, B., Yang, S., Schaumont, P., & Verbauwhede, I. (2005). A Side-Channel Leakage Free Coprocessor IC in 0.18 μm CMOS for Embedded AES-based Cryptographic and Biometric Processing. In *Proceedings of the 42nd Design Automation Conference* (pp. 222-227).

Tuyls, P., Schrijen, G.-J., Škorić, B., Van Geloven, J., Verhaegh, N., & Wolters, R. (2006). Read-Proof Hardware from Protective Coatings. In *Proceedings of the International Workshop on Cryptographic Hardware and Embedded Systems* (pp. 369-383).

Ukil, A., Bandyopadhyay, S., Bhattacharyya, A., Pal, A., & Bose, T. (2014). Lightweight security scheme for IoT applications using CoAP. *International Journal of Pervasive Computing and Communications, 10*(4), 372–392. doi:10.1108/IJPCC-01-2014-0002

Urbina, D. I., Giraldo, J. A., Cardenas, A. A., Tippenhauer, N. O., Valente, J., Faisal, M., & Sandberg, H. et al. (2016). Limiting the Impact of Stealthy Attacks on Industrial Control Systems. In *Proceedings of the 2016 ACM SIGSAC Conference on Computer and Communications Security* (pp. 1092-1105). doi:10.1145/2976749.2978388

Vasudevan, A., Owusu, E., Zhou, Z., Newsome, J., & McCune, J. M. (2012). Trustworthy Execution on Mobile Devices: What Security Properties Can My Mobile Platform Give Me? In *Proceedings of the International Conference on Trust and Trustworthy Computing* (pp. 159-178). Springer Berlin Heidelberg. doi:10.1007/978-3-642-30921-2_10

Vinoski, S. (2006). Advanced Message Queuing Protocol. *IEEE Internet Computing*, 10(6).

Vuković, O., & Dán, G. (2014). Security of Fully Distributed Power System State Estimation: Detection and Mitigation of Data Integrity Attacks. *IEEE Journal on Selected Areas in Communications*, *32*(7), 1500–1508. doi:10.1109/JSAC.2014.2332106

Wallgren, L., Raza, S., & Voigt, T. (2013). Routing Attacks and Countermeasures in the RPL-based Internet of Things. *International Journal of Distributed Sensor Networks*, *9*(8), 794326. doi:10.1155/2013/794326

Weingart, S. H. (2000). Physical Security Devices for Computer Subsystems: A Survey of Attacks and Defenses. Advanced Message Queuing Protocol*International Workshop on Cryptographic Hardware and Embedded Systems* (pp. 302-317). doi:10.1007/3-540-44499-8_24

Weiser, M. (1991). The Computer for the 21st Century. *Scientific American*, *265*(3), 94–104. doi:10.1038/scientificamerican0991-94

Whitman, M. E., & Mattord, H. J. (2011). *Principles of Information Security*. Cengage Learning.

Winter, J. (2008). Trusted Computing Building Blocks for Embedded Linux-based ARM TrustZone Platforms. In *Proceedings of the 3rd ACM workshop on Scalable trusted computing* (pp. 21-30). doi:10.1145/1456455.1456460

Wurster, G., van Oorschot and Paul, C., & Somayaji, A. (2005). A generic attack on checksumming-based software tamper resistance. In *Proceedings of the 2005 IEEE Symposium on Security and Privacy (S\&P'05)*, (pp. 127-138). doi:10.1109/SP.2005.2

Xue, M., Wang, W., & Roy, S. (2014). Security Concepts for the Dynamics of Autonomous Vehicle Networks. *Automatica*, *50*(3), 852–857. doi:10.1016/j.automatica.2013.12.001

Zhang, X., van Doorn, L., Jaeger, T., Perez, R., & Sailer, R. (2002). Secure Coprocessor-based Intrusion Detection. In *Proceedings of the 10th workshop on ACM SIGOPS European workshop* (pp. 239-242). doi:10.1145/1133373.1133423

Zhou, Z., Gligor, V. D., Newsome, J., & McCune, J. M. (2012). Building Verifiable Trusted Path on Commodity x86 Computers. In *Proceedings of the 2012 IEEE Symposium on Security and Privacy* (pp. 616-630). doi:10.1109/SP.2012.42

Zhu, Q., & Basar, T. (2015). Game-Theoretic Methods for Robustness, Security, and Resilience of Cyberphysical Control Systems: Games-in-Games Principle for Optimal Cross-Layer Resilient Control Systems. *IEEE Control Systems*, *35*(1), 46–65. doi:10.1109/MCS.2014.2364710

Zorzi, M., Gluhak, A., Lange, S., & Bassi, A. (2010). From Today's Internet of Things to a Future Internet of Things: A Wireless-and Mobility-Related View. *IEEE Wireless Communications*, *17*(6), 44–51. doi:10.1109/MWC.2010.5675777

Zuehlke, D. (2010). SmartFactory - Towards a factory-of-things. *Annual Reviews in Control*, *34*(1), 129–138. doi:10.1016/j.arcontrol.2010.02.008

KEY TERMS AND DEFINITIONS

CIA: Security attributes confidentiality, integrity, and availability that need to be protected. Many attacks target one or multiple of these attributes.

Industrial IoT: Inspired by initiatives such as Industry 4.0 or Smart Manufacturing, IoT concepts are applied to industrial machinery. These machines are connected to the Internet, thus making them accessible from everywhere.

Intrusion Detection System: Used to monitor networks or devices to detect ongoing attacks. In combination with other measures, also successfully defeated attacks should be detected by IDSs.

Logical Attack: Logical attacks can be conducted using existing interfaces to a device, such as network interfaces or a debug interface. This type of attack can be done remotely without physical access to the device.

Network Security: Due to IoT devices and even CPS being connected with other devices and even the Internet, security at the network layer needs to be provided. Security measures can be applied at different network layers such as the transport layer.

Physical Attack: Physical attacks require physical access to the device under attack. This type of attack can be invasive, semi-invasive or non-invasive, which denotes the severity of modifications an attacker performs with the attacked device.

Tamper Resistance: Devices that should not reveal any confidential information need to be tamper resistant. Tamper resistance is achieved mostly through hardware measures but can also be realized in software only.

Chapter 11
Where Do All My Keys Come From?

Andreas Daniel Sinnhofer
Graz University of Technology, Austria

Christian Steger
Graz University of Technology, Austria

Christian Kreiner
Graz University of Technology, Austria

Felix Jonathan Oppermann
NXP Semiconductors Austria GmbH, Austria

Klaus Potzmader
NXP Semiconductors, Austria

Clemens Orthacker
NXP Semiconductors, Austria

ABSTRACT

Nowadays, cyber-physical systems are omnipresent in our daily lives and are increasingly used to process confidential data. While the variety of portable devices we use excessively at home and at work is steadily increasing, their security vulnerabilities are often not noticed by the user. Therefore, portable devices such as wearables are becoming more and more interesting for adversaries. Thus, a robust and secure software design is required for the implementation of cryptographic communication protocols and encryption algorithms. While these topics are well discussed and subject to further research activities, the issue of provisioning the initial device setup is widely uncovered. However, the protection of the initial setup is as important as the protection of the confidential data during the time in use. In this work, the authors will present solutions for a secure initialization of security critical integrated circuits (ICs).

DOI: 10.4018/978-1-5225-2845-6.ch011

INTRODUCTION

Cyber-physical systems (CPS) and Internet of Things (IoT) devices are increasingly used in our daily lives. Generally speaking, IoT refers to the connection of our everyday objects with a network like the internet. Each of these devices is usually equipped with different kind of sensors to observe its environment, making the device a smart object. In combination with embedded systems, IoT promises to increase the quality of our daily lives by taking over simple tasks like controlling the room temperature and cooking coffee (Nest Labs, 2016). On the other hand, smart objects like wearables are becoming more and more interesting for adversaries due to their increasing functionalities like internet capabilities, cameras, microphones, GPS trackers and other senor devices.

Furthermore, such smart objects are often deployed in unsupervised and untrusted environments raising the question about privacy and security to a crucial topic. Thus, a robust and secure software design is required for the implementation of cryptographic communication protocols and encryption algorithms. Moreover, tamper-proof solutions like secure elements and trusted platform modules are necessary to securely calculate cryptographic functions and to store confidential data or cryptographic keys. While cryptographic protocols and secure hardware architectures are well discussed and subject to further research activities, the issue of provisioning the initial confidential device setup is widely uncovered. However, the protection of this initial setup is as important as the protection of the confidential data during the time in use. Especially the protection of master keys is essential, because otherwise all security measures, which are based on such keys, are futile.

Due to the high quantity of produced chips – e.g. 8.8 billion secure elements for smartcard chips in 2014 (IHS Markit, 2014) – it is obvious that automatic methods are required to generate the trusted data needed for each chip. Otherwise an economical and practical production is infeasible. On the one hand, the system creating this data has to be designed flexible since every product can support different cryptographic protocols and thus, require different keys. On the other hand, the personalization system needs to fulfil high security requirements to prevent the risk that the generated data leaks during the production process to an operator – or even worse – to an adversary.

As revealed in 2015 by Edward Snowden, the secret master key of SIM cards, securing the 3G and 4G mobile communication channels was subject to such an attack (Begley & Scahill, 2015; Scahill, 2015):

The American "National Security Agency" (NSA) and the British spy agency "Government Communications Headquarters" (GCHQ) perpetrated an attack and hacked into the network of Gemalto. Gemalto produces, amongst other things, Smart Cards in the form of SIM cards and EMV (Europay, MasterCard, and Visa) chip cards. More precisely, the company generates and inserts an individual cryptographic key (a symmetric encryption key) into each SIM card during the personalization process of the manufacturing process. The inserted cryptographic key is used to secure the communication between the mobile phone and the cell tower of the mobile network operator. Mobile network operators purchase SIM cards in bulks with pre-loaded keys by Gemalto. Additionally, the mobile network operators get a copy of each key from Gemalto in order to allow their networks to recognize an individual's phone. For this purpose, Gemalto provided a file containing the cryptographic keys for each of the new SIM cards to the mobile network operator. The primary goal of this hack was to steal millions of such symmetric encryption keys to wiretap and decipher the encrypted mobile phone communication. By using the stolen symmetric encryption keys, the national agencies can decrypt any mobile phone conversation or text message sent by a mobile phone having a Gemalto SIM card. With this heist, no assistance from the mobile operators, or permission from the legal official court was necessary. To get inside Gemalto's network, social engineering attacks like phishing and scouring Facebook posts where used to take over the employee's PCs (Begley & Scahill, 2015). Once inside the network, the agencies were able to retrieve the cryptographic keys because Gemalto sent them via unencrypted FTP to the Smart Card manufacturing factories. According to Begley & Scahill (Begley & Scahill, 2015), millions of keys where stolen by GCHQ in a three-month period in 2010. This is a good example showing the impact of insecure data handling and how many users can be affected by hacking the personalization system of secure integrated circuits.

In this chapter, the authors will present state of the art solutions for the secure generation and distribution of security critical data during the production of secure integrated circuits. The presented solutions are based on techniques form the Smart Card industry, since those processes have already evolved over the past decades. The reminder of this chapter is structured in the following way Section "BACKGROUND" gives an overview about the lifecycle of secure CPS devices and more generally of secure integrated circuits. Security Certification is an essential topic in the domain of consumer products. Thus, concepts for security certification are summarized as well. Section "Personalization Of Secure Integrated Circuits" describes the whole personalization process of secure integrated circuits during the production process. The Section gives information about how to generate the data, how the data is loaded and defines generic protection mechanisms that can be used to protect the process. Further, the authors summarize which data is generally personalized during the production and who is responsible for generating / protecting it. The Section is concluded with potential attack vectors and attackers which may be interested in hacking the personalization system. Finally, this Chapter is summarized and concluded with future research trends.

BACKGROUND

From a high-level perspective, a secure CPS or IoT device – or more general a secure system – consists of two separated system components. The first system component consists of all non-security critical components like peripherals or processing units. The second component is the security critical equipment which consists in most cases of a secure microcontroller and a tamper-proof memory which are usually combined in a single chip. This ensures that cryptographic functions can be securely processed and confidential data is stored in a secure manner. The second component can consist of multiple microcontrollers or co-processors, optimized for special purposes. The authors will use the term secure Integrated Circuit (IC) in the following as an abbreviation for all security critical modules, controllers, and memory.

The aforementioned two component structure is similar to the structure of secure Smart Cards (Rankl & Effing, 2010) where the Smart Cards consists of two independent components; the card body including the printing and the external interface, and the card module for cryptographic operations and secure storage. Since there is no standard which defines the lifecycle for secure ICs, the authors will adapt the lifecycle of Smart Cards, which is defined in ISO-10202-1 (ISO 10202-1, 1991). The domain of Smart Cards is an ideal example for requirements of future IoT devices: Smart Cards need to fulfill high security requirements, are produced in mass production processes, and are cheap for the end-customer.

The focus of this chapter is the secure personalization process of secure ICs. In case of consumer products, it is likely that those secure ICs are evaluated in a security certification. During such security certification audits, the countermeasures of the IC are evaluated against possible attacks. Further, the production process is investigated to ensure, that the countermeasures of the IC are not circumvented during the production. Thus, the personalization process is subject of investigation during security certification audits. In the domain of secure information technology, the Common Criteria (Common Criteria, 2012) standard is widely used to evaluate the security mechanisms of IT products. To avoid costly re-evaluation of the personalization process for different products, the authors will present state of the art concepts for an incremental and modular certification process at the end of this Section.

Lifecycle of Secure Integrated Circuits

Over the last decades, the development and production processes of secure Smart Cards were continuously improved with respect to security and costs. Since the market of IoT devices is expected to grow substantial over the next years (Manyika et al., 2015), the findings of the Smart Cards domain build a good foundation for the processes of securing IoT devices. For Smart Cards, the ISO-10202-1 standard attempts to define a lifecycle which is valid independent of the manufacturing process and the application of the card. It is strongly biased by financial transaction applications, but the lifecycle is described generic and independent of the use-cases. As a consequence, the defined lifecycle is used as a basis and adopted to be used for secure CPS or IoT devices. The lifecycle can be separated into 6 phases which are illustrated in Figure 1 and shortly described in the following enumeration (Rankl & Effing, 2010; Markantonakis, Mayes, Sauveron, & Tunstall, 2010):

- **Production of Components (Phase 1):** During this phase, all components of the secure CPS or IoT device are designed and manufactured. For example, in case of a Smart Card, usually components like the Operating System, the Secure Element and the card body are manufactured. In many cases, the development and production of the individual components is done by different vendors. With respect to security, the production is an essential step since no matter how high the quality of the system and its cryptographic protection mechanisms are they are of little help if all the confidential data is leaked during the production process. Besides security consideration, also functional testing is an important topic, since the production yields of chips can be rather low for new processes. Thus, excessive testing is used on chip level to ensure the proper operation of the IC with respect to the electrical operation as well as its functionality.

Figure 1. Lifecycle of secure CPS or IoT devices adopted from the Smart Card standard ISO 10202-1, 1991.

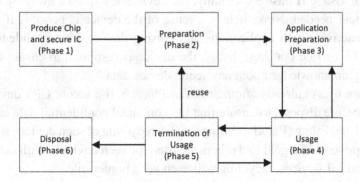

281

- **Preparation (Phase 2):** Here, all manufactured components are assembled together to the final device and the common device data is loaded. This includes configuration settings, files, and secret keys which are shared between all devices in a batch. In contrast to Phase 1, this phase is usually carried out by a single company (see (Rankl & Effing, 2010) or (Markantonakis, Mayes, Sauveron, & Tunstall, 2010)) called personalization company. In the case of Smart Cards, usually the Operating System and the applications (e.g. a banking app) are loaded to the device during this phase. For security reasons, the manufacturing of the hardware must be kept completely separated from loading the device data. Since the device data for secure devices usually always contains sensitive data, it has to be protected properly. This means that the data is encrypted and the encryption key is loaded to the device via a separate process. The authors will discuss this issue in more detail in Section "Personalization Of Secure Integrated Circuits"

- **Application Preparation (Phase 3):** In contrast to Phase 2, Phase 3 deals with the personalization of the device individual data. This can also include the visual personalization of the device if for example unique identifiers are engraved to the body housing. During this process, device individual secret keys are generated and loaded. As in Phase 2, this data has to be encrypted such that it is not exposed to any operator or third party during the production. In case of symmetric key material, the personalization company is further responsible for a secure distribution of the generated data to the according stakeholder. For example, in case of SIM cards (which was briefly discussed in the introduction), symmetric master keys are generated for each individual SIM card and loaded to the chips as well as distributed to the mobile network operator. In general, the process of loading additional applications require authentication to the device to ensure that only authorized persons can load the according data. This phase can be carried out from an external company or even from the customer in the field (see Phase 4) if the authentication tokens are shared with the customers.

- **Usage (Phase 4):** During this phase, the secure CPS or IoT devices are used by the end-customer. Depending on the use-case this phase also includes loading of additional applications, or the deactivation or deletion of applications. Thus, confidential data may be generated and loaded by the customer to the system. To ensure that this mechanism is protected, the customer needs to be aware of cryptographic keys which are used to securely communicate with the device. In case of symmetric channel encryption, there are two possible ways to personalize the according key. The first way is that a key is generated by the personalization company and securely shipped to the product issuer who further distributes it to the end-customer. The second approach is that the encryption key is sent by the product issuer to the personalization company. Either way, it has to be ensured that no single operator gets knowledge about this key during the personalization process.

- **Termination of Usage (Phase 5):** Usually, the devices are thrown away by the end-customer if they are no longer needed. Nevertheless, a reuse of the device is possible if it is returned to the vendor after deactivating all applications and erasing the sensitive confidential data. The latter should always be carried out even though the device is disposed, to ensure that malicious third parties cannot gain knowledge about any secret device data.

- **Disposal (Phase 6):** As already summarizes in Phase 5, the secure CPS device should be completely erased before disposal to ensure that the contained confidential data cannot be leaked. As stated by Rankl and Effing (Rankl & Effing, 2010), recycling of such devices is an interesting topic since rare components like gold and others are used for such devices. With the increasing number of built CPS and IoT devices, recycling will even get a bigger role.

Additionally, secure CPS or IoT devices need to be developed and produced by using appropriate quality assurance methods. In the domain of security critical devices, the ISO 9000 family is usually applied to guarantee the traceability of the manufacturing process. To ensure this traceability, each individual process step is recorded. In most cases, unique identifiers (IDs) are used to track the personalizer or manufacturer of the device and every individual process step. In case of failures during the production process, the IDs are used to identify the cause and the possible impacts to other devices.

Security Certification of Secure CPS or IoT Devices

Security Certification is an essential step during the development of secure CPS or IoT devices. This ensures that customers gain trust in the developed security measures of the device. Further, this security evidence may be an important selling point for customers. In the domain of secure information technology, the Common Criteria (CC) standard (Common Criteria, 2012) is widely used to evaluate the security measures. The CC defines a common set of requirements that need to be implemented by the security functionality of the Target of Evaluation (ToE). As a consequence, the evaluation process creates a level of confidence into the security functionality which is implemented in hardware, software, or both. The CC evaluation also considers the maturity of the development processes, the production processes and the used toolchains in case of high security levels. This includes also the personalization process of secure systems, because every cryptographic protection mechanism is futile if a secret key is leaked during the personalization process. The assurance level of the CC is rated from a scale from EAL 1 to EAL 7 (Evaluation Assurance Level), where EAL 1 is the lowest level and EAL 7 is the highest level. A higher level does not necessarily mean a higher security level, but indicates that more effort was invested during the development and evaluation of the implemented security mechanisms. The key components and stakeholder of such an evaluation are listed in the following enumeration:

- **Evaluation Facility:** Is responsible for testing and evaluating the implemented security functionalities of a Target of Evaluation. Tests and evaluation methods are derived based on a Security Target (see below). The results of the evaluation are collected in form of an Evaluation Technical Report (ETR). Based on this report, a certification body will issue the CC certificate.
- **Target of Evaluation (ToE):** Is defined 'as a set of software, firmware and/or hardware' (Common Criteria, 2012) that is target of a CC evaluation. The ToE describes the whole system and the according configuration. This configuration freedom may lead to problems during the evaluation process, since all possible configurations of the ToE must meet the defined security requirements. As a consequence, it is often the case that this configuration freedom is limited to "meaningful" configurations. These limitations are documented within the ToE in form of guidance documents. Using the ToE beyond the defined guidance, leads to a loss of the certificate. The ToE is compiled from the vendor(s) of the system.
- **Security Target (ST):** The ST is a description of the 'implementation-specific statement of security needs for a specific identified Target of Evaluation' (Common Criteria, 2012). It describes the assets, their threats and the implemented countermeasures. During the evaluation process, it is determined if the stated countermeasures are sufficient to counter the threats. Countermeasures can be divided into two separate groups (Common Criteria, 2012):

- ○ **Security Objectives for the Target of Evaluation:** These countermeasure(s) are directly implemented by the system. The correctness with respect to the threats and risks will be determined during the evaluation process.
- ○ **Security Objectives for the Operational Environment:** These countermeasure(s) are not implemented by the system, but need to be provided by the operational environment. The correctness of these countermeasures is not determined during the evaluation process.

The ST is written by the vendor(s) of the system.

- **Protection Profile (PP):** To allow groups and communities of interest to express their security requirements, the CC defines the concept of Protection Profiles (Common Criteria, 2012). While the ST always describes a specific ToE, a PP is designed to describe a group of ToE such that it can be reused in different STs. As a consequence, being compliant to a PP does not necessarily mean that a specific EAL is reached. A ToE is either fully compliant to a PP or non-compliant.
- **Evaluation Technical Report (ETR):** It is a document which is assembled by the evaluation facility during the evaluation process. It documents the overall verdict of the evaluation facility and justifies this decision based on the collected evidence of the implemented security mechanisms. It is submitted to a certification body which issues the certificate in case of a positive attestation.
- **Evaluation Processes:** The CC standard and its supporting documents defines formal and informal evaluation processes. Formal processes are explicitly defined in the standard, whilst informal processes are not defined explicitly. Thus, informal processes strongly depend on the instructed evaluation facility.

With respect to the personalization process, evaluation facilities will investigate the tools and the process flow. The used tools are usually developed by the personalization company and are designed to be compatible with a wide variety of different products. Since security requirements changes over the time, agile and modular product development techniques are widely used for a rapid and steady progression of incremental product developments, based on common parts and a modular architecture (Anderson D., 1997). On the one hand, this leads to a faster time to market, but on the other hand it raises big challenges in terms of security certification. At present, a security certification is usually started in a late phase of the development, which can lead to a big delay between the release of the product and the date the certificate is issued (Sinnhofer A. D., Raschke, Steger, & Kreiner, 2015). Further, the personalization processes should be flexible such that it can be easily integrated into the production process of secure systems independent from the involved companies. As a consequence, a modular certification scheme is required such that the personalization process can be easily integrated into the production process of the device. This is important to ensure, that costly re-evaluations can be avoided to guarantee low production costs. The following formal or informal evaluation processes are defined in the CC standard to support modular certification processes (Sinnhofer A. D., Raschke, Steger, & Kreiner, 2015):

- **Delta Evaluation (Informal Process):** The delta evaluation is a CC certification process used to maximize the reuse of previously compiled evidences. To do so, the standard specifies that the following documents need to be shared between the evaluation facilities (Common Criteria, 2002):

- ○ Product and supporting documentation
- ○ New security target(s)
- ○ Original evaluation technical report(s)
- ○ Original certification/validation report(s)
- ○ Original Common Criteria certificate(s)
- ○ Original evaluation work packages (if available)

Providing these data enables that the current evaluation facility should not have to repeat the analysis of parts of the system, where the requirements have not changed nor been impacted by any other changes. Such changes are identified by performing a delta analysis. The delta analysis is an analysis between the new security target and the original security targets(s) to identify the impact of changes. A drawback of this approach is that the evaluation technical reports contain information about the evaluation process and the applied measure to proof the security objectives of the target of evaluation. As a consequence, these reports are usually considered as proprietary to the evaluation facility, which are usually not interested in sharing this knowledge with other – competing – facilities. Thus, performing a delta evaluation is a tough challenge if the evaluation facility was changed between different certifications.

- **Composite Evaluation (Formal Process):** Although the composite evaluation was designed for Smart Card products, it can be applied to a wide variety of products which fulfill the condition that 'an independently evaluated product is part of a final composite product to be evaluated' (Common Criteria, 2012). The only restriction is that the already certified product builds the underlying platform of the composite product. This means that a layered pattern is used for the overall system architecture. Thus, it is applicable for example for an embedded system, whereas an application is running on a certified operating system which is running on a certified hardware platform. Compositional evaluations are technically similar to delta evaluations but with additional restriction to the overall structure of the product. Due to these additions, it is not necessary to share the evaluation technical reports. The lowest EAL of all components is the limiting factor of the composite evaluation. Further, the validity of the overall product certificate depends on the validity of each individual component. As a consequence, if the validity of one component expired, the whole product certificate is invalidated.
- **Composed Evaluation (Formal Process):** The composed evaluation is used to certify products which consists of independently certified (or going through an independent certification process) products/modules which are assembled to a new final product. It is similar to the composite evaluation but with the difference that the overall system architecture is not limited. Further, it is applicable for situation in which a delta evaluation is not possible since the evaluation technical reports are not shared. Since the individual components are already certified, the composed evaluation mainly focuses on the interface between the components and their according interaction(s). As a consequence, new evaluation assurance levels were introduced. These levels range from CAP-A to CAP-C (Composed Assurance Packages), where A is the lowest level and C is the highest level. The assurance level CAP-C stands for Attack potential "Enhanced Basic" which is approximately comparable with EAL-4 (see (Common Criteria, 2012); Part 3 pages 38 and 47). Due to this limitation, the composed evaluation has been performed much less successful than other modular CC certification processes.

The above certification processes all rely on delta analysis to identify the impact of changes. As such, traceability is required to explicitly state the dependencies of security requirements and the actual implementation artifacts and tests. To incorporate these requirements, Raschke et al. (Raschke, et al., 2014) introduced two processes to support an agile and modular development and certification process. The impact analysis is based on a change detection analysis in combination with a traceability impact analysis. A security model is used to describe the properties and dependencies. This model is based on the CC security target, the design documentation, the implementation artefacts and the tests.

To summarize, in the context of personalization processes, usually the Delta – or Composite evaluation is used to evaluate the tools, the process, and the configuration space.

PERSONALIZATION OF SECURE INTEGRATED CIRCUITS

The personalization process covers the phases 2 and 3 of the secure IC lifecycle which was described in Section "Lifecycle of secure Integrated Circuits". These phases are usually carried out by the same company which is usually referred to as the personalization company (Markantonakis, Mayes, Sauveron, & Tunstall, 2010). During Phase 2, the application and data is loaded which is common for every single device. In contrast, Phase 3 is dedicated for loading device individual applications or settings. This separation is required, since loading individual data to the devices is much more complex and time intensive than loading the common data (Rankl & Effing, 2010). As a consequence, the personalization company will try to minimize the size of the loaded data during Phase 3 as much as possible.

For secure applications, confidential data needs to be generated and loaded to the cards. Therefore, several security requirements need to be fulfilled by the process: On the one hand, it requires encryption such that confidential data is not leaked to any third party, including also the operator of the personalization equipment; on the other hand, it needs to be ensured that only authorized data or applications can be loaded to the system. In case that symmetric key material is generated that needs to be shared with the product issuer, the personalization company needs to take care of securely distributing the keys to the issuer.

Since the personalization process is operated in an automated high volume production process, all implemented security requirements need to be able to be operated in – at least – near real time.

Generation of the Personalization Data

For key management purposes, various standardization organizations (like (NIST FIPS PUB 140-2, 2001; NIST SP 800-57-1, 2016; PCI Security Standards Council, 2016)) recommend the use of dedicated hardware security modules (HSM) to protect the data. Hardware security modules are tamper-resistant hardware modules, designed for generating random numbers and calculating cryptographic functions. Furthermore, the hardware is optimized to accelerate the computation of the cryptographic functions, to ensure that a large amount of data can be processed efficiently by such systems. Thus, HSMs are a natural consequence for generating the required confidential personalization data in a secure and efficient way.

Figure 2 illustrates the basic components of a personalization system (adapted from (Chan & Ho, 2003)). The "Issuer System" contains the product and order specific data that is required by the personalization company to generate the data. This may also include static (confidential) data that is provided

Figure 2. Principal Structure of a personalization system
Adapted from (Chan & Ho, 2003).

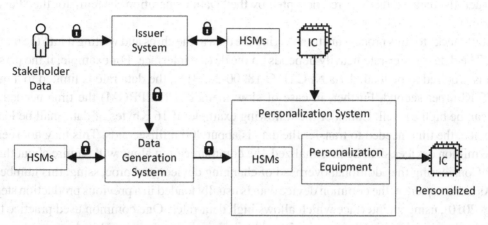

by a stakeholder (e.g. a mobile network operator). As illustrated in the Figure, external Stakeholder data is sent via a secure channel between the Stakeholder(s) and the "Issuer System". Usually, HSMs are used to secure the communication channel. This means that the sent data is encrypted with a key that is only available within the HSM. Typically, protocols using asymmetric cryptography are used to protect the communication channel (like TLS), but also other domain specific protocols may be used for this purpose (see (Sinnhofer et al., 2016)). In case of symmetric encryption, the corresponding protection key needs to be separately transported from the data. Recommendations foresee, that symmetric keys are split onto multiple shares which are sent on multiple independent ways (PCI Security Standards Council, 2016). Only after successful reception of one share, the next share is sent.

The HSMs of the "Data Generation System" are used to generate the required device data. This includes for example the generation of random keys, or the derivation of keys based on master key data that was sent by a Stakeholder. But also, non-confidential data like unique chip identifiers may be generated by the system. To be able to generate data that is based on Stakeholder data, a secure communication channel between the HSMs of the "Issuer System" and the "Data Generation System" is required.

The "Personalization Equipment" in general consists of special hardware which ensures that the data is sent cryptographically protected and authenticated to the system (Hautier, Macchetti, & Perrine, 2012; Chen, 2007). The data which is exchanged between the "Data Generation System" and the "Personalization Equipment" is again protected through a secure communication channel between the HSMs. For performance reasons, this channel is usually based on symmetric cryptography. Since such key exchange processes take up to several working days, it is usually executed several days or weeks in advance of the production. Re-keying is recommended for every separate production, even if the same products are manufactured.

The personalization equipment is a special device, to which the secure ICs, or the whole devices, are automatically mounted. In practice, many personalization devices are used in parallel to increase the throughput of the product line (Rankl & Effing, 2010). The Personalization equipment is usually executing scripts (Graham, Jr., Nablo, & Haeuser, 2002) that are prepared in advance from the personalization company based on the order. The script contains placeholder for the data that is either generated from the

"Data Generation System", or directly provided by the issuer. In case that the data is directly provided by the issuer, the data needs to be re-encrypted by the "Data Generation System" for the "Personalization System".

The bottlenecks for this process are transferring the data to the chips and writing it into the non-volatile memory. The data transfer-rate heavily depends on the device interface. For example, if the personalization data is required to be loaded via NFC (ISO 18000-3, 2010), the data rate is limited to a maximum of 423,75 Kbit per second. Further, in case of slow memories (EEPROM) the time needed to write the data can be high as well. Consider the following example: if 16 Kbytes of data shall be loaded to a single device, the time needed to transfer the data is about 300 milliseconds. This may not seem much, but if one million devices shall be personalized, the communication alone will require about three and a half day! Considering the additional overhead of changing devices and processing, this number is even higher. As a consequence, the common device data is usually loaded in a previous production step (Rankl & Effing, 2010), using an interface which allows high data-rates. One common used practice to ensure short personalization times is 'hard-wiring' applications such that they are already programmed during the lithography process in Phase 1. As a consequence of this, updating such 'hard-wired' applications may require additional effort since the ROM-Code cannot be updated during the time in use. Another drawback of ROM based products is, that the ROM mask itself has to be prepared several weeks before the start of the production. An alternative option to ROM-Code based products is the trend towards Flash based products: a Flash memory is used to store the applications that were previously loaded to the ROM code. As such, 'hard-wiring' an application does not require a time-consuming preparation of a ROM-mask.

Usually, the "Data Generation System" (as illustrated in Figure 2) is using a fixed and certified HSM firmware to generate the actual personalization data. This is required by security certifications to ensure, that the confidential data is not leaked during the data generation process. As a consequence, this firmware is in most cases suited for one dedicated product. If other products need to be supported, a new firmware needs to be developed and certified. In case of complex multi-application products, this is a considerable amount of development and certification effort. In the domain of secure ICs, the required data is similar for different use-cases or applications. Having a mature, modular development and certification processes can significantly reduce the required effort and costs. As described in Section "Security Certification of secure CPS or IoT devices", a security model can be used to trace the requirements of the personalization system to the implementation artifacts of the HSM firmware implementation. Thus, changes can be easily tracked and evaluated by the according evaluation facility.

For traditional software development, the problem of flexibility is usually solved by introducing a dedicated API that can be called arbitrarily. As identified by Anderson (Anderson, 2001), the most common API failure mode of secure systems is that functions / transactions that are secure in isolation become insecure in combination. The cause of such errors is usually application syntax, feature interactions, slow leakage, or concurrency problems. Developers of such system have to be aware, that an attacker could use any unexpected combination of function calls in order to break the trusted system. To solve the issue of leaking information, security APIs are usually designed simple such that they can be formally analyzed during the evaluation process. This is an open research challenge and thus, the authors will discuss this topic in Section "Future Research Directions" in more detail.

Authentication Methods

During the personalization process, random session keys are usually used to communicate with the individual chips. To start this process, the personalization system needs to be aware of an authentication token. This is necessary to ensure a unilateral or mutual authentication between the personalization equipment and the secure IC. There are many different methods that can be used, but the following describes a simple but common approach from the Smart Card domain (Rankl & Effing, 2010).

During the production of the secure IC, the producer of the operating system (OS) incorporates a secret value to the ROM (Read Only Memory) code of the IC. The ROM usually contains the static functions and data which are already programmed during the manufacturing of the chip. This is done by preparing a ROM mask from the program code which is applied to the chip using lithographic processes. Thus, the code is "hard-wired" to the memory. To prevent attacks on the ROM code, it is usually protected against optical attacks, including etching attacks.

The secret ROM value is combined with a value which is written to the non-volatile memory (EEPROM or Flash) of the chip by the semiconductor manufacturer to create an authentication token. The idea is that neither the OS producer, nor the semiconductor manufacturer has enough knowledge to generate this authentication token by his own. The parts of this token are sent encrypted to the personalization company. The described method can be used to generate authentication tokens which are valid for one production batch. The method can be refined if a chip individual number is combined with the secret values. Thus, the authentication tokens are only valid for a single specific chip. This increases the security in case that the chips are compromised before being completed. This method – or a similar method – is commonly used in practice.

Another attack that has to be prevented during the personalization process is the manipulation of the software of the IC during the production process. An attacker with sufficient resources (e.g. a national agency or a competitor) may be able to smuggle a manipulated IC to the personalization process. This manipulated IC basically acts like the real product, but has additional functionality like dump routines which can be used to retrieve the plain confidential data that was loaded during the personalization process. Again, a large variety of methods can be used to ensure the integrity and authenticity of the secure IC, but the following method is commonly used in practice (Rankl & Effing, 2010):

The semiconductor manufacturer stores a chip individual key into the non-volatile memory during the production process. The chip individual secret key and the unique chip identifier are securely shared with the personalization company. Before sending the personalization data to the card, the personalization system sends a challenge consisting of a random number to the chip. The chip answers this request by computing a keyed-hash message authentication code (HMAC) using the secret key. The message that is hashed consists of the ROM code and the received random number. The random number is necessary to prevent replay attacks. Further the unique chip identifier is retrieved from the card, such that the personalization system can identify the secret HMAC key. With the knowledge of the key and the contents of the ROM code, the personalization system is able to verify the retrieved HMAC. Thus, manipulation to the ROM code – and respectively to the operating system – can be detected. The verification is done in the HSM of the personalization system and thus, the secret HMAC key is never exposed to any operator.

Exemplary Personalization Process

To illustrate the application of the introduced personalization System (see Figure 2), the authors will elaborate the process in an exemplary case study showing the production of SIM cards for 3G. This requires the personalization of two unique identifiers and a symmetric encryption key: the International Mobile Subscriber Identity (IMSI), the International Mobile Station Equipment Identity (IMEI) and the Authentication and Key Agreement (AKA) key. In the following, the authors will use the term "shared" for data that is shared between the different stakeholders in an encrypted way. The plain data is only accessible by the HSMs of the Stakeholder.

SIM cards are usually ordered by a mobile network operator from a SIM card manufacturer in batches of several thousand devices. For simplicity, it is assumed that the SIM card manufacturer is responsible for the Hardware and Software development, while a dedicated Personalization company is conducted for the personalization. For illustration purposes, it is assumed that the AKA key is derived from a Master Key that is generated by the personalization company and that the IMSI and IMEI are provided by the mobile network operator.

To start the process, a secure communication channel has to be established between the mobile network operator and the SIM card manufacturer (e.g. using TLS) via which the IMSI and the IMEI is shared. Since the IMSI and IMEI are in general not confidential, the data can be sent in plain, but it has to be authenticated. The authentication is required to ensure that the provided data is not manipulated, or sent from an untrusted entity.

The SIM card manufacturer orders the personalization of the SIM cards from a dedicated personalization company. As such, another secure channel has to be established between the SIM card manufacturer and the personalization company. Via this channel, the data of the mobile network operator is forwarded as well as an authentication token such that the personalization company is able to authenticate to the manufactured SIM cards. The "Data Generation System" of the personalization company is used to generate the master key for the AKA key hierarchy, as well as to derive the actual keys for the individual chips. During the personalization process itself, the personalization equipment makes use of the generated data. Usually, symmetric encryption is used to protect the generated data to reduce the computational overhead.

After the personalization, the personalization company shares the generated master key as well as a list containing the derivation parameters of the individual chips with the SIM card manufacturer. This data is forwarded to the mobile network operator. The list of derivation parameter is required such that the mobile network operator is able to compute the device individual key if a SIM card is trying to access the services of the network. The derivation data usually contains the device individual unique identifier as well as other data.

As a consequence of the described system, the personalization company is fully transparent to the mobile network operator (and vice versa) since the whole communication is carried out through the SIM card manufacturer.

Classification of Personalization Data

A wide variety of different data is usually personalized. This Section tries to summarize and classify the most common types of data that is loaded during this process. Generally speaking, keys which are described in the following as "known" to a production system (e.g. the personalization equipment) means, that the according key is located in a Hardware Security Module. Operators or other involved persons must not be able to retrieve such keys in plain. As illustrated in Figure 2, a secure channel exists between the issuer system and the data generation system. Thus, data or keys which are shared with the issuer can be forwarded by re-encrypting the data for the personalization system.

- **Operating System:** The operating system of the secure IC is usually provided as ROM code during the production of the IC. Since the ROM code needs to be prepared several months before production, it may happen that updates need to be applied during the personalization process. These updates are generally loaded to the non-volatile memory (EEPROM or Flash) of the chip during Phase 2 of the lifecycle.
  - **Type of Data:** Updated OS routines or code is usually provided as a binary which is signed from the OS producer. Further, encryption can be used to prevent reverse engineering or to protect hard-coded confidential data.
  - **Owner of the Involved Keys:** The signature creation key (private part of an asymmetric key pair) is owned by the OS producer and is not shared with any other party. The signature verification key (public part of the asymmetric key pair) is either hard coded into the ROM-code of the OS, or personalized by the personalization company. In the latter case, the public key needs to be sent at least authenticated to the issuer. If the OS code is encrypted, the protection key needs to be known by the issuers HSM and shared with the OS producer (or vice-versa).
- **Applications:** Like for the operating system, applications may also be part of the ROM code which was burned to the IC during the production process (Phase 1). For Flash based products, this can also include the applications which are loaded to the Flash during the production process (Phase 1). The advantage of having such rom-ized or pre-loaded applications is that less data needs to be sent during the personalization process, which saves time and money. As before, updates or additional application(s) may need to be loaded during the process since the final application(s) were not available when the ROM-code was created.
  - **Type of Data:** Applications are usually provided as binary. Dependent on the use case, the operating system may require that the applications are signed. This may also be required from a security certification to ensure that only valid applications are loaded. Optionally, encryption can be used to prevent reverse engineering or to protect hard-coded confidential data.
  - **Owner of the Involved Keys:** In case of signed binaries, the signature creation key is usually owned by the OS producer. Certificate hierarchies may also be used to separate the individual application provider. The signature verification key (public key) is either hard coded into the ROM-code of the OS, or personalized by the personalization company. If the application is encrypted, the protection key needs to be known by the issuers HSM and shared with the application developer (or vice-versa). For security reasons, the protection key should be different for every individual application developer and also different of the OS protection key.

- **Application Keys:** For security relevant applications, different cryptographic keys are required to ensure the proper functionality. For example, if the application is sending confidential data to a web-server in the internet, an encryption key is required that protects the communication. This can be achieved by using symmetric or asymmetric cryptography.
  - **Type of Data:** The generated key material can be either symmetric or asymmetric. Usually, symmetric encryption keys are used if the encryption operation needs to be calculated within a limited time frame. Such symmetric encryption keys can be categorized in three groups:
    - **Static Keys:** Every chip will use the same static key.
    - **Derived Key Hierarchy:** State of the art key derivation functions (KDFs) are applied during the data generation process to generate chip individual keys based on a derivation master key. This process typically uses the unique identifier of the chip to derive the device key which is loaded during the personalization process. KDFs are cryptographic one way functions to ensure that an attacker cannot break the secret derivation master key by knowing the derived keys. In general, the data that is used during the derivation process has to be shared with the involved stakeholder. The derivation master key that is used for the key derivation may be provided by a Stakeholder, or generated in behalf of the Stakeholder from the personalization company.
    - **Random Keys:** As the name suggest, the keys are purely random for every individual device. Depending on the use case, this key material can be generated by the issuer or by the personalization system.

    Asymmetric Keys can be categorized into two groups:
    - **Encryption Keys:** The device is communicating with an external system using asymmetric encryption for a secure channel establishment. As a consequence, the encryption key (public key) of the destination needs to be personalized. This is usually done using certificates. The key-pair of the device can either be static or randomly generated.
    - **Signature Keys:** Either the device needs to verify the signature of message or data, or an external system needs to verify that the data was sent from a trusted device. In case that the device needs to verify a signature, the signature verification key (public key) needs to be personalized. This is usually done using certificates. If the device needs to compute the signature.

  Generally, from a security perspective static keys are the most critical use-case, since breaking one device automatically breaks all other devices.
  - **Owner of the Involved Keys:**
    - **Symmetric Keys:** Independent of the category (Static, Derivation Master Key, or Random), the key can either be provided by the application developer or generated by the personalization company on behalf of the application developer. In the latter case, the key(s) may need to be shared with the application developer or other system components in a secure manner. In any case, the protection key needs to be shared with the issuer. Whether to generate or import keys needs to be decided on a case by case basis considering all product and security requirements.
    - **Asymmetric Keys:** Public keys are usually provided via a certificate which is signed by a CA that is trusted by the device (i.e. the signature verification key was personalized or hard coded). The device key pair is usually randomly generated by the personalization company and loaded to the device. In rare cases, the key-pair was provided by the

application developer. In case that the key-pair was generated, the public key is usually exported as a certificate and is shared with the application developer, or any other system component that needs to be aware of the public key. The resulting certificate can be self-signed or trusted-root signed. In case that a trusted-root is used, a secure process needs to be established, such that operators are not able to issue valid certificates for misuse. Further, fake devices have to be reliably detected. The protection key used for importing static key-pairs needs to be shared with the issuer.

- **Device and/or Application Settings:** Every device and/or application may require additional configuration data to be loaded. For example, an application which communicates with a different application or process need to know the identifier of the application or process.
  - ○ **Type of Data:** In general, proprietary binary formatted data is preferred since it can be efficiently compressed and loaded on small embedded systems. But of course, any arbitrary data can be loaded like strings, files and others. In most cases, this data is not confidential and thus, not encrypted. The data can be signed if the origin of the data needs to be verified, which could be a requirement of the security certification process.
  - ○ **Owner of the Involved Keys:** In case of signed data, the signature creation key (private part of an asymmetric key pair) is owned by the according provider of the data (e.g. Customer, OS provider, etc.). The public key can either be hard coded into the ROM code, or personalized from the personalization company. In the latter case, the public key needs to be sent at least authenticated to the issuer. If the data is sent encrypted, the protection key needs to be known by the issuer's HSM and shared with the data provider (or vice-versa). For security reasons, it is important to use different encryption keys for the individual provider of the data.

Loading Personalization Data to the Chips

In principal, there are various ways for loading the personalization data to the secure ICs. The methods can be categorized into two main groups: The first category requires that the secure IC is able to perform basic file and data management commands such as Create, Install and Update. Thus, the personalization process makes use of these commands to send the data to the chip. The second category requires that the secure IC is able to load the personalization data from a defined memory region which was written during the production of the IC. The following methods are currently state of the art:

- **Category 1: Loading Personalization Data Using Logical Addresses (Rankl & Effing, 2010):** This method tries to avoid physical addresses using basic file and data management commands. The individual datasets are identified with a symbolic name such that the secure IC is able to determine the according physical address. The sent data can be independent from the used microcontroller if the API is written in a platform independent way. The drawback of this method is that the personalization process will take more time since the secure IC needs to resolve the symbolic identifier before the data is written. This overhead is only small but in a high-volume production process this may be to cost intensive.

- **Category 1: Loading Personalization Data Using Physical Addresses (Rankl & Effing, 2010; Atsumi, Kondo, & Shona, 1995):** In opposite to the first method, this method makes use of the real physical addresses of the individual datasets. Consequently, the overhead for writing the data can be kept as small as possible. In order to write this data to the real physical addresses, the personalization system needs to be aware of how the data is expected by the secure IC. This is a huge drawback since it is an additional source of error which can render all produced chips unworkable. To be able to generate the data as expected, usually a sample device is used which contains a dump memory functionality. The sample device is configured as the final product, but with the difference, that specific pattern values are used for the device individual and/or confidential data. After the initialization was done, the memory content is dumped and the physical addresses are identified by searching the according pattern values. The memory dump is used as a template during the production of the secure ICs. Only the placeholder data is replaced during the personalization process with the real data. The critical aspect is that the process needs to assure, that it is not possible to manufacture a production device having the dump memory functionality inside. Otherwise, an attacker is able to read the confidential data from the dumped memory.
- **Category 2: Loading Personalization Data Using a Dedicated Personalization Memory Region:** Another possibility for loading the personalization data is using a dedicated memory region to which the personalization data is written as a whole block. As such, no specific device API is required which is able to load / update individual data. The personalization data could be loaded to the secure IC during the last stages of the production. To actually load the data, the personalization system authenticates to the IC and sends the decryption key, necessary to decrypt the personalization data. Additional meta-information is necessary such that the IC can determine the purpose of the data. Usually, the meta-information uses symbolic names which can be interpreted by the secure IC, but also real physical addresses could be used in this process. The personalization company needs to agree with the OS producer on the format of the data which is one of the main drawbacks of this approach. An additional drawback is the computational overhead which leads to higher costs during the production process. Further, the memory region for the personalization data needs to be allocated by the secure IC which can be a problem for small low cost ICs. Of course, this additional memory can be used for customer data during the in-field use, but during the production process this may be a limiting factor.

If certified products are manufactured, it is further necessary to log every production step and to validate that the correct data was loaded. Independent from the method which was used during the personalization process, the following data is usually logged in practice:

- Unique chip identifier.
- Checksum or hash values of non-confidential data like applications or configuration settings.
- Key Check Values (KCVs) or secure cryptographic one way hashes of confidential data.

The important point is that one way functions have to be used for logging verification values of confidential data. This ensures that an attacker is not able to obtain the plain key values by observing the logged verification values. The verification values can be verified using the HSMs of the personalization system. Thus, the plain confidential data is never exposed to any operator.

Classification of Attacks and Attackers

In general, information technology systems are vulnerable to multiple possible threat vectors. On the one hand, design weaknesses of the hardware, as well as the software, can lead to a break of the system. On the other hand, cryptographic protocols which were consider as secure today may be broken in the future. One such example is the cryptographic strength of different key types. With the increasing computational power of personal computers, brute force attacks on short keys are getting more interesting. While several years ago, RSA-768 was considered as being sufficiently secure, nowadays RSA-2048 is recommended.

With respect to the scope of this chapter, the authors will focus on possible attack vectors which aim to break the system due to weaknesses in the personalization process. This is an essential topic, since breaking the personalization system leads to breaking every single produced IC! Possible attacks can be classified as follows:

- **Hardware Attacks:** As described in Section "Generation of the personalization data", the system for generating and importing confidential data consists of hardware security modules and the personalization equipment. Since these hardware components are only storing temporary data, which is used for the processing of the current batch, invasive attacks can be neglected due to operational measures. Nevertheless, these hardware components are still vulnerable to side-channel attacks like timing analysis or power analysis (Demaertelaere, 2010; Sanchez-Reillo, Sanchez-Avila, Lopez-Ongil, & Entrena-Arrontes, 2002). Furthermore, manipulated hardware devices could be used to leak generated device data.
- **Software Attacks:** As already mentioned in Section "Generation of the personalization data", the API of the hardware security modules may have vulnerabilities which can be used to leak confidential data (Anderson, 2001) by combining specific functions.
- **Social Engineering Attacks:** This sort of attack mainly aims at the people who are involved in operating the production equipment, or in developing software for the production equipment. In case that symmetric keys are shared via paper forms (as described in (PCI Security Standards Council, 2016)) between the personalization company and any other involved stakeholder, the companies responsible for dispatching the mail are also of interest to such kind of attacks.

In order to estimate the strength of attackers, the type of attackers has to be classified as well. The basic motivation behind attackers is usually the gain of financial benefit or knowledge (Rankl & Effing, 2010). National agencies for instance, are not interested in gaining financial profit, but are interested in gaining knowledge about the users, or the environment to which the system is deployed to. If details of such attacks become public, the reputation of the involved companies is damaged dramatically. Thus, another potential attack vector includes a competitor, who either wants to gain knowledge about the processes, or wants to harm the reputation.

Similar damage to the reputation can be caused by scientific researchers, which aim to break the system to gain reputation in their specific scientific field. As such, these attackers are only satisfied if their successful hacking attempt is published in scientific publication. But also, individual hackers may only be motivated in being the first, breaking the system.

In the domain of the personalization process, a few potential attackers and attack vectors can be neglected: Since the production environment is secured, it is not possible for hackers to place specific hardware devices into the production environment. This may only be possible by competitors who are using the same production facilities, or organizations with a high amount of resources they could spent to manipulate the production equipment. Further, the control logic of the personalization equipment and the equipment itself is in general disconnected from any external network. As a consequence, malicious software cannot be loaded to such devices via the internet. Thus, attacks during the personalization process are mainly carried out either by insiders or organizations like competitors, national agencies, or research institutions.

In practice, the following techniques are used to minimize the risk of hacks from the above-mentioned attackers:

- **Authentication:** As already discussed in Section "Generation of the personalization data", every single personalization operation needs to be authenticated, to ensure that only valid data is loaded to the chips. Further, authentication of the secure IC is required such that it is not possible to replace the chip with a dummy IC. As already explained, such dummy ICs could contain code which can be used to export the personalized confidential data in plain. This is especially critical with respect to static confidential data.
- **Encryption:** Only if data is stored in dedicated Hardware Security Modules – or the final secure IC – the data can be stored in plain. Whenever data is transferred between system components, the data has to be encrypted with reasonable strength. Recommendations for the required key length are usually published by standardization organizations like the NIST (NIST SP 800-57-1, 2016) and frequently updated according to the state of the art.
- **Split Knowledge:** During the production process, at least a two-man rule should be used to ensure that no single operation can be performed by a single person. Otherwise, this single individual may be subject of attacks like social engineering. The two-man rule is also reflected in the security measures described in Section "Generation of the personalization data", where the authentication token for the personalization company is split into two parts. One is delivered by the OS producer and one is delivered by the semiconductor manufacturer. Further, split knowledge is also used during development of the software that is deployed onto the hardware security modules, or developed for other production equipment. In general, multiple people are involved in the development of the software; code reviews are mandatory for code releases, which are performed by people that are not involved into the development process. Further, it is required that multi-person authentication mechanisms are used to deploy new software onto the production equipment.

Table 1 summarizes typical attacks during the personalization process and their according countermeasures.

FUTURE RESEARCH DIRECTIONS

As mentioned in Section "Generation of the personalization data", the API of the HSMs, that are responsible for generating the personalization data, is still an open research question; although the topic of API security is subject to research since the 1990s. There is a growing literature about formal verification tools which are used to analyze the security API of a system and to detect security flaws. The problem with these tools is that they are usually designed to analyze rather simple APIs. Additionally, they require a

Table 1. Non-exhaustive list of typical attacks during the personalization process

Attack	Attacker	Description/Typical Countermeasure
Tapping Data Communication	Insider, Organizations, Hackers	**Description**: During the whole process, confidential data is transferred between multiple stakeholders. This includes also the communication channels between the personalization equipment and the actual device during the production. **Countermeasure**: Secure messaging has to be used throughout the whole personalization process.
Manipulation of Data transfers	Insider, Organizations, Hackers	**Description**: Related to the previous attack. Proper origin of data streams has to be ensured throughout the whole process since otherwise, devices may be compromised (e.g. by loading dummy key data). **Countermeasures**: Authentication methods have to be used throughout the whole process to ensure the proper origin of the data, as well as message authentication methods to ensure that the data was not manipulated during the transfer.
"Fake" devices	Organizations, Insiders	**Descriptions**: Fake devices could be used to leak data that is loaded during the personalization process. In case that static keys are used, all devices can be broken if a fake device is integrated into the personalization process. Even worse, if faked HSMs are used to generate the data, all the confidential data could be leaked. **Countermeasures**: Bi-Directional authentication of the personalization equipment and the actual devices. Further, multiple eye principal for the deployment and the maintenance of the personalization equipment as well as the HSMs.
Manipulation of the Personalization Equipment	Organizations, Insiders	**Description**: Manipulated software could be loaded to the personalization equipment – including also the HSMs, to leak confidential data. **Countermeasure**: Operational measures are required to restrict the access to the personalization equipment. Further, multiple eyes principals have to be applied to ensure that only multiple operators are able to load software to the equipment. Authentication methods have to be used such that only authorized operators can execute functions of the personalization equipment.
Social Engineering	Organizations, Hackers	**Description**: Attacks on the social level can be carried out to gain access to company networks, or to establish backdoors for other attacks. **Countermeasures**: Split knowledge such that no single person is able to break the whole system. Secure messaging and secure storage of confidential data, as well as separation of networks. Increase the security awareness of all involved employees.

lot of resources in terms of computational power and memory consumption. Thus, formal analysis tools are in general not suitable to be run on HSMs to ensure runtime protection against API attacks. It is an open research challenge to adopt formal analysis tools for the requirements of a personalization system.

The current alternative approach is to come up with robustness principles to guide the designers of such systems (Anderson, 2001). Instead of providing a sequential API of the HSMs, which requires a steady interaction with the system, a set of function calls could be grouped to a single execution unit. This execution unit can be verified in advance to ensure that this sequence of function is valid with respect to the defined robustness principles. In case that the sequence of functions was verified as secure, the developer can sign the execution unit such that the HSMs are only executing verified sequences of functions. Besides this, security principals which were considered to be secure in the past are now identified to be a big security problem. For example, as Anderson pointed out (Anderson, Bond, Clulow, & Skorobogatov, 2006), the use of exclusive-or to combine a key with a PIN leads to a huge security flaw, although it was used by every VISA security module. It is up to now an open research challenge on how to systematically identify such vulnerabilities in existing systems.

Our today's organizations are driven by fast changing markets and requirements. Thus, agile and incremental development techniques are used to cope with these problems. As of today, security certification is contradicting to such development strategies. As a consequence, certification is usually carried out at a late stage of the development. Current research aims on integrating the security certification process into the development process such that the evaluation facility is able to gain trust already during the development of the system. Further attempts are made to ease the certification process by reusing previously collected evidences. But still, a lot of research and standardization activities are required to develop mature development processes that integrate security requirements. The aim of this integration should be a bilateral traceability of the security requirements to the according implementation artifacts and tests to ensure an automatic detection of the impact of changes.

CONCLUSION

The personalization of secure CPS or IoT devices is a crucial step during the production process. Every security measure which is employed during the in-field use is futile, if data is leaked during this personalization process. Especially in the domain of IoT devices, which are observing our daily activities, it is essential to protect the devices against malicious manipulations. The past has shown that hacks of such IoT devices are valuable aims for hackers. As the Mirai malware showed, one of the main problems was the careless handling of the user name and password of the webcams manufactured by Hangzhou Xiongmai Trading (Hautala, 2016). These credentials were static for every hacked webcam. Thus, every manufactured webcam of this producer can be taken over via the internet without any hint to the customer that his device was hacked by trying the default user name and password. Even worse, after changing the user name and password, the devices were still vulnerable via the remote web based administration panel (Krebs, 2016). With a mature an established personalization process, these vulnerabilities could be mitigated since every produced device could use dedicated user credentials.

As a consequence, mature personalization processes need to be established, which enables a low-cost but secure personalization for CPS or IoT devices. Thus, the developed processes need to be flexible such that they can be used for a wide variety of different products, independent of the use-case of the devices. Flexibility is also required to ensure that the personalization process can be integrated into the production process of secure systems independent of the manufacturer of the devices. As a result, the costs for such processes can be kept as low as possible. This chapter summarized generic and state of the art concepts for secure personalization processes to get a step closer to a low-cost personalization process for secure systems.

REFERENCES

Anderson, D. (1997). *Agile Product Development for Mass Customization: How to Develop and Deliver Products for Mass Customization, Niche Markets, Jit, Build-To-Order and Flexible Manufacturing*. Irwin Professional Pub.

Anderson, R. J. (2001). API Attacks. In *Security Engineering: A Guide to Building Dependable Distributed Systems*. New York, NY, USA: John Wiley & Sons, Inc.

Anderson, R. J., Bond, M., Clulow, J., & Skorobogatov, S. (2006). Cryptographic Processors-A survey. Proceedings of the IEEE, 94(2), 357-369.

Atsumi, S., Kondo, T., & Shona, Y. (1995). *Patent No. 5,442,165*. US.

Begley, J., & Scahill, J. (2015, February 19). Retrieved from The Intercept - The Great SIM Heist. Retrieved from https://theintercept.com/2015/02/19/great-sim-heist/

Chan, V., & Ho, F. (2003). *Patent No. 6588673 B1*. United States of America.

Chen, X. (2007). *Patent No. 1983466 A2*. European Union.

Common Criteria. (2002). *Common Criteria Information Statement. Reuse of Evaluation Results and Evidence*.

Common Criteria. (2012). *Common Criteria for Information Technology Security Evaluation Part 1 - 3; Version 3.1*.

Common Criteria. (2012, April). Common Criteria Supporting Document Mandatory Technical Document - Composite product evaluation for Smart Version 1.2.

Demaertelaere, F. (2010). *Hardware Security Modules*. SecAppDev.org - Secure Application Development.

Graham, H. E., Jr. M. B., Nablo, R. J., & Haeuser, W. W. (2002). *Patent No. 6402028 B1*. United States of America.

Hautala, L. (2016, October 24). *Why it was so easy to hack the cameras that took down the web*. Retrieved from https://www.cnet.com/how-to/ddos-iot-connected-devices-easily-hacked-internet-outage-webcam-dvr/

Hautier, R., Macchetti, M., & Perrine, J. (2012). *Patent No. 2720167 A1*. European union.

ISO 10202-1. (1991). Financial transaction cards -- Security architecture of financial transaction systems using integrated circuit cards -- Part 1: Card life cycle. International Organization for Standardization.

ISO 18000-3. (2010). Information technology — Radio frequency identification for item management — Part 3: Parameters for air interface communications at 13,56 MHz. International Organization for Standardization.

Krebs, B. (2016, October 21). *kresbonsecurity.com*. Retrieved January 4, 2017, from https://krebsonsecurity.com/2016/10/hacked-cameras-dvrs-powered-todays-massive-internet-outage/

Manyika, J., Chui, M., Bisson, P., Woetzel, J., Dobbs, R., Bughin, J., & Aharon, D. (2015, June). *Unlocking the potential of the Internet of Things*. Retrieved from http://www.mckinsey.com/business-functions/digital-mckinsey/our-insights/the-internet-of-things-the-value-of-digitizing-the-physical-world

Markantonakis, K., Mayes, K., Sauveron, D., & Tunstall, M. (2010). Smart Cards. In H. Bidgoli (Ed.), Handbook of Technology Management (Vols. 2, pp. 248-264). Wiley.

Markit, I. H. S. (2014, August). *Smart Card Shipments to Rise by 2.1 Billion Units by 2019*. (IHS Markit Newsroom) Retrieved October 2016, from http://press.ihs.com/press-release/design-supply-chain-media/smart-card-shipments-rise-21-billion-units-2019

Nest Labs. (2016). *Nest*. Retrieved 11 7, 2016, from https://nest.com

NIST FIPS PUB 140-2. (2001). *Security Requirements for Cryptographic Modules*. National Institute of Standards and Technology Federal Information Processing Standards Publications 140-2.

NIST SP 800-57-1. (2016). *Recommendation for Key Management - Part 1: General*. National Institute of Standards and Technology Special Publication 800-57-1.

PCI Security Standards Council. (2016). *Data Security Standard - Requirements and Security Assessment Procedures*. Payment Card Industry Security Standards Council.

Rankl, W., & Effing, W. (2010). *Smart Card Handbook* (4th ed.). Wiley. doi:10.1002/9780470660911

Raschke, W., Massimiliano, Z., Baumgartner, P., Loinig, J., Steger, C., & Kreiner, C. (2014). *Supporting evolving security models for an agile security evaluation*. IEEE. doi:10.1109/ESPRE.2014.6890525

Sanchez-Reillo, R., Sanchez-Avila, C., Lopez-Ongil, C., & Entrena-Arrontes, L. (2002). Improving Security in Information Technology using Cryptographic Hardware Modules. In *Proceedings of the International Carnahan Conference on Security Technology* (pp. 120-123). IEEE. doi:10.1109/CCST.2002.1049236

Scahill, J. (2015, February 25). What Gemalto doesn't know what it doesn't know. The Intercept. Retrieved from https://theintercept.com/2015/02/25/gemalto-doesnt-know-doesnt-know/

Sinnhofer, A., Oppermann, F., Potzmader, K., Orthacker, C., Steger, C., & Kreiner, C. (2016). Patterns to Establish a Secure Communication Channel. In *Proceedings of the 21st European Conference on Pattern Languages of Programs* (pp. 13:1-13:21). doi:10.1145/3011784.3011797

Sinnhofer, A. D., Raschke, W., Steger, C., & Kreiner, C. (2015). Evaluation paradigm selection according to Common Criteria for an incremental product development.

Sinnhofer, A. D., Raschke, W., Steger, C., & Kreiner, C. (2015). *Patterns for Common Criteria Certification*. ACM. doi:10.1145/2855321.2855355

Chapter 12
Secure and Trusted Open CPS Platforms

George Kornaros
Technological Educational Institute of Crete, Greece

Ernest Wozniak
fortiss GmbH, Germany

Oliver Horst
fortiss GmbH, Germany

Nora Koch
fortiss GmbH, Germany

Christian Prehofer
fortiss GmbH, Germany

Alvise Rigo
Virtual Open Systems, France

Marcello Coppola
STMicroelectronics, France

ABSTRACT

Cyber-physical systems (CPS) are devices with sensors and actuators which link the physical with the virtual world. There is a strong trend towards open systems, which can be extended during operation by instantly adding functionalities on demand. We discuss this trend in the context of automotive, medical and industrial automation systems. The goal of this chapter is to elaborate the research challenges of ensuring security in these new platforms for such open systems. A main problem is that such CPS apps shall be able to access and modify safety critical device internals. Cyber-physical attacks can affect the integrity, availability and confidentiality in CPS. Examples range from deception based attacks such as false-data-injection, sensor and actuator attacks, replay attacks, and also denial-of-service attacks. Hence, new methods are required to develop an end-to-end solution for development and deployment of trusted apps. This chapter presents the architecture approach and its key components, and methods for

DOI: 10.4018/978-1-5225-2845-6.ch012

open CPS apps, including tool chain and development support.

INTRODUCTION

Cyber-physical systems (CPS) are devices with sensors and actuators, which link the physical with the virtual world. In many application areas of CPS such as automotive or medical, devices are long-lived and users depend on them in their daily lives. In the past, many of these systems have been operating unchanged for years or even decades in a well-defined context. With the rapid innovation cycles in many IT services and technologies, there is also a need to extend or update these services. For instance, functionality in cars has been used as originally shipped for the full lifetime of a car. With the latest innovations in infotainment and autonomous driving, it is expected that this functionality is outdated after a few years. Thus, there is a strong trend towards open cyber-physical systems, which can be extended by instantly adding functionalities on demand.

Cyber-physical attacks can affect the integrity, availability and confidentiality in such CPS. Examples range from deception based attacks such as false-data-injection, sensor and actuator attacks, replay attacks, and denial-of-service attacks. Attacks penetrating the integrity of vehicular systems and medical devices have brought to sharp focus the urgency of securing cyber-physical systems. For networked CPS systems, a number of external and internal attacks can threaten the correct and safe operation of the system. For instance, internal CPS nodes or networks may be compromised, which may affect the safety and reliability of the overall system.

This chapter presents the research challenges and solutions of ensuring security and safety in such open systems. Today CPS apps support openness for updates of existing functionality. A main issue though, is that such CPS apps are able to access and modify safety critical device internals. Thus, it is not sufficient to isolate the apps from other parts of the system, as they typically need to access and control parts of the system. The apps must not be able to interfere or compromise proper operation of the system at any time. For the new apps, there can be different levels of trust. Yet, even for fully trusted software components, programming errors, software weaknesses or failures can lead to a compromised situation. The focus of the chapter is to show how different technologies that span different architectural levels can be used and combined to provide the required security and trustworthiness.

New methods and technologies are required to develop an end-to-end solution for development and deployment of trusted apps (Prehofer, Kornaros, & Paolino, 2015). Such methods and technologies are the building blocks for a new architectural approach. The overall idea is to provide a layered approach, consisting of multiple, independent defense mechanisms. In conjunction with the layered architecture, different classes of applications are defined, depending on their criticality.

An overview organization of an open cyber-physical system is shown in Figure 1. This figure shows a network of CPS nodes, which are orchestrated to perform distributed control services, commonly monitoring and actuation services, and user interaction tasks. For these kind of networks, there is often a need for real-time communication, hence networks like CAN or deterministic Ethernet are used. In an open cyber-physical system architecture, usually an Open Apps Platform device is acting as a gateway that connects to external untrusted networks. Besides its gateway functionality, this device also provides an open platform for adding new application software, hereby called as "apps". The gateway functionality of the device is needed for many applications that execute in the gateway or in the CPS nodes, but also for managing the applications themselves on the gateway. As CPSs' functionality becomes more and more software dominated and the interaction between the physical and cyber systems increases, CPSs become more susceptible to external and internal attacks.

Figure 1. Open CPS Architecture

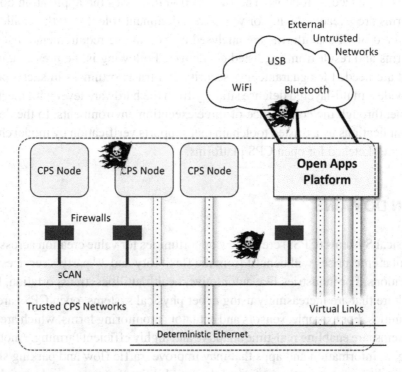

This work reviews current state-of-the-art challenges and solutions in support of open cyber-physical systems and presents a set of building blocks for a secure and trusted architecture, which comprises independent solutions that range from extensions of communication protocols and creation of Execution Environments (EE), to securing real-time resource management and model-based development. Specifically, this work makes the following contributions:

- It introduces the concept of Execution Environments (EE) and Apps Platform (AP), which is an isolated context of execution: CPS is enabled to execute its code inside isolated partitions, while a "special" EE is introduced for real-time-like and safety-critical applications. EEs address sensitive code execution and secure exposed networking functions and at the same time provide transparency with respect to the way the apps are created and certified.
- Protocols and mechanisms are surveyed and secure extensions by design are proposed to strengthen security in distributed CPS devices and networks at the same time. This work is motivated by the need to ensure safety and trust due to augmented attack surface of CPS networks, due to the integration of larger number of interoperable devices, and most importantly due to increased software components and open-ness.
- An overview is presented on the challenges posed by the integration of real-time tasks within an open CPS on multi-core platforms, and then this work presents the high-level concept of a safety integration layer as a solution to guarantee real-time properties in an open CPS.
- In the scope of open CPS we introduce the concept of model-based development, via combining the standard development practices in C/C++ programming with the modeling approach. The integration of formal verification in the development of apps is proposed to ensure safety and security related properties of open CPS functions.

This chapter is organized as follows: The first section discusses the application domains in which open CPS platforms are already playing or will play a dominant role. Next, the challenges that imply openness in this kind of CPS platforms are analysed as well as the requirements that are imposed by open CPS platforms and result from the listed challenges. Following is the presentation of innovative technologies that are needed for guaranteeing security and trustworthiness in such open CPSs. These technologies provide a multi-layered defense strategy from the hardware level with mechanisms such as ARM's TrustZone, through the coexistence of three execution environments, to the development support for critical applications by a trusted toolchain that supports verification by model checking. Finally, future directions are sketched for open CPS platforms.

APPLICATION DOMAINS

Open Cyber Physical Systems (CPSs) create new opportunities for value creation across the whole society and in particular enterprises will benefit from the flexibility and 3rd party's services developing and providing applications. For industries like automotive, health, utilities, transportation, home entertainment and agriculture that are increasingly using cyber physical systems, open CPSs are providing new business opportunities. For example, sensors and actuators monitoring farms, which are connected with management systems, are enabling real-time adaptive and highly efficient farming. Another example are vehicles exchanging information and apps that may improve traffic flow and parking slots assignment. These examples are just scratching the surface of the possibilities that secure and trusted apps, operating in open CPS platform context, can provide. Extensions and updates of functionality during operation using apps for CPS devices, like vehicles and medical devices, that have a long lifetime when compared to innovations in the ICT area, has the additional benefit of extending the CPSs usage.

The trend towards open CPS devices and apps-based platforms for vehicles is currently a highly active topic in the automotive domain. Traditionally, protection in this domain has been achieved by partitioning components across distributed modules, which communicate over a network such as a CAN bus. However, when applications are able to access that network, there are several ways to break the protection. Therefore, new concepts and implementations are needed at hardware and software level to enforce security and safety for the driver when using open CPSs as envisaged by Stankovic (2014). Here it has to be distinguished between apps that interface with external, well known Internet services and access only status information of vehicles, and highly trusted apps (or so called critical apps), which can also access critical information and settings. An example for the first app category is the check of the route based on traffic and battery condition of the e-vehicle. On the other side, an app that changes settings in the engine control of a vehicle like brakes or gears according to environment conditions such as weather and terrain is highly critical.

Also in the healthcare market, medical devices require high-level secured architecture and trusted apps due to the increasing risk of cyberattacks. Such attacks can cause critical and physical damages if the targets are e.g. wearable and implantable CPSs, surgical robots or drug delivery systems, threatening people health and/or producing concrete economic damages to healthcare systems, especially in terms of patient safety. Although it is not possible to quantify the impact of cyberattacks on healthcare devices, there are many reports on damages already caused (Burns, Johnson, & Honeyman, 2016). It is therefore evident that healthcare devices must include strong security mechanisms to ensure, on the one hand, patients' safety, and on the other hand, privacy and security of data. Once security mechanisms can be guaranteed through a trusted platform, the medical device producers in the healthcare domain will benefit from the use of trusted apps for updating and improving functionality of their devices.

Other domains like those in the context of Industry 4.0 and avionics are addressing security and trustworthiness of open CPSs, too. New approaches and technologies are being developed or existing ones are adapted and/or extended to be used in the areas of factory automation and cyber-physical production systems. In the aerospace field, the trends are the increasing complexity of the mixed-criticality systems and the need of less weight and volume. These challenges are addressed among others using multi-core platforms and the co-hosting of applications of different criticalities like the proposal of Anderson, Baruah, & Brandenburg (2009).

An analysis of the requirements in the different domains regarding support for open cyber physical systems will provide the basis for the development of a domain-independent platform for trusted open CPSs.

OPEN CPS REQUIREMENTS

Authors of (Stankovic, 2014) sketch a very futuristic vision of new applications enabled by the sensing and actuation utility and plethora of embedded devices (such as mobile phones, vehicles, etc.) connected altogether to the Internet. Cars as well as aircrafts talking to each other to avoid collisions or uploading of a physiological data to doctors in real-time with real-time feedback are examples of such vision. It is not just the applications themselves that will change but also their installation and execution which will become much easier. To reach these benefits, the provision of an open platform is necessary. These benefits of an open platform are however challenged with the new problems that span across many aspects.

1. Extension and definition of new communication interfaces and contracts for specifying interactions will be needed, to enable the exchange of information of diverse systems cooperating within the sensing and actuation utility. This is important, especially if considering the flexibility of an open platform to accept new applications during its operation, where applications might have to communicate not only between themselves, but also directly with different resources which in many cases are highly critical (e.g. physical brakes).
2. An important challenge of future open CPS platforms is to allow the execution of multiple applications of different criticality, essentially supporting mixed-criticality environments. This poses an even larger challenge for multi-core based platforms. The integration of mixed-criticality subsystems can lead to a significant and potentially unacceptable increase of engineering and certification costs if proper preconditions specification isn't put in place. For example, in order to prevent consolidated applications that run on a multi-core platform from interfering with each other, spatial and temporal isolation of the shared resources is mandatory (Richter, Herber, Rauchfuss, Wild, & Herkersdorf, 2014).
3. Analysis techniques such as response time analysis to validate real-time properties will have to be tailored, or elaboration of new types of analysis will be necessary. For example, in the context of an open platform, extensive checks before a new application is accepted for running will have to be made to determine whether real-time properties of already deployed apps will not be affected.

4. In many cases, concepts of futuristic applications directly or indirectly influence safety-critical parts of the CPS devices or exchange large amount of sensitive data. Consequently, the main challenge is to ensure security and safety. Malicious activity has continued to follow advances in technology, as it can now be seen with exploitation of mobile devices and infrastructure. Unfortunately, it might be impossible to reuse some of the currently existing security solutions as they consume lots of memory and require heavyweight computational power. Hence new, lightweight algorithms might be needed to find the balance between security and for instance power consumption of devices that will employ them (Jing, Vasilakos, Wan, Lu, & Qiu, 2014).
5. The techniques for design, integration and deployment of applications in such highly distributed ecosystem have to be considered as well. For instance, programming languages must allow inherent integration of time-based computation with event-based computation, which will enable to effectively model asynchronous dynamics that take place at different temporal and spatial scales (Khaitan and McCalley, 2015).
6. Software development itself for CPS is a sophisticated endeavor which yields many challenges (Stankovic, 2014). Therefore, new development tools will be needed to address the new philosophy of apps development, integration and deployment and to support techniques for their analysis.

Accordingly, when considering the highlighted challenges, a successful approach for open CPS platform should guarantee the integrity, safety, security of the system and additionally guarantee some non-functional properties such as real-time requirements. In that respect the key requirements, which need to be addressed by the open CPS platform, are:

1. **App Middleware:** Which will comprise solutions for communicating apps that are loaded dynamically. Apart from the inter-app communication, it should also secure the access to critical resources. This mainly results from the challenge (i).
2. **App Isolation:** Which results from the challenge (i) and (ii). Spatial as well as temporal separation is required so the applications can be executed in parallel, without any undesirable influence from the outside apps. Unless intended, any influence on app data or its execution behavior should be prevented.
3. **Access Control and Resource Management:** Yields another solution to the (i) challenge. Access to crucial resources and functions offered by the platform should be controlled. For example, entry to the critical communication interface such as the CAN bus should be restricted to apps which are certified or require real-time execution. Also, proper management or safeguarding of resources through the execution platform is required. This is to prevent from possible damage of the resource or its unlimited blocking by one app, causing violation of real-time properties of other applications which also require an access to it.
4. **Real-Time Support and Analysis Techniques:** To prevent timing delays is a response to challenge (iii). Apps running on the CPS platform in many cases need to perform real-time computation, e.g. real-time traffic update or even live video feed of a planned route for the vehicle driver (Wan, Zhang, Zhao, Yang, & Lloret, 2014). Guarantees for real-time behavior needs to be given considering parallel execution of other applications on the same platform, which might equally be real-time oriented. For this, platform should offer real-time support, e.g. via usage of a real-time operating system, whereas development tools can offer analysis techniques (e.g. schedulability analysis) to verify observance of real-time properties even before the deployment.

5.   **Reliability Regimes and Privacy Policies:** To deal with safety and security challenges as presented in (iv). CPS platform should support several reliability regimes for safe and secure operation of safety critical applications. Modes such as fail-operational, fail-safe or fail-secure fall within this group. Concerning privacy policies, apps deployed on the platform might have to include specification of them so that the requests handled by the app can be first evaluated in respect to them.

6.   **App Development:** New ways for developing applications as specified in challenge v) might be needed. A good practice is to support the standard development methods (e.g. C or C++ programming) to attract a wide community of developers but on the other side elaboration of new approaches, such as those based on the model based development, is necessary. The last provides more abstract and hence clearer perspective on system architecture, delivers a set of reusable components and enable several kinds of analysis methods to be run on the models (e.g. model checking or schedulability analysis) which contributes as well to safety and security challenges, i.e. (iii), (iv).

Fulfillment of the aforementioned requirements, which has a direct impact on the critical, two non-functional properties, i.e. safety and security of such open CPS platforms, can be accomplished by incorporating multiple safety/security layers, spanning from the trusted hardware, through computing and network virtualization, communication middleware, up to the point in which apps are developed. Usage of specific technologies might be required to support such multiple lines of defense constituting an end-to-end approach. Each of the technologies that is described in more details below, and constitute our set of contributions, could be used in a standalone manner. However, their combination forming multiple lines of defense, increases the assurance for fulfillment of the discussed requirements.

END-TO-END SOLUTION

In next generation, open cyber-physical systems, where malfunctions could cost lives, security concerns increasingly raise, with largely evolving communication, system and software architecture, to guarantee a trusted app infrastructure it is mandatory to provide multiple safety-security layers to prevent malicious behavior and external attacks. Several technologies are identified as imperative installments into a multi-layered defense strategy of an open CPS. On the hardware level, mechanisms such as memory management units, or ARM TrustZone (ARM Limited, 2009) is widely used in order to separate different execution environments. Additionally, Virtualization is recently used to provide virtual execution environments, isolation and protection of resources and spatial plus temporal isolation of apps. Next is communication middleware for securing and controlling the inter app communication as well as for controlling access to different resources. Lastly, the support for the safety and security concept can be achieved by employing a specific toolchain. The development of critical applications might be restricted to the usage of such a trusted toolchain. Through incorporating of analysis and verification techniques, a toolchain might certify safe and secure operation of an application regarding monitoring of non-functional constraints and correct execution behavior, even before the deployment. Finally, the critical apps developed with a trusted toolchain can be checked by trusted third-party that will issue a certificate acknowledging their safe and secure behavior.

A Trusted apps platform needs to ensure strong isolation and real-time properties for some apps. This cannot be assured by existing non-real-time operating systems. Moreover, existing platforms are characterized by high complexity and support for many different APIs, which is a potential loophole for security threats. It is easier to assure safety and security of operation when considering more limited operating systems. On the other side, to attract app developers it is essential that the platform offers features, such as feature-rich developer support, or simply compatibility with existing platforms and tools. This opens up a possibility for reusing currently existing tools, already developed applications or simply developers' knowledge. These contradictory concerns pose an interesting research challenge for developing execution platform that can provide multiple execution environment (EEs) intended for apps of different types and needs. Applications with a lower criticality can be run on systems like Linux or Android but enhanced with protection mechanism discussed above. High criticality apps can on the other hand be executed on the smaller, real-time operating system. This of course means less support in terms of APIs but on the other side it can assure more timely behavior of safety-critical and real-time use-cases.

EXECUTION ENVIRONMENTS AND APPS PLATFORM

As mentioned earlier in this chapter, it is of crucial importance that open CPS platforms are able to address security and safety requirements. In the Section "Application Domains" different app categories have been envisioned, each of them associated to a different level of criticality. This concept has been later formalized in Section "Open CPS Requirements" as requirement (ii). On the other hand, as discussed in Section "End-to-End Solution", these apps cannot just be executed in some operating system. The context of execution, or EE, (including CPU, RAM, operating system and peripherals) of such apps has to be selected carefully and differentiated accordingly to the apps being run. For instance, as stated by the requirement (vi), some of these EEs might need to provide real-time support, constraining considerably the characteristics of the EE. This section gives an overview of architectures and techniques used to realize systems capable of running multiple EEs, ranging from common solutions like virtualization, to more complex, hardware dependent, solutions.

Hardware manufacturers are now proposing an increasing number of SoCs that fit the open CPS platforms use case, i.e. they support real-time execution and strong isolation for non-interfering applications of mixed levels of criticality. For instance, ARMv8 processors are examples of commonly used CPUs that include, in one package, virtualization and TrustZone extensions, two technologies presented in the "End-to-End Security" Section combination of which can have interesting applications in the context of open CPSs, as will be discussed in the following lines.

The use of virtualization for instantiating Virtual Machines is nowadays a widely-used technique, which allows to flexibly deploy almost any operating system, the guest OS, on top the host OS, offering to the former an isolated partition in which to execute. The host OS is usually a general-purpose OS like Linux which, together with KVM, offers a solid virtualization infrastructure used in millions of servers out there, sustaining most of the cloud services running nowadays.

Considering an OS the only possible "guest" of a Virtual Machine is too limiting: virtualization can also be used to secure single applications that run alone inside a Virtual Machine, on top of a very simple OS (Kivity et al., 2014). In essence, a Virtual Machine can either be a self-sustained system that serves one or more functions, or it can be as well a component in a disaggregated architecture which exploits virtualization to distribute applications and services to different Virtual Machines according to some design choices. In CPS contexts, virtualization can therefore find a viable solution for running non-interfering applications in one unique platform, by confining to different execution environments the applications of the CPS. As a matter of fact, the high degree of isolation brought by virtualization comes with a cost. In fact, the more Virtual Machines are running in the system, the higher is the emulation overhead, which translates to higher resources usage of the host OS.

Clustering applications to Virtual Machines according to their criticality can be the best compromise between isolation and overhead: an application running in one Virtual Machine will be closer to applications of similar criticality, allowing for faster communication with its siblings. On the other hand, two applications of different criticality will necessarily run in different Virtual Machines, with a more complex communication mechanism interposed between them. With no surprise, such a communication introduces additional overhead: no matter what protocol will be used to allow information passing between the Virtual Machines, the communication will necessarily require at some point a device to be used, involving additional emulation. Luckily, modern virtualization techniques are able to alleviate emulation overhead, consequently lowering communication costs. As an example, paravirtualized devices, using at their own advantage the awareness of running on a virtual environment, permit to shorten the long code paths that are typically required by a faithful emulation of real devices (Russel, 2008). Low-latency communication is also possible between Virtual Machines. In fact, the implementation of ad-hoc devices and corresponding drivers for the guest OSes allow to have performance comparable to shared memory-based communication mechanisms (Macdonell et al., 2011). In essence, virtualization is now able to offer high isolation at a relatively low price, assuming that state-of-the-art solutions are employed and tuned to the specific use case.

Virtualization can therefore be used to instantiate corresponding Virtual Machines, each of them, for one "execution environment", which hosts services and applications of a given criticality. For everything which is not safety critical, an OS like Linux, Windows or Android can fit and be deployed in these execution environments; this would allow to cover use cases from the execution of the IVI system in a car to the provisioning of web services in a connected device.

The architecture depicted so far does not fit the use cases of CPS executing applications that have to obey the safety-critical requirements. Such applications come often with real-time constraints that have to be fulfilled as well. Moreover, in the most demanding cases, those safety-critical applications require

Figure 2. Open CPS example architecture

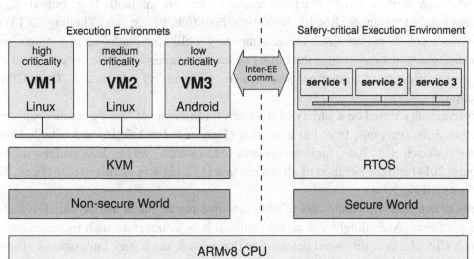

also to be certified according to some safety standard (for instance, ISO 26262 in the automotive domain, or the EN 50128 for the railway systems). In these cases, general-purpose OSes can't be considered as viable solutions, in that they are not real-time, nor certified.

It has been demonstrated (Prehofer et al., 2016) that the ARM Trust-Zone extension can be used to run simultaneously in the same CPU two different OSes, a general-purpose and a real-time one. The so-called Secure side in the CPU, which is normally used to implement secure services, is instead used as isolated compartment to run the real-time OS, adding in this manner a new execution environment for safety-critical applications and services. By using in a clever way, the capabilities of the ARMv8 architecture, it is possible to guarantee that the real-time OS is periodically and deterministically scheduled, if needed at the expenses of the general-purpose OS which has lower priority. The safety critical execution environment keeps nevertheless its secure connotation since it runs in a secure segment of the system RAM and uses secure devices that are not shared with the general-purpose OS. This makes the safety-critical execution environment ideal to host trusted services (encryption, decryption, fingerprint validation, etc.), addressing once more another requisite of modern CPS systems.

SECURE AND REAL-TIME RESOURCE MANAGEMENT

One big challenge of future Open CPSs is to allow the execution of multiple applications of different criticality, so called mixed-criticality environments. Anderson, Baruah, and Brandenburg (2009) and Mollison, Erickson, Anderson, Baruah, and Scoredos (2010) presented that this poses an even larger challenge for multi-core based platforms. In mixed-criticality environments it is of special interest to manage the information flow, i.e., communication, between low-critical and high-critical apps, as otherwise provided information from a low-critical app could compromise a receiving high-critical task (Sha, 2009). Furthermore, Pellizzoni et al. (2009) demonstrated that integrated mixed-criticality systems can be made safer by enforcing application specific constraints. Guaranteeing a safe integration of mixed-criticality tasks on one platform is also a matter of guaranteeing a proper real-time behavior for critical apps, even though low-critical apps are executed in parallel. Determining valuable worst case execution bounds for applications on multi-core platforms, however, is an own research challenge (Jacobs, 2013; Mushtaq, Al-Ars, & Bertels, 2013). The main reason for that are implicitly (e.g., buses) and explicitly (e.g., memory) shared resources. Kotaba, Nowotsch, Paulitsch, Petters, and Theiling (2013) provide a comprehensive list of shared resources on contemporary multi-core platforms in conjunction with the possible interferences that can change the timing of resource accesses. These concerns and challenges has led to the specification of requirements such as (ii), (iii) and (iv) presented in "Open CPS Requirements" section.

Many researchers focused on a variety of solutions for the issue of sharing resources in mixed criticality systems. Solutions range from bus arbitering (Hassan & Patel, 2016) and bounded interference approaches (Nowotsch et al., 2014) for interconnects, to resource servers as dedicated resource managers (Brandenburg, 2014) and the isolation of all critical tasks to a higher prioritized core (Ecco, Tobuschat, Saidi, & Ernst, 2014).

The authors consider the secure and reliable resource management as one curial aspect of future Open CPS platforms. Accordingly, the authors studied how to integrate such management structures into the open CPS platform discussed before. For that reason, the Safety Integration Layer (SIL) was developed. The SIL is a pivotal component that ensures a safe behavior of the overall system; it shall perform three main actions:

1. Protect critical platform interfaces/APIs.
2. Guarantee the overall system integrity and the assured service levels for apps.
3. Guarantee a reliable real-time behavior for the communication among apps, as well as their resource accesses.

Figure 3 illustrates the placement of the SIL and its components with respect to the previously presented platform for open CPS.

It can be seen that the SIL concept introduces three new components. Beside the Safety Integration Layer itself, these are the Integrity Manager and the SIL Client. The Integrity Manager shall ensure that all critical apps can access there declared resources at any time without interference by other apps and in accordance to their timing requirements. This includes schedulability tests during the deployment of new applications, as well as calculating new schedules for the different resources of the platform that conform with all requested real-time behaviors of the installed apps. In case no feasible schedule can be found the Integrity Manager can also reject an app during the deployment process. The SIL Client, on the other hand, extends the control range of the SIL to the non-secure world. As part of the KVM hypervisor, the SIL client moderates the resource accesses of the various virtual machines on behalf of the SIL. Communication between execution environments in the two worlds, as well as between the SIL and its client is done via the cross-world communication interface, which uses the Secure Monitor of the ARM TrustZone technology to switch worlds and safely exchange data between the two worlds.

To guarantee the overall system integrity, the assured service levels, and a reliable real-time behaviour, the SIL and its client in the KVM hypervisor coordinate the communication and resource accesses of all apps with a globally enforced schedule. The Integrity Manager ensures that there is always a feasible schedule. Furthermore, the SIL creates isolation domains in hardware and software. On the one hand, it partitions the hardware (i.e., memory and interconnects), and on the other hand, it isolates apps in their own software fault domain. The latter is done with the help of Software Fault Isolation (SFI) techniques (Ruhland, Prehofer, & Horst, 2016). The SFI technology isolates even faulty apps within their own fault domain, and specifically controls the utilized instruction set and calls to the underlying platform within each app. The SIL then operates on these defined APIs and enforces the requested service levels per app.

Figure 3. Resource management example architecture

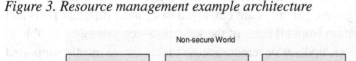

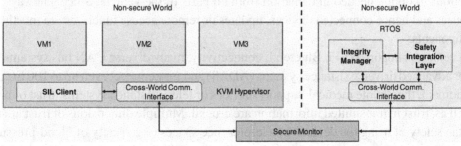

Due to its supervising characteristic and the focus on resource management, as well as communication, the authors propose to implement the SIL as an extension to an existing middleware. This middleware guarantees real-time constraints for the communication on the platform by globally coordinating bus and memory accesses. Additional resource managing components in the SIL are responsible for implementing a globally coordinated schedule on the resources. Thus, each request to a resource is supervised by the SIL, either in the sense of a middleware, or a resource arbiter.

SECURE AND TRUSTED CPS NETWORKING

Cyber-security-safety issues are undoubtedly crucial for CPSs since the entities within these systems interact not only with each other, but also interact with the environment. CPSs integrate embedded computing devices, physical processes and networks, which makes it necessary to develop safety protection mechanisms at multiple layers beyond computing, in order to consider distributed networked devices. Modern CPSs today present an increased attack surface, due to its networking and coordination functionalities, due to the integration of larger number of interoperable devices (such as medical devices), and most importantly due to increased software components and open-ness (such as modern automobiles, vehicle-to-vehicle (V2V) and machine-to-machine (M2M) communication trends) (Weimerskirch, 2014). Safeguard infrastructures need to detect and subsequently prevent threats and vulnerabilities of open CPSs that may cause corruption of sensor and control information and disruption of the physical system, or exposure of confidential information. In addition to data security, aggressors may initiate attacks that target the real-time properties of a CPS. Real-time accessibility gives a stricter operational environment than conventional CPSs.

Major concerns in CPS communication include keeping the data private and allowing only authorized access. Attackers may not only attempt to physically probe the devices, altering their behavior or intercepting the physical properties of power consumption and timing behaviors to analyze the secrets and masquerade them, but can also implement network intrusion at the physical layer as well as the software layer. All relevant safety standards assume that a system's usage context is completely known and understood at development time. This assumption is no longer true for open CPSs, meaning that their security vulnerabilities could be faults leading to life-endangering safety hazards. As many CPSs are becoming open systems, they are the target of cyber-attacks. Interconnectivity removes boundaries and the need for physical presence to gain access. For instance, automotive architectures today include features that involve both remote diagnosis and maintenance functionality. Such systems enable Over-the-Air (OTA) updates and the management of vehicle functions over communication links. As many diverse communication networks are integrated, gateways are employed to connect different parts and enable functions to obtain needed information from all parts of the vehicle. Since gateways are able to access all buses and hence connected devices, updates or remote access functions are mostly supported in such components.

Modern vehicles support Wi-Fi, Bluetooth connectivity, many diverse CAN bus systems, dedicated networks for advanced driver assistance systems (ADAS) and may connect even up to 100 ECU modules. In another domain, the remote medical-support services or tele-assistance systems' trust of personal devices, as well as, trust in transmitted information are crucial. Multiple dimensions of trust are important, such as (i) the safety of using the devices in tele-presence spaces (e.g., safety of blood-pressure devices attached to a user or safety of a sensory instrument), (ii) reliable and timely information delivery, (iii) stability of the overall system, (iv) low risk in receiving wrong information, and (v) privacy guarantees. Current systems still do not have this level of sophistication, and an appropriate trust configuration remains a challenge; especially since the verification and validation of a cyber-physical-system is not a one-time event. Instead, intra- and inter- CPS communications to support not only internal connectivity but also over-the-air connectivity, it is essentially a life-cycle process continuously ensuring the certification of safety critical services. In addition to trusted platform modules (TPMs) that can be used to enable trusted boot, where each piece of code loaded from boot-time is measured via cryptographic hash before loading, CPS communications need to be secure, taking measures to ensure trusted communication from both active (interferers) and passive (eavesdroppers) adversaries. Therefore, to guarantee secure and trusted networking in these emerging CPSs, methods are discussed next to address enhancing network protocols in terms of security and towards designing CPS devices with security in mind. Next generation open CPSs framework that we present provides integrated security assurance to allow networking self-protection at runtime.

CPS DEVICE-LEVEL SUPPORT FOR DETECTION AND PREVENTION

In addition to ensuring secure communication, modern open CPSs also involve hardware primitives for security and authenticating the CPS device itself and mechanism to ensure its own underlying binary code is trusted. ARM's TrustZone Security Extensions discussed by ARM Limited. (2009), enable processor and memory isolation effectively creating two distinct "worlds"—the secure world for security sensitive application code and the normal world for non-secure applications. Hardware solutions also offer support in on-chip networks for logically isolated multi-compartments (Kornaros et al., 2015) and hardware monitors for secure embedded devices (Mao and Wolf, 2010), or hardware support for virtualization of I/O devices such as the CAN controller in automotive and extensions that guarantee a spatial and temporal isolation of virtual controllers (Herber et al., 2014). To ensure trusted communication, proposals include for instance methods of integrating physically unclonable functions (PUFs) (A PUF is a complex physical system with a large number of inputs and outputs, where the mapping from the inputs to the outputs cannot be predicted in any reasonable time, and the system cannot be reproduced due to scientific or technological difficulties) along with existing hardware in the design to create a trusted information flow within the system (Potkonjak et al., 2010). Digital PUFs have been designed for enabling remote secret key exchange protocol and communication tasks, because both communicating parties experience very low overhead in terms of both time and energy.

Finally, software methodologies can provide enhanced security in deeply embedded real-time CPS systems. Various methods employ application instrumentation to detect anomalies, such as timing dilations exceeding worst-case execution time (WCET) bounds in order to attain elevated security assurance. Static timing analysis is performed on selected code sections to obtain bounds during the right timing for the required schedulability analysis, and the bounds are subsequently utilized to monitor execution during run-time (Zimmer et al., 2015). Intrusion Detection Systems (IDS) are also widely deployed to detect unwanted entities into a system by using signature-based, specification- based, or anomaly-based techniques. To achieve vehicular bus communication security authentication of all senders in the gateways, encryption of data transmissions and network firewalling are fundamental techniques (Kleberger et al., 2011).

Existing techniques for securing CPS networking have various drawbacks, especially in broadcast and distributed systems with limited computing power and data storage. However, the vast majority of cyber-attacks can be prevented through optimizing communication standards, incorporating hardware security attributes in device designs, upgrading firmware to support trusted root of trust, etc. By considering the implications of intercepted, deleted, modified and forged information from all components of a networked CPS, designers increasingly need to employ methods relying on communication security-by-design and integrated security assurance to protect the system end-to-end against such attacks.

NETWORK-LEVEL SUPPORT DETECTION AND PREVENTION

The networking of gateways, switches, and firewalls components for wired, wireless and sensor networks in CPSs should ensure routing security, traffic control on information flow, and the necessary network separation (demilitarized zones (DMZs). Moreover, in order to fulfill authentication requirements, developers propose more efficient schemes during the design or upgrade of communication protocols (Wang et al, 2009). A CPS network protocol should ensure that a transmitted message is authentic and determine if the integrity of the message has been compromised. An authentic message indicates that the device alleged to be the sender of the message is actually the device that sent the message. Message integrity denotes that the contents of the message received by a recipient device have not been altered after having been sent from the alleged sender. Cyber threats can involve forging communication messages that appear to be from a trusted sender, but that are not actually from the sender, or eavesdropping on legitimate messages from the sender and attempt to spoof the receiver with copies of the legitimate messages. Detection and prevention protocols must prevent the attacker from convincing the recipient that the message is from a trusted device or that the contents of a copied message can be trusted.

Previous works employ behavior-based techniques for intrusion detection (Sun et al., 2008), optionally using domain-specific knowledge and are often targeted at wireless communication. Protocol extensions towards intrusion prevention protocol can utilize different key establishment with regard to the cases of deployment of networks and establishes different types of keys according to the role of a sensor node. The prevention protocol also enables to encrypt a message selectively or to append a message authentication code to its related critical proprietary information of CPSs applications.

Gateways, switches, firewalls and components are critical for cyber-security, as they can contribute to the necessary network separation. The networking of these components for wired, wireless and sensor networks should ensure routing security and improved resiliency against cross-layer traffic injection as specified by National Institute of Standards and Technology (2014). In modern and future vehicles for example, to address increasing complexity due to the large number of Electronic Control Units (ECUs) and their software code, a promising solution is domain-based networking. In such a set-up, a domain controller isolates a number of devices (cost reduced "light" ECU) using for instance standardized Software (AUTOSAR). From a threat perspective, communication segmentation both on-chip and off-chip allows better visibility, management and isolation. Essentially, as Figure 4 shows an automotive example, the division of the network into security zones advances monitoring of internal traffic and devices, prevents unauthorized access to restricted data and resources, and controls the spread of intruders and malware, as well as error propagation.

To tackle secure networking of an open CPS the developed secure framework provides co-operative dynamic firewalling between internal and external communications through the gateway components.

Figure 4. Example of an automotive networked CPS with various Electronic Control Units (ECUs) supporting segmented on- and off-chip networks. Firewalling mechanisms located at each domain bridge enable isolation and authenticated communication.

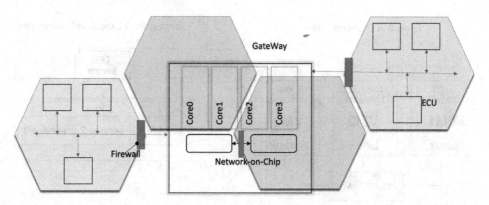

The gateway creates secure isolated on-device compartments and in-system secure network segments through embedding integrity and authentication control for each data transfer. At the same time the root-of-trust boot protocol is extended with one-time-programmable on-chip routing paths and access control rules. The developed framework enables a physical communication link among CPS devices to essentially support a secure physically separate channel and a non-secure physically separate channel that conveys untrusted data.

In addition, the distributed approach employed involves the use of a challenge response system for authentication between the gateway node and each transmission node (ECU). Hence, considering a robust open CPS, the gateway controls not only detachable devices that connect to the system, for instance such as through an OBD port, but additionally the gateway performs periodic sanity checks to ensure trusted communication with low-overhead, e.g., in CAN-based systems that require real-time data processing.

SECURE AND TRUSTED INTER-EE AND INTER-APP COMMUNICATION

In Section "Execution Environments and Apps Platform" the concept of EE has been detailed as isolated context of execution, characterized by a level of criticality. However, as pointed out by the requirement (i), such an isolation should not to prevent them from communicating with each other.

The information sharing between heterogeneous contexts of execution is one of the key feature to implement functional and full featured CPS systems. However, the trustworthiness of this communication, both between apps running on the same execution environment (Inter-App) and running on difference execution environments (Inter-EE), is of pivotal importance for the safety and security of the entire architecture. For this reason, the techniques that are used by apps to communicate need to be supervised by software, as well as by hardware. In the remaining part of this section, a review of the available techniques that allow communication between applications, virtual machines and, more generally, execution environments will be given, proposing as well ideas for novel approaches.

The communication between Virtual Machines is a topic that has been vastly explored in the past, since it introduced room for improving the canonical communication based on physical network cards

Figure 5. Communication scheme between Execution Environments: Inter-EE refers to the communication between the Safety-critical execution environments and the others. The communication between the non-safety-critical execution environments is represented by the Virtual Switch interconnection.

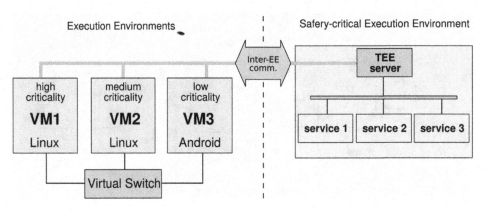

and physical switches. The emerging paradigm of Software Defined Network (SDN) and the subsequent creation of the Network Function Virtualization (NFV), made this interest even stronger. The concept of NFV is about decoupling the software implementation of network functions from the underlying hardware (Azodolmolky et al., 2013), confining the former in Virtual Machines. All this attention allowed to burst significantly the development towards highly efficient and fast solutions aimed at switching network packages between Virtual Machines. Relaying on the Linux subsystems, it was already possible to implement decent switching mechanisms between VMs' network interfaces. In fact, assigning one TAP device to every VM it is possible to benefit from the in-kernel packet switching, technique which is normally used when Linux serves as a router/switch OS. This is not an ideal solution in the context of virtualization, since the handling of incoming/outgoing packets require expensive exits from the VM which will eventually bring the execution to kernel space, where the actual packet switching happens. The packets passing though the in-kernel switching modules can be, therefore, filtered by Linux modules such as netfilter, the Linux packets filtering solution. This, together with iptables, offers a full-featured firewall solution. Other types of packets analysis (e.g.: packets inspection) are difficult to achieve in these situations from a regular user space application for security reasons.

Avoiding the commutation to kernel mode during the packet switching would bring performance and latency improvements; this is the starting point of several virtual switches that have been implemented in the past and that are still heavily used as virtual functions. Example of virtual switches are VOSYSwitch (Paolino et al., 2016), Snabb, VALE (Rizzo et al., 2012) and OVS-DPDK: all these solutions implement in user space the switching functionality, reducing the costs associated to virtualization, requiring less context switches. Flexibility-wise, these solutions are much more convenient than the in-kernel solutions: project like VOSYSwitch provides the API and the needed infrastructure to enrich the virtual switch with plug-ins, it also provides extended functionalities like virtual LANs, firewall, packets inspection and so on. Such a flexibility finds application in the CPS architecture, enforcing security policies between VMs.

The virtual switches, although being ideal solutions as communication between VMs (and so to non-safety-critical execution environments), do not address the communication between an execution environment in the Normal-world, and the RTOS (or safety-critical execution environment). The hardware partitioning of the two worlds makes impossible to use conventional communications methods:

the link between a process running on the Secure world and the Normal world requires an ad-hoc solution. Offering the insights for such a solution is the GlobalPlatform (https://www.globalplatform.org/specifications.asp) program, which aims at standardize the interoperation between multiple applications on secure chips. Specifically, the GlobalPlatform API were designed to standardize the communication protocol between these applications, called the Trusted Applications (TA), and the user (client applications running in the Non-secure side). The Secure side, according to the GlobalPlatform naming, is called Trusted Execution Environment (TEE). These API suit particularly well the Open CPS use case, giving a ready-to-use design for the cross-worlds communication. Every application which wants to initiate a trusted communication with a TA, has to first initialize the context of execution with the desired service running in the TEE (TEE Server). Such a context provides all the necessary resources to properly execute the TA, configuring for instance the shared memory between the two processes if needed. Figure 4 depicts the overall scheme of communication between execution environments.

GlobalPlatform does not address only the communication part, but also covers the characterization of the applications running on the Secure side as well as their properties. This gives valuable guidelines for the development of the Secure eservices.

Overall, GlobalPlatform offers the technology to exploit the ARMv8 TrustZone extension towards secure communication between execution environments, ensuring the integrity of the Secure services and the confidentiality of the Secure assets.

Other solutions have been explored that, relying on TrustZone, provide a framework to implement a secure communication channels between the TEE and the Normal world. Jang et al. (2015) presented a framework which, although not following the GlobalPlatform design, provides a mechanism of secure sessions, where the TEE provides the session key to the requestor only if its code and control flow have been successfully verified.

The secure provision of a key to a process running in the Non-secure side introduces powerful possibilities, like the initialization of a crypted channel between non-safety critical processes running in the same or different execution environments. In this case, it is of fundamental importance that the session key is treated with the due measures to not jeopardize the security of the system. In fact, an improper handling of such keys can greatly extend the attack surface for malicious software (like, for instance, copying the key to non-secure memory).

MODEL-BASED TOOLCHAIN

Provision of an open platform should go in pair with the specification of an approach for developing applications and/or recommendations of tools that can be used to develop applications intended to run on such platform. This is stated by one of the requirements mentioned in the "Open CPS Requirements" section, i.e. vi). Most common and a natural choice is a usage of programming languages, such as C or C++. The fact that these are the languages well known among the software engineers increases the chances of building potentially large community of developers. Indeed, the last is one of the most important objectives of open platform hence technologies which are advertised should be well recognized. Nevertheless, in the area of CPS development, there is a trend of going towards model based design (MBD) that supports the construction of abstract models and the transformation into concrete implementations. MBD is a further step in the direction of increasing the abstraction levels in the development process, offering more high-level, reusable and maintainable software components, with a main goal to speed up an entire development process, improving at the same time overall software quality as models might be a subject to formal analysis. Evaluation of properties through formal checks has a meaningful impact on the security and safety, therefore it relevantly contributes to the main concern of open CPS platforms. At the code level, software quality can be improved by unit testing, complex integration process and checks or usage of a coding standards. These are the ways to proceed when delivering the code supposed to provide certain level of quality. When moving with the development to the modeling level, additional techniques, such as model checking can be employed to check that formal defined properties of a model hold. Consequently, it is of a high interest to have a toolchain which incorporates support for programming but also exceeds the functionality of an ordinary, programming tool with the model-based design in which models are not just an artefact for code generation but also an input for verification via model checking.

The approach presented in this chapter tries to respond to such demand by providing a toolchain in which trusted apps can be developed and packaged using standard ARM toolchain and posted in the container, whereas critical apps can either be written entirely in native languages, i.e. C/C++, or can be modeled using tools such as 4DIAC modeling tool (4DIAC, Eclipse Incubation Project, 2016). 4DIAC is an IEC 61499 (IEC 61499, 2015) compliant integrated development environment (IDE) that provides an engineering environment to model distributed control applications. The development approach in 4DIAC follows the application centric design approaches as of IEC 61499 based systems. Overall systems are created by modeling the required applications. Out of the 4DIAC model machine deployable C code can be then generated. Thus, there are three basic ways in which apps can be deployed in the app container, all summarized in the Figure 6. The app container itself apart from the App Binary might include as

Figure 6. Components of apps verification and development toolchain

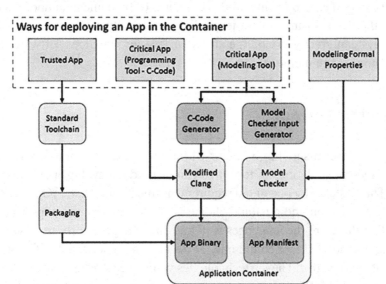

well the App Manifest. The last might be for instance formatted in JSON, and for critical apps it can store special, additional information such as:

- Signed certificate, which was created by an entity that can guarantee the safety of the app. Consequently, only certified apps may be permitted to run within the Critical Execution Environment (CEE) which eliminates situations in which end user downloads faulty or malicious software.
- Resources required by the app, for example memory, exclusive hardware access and required permanent space.
- Application manifest with Plug & Play information.

Having such information, the toolchain should be able to limit and analyze the features of an app, even before deployment and on the source level, without having to disclose the source code.

Furthermore, to ensure higher level of trust, security and safe operation, critical apps developed using a modeling tool can be verified if they are conforming to the platform API requirements and constraints. For instance, an app behavior in 4DIAC is specified using asynchronously interacting state-machines. Given a finite model of an application, it is now possible to systematically check if a formal property holds for the model, by using model checking technique. Example of a property that could be model checked for a vehicle app responsible for cruise control (CC) functionality, is that it will never operate for the vehicle speed lower than 15km/h. For that an existing model checking tool can be integrated. For example, NuSMV(Cimatti et al., 2002) has an open architecture for model checking and is reliable to be used in verifying industrial designs. The NUSMV project aims at the development of a state-of-the-art symbolic model checker, designed to be applicable in technology transfer projects: it is a well-structured, open, flexible and documented platform for model checking, and is robust and close to industrial systems standards. Seamless integration of the NuSMV checker can be done through the generation of the NuSMV input language (Cimatti & Roveri, 1998) (which is essentially the same as the CMU SMV input language (Clarke, McMillan, Campos, & Hartonas-Garmhausen, 1996)) out of the 4DIAC model (as shown on the Figure 6) or any other kind of modeling language used or tailored for designing CPS applications. Therefore, only apps modeled with 4DIAC can be verified. The results of the model checker are then bound with the app binary as a manifest of the application container.

Provision of mentioned features (e.g. support for formal verification) within the toolchain adds to the desire of securing the operation of apps within the open CPS platform context. There are however further ways in which the toolchain will support that concept. Guidelines for verification of a common security threats might be one of them.

SUMMARY AND FUTURE DIRECTIONS

The market of open CPSs is rapidly growing and evolving and at the same time security and trust are getting more and more important. Although many standard IT security concepts can be applied to open CPSs, dynamic, run-time update of critical devices should be considered explicitly in the deployment of open systems, while addressing security concerns for such devices at the same time. Open cyber-physical systems are becoming susceptible to a wider range of attacks and need to build resiliency against system compromise. The open CPS paradigm as an ensemble of diverse software-dominated components that involve feature interaction, multi-rate distributed networked subsystems, and collaborative control, requires synergistic mechanisms across hardware and software layers to ensure security. Design approaches that enable correct by construction mechanisms are important in safety-critical networked components, much like the challenge of making formal methods accessible to aid in establishing a next-generation certification process. In open CPSs it is not enough simply to add security features on to the system at some later point in time. Strategies relating to safety, and in particular security of CPS apps platform, need to be designed into the system from the outset.

The main domains – aerospace, automotive, healthcare, industrial automation – are analyzing and providing hardware and software-based technologies for addressing these security issues in their areas. But the whole CPS industry would benefit from more general domain-independent platforms and development processes, which would allow for building industrial devices and developing software services with security requirements in mind from the first step on. For example, introducing verification and model-driven development techniques such as those outlined in the previous section, in order to detect the possibility of an execution of unauthorized instructions in real-time CPS environments. By introducing early warning systems should raise intrusion detection capabilities but also might provide several steps of reduced functionality (Zimmer, Bhat, Mueller, & Mohan, 2015).

Security professionals will play a large role in the development process of open CPSs evaluating risks for organizations and deciding about solutions and tools to be applied in each individual case. Security vendors and cyber physical system vendors should cooperate for a better detection of threats and mitigation of successful attacks. Lessons learned in other industries such as personal computers, tablets and smartphones producers should be analyzed and applied in the CPS area alike to build software security on top of hardware security modules and secure communication. CPS features like real-time, distributed components and loss of physical devices should not provide any leak to attackers. But this is not enough, security of CPS needs to be built into the design of the system itself (Moholkar, 2014).

ACKNOWLEDGMENT

The research leading to these results has received funding from the European Union (EU) Horizon 2020 project TAPPS (Trusted Apps for open CPSs) under RIA grant n° 645119.

REFERENCES

4DIAC, Eclipse Incubation Project. (2016). Retrieved from https://eclipse.org/4diac

Anderson, J., Baruah, S., & Brandenburg, B. (2009). Multicore operating-system support for mixed criticality. In Proceedings of the workshop on mixed criticality: Roadmap to evolving UAV certification. San Francisco, CA, USA.

Azodolmolky, S., Wieder, P., & Yahyapour, R. (2013). Cloud computing networking: Challenges and opportunities for innovations. *IEEE Communications Magazine*, *51*(7), 54–62. doi:10.1109/MCOM.2013.6553678

Brandenburg, B. B. (2014, December). A synchronous IPC protocol for predictable access to shared resources in mixed-criticality systems. In Proceedings of the IEEE real-time systems symposium (pp. 196–206). doi:10.1109/RTSS.2014.37

Burns, A. J., Johnson, M. E., & Honeyman, P. (2016, October). A brief chronology of medical device security. *Communications of the ACM*, *59*(10), 66–72. doi:10.1145/2890488

Cimatti, A., Clarke, E., Giunchiglia, E., Giunchiglia, F., Pistore, M., Roveri, M., . . . Tacchella, A. (2002, July). NuSMV 2: An opensource tool for symbolic model checking. In E. Brinksma & K. G. Larsen (Eds.), *Computer aided verification: 14th international conference, Proceedings* (pp. 359–364). Berlin, Heidelberg: Springer Berlin Heidelberg.

Cimatti, A., & Roveri, M. (1998, December). NuSMV 1.0: User manual (Tech. Rep. Nos. Technical report, ITC-IRST, Trento, Italy.)

Clarke, E., McMillan, K., Campos, S., & Hartonas-Garmhausen, V. (1996). Symbolic model checking. In R. Alur & T. A. Henzinger (Eds.), *Computer aided verification* (pp. 419–422). Berlin, Heidelberg: Springer Berlin Heidelberg. doi:10.1007/3-540-61474-5_93

Ecco, L., Tobuschat, S., Saidi, S., & Ernst, R. (2014, August). A mixed critical memory controller using bank privatization and fixed priority scheduling. In *Proceedings of the IEEE 20th international conference on embedded and real-time computing systems and applications* (pp. 1–10). doi:10.1109/RTCSA.2014.6910550

Hassan, M., & Patel, H. (2016, April). Criticality- and requirement-aware bus arbitration for multi-core mixed criticality systems. In *IEEE real-time and embedded technology and applications symposium* (pp. 1–11). RTAS. doi:10.1109/RTAS.2016.7461327

Herber, C., Richter, A., Rauchfuss, H., & Herkersdorf, A. (2014, September). Spatial and temporal isolation of virtual CAN controllers. *SIGBED Rev.*, *11*(2), 19–26. doi:10.1145/2668138.2668141

IEC 61499. (2015). Retrieved from http://www.iec61499.de/

Jacobs, M. (2013). Improving the precision of approximations in WCET analysis for multi-core processors. In *Proceedings of the 7th junior researcher workshop on real-time computing* (pp. 1–4).

Jang, J. S., Kong, S., Kim, M., Kim, D., & Kang, B. B. (2015). SeCReT: Secure channel between rich execution environment and trusted execution environment. In NDSS.

Jing, Q., Vasilakos, A. V., Wan, J., Lu, J., & Qiu, D. (2014). Security of the internet of things: Perspectives and challenges. *Wireless Networks*, *20*(8), 2481–2501. doi:10.1007/s11276-014-0761-7

Khaitan, S. K., & McCalley, J. D. (2015, June). Design techniques and applications of cyberphysical systems: A survey. *IEEE Systems Journal*, *9*(2), 350–365. doi:10.1109/JSYST.2014.2322503

Kivity, A., Laor, D., Costa, G., Enberg, P., Har'El, N., Marti, D., & Zolotarov, V. (2014). OSv—optimizing the operating system for virtual machines. In *Proceedings of the USENIX annual technical conference (USENIX ATC)* (pp. 61–72).

Kleberger, P., Olovsson, T., & Jonsson, E. (2011, June). Security aspects of the in-vehicle network in the connected car. In Proceedings of the IEEE intelligent vehicles symposium (IV) (pp. 528–533). doi:10.1109/IVS.2011.5940525

Kornaros, G., Christoforakis, I., Tomoutzoglou, O., Bakoyiannis, D., Vazakopoulou, K., Grammatikakis, M., & Papagrigoriou, A. (2015, August). Hardware support for cost-effective system-level protection in multi-core SoCs. In Proceedings of the Euromicro conference on digital system design (pp. 41–48). doi:10.1109/DSD.2015.65

Kotaba, O., Nowotsch, J., Paulitsch, M., Petters, S. M., & Theiling, H. (2013). Muticore in real-time systems - temporal isolation challenges due to shared resources. In *Proceedings of the workshop on industry-driven approaches for cost-effective certification of safety-critical, mixed-criticality systems (WICERT)*.

ARM Limited. (2009, April). ARM security technology: Building a secure system using TrustZone technology (tech. report No. PRD29-GENC-009492C).

Macdonell, C., Ke, X., Gordon, A. W., & Lu, P. (2011). Low-latency, high-bandwidth use cases for nahanni/ivshmem. In Proceedings of the Kvm forum (Vol. 2011).

Mao, S., & Wolf, T. (2010, June). Hardware support for secure processing in embedded systems. *IEEE Transactions on Computers*, *59*(6), 847–854. doi:10.1109/TC.2010.32

Moholkar, A. V. (2014, July). Security for cyber-physical systems. *International Journal of Computing and Technology*, *1*(6).

Mollison, M. S., Erickson, J. P., Anderson, J. H., Baruah, S. K., & Scoredos, J. A. (2010, June). Mixed-criticality real-time scheduling for multicore systems. In *Proceedings of the 10th IEEE international conference on computer and information technology* (pp. 1864–1871). doi:10.1109/CIT.2010.320

Mushtaq, H., Al-Ars, Z., & Bertels, K. (2013, December). Accurate and efficient identification of worst-case execution time for multicore processors: A survey. In *Proceedings of the 8th IEEE design and test symposium* (pp. 1–6). doi:10.1109/IDT.2013.6727080

Nowotsch, J., Paulitsch, M., Bühler, D., Theiling, H., Wegener, S., & Schmidt, M. (2014, July). Multi-core interference-sensitive WCET analysis leveraging runtime resource capacity enforcement. In *Proceedings of the 26th euromicro conference on real-time systems* (pp. 109–118). doi:10.1109/ECRTS.2014.20

Panel, S. G. I. (2010). *Guidelines for smart grid cyber security (tech. report No. 7628). Cyber Security Working Group*. NIST.

Paolino, M., Fanguede, J., Nikolaev, N., & Raho, D. (2016). Turning an open source project into a carrier grade vSwitch, for NFV: VOSYSwitch challenges & results. In *Proceedings of the 5th IEEE international conference on network infrastructure and digital content (NIDC)*.

Pellizzoni, R., Meredith, P., Nam, M.-Y., Sun, M., Caccamo, M., & Sha, L. (2009). Handling mixed-criticality in SoC-based real-time embedded systems. In *Proceedings of the 7th ACM international conference on embedded software* (pp. 235–244). New York, NY: ACM. doi:10.1145/1629335.1629367

Potkonjak, M., Meguerdichian, S., & Wong, J. L. (2010, November). *Trusted sensors and remote sensing. In IEEE Sensors* (pp. 1104–1107).

Prehofer, C., Horst, O., Dodi, R., Geven, A., Kornaros, G., Montanari, E., & Paolino, M. (2016). Towards trusted apps platforms for open CPS. In *Proceedings of the 3rd international workshop on emerging ideas and trends in engineering of cyber-physical systems (EITEC)* (pp. 23–28). doi:10.1109/EITEC.2016.7503692

Prehofer, C., Kornaros, G., & Paolino, M. (2015). TAPPS - trusted apps for open cyber-physical systems. In S.K. Katsikas & A.B. Sideridis (Eds.), E-*democracy – citizen rights in the world of the new computing paradigms* (pp. 213–216). Cham: Springer International Publishing.

Richter, A., Herber, C., Rauchfuss, H., Wild, T., & Herkersdorf, A. (2014, February). Performance isolation exposure in virtualized platforms with PCI passthrough I/O sharing. In E. Maehle, K. Römer, W. Karl et al. (Eds.), *Architecture of computing systems – ARCS 2014* (pp. 171–182). Lübeck, Germany: Springer International Publishing.

Rizzo, L., & Lettieri, G. (2012). Vale, a switched Ethernet for virtual machines. In *Proceedings of the 8th international conference on emerging networking experiments and technologies* (pp. 61–72). doi:10.1145/2413176.2413185

Ruhland, A., Prehofer, C., & Horst, O. (2016, December). embSFI: An approach for software fault isolation in embedded systems. In M. Völp, P. Esteves-Verissimo, A. Casimiro, & R. Pellizzoni (Eds.), *Proceedings of the 1st workshop on security and dependability of critical embedded real-time systems*, Porto, Portugal (pp. 6–11). Retrieved from https://certs2016.uni.lu/Media/certs2016.uni.lu/Files/CERTS-2016-Ruhland-embSFI

Russell, R. (2008). virtio: Towards a de-facto standard for virtual I/O devices. *Operating Systems Review*, *42*(5), 95–103. doi:10.1145/1400097.1400108

Sha, L. (2009, September). Resilient mixed-criticality systems. *Crosstalk*, *22*(9-10), 9–14.

Stankovic, J. A. (2014, February). Research directions for the internet of things. *IEEE Internet of Things Journal, 1*(1), 3–9. doi:10.1109/JIOT.2014.2312291

Sun, Y., Han, Z., & Liu, K. J. R. (2008, February). Defense of trust management vulnerabilities in distributed networks. *IEEE Communications Magazine, 46*(2), 112–119. doi:10.1109/MCOM.2008.4473092

Wan, J., Zhang, D., Zhao, S., Yang, L. T., & Lloret, J. (2014, August). Context-aware vehicular cyber-physical systems with cloud support: Architecture, challenges, and solutions. *IEEE Communications Magazine, 52*(8), 106–113. doi:10.1109/MCOM.2014.6871677

Wang, Q., Khurana, H., Huang, Y., & Nahrstedt, K. (2009, April). Time valid one-time signature for time-critical multicast data authentication. In IEEE INFOCOM (pp. 1233–1241). doi:10.1109/INFCOM.2009.5062037

Weimerskirch, A. (2014). V2V communication security: A privacy preserving design for 300 million vehicles. In *Proceedings of the workshop on cryptographic hardware and embedded systems (CHES)*, Busan, Korea.

Zimmer, C., Bhat, B., Mueller, F., & Mohan, S. (2015). Intrusion detection for CPS real-time controllers. In S. K. Khaitan, J. D. McCalley, & C. C. Liu (Eds.), *Cyber physical systems approach to smart electric power grid* (pp. 329–358). Berlin, Heidelberg: Springer.

Chapter 13
Side–Channel Attacks in the Internet of Things:
Threats and Challenges

Andreas Zankl
Fraunhofer AISEC, Germany

Hermann Seuschek
Technical University of Munich, Germany

Gorka Irazoqui
Nagravision, Spain

Berk Gulmezoglu
Worcester Polytechnic Institute, USA

ABSTRACT

The Internet of Things (IoT) rapidly closes the gap between the virtual and the physical world. As more and more information is processed through this expanding network, the security of IoT devices and backend services is increasingly important. Yet, side-channel attacks pose a significant threat to systems in practice, as the microarchitectures of processors, their power consumption, and electromagnetic emanation reveal sensitive information to adversaries. This chapter provides an extensive overview of previous attack literature. It illustrates that microarchitectural attacks can compromise the entire IoT ecosystem: from devices in the field to servers in the backend. A subsequent discussion illustrates that many of today's security mechanisms integrated in modern processors are in fact vulnerable to the previously outlined attacks. In conclusion to these observations, new countermeasures are needed that effectively defend against both microarchitectural and power/EM based side-channel attacks.

DOI: 10.4018/978-1-5225-2845-6.ch013

INTRODUCTION

Currently, we experience exciting times for the advancement of computing technology. Driven by ubiquitous connectivity, miniaturization of devices, and new developments in sensor technology, the gap between the virtual and the physical world is rapidly closing in what is known today as the Internet of Things (IoT). Devices that operate as part of the IoT must often meet strict requirements regarding energy consumption, complexity, and cost per unit. While computational resources and performance are often limited, many IoT ecosystems deploy backend servers that collect information for in-depth analysis, advanced customer services, or feedback to actuators in the field. While this symbiosis of smart devices and backend systems enables innovative business models, it also raises concerns over the privacy of data and the security of the devices processing it. Among the most critical components in this ecosystem are the main processing units. Due to an ever-growing number of transistors, processor designers are able to implement sophisticated mechanisms that continuously improve performance for every product generation. However, the secure execution of sensitive applications can often not be assured when these performance enhancements are active. This is because execution properties, e.g. the program runtime or the accompanying power consumption, heavily depend on the specific data and instructions that are processed. Anyone that observes the execution can therefore infer what is being processed. For security applications, this eventually means that confidential information is leaked to outside observers. Such information leaks are generally studied in the area of side-channel attacks, a subset of which will be addressed in this chapter. In literature, the field of *microarchitectural attacks* (Acıiçmez & Koç, 2009) studies how the properties of a processor's instruction set implementation affect the security and privacy of executed applications. Typical targets are resources shared by processor cores or execution threads, such as caches, branch prediction and shared functional units like arithmetic logic units (ALUs). By observing, manipulating or competing for these shared resources, adversaries can learn critical details of programs running on the processor. This can quickly become a serious issue when multiple customers share a backend system or when multiple applications are running concurrently on an IoT device. If one customer has malicious intents or if one application is compromised, the security of everyone else is suddenly at stake. In addition, IoT devices face another threat. Since they are deployed in great numbers, it is feasible in many cases to get physical access to them. This enables an adversary to exploit yet another type of side-channel. With the appropriate measurement equipment, it is possible to observe the power consumption and the closely related electromagnetic (EM) emanation of a device, while it is working on a task. In literature, the fields of *power analysis* (Kocher et al., 1999; Mangard et al., 2008) and *electromagnetic analysis* (Quisquater et al., 2001; Gandolfi et al., 2001) study physical properties of devices to learn about their inner workings and to infer the information processed by them. Due to the implementation of modern electronics, the power consumption varies depending on the data that is being processed. This inevitably leaks information to adversaries observing the power and EM side-channels of the device.

In response to these threats, this chapter gives a comprehensive overview of state of the art literature in the field of microarchitectural attacks. In addition, it outlines the capabilities of power and EM based attacks, and shows how they might be combined with microarchitectural observations to derive new threats once physical access to IoT devices is obtained. After establishing the state of the art, a selection of security features on modern processors and their utility against the previously described attacks is discussed. In particular, trusted execution environments are described, which are used to encapsulate security critical computations in enclaves that are separated from the rest of the system with the help of the processor hardware. Then, instruction set extensions for cryptographic operations are discussed, which are known from x86 processors and which have recently been integrated into the latest ARMv8 processor architecture. The discussion also comprises cryptographic hardware accelerators, which have emerged in the smart card domain and are part of numerous systems-on-chips sold today. The chapter is concluded with a summary of how recent developments in side-channel attack literature affect current security trends on IoT systems, followed by a brief outlook of tomorrow's challenges in securing them.

STATE OF THE ART

This section gives a comprehensive overview of previous works in the field of microarchitectural attacks. Subsequently, the area of power and EM based analysis is introduced to illustrate that physical access to devices not only enables dangerous attacks by itself, but also allows adversaries to exploit microarchitectural events in new ways. Throughout the section, publications are grouped and discussed to establish an understanding of scenarios, components, and features that have been exploited in the past.

Microarchitectural Attacks

The microarchitecture of a processor is the implementation of its instruction set architecture (ISA), which defines the fundamental interface between software and hardware. Attacks that target this implementation are called microarchitectural attacks. In general, they exploit implementation features without requiring physical access to the device. They enable adversaries to break confidentiality and privacy by inferring information from other processes across software based boundaries established by operating systems or hypervisors. They are a threat to users on a wide range of systems, from server and cloud computing to mobile and IoT devices. Although microarchitectures are considerably divers, some components are used in most modern processors as they add well-known performance benefits.

A high-level layout of modern computer systems is shown in Figure 1. They typically consist of one or more processor (CPU) sockets, each containing several CPU cores. Multiple applications are executed on the cores at the same time. The memory hierarchy is an important part of the processor design and

Figure 1. High-level layout of modern computer systems and their memory hierarchy

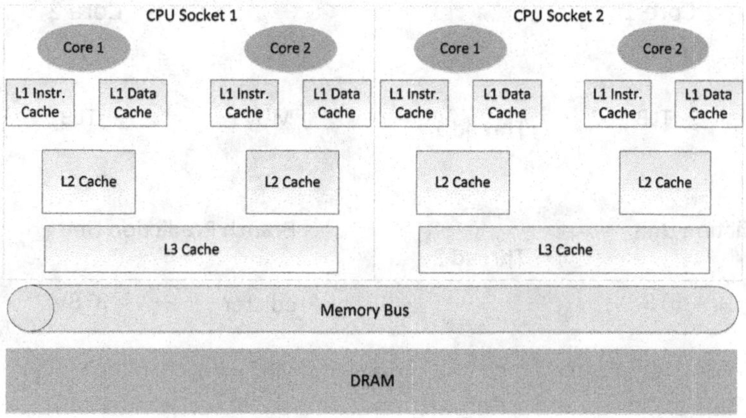

a common target in microarchitectural attacks. Closest to the processor cores, the caches store data and instructions that have recently been used, because they are very likely to be utilized again. This avoids costly DRAM accesses and speeds up code execution. The cache hierarchy is split into core-private cache levels (L1 and L2) and shared cache levels (L3). The last-level cache (LLC) is typically shared among all CPU cores. Each level can either be explicitly separated into data and instruction side (L1) or unified (L2 and L3). The memory bus is in charge of the communication between the cache hierarchy and the DRAM, and further communicates the state of shared memory across CPU sockets. Finally, the DRAM holds all data and instructions necessary for the execution of the operating system and all applications.

Within each CPU core, several performance-improving components are implemented. A selection of common attack targets is illustrated in Figure 2. The Branch Prediction Unit (BPU) predicts the outcome of conditional branches based on observations of previous ones. It is divided into a predictor and a Branch Target Buffer (BTB), which holds information about the most recently executed branches. Additionally, processes have access to Performance Monitoring Units (PMU), i.e., special hardware registers that count specific hardware events (e.g. cache misses). PMUs allow detailed insight into a CPU core's state and performance metrics. They operate in real time and without the need of attaching additional debugging hardware. Another component, the Translation Lookaside Buffer (TLB), is speeding up the translation between virtual and physical memory addresses. By storing recently performed translations, the TLB helps to avoid repeated and costly conversions. Finally, CPU cores can support parallel execution of multiple processes by cleverly assigning and scheduling unused execution units within the core. This is called simultaneous multithreading (SMT) and introduces the notions of physical and logical CPU cores. The number of logical cores matches the number of hardware threads, whereas physical cores refer to the (smaller) number of actual CPU cores.

All of the components mentioned above have been exploited in microarchitectural attacks. While the term attack implies the existence of an aggressor and a victim, it is important to note that all exploited components can also be used to establish traditional communication channels. If adversary and victim collaborate, they can communicate via the microarchitecture and thereby bypass any logical boundaries enforced by operating systems or hypervisors. This is called a covert channel, which is particularly useful for leaking sensitive information to unauthorized users. Attacks and covert channels can be instantiated on one CPU core (single-core), across CPU cores (cross-core), and even across CPU sockets (cross-CPU).

Figure 2. Typical core-internal components exploited in microarchitectural attacks

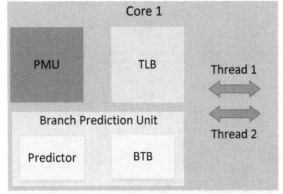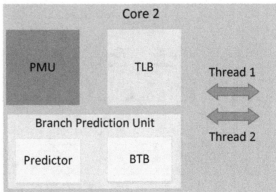

Components in Figure 2 are targets in single-core scenarios. LLCs that are shared among all cores are a promising target for cross-core scenarios. The memory bus and DRAM enable attacks and covert channels in cross-CPU scenarios. The following sections provide an overview of hardware components and features that have been exploited in different scenarios to launch attacks or establish covert channels.

Simultaneous Multithreading

Simultaneous multithreading (SMT) is a technique to execute multiple threads in parallel on one processor core. Each stage in the instruction pipeline is thereby designed to serve more than one thread. This results in multiple instructions being executed from multiple threads in one clock cycle. SMT is for instance implemented in Intel (Intel Corporation, 2017) (named Hyper-threading) or AMD processors (Advanced Micro Devices, Inc., 2017). In literature, Percival (2005) exploits this technology to steal cryptographic keys via the L1 data cache. A spy and a victim process, the latter of which is generating digital signatures with RSA, run on the same core, but in different threads. Because of SMT, the spy is able to observe the cache concurrently to the victim and consequently to retrieve a significant fraction of the private exponent's bits. Acıiçmez and Seifert (2007) propose another method to steal cryptographic keys using Hyper-threading on Intel processors. The authors attack a square-and-multiply implementation of modular exponentiation that is used during RSA signature generation. As the large parallel integer multiplier of the arithmetic logic unit (ALU) is shared between the two hardware threads, a spy thread issuing and timing multiplication instructions can infer when the other thread is using the integer multiplication. An increase in time indicates that the hardware multiplier is used by the other thread. This is sufficient to retrieve the secret exponent and suggests that also other shared function units might be targets on processors implementing SMT.

Branch Prediction Unit

Instruction pipelines are used to increase the throughput of a processor by splitting up fetch, decode, execute, memory-access and write-back steps into several pipeline stages. As the pipeline fetches instructions sequentially, conditional branches force the pipeline to be flushed and loaded with the new target instructions. This is called a control hazard. The more stages a pipeline has, the bigger the impact is on the performance of the CPU. Speculative execution of instructions is a useful solution against control hazards. The main challenge is predicting the most likely execution path, i.e., the most likely outcome of a branch condition. This is handled by Branch Prediction Units (BPU), which are usually divided into two components: Branch Target Buffers (BTB) and the predictor. The BTB is a buffer that stores the addresses of the most recently processed branches, while the predictor is responsible for choosing the most likely path.

As BPUs are active for any process within the same core, the BTB has been targeted in microarchitectural attacks to infer secret branch conditions from a victim process. Since the BPU relies on a history of branches that have previously been taken, a malicious spy process can manipulate the predictions of the BPU by filling all entries of the BTB with own branch information. Any prediction for the targeted victim process will automatically result in a negative prediction, i.e., the branch will not be taken. If the prediction is correct (and the branch is indeed not taken), the victim process will be fast, as the pipeline stays filled. If a misprediction occurs (and the branch is taken), the pipeline is flushed and the victim process is slowed down. If this runtime difference can be observed, the actual (and possibly secret) value of the branch condition can be inferred.

Instead of measuring the runtime of the victim process, the spy process can also measure the execution time of its own branches. The spy therefore fills up the BTB again and lets the victim execute a conditional branch instruction. The spy then measures the time it takes to execute its own branches. If the victim actually took the branch, one of the spy's BTB entries has been replaced, which causes the runtime of the corresponding branch to increase due to a misprediction. If the victim process did not take the branch, the spy's branches are correctly predicted and no slow down occurs.

Both of the attack strategies described above have been proposed by Acıiçmez, Koç, and Seifert (2006; 2007). In contrast to other microarchitectural targets, BPUs have one disadvantage in an attack, because they are core-private resources. Attacks are therefore only applicable, if spy and victim run on the same CPU core. In practice, this can only be assumed to be given in specific scenarios, such as when attacking a trusted execution environment (TEE). TEEs are protected runtime environments that are separated from the rest of the system, which is assumed to be untrusted. Despite the isolation, the untrusted operating system can typically determine the CPU affinity of TEE protected processes. As a consequence, it can schedule spy and victim (running in the TEE) on the same CPU core. Exploiting BPUs in this attack scenario has been proposed by Lee et al. (2016).

Out-of-Order Execution

Out-of-order execution relaxes the requirement that instructions are executed strictly sequentially and allows finishing an instruction while the processor still waits for the result of a previous one. A first discussion of out-of-order execution in the context of timing based attacks is given by Coppens, Verbauwhede, Bosschere, and Sutter (2009). D'Antoine (2015) demonstrates an out-of-order execution based covert channel between two virtual machines separated by a hypervisor. To construct the channel, two threads execute interdependent load and store operations in two variables (i.e. one thread stores the value loaded by the other one). If the threads run in parallel, three cases can occur: (i) both threads are executed in order and at the same time; (ii) both threads are executed in order but one is executed faster; (iii) or both threads execute out of order. Note that the result of the operations will be different for each of the cases. A covert channel can be established by transmitting a '0' with out-of-order execution and a '1' with in-order execution. A collaborator can enforce in-order execution by utilizing memory barrier instructions.

Performance Monitoring Unit

The performance monitoring unit (PMU) is a dedicated hardware component within a processor that counts a broad spectrum of low-level events related to code execution. It is typically realized in the form of a co-processor or a set of special-purpose registers that store the event counts. The selection of observable events is usually larger than the number of actual counters; hence, counters must be configured in advance. All events associated with a counter are recorded in parallel. As the PMU allows detailed insight into the state of the processor in real-time, it is a valuable tool for debugging applications and their performance. The list of available events consequently focuses on waiting periods (e.g. clock cycles the processor is stalled), memory or bus accesses (e.g. cache misses or DRAM requests), and other performance-critical metrics like branch prediction or TLB events.

The available details through the PMU can also be leveraged in microarchitectural attacks. In early work, Ammons, Ball, and Larus (1997) conduct a study in which the logical structure of hardware counters are explained to profile different benchmarks. Uhsadel, Georges, and Verbauwhede (2008) show that hardware performance counters can be used to mount cache attacks. By looking at the L1 and L2 data cache miss events it is possible to recover an AES key on AMD processors. Weaver, Terpstra, and Moore (2013) investigate x86 systems regarding event determinism and over-counts. They conclude that most events on their tested hardware suffer from non-determinism and over-counts. Bhattacharya and Mukhopadhyay (2015) show how to use branch prediction counters to recover a 1024-bit RSA key on Intel processors. In contrast, performance counters can also be used to detect cache attacks and evaluate software against them. Chiappetta, Savaş, and Yilmaz (2015) employ machine-learning techniques to detect a cache attack in real-time on an Intel processor. Zankl, Miller, Heyszl, and Sigl (2016) show that a wide selection of performance events related to memory accesses are applicable to evaluate cryptographic software with respect to cache attacks on ARM processors.

Security Critical Instructions

The instruction set defines all instructions that a processor can execute and that software may be composed of. While many types of instructions such as memory, logic or control flow operations are common, some instructions implement very specific functionality and are consequently available only on a selection of processors.

The x86 instruction set defines an instruction called `clflush`, which evicts a given memory address from the cache hierarchy of the processor and ensures that the next data fetch from this address will be served from DRAM. The `clflush` instruction is part of the Streaming SIMD Extensions 2 (SSE2), an instruction set extension that enables efficient single instruction, multiple data (SIMD) operations. If a processor does not feature SSE2, it can still implement just `clflush`. With the introduction of the ARMv8 processor architecture, ARM CPUs provide similar cache flush instructions. But unlike `clflush`, which is available to all privilege levels, access to cache flush instructions on ARM can be limited to privileged code.

Although cache flush instructions serve a valid purpose, e.g. executing self-modifying code, they also enable microarchitectural attacks targeting the memory hierarchy of the processor. Adversaries can determine the use of a memory address by flushing it from cache, reloading it after a certain waiting period, and measuring the time it takes to reload. This technique is called Flush+Reload and has been demonstrated on x86 by Yarom and Falkner (2014) as well as on ARM processors by Lipp, Gruss, Spreitzer, Maurice, and Mangard (2016). The use of a memory address can also be determined by only measuring the time it takes to execute a flush command. If the address is somewhere in the cache hierarchy, the flush instruction will take longer to complete. This has been demonstrated by Gruss, Maurice, Wagner, and Mangard (2016). If an adversary constantly flushes an address from cache, all accesses to it will be served from DRAM. This has been leveraged by Kim et al. (2014) to stress DRAM cells and flip bits in them. This forms the basis of so-called Rowhammer attacks. If `clflush` is not available, cache lines can still be evicted by filling the cache sets they are stored in. Although not as efficient, Gruss, Spreitzer, & Mangard (2015) demonstrate the feasibility of this approach and introduce Evict+Reload, a substitute attack for Flush+Reload that does not require a flush instruction.

Another x86 instruction investigated in literature is `rdseed`. It allows all privilege levels to retrieve random bits generated by the processor hardware. Due to the limited pool of entropy and the consequently low throughput of the instruction, a covert channel can be implemented. '0's and '1's are transmitted between two collaborating processes by exhaustively using `rdseed` or not using it at all. This has been demonstrated by Evtyushkin and Ponomarev (2016).

Instruction and Data Caches

The instruction cache, or I-cache, is responsible of storing instructions executed by the processor. While higher cache levels are often separated into instruction and data side, lower levels and especially the last-level cache are typically unified, mixing the storage of instructions and data. In literature, Acıiçmez (2007) demonstrates that instruction caches can be monitored to learn the execution flow of a target program. The author monitors the I-cache to observe square-and-multiply function calls in a modular exponentiation implementation of RSA. With the observations, it is possible to recover the secret RSA key. The attack works by evicting cache lines holding the target functions, which is achieved by filling their corresponding cache sets with dummy instructions. After a while, the dummy instructions are reloaded and their execution time is measured. If they still resided in I-cache, i.e., the target function was not called, the execution time is low. Acıiçmez and Schindler (2008) continue this work and target a windowed modular exponentiation implementation. The authors observe extra reduction steps in the Montgomery multiplication routine via the instruction cache. These extra reductions reveal sufficient bits of the private exponent to entirely recover it. This attack works despite the enabled base blinding countermeasure. Acıiçmez, Brumley, and Grabher (2010) further improve the recovery of secret exponents from I-cache observations of modular exponentiation implementations by using Hidden Markov Models (HMM) and vector quantization. With this new technique, the authors target a Digital Signature Algorithm (DSA) implementation and successfully recover a key in a practical scenario. Given that the I-cache leaks the execution flow, thorough evaluation of software can reveal code sections that may be exploited in an attack. Doychev, Feld, Köpf, Mauborgne, and Reineke (2013) propose a static code analysis tool that allows testing software against different cache based attacker models. Zankl, Heyszl, and Sigl (2017) propose a dynamic analysis tool to automatically scan implementations of modular exponentiation for instruction cache leaks. Their results show that despite previous attacks, several modern cryptographic libraries still employ unprotected implementations that are all potentially vulnerable to I-cache attacks.

Similar to instructions, data is cached in dedicated D-caches or unified cache levels. The handling of data and instructions in caches is very similar and follows the same fundamental principles in both cases. Consequently, most cache manipulation techniques apply to both instruction and data targets, or can be adopted with moderate effort. Although the following overview focuses on data cache attacks, the majority of approaches also affect the instruction side of the cache hierarchy. In early literature, Percival (2005) introduces a method to observe L1 data cache accesses. The author uses it to retrieve an RSA key by observing the execution of a sliding window modular exponentiation implementation. While monitoring function calls in the I-cache reveals a significant fraction of the key, observing the pre-computed multipliers in the D-cache allows recovering the entire key. The multipliers reside in an array that is spread over the data cache. Their location within the array directly reveals the bits of the secret exponent. This location information can be recovered with cache observations. While Percival relies on simultaneous multithreading, Neve and Seifert (2007) show that it is possible to exploit data cache observations also in single-threaded processors. The authors leverage the ability of a process to voluntarily yield its processor time to affect the scheduling of spy and victim threads. The authors apply this technique to attack an AES implementation using precomputed T-tables. These tables speed up the execution of AES in software, but introduce key-dependent memory accesses that can be observed in the data cache. With only 20 encryptions and a new attack method that targets the last encryption round, the authors are able to recover the entire AES key. Osvik, Shamir, and Tromer (2006) introduce two new attack strategies called Evict+Time and Prime+Probe, and apply them to the T-table based AES implementation used by the Linux kernel. Both strategies evict target cache lines by filling their corresponding cache sets with dummy data. For Evict+Time, the adversary encrypts a plaintext with AES, evicts one cache line storing T-table entries, re-encrypts the plaintext, and then measures whether the target cache line is cached again or not (i.e., was used or not). For Prime+Probe, all cache sets storing T-table parts are filled prior to encryption. After the encryption, the adversary checks which sets contain T-table data (i.e. were used during encryption). With Prime+Probe, the authors are able to recover an entire AES key with 300 encryptions. Brumley and Hakala (2009) present a new type of attack in which L1 data cache templates are used to recover an Elliptic Curve DSA (ECDSA) key. Similar to Acıiçmez et al. (2010), the authors apply HMM and vector quantization. Zhang, Juels, Reiter, and Ristenpart (2012) combine HMM with Support Vector Machines (SVM). In their work, two virtual machines (VMs) reside on the same core of a processor and share the L1 data and instruction cache. The victim VM performs ElGamal decryptions using a square-and-multiply based modular exponentiation implementation. The SVM is used to eliminate noise in the cache observations and to correctly classify square, multiplication, and modular reduction operations. The errors in the output sequence of the SVM are reduced with a HMM. With this approach, the authors are able to recover an ElGamal key across VM boundaries.

In 2011, Gullasch, Bangerter, and Krenn present the first last-level cache attack on AES. Although virtual address spaces of processes are separated, victim and spy can share the physical memory where the T-tables are stored. This is possible due to memory deduplication, a memory saving technique that maps identical copies of virtual memory to the same physical location. As soon as both spy and victim have mapped the T-tables to their respective virtual address spaces, only one copy will exist in RAM. The spy then uses the flush instruction `clflush` to evict parts of the T-tables from cache. Due to deduplication, this removes the parts also for the victim. The authors then exploit the Completely Fair Scheduler (CFS) under Linux to repeatedly preempt the victim and consequently control when it is running. The spy flushes T-table entries, lets the victim run for a certain time span, and checks whether the victim used the flushed entries. With this technique, the spy is able to retrieve the entire AES key without knowing plain- or ciphertext. A neural network is used in addition to reduce the noise in the cache observations. In contrast to Prime+Probe, this technique is not affected by address space layout randomization (ASLR). If necessary, cache observations can also be used to defeat ASLR both on kernel level, as demonstrated by Hund, Willems, and Holz (2013), and on user level, as illustrated by Gras, Razavi, Bosman, Bos, and Giuffrida (2017).

Based on the work by Gullasch et al. (2011), Yarom and Falkner (2014) present another last-level cache attack called Flush+Reload. The authors rely on memory deduplication between victim and spy, but do not require any manipulation of the CFS or any noise reduction using neural networks. They employ the technique to demonstrate the feasibility of recovering an RSA key from a square-and-multiply modular exponentiation implementation in native and multiple virtual machine based settings. The work of Yarom and Falkner significantly increased the popularity of the technique by Gullasch et al. (2011), hence Flush+Reload was subsequently studied in a variety of scenarios and the name is mainly used to refer to the general technique. In follow-up work, Benger, van de Pol, Smart, and Yarom (2014) present a Flush+Reload attack on an ECDSA implementation. With the help of a lattice based key recovery algorithm, the authors are able to recover the private key by observing ECDSA signatures. Irazoqui, İnci, Eisenbarth, and Sunar (2014) use Flush+Reload to recover an AES key across Xen and VMware based virtual machines. This work emphasizes the strength of the method in virtualized environments. By collecting 400,000 ciphertext timing pairs the last round key can be recovered. Zhang, Juels, Reiter, and Ristenpart (2014) use the Flush+Reload technique to detect the co-location of virtual machines on the same server hardware. The authors also demonstrate a cross-VM attack with which the spy can obtain the number of items in the victim's shopping cart while the victim is browsing an e-commerce site. Irazoqui, İnci, Eisenbarth, and Sunar (2015) use the Flush+Reload technique to implement a modified Lucky 13 attack on connections using Transport Layer Security (TLS). The original attack by AlFardan and Paterson (2013) exploits timing variances to recover the protected plaintext in TLS connections. Irazoqui et al. show that although TLS implementations were subsequently made constant-time, they are still vulnerable to cache observations, even across virtual machines. Gruss, Spreitzer, & Mangard (2015) propose template attacks using Flush+Reload. The idea is to profile the cache patterns of software for known inputs and store them in templates. As soon as an unknown input is processed, the adversary looks up the observed patterns and matches them with the templates to retrieve the most likely input. Eventually, hypervisors disabled memory deduplication to prevent Flush+Reload attacks between their virtual machines. While Prime+Probe does not require memory deduplication, its cache evictions are more complex to implement. In order to efficiently fill a cache set and subsequently evict all previously stored cache lines, it is mandatory to know how addresses in user space map to cache sets. As last-level caches on Intel processors derive the set number from the physical address, the adversary needs to know the conversion between virtual and physical addresses. As this information is often only accessible to privileged code, Irazoqui, Eisenbarth, and Sunar (2015b) and Liu, Yarom, Ge, Heiser, and Lee (2015) propose the use of so-called Huge Pages. While standard memory pages are typically a few kiB in size, Huge Pages can be up to several MiB. As the least significant bits of virtual and physical addresses are identical, Huge Pages reveal enough bits to derive the cache set number, even when only virtual addresses are available. While Irazoqui et al. (2015b) use this method to retrieve AES keys across virtual machine boundaries, Liu et al. (2015) recover ElGamal keys from a square-and-multiply modular exponentiation implementation across virtual machines. İnci, Gulmezoglu, Irazoqui, Eisenbarth, and Sunar (2015) apply the same technique on Amazon's EC2 cloud and demonstrate the viability of the method even on commercial cloud systems.

Attacks on data and instruction caches are not only practical in native desktop and server, or cloud computing scenarios. Oren, Kemerlis, Sethumadhavan, and Keromytis (2015) demonstrate that cache attacks can also be mounted from within the web browser. The attack code is hosted on a web server and executed remotely on each visiting client's machine. The attack is implemented in JavaScript and allows recovering the browsing activity of clients, even if a separate browser is used on the same machine in incognito mode. Recently, cache attack techniques have also been ported to mobile, i.e., ARM based systems. Lipp et al. (2016) demonstrate the general feasibility of Prime+Probe, Flush+Reload, and Evict+Reload on ARM application processors found in mobile phones. The authors show covert channels on several platforms, implement a full key recovery attack on AES, and spy on a program running in ARM TrustZone, a trusted execution environment that isolates sensitive applications.

Cache Internals

Caches provide significant execution speed-ups to applications and are therefore a vital part of the processor implementation. They operate transparently to user applications, which leaves little incentive for manufacturers to publicly document details of the cache implementations. Yet, attack techniques like Prime+Probe require detailed knowledge of the cache to efficiently evict data and instructions. Therefore, several publications have been dedicated to reverse-engineering cache implementation details.

On Intel processors, the last-level cache is separated into slices, each of which manages a part of the cache. The concept of slices allows to evenly distribute the load on the LLC and to reduce cache contentions. Evicting a cache line from a given cache set, however, now requires knowing which slice the set belongs to. This decision is implemented by a hash function that takes the physical address as input and returns the slice number as output. Note that this hash function is not equivalent to a cryptographic hash function. In literature, Irazoqui, Eisenbarth, and Sunar (2015c) reverse engineer this function for a total of six Intel desktop and server processors. The authors use an iterative approach where a large set of addresses is grouped according to their slice number by using memory access timing measurements. Once the addresses are grouped, the bits of the physical address influencing the slice selection can be determined. Maurice, Le Scouarnec, Neumann, Heen, and Francillon (2015) demonstrate a different method to reverse engineer the slice selection. The authors use performance counters to count accesses to each individual cache slice and thereby map physical addresses to the slices. After all addresses have been assigned a slice, the bits responsible for slice selection are recovered. The authors present results for 2-, 4-, and 8-core Intel desktop and server processors. Yarom, Ge, Liu, Lee, and Heiser (2015) propose yet another method to reverse engineer cache slice selection by comparing access times to cache sets from different processor cores. Given that each core is assigned a slice to which its access is faster than to any other slice, these measurements again allow assigning physical addresses to slices and subsequently recovering the slice selection. The authors finally present the slice selection of a 6-core Intel processor. Knowing the slice selection allows to implement efficient attacks in practice. İnci et al. (2015) use the method by Irazoqui et al. (2015c) to learn the slice selection of a 10-core Intel server processor found in Amazon's EC2 cloud. The authors then demonstrate co-location between virtual machines and recover a full RSA key across VM boundaries.

Another concept of improving cache performance is a cache bank. Each bank serves a part of each cache line and thereby enables accesses in parallel. Hence, if multiple accesses are made to the same cache line but to different offsets on that line, they can be fulfilled simultaneously. On the contrary, if multiple accesses are made to the same location on the cache line, only one access is served at a time and contentions occur. These so-called cache bank conflicts have been leveraged by Yarom, Genkin, and Heninger (2016) to construct a cache attack against a hardened fixed window exponentiation implementation that is normally immune to cache attacks. The implementation spreads the pre-computed multipliers over a set of cache lines, thus requiring that all lines are accessed when retrieving any of the multipliers. However, as each bank serves only a sub-set of multipliers, it is possible to artificially saturate a bank and subsequently distinguish between accesses to different multipliers. The authors implement this attack on an Intel processor with SMT and retrieve a full RSA key via the L1 data cache.

Cache Prefetching

Prefetching is a common mechanism in processor architectures that speeds up access to uncached instructions or data that are likely to be used by the processor. Cache prefetching can be triggered from hardware and software. Hardware based prefetching transparently detects memory at runtime that is possibly used next by the executed program. Software based prefetching is done by inspecting the code prior to execution and adding additional prefetch instructions. Both concepts can be exploited in microarchitectural attacks. Rebeiro and Mukhopadhyay (2015) present an analysis of sequential and arbitrary-stride prefetching in profiled cache timing attacks. The authors conclude that for block ciphers with smaller tables the leakage exploited in attacks is higher than for ciphers using larger tables. Gruss, Maurice, Fogh, Lipp, and Mangard (2016) demonstrate that prefetch instructions can be abused to retrieve address information of objects in memory. With their technique, the authors defeat address space layout randomization and bypass several execution prevention mechanisms.

Memory Bus

Traditional attacks on the cache hierarchy are often based on contentions in the cache. This concept can also be adapted to the memory bus of a processor, which introduces an entirely new microarchitectural attack vector. When two threads on two different processor cores operate on the same shared variable, race conditions can occur. Modifications of the variable by one thread might not be consistently and immediately visible to the other thread, as modifications might only affect core-private caches. In order to avoid any incoherency, atomic operations allow a thread to exclusively operate on a shared variable and essentially prevent that changes in the variable are visible half-way through. To implement atomic operations, lock prefixes are used to ensure that a shared variable is locked in cache until the thread has finished updating the value. These lock instructions work well, if the target data fits on one cache line. However, for data spanning more than one line, it is not possible to issue multiple lock instructions simultaneously. Instead, modern processors lock the memory bus temporarily to prevent the introduction of new race conditions. This bus locking slows down other users, which can be detected. Consequently, it can enable covert channels or serve as a preparation or extension to existing microarchitectural attacks.

In literature, Varadarajan, Zhang, Ristenpart, and Swift (2015), Xu, Wang, and Wu (2015), and İnci, Gulmezoglu, Eisenbarth, and Sunar (2016) exploit memory bus locking to detect co-residency in IaaS clouds by observing the performance degradation in HTTP queries to the victim. Allan, Brumley, Falkner, van de Pol, and Yarom (2016) use the technique as a side-channel attack amplifier, i.e., to obtain a higher resolution when performing cache attacks. Finally, İnci, Irazoqui, Eisenbarth, and Sunar (2016) and Zhang, Zhang, and Lee (2016) utilize memory bus locking effects as a Quality of Service (QoS) degradation mechanism in IaaS clouds.

DRAM and Rowhammer Attacks

Dynamic random-access memory (DRAM) is a high-density storage technology that provides large capacity volatile memories at low cost. It is commonly used as main memory on modern desktop, server, and embedded systems. A channel is the link between a DRAM module and the memory controller. Multiple DRAM modules can be mounted to the ranks, i.e. back and front, of a dual in-line memory module (DIMM). Synchronous DRAM, or SDRAM, modules feature a clock signal and are comprised of banks. Each bank stores a block of memory on a set of rows. While different banks can be accessed in parallel, only one row can be accessed per bank at a time. Typically, row buffers cache recently used rows in each bank. DRAMs periodically read and re-write stored data to preserve it. This is called memory refreshing and is done at a defined refresh rate as a background task. As bits are stored in the presence or absence of an electric charge, bits can corrupt if the charges vanish or leak. Refreshing therefore prevents the corruption of the stored data. If two addresses are physically adjacent, they share the same channel, DIMM, rank and bank. From the perspective of the processor, DRAM is an external memory with significantly slower access times compared to the cache. Apart from exploiting these timing differences, DRAM has also been targeted directly in attacks.

In literature, Kim et al. (2014) describe that due to the high density of DRAM memory, repeated accesses to the same row can corrupt data stored on adjacent rows. This is because the continuous access to a DRAM row increases the charge leak rate of adjacent rows. The refresh rate of DRAMs is therefore chosen such that a refresh occurs before a corruption takes place. However, if a malicious program generates repeated accesses to the same row, chances increase that adjacent rows leak their charges before a refresh occurs. While Kim et al. demonstrate the general feasibility of inducing bit flips in a wide range of available DRAM modules, Seaborn (2015) shows that this is also a security problem. The author publishes two exploits using DRAM bit flips to escape the Native Client (NaCl) sandbox and to gain elevated privileges on Linux. From there on, the technique gained more attention under the name of Rowhammer. So-called Rowhammer attacks have been demonstrated by Gruss, Maurice, and Mangard (2016) in JavaScript, by van der Veen et al. (2016) on mobile devices, and by Xiao, Zhang, Zhang, and Teodorescu (2016) on IaaS hypervisors. Bhattacharya and Mukhopadhyay (2016) demonstrate that also well-known fault attacks on cryptographic primitives can be mounted with Rowhammer. Pessl, Gruss, Maurice, Schwarz, and Mangard (2016) show that the access time differences introduced by the row buffers can be exploited to establish covert channels, even across virtual machine boundaries, or to infer information from running processes similar to Prime+Probe based attacks. The authors also provide methods to determine the mapping between memory addresses and channels, ranks, and banks.

Evolution of Microarchitectural Attack Scenarios

Early microarchitectural attacks focused on shared resources that are private to every processor core. The branch prediction unit (Acıiçmez et al., 2006) and core-private cache levels (Percival, 2005) have both successfully been exploited to launch attacks between processes sharing the same core. In scenarios where the adversary cannot influence the processor core affinity, the success of these attacks is considerably limited. While multiple processor cores became common among desktop, server, and embedded systems, literature increasingly focused on microarchitectural attack vectors that work cross-core. The last-level cache, which is shared among all cores, has emerged as a particularly popular target. About a decade after the first single-core cache attacks have been proposed, multiple new attack vectors were introduced. They can be grouped into attacks requiring shared memory between victim and spy as well as a memory deduplication mechanism (Yarom & Falkner, 2014; Gruss, Maurice, Wagner, & Mangard, 2016), and attacks working without these requirements (Irazoqui, Eisenbarth, & Sunar, 2015b; Liu et al., 2015; Maurice, Neumann, Heen, & Francillon, 2015). With the increasingly dense integration of resources on a single die, state of the art systems nowadays contain multiple processor sockets, each of which are comprised of multiple processor cores. If an adversary is not able to influence the processor socket affinity, even cross-core cache attacks have limited usability. In response, literature focused on resources shared across all sockets or mechanisms that have mutual effects between sockets. Cache coherency protocols ensure that memory can be used on any socket or shared between sockets without sacrificing coherency. Consequently, these protocols have been exploited to mount cross-CPU attacks (Irazoqui, Eisenbarth, & Sunar, 2015a; Lipp et al., 2016). Memory bus locking has been exploited to induce significant performance degradation across CPU sockets (Zhang et al., 2016). The row buffers of DRAM modules have been targeted in cross-CPU attacks (Pessl et al., 2016) and also Rowhammer based attacks are in general not CPU bound (Kim et al., 2014). The publications over the past decade show that hardware level processor attacks developed from single-core scenarios to complex multi-core and multi-CPU systems. As a result, these attacks continue to be a considerable threat on low- as well as high-end processing systems.

Power- and EM-Based Side-Channel Attacks

The field of power based side-channel attacks was introduced by Kocher (1996) and Kocher, Jaffe, and Jun (1999) almost two decades ago. Subsequently, Quisquater et al. (2001) and Gandolfi et al. (2001) illustrated the practicality of electromagnetic emanation based side-channels. With their seminal works, these authors showed that even if cryptographic algorithms are secure in theory, their implementations can still be attacked in practice. Before the introduction of side-channel attacks, the security of cryptographic algorithms was studied by assuming that adversaries have only black box access to a target device. As it turned out, this model is not sufficient in practice, because adversaries have also access to some internal state information which is leaked through side-channels. Over the past years, multiple attacks exploiting these side-channels have been proposed. The following paragraphs describe the steps required to perform successful attacks.

- **Measurements:** In the first step, the acquisition of one or more side-channel traces, which are discrete time series, is performed. The resulting traces represent physical properties of the device during execution such as the power consumption or electromagnetic field strength on a certain position.
- **Pre-Processing:** In the second step, the raw time series are improved for further analysis. This step is optional, but can significantly increase the success of the attack. During pre-processing, several techniques can be employed to reduce noise, to remove redundant information (by compressing data), to align traces, or to transform them into different representations (e.g. into frequency domain).
- **Analysis:** The analysis step extracts information from the acquired traces about the (secret) data that has been processed by the target device. Over time, multiple methods have been proposed, which can be categorized using two orthogonal criteria. The first one defines whether multiple side-channel traces are needed or whether a single trace is sufficient to perform an attack. The second criterion defines whether a training device is available to obtain the leakage characteristics (profiled) or whether the attack is based on assumptions regarding the leakage characteristics (not profiled).

Table 1 shows the four possible combinations of these criteria. The most basic analysis methods are the simple power analysis (SPA) and its electromagnetic counterpart SEMA, which only require one side-channel trace and do not require profiling. The common way to perform such a simple analysis is to

Table 1. Side-channel attack classification according to trace acquisition and device profiling

	Single Measurement	**Multiple Measurements**
Not Profiled	Simple Analysis (SPA, SEMA)	Differential Analysis (DPA, DEMA, CPA, MIA, KSA)
Profiled	Template Attacks (TA)	Stochastic Approach (SA)

visually inspect a plotted trace. The goal is to find patterns in the trace caused by conditional branches that depend on a processed secret. These attacks work well with computations on large numbers as used by public key cryptography.

The differential analysis methods exploit statistics of multiple side-channel traces. They do not necessarily require a profiling step and use leakage assumptions based on hypothetical internal values that are related to a processed secret. An adversary simply guesses part of the secret and compares the corresponding leakage assumptions with the observed side-channel trace. The comparison is done using statistical methods, which are referred to as distinguishers in side-channel literature. Extensions to the initial differential methods (DPA, DEMA) are based on Pearson correlation (CPA) (Brier, Clavier, & Olivier, 2004), mutual information (MIA) (Batina et al., 2010), and the Kolmogorov-Smirnov test (KSA) (Whitnall, Oswald, & Mather, 2011). Attacks with a profiling step are based on the assumption that the leakage characteristics of different devices of the same type are similar. An adversary can therefore learn the leakage characteristics of a training device and then use them to attack the target device. The first profiled attack was the template attack (TA) (Chari, Rao, & Rohatgi, 2003). This method is based on multivariate Gaussian models for all possible parts of the secret. Template attacks can recover secrets with only one side-channel trace after proper characterization of a training device. The stochastic approach (SA) (Schindler, Lemke, & Paar, 2005; Kasper, Schindler, & Stöttinger, 2010) approximates the leakage function of the device using a linear model. The subsequent secret extraction can be performed with various methods. For example, Schindler et al. (2005) use the maximum likelihood principle. The linear model parameters can also be used to identify leakage sources in a design as described by De Santis et al. (2013).

Combined Attacks

In the traditional threat model of microarchitectural attacks an adversary can either be external, e.g. interacting with the target system over the network, or internal, e.g. executing code on the target system. Physical proximity to the target is typically not required. In contrast, power and EM based side-channel attacks require access to the target system in order to measure its power consumption or electromagnetic emanation. Combined attacks leverage both microarchitectural and power/EM based side-channel aspects. They capture the power consumption or EM emanation of a device and infer the microarchitectural activity from the measurements. As such they require physical proximity, but allow for both internal and external microarchitectural adversaries. In literature, the combination of microarchitectural and power/ EM based side-channels has been studied from both sides of the spectrum. On the one side, attacks have been proposed that recover the sequence or occurrence of cache hit and miss events in the power profile and infer secrets from this cache activity. On the other side, leakage characteristics of instructions and functional units have been investigated to infer processed secrets from power and EM traces. Both of these aspects of combined attacks are briefly described in the following paragraphs.

- **Cache Event Detection:** Bertoni, Zaccaria, Breveglieri, Monchiero, and Palermo (2005) propose a combined attack on an AES software implementation, in which the adversary is able to measure the power consumption of the target device. The attacker implements a strategy similar to Evict+Time: encrypt a plaintext, execute code on the device that evicts one cache line of the AES S-box, and encrypt the previous plaintext again. In contrast to the original Evict+Time attack, the adversary monitors the power consumption of the second encryption. If a cache miss is visible, then the current key relied on the evicted line to encrypt the given plaintext. This knowledge enables the adversary to infer the key. With the help of a power consumption simulation, the authors demonstrate that a cache miss has a distinct power profile that is different from cache hits. Lauradoux (2005) also proposes a combined attack on an AES software implementation. In contrast to Bertoni et al., the author describes a chosen-plaintext attack in which the adversary modifies the plaintext and observes the corresponding sequence of cache hits and misses in the power consumption measurement. Lauradoux also argues that hits and misses have distinct power consumption profiles, but does not execute the attack on an actual processor. Poddar, Datta, and Rebeiro (2011) propose a similar combined attack on a software implementation of CAMELLIA. The authors demonstrate that their chosen-plaintext attack successfully recovers the secret key after monitoring around 214 encryptions. Rebeiro and Mukhopadhyay (2011) propose a combined attack on a CLEFIA software implementation. The authors demonstrate that their chosen-plaintext attack can reliably recover the secret key after observing the sequences of cache hits and misses of 217 encryptions. Gallais, Kizhvatov, and Tunstall (2011) propose multiple combined attacks on an AES software implementation. The authors observe sequences of cache hits and misses in the power consumption measurements while conducting known- and chosen-plaintext attacks. With a key recovery algorithm that is tolerant to wrong observations of cache hits and misses, the authors are able to recover the full key with approximately 30 encryptions.

- **Data-Path Leakage:** The utilization of functional units in the data-path of microarchitectures by certain code sequences highly influences the observable power or electromagnetic leakage of the devices. Especially for resource-constrained microcontrollers like Atmel AVR or ARM Cortex-M, the knowledge about leakage characteristics is important when it comes to the secure implementation of cryptographic algorithms. Due to the deterministic execution of code on these devices, extracting keys from implementations by using power or EM based side-channel attacks is a feasible task. Therefore, proper side-channel countermeasures are essential in many cases. However, also the effectiveness of countermeasures is adversely affected by the leakage characteristics of the data path. This leakage can be described by a leakage function $L_\theta(\cdot) = L_{\theta,d}(\cdot) + N_\theta$, which is composed of a deterministic part $L_{\theta,d}(\cdot)$ and a noise part N_θ. Following Balasch, Gierlichs, Grosso, Reparaz, and Standaert (2014), the deterministic part can be categorized, among other criteria, in value based leakage functions and transition based leakage functions. Value based leakage means that processed values are leaked directly by the device. Therefore, the leakage function takes $v \in V$ from the set of processed values V. For transition based leakage, two values are exposed in a combined way which is modeled by a function that takes a transition between two values $t \in T$, where $T = \{v \oplus v' \mid v, v' \in V\}$. The authors also give an explanation to which extent masking countermeasures are weakened by wrong assumptions about the leakage characteristics. They show by theoretical reasoning and experimental confirmation that masking countermeasures claiming d^{th}-order security under value based leakage degenerate to $d/2^{th}$-order security. Depending on the executed code, the leakage of a device is either value based and/or transition based. Seuschek, De Santis, and Guillen (2017) show that if the transition based leakage can be prevented for certain combinations of computed values, it is possible to preserve the security level of a masking countermeasure. In order to achieve this goal, the authors analyze the typical high-level leakage patterns of an ARM Cortex-M0 processor by leveraging assumptions about the microarchitecture combined with results from an EM analysis. The authors demonstrate that ALU instructions leak combined values from consecutive instructions. In contrast, memory access instructions have more complex leakage characteristics and the contribution to leakage is many times higher than for typical ALU instructions. The store instruction, for example, has the special property that it influences the leakage of several following instructions. Although these leakage characteristics describe high level phenomena for ARM Cortex-M0, the results are not necessarily restricted to this particular processor and might also be found on similar architectures. The gained knowledge about the leakage can be used by compilers to schedule the instructions in a way that the resulting leakage is reduced, and the effectiveness of implemented countermeasures is preserved.

Although powerful, combined attacks exhibit a main difference compared to traditional microarchitectural attacks: they require physical proximity to the target system. While this has long been considered to render combined attacks less practical, the perception is starting to change with the introduction of the Internet of Things, in which physical proximity to target devices is becoming increasingly realistic.

Other Physical Attacks

In literature, several attacks have been proposed that exploit the physical properties of processor implementations. Kong, John, Chung, Chung, and Hu (2010) present a thermal attack on the instruction cache. The authors show that I-caches are often neglected in on-chip thermal management and are therefore vulnerable to thermal attacks. With a malicious program, they practically demonstrate that it is possible to overheat the instruction cache, which may lead to malfunction and reliability problems. Masti et al. (2015) exploit the heat development of Intel Xeon processors to build a covert channel. By stressing a processing core and subsequently increasing its temperature, a process can communicate information to any other process on the system that has access to the processor's temperature information. The channel provides a throughput of 12.5 bits per second. Another attack vector is investigated by Riviere et al. (2015). The authors study electromagnetic fault injection (EMFI) and its effects on the instruction cache and control flow using an ARMv7-M platform. They conclude that faults can be injected with high control and reliability, and that cryptographic implementations secured against previous fault attacks would still be vulnerable to the proposed EMFI attack vector. Rathi, De, Naeimi, and Ghosh (2016) demonstrate physical attacks on so-called Spin-Transfer Torque RAMs (STTRAM), a promising new technology for cache implementations. The authors study external magnetic field and temperature attacks on STTRAMs and propose corresponding mitigation techniques including stalling the processor or bypassing caches while under attack. Furthermore, they identify a power consumption based side-channel that allows inferring information about cached data that is read or written.

CHALLENGING THE SECURITY OF IoT DEVICES

Microarchitectural as well as power and EM based side-channel attacks are fundamental attack vectors that an adversary can leverage to compromise an IoT device. The following section illustrates how some of these attacks threaten security measures that are integrated into modern processors.

Trusted Execution Environments

A trusted execution environment (TEE) is a security feature that provides enhanced isolation of security-critical applications within an untrusted operating system (often called Rich OS). The main goals are ensuring confidentiality and integrity of executed code and processed data. Applications running within TEEs are typically smaller in scope than operating systems, but offer more functionality than secure elements (SE). TEE software can leverage the full computational power of the processor while still profiting from a high level of isolation from the rest of the system. Figure 3 shows a comparison of a typical TEE to a full-scale embedded operating system and a secure element. The operating system offers basic software-level protection and separation mechanisms, but has its focus on functionality. For wide-spread mobile operating systems such as Android, software exploits are found on a regular basis (The MITRE Corporation, 2016). The TEE adds an isolation and protection layer that is rooted in hardware to effectively separate software on the processor. Exploits in the Rich OS do not automatically compromise applications running in the TEE. A secure element offers further protection by outsourcing applications onto separate, tamper-resistant hardware. SEs physically isolate software from the rest of the system. This offers the highest level of protection, but also reduces the computational resources available to the software. TEEs are a hybrid model between an operating system and a secure element that offers hardware-backed isolation while still maintaining access to most of the processors computational resources.

Standardization efforts regarding trusted execution environments have mainly been driven by GlobalPlatform (2016a), a non-profit organization working on facilitating the secure and interoperable deployment and management of multiple embedded applications on secure chip technology.

Figure 3. Comparison of a trusted execution environment to an operating system and a secure element

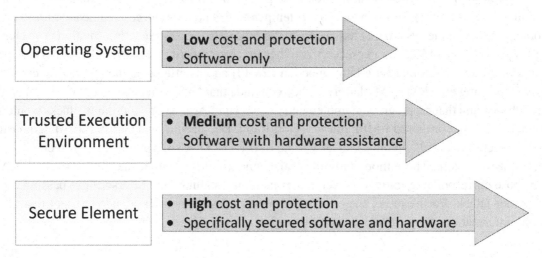

Multiple industry partners and government bodies are taking part in these standardization efforts, which are mainly motivated by content protection, mobile payment, authentication and BYOD (bring-your-own-device) applications (GlobalPlatform, 2016a, 2016b). Despite this standardization process, several proprietary solutions have been established in industry. Due to its wide-spread application to IoT devices, this section focuses in particular on ARM TrustZone.

The main concept of ARM TrustZone is that any part of the system can either operate in a Secure, i.e. trusted, or a Normal, i.e. untrusted, world (ARM, 2009). The separation of the two worlds affects the fabric of the processor in different ways. First, all available hardware resources, e.g. peripherals, can be attributed to one of the two worlds. This hardware level separation is enforced by the AMBA AXI bus and works in a one-way fashion. Normal world resources cannot access components belonging to the Secure world, but trusted resources in the Secure world can access any component of the system. Second, the separation in two worlds also affects code execution. In order to run Secure and Normal world applications side-by-side, ARM processors implement the so-called security extensions (ARM, 2009). They essentially allow each component of the processor to switch between both worlds in a time-sliced fashion, hence removing the need for separate hardware to execute Secure world code. Third, the separation also affects the debug interface, which can be configured independently for both worlds, e.g. allowing debug access for the Normal world but blocking it for the Secure one. In order to switch between Secure and Normal world execution, a monitor mode must be entered. This can be achieved from the Normal world with an interrupt, an external abort or a direct call using the Secure Monitor Call (SMC) instruction. The software running in monitor mode is supposed to perform the transition between the two worlds. It saves and restores processing states, and exclusively controls the Not Secure bit (NS- bit) of the Secure Configuration Register (SCR) in co-processor 15. At all times, the NS-bit signals whether the processor currently operates in the Normal or Secure world. For instance, the memory management unit (MMU) keeps mappings for both worlds and selects the right one depending on the NS-bit. Translation lookaside buffer (TLB) entries of both worlds can be tagged with the NS-bit and can therefore co-exist simultaneously in the TLB. This removes the need for a TLB flush when transitioning between the worlds. Similarly, cache entries can be tagged with the NS-bit, thus allowing cache lines of both worlds to reside in the caches at the same time. This removes the need for a cache flush when switching between worlds. Note that there is no separation enforced regarding TLB or cache evictions. Normal world entries in both buffers are allowed to evict Secure world entries and vice versa. Furthermore, Secure world code can directly access Normal world data from any cache level, a concept described by ARM as World-shared memory (ARM, 2009).

The weak separation of Normal and Secure world in the processor cache and particularly the ability of Normal world applications to evict cache lines belonging to Secure world processes enable the execution of cache attacks. Guanciale, Nemati, Baumann, and Dam (2016) describe a scenario in which the adversary has compromised the Rich OS kernel space and launches the attack proposed by Neve and Seifert (2007) on an application performing AES encryptions within the TrustZone. The idea behind the attack is to create a so-called memory alias: two virtual address pointers that point to the same physical address but have different cacheability attributes. As the adversary controls the kernel of the Rich OS, it is possible to create a set of cacheable virtual addresses $VA_{c,i}$ that map to the physical addresses PA_i residing in cache sets i. These sets contain the cache lines that store the AES T-tables within the TrustZone. In addition, a set of non-cacheable virtual addresses $VA_{nc,i}$ is created that points to the same set of physical addresses. The adversary then invalidates all virtual addresses $VA_{c,i}$, writes '0's to all addresses $VA_{nc,i}$ and reads all addresses $VA_{c,i}$. Since addresses $VA_{nc,i}$ are non-cacheable, the '0's are written directly to physical memory and brought into cache after invalidating and reading all addresses $VA_{c,i}$. Now that all cached values of $VA_{c,i}$ are zero, the adversary writes '1's to all addresses $VA_{nc,i}$. While the cache contains '0's, the physical memory now contains all '1's. Then an encryption is requested from the TrustZone application, which depending on the secret key brings new lines into some of the i sets. These lines will evict the lines corresponding to addresses $VA_{c,i}$. After the encryption, the adversary reads all addresses $VA_{c,i}$. Reading a '0' indicates that the cache value has been read and therefore that the corresponding cache set has not been used by the TrustZone application. Reading a '1' indicates that the physical memory value has been read and therefore that the corresponding cache set has been used by the TrustZone application. Using this attack strategy, the authors are able to extract the secret AES key after less than 850 observed encryptions on an ARM Cortex-A7 processor.

Zhang, Sun, Shands, Lou, and Hou (2016) propose another cache attack on ARM TrustZone. An application within the TrustZone is again offering an AES encryption service to the Rich OS. The authors describe how the Prime+Probe attack by Osvik et al. (2006) can be launched from a compromised Rich OS kernel as well as from a malicious user-space application. The main advantage for a kernel based attack is that virtual-to-physical address mappings and high precision timers are readily available. During the prime step, the entire cache hierarchy is filled with data from the adversary in order to evict all cache lines belonging to the Secure world. Then, the entire cache is cleaned and invalidated with cache maintenance operations, which are only available to privileged code. Note that cache maintenance operations only affect the corresponding world, i.e., the Rich OS kernel cannot clean and invalidate lines from the Secure world. Hence, the cache is initially filled with Rich OS data. After the entire cache has been cleaned and invalidated, the L1 data cache is filled with the actual data of the prime step. After the encryption, the adversary probes all L1 data cache sets and measures the probing times using the cycle count register `PMCCNTR`, which by default is only accessible from privileged code. If the adversary has only compromised a Rich OS user-space application, memory mappings and high precision timers are not necessarily available. To obtain a prime and probe memory set, the authors suggest allocating a large chunk of memory and selecting appropriate pages by observing the AES encryption pattern through access timing measurements of the page. Alternatively, a kernel function with known physical offset can be invoked repeatedly and its impact on a selected page can be measured through access times. This way, the physical address offset of the selected page can be determined. To replace the high precision clock cycle counter, the `perf` subsystem of the Linux kernel is used via the `perf_event_open` system call. Even though the acquired clock cycle event is significantly noisier than read-outs from the `PMCCNTR`, the authors manage to distinguish between cache hit and reload from memory by enhancing the noisy measurements with the original timing population mean of the `PMCCNTR` readings. The authors assume that this mean can be obtained from datasheets or test devices. The final attack that is executed by Zhang et al. is based on the work by Irazoqui, İnci, Eisenbarth, and Sunar (2014). With the attack launched from the Rich OS kernel, the authors are able to extract the secret AES key from the TrustZone application with 3,000 encryptions. The attack from the Rich OS user-space takes 9,000 encryptions. The hardware used to perform the attacks is an ARM Cortex-A8.

Lipp et al. (2016) use the Prime+Probe technique to attack the TrustZone based key storage on Android mobile phones. The authors are able to use cache observations and requests to the application running in the TrustZone to learn whether a given RSA key is valid, i.e., stored in the TrustZone based key storage. This is possible, because the cache profiles for valid (i.e. stored) and invalid (i.e. not stored) keys are different and thus observable by an adversary. Brumley (2015) describes a cache storage attack that retrieves information leaking from the TEE to the Rich OS. The approach differs from others, as it requires that the Rich OS can directly access data on cache lines. To achieve this, the author describes two debug operations that can be performed via the co-processor 15. Since access to these operations is restricted to privileged code, the attack has to be launched from the Rich OS kernel space. The attack itself is based on the work by Neve and Seifert (2007), who target an AES implementation using T-tables. In the first step of Brumley's attack, the adversary pollutes all cache sets corresponding to the AES T-tables with its own data. Again, this is possible, because the cache allows evictions from both worlds. The adversary then triggers an encryption that is executed within the TEE, which replaces some of the previously placed data. By systematically reading the content of the cache lines in the AES related sets, the adversary will at some point access a line that is part of the TEE, i.e. having the NS-bit set to '0'. This causes a processor exception due to a security policy violation, because the content of Secure world cache lines cannot be read from the Normal world. By detecting the exception, the adversary knows that the accessed line corresponds to T-table data from within the TEE. By systematically probing all entries of the T-tables, the adversary can infer the secret key used during encryption. However, the attack is not demonstrated in practice by the author.

Attacks on trusted execution environments often assume that the operating system is compromised. This gives an adversary full control over virtual-to-physical address mappings, high precision timers, and process scheduling. The control over the scheduler enables the attacker to dictate when and on which processor core the TEE application is running. This essentially re-enables microarchitectural attacks that only work in a single-core scenario. Lee et al. (2016) demonstrate such an attack using the TEE technology Software Guard Extensions (SGX) that is implemented on Intel processors from the Skylake microarchitecture onwards (Schunter, 2016). The authors exploit the core-private branch prediction unit to infer the control flow of SGX applications. This is possible, because the branch history is not cleared upon switching between SGX and untrusted programs. Together with previous attacks on ARM TrustZone, this shows that commercially available trusted execution environments still fail to properly isolate applications on the microarchitectural level.

Instruction Set Extensions

With the rapid spread of cryptographic applications, many modern processors started to integrate extensions to their instruction set that speed up the execution of cryptographic ciphers. The AES New Instructions (AES-NI) extension, for instance, accelerates AES on x86 hardware. In particular, the AESENC and AESDEC instructions implement one en- respectively decryption round of the cipher. AESENCLAST and AESDECLAST implement the corresponding last rounds, which are treated differently in the cipher. AESKEYGENASSIST can be used to generate the round keys required for encryption. If it is combined with AESIMC, the decryption round keys are derived. Another instruction facilitating cryptographic operations is PCLMULDQ. It is used to speed up carry-less polynomial multiplications, as needed by the Galois Counter Mode (GCM), a block cipher mode of operation (Gueron, 2009). Next to a significant performance improvement, the AES-NI extension allows implementations to run in constant-time without exhibiting key-dependent execution flow or key-dependent memory accesses. This essentially eliminates the cache based attack vector used in literature to recover the secret AES key from side-channel observations (Osvik et al., 2006). However, Saab, Rohatgi, and Hampel (2016) demonstrate an EM based side-channel attack against AES-NI. The authors describe a measurement setup targeting an Intel Core i7 Ivy Bridge processor. It runs a full-scale Ubuntu operating system and an AES-NI implementation of AES-256 in cipher-block-chaining (CBC) mode. By measuring less than 1.5 million EM traces the authors are able to clearly identify a Hamming distance leak between two consecutive round states generated with `AESENC` instructions. The authors then describe a way how the detected leakage can be used to recover the full AES key. Similar results have been obtained by Longo, Mulder, Page, and Tunstall (2015). The authors investigate the EM side-channel leakage of three different AES implementations on an ARM Cortex-A8 processor. One of the implementations is using the ARM NEON instruction set extensions, a single instruction, multiple data (SIMD) extension originally intended for media and signal processing applications. The wide registers of the NEON co-processor are used to realize a bit-sliced implementation of AES, which processes multiple AES operations bit by bit in parallel. Although the employed implementation is constant-time and performs no data-dependent branches or table lookups (Käsper & Schwabe, 2009), Longo et al. still manage to successfully extract the secret AES key from approximately 5,000 EM side-channel traces. The ARMv8 instruction set architecture also offers extensions for the AES cipher (Gouvêa & López, 2015). The instruction `AESE` implements the add-round-key, sub-bytes and shift-rows operations, while the mix-column step can be performed separately with `AESMC`. The instructions `AESD` and `AESIMC` implement the same functionality for AES decryption. Polynomial multiplications are accelerated with `PMULL` and `PMULL2` instructions. In addition, and in contrast to the AES-NI extension, ARMv8 also offers instructions to accelerate the Secure Hash Algorithm (SHA), in particular SHA-1 and SHA-256. For these ARMv8 instruction set extensions, literature still lacks a comprehensive power or EM based side-channel evaluation. Further instruction set extensions enabling speed ups of AES are proposed by Tillich and Großschädl (2006), Kocabaş, Savaş, and Großschädl (2008), and Lee and Chen (2010).

Cryptographic Accelerators

Another way of protecting the execution of cryptographic ciphers on IoT devices is to outsource them to dedicated hardware. Since these accelerators are essentially the same hardware implementations that are also found in smart cards and microcontrollers, they are susceptible to the same power or EM based side-channel attacks that have been described in the State of the Art section. However, the location of the accelerator hardware with respect to the main processor is critical to an adversary. If an accelerator is placed outside of the processor package, an adversary can mount several attacks with lower effort compared to a power or EM based side-channel attack. If the communication between processor and accelerator is not protected, an adversary can sniff plain- and ciphertexts going back and forth on the bus. Also, an adversary can desolder the accelerator and use it for more advanced attacks, e.g., simulating a legitimate device or extracting keys with invasive methods. Consequently, if an accelerator is placed outside of the main processor's package, the communication channel must be thoroughly protected.

Cryptographic accelerators that are placed within the package of the main processor are still susceptible to power and EM based side-channel attacks. However, it has been unclear in the past, whether attacking an accelerator is feasible in this scenario because of the interferences from the processor and other components contained in the same package. While integrated cryptographic accelerators on microcontroller systems have been successfully attacked in the past (Heinz, Heyszl, & Stumpf, 2014), Longo et al. (2015) have been the first to show that attacks are also feasible on full-scale application processors running in the gigahertz range. In their work, the authors target an ARM Cortex-A8 processor featuring an on-chip AES hardware accelerator. After acquiring 500,000 EM traces, the authors are able to successfully recover the AES key used by the accelerator. Nevertheless, the main challenges are finding a sufficiently precise trigger and an appropriate leakage model, since details about on-chip accelerators are often not publicly available.

DISCUSSION AND OUTLOOK

While the interconnection of smart devices offers great opportunities for businesses, governments, and consumers, it remains a substantial challenge to ensure the confidentiality of processed information and the privacy of users. One of the reasons is that current processor generations fail to securely execute critical software due to an overwhelming arsenal of microarchitectural performance enhancements. While commodity software significantly benefits from runtime optimizations and speed improvements at the hardware level, these performance enhancements have repeatedly been shown to compromise security critical applications. All that is required in most cases is one application or user with malicious intent. With an increasing complexity of IoT devices and backend services, the risk of introducing a malicious entity to the system has become significant. Example scenarios are customers sharing cloud servers, software developers contributing to app stores, or even closed systems that run applications with different protection levels and security requirements. Once an adversary manages to execute code on a device, it becomes feasible to exploit the microarchitecture of the processor. Literature provides a wide spectrum of attacks that, although initially studied on desktop and server systems, are ported to embedded processors step by step. As a result, microarchitectural attacks are a substantial risk to IoT devices in the field and servers in the back end.

Due to the ubiquitous deployment of IoT devices, getting physical access to a device has never been easier. While this generally enables hardware attacks like probing debug interfaces or sniffing on-board buses, it also facilitates side-channel attacks that leverage secret-dependent variations in the power consumption or electromagnetic emanation of the device. This type of attacks has been thoroughly studied in literature, although on much simpler processing devices such as smart cards or microcontroller. It has long been unclear whether power or EM based side-channel attacks can also be mounted on IoT devices that feature more powerful processing units. Recent literature indicates that even though these processors run in the gigahertz range and are accompanied by a large set of peripherals and on-chip components, side-channel attacks are still a viable threat. Even more so, the combination of microarchitectural attacks with power consumption or electromagnetic emanation traces enables new and powerful threat scenarios.

This leaves IoT devices in a unique and worrisome position, facing substantial threats from two well-studied areas of side-channel attack literature. Protection mechanisms are therefore of utmost importance. Critical developments in IoT security features comprise trusted execution environments, instruction set extensions for cryptographic operations, and standalone hardware accelerators for cryptographic ciphers. While all of these features add additional layers of security to the overall system, all of them have been shown to be vulnerable to either power/EM based or microarchitectural side-channel attacks. Trusted execution environments fail to provide sufficient isolation at the microarchitectural level and are vulnerable to traditional cache attacks. It is important to note that the reason is not a failure in the design but rather a conscious choice that was made in favor of performance (ARM, 2009). The direct consequence for a security engineer is to implement yet another protective layer (Kong, Acıiçmez, Seifert, & Zhou,

2013) to thwart cache based side-channel attacks or, if possible, to rely on more comprehensive TEE designs (Costan, Lebedev, & Devadas, 2016). As literature is just beginning to uncover the details of current IoT processor microarchitectures, more sophisticated attacks can be expected to be proposed. Especially critical system components such as TEEs have not yet seen a fully comprehensive analysis regarding microarchitectural attack vectors.

Instruction set extensions provide considerable speed-ups and at the same time enable developers to eliminate microarchitectural leakage. Today, a substantial number of x86 and ARM processors support the execution of AES in a way that is resistant to cache based attacks. However, only a very limited number of cryptographic algorithms and operations can be protected in such a way. And those algorithms that can be protected have been shown to be vulnerable to power and EM based side-channel attacks, even though they are executed on powerful application processors running in the gigahertz range. Standalone cryptographic accelerators find themselves in a similar situation. While they typically support a broader range of cryptographic algorithms and offer better separation from the main processor, they also have been shown to be vulnerable to power and EM based side-channel attacks, even when located within the processor package. This clearly suggests that on-chip hardware accelerators, whether part of the instruction set or not, must thoroughly be protected against side-channel attacks.

The consequence of the successful attacks on instruction set extensions and hardware accelerators is to target the power and EM based leakage of the main processing unit itself. Recently, Unterluggauer and Mangard (2016) demonstrated a differential power analysis attack on the disk encryption of an ARM Cortex-A9. The AES encryption algorithm ran entirely in software, as part of the Linux operating system kernel, and leveraged the full computational power of the processor. This attack illustrates that the complexity of application processors is no longer an obstacle for power and EM based side-channel attacks. As the quality of these attacks on IoT devices improves and as the understanding of their microarchitecture deepens, combined attacks might add an entirely new dimension to the threats that IoT devices are facing at the moment. After all, this field remains largely uninvestigated today. And as attacks are becoming more sophisticated, the need for systematic countermeasures is going to grow accordingly. Unlike before, however, their effectiveness and success will be measured by how well they will defend against both microarchitectural as well as power and EM based side-channel attacks.

REFERENCES

Acıiçmez, O. (2007). Yet another microarchitectural attack: Exploiting i-cache. In *Proceedings of the 2007 acm workshop on computer security architecture* (pp. 11–18). ACM. doi:10.1145/1314466.1314469

Acıiçmez, O., Brumley, B. B., & Grabher, P. (2010). *New Results on Instruction Cache Attacks* (Vol. 6225, pp. 110–124). Ches.

Acıiçmez, O., & Koç, Ç. K. (2009). In Ç. K. Koç (Ed.), *Cryptographic engineering* (pp. 475–504). Boston, MA: Springer US. doi:10.1007/978-0-387-71817-0_18

Acıiçmez, O., Koç, Ç. K., & Seifert, J.-P. (2006). Predicting secret keys via branch prediction. In M. Abe (Ed.), *Topics in cryptology – CT-RSA 2007* (Vol. 4377, pp. 225–242). Springer Berlin Heidelberg. doi:10.1007/11967668_15

Acıiçmez, O., Koç, Ç. K., & Seifert, J.-P. (2007). On the power of simple branch prediction analysis. In *Proceedings of the 2nd acm symposium on information, computer and communications security* (pp. 312–320). New York, NY, USA: ACM.

Acıiçmez, O., & Schindler, W. (2008). A vulnerability in rsa implementations due to instruction cache analysis and its demonstration on openssl. In *Topics in cryptology– ct-rsa 2008* (pp. 256–273). Springer. doi:10.1007/978-3-540-79263-5_16

Acıiçmez, O., & Seifert, J.-P. (2007). Cheap hardware parallelism implies cheap security. In Fault diagnosis and tolerance in cryptography, 2007. fdtc 2007. workshop on (pp.80–91). doi:10.1109/FDTC.2007.16

Advanced Micro Devices, Inc. (2017). *The "Zen" Core Architecture.* Retrieved from https://www.amd.com/en-gb/innovations/software-technologies/zen-cpu

AlFardan, N. J., & Paterson, K. G. (2013). Lucky thirteen: Breaking the TLS and DTLS record protocols. In *Proceedings of the 2013 IEEE symposium on security and privacy* (pp. 526–540).

Allan, T., Brumley, B. B., Falkner, K., van de Pol, J., & Yarom, Y. (2016, December). Amplifying side channels through performance degradation. In *Proceedings of the Annual computer security applications conference,* Los Angeles, CA. doi:10.1145/2991079.2991084

Ammons, G., Ball, T., & Larus, J. R. (1997). Exploiting hardware performance counters with flow and context sensitive profiling. *ACM Sigplan Notices, 32*(5), 85–96. doi:10.1145/258916.258924

ARM. (2009, April). *ARM Security Technology - Building a Secure System using Trust- Zone Technology.* Retrieved from http://infocenter.arm.com/help/topic/ com.arm.doc.prd29-genc-009492c/PRD29-GENC-009492C_trustzone_security_whitepaper.pdf

Balasch, J., Gierlichs, B., Grosso, V., Reparaz, O., & Standaert, F.-X. (2014, June 2). *On the Cost of Lazy Engineering for Masked Software Implementations.* Cryptology ePrint Archive, Report 2014/413. Retrieved from http://eprint.iacr.org

Batina, L., Gierlichs, B., Prouff, E., Rivain, M., Standaert, F.-X., & Veyrat-Charvillon, N. (2010, October 21). Mutual Information Analysis: A Comprehensive Study. *Journal of Cryptology,* 1–23.

Benger, N., van de Pol, J., Smart, N. P., & Yarom, Y. (2014). "ooh aah... just a little bit": A small amount of side channel can go a long way. In *Proceedings of the International workshop on cryptographic hardware and embedded systems* (pp. 75–92).

Bertoni, G., Zaccaria, V., Breveglieri, L., Monchiero, M., & Palermo, G. (2005). Aes power attack based on induced cache miss and countermeasure. In *Proceedings of the international conference on information technology: Coding and computing (itcc'05)* (Vol. 1, pp. 586–591). Washington, DC, USA: IEEE Computer Society. doi:10.1109/ITCC.2005.62

Bhattacharya, S., & Mukhopadhyay, D. (2015). Who watches the watchmen?: Utilizing performance monitors for compromising keys of rsa on intel platforms. In *Proceedings of the International workshop on cryptographic hardware and embedded systems* (pp. 248–266). doi:10.1007/978-3-662-48324-4_13

Bhattacharya, S., & Mukhopadhyay, D. (2016). Curious case of rowhammer: Flipping secret exponent bits using timing analysis. In B. Gierlichs & A. Y. Poschmann (Eds.), *Cryptographic hardware and embedded systems – CHES 2016* (pp. 602–624). Berlin, Heidelberg: Springer Berlin Heidelberg.

Brier, E., Clavier, C., & Olivier, F. (2004). Correlation Power Analysis with a Leakage Model. In M. Joye & J.-J. Quisquater (Eds.), *Cryptographic hardware and embedded systems - CHES 2004* (Vol. 3156, pp. 16–29). Springer Berlin Heidelberg. doi:10.1007/978-3-540-28632-5_2

Brumley, B. B. (2015). Cache storage attacks. In K. Nyberg (Ed.), *Topics in cryptology— CT-RSA 2015* (Vol. 9048, pp. 22–34). Springer International Publishing.

Brumley, B. B., & Hakala, R. M. (2009). Cache-timing template attacks. In *Proceedings of the International conference on the theory and application of cryptology and information security* (pp.667–684).

Chari, S., Rao, J. R., & Rohatgi, P. (2003). Template Attacks. In Kaliski B.S., Koç. K., Paar C. (Eds.) Cryptographic Hardware and Embedded Systems - CHES 2002. CHES 2002. Lecture Notes in Computer Science, 2523. Berlin, Heidelberg: Springer Berlin Heidelberg.

Chiappetta, M., Savaş, E., & Yilmaz, C. (2015). *Real time detection of cache-based side- channel attacks using hardware performance counters* (Tech. Rep.). Cryptology ePrint Archive, Report 2015/1034. Retrieved from http://eprint.iacr.org

Coppens, B., Verbauwhede, I., Bosschere, K. D., & Sutter, B. D. (2009). Practical mitigations for timing-based side-channel attacks on modern x86 processors. In *Proceedings of the 2009 30th IEEE symposium on security and privacy* (pp. 45–60). Washington, DC, USA: IEEE Computer Society. doi:10.1109/SP.2009.19

Costan, V., Lebedev, I., & Devadas, S. (2016, August). Sanctum: Minimal hardware extensions for strong software isolation. In *Proceedings of the 25th USENIX Security Symposium* (pp. 857–874). Austin, TX: USENIX Association.

D'Antoine, S. (2015, Aug). *Exploiting out of order execution for covert cross vm communication.* Las Vegas: Blackhat.

De Santis, F., Kasper, M., Mangard, S., Sigl, G., Stein, O., & Stöttinger, M. (2013). On the Relationship between Correlation Power Analysis and the Stochastic Approach: An ASIC Designer Perspective. In G. Paul & S. Vaudenay (Eds.), *Progress in cryptology – INDOCRYPT 2013, LNCS* (Vol. 8250, pp. 215–226). Springer International Publishing. doi:10.1007/978-3-319-03515-4_14

Doychev, G., Feld, D., Kopf, B., Mauborgne, L., & Reineke, J. (2013). Cacheaudit: A tool for the static analysis of cache side channels. In *Presented as part of the 22nd USENIX Security Symposium (USENIX Security 13)* (pp. 431–446). USENIX, Washington, D.C.

Evtyushkin, D., & Ponomarev, D. (2016). Covert channels through random number generator: Mechanisms, capacity estimation and mitigations. In *Proceedings of the 2016 ACM SIGSAC conference on computer and communications security* (pp. 843–857). New York, NY: ACM. doi:10.1145/2976749.2978374

Gallais, J.-F., Kizhvatov, I., & Tunstall, M. (2011). Improved trace-driven cache-collision attacks against embedded aes implementations. In Y. Chung & M. Yung (Eds.), *Information security applications* (Vol. 6513, pp. 243–257). Springer Berlin Heidelberg. doi:10.1007/978-3-642-17955-6_18

Gandolfi, K., Mourtel, C., & Olivier, F. (2001). Electromagnetic analysis: Concrete results. In K. Çetin, D. Naccache, C. Paar et al. (Eds.), Cryptographic Hardware and Embedded Systems - CHES 2001, LNCS (Vol. 2162, pp. 251–261). Springer Berlin Heidelberg.

GlobalPlatform. (2016a). *About globalplatform. our mission.* Retrieved from http://www.globalplatform. org/aboutusmission.asp

GlobalPlatform. (2016b). *Globalplatform made simple guide: Trusted execution environment (tee) guide.* Retrieved from http://www.globalplatform.org/mediaguidetee.asp

Gouvêa, C., & López, J. (2015). Implementing gcm on armv8. In K. Nyberg (Ed.), *Topics in cryptology — CT-RSA 2015, LNCS* (Vol. 9048, pp. 167–180). Springer International Publishing.

Gras, B., Razavi, K., Bosman, E., Bos, H., & Giuffrida, C. (2017). Aslr on the line: Practical cache attacks on the mmu. In Proceedings of NDSS symposium 2017.

Gruss, D., Maurice, C., Fogh, A., Lipp, M., & Mangard, S. (2016). Prefetch side-channel attacks: Bypassing smap and kernel aslr. In *Proceedings of the 2016 ACM SIGSAC conference on computer and communications security* (pp. 368–379). doi:10.1145/2976749.2978356

Gruss, D., Maurice, C., & Mangard, S. (2016). Rowhammer.js: A remote software- induced fault attack in javascript. In *Proceedings of the 13th international conference on detection of intrusions and malware, and vulnerability assessment, LNCS* (Vol. 9721, pp. 300–321). New York, NY: Springer-Verlag. doi:10.1007/978-3-319-40667-1_15

Gruss, D., Maurice, C., Wagner, K., & Mangard, S. (2016). Flush+flush: A fast and stealthy cache attack. In *Proceedings of the 13th conference on detection of intrusions and malware & vulnerability assessment (DIMVA).* doi:10.1007/978-3-319-40667-1_14

Gruss, D., Spreitzer, R., & Mangard, S. (2015). Cache template attacks: Automating attacks on inclusive last-level caches. In *Proceedings of the 24th USENIX Security Symposium (USENIX Security 15)*(pp. 897–912).

Guanciale, R., Nemati, H., Baumann, C., & Dam, M. (2016). Cache storage channels: Alias-driven attacks and verified countermeasures. In Proceedings of the IEEE symposium on security and privacy.

Gueron, S. (2009). Intel's new AES instructions for enhanced performance and security. In O. Dunkelman (Ed.), *Fast software encryption: 16th international workshop, FSE 2009* (pp. 51–66). Berlin, Heidelberg: Springer Berlin Heidelberg. doi:10.1007/978-3-642-03317-9_4

Gullasch, D., Bangerter, E., & Krenn, S. (2011). *Cache games–bringing access-based cache attacks on aes to practice. In Proceedings of the 2011 IEEE symposium on security and privacy* (pp. 490–505). doi:10.1109/SP.2011.22

Heinz, B., Heyszl, J., & Stumpf, F. (2014, Dec). Side-channel analysis of a high-throughput AES peripheral with countermeasures. In *Proceedings of the 2014 14th international symposium on Integrated circuits (ISIC)* (p. 25-29).

Hund, R., Willems, C., & Holz, T. (2013). Practical timing side channel attacks against kernel space aslr. In Proceedings of the 2013 IEEE symposium on Security and privacy (pp. 191–205). doi:10.1109/SP.2013.23

İnci, M. S., Gulmezoglu, B., Eisenbarth, T., & Sunar, B. (2016). Co-location detection on the cloud. In F.-X. Standaert & E. Oswald (Eds.), *Constructive side-channel analysis and secure design: 7th international workshop* (pp. 19–34). Cham: Springer International Publishing. doi:10.1007/978-3-319-43283-0_2

İnci, M. S., Gulmezoglu, B., Irazoqui, G., Eisenbarth, T., & Sunar, B. (2015). *Seriously, get off my cloud! cross-vm rsa key recovery in a public cloud* (Tech. Rep.). Cryptology ePrint Archive. Report 2015/898. Retrieved from http://eprint.iacr.org

İnci, M. S., Irazoqui, G., Eisenbarth, T., & Sunar, B. (2016, December). Efficient adversarial network discovery using logical channels on Microsoft Azure. In *Proceedings of the Annual computer security applications conference,* Los Angeles, CA, US.

Intel Corporation. (2017). *Intel Hyper-Threading Technology.* Retrieved from https://www-ssl.intel.com/content/www/us/en/architecture-and-technology/hyper-threading/hyper-threading-technology.html

Irazoqui, G., Eisenbarth, T., & Sunar, B. (2015a). *Cross processor cache attacks.* Cryptology ePrint Archive Report 2015/1155. Retrieved from http://eprint.iacr.org/

Irazoqui, G., Eisenbarth, T., & Sunar, B. (2015b). *SSA: A shared cache attack that works across cores and defies VM sandboxing–and its application to AES. In Proceedings of the 2015 IEEE symposium on security and privacy* (pp. 591–604).

Irazoqui, G., Eisenbarth, T., & Sunar, B. (2015c). Systematic reverse engineering of cache slice selection in intel processors. In Proceedings of the 2015 Euromicro conference on Digital system design (pp. 629–636). doi:10.1109/DSD.2015.56

Irazoqui, G., İnci, M. S., Eisenbarth, T., & Sunar, B. (2014). Wait a minute! a fast, cross-vm attack on aes. In *Proceedings of the International workshop on recent advances in intrusion detection* (pp. 299–319). doi:10.1007/978-3-319-11379-1_15

Irazoqui, G., İnci, M. S., Eisenbarth, T., & Sunar, B. (2015). Lucky 13 strikes back. In *Proceedings of the 10th acm symposium on information, computer and communications security* (pp. 85–96).

Käsper, E., & Schwabe, P. (2009). Faster and timing-attack resistant aes-gcm. In C. Clavier & K. Gaj (Eds.), *Cryptographic hardware and embedded systems – CHES '09* (Vol. 5747, pp. 1–17). Springer Berlin Heidelberg. doi:10.1007/978-3-642-04138-9_1

Kasper, M., Schindler, W., & Stöttinger, M. (2010, December). A stochastic method for security evaluation of cryptographic FPGA implementations. In Proceedings of the 2010 international conference on Field-programmable technology (pp. 146–153). IEEE. doi:10.1109/FPT.2010.5681772

Kim, Y., Daly, R., Kim, J., Fallin, C., Lee, J. H., Lee, D., & Mutlu, O. (2014). Flipping bits in memory without accessing them: An experimental study of dram disturbance errors. In *Proceeding of the 41st annual international symposium on computer architecture* (pp. 361–372). Piscataway, NJ, USA: IEEE Press. doi:10.1145/2678373.2665726

Kocabaş, O., Savaş, E., & Großschädl, J. (2008, Dec). Enhancing an embedded processor core with a cryptographic unit for speed and security. In Proceedings of the international conference on Reconfigurable computing and fpgas RECONFIG '08. (p. 409-414). doi:10.1109/ReConFig.2008.59

Kocher, P. (1996). Timing Attacks on Implementations of Diffie-Hellman, RSA, DSS, and Other Systems. In N. Koblitz (Ed.), *Proceedings of CRYPTO '96* (Vol. 1109, pp. 104–113). Springer-Verlag. doi:10.1007/3-540-68697-5_9

Kocher, P., Jaffe, J., & Jun, B. (1999). Differential Power Analysis. In M. J. Wiener (Ed.), *Proceedings of CRYPTO '99* (Vol. 1666, pp. 388–397). Springer-Verlag.

Kong, J., Acıiçmez, O., Seifert, J.-P., & Zhou, H. (2013, July). Architecting against software cache-based side-channel attacks. *IEEE Transactions on Computers, 62*(7), 1276–1288.

Kong, J., John, J. K., Chung, E.-Y., Chung, S. W., & Hu, J. (2010). On the thermal attack in instruction caches. *IEEE Transactions on Dependable and Secure Computing, 7*(2), 217–223. doi:10.1109/TDSC.2009.16

Lauradoux, C. (2005). Collision attacks on processors with cache and countermeasures. In Weworc'05 (p. 76-85).

Lee, R., & Chen, Y.-Y. (2010, June). Processor accelerator for AES. In *Proceedings of the 2010 IEEE 8th symposium on Application specific processors* (pp. 16-21). doi:10.1109/SASP.2010.5521153

Lee, S., Shih, M., Gera, P., Kim, T., Kim, H., & Peinado, M. (2016). Inferring fine-grained control flow inside SGX enclaves with branch shadowing. CoRR, abs/1611.06952

Lipp, M., Gruss, D., Spreitzer, R., Maurice, C., & Mangard, S. (2016, August). Ar- mageddon: Cache attacks on mobile devices. In *Proceedings of the 25th USENIX security symposium (USENIX security 16).* Austin, TX: USENIX Association.

Liu, F., Yarom, Y., Ge, Q., Heiser, G., & Lee, R. B. (2015). Last-level cache side-channel attacks are practical. In IEEE symposium on security and privacy (pp. 605–622). doi:10.1109/SP.2015.43

Longo, J., Mulder, E. D., Page, D., & Tunstall, M. (2015). *Soc it to em: electromagnetic side-channel attacks on a complex system-on-chip.* Cryptology ePrint Archive Report 2015/561. Retrieved from http://eprint.iacr.org

Mangard, S., Oswald, E., & Popp, T. (2008). Power Analysis Attacks: Revealing the Secrets of Smart Cards. In Advances in information security. Springer.

Masti, R. J., Rai, D., Ranganathan, A., Müller, C., Thiele, L., & Capkun, S. (2015). Thermal covert channels on multi-core platforms. In Proceedings of the 24th USENIX Security Symposium (USENIX Security 15) (pp. 865–880).

Maurice, C., Le Scouarnec, N., Neumann, C., Heen, O., & Francillon, A. (2015). Reverse engineering intel last-level cache complex addressing using performance counters. In *Proceedings of the International workshop on recent advances in intrusion detection* (pp. 48–65). doi:10.1007/978-3-319-26362-5_3

Maurice, C., Neumann, C., Heen, O., & Francillon, A. (2015, July 9-10). C5: Cross-cores cache covert channel. In *Proceedings of DIMVA 2015, Detection of Intrusions and Malware, and Vulnerability Assessment*, Milano, Italy.

Neve, M., & Seifert, J.-P. (2007). Advances on access-driven cache attacks on aes. In E. Biham & A. Youssef (Eds.), *Selected areas in cryptography* (Vol. 4356, pp. 147–162). Springer Berlin Heidelberg. doi:10.1007/978-3-540-74462-7_11

Oren, Y., Kemerlis, V. P., Sethumadhavan, S., & Keromytis, A. D. (2015). The spy in the sandbox: Practical cache attacks in javascript and their implications. In *Proceedings of the 22nd ACM SIGSAC Conference on Computer and Communications Security* (pp. 1406–1418). doi:10.1145/2810103.2813708

Osvik, D. A., Shamir, A., & Tromer, E. (2006). Cache attacks and countermeasures: the case of AES (extended version). In *Topics in cryptology - CT-RSA 2006, the cryptographers' track at the RSA conference 2006* (pp. 1–20). Springer-Verlag.

Percival, C. (2005). Cache missing for fun and profit. In Proc. of BSDCAN '05.

Pessl, P., Gruss, D., Maurice, C., Schwarz, M., & Mangard, S. (2016, August). Drama: Exploiting dram addressing for cross-cpu attacks. In Proceedings of the 25th USENIX Security Symposium (USENIX Security 16). Austin, TX: USENIX Association.

Poddar, R., Datta, A., & Rebeiro, C. (2011). A cache trace attack on camellia. In M. Joye, D. Mukhopadhyay, & M. Tunstall (Eds.), *Security aspects in information technology* (pp. 144–156). Berlin, Heidelberg: Springer Berlin Heidelberg. doi:10.1007/978-3-642-24586-2_13

Quisquater, J. J., & Samyde, D. (2001). Electromagnetic analysis (ema): Measures and counter-measures for smart cards. In *Proceedings of the International Conference on Research in Smart Cards: Smart Card Programming and Security E-SMART '01* (pp. 200–210). London, UK: Springer-Verlag. doi:10.1007/3-540-45418-7_17

Rathi, N., De, A., Naeimi, H., & Ghosh, S. (2016). Cache bypassing and checkpointing to circumvent data security attacks on sttram. CoRR, abs/1603.06227.

Rathi, N., Naeimi, H., & Ghosh, S. (2016). Side channel attacks on sttram and low-overhead countermeasures. CoRR, abs/1603.06675.

Rebeiro, C., & Mukhopadhyay, D. (2011). Cryptanalysis of clefia using differential methods with cache trace patterns. In A. Kiayias (Ed.), *Topics in cryptology – CT-RSA 2011* (pp. 89–103). Springer Berlin Heidelberg. doi:10.1007/978-3-642-19074-2_7

Rebeiro, C., & Mukhopadhyay, D. (2015). *A formal analysis of prefetching in pro- filed cache-timing attacks on block ciphers*. Cryptology ePrint Archive, Report 2015/1191. Retrieved from http://eprint.iacr.org

Riviere, L., Najm, Z., Rauzy, P., Danger, J.-L., Bringer, J., & Sauvage, L. (2015). High precision fault injections on the instruction cache of armv7-m architectures. In Hardware oriented security and trust (host), 2015 ieee international symposium on (pp. 62–67). doi:10.1109/HST.2015.7140238

Saab, S., Rohatgi, P., & Hampel, C. (2016). *Side-channel protections for cryptographic instruction set extensions.* Cryptology ePrint Archive, Report 2016/700. Retrieved from http://eprint.iacr.org

Schindler, W., Lemke, K., & Paar, C. (2005). A Stochastic Model for Differential Side Channel Cryptanalysis. In J. Rao & B. Sunar (Eds.), *Cryptographic hardware and embedded systems – ches 2005* (Vol. 3659, pp. 30–46). Springer Berlin Heidelberg. doi:10.1007/11545262_3

Schunter, M. (2016). Intel software guard extensions: Introduction and open research challenges. In *Proceedings of the 2016 ACM workshop on software protection.* New York, NY: ACM. doi:10.1145/2995306.2995307

Seaborn, M. (2015). *Exploiting the dram rowhammer bug to gain kernel privileges* (Tech. Rep.). Google Project Zero. Retrieved from https://googleprojectzero.blogspot.de/2015/03/exploiting-dram-rowhammer-bug-to-gain.html

Seuschek, H., De Santis, F., & Guillen, O. M. (2017). Side-channel Leakage Aware Instruction Scheduling. In *Proceedings of the fourth workshop on cryptography and security in computing systems* (pp. 7–12). New York, NY: ACM. doi:10.1145/3031836.3031838

The MITRE Corporation. (2016). *Common vulnerabilities and exposures. the standard for information security vulnerability names.* Retrieved 05.12.2016 from https://cve.mitre.org/cgi-bin/cvekey.cgi?keyword=Android

Tillich, S., & Großschädl, J. (2006). Instruction set extensions for efficient aes implementation on 32-bit processors. In L. Goubin & M. Matsui (Eds.), *Cryptographic hardware and embedded systems - ches 2006* (Vol. 4249, pp. 270–284). Springer Berlin Heidelberg. doi:10.1007/11894063_22

Uhsadel, L., Georges, A., & Verbauwhede, I. (2008). Exploiting hardware performance counters. In Proceedings of the 5th workshop on Fault diagnosis and tolerance in cryptography FDTC'08. (pp. 59–67). doi:10.1109/FDTC.2008.19

Unterluggauer, T., & Mangard, S. (2016). Exploiting the physical disparity: Side-channel attacks on memory encryption. In F.X. Standaert & E. Oswald (Eds.), *Constructive side-channel analysis and secure design* (pp. 3–18). Cham: Springer International Publishing.

van der Veen, V., Fratantonio, Y., Lindorfer, M., Gruss, D., Maurice, C., Vigna, G., & Giuffrida, C. (2016). Drammer: Deterministic rowhammer attacks on mobile platforms. In *Proceedings of the 2016 ACM SIGSAC conference on computer and communications security* (pp. 1675–1689). New York, NY, USA: ACM. doi:10.1145/2976749.2978406

Varadarajan, V., Zhang, Y., Ristenpart, T., & Swift, M. (2015, August). A placement vulnerability study in multi-tenant public clouds. In Proceedings of the 24th USENIX Security Symposium (USENIX Security 15) (pp. 913–928). Washington, D.C.: USENIX Association.

Weaver, V. M., Terpstra, D., & Moore, S. (2013). Non-determinism and overcount on modern hardware performance counter implementations. In Proceedings of the 2013 IEEE international symposium on Performance analysis of systems and software (ISPASS) (pp. 215–224). doi:10.1109/ISPASS.2013.6557172

Whitnall, C., Oswald, E., & Mather, L. (2011). An Exploration of the Kolmogorov-Smirnov Test as a Competitor to Mutual Information Analysis. In E. Prouff (Ed.), *Smart card research and advanced applications* (Vol. 7079, pp. 234–251). Springer Berlin Heidelberg. doi:10.1007/978-3-642-27257-8_15

Xiao, Y., Zhang, X., Zhang, Y., & Teodorescu, R. (2016, August). One bit flips, one cloud flops: Cross-vm row hammer attacks and privilege escalation. In Proceedings of the 25th USENIX Security Symposium (USENIX Security 16) (pp. 19–35). Austin, TX: USENIX Association.

Xu, Z., Wang, H., & Wu, Z. (2015). A measurement study on co-residence threat inside the cloud. In Proceedings of the 24th USENIX Security Symposium (USENIX Security 15) (pp. 929–944). Washington, D.C.: USENIX Association.

Yarom, Y., & Falkner, K. (2014). Flush+ reload: a high resolution, low noise, l3 cache side-channel attack. In *Proceedings of the 23rd USENIX Security Symposium (USENIX Security 14)* (pp.719–732).

Yarom, Y., Ge, Q., Liu, F., Lee, R. B., & Heiser, G. (2015). *Mapping the intel last-level cache* (Tech. Rep.). IACR Cryptology ePrint Archive, Report 2015/905. Retrieved from http://eprint.iacr.org

Yarom, Y., Genkin, D., & Heninger, N. (2016). Cachebleed: A timing attack on openssl constant time rsa. In *Proceedings of the International conference on cryptographic hardware and embedded systems* (pp. 346–367). doi:10.1007/978-3-662-53140-2_17

Zankl, A., Heyszl, J., & Sigl, G. (2017). Automated detection of instruction cache leaks in modular exponentiation software. In K. Lemke-Rust & M. Tunstall (Eds.), *Smart card research and advanced applications* (pp. 228–244). Cham: Springer International Publishing. doi:10.1007/978-3-319-54669-8_14

Zankl, A., Miller, K., Heyszl, J., & Sigl, G. (2016). Towards efficient evaluation of a time-driven cache attack on modern processors. In I. Askoxylakis, S. Ioannidis, S. Katsikas et al. (Eds.), *Computer security – esorics 2016* (pp. 3–19). Cham: Springer International Publishing. doi:10.1007/978-3-319-45741-3_1

Zhang, N., Sun, K., Shands, D., Lou, W., & Hou, Y. T. (2016). *Truspy: Cache side- channel information leakage from the secure world on arm devices.* Cryptology ePrint Archive, Report 2016/980. Retrieved from http://eprint.iacr.org

Zhang, T., Zhang, Y., & Lee, R. B. (2016). Memory dos attacks in multi-tenant clouds: Severity and mitigation. CoRR, abs/1603.03404

Zhang, Y., Juels, A., Reiter, M. K., & Ristenpart, T. (2012). Cross-vm side channels and their use to extract private keys. In *Proceedings of the 2012 acm conference on computer and communications security* (pp. 305–316). doi:10.1145/2382196.2382230

Zhang, Y., Juels, A., Reiter, M. K., & Ristenpart, T. (2014). Cross-tenant side-channel attacks in paas clouds. In *Proceedings of the 2014 acm sigsac conference on com- puter and communications security* (pp. 990–1003). doi:10.1145/2660267.2660356

KEY TERMS AND DEFINITIONS

Branch Prediction Unit: Microarchitectural component that predicts the outcome of conditional branches to avoid stalling the instruction pipeline.

Combined Attacks: Mixture of power and EM based side-channel and microarchitectural attacks. They typically exploit observations of microarchitectural events in power or EM measurements.

Instruction Set Architecture: The fundamental interface between software and hardware on a processor. It defines data types, instructions, registers, memory addressing, interrupts and more.

Microarchitecture: Implementation of a processor's instruction set architecture (ISA). The same ISA can be implemented using different design strategies like energy efficiency or space minimization.

Out-of-Order Execution: Optimization that relaxes the requirement of instructions being executed strictly sequentially. It allows an instruction to finish while the processor still waits for the result of a previous one.

Performance Monitoring Unit: Dedicated hardware component within a processor that counts a broad spectrum of low-level events related to code execution.

Side-Channel: A physical characteristic of a device executing an algorithm. Side-channels include execution time, power consumption, and electromagnetic emanation.

Simultaneous Multithreading: Technique to execute multiple separate threads in parallel on one processor core. It enables the execution of multiple instructions from multiple threads in one clock cycle.

Trusted Execution Environment: Security feature that provides enhanced isolation of security-critical applications from an untrusted operating system.

Chapter 14
Integrating Integrity Reporting Into Industrial Control Systems:
A Reality Check

Tobias Rauter
Graz University of Technology, Austria

Johannes Iber
Graz University of Technology, Austria

Christian Kreiner
Graz University of Technology, Austria

ABSTRACT

Due to the need of increased cooperation and connectivity, security is getting a vital property of industrial control systems. Besides system hardening, the detection of security breaches in different subsystems has been becoming a research-focus recently. This chapter summarizes the work concerning anomaly detection at different system levels. The, a system that maintains availability and integrity of distributed control systems through automated reconfiguration in case of integrity violations is proposed. We aim to detect such integrity violations through integrity reporting. This is a well-known technology, albeit not widely used in real system because of scalability problems. In this chapter, three different remote attestation methods (binary, privilege and signature-based) are integrated into a remote terminal unit to analyze and discuss the benefits and drawbacks of each method. Depending on the actual RTU architecture and already in-place development and deployment processes, the integration of remote attestation may be feasible for industrial control systems.

INTRODUCTION

The growth of the renewable energy sector has a high impact on the technology of hydro-power plant unit control systems (Liserre, Sauter, & Hung, 2010a). Nowadays, these have to react to power grid changes in time to achieve overall grid stability. As a consequence, control devices (depending on the provided

DOI: 10.4018/978-1-5225-2845-6.ch014

functionality, they are also referred to as Remote Terminal Unit (RTU) or Programmable Logic Controller (PLC)) in single power plants, as well as control devices of different power plants have to cooperate in order to achieve the system-wide control goal. These requirements lead to networks of small, embedded control devices and heavyweight Supervisory Control and Data Acquisition (SCADA) servers and clients. At the same time, these power plants represent critical infrastructures that have to be protected against security attacks that have occurred lately (Miller & Rowe, 2012).

Analyzing attacks such as the recent Ukrainian blackout, reveals complex long-term attacks on multiple system levels (Electricity Information Sharing and Analysis Center, 2016). More and more countries are starting to obligate operators and suppliers of critical infrastructure to protect security properties of such systems. Both industry and academia are focusing on security properties of RTUs and their communication.

This chapter shows how availability and integrity of a distributed control system can be maintained in case of single compromised system components through automated reconfiguration. In order to do so, the compromise will be identified through integrity reporting. This means that one entity (the prover), proves its configuration state to another entity (the challenger). While this technology is well known and still a research topic, its application in real world systems, especially in embedded devices, is limited. The main problems concern the maintenance of a reference configuration the challenger needs to store to verify the integrity of the prover's configuration. Especially in distributed embedded systems, such as typical Industrial Control System (ICS) architectures, these references have to be distributed to all possible communication partners of each proving device. Moreover, every time the prover's configuration gets updated, all references have to be redeployed. This is tedious and not feasible in real-world distributed systems.

First, this chapter will discuss the specific needs of an ICS with regards to security and how existing work aims to detect compromise through anomaly detection at different system levels. Moreover, an overview of trusted computing and how dedicated security modules such as a Trusted Platform Module (TPM) can be used to enable secure integrity reporting is given. Based on a real RTU architecture, problems that prevent such technologies from being used in real systems nowadays are discussed. We then show how three remote attestation methods, namely binary attestation, privilege-based attestation and signature-based attestation can be integrated in order to analyze their applicability in the ICS domain. In the last section, we discuss our findings and compare the benefits and drawbacks of each method.

BACKGROUND AND RELATED WORK

This section starts with a discussion of the basic structure and terminologies used in a SCADA system. Subsequently, the security objectives, especially the differences compared to conventional IT systems are described. Then, we provide an overview of existing Intrusion Detection System (IDS) solutions that target the ICS domain and motivate the need of device-level configuration integrity verification and reporting (attestation) capabilities. In our work, this is achieved by trusted computing methodologies. Therefore, we give an overview of trusted computing basics and existing integrity attestation methodologies.

Industrial Control Systems

The National Institute of Standards and Technology (NIST) defines an ICS as a general term that comprises different types of control systems such as SCADA systems, Distributed Control System (DCS) or PLC (Stouffer, Falco, & Scarfone, 2015). In general, an ICS is in charge of controlling a physical process. A control device (i.e., a computing device) reads physical values and decides how to manipulate the process. In order to do so, sensors and actuators are needed. Moreover, a Human-Machine-Interface (HMI) may be provided to allow operators to control the algorithms, supervise the process or processing the data. While such HMIs are often local, the need for remote access and maintenance or cooperation of controllers has been rising recently due to the increased connectivity and distribution of processes.

SCADA systems are used to control, supervise and manage distributed control systems centrally. Figure 1 shows the basic building blocks of a SCADA system used to supervise and control power plants at different geographic locations. At bus or process level, the controlled physical process is measured and manipulated through sensors and actuators. On the device level, RTUs (or PLCs) are the actual control devices that execute the control strategy and interface with the environment (i.e., communicate with sensors and actuators). Since the control strategy could be distributed, the RTUs have to communicate directly with each other. In addition to the normal client that is used to supervise the system, a maintenance terminal exists to configure and deploy the control tasks to the RTUs. Each location maintains

Figure 1. General SCADA system structure

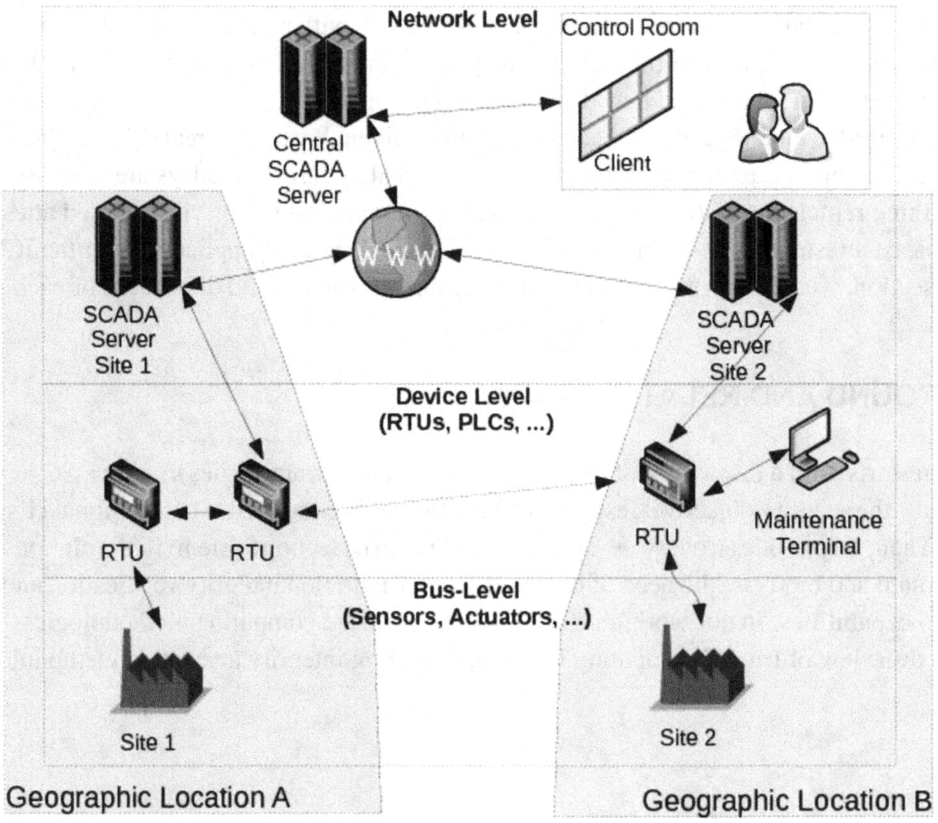

its local SCADA server that collects the information from all RTUs. All local servers synchronize with the central SCADA server in order to enable the central SCADA client to supervise all plants. A real system would contain additional clients at the different sites and also HMI panels which are directly mounted on the control devices. However, they provide similar (although degraded) functionality and are therefore not considered here for simplicity.

Traditionally, ICS were not comparable to usual IT systems. Proprietary protocols, hardware and software were used to control a physical process locally. The devices and interfaces were physically secured and not connected to any open network, which reduced the need for IT security solutions. Nowadays, low-cost IP devices usually replace these proprietary solutions (Stouffer et al., 2015) and new requirements, for example in the field of energy generation (Liserre, Sauter, & Hung, 2010b), demand the cooperation of geographically distributed control systems. This leads to new attack vectors which are already exploited actively (Miller & Rowe, 2012). In contrast to usual IT systems which handle data, ICS handle physical processes within particular environments. A malfunction could cause risk to health and safety of human lives, serious damage to the environment or a breakdown of critical infrastructure such as the power grid. For that reason, national governments start forcing the operators of critical infrastructure by law to implement state-of-the-art security measures (ITSG, 2015).

The main difference between traditional IT systems and ICS is the priority of security properties (Stouffer et al., 2015). For most IT systems, the importance of confidentiality exceeds that of integrity and availability. In ICS, however, a loss of the function's availability is often safety-relevant or may have a huge (financial) impact on companies or even society (e.g., critical infrastructure). Therefore, availability is the main goal in such systems. Since component integrity is a requirement for ensured availability of the expected function, integrity is just as important. Confidentiality is, although important, typically considered a second priority. Information leakage is usually not as critical as the loss of functionality (Stouffer et al., 2015). This change of priority is the main reason why security solutions in the ICS domain are often different to general IT systems.

Intrusion Detection Systems (IDS)

While hardening an ICS with regard to security is an important task, neither remote attacks (e.g., exploiting software bugs or using social engineering) nor insider attacks can be prevented completely (e.g., (Lee, Assante, & Conway, 2014, Langner (2011), Electricity Information Sharing and Analysis Center (2016))).

Intrusion detection or prevention systems are used to analyze information systems and detect signs of intrusion (Amoroso, 1999). Concerning the layer of application, IDS can roughly be separated into two groups. Network-based IDS monitor network traffic and may run on dedicated devices without directly affecting the actual system components. Host-based IDS are located at the host computer, server or control device to monitor ongoing events on the equipped device at the cost of performance overhead. Independently from the system layer, these solutions can be grouped into three categories regarding the type of analysis (Amoroso, 1999): signature, integrity and statistical analysis.

Signature analysis is probably the most known type. Pattern matching is used to identify suspicious programs, data or activities. Network-based IDS compare network traffic on different protocol levels to known attack patterns. Snort (Roesch, 1999), for example, provides rules for common protocols such as HTTP and TCP but also for domain-specific protocols such as Modbus or DNP3. Host-based IDS can check configuration files or executables against known adverse programs or configurations.

Integrity analysis identifies whether a specific component has been altered in an unauthorized or unintended way. Usually, cryptographic mechanisms such as hashes or signatures are used to verify the integrity of a message, a configuration file or an executable.

Statistical analysis (often referred to as anomaly-based analysis) tries to identify deviations from normal behavior. Signature analysis can only identify known attacks, while integrity analysis relies on a known reference state. By inspecting the behavior of a component, it is possible to identify attacks that have not been known before. However, depending on the actually used metrics, statistical analysis may be tricked very simply or produce a significant amount of false positives (Urbina et al., 2016).

Intrusion Detection in Industrial Control Systems

Due to the specific constraints in the ICS field (availability comes before integrity and confidentiality) and the frequent use of performance-constrained devices for the control task, many domain-specific intrusion detection mechanisms have been proposed. Since SCADA systems integrate classical IT systems, control systems and physical processes, solutions for the process, the device and the network level exist (Mitchell & Chen, 2014; Urbina et al., 2016).

Anomaly Detection on the Process Level

Intrusion detection systems that try to detect intrusions on the process level are mainly concerned with false data injection or false control commands (Liu, Ning, & Reiter, 2009). While many systems integrate basic integrity checks such as threshold or state estimation to identify false values arising from wrong measurements, these techniques are not sufficient to detect malicious attackers being able to control sensor readings.

In a typical control loop, a physical process is measured by sensors. The controller uses these measurements, usually together with state information, to calculate the excitation of actuators. Since this process follows physical laws, anomaly detection on the process level uses a model of the physical process and compares measured values with an estimation based on the actuator excitation. In (Mitchell & Chen, 2014), the authors show that most IDS for control systems use behavior-based detection (statistical analysis) and nearly half of all surveyed IDS use information about the physical process model to identify intrusions.

In (Urbina et al., 2016), the authors identified two main model types: auto-regressive models basically predict the next sensor value based on the last N measured values. Linear dynamic state-space models, on the other hand, also take into account control inputs and internal states. Whenever the measured value significantly deviates from the expected one (generated by the model), an event occurs. Stateless anomaly detection systems raise an alarm at the first event, while stateful systems take track of such events and combine historical deviations to decide whether an alarm should be given. While most surveyed methods use stateless detection, stateful approaches generally perform better.

Another class of contributions try to use more general models to identify anomalies independent from the underlying physical process. Such methods use clustering of correlated sensor signals to react to entropy changes (Krotofil, Larsen, & Gollmann, 2015) or Gaussian mixture models (Kiss, Genge, & Haller, 2015). Also, multivariate statistical approaches are used to distinguish between normal process disturbances and intrusions (Iturbe, 2016).

Anomaly Detection on the Network Level

Since the network level which is composed of the SCADA servers and the connections to the control devices is similar to 'normal' IT systems, at this level IDS are also comparable (Mitchell & Chen, 2014). Most ICS/SCADA-specific IDS provide rules for special protocols such as CAN, DNP3 or Modbus. While network-based IDS are a good substitution since they do not interfere with the system function, they suffer from visibility problems: The IDS nodes only see a subset of the system (i.e., accessible network packets) and, therefore, cannot make strong statements about the overall system integrity. Due to the high amount of legacy devices in SCADA networks, network-based IDS are nevertheless important to detect a compromised device that do not provide state-of-the-art security measures. Therefore, much research is currently done in this field. Bro (Paxson, 1999), for example, is extended to support automated white-listing for the IEC-61870 protocol what leads to reasonable small false-positive rates (Udd, Asplund, Nadjm-Tehrani, Kazemtabrizi, & Ekstedt, 2016). Other approaches try to combine process level and network level IDS to increase detection rates (Ghaeini & Tippenhauer, 2016, Hadžiosmanović, Bolzoni, & Hartel (2012)).

Anomaly Detection on the Device Level

IDS on the device level try to identify intrusions or integrity violations of single devices. Similar to the process level methodologies, for example, one could create a plausibility checker to verify the decisions (i.e., the calculated actuator stimuli) of a control device. Also, specific malware detection tools for PLC code have been proposed (Zonouz, Rrushi, & McLaughlin, 2014). In (Formby, Srinivasan, Leonard, Rogers, & Beyah, 2016), the authors use fingerprinting techniques to detect intrusions on the device and network level. They measure the cross-layer response time (i.e., the time difference between a TCP ACK and the actual application layer response) and operation time (i.e., the time a device needs to execute a command) to fingerprint devices and software. Significant deviations from these fingerprints would indicate the existence of an intrusion.

SUMMARY

A variety of IDS have been proposed on each level of ICS. Each layer covers a set of possible attacks. The vast majority of ICS-specific intrusion detection solutions take into account the physical process or work on the network level, which is important to deal with legacy devices and resource-constrained hardware. In this chapter, we focus on the device level to explore one possible method that can be used in future generations of control devices in ICS.

Trusted Computing

The Merriam-Webster dictionary defines the term trust as

1. Assured reliance on the character, ability, strength, or truth of someone or something, or
2. One in which confidence is place.

Thus, trust means that some entity can rely on a property of another entity in a guaranteed (assured) way. Generally, the term trust is ambiguous for many people. In trusted computing, trust is used in the sense of behavioral reputation. Something is trusted if it behaves as anticipated. In distributed computing systems, trust is a very important property since the function of one entity depends on the assumption that other entities behave as expected.

In computing systems, one can trust another person or a device under the following presumptions (Proudler, 2005):

- It can be identified unambiguously
- It operates unhindered and
- There is known, consistent good behavior of the entity (OR some third person who is trusted attests such good behavior).

The first premise to trust an entity is identification. You can only expect a certain behavior of someone/ something you know. Second, you have to assure that this entity works unhindered. Even if the entity would work as expected for itself, you have to ensure that there is no external (or internal) force that hinders the entity from doing so. Third, you have to have some reference value, some 'reason' why you trust the entity -- either by experience (e.g., the entity has been behaving 'good' for a long time), or someone

Trusted Computing Group

In 1999, the Trusted Computing Platform Alliance (TCPA), a consortium of different industry vendors, aimed at generating an open specification to build a solid foundation to increase trust in PCs (Alliance, 2000). In their first white paper, they discuss the seeming contradiction of open platforms and trust as also the limitations of software-based trust. They advocated the TCPA subsystem, a mechanism that is used to provide evidence for trust in the whole platform. The subsystem comprises two building blocks:

- A dedicated hardware module, the TPM (Trusted Computing Group, 2006), which is the anchor to prevent all software-based attacks.
- Software that performs integrity metrics in conjunction with the TPM.

With the help of this subsystem, the TCPA aims at creating a hardware-based foundation for trust based on the integrity metrics. These are platform characteristics that can be used to establish a platform identity. Basically, they propose to hash all components and extend these so-called 'measurements' to the TPM prior to the execution of every component. This process prevents software components from hiding the fact of their execution and is nowadays known as 'Authenticated Boot' or 'Measured Boot'.

In 2003, the Trusted Computing Group (TCG) (TCG, 2016) developed out of the TCPA and continued TCPA's work. The TCG defines trust as (Trusted Computing Group, 2007):

Trust is the expectation that a device will behave in a particular manner for a specific purpose. A trusted platform should provide at least three basic features: protected capabilities, integrity measurement and integrity reporting. (Trusted Computing Group, 2007)

This definition is similar to the previously introduced behavior-based definition of trust. Also, the integrity property of a computer system is seen as guarantee that the system will perform as intended by the creator (Biba, 1977). In other words, the system meets its specification in the first place and has not been modified in an unauthorized or unintended way. Thus, one can trust a system if the initial system state is trusted and it is ensured that its integrity has not been not violated. In order to trust the initial system state, one has to know the system's specification and it has to be assured that the system fulfills this specification. Moreover, the specification must reflect the behavior that is expected from the system. Additionally, processes in the development (and even in the production and deployment) phases of a system have to be in place to ensure the trustworthy initial system. We do not consider these requirements in this chapter but it is important to keep in mind that there are important prerequisites when using the TCG's approach.

The TCG defines three features a trusted platform has to encompass. Similar to the previous proposal of the TCPA, a trusted platform has to provide protected capabilities (which means a TPM in the TCG's specification) and hardware-backed software mechanisms to measure and report (attest) the integrity of the platform.

Protected Capabilities

Protected capabilities are a set of commands with exclusive permission to access shielded locations. A TPM is a hardware module that implements such protected capabilities. It implements key management, authenticated integrity measurement reporting and shielded locations (e.g., the Platform Configuration Register (PCR)) to protect the measurements. The basic blocks of a TPM are:

- A Non Volatile Memory (NVM) which is utilized to store the Storage Root Key (SRK) and the Endorsement Key (EK) as well as user-defined values. This memory is physically located in a shielded location where it is protected against interference from the outside and exposure.
- An RSA engine which is used for asymmetric encryption/decryption of keys/data and for creating and verifying digital signatures.
- An SHA-1 engine employed for Hashed Message Authentication Code (HMAC).
- A True Random Number Generator (TRNG) which is used for key generation.

Platform Control Register (PCR)

PCRs are used to save measurements on the TPM. It is necessary to prevent arbitrary write access for these registers. Otherwise, a malicious software with privileged access would be able to write false measurement states and, therefore hide the fact of its execution. In order to handle this problem, a TPM only provides an ordinary read and an extend command. The extension of a PCR is a function that hashes the concatenation of the previous value (in the register) and the new value (the new measurement). This process is non-commutative. Consequently, writing an arbitrary value into such registers (i.e., hiding the fact of execution) is protected through the first pre-image resistance of the used cryptographic hash.

TPM Keys

In order to implement different types of functions, the TCG defines different key types for TPMs (Trusted Computing Group, 2006).

- **Endorsement Key (EK):** This key is the unique platform identity key. Some manufacturers create the key during production and sign it to certify that it comes from a TPM. It cannot leave the TPM and cannot be used for signing.
- **Storage Root Key (SRK):** The SRK is the root element of the key hierarchy and used to generate keys of the next three key types.
- **Storage Key:** Used to encrypt other elements in the hierarchy.
- **Signature Key:** Used for signing operations.
- **Binding Key:** Used to encrypt small amounts of data (like keys used for symmetric cryptography).
- **Attestation Identity Key (AIK):** These keys are used as aliases for the EK to sign PCR values for remote attestation as will be described later in this section.

Since the NVM of the TPM is very limited, only the EK and SRK are stored permanently. All other keys are managed in a tree structure and encrypted by their parent.

Integrity Measurement and Reporting

Besides protected capabilities, a trusted platform according to the TCG has to provide integrity measurement and reporting features. Integrity measurement is defined as (Trusted Computing Group, 2007)

... the process of obtaining metrics of platform characteristics that affect the integrity (trustworthiness) of a platform and putting digests of those metrics in PCRs. (Trusted Computing Group, 2007)

The starting point for measurements is the Root of Trust for Measurement (RTM). A Static Root of Trust for Measurement (RTM) starts the measurement at a well-known starting state (i.e., power on). Each subsequently executed component has to be measured and extended to a PCR prior to its execution. This builds up the so-called chain of transitive trust and enables the verification of the system's state at a later point.

Remote attestation (integrity reporting) is the process of proving the integrity of the configuration of one system (prover) to another entity (challenger). The prover (also referred to as appraiser (Coker et al., 2011)) supplies evidence for its claim (the integrity measurements). A challenger has to store a policy or reference that enables the verification of whether the measured configuration represents a non-compromised system. Additionally, a protocol for securely sharing this information has to be in place. Usually, the challenger sends a random value, called nonce, to request the prover's configuration. The prover signs the measurement together with the nonce. This is done by the TPM with an AIK. The challenger is now able to verify whether the retrieved measurement complies to its policy to check the signature with the public part of the AIK in order to ensure the integrity of the reported values.

Methods for Integrity Measurement and Reporting

A system's configuration is represented by the software components running on the device and their configurations. Remote attestation methods for binaries, properties, security policies and platform-specific permission systems have already been introduced. Two of the most common methods are binary and property-based attestation.

The Integrity Measurement Architecture (IMA) (Sailer, Zhang, Jaeger, & Doorn, 2004) generates a measurement list of all binaries and configuration files loaded by the system. The cumulative measurement (i.e., hash) of the measurement list is extended into a PCR. To attest the system's state, the prover sends the measurement list to the challenger and proves its integrity with the help of the TPM. Binary measurement approaches are not suitable for systems with different or dynamic configurations because each challenger has to maintain a comprehensive list of known `good' configurations. Especially when system updates or backups are taken into account, the set of possible configurations may grow to an unmaintainable size. Moreover, the verification of all binaries is not necessary every time. The challenger might only be interested in modules which may affect the integrity of the target software. Our work uses IMA for the attestation of highly privileged software components.

Property-based attestation (Sadeghi & Stüble, 2004, Ceccato, Ofek, & Tonella (2008)) overcomes some issues of binary-based methods. A challenger is only interested in whether the prover fulfills particular security properties or not (e.g., strict isolation of processes). Therefore, a set of possible platform configurations is mapped to different properties. This approach eliminates the need for comprehensive lists of reference configurations on the challenger by introducing a Trusted Third Party (TTP), which is in charge of the mapping. Similar approaches focusing on privacy-preserving features (L. Chen, Löhr, Manulis, & Sadeghi, 2008) do not need a TTP and use ring signatures to protect the prover's configuration from exposure. This chapter discusses privilege-based attestation (besides others) which uses the absence of privileges that enable specific components to harm other component's integrity as attestation property.

Another group of approaches use information flow analysis based on security policies (Jaeger, Sailer, & Shankar, 2006), (Xu, Zhang, & Hu, 2012). These approaches model all possible communications between processes. The basic idea is that a high-integrity process is successfully attested if all binary measurements are valid and there is no possible information flow from low-integrity to high-integrity processes. These approaches reduce the number of platform configurations since only a small set of system and high-integrity applications has to be measured. However, they rely on well-defined security policies and the generation of additional filter-components. Privilege-based attestation does not rely on existing policies or descriptions. They are generated at execution time.

Similar to policy-based and information flow based methods, PRIvilege-Based remote Attestation (PRIBA) (Rauter, Höller, Kajtazovic, & Kreiner, 2015) tries to reduce the information needed by the challenger by using privileges of software modules as trust properties. For software modules that have privileged access on the executing prover, binary measurement is used. All other modules are parsed for privileged calls to the system library to generate a privilege measurement of the module. The challenger is able to decide whether the measured module violates the prover's integrity by checking the measurement against a policy. The presented approach potentially reduces the size and the update frequency of the challenger's reference measurements. However, until now only the basic concept has been presented and no implementation exists. Neither the measurement of a module's privileges nor the verification against the policy has been investigated.

In (Rein, Rieke, Jäger, Kuntze, & Coppolino, 2015), similar problems in the same domain are discussed. The authors analyze how to use trusted computing and remote attestation in hydro-electric power plants to verify the integrity of sensor data. These sensors are often placed in physically unprotected locations and adversaries may be able to tamper with their data. Since the control decisions are taken based on the sensor values, their integrity has to be protected. The authors integrated verified boot into the sensor's controller to prove their integrity to other network participants. They built a prototypical implementation based on IMA and proposed to distribute their integrity measurement entries incrementally. This approach reduces the network and verification overhead for remote attestation because this does not seem to be a big problem when attesting small devices like sensors to more complex and connected devices.

MAINTAINING AVAILABILITY AND INTEGRITY IN INDUSTRIAL CONTROL SYSTEMS

As mentioned in the last section, availability and integrity are the main security goals in ICS. Also, the concept of trusted computing was discussed. In computing systems, trust is established through assurance of integrity. Other devices in the same network have to behave as expected, otherwise the functionality of its peers may be compromised. This would be a loss of availability through an integrity violation.

The first problem seems to be the detection of integrity violations. We will discuss how to use integrity attestation and trusted computing technologies. But how should the whole system behave, when a compromise of a single component is detected? Usually, a compromised system is isolated and/or shut down to prevent the attacker from spreading through the system. But this would cause a loss of availability. Before we examine how to detect integrity violations in ICS, we have to reflect on what to do with this information.

System Reconfiguration

Figure 2 shows an exemplary distributed control system with three PLCs. Each control device has access to a specific set of sensors and actuators and altogether four control tasks are distributed over these devices. Now, let us assume that an attacker is able to compromise *RTU-A* and execute malicious software on this device. The correct functionality of *RTU-A* cannot be guaranteed, it might behave unexpected and cannot be trusted anymore. An IDS based on integrity analysis would recognize this integrity violation and report it to the system. In order to maintain availability and integrity of the overall system, the functionality provided by *RTU-A* has to be retained while the compromised component *RTU-A* has to be isolated from the rest of the system. In order to dissolve this apparent contradiction, some kind of hypervisor has to re-configure the overall system. This hypervisor may be executed on a dedicated machine or distributed over all devices in the network.

Now, there are two possibilities: Either the hypervisor resolves the integrity violation of *RTU-A*. This could be done, for example, by resetting the device to a known good state (e.g., rollback to a backup). An attacker, however, could potentially simply re-play the same attack and compromise the system again. The second possibility is to migrate the function of the compromised device and isolate it afterwards. This approach would also enable a forensic analysis of the device to learn about the attacker.

Figure 2. Exemplary system before reconfiguration

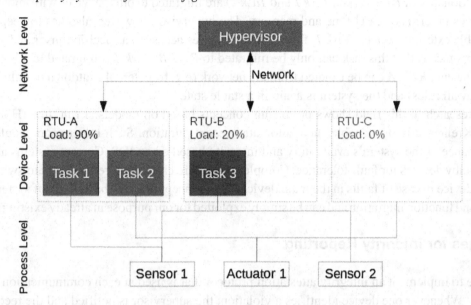

All in all, the second approach sounds more promising. The function of the compromised device is reflected in the tasks it is executing. In this case *Task 1* and *Task 2*. These tasks require different types of resources. On one hand, the tasks require memory and CPU resources on the machine which executes the tasks (often including real-time requirements). On the other hand, the task may also require access to external devices such as specific sensors and actuators. An ideal hypervisor would have knowledge of the overall system and how the devices are interconnected. Based on this knowledge, it would re-configure the exemplary system as shown in Figure 3.

Figure 3. Exemplary system after reconfiguration

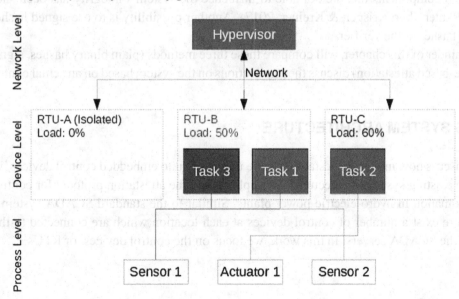

The functionality of *RTU-A* (i.e., *Task 1* and *Task 2*) are migrated to other devices with enough available resources in terms of CPU-time and memory. The hypervisor, however, also has to keep track of the accessable external devices. *Task 1*, for example, requires access to a specific sensor and a specific actuator. This means that this task can only be migrated to *RTU-B*. *Task 3* is migrated to a hot-standby device. At the end, *RTU-A* can be isolated from the network (e.g. by external shutdown or only logically through firewall rules) and the system is again in a stable state.

Recent research in this field shows promising concepts based on models at run time (Höller, Iber, Rauter, & Kreiner, 2016) to enable such automated reconfiguration. Such hypervisors would enable the maintenance of the system's availability and integrity based on an IDS. Current systems also often use hot-standby devices for fault-tolerance. Complete PLCs are carried out redundantly to switch to the secondary device in case of faults in the main device. This concept is a very basic form of system reconfiguration and function migration and can be simply exploited for our purpose in already existing systems.

Challenges for Integrity Reporting

We propose to implement an integrity attestation protocol that is used at each communication between the devices. Whenever one device identifies a violation, the supervisor is notified and the reconfiguration is triggered.

As described before, there exists many methods for remote attestation. While this technology is well known and still a research topic, its application in real world systems, especially in embedded devices, is limited. The main problems concern the maintenance of the reference measurements. Especially in distributed embedded systems, such as in typical ICS architectures, these references have to be distributed to all possible communication partners of each proving device. Moreover, every time the prover's configuration gets updated, all references have to be redeployed. This is tedious and not feasible in real-world distributed systems. This is especially true when connectivity and resources in terms of computing power are constrained, as in control systems for power plants. A lot of research is focusing on reducing the complexity and dynamics of the reference measurements. One approach of ignoring low-privileged components that are not able to influence the system's integrity has been shown to be promising (Rauter, Iber, Krisper, & Kreiner, 2017). Another possibility is to use signed hashes instead of reference hashes at the verifier.

The remainder of this chapter, will compare these three methods (plain binary hashes, signed hashes and privilege-based attestation) discuss the implications on the system based on an actual control device.

EXISTING SYSTEM ARCHITECTURE

Before we discuss how integrity attestation can be integrated into embedded control devices, we briefly illustrate the existing system architecture. We implemented the attestation protocol for control devices used for automation in hydro-electric power plants. Similar to the standard SCADA system shown in Figure 1, there exist a number of control devices at each location which are connected to the process layer and to the SCADA servers. In this work, we focus on the control devices, or RTUs.

Figure 4. The existing system architecture

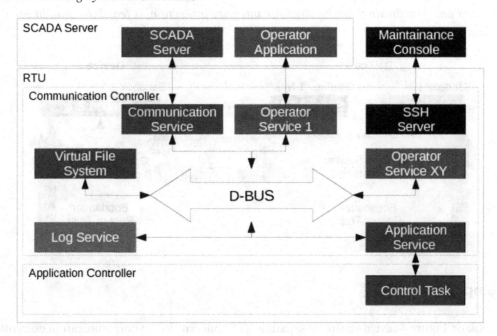

Overview

Figure 4 shows the architecture of the already existing control system, focusing on one RTU and its interfacing components. The RTU is in charge of executing the control task, which interfaces the sensors and actuators on the process level. Additionally, the RTU provides an interface to the outer world. It consists of one central module and different interface modules. The interface modules provide the actual digital and analog I/Os that are connected to the process layer. The central module consists of two subsystems with dedicated controllers.

The application controller is executing the control task on top of a real-time operating system. This controller is inspired by the IEC 61131 (IEC, 1995) standard for programmable logic controllers. There exist a number of tasks that are executed periodically. At the start of each cycle, input data (so called datapoints) are read into the process space. These datapoints contain actual sensor values, internal states or computed variables. After the computation is finished for each cycle, the internal data are written to output-datapoints. Again, these datapoints may represent internal data structures or states, but also output values for actuators.

The communication controller is in charge for providing the communication interfaces and is separated from the application controller to minimize the possibility of interference from the outer world. Moreover, the requirements for the components running on these parts differ extremely. While the tasks on the application controller have strong real-time requirements, but run mostly isolated, the tasks on the communication controller require sophisticated inter-process communication capabilities and other features such as simple maintenance access and different network stacks. For this reason, the communication controller provides a full linux operating system. With this architecture, it is also possible to separate different priorities concerning dependability. The availability and safety critical control task can be managed separated from the security critical communication tasks.

Figure 5. Overview of the integrity verification at device level; while state-of-the-art technologies such as Secure Boot and Sandboxing can be used for integrity protection, a feasible solution for integrity reporting has to be found.

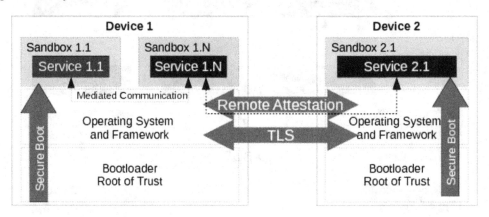

RTU Components

A closer look on Figure 4 reveals a strong separation of concerns in the communication controller. The SCADA-server collects and modifies datapoints from different RTUs (and other SCADA-servers). Since every plant operator has individual needs, the OEM of the SCADA server allows operator specific applications with limited privileges to be executed on the server. Moreover, for other tasks such as firmware updates, a maintenance console is used.

The communication controller executes different services that provide the required interfaces. The most important services are the communication service and the application service, which are in charge of enabling the access of datapoints from the control task on the application cpu to the outer world (i.e., the SCADA-server). The file system is mediated through the virtual file system component. All other services access their files via this service and therefore do not need to access the file resources directly. Additionally, there exist some operator specific services such as generation of curves based on control datapoints that also provide interfaces to the outer world. In the next section, we will show how this already implemented separation of concerns and the mediated file system access will help us to implement security features.

IDS BASED ON INTEGRITY REPORTING FOR DEVICES IN ICS

To enable a further evaluation, this section describes how different methods of integrity reporting are integrated into the existing system architecture described before. We integrate plain IMA (Sailer et al., 2004), an adoption of privilege-based attestation for control systems (Rauter et al., 2017) and a signature-based approach that uses signatures of binaries as attestable properties. Since the integrity reporting methods are only useful in the context of a generally protected system, we start with a brief overview of the security concepts that are implemented in the RTUs.

RTU Security Concept Overview

Figure 5 shows the overall security concept for RTUs. Basically, integrate integrity enforcement (i.e., devices try to prevent transitions that would lead to inconsistent states) and integrity reporting (i.e., devices assure their integrity to their peers) technologies are integrated. As mentioned above, there exist three preconditions for a trusted system: Unhindered operation, reference behaviour and unambiguously identification. Unhindered operation and reference behaviour will be supported by the integrity enforcing and reporting technologies. Identification is done based on TLS.

Whenever two devices (RTUs, RTU and SCADA-server, etc.) communicate with each other, they set up a secure connection based on Transport Layer Security (TLS). Beside message integrity and confidentiality, this protocol enables mutual authentication based on public-key cryptography. During the production process, each device is provisioned with its own private key that is certified by the Original Equipment Manufacturer (OEM) to enable identification during run-time. The private keys are generated and stored on a TPM to prevent potential malicious software from reading the key.

Each device implements a set of security features to prevent malicious attacks or at least mitigate the consequences of a successful exploit. Beside usual system-hardening components such as firewalls, all RTUs implement secure boot to prevent unknown or compromised software components from being executed at all. During the development process, the OEM signs and certifies released binaries and only such binaries are allowed to be executed on the RTU. In order to mitigate the attack potential of compromised components due to exploited security relevant bugs, sandboxing is used. Each component is executed in its own sandbox, confined to the privileges it actually needs to work properly. An adversary that is able to exploit a bug is thus also confined to these privileges.

The technologies described so far can be used to identify devices and to harden themselves against attacks. In a distributed system, however, the chance of successful attacks cannot be fully eliminated. Therefore, integrity attestation is used to ensure the integrity of the peer. Without support of authentication and the other integrity enforcing technologies in place, remote attestation would not work at all or would be at least not as useful as expected. The remainder of this section describes the integration of different attestation methods in the RTU architecture.

Integrity Attestation Between RTUs

In order to enable integrity attestation, the following building blocks have to be integrated:

- A secure underlying network connection that enables authentication and identification. This is done by TLS.
- A protocol that enables a secure generation and exchange of the integrity proof.
- A method that defines the semantics of the integrity proof. This method defines how integrity is represented in the 'measurement'. It thus defines what the prover has to store and what information the challenger needs to know to understand and verify the prover's state.

Attestation Protocol

The attestation protocol assumes that all used keys are certified by a common Certification Authority (CA) (i.e., the OEM, during the production or installation process) and that the prover has generated a representation of its configuration (i.e., the 'measurement list') by one of the methods described later in this section. Moreover, the prover has used a TPM to protect the measurement list (e.g., by extending all changes to a PCR). The integrity of the measurement list is thus attestable with the help of the TPM.

The prover initiates a TLS connection with the challenger. Both peers are authenticated and the channel is secured. The challenger generates a nonce to prevent replay-attacks and requests a proof of the prover's platform state. A TPM is used to generate this proof by issuing the TPM-Quote command. The PCRs used to protect the measurement list are signed with an AIK directly on the TPM. The challenger verifies the proof by checking the signature and verifying whether the AIK is certified by the CA. Now the challenger requests the semantics of the proof (i.e., the measurement list) and checks it against its local policy and reference value. This last step can be omitted whenever the state of the prover did not change since the last attestation (i.e., the PCR values did not change). In this case, only the freshness of the PCR value by checking the quote response has to be verified.

Integrity Attestation Methods

As mentioned before, we integrated three different methods of integrity attestation to examine their applicability for our RTUs. Each method uses different properties (e.g., binary hashes) to generate the measurement list and to prove the state of the system. While we can use the same protocol, independent from the method, the following difference have to be considered:

- **Measurement List Generation and Storage:** The prover has to generate the measurement list. Depending on what properties are used for the measurement, this may add significant overhead in terms of CPU or memory for the prover. Moreover, the measurements have to be stored.
- **Protocol Overhead:** Depending on the attestation method, the measurement list and possible additional information has to be sent over the network during the attestation process to enable the verification of the prover's state.
- **Verification Process:** After verifying the integrity of the measurement list (e.g., by verifying whether the measurement list correlates with the signed PCR value), the challenger has to verify whether the measurement list represents a valid system state. The complexity and needed information for this step depends on the used attestation method.

Plain Binary Attestation With IMA

The first method is plain binary attestation based on IMA (Sailer et al., 2004). Here, the hashes of the binaries of all executed programs (and their configurations) represent the system state.

- **Measurement List Generation:** The prover generates a hash of each binary or configuration file prior its execution. Each measurement is added to the measurement list and extended to the PCR.
- **Protocol Overhead:** During the attestation process, the prover has to provide the measurement list that contains the names (i.e., full paths) of all executed applications and their hash values.
- **Verification Process:** The challenger verifies all hash values against a reference list. This reference list has to be pre-deployed.

Privilege-Based Attestation

The second method is privileged-based attestation, as discussed in (Rauter et al., 2017). If one can ensure that there is no writeup and no read-down (e.g. write from a reduced privileged service to a privilege service), one can ensure that the lesser privileged services are not able to harm the integrity of the higher privileged services (Biba, 1977). Compared to IMA, this method reduces the number of potential reference measurements for the verification, because the challenger can simply ignore applications that have not enough privileges to violate the integrity of the targeted service.

- **Measurement List Generation:** Similar to IMA, the prover generates binary measurements for all executed applications. Moreover, all applications have to be classified regarding their privileges. The classification has also to be 'measured' prior to the execution of an application. This is achieved by detecting used libraries and enforcing the identified privilege class of the service with sandboxes. Since the existing architecture enforces a seperation of concerns, this part can be implement relatively easily (Rauter et al., 2017). Both type of measurements, the binary and the privilege measurements, have to be extended to a PCR.
- **Protocol Overhead:** During the attestation process, the prover has to provide the measurement list that contains the names (i.e., full paths) of all executed applications, their hash values and their privilege classification.
- **Verification Process:** The challenger removes all under-privileged applications from the measurement list and verifies the remaining hash values against a reference list.

Signature-Based Attestation

The third method uses the authority of the OEM to sign the hash values of the executables. Basically, the OEM represents a TTP that certifies the property of a 'known good software' for each binary hash. The challenger has to trust the CA that certifies these properties for all applications.

- **Measurement List Generation:** The prover generates a hash of each binary or configuration file prior its execution. Each measurement is added to the measurement list and extended to the PCR.
- **Protocol Overhead:** During the attestation process, the prover has to provide the measurement list that contains the names (i.e., full paths) of all executed applications and their hash values. Moreover, the prover has to provide certificates for the hash values.
- **Verification Process:** The challenger verifies whether there exists a good certificate for all hash values.

EVALUATION

Integrating integrity attestation into a distributed computing system introduces additional challenges in all lifecycle stages of the system. Integrity measurements have to be taken, the attestation protocol introduces communication overhead and the challenger has to verify the measurement. Moreover, the policy which is used to verify a measurement list has to be updated each time, the software configuration of the prover changes. Another way is to formulate a policy in such a way that at least minor updates of the prover do not require an update of the reference values without degrading the quality of the integrity verification. In order to achieve this in a feasible way, the development and deployment process of the software components have to be adapted. Moreover, secure provisioning is needed to distribute and certify secrets that enable identification.

Based on the three implement attestation methods in the RTU described before, we examined especially the following properties:

- **Operational Overhead:** What is the introduced overhead during the operation phase by implementing the methodology? This comprises the overhead for generating the measurement list, the communication overhead in the attestation protocol and the verification overhead at the challenger's side.
- **Configuration Updates:** What are the implications of software updates on the prover for all other devices in the system?
- **Development Process:** Are there some necessary adaptions of the development and distribution process of the software components?
- **Secure Provisioning:** What are the requirements regarding secure provisioning?

After evaluating these questions for each method, we compare the benefits and drawbacks of each and discuss what constraints and circumstances would support which methodology.

Plain Binary Attestation With IMA

- **Operational Overhead:** On the presented system, IMA is configured to hash all executables, linked libraries and configuration files (i.e., file opened for read). The accumulated size of the 267 measured files is about 50 MB. For each file, one entry in the measurement list is taken. Each entry contains the file name (fixed size: 255 Byte) and a SHA-1 hash (20 Byte). Usually, one has to maintain all measurement entries separately since the PCR extension is non-commutative. In the used system, however, the order of execution of the base system and libraries can be controlled. Therefore, the size of the measurement list can be reduced to 42 entries, similar as shown in (Rauter et al., 2017). The boot-composite (i.e., kernel measurement), the platform-composite (system services and system libraries), and the remaining 40 measurements that represent the actual running application services, its libraries and configurations.

The overhead for computing the measurements and extension to the PCR register increases the boot-time from 21s to 49s. This is a huge overhead for the boot process. During runtime, however, there are no additional measurements because all applications are already started. Only software updates or malicious software components would cause an additional measurement. Since the boot-time still complies with the requirements (only the boot-time of the independent application controller is critical), the overhead is acceptable.

The measurement list with all entries has to be sent during the attestation process each time the configuration changes. As discussed before, the list is relatively stable except in case of software updates. Therefore, also this overhead is acceptable.

The verification for the challenger is basically a re-computation of the PCR value and consists a couple of hash operations. Moreover, the challenger has to store the reference values for all applications. Both, the computing and memory overhead are manageable, even for lightweight systems.

- **Configuration Updates:** Each update of any software component (or configuration) on the prover requires an update of all reference lists at each possible communication partner (challenger). The update process is thus more complex, especially when a sophisticated re-verification of the function of devices is needed after each update. Moreover, software updates often introduce, albeit short, downtimes for each device what may not be acceptable for the operator of the system. Additionally, a software update triggers a new measurement and a re-transmission of the measurement list.
- **Development Process:** The reference measurement lists have to be created during the development process. This means that a list of hashes for each application has to be maintained. The overhead of integration of this additional step into an existing build and deployment infrastructure is, however, limited.
- **Secure Provisioning:** The generation and certification of AIKs has to be done securely during the production or deployment process of the devices. Since this step is already done for the private keys used for identification and authentication for devices during the production process, the infrastructure already exists and the overhead is also limited. Moreover, the distribution of reference measurements has to be done in a secure way. This is, however, similar to a normal software update and can be done with the already in-place authenticated software update process.

Privilege-Based Attestation

- **Operational Overhead:** Since privilege-based attestation also requires binary measurement for same-and higher privileged components, all considerations regarding measurement and protocol overhead of plain binary attestation are also true for this method. Additionally, privilege measurements (i.e., the privilege classification) for each entry have to be taken and communicated. In the presented system, this is done by analyzing the linked libraries. Each library allows access to a specific set of critical system functions. The overhead in the linking process is negligible (Rauter et al., 2017). The classification is added to the measurement list and encoded as label in a 4 Byte integer. Moreover, a sandboxing mechanism has to be in place that mediates all accesses to critical system functions and resources to ensure that each application stays in its classified privilege level.

The verification on the challenger is now more complex. First, the challenger has to know its 'target service' (i.e., the service it is actually using on the prover). Then, all services with lower privilege classification are ignored in the measurement list. Technically, this reduces the Trusted Computing Base (TCB) (i.e., the set of software components which are critical to the integrity of the targeted service). For the remaining entries, the same verification method as before is used.

- **Configuration Updates:** As shown in (Rauter et al., 2017), this approach can significantly reduce the size of the TCB, especially if the targeted service has high privileges (about 50%). Therefore, the frequency of updates of the reference lists is also reduced for a potentially high number of devices.
- **Development Process:** This approach requires the possibility to determine the privilege classification at library-level. Therefore, each library has to be designed in such a way, that it exports a set of accessor functions within the same classification. In the used system, for example, there exist li-

braries that allow access to system functions (system-privilege: access all system resources), control functions (control-privilege: access to resources and functions which are critical to the control task) and additional lower privileged functions (e.g., only read access to datapoints). While this raised relatively little changes in the used system architecture (the service oriented architecture separated the privileges from the beginning), this may require a significant architectural change for other systems that may not be feasible at all.

- **Secure Provisioning:** There are no additional secrets that have to be provided compared to plain binary attestation.

Signature-Based Attestation

- **Operational Overhead:** The measurement and protocol overhead is the at least the same as for plain binary attestation. The challenger, however, does not have a list of reference measurements now. Instead, it requests certificates for each measurement entry from the prover. These certificates have to be created by the OEM and distributed to the prover with each software update. The challenger now has to verify the signatures, what includes public-key cryptography. Consequently, the computing overhead on the challenger may be significant and the process is not feasible for lightweight devices.
- **Configuration Updates:** A configuration update on the prover requires also the update of the certificate. The distribution to the challengers, however, can be done during the normal attestation process, since the challenger simply requests the new certificate from the prover when an unknown measurement appears in the list.
- **Development Process:** In addition to the generation of the application's binary hash, the OEM has to sign these hashes during the build or deployment process. This may require some changes in the build policy of the company, since the private key used to generated these signatures has to be protected and the builds that are actually signed have to be selected carefully (e.g., only builds that are meant for deployment).
- **Secure Provisioning:** The challenger requires knowledge of the CA that signs the software components. In this case, this is the same entity that certifies the identification keys and the AIK. Therefore, no additional overhead is required here.

Overview and Discussion

Table 1 summarizes the benefits and drawbacks of each examined method. While plain binary attestation suffers from the potential unacceptable problem of updates the reference measurements, the other methods may be feasible, depending on the actual system.

The privilege-based method potentially significantly reduces the quantity and the dynamics of the measurement lists in case of software updates. However, it raises significant requirements concerning the system architecture and the development process. The identification of useful privilege classification levels is non-trivial. And even in the used architecture, which was built with privilege separation in mind, some architectural adoptions and instructions to raise the awareness of developers is needed.

The signature-based approach is less invasive but it requires all software modules to be certified. In case a secure-boot process is already in place, these signatures could be, however, re-used. Additionally,

Table 1. Evaluation summary

	Binary-Based	Privilege-Based	Signature-Based
Prover Overhead			
Time Overhead	- (boot)	- (boot)	- (boot)
Entry Size[B]	275	279	275
Entry Count	42	42	42
Communication Overhead			
Additional Information	Measurement List	Measurement List	Measurement List, Signatures
Challenger Overhead			
Reference Measurement	42	20-42	0 0
Additional Information		Target Service	CA, Singnature-Cache (optional)
Computing Overhead	++	++	-- (public-key-crytography)
Software Update on Prover			
Challenger-Updates	--	+-(depends)	++ (no dedicated updates)
Development Process			
Potential Impact	-	--	-
Secure Provisioning			
Potential Impact	-	-	-

the challenger has to compute cost-intensive signature verification based on public key cryptography, that may not be feasible for some types of lightweight devices such as smart sensors or actuators.

Depending on the actual system and already in-place security enhancing subsystems, integrity reporting could be a practicable analysis method to detect compromised components to further ensure system integrity and availability.

CONCLUSION AND FUTURE OUTLOOK

In this chapter, we discussed the specific security requirements in the field of ICS due to the changing requirements that emerge from the need of increased connectivity and cooperation of control systems at different geographic locations. We described how IDS can be used to improve availability and integrity in such systems and summarized methods of anomaly detection at different system levels.

We motivated the need for IDS based on integrity analysis to design a distributed control system with automated reconfiguration capabilities in case of compromise of single components. Integrity reporting technologies, as proposed by the TCG, are a promising candidate as basis for such anomaly detection systems. Due to the problem of the distribution of reference measurements, such systems are not yet widely used.

We investigated three methods based on an actual RTU architecture to examine their practicability in this domain. While plain binary attestation does not seem to fit the requirements, we have shown that privilege-based and signature-based attestation could be promising candidates in this domain, depending on the existing system architecture.

Future research topics include the integration of not-yet discovered or adapted attestation methodologies but also investigations concerning a better applicability of existing methods. Moreover, the requirements regarding the secure hardware backends should be explored to get a better understanding of the features that are actually used.

REFERENCES

Alliance, T. C. P. (2000). *Building A Foundation of Trust in the PC*.

Amoroso, E. G. (1999). *An Introduction to Intrusion Detection*.

Biba, K. J. (1977). *Integrity Considerations for Secure Computer Systems*.

Ceccato, M., Ofek, Y., & Tonella, P. (2008). A Protocol for Property-Based Attestation. *Theory and Practice of Computer Science*, 7.

Chen, L., Löhr, H., Manulis, M., & Sadeghi, A. (2008). *Property-Based Attestation Without a Trusted Third Party*. Information Security. doi:10.1007/978-3-540-85886-7_3

Coker, G., Guttman, J., Loscocco, P., Herzog, A., Millen, J., OHanlon, B., & Sniffen, B. et al. (2011). Principles of Remote Attestation. *International Journal of Information Security*, *10*(2), 63–81. doi:10.1007/s10207-011-0124-7

Electricity Information Sharing and Analysis Center. (2016). *Analysis of the Cyber Attack on the Ukrainian Power Grid*.

Formby, D., Srinivasan, P., Leonard, A., Rogers, J., & Beyah, R. (2016). Who's in Control of Your Control System? Device Fingerprinting for Cyber-Physical Systems. In Network and distributed system security symposium (pp. 21–24). doi:10.14722/ndss.2016.23142

Ghaeini, H. R., & Tippenhauer, N. O. (2016). HAMIDS: Hierarchical Monitoring Intrusion Detection System for Industrial Control Systems. In *Proceedings of the Workshop on cyber-physical systems security and privacy* (pp. 103–111). doi:10.1145/2994487.2994492

Hadžiosmanović, D., Bolzoni, D., & Hartel, P. H. (2012). A Log Mining Approach for Process Monitoring in SCADA. *International Journal of Information Security*, *11*(4), 231–251. doi:10.1007/s10207-012-0163-8

Höller, A., Iber, J., Rauter, T., & Kreiner, C. (2016). Poster: Towards a Secure, Resilient, and Distributed Infrastructure for Hydropower Plant Unit Control. In *Adjunct Proceedings of the 13th International Conference on Embedded Wireless Systems and Networks (EWSN) [Poster]*.

IEC. (1995). *Application and implementation of IEC 61131-3*.

ITSG. (2015). *Gesetz zur Erhöhung der Sicherheit informationstechnischer Systeme*. IT-Sicherheitsgesetz.

Iturbe, M. (2016). On the Feasibility of Distinguishing Between Process Disturbances and Intrusions in Process Control Systems using Multivariate Statistical Process Control. In Dependable systems and networks workshop. doi:10.1109/DSN-W.2016.32

Jaeger, T., Sailer, R., & Shankar, U. (2006). Policy-Reduced Integrity Measurement Architecture. In *Symposium on access control models and technologies.*

Kiss, I., Genge, B., & Haller, P. (2015). A Clustering-Based Approach to Detect Cyber Attacks in Process Control Systems. In *Proceedings of the 2015 IEEE 13th International Conference on Industrial Informatics (INDIN)* (pp. 142–148).

Krotofil, M., Larsen, J., & Gollmann, D. (2015). The Process Matters: Ensuring Data Veracity in Cyber-Physical Systems. In Proceedings of the ACM symposium on information, computer and communications security.

Langner, R. (2011). *Stuxnet: Dissecting a Cyberwarfare Weapon. Security Privacy.* IEEE.

Lee, R. M., Assante, M. J., & Conway, T. (2014). *German Steel Mill Cyber Attack* (pp. 1–15).

Liserre, M., Sauter, T., & Hung, J. (2010a). Future Energy Systems: Integrating Renewable Energy Sources into the Smart Power Grid Through Industrial Electronics. *IEEE Industrial Electronics Magazine, 4*(1), 18–37. doi:10.1109/MIE.2010.935861

Liserre, M., Sauter, T., & Hung, J. Y. (2010b). Future Energy Systems: Inegrating Renewable Energy into the Smart Power Grid Through Industrial Electronics. *IEEE Industrial Electronics Magazine,* (March), 18–37.

Liu, Y., Ning, P., & Reiter, M. K. (2009). False Data Injection Attacks Against State Estimation in Electric Power Grids. In *Proceedings of the Conference on Computer and Communications Security, 14*(1), 1–33. doi:10.1145/1653662.1653666

Miller, B., & Rowe, D. (2012). A Survey SCADA of and Critical Infrastructure Incidents. In *Proceedings of the Annual Conference on Research in Information Technology,* 51. doi:10.1145/2380790.2380805

Mitchell, R., & Chen, I.-r. (2014). A Survey of Intrusion Detection Techniques for Cyber-Physical Systems. *ACM Computing Surveys (CSUR), 46*(4).

Paxson, V. (1999). Bro: A System for Detecting Network Intruders in Real-Time. *Computer Networks, 31*(23-24), 2435–2463. doi:10.1016/S1389-1286(99)00112-7

Proudler, G. (2005). Concepts of Trusted Computing. In C. Mitchell (Ed.), *Trusted computing. Proudler2005.* doi:10.1049/PBPC006E_ch2

Rauter, T., Höller, A., Kajtazovic, N., & Kreiner, C. (2015). Privilege-Based Remote Attestation: Towards Integrity Assurance for Lightweight Clients. In *Proceedings of the Workshop on ioT privacy, trust, and security.* doi:10.1145/2732209.2732211

Rauter, T., Iber, J., Krisper, M., & Kreiner, C. (2017). Integration of Integrity Enforcing Technologies into Embedded Control Devices: Experiences and Evaluation. In *The 22nd IEEE pacific rim international symposium on dependable computing*.

Rein, A., Rieke, R., Jäger, M., Kuntze, N., & Coppolino, L. (2015). Trust Establishment in Cooperating Cyber-Physical Systems. In Security of industrial control systems and cyber physical systems.

Roesch, M. (1999). Snort: Lightweight Intrusion Detection for Networks. In *Proceedings of LISA '99: 13th Systems Administration Conference* (pp. 229–238).

Sadeghi, A., & Stüble, C. (2004). Property-based Attestation for Computing Platforms: Caring About Properties, not Mechanisms. *Proceedings of the 2004 Workshop on New Security Paradigms* (pp. 67–77).

Sailer, R., Zhang, X., Jaeger, T., & van Doorn, L. (2004). Design and Implementation of a TCG-based Integrity Measurement Architecture.

Stouffer, K., Falco, J., & Scarfone, K. (2015). Guide to Industrial Control Systems (ICS) Security. Nist Special Publication, 800(82).

TCG. (2016). Trusted Computing Group. Retrieved January 1, 2016, from https://www.trustedcomputinggroup.org/

Trusted Computing Group. (2006). TPM Main Specification Level 2 Version 1.2.

Trusted Computing Group. (2007). *TCG Specification Architecture Overview* (pp. 1–24). No. August.

Udd, R., Asplund, M., Nadjm-Tehrani, S., Kazemtabrizi, M., & Ekstedt, M. (2016). Exploiting Bro for Intrusion Detection in a SCADA System. In *Proceedings of the Cyber-Physical System Security Workshop* (pp. 44–51). doi:10.1145/2899015.2899028

Urbina, D. I., Giraldo, J., Cardenas, A. A., Tippenhauer, N. O., Valente, J., & Faisal, M. … Sandberg, H. (2016). Limiting the Impact of Stealthy Attacks on Industrial Control Systems. In *Proceedings of the 23rd aCM conference on computer and communications security*.

Xu, W., Zhang, X., & Hu, H. (2012). Remote Attestation with Domain-Based Integrity Model and Policy Analysis. In *Dependable and Secure Computing* (pp. 429–442).

Zonouz, S., Rrushi, J., & McLaughlin, S. (2014). Detecting Industrial Control Malware using Automated PLC Code Analytics. *IEEE Security and Privacy, 12*(6), 40–47. doi:10.1109/MSP.2014.113

Chapter 15
Integration of Security in the Development Lifecycle of Dependable Automotive CPS

Georg Macher
AVL List GmbH, Austria

Christoph Schmittner
Austrian Institute of Technology, Austria

Eric Armengaud
AVL List GmbH, Austria

Zhendong Ma
Austrian Institute of Technology, Austria

Christian Kreiner
Graz University of Technology, Austria

Helmut Martin
Virtual Vehicle Research Center, Austria

Eugen Brenner
Graz University of Technology, Austria

Martin Krammer
Virtual Vehicle Research Center, Austria

ABSTRACT

The exciting new features, such as advanced driver assistance systems, fleet management systems, and autonomous driving, drive the need for built-in security solutions and architectural designs to mitigate emerging security threats. Thus, cybersecurity joins reliability and safety as a cornerstone for success in the automotive industry. As vehicle providers gear up for cybersecurity challenges, they can capitalize on experiences from many other domains, but nevertheless must face several unique challenges. Therefore, this article focuses on the enhancement of state-of-the-art development lifecycle for automotive cyber-physical systems toward the integration of security, safety and reliability engineering methods. Especially, four engineering approaches (HARA at concept level, FMEA and FTA at design level and HSI at implementation level) are extended to integrate security considerations into the development lifecycle.

DOI: 10.4018/978-1-5225-2845-6.ch015

INTRODUCTION

Before the introduction of wireless connections and automated driving functionalities, vehicles were physically isolated machines with mechanical controls. Extra-functional properties of concern were mainly timing, reliability and functional safety. The emergence of cyber-physical automotive systems over the last decades has affected the development of vehicles, promising to improve the safety of drivers and support new applications. The deployment of connected CPS especially is leading to a strong re-organization of the automotive market, moving from "vehicle as a product" to "transportation as a service". Hence, the availability of information (e.g., powertrain control strategy, traffic information, as well as infotainment and connectivity) is shifting the customer added value of the passenger car.

In this context, the rising vehicle-to-vehicle and vehicle-to-infrastructure connectivity causes multiple inter-vehicle connections as well as capabilities for (wireless) networking with other vehicles and non-vehicle entities. Automotive systems are developing from stand-alone systems towards systems of systems, interacting and coordinating with each other and influencing vehicle actions. Connections are not restricted to internal systems (e.g. steering, sensor, actuator, and communications) but also include other road users and the infrastructure. Current vehicles already utilize connectivity for over-the-air updates, smart maintenance, remote tracking or insurance services.

A well-known demonstration of security risks was the hack of a Jeep Cherokee (Miller & Valasek, Remote Exploitation of an Unaltered Passenger Vehicle, 2015). The intrusion started through a vulnerability in the cellular network configuration, progressed from the telematic system and ultimately affected even safety-critical control units. The Attackers were able to influence braking, steering and acceleration. A similar weakness was also found by the German automotive club ADAC in the ConnectedDrive system installed in BMW vehicles. A vulnerability in the communication configuration allowed an attacker to access the communication.

Audi and Corvette examples demonstrated that attacks are not always triggered by direct remote connectivity. The CrySyS Lab of the Budapest University of Technology and Economics demonstrated that an infected USB stick was sufficient to deactivate the Airbags in an Audi TT without giving either the rest of the system or the driver notice of the deactivation (Szijj, Buttyan, & Szalay, 2015).

In the case of the Corvette the attack was conducted through an insurance OBD-dongle. While the on-board diagnosis (OBD) interface is intended for maintenance and error reports, it also allows monitoring of the vehicle speed and location. The insurance company offered personalized insurance deals, based on driving behavior. The OBD dongle monitored speed and location and transmitted the data to the insurance company. Researchers were able to misuse the same connection to perform a proof-of-concept attack on the braking system of the vehicle.

After 2018, all vehicles sold in the EU, are required to be able to send GPS coordinates, impact sensor and airbag deployment information in the case of an accident. This so-called eCall functionality requires wireless connectivity. GM offers in North America already a similar service through the OnStar Network, which was successfully attacked (Baldwin, 2015).

While wireless connections open the attack surface, increased automated driving functionalities and data collection have introduced further valuable targets for attacker. Motivation for such attacks range from inflicting financial damage on a competitor (e.g., loss of image), loss of confidentiality or privacy with respect to driver (e.g., profile) or car manufacturer (e.g., sensitive vehicle information), or operational or safety impacts. Taking into account the fact that worldwide over a million people fall victim to cybercrime every day and that the global cost of cybercrime was assessed at 313 billion Euros in 2011

(Cercone & Ernst, 2012), security is a high priority requirement for automotive CPS. As a result, the automotive domain is starting to adapt established processes and methods for security engineering (e.g. the recently available SAE J3061 (SAE Vehicle Electrical System Security Committee, 2016) and new work item proposals for automotive cybersecurity ISO standards).

While reliability and now functional safety are well accepted in the automotive domain, security engineering is a novel aspect for this industry. Even if the hand-over of know-how and best practice from other application domains can be performed successfully, a major aspect here is the efficient integration of reliability, safety and security engineering into a common lifecycle for the development of dependable automotive cyber-physical systems. The main contributions this paper makes are (a) the introduction of differential analysis covering both safety and security aspects over the lifecycle (SAHARA at concept level, FMEVA and ATA at design level and HSI trust-boundary method at implementation level, all having the target of integrating the security consideration in safety analysis), (b) the enhancement of safety assurance cases as an advance towards case dependability for the integration of security considerations, and (c) the application of the proposed methods for an automotive use case in order to evaluate the benefits of the proposed approach.

The paper is organized as follow: first, the challenges and the impact of cyber-physical systems and connected vehicles in the automotive sector are highlighted. Subsequently, automotive engineering approaches and best practices from other domains are reviewed. In the third section, an extension of the state-of-the-art lifecycle in automotive system development for comprehensive dependability features (taking into consideration cooperative safety, security and reliability features) is proposed, followed and concluded by an application of the proposed dependability feature engineering approach based on an automotive use-case example of a battery management system.

DEPENDABILITY FEATURE ENGINEERING

The term "dependability" can be defined as follows: Dependability of a system is the ability to avoid service failures that are more frequent and more severe than is acceptable. A service failure (abbr. failure) is an event that occurs when the delivered service deviates from correct service. Correct service is delivered when a service implements the system function. Since a service is a sequence of the system's externally visible states, a service failure means that at least one (or more) externally visible state of the system deviates from the correct service state. The deviation is termed an error. The adjudged or hypothesized cause of an error is termed a fault. System's faults can occur internal or external. For this reason the definition of an error is: the part of the total system state that may lead to its subsequent service failure. (Avizienis, Laprie, & Randell, Dependability and its Threats - A Taxonomy, 2004)

"Dependability" is a holistic term for combining different concepts in the context of threats, attributes, and means (see Figure 1).

Dependability can be introduced in general terms as a global concept that subsumes usual attributes such as reliability, availability, safety, integrity, maintainability, etc. The security consideration also includes and comprises additional concerns for confidentiality.

Over the past centuries many means have been developed to attain the various attributes of dependability and security. Those means can be grouped into following major categories:

Figure 1. Dependability and security tree
Source: Avizienis, Laprie, & Randell, 2004.

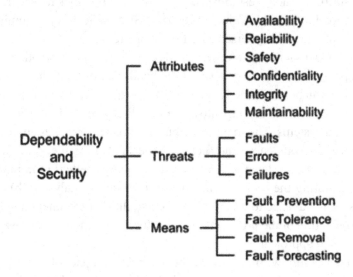

- **Fault Prevention:** Means to prevent the occurrence or introduction of faults;
- **Fault Tolerance:** Means to avoid service failures in the presence of faults;
- **Fault Removal:** Means to reduce the number and severity of faults;
- **Fault Forecasting:** Means to estimate the present number, the future incidence, and the likely consequences of faults.

Fault prevention and fault tolerance aim to provide the capability to deliver a service that can be trusted, while fault removal and fault forecasting aim to reach confidence in that ability by justifying that the functional and the dependability & security specifications are adequate and that the system is likely to meet them.

Dependability Feature Nomenclatures and Relation

The trend of replacing traditional mechanical systems with modern embedded systems is leading to new challenges in the degree of integration and criticality of the control application, electronics hardware, in addition to mechanical subsystems. System dependability features have mutual impacts, similarities and interdisciplinary values in common and a considerable overlap among existing methods. Further to this, specialized, separated standards, such as ISO 26262 (ISO 26262 Road vehicles Functional Safety Part 1-10, 2011) for functional safety, and SAE J3061 (SAE Vehicle Electrical System Security Committee, 2016) respective Common Criteria (The Common Criteria Recognition Agreement Members, 2014) in the security domain, have been established to provide requirements and guidance for development in the corresponding domain. However, future automotive systems will require appropriate systematic approaches to support comprehensive integrated dependable system engineering, rather than traditional engineering approaches treating and managing safety, security, or reliability features separately.

A contemporary integrated automotive dependability approach, as depicted in Figure 8 and according to (Macher G., Hoeller, Sporer, Armengaud, & Kreiner, 2015) should encompass at least the following attributes:

- **Safety:** Absence of catastrophic consequences for users and environment.
- **Security:** The concurrent existence of availability for authorized users only, confidentiality, and integrity with a clearly defined improper unauthorized access profile.
- **Serviceability:** The combination of reliability (continuity of correct service) and maintainability (ability to undergo modifications and repairs).

Table 1 provides a mapping of dependability features and their corresponding analysis concepts in early design phases of an embedded automotive system. The integrated approach is based on a combination of security threats analysis using STRIDE (Microsoft Corporation, 2005), functional safety hazards analysis and risk assessment (HARA) called SAHARA (Macher G., Sporer, Berlach, Armengaud, & Kreiner, 2015). A further extension by a service deterioration analysis (SDA) (Macher G., Hoeller, Sporer, Armengaud, & Kreiner, 2015) yields an integrated dependability analysis approach for the aforementioned attributes.

While engineering one individual technical (dependable) system alone, it becomes evident during these criticality analysis stages that the system boundaries to be analyzed differ significantly when analyzing different dependability attributes viz. functional safety, Cybersecurity, reliability, and more.

Table 1. Mapping of safety, security, and service oriented engineering terms

		Safety Engineering ISO26262 (IEC61508)	Security Engineering STRIDE, SAHARA, SAE J3061	Service-Oriented Engineering SDA, RAMS
Analysis Subjects	Risk	hazard	threat	warranty claim, unplanned maintenance
	system inherent deficiency	malfunction	vulnerability	service loss or degradation
	external enabling condition	hazardous situation	attack	(mis)usage profile
Analysis Categories	impact analysis	severity	threat criticality	reputation loss, deterioration impact
	external risk control analysis	controllability	attacker skills, know-how	repair efforts, repair aggravation
	occurrence analysis	Exposure (frequency)	point of attack, attack resources	operation condition spectrum
Analysis Results	Design goal	safety goal	security target	dependability target
	Design goal criticality	ASIL (Automotive Safety Integrity Level), (SIL)	SecL (Security Level)	deterioration resistance level (DRL), system reliability, service level agreement

Source: Macher G., Hoeller, Sporer, Armengaud, & Kreiner, 2015.

According to ISO26262, in Functional Safety we need to define and analyze the so called "Item" stressing the potentially dangerous functional aspect. The definition by the standard: "…an Item is a system or an array of systems to implement a function at the vehicle level, to which ISO 26262 is applied." Further safety analysis is then based on this Item, covering only a subset of the overall system and system context.

The corresponding concept for vehicle cybersecurity is called "Feature." The SAE J3061 definition: "The feature definition identifies the physical boundaries, Cybersecurity perimeter, and trust boundaries of the feature, including the network perimeter of the feature." And furthermore, to point out its importance: "This feature definition is important since it defines the scope of the feature. Analysis activities performed on the feature are restricted to the described scope and perimeters defined in the feature definition."

The general architecture integration concept is highlighted by the *Trident Architectural Views* pattern (Kreiner, 2015). This considers three essential architectural viewpoints (function, elements, and composition) and their relations as shown in Figure 2. System architecture is approached from these three viewpoints. Following the relations makes inconsistencies and omissions in the view models visible. In a way, these nine relationships also yield nine additional consistency sub views. While Elements (E) and composition (C) are of course the elements of the system developed AND its environment, the Function view (F) - i.e. the dependability attribute under investigation - guides the selection of the corresponding Elements and Composition for a specific dependability attribute

Figure 2. Trident architectural views: three essential architectural viewpoints with nine relations for engineering of dependable systems
Source: Kreiner, 2015.

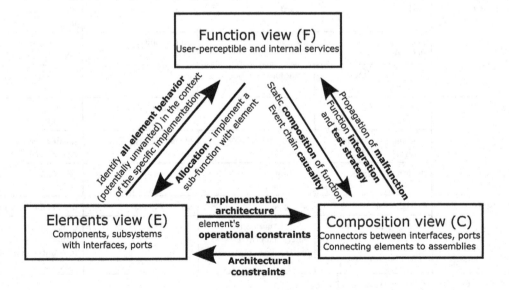

Cooperative Safety and Security Process Framework

Each area of development has its own types of processes. An extensive development process needs to be well defined and systematic to overcome its complexity. Quality management and quality assessment become important in complex processes. An example for a project management methodology is the V-Modell XT®. It defines activities to minimize process risks, improve quality, reduce costs and improve communication between all stakeholders. Additionally, it defines quality requirements for functionality, reliability, efficiency, changeability and roles which determine who is responsible for specific results. These requirements are verified and validated during an evaluation (Verein zur Weiterentwicklung des V-Modell XT e.V., 2015).

Safety and security activities are part of the V-Modell XT but for the automotive domain ISO 26262 and SAE J3061 define a more specific safety lifecycle and a cybersecurity lifecycle. ISO 26262 defines a safety life cycle but presupposes that special quality standards such as Automotive SPICE are used additionally. It demands evidence to show that the established processes perform appropriately. Reviews (e.g. review of the safety analysis), audits (e.g. functional safety audit) and assessments (e.g. functional safety assessment) are included requirements. That is why the necessary supportive arguments should be available.

Automotive SPICE (The SPICE User Group, 2015) provides a process reference and a process assessment model to improve the quality of development processes. Its focus is on process improvement and assessment. An assessment leads to a "Process capability Level".

SAE J3061defines "a complete lifecycle process framework that can be tailored and utilized within each organization's development processes to incorporate Cybersecurity into cyber-physical vehicle systems" (SAE Vehicle Electrical System Security Committee, 2016).

We will present the interaction between the two domains safety and cybersecurity, as provided in the SAE J3061 guidebook. A well-defined and well-structured cooperative safety and security process framework is needed, because system safety and cybersecurity should be built into the system rather than added on at the end of development.

The cooperative process framework needs to apply a discipline specific process (e.g. cybersecurity), which has its focus on domain specific aspects, separately to any other discipline specific process (e.g. functional safety). But it is vital to identify, establish and distribute the various communication paths between all disciplines. Figure 3 shows an example for the concept phase for cybersecurity and safety, which highlights the required interaction during the elaboration of the risk assessment, the functional concept, the functional requirements and the concept phase review. For all lifecycle phases (concept phase, system development, hardware and software development, production, operation and decommissioning) it is important to harmonize the specific outcomes of analysis activities and the derived counter measures between the relevant disciplines.

Consideration of a number of different standards may cause repetition of activities. Tailoring of standards to company- and project- specific processes as well as definition of a harmonized terminology demand enormous effort and work input. A special process management methodology may be useful for dealing with this workload. For example, "Security-informed Safety-oriented Process Line Engineering", is used to identify commonalities in different processes. During the integration of different standards to an integrated process a developer must map different terms to gain a common terminology. A vital step to maximize the commonality level is to go beyond irrelevant terminological differences. The identification

Figure 3. Concept phase activities with potential communications paths between cybersecurity and safety activities
Source: SAE Vehicle Electrical System Security Committee, 2016.

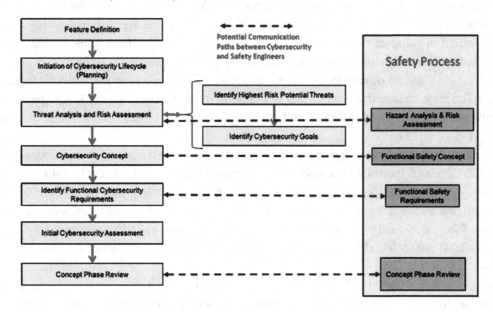

of commonality leads to a smaller development process because repetitions are prevented. This saves time and money (Gallina, Kashiyarandi, Martin, & Bramberger, 2014) and (Gallina & Fabre, 2015).

In a manner similar to the original methods, each safety and security method is aimed at a different phase of the lifecycle and will generate the best results in this phase (see Figure 4). SAHARA can be already used during concept phase, based on first functions and features and identify safety & security goals. For the application of FMVEA a first system architecture is required in order to identify potential attack paths and system or design vulnerabilities. The Attack Tree Analysis (ATA) requires an even more detailed design and can also consider concrete and known software vulnerabilities. The HSI trust boundary method provides a way to identify trust boundaries and attack vectors on complex systems via signal interfaces based on the hardware-software interface (HSI). This central development artefact of the ISO 26262 functional safety development process helps further in supporting the cybersecurity engineering process on the interface layer. The Dependability Case can be seen as a collection of all required evidences supported by different engineering approaches for the argumentation that the system is dependable.

RELATED ENGINEERING APPROACHES

This section provides an overview of industrial established practices in relation to comprehensive dependability engineering. More especially, the methods for systematic risk management and for system validation (risk management, SAHARA, FMVEA, and ATA) and for comprehensive dependability evidence provisioning (assurance case), especially in context of ISO 26262 process landscape, are described as a comprehensive approach for managing the safety and security attributes during system development.

Figure 4. Mapping of methods to specific development phases

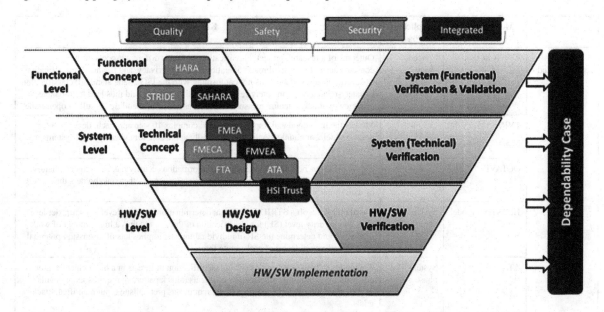

Overview of Risk Management Methods

While the hazard analysis and risk assessment (HARA) method in the context of automotive functional safety is standardized and mandated by the ISO 26262 standard, several candidates for a cybersecurity threat analysis and risk assessment (TARA) method exist. While some of these are mentioned in the SAE J3061 cybersecurity guidebook, there are more in existence than those in this listing. SAE J3061 states on the collection of cybersecurity analysis techniques "Appendix A (Description of cybersecurity analysis techniques) is provided as a reference to further research and to facilitate design and process improvements. Appendix A is not a comprehensive listing of Cybersecurity analysis techniques." (SAE Vehicle Electrical System Security Committee, 2016)

An overview and review of available threat analysis methods and their automotive applicability is given in (Macher, Armengaud, Brenner, & Kreiner, 2016). In particular, this review also includes an analysis of the development phases in which these methods can be sensibly applied (see Table 2 and Table 3). While only a few are suited as TARA for early concept stages, some others have properties which are highly desirable at later development stages. Based on this analysis we selected the sequel of methods described in detail further down. Notable methods are:

- TARA methods listed in SAE J3061 Appendices A-C:
  - EVITA method
  - Threat, vulnerabilities, and implementation risks analysis (TVRA)
  - Operationally critical threat, asset, and vulnerability evaluation (OCTAVE)
  - HEAVENS security model
  - Attack tree Analysis (ATA)
  - Software vulnerability analysis

Table 2. Evaluation of TARA Methods recommended by SAE J3061

	Method Name	Applicable Phase	Key Facts
SAE J3061 recommended	EVITA method	Concept phase	Outcome of a research project; classification separates different aspects of the consequences of security threats (operational, safety, privacy, and financial) classification of severity is adopted and thus not conforming with the ISO 26262 standard; classification of safety-related and non-safety-related threats differs and could thus lead to in-balances; accuracy of attack potential measures and expression as probabilities is still an open issue
	TVRA	---	Models the likelihood and impact of attacks; complex 10 step approach; developed for data - and telecommunication networks; hardly applicable for cyber physical systems in vehicles
	OCTAVE	---	This approach is best suited for enterprise information security risk assessments; hardly applicable for cyber physical systems in vehicles; brings together stakeholders thru series of workshops
	HEAVENS model	System phase	Based on Microsoft's STRIDE approach; determination of threat level (TL), impact level (IL), and security level (SL) for classification of threats; requires a high amount of work to analyze and determine the SL of individual threats; implies lots of discussion potential for each individual factor of each single threat.
	ATA	System phase	Analogous to fault tree analysis (FTA); identification of threats in a hierarchical manner; adequate for exploiting combinations of threats (attack patterns); requires more details of the system design to be more accurate, requires as prerequisite input identified attack goals.
	SW vulnerability analysis	SW phase	Examines software code to prevent occurrence of potential vulnerabilities; focuses on SW development level

Based on (Macher, Armengaud, Brenner, & Kreiner, 2016).

Table 3. Evaluation of TARA Methods not mentioned by SAE J3061

	Method Name	Applicable Phase	Key Facts
Not in SAE J3061	FMVEA	System phase	Based on the FMEA; identify threat modes (via e.g. STRIDE model) for each component/function of the system, identify system level effects and risks, categorizes risks via quantification of attacker effort, system properties for attack likelihood and threat effects.
	SAHARA	Concept phase	Threat analysis via STRIDE model; security and safety analysis possible in a combined and independent manner; easy quantification scheme; no adaptation of standardized quantification scheme for safety; requires less analysis efforts and details of the analyzed system
	SHIELD	System phase	Evaluates multiple system configurations; only evaluates system's security, privacy and dependability level; implies a high discussion potential for each classification, due to the lack of guidance on how to estimate the security, privacy, and dependability values.
	CHASSIS	Concept phase	Combined safety and security assessments; relies on modelling of misuse cases and misuse sequence diagrams; implies additional modelling expenses for the early development phase; structures the harm information in the form of HAZOP tables and in combination with the BDMP technique.
	BDMP	System phase	Based on ATA and FTA; fault tree and attack tree analysis are combined and extended with temporal connections.
	Threat Matrix	System phase	Proposed by US Department of Transportation; used to consolidate threat data; threat matrix is spreadsheet based; variation of the FMEA approach; geared towards the establishment of a threat database; not a preferable approach for concept analysis.
	BRA	Concept phase	Threat impact determination via 10 yes/no questions; quick risk conversations to enable discussion of a specific risk; not a full risk management methodology; quantitative analysis not based on statistics or monetary values; not a threat discovery or threat risk assessment technique on its own.
	STPA-SEC	---	Control model based analysis, originally developed for safety and later extended for security. A mixture of a system engineering approach and analysis technique, compatibility with ISO 26262 lifecycle still in discussion, modelling based on control loops which can mask security relevant issues.

Based on (Macher, Armengaud, Brenner, & Kreiner, 2016).

- TARA methods beyond SAE J3061:
  - ○ Failure mode and failure effect model for safety and security cause-effect analysis (FMVEA)
  - ○ Security aware hazard analysis and risk assessment (SAHARA)
  - ○ SHIELD
  - ○ CHASSIS
  - ○ Boolean Logic Driven Markov Processes (BDMP)
  - ○ Threat Matrix
  - ○ Binary Risk Analysis (BRA)
  - ○ STAMP Based Process Analysis (STPA-SEC)

SAHARA Method

The SAHARA method (Macher G., Sporer, Berlach, Armengaud, & Kreiner, 2015) was developed in cooperation with SoQrates working parties (Initiative, 2015) and combines the automotive hazard analysis and risk assessment (HARA) with the security domain STRIDE approach (Microsoft Corporation, 2005) to quantify impacts of security threats and safety hazards on system concepts at initial concept phase. STRIDE is a threat modelling approach and an acronym for spoofing, tampering, repudiation, information disclosure, denial of service, and elevation of privileges. The key concept of the STRIDE approach is the systematic analysis of system components for susceptibility of threats and mitigation of all threats to enable argumentation of a certain security of the system.

Figure 5 shows the conceptual overview of the SAHARA method and coupling of the safety and security analysis methods involved. For the initial stage, an ISO 26262 (ISO 26262 Road vehicles Func-

Figure 5. Conceptual overview of the SAHARA method
Source: A Combined Safety-Hazards and Security-Threat Analysis Method for Automotive Systems (Macher, Hoeller, Sporer, Armengaud, & Kreiner, 2015)

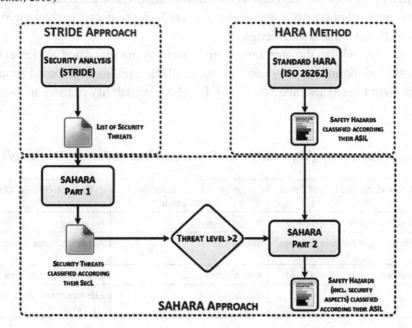

tional Safety Part 1-10, 2011) conform HARA analysis (see the right side of Figure 5) can be performed in a conventional manner. This means that the functions provided by the system are analyzed for their possible malfunction (hazards) and the worst possible situation in which this malfunction may happen. The hazard and situation combinations (hazardous event) are analyzed and quantified according to the ISO 26262 standard regarding their severity (S) and controllability (C) by the driver in the event of an occurrence. Further, the frequency and duration of exposure (E) in which this hazardous situation may occur is quantified. These factors (S, C, and E) determine the automotive safety integrity level (ASIL), the central metric for determination of development efforts required for the rest of the development process.

The security-focused analysis of possible attack vectors of the system can be done independently by specialists of the security domain (see the left side of Figure 5). For this analysis, the STRIDE threat model approach is used to expose security design flaws of the system design by methodically reviewing the system design. This is done in five steps: 1) the identification of security objectives; 2) a survey of the application; 3) the decomposition of the application; 4) the identification of threats; and 5) the identification of vulnerabilities. This threat modelling approach does not prove a given design secure, but helps to learn from mistakes and avoid repeating them. The two loosely coupled analysis steps (security analysis and safety analysis) can either be performed by individual teams or in cooperation with safety and security experts.

After this identification of possible security threats and safety hazards, the SAHARA method combines the outcomes of the security analysis with the outcomes of the safety analysis. The ASIL concept of the safety analysis is thus adopted and applied to the security analysis outcomes. In order to quantify the security level (SecL) of a threat, the required knowledge (K) and resources (R) to pose the threat, as well as the impact of the successful attack (T), are estimated (see Table 4). The factor T also implies impacts on human life (quality of life) as well as possible impacts on safety features. This information on security threats that may lead to a violation of safety goals is passed on for further safety analysis (depicted as SAHARA part 2 in Figure 5).

The required know-how - 'K' - is classified as: Level 0 - no prior knowledge required (the equivalent of black-box approach). Level 1 - covers persons with technical skills and basic understanding of internals (representing the equivalent of grey-box approaches). Level 2 – represent white-box approaches, persons with focused interests and domain knowledge.

Required resources - 'R' - to threaten the system's security are classified as: Level 0 - threats not requiring any tools at all or an everyday commodity, available even in unprepared situations. Level 1 - tools that can be found in any average household. Level 2 - availability of these tools is more limited

Table 4. Classification examples of Knowledge 'K', Resources 'R', and Threat 'T' value of security threats

Level	Required Knowledge (K) Classification	Required Resources (R) Classification	Threat Criticality (T) Classification
0	Unknown internals (black-box approach)	No tools required	No impact
1	Basic understanding of internals (grey-box approach)	Standard tools	Annoying, partial reduced service
2	Internals disclosed (white-box approach)	Non-standard tools	Damage of goods, privacy intrusion
3	---	Advanced tools	Life-threatening possible, maximum security impact

(such as special workshops). Level 3 - are advanced tools whose accessibility is very limited and are not widespread.

The criticality of the successful attack - 'T' - is classified as: Level 0 - indicates in this case a security irrelevant impact. Level 1 - is limited to annoying, possibly reduced availability of services. Level 2 - implying damage of goods or manipulation of data or services. Level 3 – represents the highest criticality (affecting car fleets) and also implies impacts on human life (quality of life) as well as possible impacts on safety features.

In general, the SAHARA quantification scheme is less complex and requires fewer analysis efforts and details of the analyzed system than other available approaches. The quantification of required know-how and tools can also be seen as equivalent to a likelihood estimation of an attack to be carried out. Nevertheless, this quantification provides the possibility to determine limits on the resources spent in preventing the system from being vulnerable to a specific threat (risk management for security threats) and the quantification of the threat impact on safety goals (threat level 3) or its non-impact on them (all others). Moreover, a combined review of the safety analysis by security and safety experts can also help to improve the completeness of security analysis. Bringing together and combining the different mind-sets and engineering approaches of safety engineers and security engineers, who are able to work independently from one another and also mutually benefit from each other's findings, is a fruitful approach that is likely to achieve higher analysis maturity standards.

FMVEA Method

The FMVEA Method (Schmittner, Gruber, Puschner, & Schoitsch, 2014) was developed in the context of the ARROWHEAD project and extends the established Failure Mode and Effect Analysis with security related threat modes.

Figure 6 gives an overview of the main steps for the standard FMEA (International Electrotechnical Commission, 2006). A system is modelled and divided into parts and all the potential failure modes are identified for each part. Depending on the detail level parts can be process steps, functions, system architecture elements or software / hardware parts. All system effects are identified for each potential failure mode and the severity is evaluated. For all failure modes with a critical severity potential failure causes and their likelihood are evaluated and the criticality is calculated.

Figure 7 gives an overview of the cause and effect model for the Failure modes, Vulnerabilities and Effects Analysis. The failure part consists, as before, of failure cause, failure mode, and effect. Security related parts are added here, including vulnerability, threat agent, threat mode and effect. Depending on the level of analysis a vulnerability can be an architectural weakness or a known software vulnerability. Compared to safety, security requires not only a weakness but also an element, which is exploiting this weakness. This can be a software or a human attacker. Different threat modelling concepts can be used for the identification of threat modes such as CIA (confidentiality, integrity, availability), summarizing

Figure 6. Main steps of FMEA

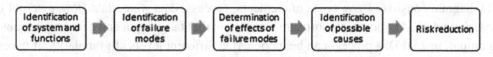

Figure 7. Depiction of the relation of cause and effect model for failures and threats

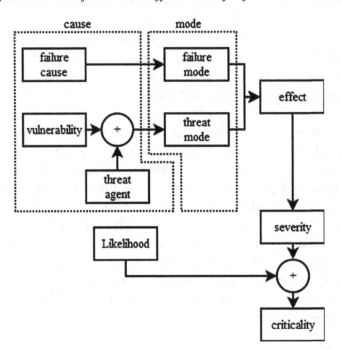

security properties an attack could exploit, or also STRIDE. Based on the severity of the effect, measured in term of financial damage, loss of confidentiality or privacy and operational or safety impact and the likelihood of the failure or threat the criticality is measured. In the likelihood context the system properties and attacker properties should be investigated.

Existing databases and domain knowledge can be used for identifying potential failure modes. Since the challenge of security for the automotive domain has emerged relatively recently, there is less knowledge about the threat modes than is the case in some other fields and domains. The analysis is based on a system model, depicting network architecture and data flows. In the practice, we currently use threat modelling to identify and analyze threat modes for each element of the system model. The main steps involved in a threat modelling process include:

1. Model a system by drawing the system architecture in data-flow diagram (DFD), adding system details to the elements in the DFD, and draw the trust boundaries.
2. Identify threats stemming from data flows by using a threat identification methodology such as the STRIDE or CIA method. An assessment of the severity of the threats can be added.
3. Address each threat by redesigning the system, adding mitigation, or ignoring it if the risk is acceptable.
4. Validate the threat modelling diagram against actual system and all identified threats are addressed.

A DFD diagram consists of five types of elements: process, data store, data flow, external interactor, and trust boundary. A process is a software component that takes input and performs actions and/or generates output. In a DFD, a process can be modelled in different levels of granularity. If necessary, a high-level process can be decomposed into more detailed low-level processes in a hierarchical manner.

For example, if we start to model all software components of a "Head Unit" at Level 0, we can further decompose it into processes of "Communication Gateway", "Linux OS", "Applications", and "HMI" at a lower level for Level 1. Depending on the available system details and threat identification needs, a process can be further decomposed into lower-level components such as specific Linux kernel modules.

Further to this a data store in the DFD represents a firmware, file system, or memory. A data flow in the DFD is a directed arrow, representing the flow of data between two elements. For example, a data flow can be a protocol specific communication link such as CAN Bus, FlexRay, or HTTPs. An external interactor is either a human user or a user agent that interacts with a process from the outside. Trust boundaries divide the elements in the diagram into different trust zones, e.g. elements reside in the in-car systems and external hosts communicated from untrusted open networks. The assumptions on the trust boundary greatly influence the result of threat identification. A data flow originated outside the trust boundary is assumed to be untrustworthy by default such that additional verification or security controls should be applied.

When identifying threats, different methodologies can be applied. As mentioned in (Macher G., Sporer, Berlach, Armengaud, & Kreiner, 2015), STRIDE is a popular methodology due to its easy-for-developer origin (Shostack, Experiences threat modeling at Microsoft, 2008) and extensive documentation of applications (Shostack, Threat modeling: Designing for security, 2014). However, depending on the granularity of the system information available and the timing of the threat modelling in the development lifecycle, alternative methodologies can also be used for optimal cost-benefit results. For example, the enumeration of potential attacks on each of the elements in a brainstorming session by domain experts will already improve the security posture of the design at the concept phase. Mitigations are technical or organizational countermeasures corresponding to the identified threats. The linking of mitigations to the threats ensures that all identified threats will be considered and addressed, and puts mitigations into perspective with the overall security architecture. Threat modelling is essentially a theoretical model of perceived threats to a system. Validating the theoretical model against the actual system will ensure the correctness of the results from the threat modelling. Validating that all identified threats are addressed provides additional layer of quality control on the security activities in the development process. Depending on the level of details for the failure modes either data from past events or generic failure modes can be used. An overview of generic failure modes which can be applied to the elements in a DFD diagram is given in (Haapanen & Helminen, 2020).

For the rating of severity, the FMVEA can either determine the severity directly or use information from previously conducted analysis such as e.g. SAHARA. Since FMVEA requires at least a basic system architecture more information for the rating of likelihood are available, like more detailed potential attack surfaces and weaknesses.

Table 5 CARE Attack Likelihood Parameter shows a likelihood rating systems, which differs between the four factors:

- Necessary capabilities of the attacker
- Availability of information about the attacked systems
- Reachability of the attacked systems
- Required attack for the easiest identified attack.

Ratings for all categories are added up and assigned to one of five Likelihood categories (Table 6: Likelihood categories).

Table 5. CARE attack likelihood parameter

Parameter	Values			
Capabilities	Amateur (3)	Mechanic, Repair shop (2)	Hacker, Automotive expert (1)	Expert team from multiple domains (0)
Availability of Information	Information publicly available (3)	Information available for maintenance of for customer / operator (2)	Information available for production, OEM, system integrator (1)	Information available in company of ECU supplier (0)
Reachability	Always accessible via untrusted networks (3)	Accessible via private networks or part time accessible via untrusted networks(2)	Part time accessible via private networks or easily accessible via physical (1)	Only accessible via physical (0)
Required Equipment	Publically available standard IT devices / SW[1] (3)	Publically available specialized IT devices / SW[2] (2)	Tailor-made / proprietary IT devices / SW[3] (1)	Multiple Tailor-made / proprietary IT devices / SW (0)

Table 6. Likelihood categories

Range	0-2			3-5			6-8			9-11			>11
Category	Improbable			Remote			Occasional			Probable			Frequent
Values	0	1	2	3	4	5	6	7	8	9	10	11	>11

This was done to be consistent with the five likelihood categories presented in IEC 60812 (International Electrotechnical Commission, 2006), Analysis techniques for system reliability – Procedure for failure mode and effects analysis (FMEA). The result is a Likelihood Rating from Improbable to Frequent.

Attack Tree Analysis

The fault tree analysis (FTA) is widely known as a state of the art methodology to analyze systems and subsystems in the context of the functional safety of systems. It is a deductive failure analysis, meaning that a known failure mode or undesired state is decomposed into a quantity of lower level events. By doing so, a tree of events and their logical combinations is constructed, giving in-depth information about the occurrence of the investigated top-level failure mode.

The fault tree analysis is a quantitative analysis, as each event or logical gate may be assigned a statistical probability. Subsystem failures occur at a failure rate λ and the logical combination with other subsystem failures leads to a quantified occurrence of the top-level failure mode. This further leads to a better understanding of the system under investigation, especially when this system is integrated into a larger system-of-systems or is part of a distributed cyber-physical system. In the automotive domain, where complex multi-level integrator-supplier relationships exist, the FTA is requested by many standards (ISO 26262, IEC 61508) and is therefore state-of-the-art.

The concept of the FTA in the field of automotive functional safety is also applicable to the field of automotive security. In this case, the top-level event expresses the occurrence of a security related incident of the system under investigation. At the lower levels, potential attacks are logically combined aggregating information about the top-level event.

Since the late 1990s a methodology evolved which uses structured data to identify threats to computer systems. While the so-called attack tree analysis (ATA) was first applied within the domain of computer networks (Tidwell, Larson, Fitch, & Hale, 2001), (Ammann, Wijesekera, & Kaushik, 2002), and (Schneier, 1999), it constantly evolved and was applied to other system categories, e.g. Supervisory Control and Data Acquisition (SCADA) systems. Conducting an ATA provides several advantages, compared to different methods. The ATA helps to understand what potential attack goals are, who the attackers are, what attacks are most likely to occur, which security assumptions apply to a given system, and finally, which investments regarding countermeasures are considered most effective.

Attackers may have different motivations, and opportunity crimes typically require less effort than well-planned operations. The kind of access to the system available to the attacker also plays a large role. Different unique skills may also be required by an attacker. The risk aversion of the attacker may heavily influence the attack execution. Acceptance of certain risks (e.g. publicity, jail time, death) leads to totally different attacks. Finally, a lack of all of these points may be compensated through the availability of appropriate funding. Attack trees help to describe the security of systems under investigation by building kind of knowledge databases. They are also a way to capture expertise, and make this knowledge available for future re-use, speeding up decisions and increasing their transparency.

Attack trees are basically data trees, where the root node represents an attack goal. An attack goal represents the violation of a security property, such as confidentiality or authenticity. The subordinate leaf-nodes represent attacks, targeting their linked attack goal. Multiple attack trees aiming at different attack goals may exist in parallel for complex systems. In this case, common attacks, which are relevant to multiple attack goals, are of special interest. When developing an attack tree, logical expressions are used to relate different applicable attacks to each other. A logical OR gate represents alternatives for attacking a system, whereas an AND gate determines attacks which are only successful in combination with each other.

Each leaf node of an attack tree may be assigned Boolean properties, e.g. to indicate the feasibility of an attack. The options in this case are "possible" and "impossible". Depending on the tree data structure, known system properties, or implemented security measures, certain tree branches may become irrelevant during analysis, as these properties are propagated up the tree. In contrast to Boolean properties, continuous node values may be assigned to leaf nodes. Typical examples are cost, time, or resource estimations, as these help to quantify the probability of occurrence of attack scenarios.

Attack trees provide valuable information to safety- and security-engineers. The consideration of Boolean properties and continuous node values within a single analysis allows complex tree evaluations, e.g. to "determine the best possible attack which costs €1000 or less". To determine if and which dedicated countermeasures against certain threats are taken, thresholds and guidelines are necessary to evaluate the selected metrics. From the automotive integrator's perspective assumptions are also subject to inclusion within an attack tree. A comprehensive list of assumptions, resulting from e.g. requirements, may influence security decisions based on attack trees.

An attack tree is built in three steps.

1. Identify the attack goals
2. Identify attacks against each goal, repeat as necessary
3. Re-use patterns of attacks for re-usable components

If attack trees for a given system have reached a mature state, impact analyses give information on how a system modification affects the selected metrics. The value of an attack goal thus needs to be calculated as described. Following on from this first step, changes are applied to the system and new leaf nodes or even a new attack must be introduced. The tree is subject to upward modification as necessary. Finally, the new attack goal values are calculated and compared to the previous ones. This approach may also be used to compare and rank different attacks to the system under investigation.

HSI Trust-Boundary Method

An unambiguous definition of the hardware-software interface (HSI) has become vital in the context of the road vehicles – functional safety standard ISO 26262 (ISO 26262 Road vehicles Functional Safety Part 1-10, 2011). In the ISO 26262 context, the HSI definition is probably the most crucial and essential work-product required by ISO 26262 related development approaches. The HSI specification no longer consists of only a single spreadsheet description of all signals from hardware to software and vice versa. It requires mutual knowledge of hardware and software components and also consists of supplementary information, such as resource consumption objectives, HW specifics, and controller module configurations.

Table 7 itemizes essential HSI attributes extracted from standards (ISO 26262 (ISO 26262 Road vehicles Functional Safety Part 1-10, 2011), AutomotiveSPICE (The SPICE User Group, 2015), SAE J3061 (SAE Vehicle Electrical System Security Committee, 2016)) and scientific papers (Sporer, Macher, Kreiner, & Brenner, 2016) and (Macher, Sporer, Brenner, & Kreiner, 2016). Security related information have been added (bold text) to support identification of attack vectors via their signal interfaces of the systems. The information in bold can be used to determine trust boundaries of specific systems.

In this context cybersecurity relevant signals inherit their security level from the threat analysis and risk assessment (TARA; as required by SAE J3061 (SAE Vehicle Electrical System Security Committee, 2016)) of the system to which they belong. Depending on the related security level the signal shall be protected against cybersecurity attacks. The enhancement of the HSI definition with supplementary cybersecurity related information to individual signals helps to determine trust boundaries and attack vectors by focusing on the system interfaces and thus identifying controllers which can directly intervene in the signals involved. All the control units, which have access to the system signals, are thus identified by analyzing all the signal interfaces of the system. These control units are within the same trust boundary and for this reason equally trusted. An access to the trust boundary is only possible via devices with connections outside the trust boundaries. These devices are referred to as gateways and are responsible for preventing attacks and the misuse of trust of the control units within a trust boundary. Accordingly, the identification of trust boundaries and gateways which protect the boundaries is both crucial and can be cumbersome for complex system and network structures.

Dependability Case

Development projects which deal with different domains are based on various standards. These standards deal with a wide spectrum of terms like dependability, safety, security, reliability, availability, maintainability, supportability, usability, testability und durability. One main problem is the harmonization of all these terms, because there are different definitions available even in standards. Such a harmonization of engineering terms and their relations will be shown in section "Dependability Feature Nomenclatures

Table 7. Essential HSI attributes, comments, and origin

	Attribute	Comment	Origin
Conceptual Layer	signal name	significant name	scientific publications
	signal description	short signal description	ISO 26262 part 6
	signal direction	input or output	scientific publications
	signal source /sink	**actuator or sensor related to signal**	**scientific publications**
	ASIL	Automotive Safety Integrity Level	ISO 26262 part 4
	security level (SecL)	**security metric**	**SAE J3061**
Physical Layer	supply voltage	-	scientific publications
	physical min value	-	**ASPICE**
	physical max value	-	**ASPICE**
	physical unit	-	ISO 26262 part 6, ASPICE
	accuracy	% range of value	ISO 26262 part 6
	HW interface type	digital, analogue, bus …	ISO 26262 part 6, ASPICE
	HW pin	pin number or identifier	ISO 26262 part 5
Data Layer	message ID	for bus communication only	scientific publications
	message offset	for bus communication only	scientific publications
	cycle time internal	xCU internal refresh rate	ISO 26262 part 6, ASPICE
	cycle time external	**cycle time of digital signal from external**	**scientific publications**
	trigger	identifier or trigger	ISO 26262 part 6
	operation mode	**required special operation modes**	**ISO 26262**
	HW diagnostic feature	**diagnostic feature description**	**ISO 26262**
	memory type	-	ISO 26262
	data protection	**special security information**	**ASPICE**
	timing dependencies /sequence order	-	**ASPICE**
Presentation Layer	SW signal name	signal identifier for ASW	scientific publications
	initial value	-	scientific publications
	SW data type	-	ASPICE
	scaling LSB	fixed-point arithmetic scaling	scientific publications
	scaling offset	fixed-point arithmetic scaling	scientific publications
	SW min value	-	**ASPICE**
	SW max value	-	**ASPICE**
	SW accuracy	% range of value	ISO 26262
	SW unit	physical unit representation	ASPICE
	default value	**default value in case of invalid signal**	**scientific publications**
	detection time	time to fault diagnosis	ISO 26262
	reaction time	reaction time after fault detection	ISO 26262

and Relation". Furthermore, the standards not only provide cover for mandatory processes. In most cases they demand a thoroughly adequate documentation.

Different types of case are used for different development goals. The following paragraph gives a short overview about some of them.

An assurance case should demonstrate that sufficient assurance has been achieved for a system. The assurance case concept is established in the automotive domain but the term "safety case" is more common. The term assurance case refers to the increasing generalization of this approach to include addressing other attributes. In many industries, the development, review and acceptance of a safety case forms a key element of regulatory processes, this includes the nuclear and defense industries as well as civil aviation, rail, and automotive industries (Hawkings, Habli, Kelly, & McDermid, 2013). IEC 15026 covers assurance case concepts and defines requirements concerning structure and components of an assurance case (International Electrotechnical Commission, 2011). An assurance case has a top-level claim and so a specific project may have multiple top level claims and multiple assurance cases. Furthermore, arguments, which support the claims must be available.

In the automotive domain the term safety case is well known because it is required for the safety management demanded by ISO 26262, but the standard does not provide detailed requirements concerning how to elaborate safety cases. It defines a safety case as "the compilation of all work products that are used as evidence to show that all requirements for an item are satisfied. ... The three principal elements are requirements, arguments and evidence". According to ISO 26262 the safety case compiles generated work products. It should provide a clear, comprehensive and defensible argument supported by evidence. Arguments should explain the relationship between evidence and requirements (ISO 26262 Road vehicles Functional Safety Part 1-10, 2011).

If we take a look at safety cases in other domains, it can be seen that they are regarded as important and are also given a great deal of attention. In the avionics domain specific safety case development manuals are available for specific stakeholders, e.g. air navigation, which is a best practice manual and describes how to use GSN for the safety argumentation for specific units or projects. The "Safety Case Development Manual" (EUROCONTROL - European Organisation for the safety of air navigation, 2006) is not only applicable to air traffic management. Its aim is to establish the link between the contents of a safety case (e.g. evidence, arguments...), which is useful in all domains where safety is a relevant topic. Depending on the context different stages of safety cases can be defined. The British "Office for Nuclear Regulation" (Office for Nuclear Regulation, 2013) defines 11 principal stages in the life cycle of a nuclear facility. Kelly (Kelly, Bate, Mc Dermid, & Burns, 1997) defines four software safety cases based on the "MoD Defence Standard 00-55" (UK Ministry of Defence, 1997) from the military domain. These are termed preliminary, intermediate, pre-operational and operational safety cases. In the automotive domain, a first approach regarding the topic of cybersecurity case was elaborated by SAE Vehicle Electrical System Security Committee and this led to the compiling of the cybersecurity guidebook SAE J3061. This recommended practice establishes a set of high-level guiding principles for cybersecurity as it relates to automotive cyber-physical systems to be utilized in series production. It defines the cybersecurity case, which provides the final argumentation and evidence that the feature as designed and developed satisfies its cybersecurity goals. It can be seen as a final cybersecurity assessment after all milestone reviews have been completed and before the feature can be released for production.

Trade-Off Approach to Cover Cooperative Dependability Cases

The international standard IEC 62741 "Demonstration of dependability requirements – The dependability case" defines that a dependability case is an "evidence-based, reasoned, traceable argument created to support the contention that a defined system does and/or will satisfy the dependability requirement" and it covers the dependability case management (International Electrotechnical Commission, 2015). Attempting to address all dependability attributes may result in competing objectives. The main problem is that the dependability attributes are non-orthogonal and can be interrelated to each other. As a consequence, there are trade-offs among the dependability attributes that need to be resolved in order to achieve the optimum dependability characteristics for the system. The trade-off represents the best possible compromise between conflicting objectives. The balance of these trade-offs can depend largely upon the context in which the system operates (Despotou & Kelly, 2004). Analysis approaches, like SAHARA, which cover possible trade-offs of different attributes and the impact and effects of security on safety are thus most welcome (see section SAHARA Method). Figure 8 depicts the non-orthogonal and interrelated nature of dependability attributes and the thus required trade-off.

Modelling of Argumentation

SACM (Structured Assurance Case Metamodel) is an OMG (Object Management Group) standard, which provides a common framework for assurance case development and information exchange. SACM is currently the only standard metamodel for creating and exchanging structured assurance cases. SACM is further aligned with GSN (Goal Structuring Notation) (Goal Structuring Notation Working Group, 2011). A mapping between the elements of these techniques and SACM has been specified (Object Management Group, 2016). Furthermore, the standard covers assurance case constructs used in practice. GSN diagrams can be represented with SACM concepts. GSN is a graphical notation, which is used to visualize and document the argumentation structure. It is a common technique for assurance case specification in industry. In GSN, an argument is defined as a series of connected claims. Strategy-elements

Figure 8. Overview of the dependability attributes with non-orthogonal and interrelated nature
Source: Macher G., Hoeller, Sporer, Armengaud, & Kreiner, 2015.

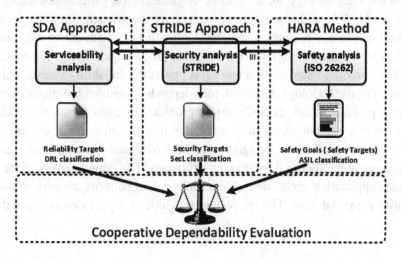

are used to explain the reasoning behind the connection between goals and sub-goals. Context-elements provide additional information to support a correct understanding of a specific argumentation part. Solutions are elements that support goals because they document pieces of evidence. The relationship between GSN elements is documented in a graphical manner using different linkage elements (arrows). Two types of linkage elements are available: 'SupportedBy' and 'InContextOf'. The former, represented by lines with solid arrowheads, indicates an inferential or evidential relationship, the latter represented as lines with hollow arrowheads, indicates contextual relationships (Martin, Krammer, Bramberger, & Armengaud, 2016).

SACM is used in practice both as a data exchange format and as a data model for assurance information structuring. In this book chapter, we focus on the graphical representation of dependability cases based-on GSN.

Methodology to Support Dependability Cases

Large projects (e.g. development of a new electric car from scratch) produce enormous quantities of work products, which are created by independent development groups. In such a development scenario, it is absolutely essential to have a well-defined methodology and a working tool to manage the documentation. Companies especially in different domains have their specific development processes with different priorities. A methodology that supports both individual argumentation related to standard compliant safety cases and cybersecurity cases is thus a vital need.

The process- and product-based safety and security argumentation (P2S2A) makes a distinction between two different types of argumentation namely process-based and product based argumentation. Process-based argumentation is directly related to (process) requirements demanded by specific standards (e.g. ISO 26262). For example, the argument supports the decision why FMEA was used instead of HAZOP for hazard identification. Product-based arguments are based on product specific requirements that lead to product specific decisions (e.g. different battery systems). The methodology must be suitable for connecting claims with related evidence and for managing the arguments belonging to them (Martin, Krammer, Bramberger, & Armengaud, 2016). The overall goal is to get a clear, complete and structured dependability argumentation (e.g. for safety and security). Traceability between argumentation fragments and relevant standards is enabled and improved by using graphical visualization.

The features of the methodology are as follows. Argumentation patterns according to the development process (e.g. for HARA) and best practices for product specific solutions are provided. They have a generic specification, provide templates, matching guidelines and cover two argumentation aspects. On the one hand process-based argumentation supports process audits (e.g. functional safety audits) and on the other hand product-based argumentation supports dependability assessment (e.g. functional safety assessments). The methodology deals with interdependent argumentation; for example, SAHARA identifies a security problem which causes a safety problem. In cases of interdependence a top-level claim may have lines of argumentation which are related to different types of evidences (e.g. security- and safety-related evidence). Process designers are able to create reusable and standard compliant argumentation patterns in parallel to development processes. The completeness of the pattern may be improved after each application cycle. Reusable templates and patterns are easy to use even for users who are not familiar with all details. The templates and guidelines provided enhance the completeness of argumentation. Complete argumentation shows a clear relationship between requirements, elaborated process outcome and related evidence. An additional advantage of patterns is that they can be instantiated to add project specific evidence if needed. Separation of different kinds of argumentation makes the methodology manageable and easy to understand.

APPLICATION EXAMPLE

This section demonstrates the application of the proposed dependability feature engineering approach based on an automotive use-case example of a connected electrified hybrid powertrain. Electrified hybrid powertrains (a combination of one or more electric motor(s) and a conventional internal combustion engine) are currently the most common variant of hybrid powertrains. Such systems allow a variety of combinations and optimization options for different application scenarios. Electrified hybrid powertrains are therefore frequently seen in various endurance race cars (e.g. ELMS and FIA World Endurance Championship), Formula 1, various supercars (e.g. BMW i8 and Porsche 918 Spyder) as well as in a growing number of passenger cars. The variety of powertrain configuration options increases the complexity of both the powertrain itself as also the required control systems (software functions and control units). Several different types of energy sources can only be utilized perfectly if the control systems are suitably designed and perfectly configured. To that aim connectivity features and external real-time data are being integrated ever more frequently into control strategy decisions.

In addition, update functionalities and novel business models can be discovered with the integration of connectivity features, over-the-air (OTA). We thus concentrate on a specific part of the connected powertrain, the battery management unit (BMS) and its functionalities related to OTA updates and battery leasing business strategies. BMS are control systems embedded in high-voltage batteries, which can potentially cause life-threatening malfunctions and if equipped with OTA functionalities and economic data, cybersecurity related attack vectors. Thus, these systems must be evaluated in a safety and security context. Figure 9 depicts the conceptual architecture of the application example powertrain. The depiction shows the elements directly related to the BMS; the full HV battery system consists of the BMS, the battery satellite modules (grouping battery cells in modules and communicating via dedicated bus), and a fan control for cooling of the battery cells. This system is connected to various powertrain control units (depicted as rest of powertrain), the charging interface (enabling the communication with battery charging stations), the on-board diagnostic interface (OBD) and via a dedicated gateway to the vehicle infotainment systems (including the driver interface (HMI) and also a wireless internet connection).

Application of the SAHARA Method

To begin the dependability feature analysis of the BMS the functions provided by the system (e.g. provide battery information and monitor high-voltage system) are analyzed for their possible malfunction (hazards) and the worst possible situation in which this malfunction may occur (depicted in Figure 10: #20 undetected short circuit outside of HV battery during normal operations and #11 voltage shock of driver at any driving situation). These hazard and situation combinations (hazardous situations) are analyzed and quantified according to ISO 26262 standard regarding their severity and controllability by

Figure 9. Overview of the Powertrain system architecture

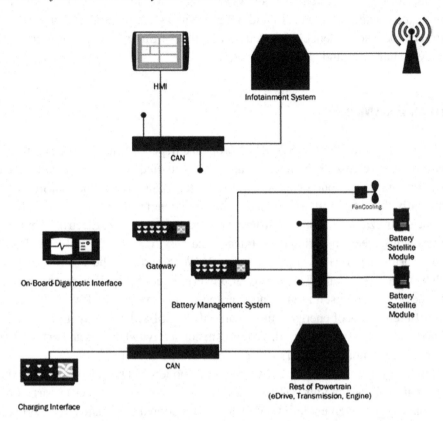

Figure 10. Excerpt of the HARA of the BMS use-case

Hazard description					Hazard classification (without				Safety goal description	
Hazard ID	Function	Assumed Hazard	General Driving Situation	General Environment al Conditions	Severity 'S'	Exposure or Frequency 'E'	Controlability 'C'	Resulting ASIL	Safety Goal	Safe State
48	store_energ	short circuit	repair	all	3	2	3	ASIL B	Detect short circuit and isolation faults, Prevent from electric shock	Disconnect HV battery, driver warning
20	prov_energ	Short circuit outside of the battery	all	all	3	4	3	ASIL D	Manual main switch off must be possible	Disconnect HV battery, driver warning
11	hv_mon	Voltage shock of driver	Parking	all	3	4	3	ASIL D	Prevent from electric shock	Disconnect HV battery, driver warning
12	hv_mon	Voltage shock of driver	Driving	all	3	4	3	ASIL D	Prevent from electric shock	Disconnect HV battery, driver warning
23	prov_energ	failure to disconnect HV battery	accident	all	3	1	3	ASIL A	Prevent from electric shock	Disconnect HV battery, driver warning
25	prov_energ	unintende closing of HV connectors	accident	all	3	1	3	ASIL A	Prevent from electric shock	Disconnect HV battery, driver warning
26	prov_energ	unintende closing of HV connectors	repair	all	3	2	3	ASIL B	Prevent from electric shock	Disconnect HV battery, driver warning
8	prov_energ	No torque provided	Parking	all	0	4	0	QM		--- not safety critical ---

the driver in event of occurrence, as also the frequency or exposure in which the car may be subjected to this specific situation. As can be seen in Figure 10, hazard #11 and #20 are considered to be maximum safety relevant (will further be analyzed and processed by safety engineering), while hazard #8 refusal to provide electric energy for torque is not considered safety relevant at all (and will be neglected by safety engineering processes, although there is potential vulnerability for security attacks, which can lead to loss of reputation).

A security focused analysis of possible attack vectors of the system can be done independently by specialists of the security domain to expose security design flaws of the BMS design. Figure 11 shows an excerpt of this security analysis of the BMS.

After the identification of possible security threats and safety hazards, the SAHARA method combines the outcomes of the security analysis with the outcomes of the safety analysis. The threats are thus quantified according to the resources (R) and know-how (K) required to exert the threat and the threat criticality (T) (depicted as SAHARA part 1 in Figure 5). The second step (depicted as SAHARA part 2 in Figure 5) is the hand-over of information of security threats that may lead to a violation of safety goals for further safety analysis. This improves the completeness of the safety analysis in terms of hazardous events initiated by security attacks, related to the ISO 26262 requirement of analysis of 'foreseeable misuse'. Moreover, a combined review of the safety analysis by security and safety experts can also help to improve its completeness. The combination of the different mind-sets and engineering approaches of safety engineers and security engineers, who are able to work independently from one another and also mutually benefit from each other's findings, is a fruitful approach that is likely to achieve higher analysis maturity standards.

In the case of the BMS example (analysis excerpt depicted in Figure 11) it can be seen that security hazards SH_2 and SH_3 are aimed at tampering with the SoH status to gain benefits on the reselling of the battery. Nevertheless, the two hazards are classified with a SecL of 0 due to the high level of required resources and know-how needed to realize the attack. As can also be seen in Figure 11, SH_1, SH_4, SH_5, SH_7, SH_8 and SH_9 have a threat level 'T' of 3, which implies also a possible impact on safety goals, regardless of their varying SecL level. The quantification of a SecL enables the possibility to determine limits to the resources spent in preventing the system from being vulnerable to a specific threat

Figure 11. Excerpt of the quantification of security risks of the BMS

Security Risk description					Security Risk classification				Security
Security Hazard ID	STRIDE Function	Attack description	General Situation	attacker generated malfunction	Required Resources 'R'	Required Know-How 'K'	Threat Level 'T'	Resulting SecL	Security Goal
SH_1	Spoofing	spoofing of HV system ready signals	all	HV system ready without ensured overall system safety	2	2	3	1	Secure HV ready signal integrity
SH_2	Tampering	tampering of SoH	reselling	SoH is higher than in reality	3	2	2	0	no
SH_3	Tampering	tampering of SoH	reselling	SoH is higher than in reality	3	2	2	0	no
SH_4	Spoofing	spoofing actual sensor readings	all	extending safe operation areas of HV battery (temp, cell current, cell voltages)	1	2	3	2	ensure sensor signal integrity
SH_5	Denial of service	DoS communication with charger	charging	communication with charger jammed	2	1	3	2	no
SH_6	Denial of service	disconnecting of LV battery	all	immobilizing of driving functionality	1	1	2	2	prevent LV battery from being removed
SH_7	Denial of service	bypass manual emergency kill switch	all	emergency kill switch without function	1	2	3	2	enclosure emergency kill switch
SH_8	Denial of service	bypass battery fuse		replace fuse with non current limiting element	1	1	3	3	prevent HV battery fuse from being removed
SH_9	Spoofing	spoofing of HV isolation monitoring signals	all	HV system ready without ensured overall system safety	3	2	3	0	no

(risk management for security threats) and the quantification of the threat impact on safety goals (threat level 3) or its non-impact on them (all others). The information of security threat impact on safety can be handed over to the safety analysis method (depicted as SAHARA part 2 in Figure 5) and thus further analyzed for the impact on safety of the system.

An excerpt from the safety and security related parts of the SAHARA analysis of the BMS example is depicted in Figure 12. As shown in this figure, the quantification of the impact the threat has on the security of the system (SecL) and the safety of the system (ASIL) may diversify greatly and cannot be deduced directly from another example.

Application of the FMVEA Method

As a first step for the FMVEA analysis, the system model is refined and a DFD is constructed. Data flows show how the system elements interact and communicate with each other and can be used in order to identify potential attack vectors or determine failure effects.

Figure 13 shows the dataflow model for the Battery Management System. The model does not contain all architectural elements and interactions, but is restricted to the scope of the analysis. Note that for the sake of simplicity, we only include the data flows related to our threat modelling in the DFD. In reality, most data flows are bi-directional. Also, note that the DFD is slightly different from the system architecture diagram in Figure 9, because it models the data flows among the automotive components. For example, the CAN bus is modelled as data flows between two DFD elements (e.g. processes or external interactors).

The FMVEA analysis and its scope build up on the previously conducted SAHARA analysis and also use the determined ASIL for the severity rating of safety-critical effects. We focus on SH_4, "extending safe operation areas of HV battery" for our analysis and identify additional causes. Accordingly, we focus on the threats related to BMS, i.e. threats targeting or originating from the BMS. The threat modes are identified based on the STRIDE method. A threat modelling tool such as Microsoft TMT (Microsoft, 2016) can partially automate the threat modelling process for the FMVEA.

Figure 12. Excerpt of safety and security related parts of the SAHARA

Security Risk description					Security Risk		Security Risk related Safety goal description				
Security Hazard ID	STRIDE Function	Attack description	General Situation	attacker generated malfunction	Threat Level 'T'	Resulting SecL	Severity 'S'	Exposure 'E'	Controlability 'C'	Resulting ASIL	Safety Goal
SH_2	Tampering	tampering of SoH	reselling	SoH is higher than in reality	2	0				QM	--- no safety impact --
SH_3	Tampering	tampering of SoH	reselling	SoH is higher than in reality	2	0				QM	--- no safety impact --
SH_4	Spoofing	spoofing actual sensor readings	all	extending safe operation areas of HV battery (temp, cell current, cell voltages)	3	2	3	4	3	ASIL D	Battery outgasing and fire shall be prevented
SH_5	Denial of service	DoS communication with charger	charging	communication with charger jammed	3	2	3	4	3	ASIL D	Battery outgasing and fire shall be prevented
SH_6	Denial of service	disconnecting of LV battery	all	immobilizing of driving functionality	2	2				QM	--- no safety impact --
SH_7	Denial of service	bypass manual emergency kill switch	all	emergency kill switch without function	3	2	3	4	2	ASIL C	Manual main switch off must be possible
SH_8	Denial of service	bypass battery fuse		replace fuse with non current limiting element	3	3	3	4	3	ASIL D	Battery outgasing and fire shall be prevented
SH_9	Spoofing	spoofing of HV isolation monitoring signals	all	HV system ready without ensured overall system safety	3	0	3	4	3	ASIL D	Detect short circuit and isolation faults, Prevent from electric shock

Figure 13. Dataflow diagram of the BMS use-case

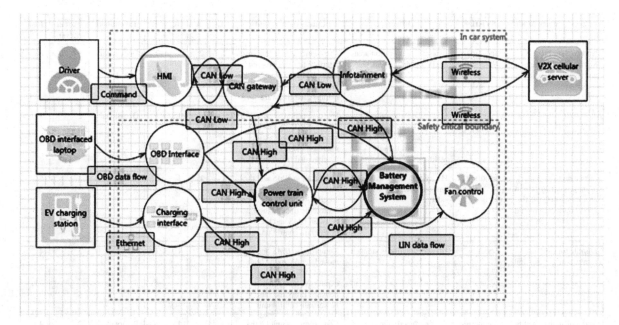

The first threat mode "Update Battery Management System with malicious software or firmware" of Table 9 relates to the STRIDE category spoofing and can cause "extend safe operation areas of HV battery" as well as "Manipulate transmitted data and try to improve resale value by transmitting a higher SoH than in reality". We focus on the first effect, because this has the higher threat level, as identified in the first step of the SAHARA.

A potential vulnerability or weakness, which could enable the threat mode is a direct access to the CAN bus from the charging unit, a summary of such an attack would be: "Use connection of charging interface to CAN bus and attack BMS via charging interface and install manipulated firmware". Using the weakness of a direct connection from the charging interface to the CAN bus would still require an automotive expert or hacker for exploitation. As demonstrated by Miller and Valasek (Miller & Valasek, Adventures in Automotive Networks and Control Units, 2013), the required information is more or less available for maintenance or customers. The system is only accessible when the vehicle is connected to a special purpose but publicly available charging station by its charging interface. This should be sufficient to conduct the attack. This leads to the CARE rating 1|2|1|2 (see Table 8 for more details), which results in 6, which is rated as: Occasional occurring (see Table 6).

The second threat mode "fake data from Battery Management System in an attempt to cause the power train control unit to have a reaction" has the effect of "HV system ready without ensured overall system

Table 8. CARE value sum vs. likelihood rating

Sum of CARE Values	0-2	3-5	6-8	9-11	>11
Likelihood Rating	Improbable	Remote	Occasional	Probable	Frequent

Table 9. FMVEA analysis of HV battery

Threat/Failure Mode	STRIDE	Effect	Cause/Vulnerability	C	A	R	E	Likelihood	Threat Level	Risk
Update Battery Management System with malicious software or firmware	Spoofing	Extend safe operation areas of HV battery	Use connection of charging interface to CAN bus and attack BMS via charging interface and install manipulated firmware	1	2	1	2	Occasional	3	6
		Manipulate transmitted data and try to improve resell Value by transmitting a higher SoH than in reality	Use connection of charging interface to CAN bus and attack BMS via charging interface and install manipulated firmware	1	2	1	2	Occasional	2	5
Fake data from Battery Management System in an attempt to cause the Power train control unit to have a reaction	Spoofing	HV system ready without ensured overall system safety	Compromise BMS and then move laterally in the high speed CAN bus network, exploit the trust relation between BMS and the Powertrain control unit	1	1	1	2	Remote	3	5
Disable function of Power train control unit	Spoofing	Driving function is stopped	Compromise BMS and then move laterally in the high speed CAN bus network, exploit the trust relation between BMS and the Powertrain control unit	1	1	1	2	Remote	2	4
Manipulate data sent to Battery Management System	Tampering	Driving function may be stopped if start charging message is sent to BMS and BMS stops to deliver power to powertrain	Compromise a unit on the CAN bus, exploit the BUS communication, tamper or replay a received messages sent on CAN bus to BMS	1	1	1	2	Remote	2	4
Brick the BMS, stop it functioning at all	DoS	Driving function and additional HV battery dependent functions are stopped immediately	Send falsified firmware update to BMS, cause it to a non-working state	1	1	3	2	Occasional	3	6
Flood the CAN bus	DoS	Communication and coordination of ECUs is impeded, Powertrain system stops	Flood the CAN bus with garbage messages via charging connection	2	2	2	2	Occasional	2	5
CAN communication disturbed		Communication and coordination of ECUs is impeded, powertrain system stops	ECU is stuck in send loop and arbitration with other messages does not work	0	0	0	0	2	2	4
Battery Management System stops working or crashes during program executions		BMS is stopped or operation crashes, HV system is unavailable	ECU is stuck in operation	0	0	0	0	2	3	5
Manipulate data sent to Battery Management System to exploit a software vulnerability or weakness	Elevation of privilege	BMS is stopped or operation crashes, HV system is unavailable	Send crafted CAN packets to BMS to exploit vulnerabilities in input parsing or others in the software stack	1	1	1	2	Remote	3	5
Disable certain functions in Battery Management System	DoS	Extend safe operation areas of HV battery	Send crafted messages to BMS to disable certain functions	1	1	1	2	Remote	3	5

safety". It shows that the information generated from SAHARA can be reused for identification and categorization of effects. A potential vulnerability is caused by the complete trust relationship between components on the same CAN bus "Compromise BMS and then move laterally in the high-speed CAN bus network to exploit the trust relationship between BMS and the Powertrain control unit".

Application of the ATA

This section demonstrates the creation of an attack tree and its analysis on system level. It focuses on the battery management system (BMS), as the intended functionality of this architectural component is required for numerous safety- and security-critical functions.

The attack goal as root node is entitled "Update battery management system (BMS) with malicious software". As already explained earlier, this allows different effects according to the SAHARA approach. One effect includes spoofing, and may cause battery operation outside its safe operation window[4]. Furthermore, another effect of this attack goal targets fraud crimes, when e.g. higher SoH values than measured are communicated by the BMS. Again, we focus on the first effect, as it has the higher threat level of 3.

In order to construct an attack tree, we carry out an architecture analysis according Figure 9 and Figure 13. One can clearly see that the BMS is not directly exposed to the outside vehicle. For this reason it makes sense to investigate attack paths according to the system architecture. The BMS is connected to a CAN bus, communicating with the charging interface, the on-board diagnostic interface, a gateway, its connected battery satellite modules, as also other powertrain components, which are not in focus here for reasons of space and legibility. It would appear to be thoroughly clear that an attacker must reach the BMS through one of these connections or subsystems. We must thus consider the CAN bus, the modular and exchangeable battery satellite modules (consider battery leasing models), and the fan cooling system for unauthorized access to the BMS. The CAN bus is connected to the gateway, the OBD, a charging interface, and any other powertrain components. Since the charging interface represents an interface to the vehicle, this provides a logical entry point for the following two attacks. First, the BMS update function must be triggered through the charging interface, as the vehicle's original equipment manufacturer may supply software updates on a regular basis through this interface. Second, the malicious software must be transmitted through the charging interface. According to the attack tree's Boolean node values, these attacks are possible to commit ("P") in general. Additionally, the attack tree has continuous node values, indicating the required special equipment (SE) necessary to launch the attacks. For the charging interface, well defined plug specifications are available in general. A wall box for charging and communicating with the vehicle may either be modified or copied/reverse engineered. The attack tree quantifies this risk using an SE value of 2 (see Table 5).

The depicted attack tree in Figure 14 clearly indicates an attack path from the charging interface to the BMS. This attack path allows the derivation of different security measures across the entire vehicle, targeting the update functionality of the BMS, e.g. protection of the charging interface connection by using cryptographic techniques or enhanced bus access schemes to ensure the authenticity of transmitted data.

Trust Boundary Definition on Signal-Level

As mentioned previously in this document, the identification of trust boundaries completely differs in safety and security engineering. In cybersecurity, trust boundaries are used to describe a boundary where program execution or data protection change their levels of "trust". Thus, trust boundaries can be related to privileges, integrity, control units or communication networks, and can also refer to points or attack surfaces where attackers can intervene.

The signal information within the HSI can be used for the systematic identification of trust boundaries. Safety or cybersecurity relevant signals inherit their ASIL from the hazard analysis and risk assessment (HARA; required by ISO 26262) and/or their security level from threat analysis and risk assessment

Figure 14. Excerpt of the BMS ATA focusing on malicious software update of the BMS

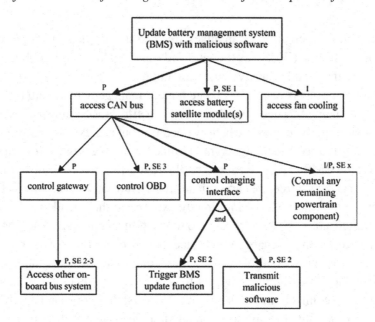

(TARA; requested by SAE J3061). Depending on the related security level / ASIL, the signal shall be protected against cybersecurity attacks according to a defense in depth pattern.

All the signals required for the system are analyzed with this aim in view. Based on this analysis, all the control units having access to these signals are then identified. These control units are within the same trust boundary and thus are equally trusted. The access to the trust boundary is enabled via dedicated devices (gateways) which also have connections outside the trust boundaries. The gateways are required to prevent the misuse of trust, and thus they protect the control units within a trust boundary from outside attacks.

Figure 15 and Figure 16 depicts two block representations of the BMS; the left figure shows the main components of the BMS and their information interfaces (yellow ports), while the right figure depicts the conceptual building blocks of the complete HV battery from sensors to actuators. The BMS requires several input sensors, sensing e.g. cell voltages, cell temperatures, output current, output voltage, and actuators (the battery main contactors).

These main building blocks of the BMS are:

- **Power Contactors:** Connection with vehicle HV system
- **Interlock:** De-energizing HV system when tripped
- **CAN:** Automotive communication interface
- **Relay:** Main contactor and output unit of the BMS
- **Temperature Sensors:** Feedback of actual cell temp
- **Voltage Sensors:** Feedback of actual cell voltages
- **Current Sensors:** Feedback of actual current flow
- **Fuse:** Protective circuit breaker in case of fault
- **Cells:** Electro-Chemical energy storage
- **BMS Controller:** Monitoring and control unit

Figure 15. Block diagram depictions of the BMS and main components (shows the main components of the BMS and information interfaces)

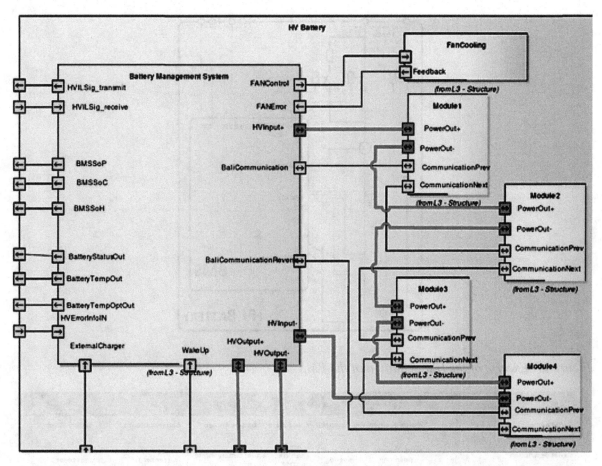

From the ISO 26262 aligned HSI of the battery management system (depicted in Figure 17) it can be seen that the SecL of the directly connected signals (battery current 1, battery current2, and battery voltage) are treated as 0 (not security relevant) while the signals provided via CAN bus (thus provided from outside of trust boundary 0 in Figure 18) are assigned a SecL = 2. This results from the fact that in order to raise a security attack, these signals would have to be manipulated in the vehicle directly at the battery management system and that these signals are within the same trust boundary 0 (see depiction of trust boundaries in Figure 18). On the other hand, the SecL=2 indicates a possible cybersecurity vulnerability and thus requires built-in security solutions exhibiting a defense-in-depth approach.

The realization of these protection mechanisms requires the coordinated design of multiple security technologies (such as isolation of safety critical systems, secure boot, tamper protection, message authentication, network encryption and many others). Currently no standardization for the coordination of security designs has been established and it is up to the manufacturers to decide how to provide a secure context. Thus, we established the design guidelines for signal security for the different security levels described in Table 10.

Based on the HSI identification of the interfaces providing the signals, devices connected to this interface can be easily identified and trust-boundaries for the specific system identified. This enables a

Figure 16. Block diagram depictions of the BMS and main components (conceptual building blocks of the HV battery)

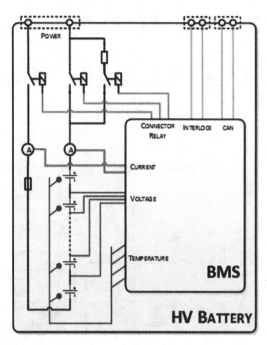

Figure 17. Excerpt of the HSI definition of the BMS

HSI		BMS					
Signal name			Throttle Position	vehicle speed	vehicle state	battery voltage	battery current 1	battery current 2
signal description		common	actual throttle position	actual vehicle speed	actual vehicle state	actual battery volate	actual battery current (sensor 1)	actual battery current (sensor 2)
Sensor/Actuator			VCU	VCU	VCU	BMS	I_sens1	I_sens2
Direction			in	in	in	in	in	in
ASIL			ASIL B(D)	ASIL B(D)	ASIL D	ASIL D	ASIL B(D)	ASIL B(D)
Secl			2	2	2	0	0	0
Source(CAN/ANA/DIG)			CAN	CAN	CAN	ANA	ANA	ANA
physical unit		physical	--	--	--	V	A	A
physical range lower limit			--	--	--	10	5	10
physical range upper limit			--	--	--	500	200	2000
supply voltage			--	--	--	--	--	--
signal tolerance	%		1	1	--	5	5	1
Interface			CAN A	CAN A	CAN A	analog	analog	analog
pin			Port B12	Port B12	Port B12	Port B33	Port A11	Port A28
refresh rate	ms	data	10	100	100	10	10	10
cycle time	ms		1	10	10	10	10	10
message ID			0x185	0x188	0x198	--	--	--
message offset			0	0	0	--	--	--
trigger						timer	timer	timer
operation mode			normal	normal	normal	normal	normal	normal / fault_1 / fault_
HW diagnostic			CRC	CRC	CRC	voltage range	redundancy	redundancy
register-type			RAM	RAM	RAM	RAM	RAM	RAM
data protection			--	--	--	--	--	--
dependency			--	--	--	--	--	--
Signaltype (V / % / deg)		SW	%	kmph	--	V	A	A
variable name			VCU_THrPos_Pctg	VCU_VehSpd_kmph	VehState_Ctl	BMS_BatActUSens	BMS_BatActiSens1	BMS_BatActiSens2
Initial value			0	0	--	0	0	0
signal range lower limit			0	0	--	10	0	0
signal range upper limit			100	400	--	450	200	2000
Scaling LSB				163	--	1	1	1
Scaling Offset				35	--	0	0	0
accuracy			0,5	0,5	--	1	1	1
default value			0	0	--	0	0	0
type			uint8	uint16	uint8	uint16	uint16	uint16
detection time	ms		50	200	200	50	50	50

Figure 18. Depiction of trust boundaries from BMS point of view

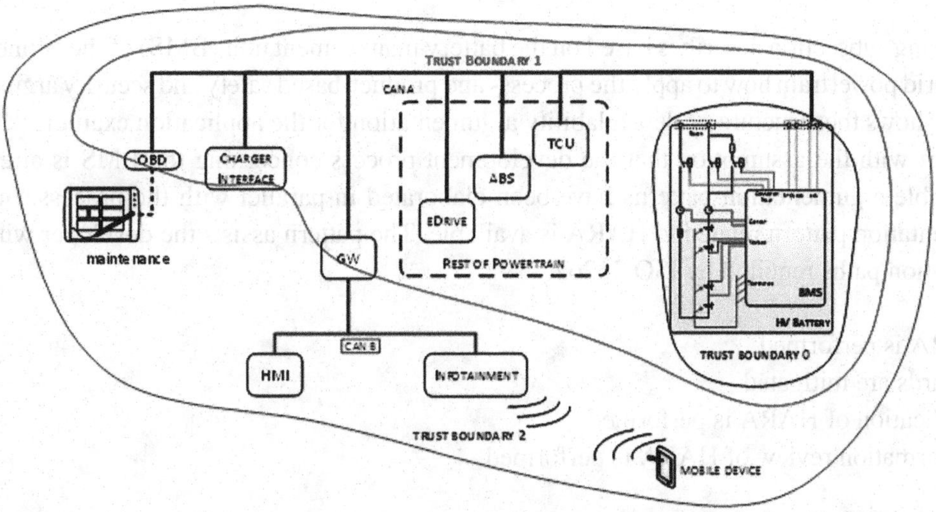

Table 10. Required protection mechanism per security classification (protection mechanisms of lower classification levels also mandatory)

Security Classification (SecL)	Required Protection Mechanism
0	No additional requirements
1	• Verify origin of message • Verify integrity of message
2	• Check frequency of message transmission • Detect abnormal behavior • Use immutable device identification • Establish intrusion detection
3	• Encrypt communication • Encrypt data
4	• Establish private communication channel • Correct cycle detection • Block unapproved and inappropriate messages

complete identification of involved controllers for a further analysis of interfaces and the establishment of barriers for cybersecurity attacks. For that aim, the first step of the approach identifies controllers which have access to the signals related to the BMS based on the HSI definition. These controllers either generate the signals directly or are connected to the same communication bus. The second step identifies the inner trust boundary 0 which includes signals directly connected to the BMS and simultaneously the gateways to the trust boundary (CAN connection of the BMS). These two steps are repeated for the remaining signals to establish further trust boundaries, as depicted in Figure 18.

Dependability Case

The following subsection describes based on the battery management unit (BMS) of the connected electrified hybrid powertrain how to apply the process- and product-based safety and security argumentation. Figure 19 shows the structure of dependability argumentation for the application example.

We start with the assumption that the development process concerning the BMS is already available. Suitable argumentation patterns have been elaborated in parallel with the process. In that case an argumentation pattern related to HARA is available. The pattern assists the developer with the four argumentation paths required by ISO 26262.

- HARA is performed
- Hazards are mitigated
- Verification of HARA is performed
- Confirmation review of HARA is performed

This type of argumentation is the process-based argumentation (see Figure 20). In addition a product-based argumentation is needed to argue product specific decisions. This example concerns to the hazard "Battery system is overheating" which has been identified in a HARA. The safety goal "Prevent overheating of the battery system" has been derived to overcome this hazard. The intention of the related argumentation is to show that the associated safety measure "Temperature monitoring" is appropriate.

Security argumentation works analogously to the safety argumentation. STRIDE is an appropriate method for conventional security analysis. An example is shown in the section "Overview of Risk Management Methods." It classifies security risks and defines security goals. For example, security hazard SH_4 "spoofing actual sensor readings" (see Figure 11) may lead to a malfunction in the HV battery. If an attacker manipulates sensor readings it may be possible to extend the operation area of the HV battery (e.g. lower temperature value allows obtaining a higher current). The detailed security risk classification can be found in Figure 12. The process- and product-based argumentation is set up based on that security analysis. On the one hand the argumentation supports the complete and standard compliant security process and on the other hand it demonstrates why product specific decisions, related to security goals, have been made in that specific manner. As shown in section "SAHARA Method" an independent analysis of safety and security is of limited use. SAHARA combines both types of analy-

Figure 19. Structure of the dependability argumentation

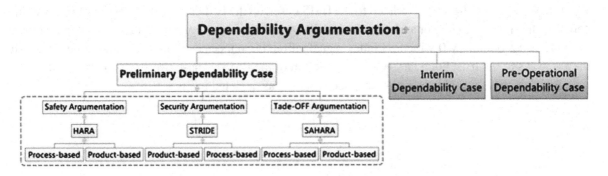

Figure 20. Process-based argumentation

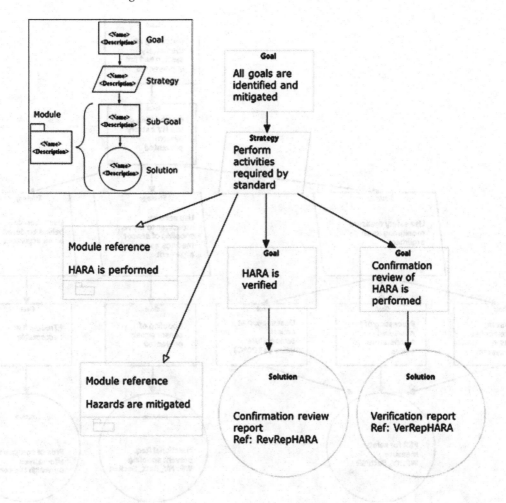

sis and considers impact to safety caused by security threats. SAHARA identifies additional hazards which lead to additional or changed safety goals. The accompanying argumentation has once again to deal with process- and product-based reasons and conclusions. Figure 12 shows the security risk related safety goal description. The security hazard SH_4 is examined again and it receives an additional ASIL classification to its existing security level. In that case ASIL C because of the possibility that "fire and battery outgasing" could occur.

Figure 21 shows the product-based argumentation related to the safety goal "Battery outgasing and fire shall be prevented" Sub goals are "Prevent overheating of the HV battery" from a safety point of view and "prevent spoofing actual sensor readings" (related to SH_4) from a security point of view. The strategy explains the decomposition of the top goal and defines the chosen argumentation paths. The solution presents the reference to the evidence, which could be a link to a specific document in a repository. In the example "functional cybersecurity requirements to prevent spoofing" are needed to overcome the top goal. The corresponding evidence is the list of functional cybersecurity requirements stored in the project related file "HV_Batt_SecReq".

Figure 21. Product-based argumentation of dependability case

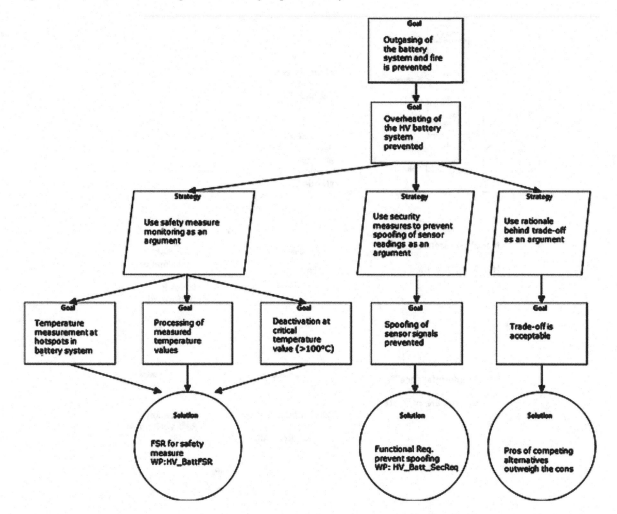

The dependability argumentation by using GSN modelling provides the possibility to present a clear dependability case by using the basic elements goal (what we want to show), strategy (why we believe the goal is true) and evidence (specific requirements, analysis results, test results, etc.). The arguments are structured hierarchically, which is supported by a graphical representation. This approach improves the discussion within the engineering team and reduces time-to-agreement on what evidence is needed and what the evidence means. Furthermore, dependability argumentation supports monitoring of project progress towards successful certification.

CONCLUSION

The intensive deployment of connected cyber-physical systems with vehicle-to-vehicle and vehicle-to-infrastructure communication is revolutionizing the automotive industry. Hence, the traditional customer value "vehicle product" is being shifted to "mobility as a service" with the combined offer for information and infotainment. At the same time this higher degree of connectivity is offering new attack surfaces. In this highly competitive market, security attacks can lead to competitive advantages in the context of financial damage to a competitor (e.g., loss of image), loss of confidentiality or privacy with respect to driver (e.g., profile) or car manufacturer (e.g., sensitive vehicle information).

Similar to the situation for functional safety, a holistic approach covering the entire lifecycle – and well-integrated with the other engineering domains – is required. Hence, the tight integration of security considerations together within the safety and reliability lifecycle is required to ensure consistent system definition, implementation and validation. The consideration of the entire product lifecycle is important in order to obtain a clear view of the entire system and tailor the dependability development accordingly. This targets the deployment of necessary and sufficient methods, which at the same time are not over-engineered (and therefore competitive for the market from a pure cost point of view).

In the course of this chapter, four different analyses integrating security with functional safety along the development lifecycle were discussed. Starting with the concept level, the SAHARA approach targets the identification of both safety goals and security threats – especially those having an impact on functional safety. This conjoint identification is important for consolidating the dependability targets at an early stage of the development. This minimizes the risk of contradictory requirements and development. During the design phase, the FMEVA and the ATA approaches were presented as enhancements of traditional FMEA and FTA in order to include security analyses in well-known engineering methods. Finally, the HSI trust boundary method is enhancing the implementation phase with security considerations.

Another contribution of this chapter is the enhancement of the safety assurance case towards the direction of a dependability case. Hence, the set-up of a documented argumentation on the appropriateness of the process and development activities is a tedious and challenging task. The focus for functional safety is fixed on the absence of hazardous situations, while the security argumentation focuses on the absence of suitable attack surfaces. In both cases a similar approach is required (GSN, product and process based argumentation), and it is certainly true that the entire argumentation for a given product needs to be kept consistent throughout the different engineering domains. The proposed approach supports building the overall argumentation and keeping this argumentation consistent.

To conclude, the convergence of several engineering methods towards the achievement of a common dependability engineering over the entire development lifecycle is a challenging task, with the challenges arising in terms of expertise, methods and company organization. Hence, the experts are focusing on different disciplines, using different methods and tools and are they are also quite possibly allocated to different teams. It will only be possible to create a dependable system in a cost effective manner by an efficient merging of the different engineering disciplines involved.

ACKNOWLEDGMENT

This work is supported by the EMC² project. Research leading to these results has received funding from the EU ARTEMIS Joint Undertaking under grant agreement n° 621429 (project EMC2).

VIRTUAL VEHICLE Research Center is funded within the COMET – Competence Centers for Excellent Technologies – programme by the Austrian Federal Ministry for Transport, Innovation and Technology (BMVIT), the Federal Ministry of Science, Research and Economy (BMWFW), the Austrian Research Promotion Agency (FFG), the province of Styria and the Styrian Business Promotion Agency (SFG). The COMET programme is administrated by FFG.

REFERENCES

Ammann, P., Wijesekera, D., & Kaushik, S. (2002). Scalable, graph-based network vulnerability analysis. In *Proceedings of the 9th ACM Conference on Computer and Communications Security - CCS '02.* doi:10.1145/586110.586140

Avizienis, A., Laprie, J.-C., & Randell, B. (2004). Dependability and its Threats - A Taxonomy. In *Proceedings of the IFIP Congress Topical Sessions* (pp. 91-120).

Avizienis, A., Laprie, J.-C., Randell, B., & Landwehr, C. (2004). Basic Concepts and Taxonomy of Dependable and Secure Computing. *IEEE Transactions on Dependable and Secure Computing, 1*(1), 11–33. doi:10.1109/TDSC.2004.2

Baldwin, R. (2015). OwnStar car hacker can remotely unlock BMWs, Benz and Chrysler. *Engadget.* Retrieved from http://www.engadget.com/2015/08/13/ownstar-hack/

Cercone, M., & Ernst, T. (2012). *An EU Cybercrime Center to fight online criminals and protect e-consumers.*

Despotou, G., & Kelly, T. (2004). Extending the safety case concept to address dependability. In *Proceedings of the 22nd International System Safety Conference.*

EUROCONTROL - European Organisation for the safety of air navigation. (2006). *Safety Case Development Manual Edition 2.2.* DAP/SSH/091.

Gallina, B., & Fabre, L. (2015). Benefits of Security-informed Safety-oriented Process Line Engineering. *Digital Avionics Systems Conference (DASC-34).*

Gallina, B., Kashiyarandi, S., Martin, H., & Bramberger, R. (2014). *Modeling a Safety- and Automotive-oriented Process Line to Enable Reuse and Flexible Process Derivation.* Västerås, Sweden: *Proceedings of the 8th IEEE International Workshop on Quality-Oriented Reuse of Software (QUORS).*

Goal Structuring Notation Working Group. (2011). *GSN Community Standard version 1.* http://www.goalstructuringnotation.info/documents/GSN_Standard.pdf

Haapanen, P., & Helminen, A. (2020). *Failure mode and effects analysis of software-based automation systems.* Helsinki: Radiation and Nuclear Safety Authority.

Hawkings, R., Habli, I., Kelly, T., & Mc Dermid, J. (2013). *Assurance cases and prescriptive software safety certification: a comparative study.*

Initiative, S. (2015). *SOQRATES Initiative.* Retrieved 31. March 2016 from http://www.soqrates.de

International Electrotechnical Commission. (2006). *IEC 60812 - Analysis techniques for system reliability - Procedure for failure mode and effects analysis (FMEA).* Retrieved from https://webstore.iec.ch/preview/info_iec60812%7Bed2.0%7Den_d.pdf

International Electrotechnical Commission. (2011). *ISO/IEC 15026-2: Systems and Software Engineering – Systems and Software Assurance – Part 2: Assurance case.*

International Electrotechnical Commission. (2015). *IEC EN 62741 – Guide to the Demonstration of Dependability Requirements –*.

International Organization for Standardization - ISO. (2009). *IEC 61508 Functional safety of electrical/ electronic / programmable electronic safety-related systems.*

ISO 26262 Road vehicles Functional Safety Part 1-10. (2011). ISO - International Organization for Standardization.

Kelly, T., Bate, I., Mc Dermid, J., & Burns, A. (1997). Building a preliminary safety case: an example from aerospace. In *Proceedings of the Australian Workshop of Industrial Experience with Safety Critical Systems*, Sydney, Australia.

Kreiner, C. (2015). *Essential architectural views for dependable systems design.* 20th European Conference on Pattern Languages of Programs, EuroPLoP 2015.

Macher, G., Armengaud, E., Brenner, E., & Kreiner, C. (2016). A Review of Threat Analysis and Risk Assessment Methods in the Automotive Context. *In Proceedings of the International Conference on Computer Safety, Reliability, and Security (SafeComp 2016)*. doi:10.1007/978-3-319-45477-1_11

Macher, G., Hoeller, A., Sporer, H., Armengaud, E., & Kreiner, C. (2015). A Comprehensive Safety, Security, and Serviceability Assessment Method. In *Proceedings of the 34th International Conference on Computer Safety, Reliability, and Security - SAFECOMP 2015*, Delft, The Netherlands. doi:10.1007/978-3-319-24255-2_30

Macher, G., Hoeller, A., Sporer, H., Armengaud, E., & Kreiner, C. (2015). Service Deterioration Analysis (SDA): An Early Development Phase Reliability Analysis Method. In *Review at 45th Annual International Conference on Dependable Systems and Networks (DSN) - RADIANCE Workshop*.

Macher, G., Hoeller, A., Sporer, H., Armengaud, E., & Kreiner, C. (2015). A combined safety-hazards and security-threat analysis method for automotive systems. In F. Koorneef & C. van Gulijk (Eds.), *SAFECOMP 2015 Workshops ASSURE, DECSoS, ISSE, ReSA4CI, and SASSUR, LNCS 9338* (pp. 237–250).

Macher, G., Sporer, H., Berlach, R., Armengaud, E., & Kreiner, C. (2015). SAHARA: A security-aware hazard and risk analysis method. In Design, Automation Test in Europe Conference Exhibition (DATE 2015), (pp. 621-624).

Macher, G., Sporer, H., Brenner, E., & Kreiner, C. (2016). Supporting Cyber-security based on Hardware-Software Interface Definition. In *Proceedings of the 23nd European Conference on Systems, Software and Services Process Improvement - EuroSPI 2016*, Graz, Austria. doi:10.1007/978-3-319-44817-6_12

Martin, H., Krammer, M., Bramberger, R., & Armengaud, E. (2016). *Process-and Product-based Lines of Argument for Automotive Safety Cases.*

Microsoft. (2016). *Microsoft Threat Modeling Tool.* Retrieved from https://www.microsoft.com/en-us/download/details.aspx?id=49168

Microsoft Corporation. (2005). The stride threat model. Retrieved from http://msdn.microsoft.com/en-us/library/ee823878/%28v=cs.20/%29.aspx

Miller, C., & Valasek, C. (2013). Adventures in Automotive Networks and Control Units. In *Proceedings of the DEF CON 21 Hacking Conference,* Las Vegas.

Miller, C., & Valasek, C. (2015). *Remote Exploitation of an Unaltered Passenger Vehicle.* Retrieved from http://illmatics.com/Remote%20Car%20Hacking.pdf

Object Management Group. (2015). *Structured Assurance Case Metamodel version 1.1.* Retrieved from http://www.omg.org/spec/SACM/1.1/

Object Management Group. (2016). Structured Assurance Case Metamodel (SACM), V2.0-Beta 1.

Office for Nuclear Regulation. (2013). *The purpose, scope, and content of safety cases, NS-TAST-GD-051 Revision 3.* Retrieved from http://www.onr.org.uk/operational/tech_asst_guides/ns-tast-gd-051.pdf

SAE Vehicle Electrical System Security Committee. (2016). *SAE J3061- Cybersecurity Guidebook for Cyber-Physical Automotive Systems.* SAE - Society of Automotive Engineers.

Schmittner, C., Gruber, T., Puschner, P., & Schoitsch, E. (2014). Security application of failure mode and effect analysis (FMEA). In *Proceedings of the International Conference on Computer Safety, Reliability, and Seucirty (SafeComp 2014).* doi:10.1007/978-3-319-10506-2_21

Schneier, B. (1999). Attack Trees. *Dr. Dobb's Journal of Software Tools for the Professional Programmer.*

Shostack, A. (2008). Experiences threat modeling at Microsoft. In *Proceedings of the Modeling Security Workshop,* Lancaster University UK.

Shostack, A. (2014). *Threat modeling: Designing for security.* Wiley & Sons.

Sporer, H., Macher, G., Kreiner, C., & Brenner, E. (2016). Resilient Interface Design for Safety-Critical Embedded Automotive Software. *In Proceedings of the Sixth International Conference on Computer Science and Information Technology, Academy & Industry Research Collaboration Center (AIRCC).* doi:10.5121/csit.2016.60117

Szijj, A., Buttyan, L., & Szalay, Z. (2015). *Hacking cars in the style of Stuxnet.* Retrieved from http://www.hit.bme.hu/~buttyan/publications/carhacking-Hacktivity-2015.pdf

The Common Criteria Recognition Agreement Members. (2014). *Common Criteria for Information Technology Security Evaluation.*

The SPICE User Group. (2015). *Automotive SPICE Process Assessment / Reference Model V3.0.*

Tidwell, T., Larson, R., Fitch, K., & Hale, J. (2001). *Modeling Internet Attacks.* Retrieved from http://citeseerx.ist.psu.edu/viewdoc/download?doi=10.1.1.108.9040&rep=rep1&type=pdf

UK Ministry of Defence . (1997). *Defence Standard 00-55, Requirements for safety related software in defence equipment.*

Verein zur Weiterentwicklung des V-Modell XT e. V. (2015). *V-Modell XT, 2.0.* Retrieved from www.v-modell-xt.de

ENDNOTES

[1]   Readily available equipment, as example simple OBD diagnostics devices, common IT device such as notebooks.

[2]   Equipment that is obtainable with little effort, as for example computing power from a cloud provider, in-vehicle communication devices (e.g., CAN cards), or costly workshop diagnosis devices.

[3]   Equipment that is not readily available, because it is either proprietary or custom made

[4]   http://www.mpoweruk.com/lithium_failures.htm

Compilation of References

3rd Generation Partnership Project (3GPP). (2016). 3GPP TS 36.211 3GPP TSG RAN Evolved Universal Terrestrial Radio Access (E-UTRA) Physical Channels and Modulation, version 13.1.0, Release 13, March 2016.

3rd Generation Partnership Project (3GPP). (2016). 3GPP TS 36.213 3GPP TSG RAN Evolved Universal Terrestrial Radio Access (E-UTRA) Physical layer procedures, version 13.1.1, Release 13, March 2016.

4DIAC, Eclipse Incubation Project. (2016). Retrieved from https://eclipse.org/4diac

Aaraj, N., Raghunathan, A., & Jha, N. K. (2008). Analysis and Design of a Hardware/Software Trusted Platform Module for Embedded Systems. *ACM Transactions on Embedded Computing Systems*, 8.

Accellera. (2015, May). *Universal Verification Methodology (UVM) 1.2 User's Guide* (Tech. rep.).

Accellera.org. (2016). SystemC- Accellera Systems Initiative. Retrieved from http://www.accellera.org/downloads/standards/systemc/

Acıiçmez, O., & Seifert, J.-P. (2007). Cheap hardware parallelism implies cheap security. In Fault diagnosis and tolerance in cryptography, 2007. fdtc 2007. workshop on (pp.80–91). doi:10.1109/FDTC.2007.16

Acıiçmez, O. (2007). Yet another microarchitectural attack: Exploiting i-cache. In *Proceedings of the 2007 acm workshop on computer security architecture* (pp. 11–18). ACM. doi:10.1145/1314466.1314469

Acıiçmez, O., Brumley, B. B., & Grabher, P. (2010). *New Results on Instruction Cache Attacks* (Vol. 6225, pp. 110–124). Ches.

Acıiçmez, O., & Koç, Ç. K. (2009). In Ç. K. Koç (Ed.), *Cryptographic engineering* (pp. 475–504). Boston, MA: Springer US. doi:10.1007/978-0-387-71817-0_18

Acıiçmez, O., Koç, Ç. K., & Seifert, J.-P. (2006). Predicting secret keys via branch prediction. In M. Abe (Ed.), *Topics in cryptology – CT-RSA 2007* (Vol. 4377, pp. 225–242). Springer Berlin Heidelberg. doi:10.1007/11967668_15

Acıiçmez, O., Koç, Ç. K., & Seifert, J.-P. (2007). On the power of simple branch prediction analysis. In *Proceedings of the 2nd acm symposium on information, computer and communications security* (pp. 312–320). New York, NY, USA: ACM.

Acıiçmez, O., & Schindler, W. (2008). A vulnerability in rsa implementations due to instruction cache analysis and its demonstration on openssl. In *Topics in cryptology–ct-rsa 2008* (pp. 256–273). Springer. doi:10.1007/978-3-540-79263-5_16

Aditya, S., Alexsandr, A. K., Dirk, A. S., & Christiaan, P. (2010). Multi-View Modeling to Support Embedded Systems Engineering in SysML. In Graph transformations and model-driven engineering (pp. 580-601).

Adler, R., Domis, D., Höfig, K., Kemmann, S., Kuhn, T., Schwinn, J. P., & Trapp, M. (2011). Integration of component fault trees into the UML. In International Conference on Model Driven Engineering Languages and Systems (pp. 312-327). doi:10.1007/978-3-642-21210-9_30

Adler, R., Schneider, D., & Trapp, M. (2010). Engineering Dynamic Adaptation for Achieving Cost-Efficient Resilience in Software-Intensive Embedded Systems. In *Proceedings of the IEEE International Conference on Engineering of Complex Computer Systems*. (pp. 21-30). Los Alamitos, California: IEEE Computer Society Press. doi:10.1109/ICECCS.2010.22

Adomavicius, G., & Tuzhilin, A. (2005). Personalization Technologies: A Process-Oriented Perspective. *Communications of the ACM, 48*(10), 83–90. doi:10.1145/1089107.1089109

Advanced Micro Devices, Inc. (2017). *The "Zen" Core Architecture.* Retrieved from https://www.amd.com/en-gb/in-novations/software-technologies/zen-cpu

Akram, R. N., Markantonakis, K., & Mayes, K. (2014). Trusted Platform Module for Smart Cards. In *Proceedings of the 2014 6th International Conference on New Technologies, Mobility and Security (NTMS)* (pp. 1-5).

Alajrami, S., Gallina, B., & Romanovsky, A. (2016). EXE-SPEM: To- wards Cloud-Based Executable Software Process Models. In *Proceedings of the 4th International Conference on Model-Driven Engineering and Software Development.*

Albers, S. (2006). Online algorithms. In D. Q. Goldin, S. A. Smolka, & P. Wegner (Eds.), *Interactive Computation: The New Paradigm* (pp. 143–164). Springer. doi:10.1007/3-540-34874-3_7

AlFardan, N. J., & Paterson, K. G. (2013). Lucky thirteen: Breaking the TLS and DTLS record protocols. In *Proceedings of the 2013 IEEE symposium on security and privacy* (pp. 526–540).

Alhakeem, M. S., Munk, P., Lisicki, R., Parzyjegla, H., Parzyjegla, H., & Muehl, G. (2015). A Framework for Adaptive Software-Based Reliability in COTS Many-Core Processors. In *Proceedings the 28th international conference on architecture of computing systems ARCS '15* (pp. 1–4).

Allan, T., Brumley, B. B., Falkner, K., van de Pol, J., & Yarom, Y. (2016, December). Amplifying side channels through performance degradation. In *Proceedings of the Annual computer security applications conference,* Los Angeles, CA. doi:10.1145/2991079.2991084

Alliance, T. C. P. (2000). *Building A Foundation of Trust in the PC.*

Alsbou, N., Henry, D., & Refai, H. (2010). R-ALOHA with Priority (PRALOHA) in Non Ideal Channel with Capture Effects. In *Proceedings of the International Conference on Telecommunications (ICT 2010).* doi:10.1109/ICTEL.2010.5478849

AMADEOS. (2015). *AMADEOS Conceptual Model. Deliverable 2.2.* Retrieved from http://amadeos-project.eu/wp-content/uploads/2015/07/AMADEOS_D2.2_v2.6-final.pdf

Ammann, P., Wijesekera, D., & Kaushik, S. (2002). Scalable, graph-based network vulnerability analysis. In *Proceedings of the 9th ACM Conference on Computer and Communications Security - CCS '02.* doi:10.1145/586110.586140

Ammons, G., Ball, T., & Larus, J. R. (1997). Exploiting hardware performance counters with flow and context sensitive profiling. *ACM Sigplan Notices, 32*(5), 85–96. doi:10.1145/258916.258924

Amorim, T., Ruiz, A., Dropmann, C., & Schneider, D. (2015). Multidirectional Modular Conditional Safety Certificates. In *Proceedings of the 4th International Workshop on Next Generation of System Assurance Approaches for Safety-Critical Systems - SAFECOMP*, Delft.

Amoroso, E. G. (1999). *An Introduction to Intrusion Detection.*

Ampère, A. M. (1838). *Essai sur la philosophie des sciences*. Paris: Bachelier.

Anderson, J., Baruah, S., & Brandenburg, B. (2009). Multicore operating-system support for mixed criticality. In Proceedings of the workshop on mixed criticality: Roadmap to evolving UAV certification. San Francisco, CA, USA.

Anderson, R., & Kuhn, M. (1997). Low Cost Attacks on Tamper Resistant Devices. In *Proceedings of the International Workshop on Security Protocols* (pp. 125-136).

Anderson, D. (1997). *Agile Product Development for Mass Customization: How to Develop and Deliver Products for Mass Customization, Niche Markets, Jit, Build-To-Order and Flexible Manufacturing*. Irwin Professional Pub.

Anderson, R. J. (2001). API Attacks. In *Security Engineering: A Guide to Building Dependable Distributed Systems*. New York, NY, USA: John Wiley & Sons, Inc.

Anderson, R. J., Bond, M., Clulow, J., & Skorobogatov, S. (2006). Cryptographic Processors-A survey. Proceedings of the IEEE, 94(2), 357-369.

Anderson, R., Bond, M., Clulow, J., & Skorobogatov, S. (2006). Cryptographic Processors - A Survey. *Proceedings of the IEEE, 94*(2), 357–369. doi:10.1109/JPROC.2005.862423

Anderson, R., & Kuhn, M. (1996). Tamper Resistance - a Cautionary Note. In *Proceedings of the second Usenix workshop on electronic commerce*, 2, pp. 1-11.

André, C., Mallet, F., Khan, A. M., & de Simone, R. (2008). Modeling SPIRIT IP-XACT with UML MARTE. In *Proc. DATE Workshop on Modeling and Analysis of Real-Time and Embedded Systems with the MARTE UML profile*.

Anthony, R., Rettberg, A., Chen, D., Jahnich, I., de Boer, G., & Ekelin, C. (2007). *Towards a Dynamically Reconfigurable Automotive Control System Architecture. In Embedded System Design: Topics, Techniques and Trends* (pp. 71–84). Springer.

Antsaklis, P. J., Goodwine, B., Gupta, V., McCourt, M. J., Wang, Y., Wu, P., . . . Zhu, F. (2013). Control of cyberphysical systems using passivity and dissipativity based methods. *European Journal of Control, 19*(5), 379-388.

Antunes, D., & Heemels, W. (2016, August). Frequency-Domain Analysis of Control Loops With Intermittent Data Losses. *IEEE Transactions on Automatic Control, 61*(8), 2295–2300. doi:10.1109/TAC.2015.2492199

ARINC. (2005). *Arinc 653, avionic application software standard interface, part 1.*

ARM Limited. (2009, April). ARM security technology: Building a secure system using TrustZone technology (tech. report No. PRD29-GENC-009492C).

ARM. (2009, April). *ARM Security Technology - Building a Secure System using Trust- Zone Technology*. Retrieved from http://infocenter.arm.com/help/topic/ com.arm.doc.prd29-genc-009492c/PRD29-GENC-009492C_trustzone_security_whitepaper.pdf

ARM. (n.d.). *Trustzone Security White Paper*. Retrieved from http://infocenter.arm.com/help/topic/com.arm.doc.prd29-genc-009492c/PRD29-GENC-009492C_trustzone_security_whitepaper.pdf

Asada, H., Kanade, T., & Takeyama, I. (1983). Control of a Direct-Drive Arm. *Journal of Dynamic Systems, Measurement, and Control, 105*(3), 136–142. doi:10.1115/1.3140645

Aßmann, U., Götz, S., Jézéquel, J.-M., Morin, B., & Trapp, M. (2014). A Reference Architecture and Roadmap for Models@run.time Systems. In *Models@run.time: Foundations, applications, and roadmaps* (pp. 1–18). doi:10.1007/978-3-319-08915-7_1

Atsumi, S., Kondo, T., & Shona, Y. (1995). *Patent No. 5,442,165.* US.

Aucsmith, D. (1996). Tamper Resistant Software: An Implementation. In *Proceedings of the International Workshop on Information Hiding,* (pp. 317-333).

Automotive Industry Action Group (AIAG). (2016).

AUTOSAR. (2016, 12 12). *Website of the autosar standard.* Retrieved 07 27, 2015, from http://www.autosar.org/

Avizienis, A., Laprie, J.-C., & Randell, B. (2004). Dependability and its Threats - A Taxonomy. In *Proceedings of the IFIP Congress Topical Sessions* (pp. 91-120).

Avizienis, A., Laprie, J.-C., & Randell, B. (2004). Dependability and its Threats - A Taxonomy. In *Proceedings of the IFIP Congress Topical Sessions,* 91-120.

Avizienis, A., Laprie, J.-C., Randell, B., & Landwehr, C. (2004). Basic Concepts and Taxonomy of Dependable and Secure Computing. *IEEE Transactions on Dependable and Secure Computing, 1*(1), 11–33. doi:10.1109/TDSC.2004.2

Azodolmolky, S., Wieder, P., & Yahyapour, R. (2013). Cloud computing networking: Challenges and opportunities for innovations. *IEEE Communications Magazine, 51*(7), 54–62. doi:10.1109/MCOM.2013.6553678

Babaoglu, O., Canright, G., Deutsch, A., Caro, G. A. D., Ducatelle, F., Gambardella, L. M., & Urnes, T. et al. (2006). Design Patterns from Biology for Distributed Computing. *ACM Transactions on Autonomous and Adaptive Systems, 1*(1), 26–66. doi:10.1145/1152934.1152937

Baheti, R., & Gill, H. (2011). Cyber-physical systems. *The impact of control technology, 12,* 161-166.

Balasch, J., Gierlichs, B., Grosso, V., Reparaz, O., & Standaert, F.-X. (2014, June 2). *On the Cost of Lazy Engineering for Masked Software Implementations.* Cryptology ePrint Archive, Report 2014/413. Retrieved from http://eprint.iacr.org

Baldwin, R. (2015). OwnStar car hacker can remotely unlock BMWs, Benz and Chrysler. *Engadget.* Retrieved from http://www.engadget.com/2015/08/13/ownstar-hack/

Bao, F., Deng, R. H., Han, Y., Jeng, A., Narasimhalu, A. D., & Ngair, T. (1997). Breaking Public Key Cryptosystems on Tamper Resistant Devices in the Presence of Transient Faults. In *Proceedings of the International Workshop on Security Protocols* (pp. 115-124).

Bar, A. R. (2014). Recent progress in road and lane detection a survey. *Machine Vision and Applications, 25*(3), 727–745.

Bard, J., Plummer, J., & Sourie, J. (1998). Determining Tax Credits for Converting Non-food Crops to Biofuels: An Application of Bi-level Programming. In Multilevel Optimization: Algorithms and Applications (pp. 23-50).

Barnasconi, M., Pêcheux, F., Vörtler, T., & Einwich, K. (2014). Advancing System Level Verification Using UVM in SystemC. In Proceedings of the DVCON 2014, San Jose, California, USA.

Baronti, P., Pillai, P., Chook, V. W., Chessa, S., Gotta, A., & Hu, Y. F. (2007). Wireless sensor networks: A survey on the state of the art and the 802.15. 4 and ZigBee standards. *Computer Communications, 30*(7), 1655–1695. doi:10.1016/j.comcom.2006.12.020

Batina, L., Gierlichs, B., Prouff, E., Rivain, M., Standaert, F.-X., & Veyrat-Charvillon, N. (2010, October 21). Mutual Information Analysis: A Comprehensive Study. *Journal of Cryptology,* 1–23.

BBC. (24. 10 2012). *BBC Ceefax, the world's first teletext service, has completed its final broadcast after 38 years on air.* Retrieved from http://www.bbc.com/news/uk-20032882

Beckmann, M. J., McGuire, C. B., & Winsten, C. B. (1956). *Studies in the economics of transportation.* Cowles Commission for Research in Economics, Yale University Press.

Beggs, C. (2006). Proposed Risk Minimization Measures for Cyber-Terrorism and SCADA Networks in Australia. In *Proceedings of the 5th European conference on information warfare and security (ECIW 2006, Helsinki). Academic Publishing, Reading, UK,* (pp. 9-18).

Begley, J., & Scahill, J. (2015, February 19). Retrieved from The Intercept - The Great SIM Heist. Retrieved from https://theintercept.com/2015/02/19/great-sim-heist/

Ben Khaled-El Feki, A. (2014). *Distributed real-time simulation of numerical models: application to power-train* [Doctoral dissertation].

Benger, N., van de Pol, J., Smart, N. P., & Yarom, Y. (2014). "ooh aah... just a little bit": A small amount of side channel can go a long way. In *Proceedings of the International workshop on cryptographic hardware and embedded systems* (pp. 75–92).

Bennaceur, A., France, R., Tamburrelli, G., Vogel, T., Mosterman, P. J., & Cazzola, W. ... Redlich, D. (2014). Mechanisms for leveraging models at runtime in self-adaptive software. In N. Bencomo, R. France, B.H.C. Cheng et al. (Eds.), *Models@run.time: Foundations, applications, and roadmaps* (pp. 19–46). Cham: Springer International Publishing. doi:10.1007/978-3-319-08915-7_2

Benvenuti, L., Balluchi, A., Bemporad, A., Di Cairano, S., Johansson, B., Johansson, R., & Tunestal, P. (2009). Automotive control. In *J. Lunze, & F. Lamnabhi-Lagarrigue (Eds.), Handbook of hybrid systems control: Theory, tools, applications* (pp. 439–470). New York: Cambridge University Press. doi:10.1017/CBO9780511807930.016

Berenbach, B., & Konrad, S. (2008). The Reinforcement Pedagogical Pattern for Industrial Training. In *REET '08 Proceedings of the 2008 Requirements Engineering Education and Training.* IEEE. doi:10.1109/REET.2008.7

Bergin, J., Eckstein, J., Völter, M., Sipos, M., Wallingford, E., & Marquardt, K. (Eds.). (2012). Pedagogical Patterns: Advice for Educators. Joseph Bergin Software Tools.

Bertoni, G., Zaccaria, V., Breveglieri, L., Monchiero, M., & Palermo, G. (2005). Aes power attack based on induced cache miss and countermeasure. In *Proceedings of the international conference on information technology: Coding and computing (itcc'05)* (Vol. 1, pp. 586–591). Washington, DC, USA: IEEE Computer Society. doi:10.1109/ITCC.2005.62

Beugnard, A., Jézéquel, J., & Plouzeau, N. (2010). Contract Aware Components, 10 years after. In Proceedings of the Component and Service Interoperability (WCSI10) (pp. 1-11).

Beugnard, A., Jezequel, J., Plouzeau, N., & Watkins, W. (1999, June). Making components contract aware. *Computer, 32*(7), 38–45. doi:10.1109/2.774917

Bézivin, J. (2004). In search of a basic principle for model driven engineering. *Novatica Journal, Special Issue, 5*(2), 21–24.

Bhattacharya, S., & Mukhopadhyay, D. (2015). Who watches the watchmen?: Utilizing performance monitors for compromising keys of rsa on intel platforms. In *Proceedings of the International workshop on cryptographic hardware and embedded systems* (pp. 248–266). doi:10.1007/978-3-662-48324-4_13

Bhattacharya, S., & Mukhopadhyay, D. (2016). Curious case of rowhammer: Flipping secret exponent bits using timing analysis. In B. Gierlichs & A. Y. Poschmann (Eds.), *Cryptographic hardware and embedded systems – CHES 2016* (pp. 602–624). Berlin, Heidelberg: Springer Berlin Heidelberg.

Biba, K. J. (1977). *Integrity Considerations for Secure Computer Systems.*

Biswas, J., & Veloso, M. (2012). Depth Camera based Localization and Navigation for Indoor Mobile Robots. In *Proceedings of IEEE International Conference on Robotics and Automation.* doi:10.1109/ICRA.2012.6224766

Blair, G., Bencomo, N., & France, R. B. (2009). Models@ run.time. *Computer, 42*(10), 22–27. doi:10.1109/MC.2009.326

Blomstedt, F. (2014). The arrowhead approach for SOA application development and documentation. In *Proceedings of the IECON 2014 - 40th Annual Conference of the IEEE Industrial Electronics Society,* Dallas (pp. 2631-2637). IEEE.

Blue, V. J., Adler, J. L., & List, G. F. (1997). Real-Time Multiple-Objective Path Search for In-Vehicle Route Guidance Systems. *Intelligent Transportation Systems and Artificial Intelligence, 1588*(3), 10–17.

Blum, A., Even-Dar, E., & Ligett, K. (2010). Routing Without Regret: On Convergence to Nash Equilibria of Regret-Minimizing Algorithms in Routing Games. *Theory of Computing, 6,* 179–199.

Boger, Y. (2016). (OSVR). Retrieved 11 21, 2016, from The VRguy's Blog: http://vrguy.blogspot.de/

Bond, M., & Anderson, R. (2001). API-Level Attacks on Embedded Systems. *Computer, 34*(10), 67–75. doi:10.1109/2.955101

Borgers, D., Geiselhart, R., & Heemels, W. (2016). *Tradeoffs between quality-of-control and quality-of-service in large-scale nonlinear networked control systems.* doi:10.1016/j.nahs.2016.10.001

Bouguet, J.-Y. (2016, 12 11). Camera Calibration Toolbox for Matlab. Retrieved from https://www.vision.caltech.edu/bouguetj/calib_doc/#start

Bowen, J., & Stavridou, V. (1993). Safety-critical systems, formal methods and standards. *Software Engineering Journal, 8*(4), 189–209. doi:10.1049/sej.1993.0025

Boyd, J. R. (1996). The Essence of Winning and Losing. Retrieved from http://dnipogo.org/john-r-boyd/

Boyd, S., El Ghaoui, L., Feron, E., & Balakrishnan, V. (1994). Linear matrix inequalities in system and control theory (15th ed.). Philadelphia: Society for industrial and applied mathematics.

Brachmann, M., Keoh, S. L., Morchon, O. G., & Kumar, S. S. (2012, July). End-to-End Transport Security in the IP-Based Internet of Things. In *Proceedings of the 2012 21st International Conference on Computer Communications and Networks (ICCCN)* (pp. 1-5). IEEE.

Braess, D. (1968). Über ein Paradoxon aus der Verkehrsplanung. *Unternehmensforschung, 12*(1), 258–268.

Brambilla, M., Cabot, J., & Wimmer, M. (2012). Model-Driven Software Engineering in Practice. *Synthesis Lectures on Software Engineering, 1*(1), 1–182. doi:10.2200/S00441ED1V01Y201208SWE001

Brandenburg, B. B. (2014, December). A synchronous IPC protocol for predictable access to shared resources in mixed-criticality systems. In Proceedings of the IEEE real-time systems symposium (pp. 196–206). doi:10.1109/RTSS.2014.37

Branicky, M. S. (2005). Introduction to hybrid systems. In *D. Hristu-Varsakelis, & W. S. Levine (Eds.), Handbook of networked and embedded control systems* (pp. 91–116). Boston: Birkhäuser. doi:10.1007/0-8176-4404-0_5

Brier, E., Clavier, C., & Olivier, F. (2004). Correlation Power Analysis with a Leakage Model. In M. Joye & J.-J. Quisquater (Eds.), *Cryptographic hardware and embedded systems - CHES 2004* (Vol. 3156, pp. 16–29). Springer Berlin Heidelberg. doi:10.1007/978-3-540-28632-5_2

Brumley, B. B., & Hakala, R. M. (2009). Cache-timing template attacks. In *Proceedings of the International conference on the theory and application of cryptology and information security* (pp.667–684).

Brumley, B. B. (2015). Cache storage attacks. In K. Nyberg (Ed.), *Topics in cryptology— CT-RSA 2015* (Vol. 9048, pp. 22–34). Springer International Publishing.

Brun, Y., Desmarais, R., Geihs, K., Litoiu, M., Lopes, A., Shaw, M., & Smit, M. (2013). A Design Space for Self-Adaptive Systems. In R. de Lemos, H. Giese, H. A. Müller, & M. Shaw (Eds.), *Software engineering for self-adaptive systems ii* (pp. 33–50). Berlin, Heidelberg: Springer Berlin Heidelberg. doi:10.1007/978-3-642-35813-5_2

Burns, A. J., Johnson, M. E., & Honeyman, P. (2016, October). A brief chronology of medical device security. *Communications of the ACM, 59*(10), 66–72. doi:10.1145/2890488

Campana, F., Moreno, A., Riano, D., & Varga, L. (2008). K4Care: knowledge-based homecare e-services for an ageing Europe. In R. Annicchiarico, U. Cortés, & C. Urdiales (Eds.), Agent Technology and E-Health (pp. 95-116). Basel: Birkhäuser Verlag. doi:10.1007/978-3-7643-8547-7_6

Campo-Jimenez, G., Martin Perandones, J., & Lopez-Hernandez, F. (2013). A VLC-based beacon location system for mobile applications. In *Proceedings of the International Conference on Localization and GNSS* (pp. 25–27). Turin: IEEE. doi:10.1109/ICL-GNSS.2013.6577276

Candence. (2017). Retrieved from https://www.cadence.com

Capossele, A., Cervo, V., De Cicco, G., & Petrioli, C. (2015). Security as a CoAP resource: an optimized DTLS implementation for the IoT. In *Proceedings of the 2015 IEEE International Conference on Communications (ICC)* (pp. 549-554). doi:10.1109/ICC.2015.7248379

Cardenas, A. A., Amin, S., & Sastry, S. (2008). Secure Control: Towards Survivable Cyber-Physical Systems. In *Proceedings of the 28th International Conference on, Distributed Computing Systems Workshops ICDCS'08* (pp. 495-500).

Cardenas, A. A., Amin, S., & Sastry, S. (2008). Secure control: Towards survivable cyber-physical systems. In *Proceedings of the International Conference on Distributed Computing Systems* (pp. 495-500). Beijing.

Cardenas, A. A., Amin, S., Sinopoli, B., Giani, A., Perrig, A., & Sastry, S. (2009). Challenges for Securing Cyber Physical Systems. In *Proceedings of the Workshop on future directions in cyber-physical systems security*, (p. 5).

Carter, W. S. (1994). The future of programmable logic and its impact on digital system design. In *Proceedings of the IEEE International Conference on Computer Design: VLSI in Computers and Processors* (pp. 10-16). Cambridge: IEEE. doi:10.1109/ICCD.1994.331842

Catrene. (2016). OpenES CATRENE Project: CA703. Retrieved from http://www.ecsi.org/openes

Cavalieri, S., Cutuli, G., & Monteleone, S. (2010, May). Evaluating Impact of Security on OPC UA Performance. In *Proceedings of the 3rd International Conference on Human System Interaction*, (pp. 687-694). doi:10.1109/HSI.2010.5514495

Ceccato, M., Ofek, Y., & Tonella, P. (2008). A Protocol for Property-Based Attestation. *Theory and Practice of Computer Science*, 7.

Celesti, A., Fazio, M., & Villari, M. (2013). SE CLEVER: A secure message oriented Middleware for Cloud federation. In *Proceedings of the 2013 IEEE Symposium on Computers and Communications (ISCC)*, (pp. 35-40). doi:10.1109/ISCC.2013.6754919

Censi, A., Strubel, J., Brandli, C., Delbruck, T., & Scaramuzza, D. (2013). Low-latency localization by Active LED Markers tracking using a Dynamic Vision Sensor. In *Proceedings of the IEEE/RSJ International Conference on Intelligent Robots and Systems 2013*. doi:10.1109/IROS.2013.6696456

Cercone, M., & Ernst, T. (2012). *An EU Cybercrime Center to fight online criminals and protect e-consumers.*

Čertický, M., Jakob, M., & Píbil, R. (2016). Simulation Testbed for Autonomic Demand-Responsive Mobility Systems. In T.L. McCluskey, A. Kotsialos, J.P. Müller et al. (Eds.), Autonomic Road Transport Support Systems (pp. 147-164). Birkhäuser Basel.

Chan, V., & Ho, F. (2003). *Patent No. 6588673 B1*. United States of America.

Chandola, V., Banerjee, A., & Kumar, V. (2009). Anomaly Detection: A Survey. *ACM Computing Surveys, 41*(3), 1–58. doi:10.1145/1541880.1541882

Chandra, A., Lewis, P. R., Glette, K., & Stilkerich, S. C. (2016). Reference Architecture for Self-aware and Self-expressive Computing Systems. In P. R. Lewis, M. Platzner, B. Rinner, J. Tørresen, & X. Yao (Eds.), *Self-aware computing systems: An engineering approach* (pp. 37–49). Cham: Springer International Publishing. doi:10.1007/978-3-319-39675-0_4

Chaojun, G., Jirutitijaroen, P., & Motani, M. (2015). Detecting False Data Injection Attacks in AC State Estimation. *IEEE Transactions on Smart Grid, 6*(5), 2476–2483. doi:10.1109/TSG.2015.2388545

Charette, R. N. (2009). This Car Runs on Code - IEEE Spectrum. Retrieved from http://spectrum.ieee.org/transportation/systems/this-car-runs-on-code

Charette, R. N. (2009). *This Car Runs on Code*. Retrieved from http://spectrum.ieee.org/transportation/systems/this-car-runs-on-code

Chari, S., Rao, J. R., & Rohatgi, P. (2003). Template Attacks. In Kaliski B.S., Koç. K., Paar C. (Eds.) Cryptographic Hardware and Embedded Systems - CHES 2002. CHES 2002. Lecture Notes in Computer Science, 2523. Berlin, Heidelberg: Springer Berlin Heidelberg.

Chen, X. (2007). *Patent No. 1983466 A2*. European Union.

Chen, Y.-K. (2012). Challenges and opportunities of internet of things. In *Proc. of the Asia and South Pacific Design Automation Conference (ASP-DAC)*, Sydney, Australia (pp. 383–388). doi:10.1109/ASPDAC.2012.6164978

Cheng, B. H. C., de Lemos, R., Giese, H., Inverardi, P., Magee, J., & Andersson, J. ... Whittle, J. (2009). Software Engineering for Self-Adaptive Systems: A Research Roadmap. In B.H.C. Cheng, R. de Lemos, H. Giese et al. (Eds.), *Software engineering for self-adaptive systems* (pp. 1–26). Berlin, Heidelberg: Springer. doi:10.1007/978-3-642-02161-9_1

Cheng, P., Zhang, H., & Chen, J. (2016). *Cyber Security for Industrial Control Systems: From the Viewpoint of Close-Loop*. CRC Press. doi:10.1201/b19629

Chen, L., Löhr, H., Manulis, M., & Sadeghi, A. (2008). *Property-Based Attestation Without a Trusted Third Party*. Information Security. doi:10.1007/978-3-540-85886-7_3

Chetverikov, D., Eichhardt, I., & Jankó, Z. (2015). *A Brief Survey of Image-Based Depth Upsampling*. KEPAF.

Chiappetta, M., Savaş, E., & Yilmaz, C. (2015). *Real time detection of cache-based side-channel attacks using hardware performance counters* (Tech. Rep.). Cryptology ePrint Archive, Report 2015/1034. Retrieved from http://eprint.iacr.org

Choi, Y. J., Park, S., & Bahk, S. (2006). Multichannel Random Access in OFDMA Wireless Networks. *IEEE Journal on Selected Areas in Communications*, *24*(3), 603–613. doi:10.1109/JSAC.2005.862422

Cimatti, A., & Roveri, M. (1998, December). NuSMV 1.0: User manual (Tech. Rep. Nos. Technical report, ITC-IRST, Trento, Italy.)

Cimatti, A., Clarke, E., Giunchiglia, E., Giunchiglia, F., Pistore, M., Roveri, M., . . . Tacchella, A. (2002, July). NuSMV 2: An opensource tool for symbolic model checking. In E. Brinksma & K. G. Larsen (Eds.), *Computer aided verification: 14th international conference, Proceedings* (pp. 359–364). Berlin, Heidelberg: Springer Berlin Heidelberg.

CISC Semiconductor GmbH. (2017). Retrieved from https://www.cisc.at/

Claes, R., Holvoet, T., & Weyns, D. (2011). A decentralized approach for anticipatory vehicle routing using delegate multi-agent systems. *IEEE Transactions on Intelligent Transportation Systems*, *12*(2), 364–373. doi:10.1109/TITS.2011.2105867

Clarke, E., McMillan, K., Campos, S., & Hartonas-Garmhausen, V. (1996). Symbolic model checking. In R. Alur & T. A. Henzinger (Eds.), *Computer aided verification* (pp. 419–422). Berlin, Heidelberg: Springer Berlin Heidelberg. doi:10.1007/3-540-61474-5_93

Cloosterman, M. (2008). *Control over communication networks: modelling, analysis and synthesis* [Doctoral dissertation]. Technische Universiteit Eindhoven. Retrieved from (https://pure.tue.nl/ws/files/3251237/200810902.pdf)

Cloosterman, M., van de Wouw, N., Heemels, W., & Nijmeijer, H. (2009, July). Stability of networked control systems with uncertain time-varying delays. *IEEE Transactions on Automatic Control*, *54*(7), 1575–1580. doi:10.1109/TAC.2009.2015543

Cockburn, D., Varga, L. Z., & Jennings, N. R. (1992). Cooperating Intelligent Systems for Electricity Distribution. In M.A. Bramer, & R.W. Milne (Eds.), BCS Expert Systems 92 Conference (Application Track), Churchill College, Cambridge, UK.

Coker, G., Guttman, J., Loscocco, P., Herzog, A., Millen, J., OHanlon, B., & Sniffen, B. et al. (2011). Principles of Remote Attestation. *International Journal of Information Security*, *10*(2), 63–81. doi:10.1007/s10207-011-0124-7

Çolak, S., Lima, A., & González, M. C. (2016). Understanding congested travel in urban areas. *Nature Communications*, *7*. doi:10.1038/ncomms10793 PMID:26978719

Common Criteria. (2002). *Common Criteria Information Statement. Reuse of Evaluation Results and Evidence.*

Common Criteria. (2012). *Common Criteria for Information Technology Security Evaluation Part 1 - 3; Version 3.1.*

Common Criteria. (2012, April). Common Criteria Supporting Document Mandatory Technical Document - Composite product evaluation for Smart Version 1.2.

COMPLEX I ECSI. (2016). Retrieved from http://ecsi.org/complex

Coppens, B., Verbauwhede, I., Bosschere, K. D., & Sutter, B. D. (2009). Practical mitigations for timing-based side-channel attacks on modern x86 processors. In *Proceedings of the 2009 30th IEEE symposium on security and privacy* (pp. 45–60). Washington, DC, USA: IEEE Computer Society. doi:10.1109/SP.2009.19

Costan, V., Lebedev, I., & Devadas, S. (2016, August). Sanctum: Minimal hardware extensions for strong software isolation. In *Proceedings of the 25th USENIX Security Symposium* (pp. 857–874). Austin, TX: USENIX Association.

Cui, A., & Stolfo, S. J. (2010). A Quantitative Analysis of the Insecurity of Embedded Network Devices: Results of a Wide-Area Scan. In *Proceedings of the 26th Annual Computer Security Applications Conference* (pp. 97-106). doi:10.1145/1920261.1920276

D'Antoine, S. (2015, Aug). *Exploiting out of order execution for covert cross vm communication*. Las Vegas: Blackhat.

Dadras, S., Gerdes, R. M., & Sharma, R. (2015). Vehicular Platooning in an Adversarial Environment. In *Proceedings of the 10th ACM Symposium on Information, Computer and Communications Security* (pp. 167-178).

Dagon, D., Gu, G., Lee, C. P., & Lee, W. (2007). A Taxonomy of Botnet Structures. In *Proceedings of the Computer Security Applications Conference, 2007. ACSAC 2007. Twenty-Third Annual* (pp. 325-339).

Dai, L., Zhang, F., Mei, X., & Zhang, X. (2015). Fast Minimax Path-Based Joint Depth Interpolation. *IEEE Signal Processing Letters*, 22(5), 623–627. doi:10.1109/LSP.2014.2365527

Daniela, T. (2011). Communication Security in SCADA Pipeline Monitoring Systems. In *Proceedings of the 2011 RoEduNet International Conference 10th Edition: Networking in Education and Research* (pp. 1-5).

David, P., Idasiak, V., & Kratz, F. (2009). Towards a better interaction between design and dependability analysis: FMEA derived from UML/SysML models. In *Proceedings of the Joint ESREL and SRA-Europe Conference* (Vol. 3, pp. 2259-2266). Retrieved from http://www.scopus.com/inward/record.url?eid=2-s2.0-78751589362&partnerID=40&md5=1e1684e4af48e5906773f66766c37201

Daws, R. (2016, 11). Akamai: IoT botnet set a record in a year when DDoS attacks increased 71 percent. IoT Tech News.

De Santis, F., Kasper, M., Mangard, S., Sigl, G., Stein, O., & Stöttinger, M. (2013). On the Relationship between Correlation Power Analysis and the Stochastic Approach: An ASIC Designer Perspective. In G. Paul & S. Vaudenay (Eds.), *Progress in cryptology – INDOCRYPT 2013, LNCS* (Vol. 8250, pp. 215–226). Springer International Publishing. doi:10.1007/978-3-319-03515-4_14

DEC. (1967). *The digital small computer handbook*. Digital equipment corp.

DECOS. (2007). Dependable Embedded Components and Systems .

Demaertelaere, F. (2010). *Hardware Security Modules*. SecAppDev.org - Secure Application Development.

Dempe, S. (2003). Annotated Bibliography on Bi-level Programming and Mathematical Programs with Equilibrium Constraints. *Journal of Optics*, 52(3), 333–359.

Denning, D. E. (2000). Cyberterrorism: Testimony Before the Special Oversight Panel on Terrorism Committee on Armed Services US House of Representatives. *Focus on Terrorism, 9*.

Denning, D. E. (2000). Cyberterrorism: The Logic Bomb versus the Truck Bomb. *Global Dialogue, 2*.

Derler, P., Lee, E. A., Tripakis, S., & Törngren, M. (2013). Cyber-physical system design contracts. *ICCPS '13 Proceedings of the ACM/IEEE 4th International Conference on Cyber-Physical Systems* (pp. 109-118). New York: ACM.

Derler, P., Lee, E. A., & Vincentelli, A. S. (2012, January). Modelling cyber-physical systems. *Proceedings of the IEEE, 100*(1), 13–28. doi:10.1109/JPROC.2011.2160929

Despotou, G., & Kelly, T. (2004). Extending the safety case concept to address dependability. In *Proceedings of the 22nd International System Safety Conference*.

Deyle, T. (2016, 12 11). Valve's "Lighthouse" Tracking System May Be Big News for Robotics. *Hizook*. Retrieved from http://www.hizook.com/blog/2015/05/17/valves-lighthouse-tracking-system-may-be-big-news-robotics

Dhome, K. M.-B.-A. (2015). Bundle adjustment revisited for SLAM with RGBD sensors. In *Proceedings of the 14th IAPR International Conference on Machine Vision Applications (MVA)*.

Dierks, T. (2008). *The Transport Layer Security (TLS) Protocol Version 1.2*. IETF. doi:10.17487/rfc5246

DO-297. (2005). *Integrated Modular Avionics (IMA)*. Development Guidance.

Dobson, S., Zambonelli, F., Denazis, S., Fernández, A., Gaïti, D., & Gelenbe, E. ... Schmidt, N. (2006). A survey of autonomic communications. *ACM Transactions on Autonomous and Adaptive Systems, 1*(2), 223–259. doi:10.1145/1186778.1186782

Dobson, S., Sterritt, R., Nixon, P., & Hinchey, M. (2010). Fulfilling the Vision of Autonomic Computing. *Computer, 43*(1), 35–41. doi:10.1109/MC.2010.14

Donkers, T., Heemels, W., van de Wouw, N., & Hetel, L. (2011). Stability analysis of networked control systems using a switched linear systems approach. *IEEE Transactions on Automatic Control. Institute of Electrical and Electronics Engineers, 56*(9), 2101–2115.

Do, T.-H., & Yoo, M. (2016). An in-Depth Survey of Visible Light Communication Based Positioning Systems. *Sensors (Basel, Switzerland), 16*(5), 678. doi:10.3390/s16050678 PMID:27187395

Doychev, G., Feld, D., Kopf, B., Mauborgne, L., & Reineke, J. (2013). Cacheaudit: A tool for the static analysis of cache side channels. In *Presented as part of the 22nd USENIX Security Symposium (USENIX Security 13)* (pp. 431–446). USENIX, Washington, D.C.

EAST-ADL Association. (2014). Retrieved from http://www.east-adl.info/

Ecco, L., Tobuschat, S., Saidi, S., & Ernst, R. (2014, August). A mixed critical memory controller using bank privatization and fixed priority scheduling. In *Proceedings of the IEEE 20th international conference on embedded and real-time computing systems and applications* (pp. 1–10). doi:10.1109/RTCSA.2014.6910550

Eclipse. (2015). Papyrus. Retrieved from https://www.eclipse.org/papyrus/

Ejaz, W., Naeem, M., Shahid, A., Anpalagan, A., & Jo, M. (2017). Efficient Energy Management for the Internet of Things in Smart Cities. *IEEE Communications Magazine, 55*(1), 84–91. doi:10.1109/MCOM.2017.1600218CM

El Salloum, C., Elshuber, M., Höftberger, O., Isakovic, H., & Wasicek, A. (2013). The ACROSS MPSoC - A new generation of multi-core processors designed for safety-critical embedded systems. *Microprocess. Microsyst., 37*, 0141-9331.

Electricity Information Sharing and Analysis Center. (2016). *Analysis of the Cyber Attack on the Ukrainian Power Grid*.

El-Tantawy, S., Abdulhai, B., & Abdelgawad, H. (2013). Multiagent Reinforcement Learning for Integrated Network of Adaptive Traffic Signal Controllers (MARLIN-ATSC): Methodology and Large-Scale Application on Downtown Toronto. *IEEE Transactions on Intelligent Transportation Systems, 14*(3), 1140–1150. doi:10.1109/TITS.2013.2255286

Ercan, A. T. (2015). Fusing Inertial Sensor Data in an Extended Kalman Filter for 3D Camera Tracking. *IEEE Transactions on Image Processing, 24*(2), 538-548.

EUROCONTROL - European Organisation for the safety of air navigation. (2006). *Safety Case Development Manual Edition 2.2*. DAP/SSH/091.

Evans, D. (2011). The Internet of Things. *How the Next Evolution of the Internet is Changing Everything* (Whitepaper). *Cisco Internet Business Solutions Group, 1*, 1–12.

EVITA. (2016, 12 12). *EVITA*. Retrieved 08 03, 2016, from http://www.evita-project.org/

Evtyushkin, D., & Ponomarev, D. (2016). Covert channels through random number generator: Mechanisms, capacity estimation and mitigations. In *Proceedings of the 2016 ACM SIGSAC conference on computer and communications security* (pp. 843–857). New York, NY: ACM. doi:10.1145/2976749.2978374

Falliere, N., Murchu, L. O., & Chien, E. (2011). W32. stuxnet dossier. *White Paper, Symantec Corp., Security Response, 5*(6).

Feller, T. (2014). Towards Trustworthy Cyber-Physical Systems. In *Trustworthy Reconfigurable Systems* (pp. 85–136). Springer.

Fenelon, P., & Hebbron, B. (1994). Applying HAZOP to Software Engineering Models. *Risk Management And Critical Protective Systems: Proceedings of SARSS*, (pp. 1/1–1/16). Altrinchan.

Fernandes, P., & Nunes, U. (2010). Platooning of Autonomous Vehicles with Intervehicle Communications in SUMO Traffic Simulator. In *Proceedings of the International IEEE Conference on Intelligent Transportation Systems (ITSC)*. doi:10.1109/ITSC.2010.5625277

Fernandez-Marquez, J. L., Marzo Serugendo, G. D., Montagna, S., Viroli, M., & Arcos, J. L. (2013). Description and Composition of Bio-inspired Design Patterns: A Complete Overview. *Natural Computing, 12*(1), 43–67. doi:10.1007/s11047-012-9324-y

Ferstl, D., Reinbacher, C., Ranftl, R., Ruether, M., & Bischof, H. (2013). Image Guided Depth Upsampling Using Anisotropic Total Generalized Variation. In *Proceedings of the IEEE International Conference on Computer Vision*, Sydney (pp. 993-1000).

Fitzgerald, J., Larsen, P. G., & Verhoef, M. (2014). From embedded to cyber-physical systems: Challenges and future directions. In J. Fitzgerald, P. G. Larsen, & M. Verhoef (Eds.), *Collaborative design for embedded systems: Co-modelling and Co-simulation* (pp. 293–303). Berlin, Heidelberg: Springer. doi:10.1007/978-3-642-54118-6_14

FORD GT - Lines of code. (2016). Retrieved from https://www.eitdigital.eu/news-events/blog/article/guess-what-requires-150-million-lines-of-code/

Formby, D., Srinivasan, P., Leonard, A., Rogers, J., & Beyah, R. (2016). Who's in Control of Your Control System? Device Fingerprinting for Cyber-Physical Systems. In Network and distributed system security symposium (pp. 21–24). doi:10.14722/ndss.2016.23142

Foxlin, G. W. (2002). Motion tracking: No silver bullet, but a respectable arsenal. *IEEE Computer Graphics and Applications, 22*(6), 24–38. doi:10.1109/MCG.2002.1046626

Fricke, A., & Völter, M. (2000). SEMINARS: A Pedagogical Pattern Language about teaching seminars effectively. In Proceedings of the EuroPLoP 2000.

Fridman, E. (2014). *Introduction to time-delay systems*. Basel, Switzerland: Springer International Publishing. doi:10.1007/978-3-319-09393-2

Gallagher, S. (2016, 10). Double-dip Internet-of-Things botnet attack felt across the Internet. *Ars Technica*.

Gallais, J.-F., Kizhvatov, I., & Tunstall, M. (2011). Improved trace-driven cache-collision attacks against embedded aes implementations. In Y. Chung & M. Yung (Eds.), *Information security applications* (Vol. 6513, pp. 243–257). Springer Berlin Heidelberg. doi:10.1007/978-3-642-17955-6_18

Gallina, B., & Fabre, L. (2015). Benefits of Security-informed Safety-oriented Process Line Engineering. *Digital Avionics Systems Conference (DASC-34)*.

Gallina, B., Kashiyarandi, S., Martin, H., & Bramberger, R. (2014). Modeling a Safety- and Automotive-oriented Process Line to Enable Reuse and Flexible Process Derivation. In *Proceedings of the 8th IEEE International Workshop on Quality-Oriented Reuse of Software (QUORS)*.

Gallina, B., Kashiyarandi, S., Martin, H., & Bramberger, R. (2014). *Modeling a Safety- and Automotive-oriented Process Line to Enable Reuse and Flexible Process Derivation*. Västerås, Sweden: *Proceedings of the 8th IEEE International Workshop on Quality-Oriented Reuse of Software (QUORS)*.

Gandolfi, K., Mourtel, C., & Olivier, F. (2001). Electromagnetic analysis: Concrete results. In K. Çetin, D. Naccache, C. Paar et al. (Eds.), Cryptographic Hardware and Embedded Systems - CHES 2001, LNCS (Vol. 2162, pp. 251–261). Springer Berlin Heidelberg.

Ganesan, G., & Li, Y. (2007). A Simple Reservation Scheme for Multicarrier Channel Aware Aloha. In *Proceedings of the IEEE Global Communications Conference (GLOBECOM 2007)* (pp. 1451-1455). doi:10.1109/GLOCOM.2007.279

García, J., Torralba, Á., Florez, J. E., Borrajo, D., López, C. L., & García-Olaya, Á. (2016). TIMIPLAN: A Tool for Transportation Tasks. In T.L. McCluskey, A. Kotsialos, J.P. Müller et al. (Eds.), Autonomic Road Transport Support Systems (Autonomic Systems) (pp. 269-286). Birkhäuser Basel. doi:10.1007/978-3-319-25808-9_16

García, J., Florez, J. E., Torralba, Á., Borrajo, D., López, C. L., García-Olaya, A., & Sáenz, J. (2013). Combining linear programming and automated planning to solve intermodal transportation problems. *European Journal of Operational Research*, *227*(1), 216–226. doi:10.1016/j.ejor.2012.12.018

Garcia-Morchon, O., Kumar, S., Struik, R., Keoh, S., & Hummen, R. (2013). *Security Considerations in the IP-based Internet of Things*. IETF.

Geisberger, E., & Broy, M. (2012). agendaCPS: Integrierte Forschungsangende Cyber-Physical Systems. Berlin Heidelberg: Springer Verlag.

Geisler. (2016). *Leon 3 SPARC*. Von Geisler: http://www.gaisler.com/index.php/products/processors/leon3?task=view&id=13

Ghaeini, H. R., & Tippenhauer, N. O. (2016). HAMIDS: Hierarchical Monitoring Intrusion Detection System for Industrial Control Systems. In *Proceedings of the Workshop on cyber-physical systems security and privacy* (pp. 103–111). doi:10.1145/2994487.2994492

Gibson, I., Rosen, D. W., & Stucker, B. et al. (2010). *Additive Manufacturing Technologies* (Vol. 238). Springer. doi:10.1007/978-1-4419-1120-9

Giese, H., Bencomo, N., Pasquale, L., Ramirez, A. J., Inverardi, P., Wätzoldt, S., & Clarke, S. (2014). Living with Uncertainty in the Age of Runtime Models. In N. Bencomo, R. France, B. H. C. Cheng, & U. Aßmann (Eds.), *Models@run.time: Foundations, applications, and roadmaps* (pp. 47–100). Cham: Springer International Publishing. doi:10.1007/978-3-319-08915-7_3

Github. (2016, 12 11). *DIY Position Tracking using HTC Vive's Lighthouse*. Retrieved 11 21, 2016, from https://github.com/ashtuchkin/vive-diy-position-sensor

GlobalPlatform. (2016a). *About globalplatform. our mission.* Retrieved from http://www.globalplatform.org/aboutus-mission.asp

GlobalPlatform. (2016b). *Globalplatform made simple guide: Trusted execution environment (tee) guide.* Retrieved from http://www.globalplatform.org/mediaguidetee.asp

Goal Structuring Notation Working Group. (2011). *GSN Community Standard version 1*. http://www.goalstructuringnotation.info/documents/GSN_Standard.pdf

Goal Structuring Notation Working Group. (2011). *GSN Community Standard version 1*. Retrieved from http://www.goalstructuringnotation.info/documents/GSN_Standard.pdf

Gödel Prize. (2012). Retrieved November 28, 2016, from http://www.acm.org/press-room/news-releases/2012/goedel-prize-2012/

Goswami, D., Schneider, R., Masrur, A., Lukasiewycz, M., Chakraborty, S., Voit, H., & Annaswamy, A. (2012). Challenges in automotive cyber-physical systems design. In *Proceedings of the 2012 International Conference Embedded Computer Systems (SAMOS)* (pp. 346-354). Samos: IEEE. doi:10.1109/SAMOS.2012.6404199

Gouvêa, C., & López, J. (2015). Implementing gcm on armv8. In K. Nyberg (Ed.), *Topics in cryptology — CT-RSA 2015, LNCS* (Vol. 9048, pp. 167–180). Springer International Publishing.

Graham, H. E., Jr. M. B., Nablo, R. J., & Haeuser, W. W. (2002). *Patent No. 6402028 B1*. United States of America.

Gras, B., Razavi, K., Bosman, E., Bos, H., & Giuffrida, C. (2017). Aslr on the line: Practical cache attacks on the mmu. In Proceedings of NDSS symposium 2017.

Grenander, S., Simpson, K., & Sindiy, O. (2009). The Autonomy System Architecture. In *Proceedings of the AIAA infotech@Aerospace conference*. Reston, Virigina: American Institute of Aeronautics; Astronautics. doi:10.2514/6.2009-1884

Grimwood, J. M. B. C. (1969). Project Gemini; Technology and Operations. Washington, D.C.: G.P.O.

Group, O. M. (2015). OMG Unified Modeling Language TM (OMG UML), Superstructure v.2.5. *InformatikSpektrum, 21*, 758. doi:10.1007/s002870050092

Gruss, D., Maurice, C., & Mangard, S. (2016). Rowhammer.js: A remote software- induced fault attack in javascript. In *Proceedings of the 13th international conference on detection of intrusions and malware, and vulnerability assessment, LNCS* (Vol. 9721, pp. 300–321). New York, NY: Springer-Verlag. doi:10.1007/978-3-319-40667-1_15

Gruss, D., Maurice, C., Wagner, K., & Mangard, S. (2016). Flush+flush: A fast and stealthy cache attack. In *Proceedings of the 13th conference on detection of intrusions and malware & vulnerability assessment (DIMVA)*. doi:10.1007/978-3-319-40667-1_14

Gruss, D., Spreitzer, R., & Mangard, S. (2015). Cache template attacks: Automating attacks on inclusive last-level caches. In *Proceedings of the 24th USENIX Security Symposium (USENIX Security 15)*(pp. 897–912).

Gruss, D., Maurice, C., Fogh, A., Lipp, M., & Mangard, S. (2016). Prefetch side-channel attacks: Bypassing smap and kernel aslr. In *Proceedings of the 2016 ACM SIGSAC conference on computer and communications security* (pp. 368–379). doi:10.1145/2976749.2978356

Guanciale, R., Nemati, H., Baumann, C., & Dam, M. (2016). Cache storage channels: Alias-driven attacks and verified countermeasures. In Proceedings of the IEEE symposium on security and privacy.

Güdermann, M., Ortmeier, F., & Reif, W. (2006). Safety and dependability analysis of self-adaptive systems. In *Proceedings of the Second International Symposium in Leveraging Applications of Formal Methods, Verification and Validation.* Paphos: IEEE. doi:10.1109/ISoLA.2006.38

Gueron, S. (2009). Intel's new AES instructions for enhanced performance and security. In O. Dunkelman (Ed.), *Fast software encryption: 16th international workshop, FSE 2009* (pp. 51–66). Berlin, Heidelberg: Springer Berlin Heidelberg. doi:10.1007/978-3-642-03317-9_4

Gullasch, D., Bangerter, E., & Krenn, S. (2011). *Cache games–bringing access-based cache attacks on aes to practice. In Proceedings of the 2011 IEEE symposium on security and privacy* (pp. 490–505). doi:10.1109/SP.2011.22

Gvero, I. (2013, August). Computers As Components 3rd Edition: Principles of Embedded Computing System Design by Marilyn Wolf. *SIGSOFT Softw. Eng. Notes, 38,* 67-68. doi:10.1145/2507288.2507292

Haapanen, P., & Helminen, A. (2020). *Failure mode and effects analysis of software-based automation systems.* Helsinki: Radiation and Nuclear Safety Authority.

Hadžiosmanović, D., Bolzoni, D., & Hartel, P. H. (2012). A Log Mining Approach for Process Monitoring in SCADA. *International Journal of Information Security, 11*(4), 231–251. doi:10.1007/s10207-012-0163-8

Hajnal, Á., Isern, D., Moreno, A., Pedone, G., & Varga, L. (2007). Knowledge Driven Architecture for Home Care. In Burkhard, H-D., Lindemann, G., Verbrugge, R., & Varga, L., (Eds.), *CEEMAS 2007. Multi-agent systems and applications V: 5th International Central and Eastern European Conference on Multi-agent Systems, Lecture Notes in Computer Science, Lecture Notes in Artificial Intelligence (Vol. 4696,* pp. 173-182). Springer Berlin Heidelberg

Hansman, S., & Hunt, R. (2005). A taxonomy of network and computer attacks. *Computers & Security, 24,* 31-43.

Han, Y. S., Deng, J., & Haas, Z. J. (2006). Analyzing Multi-Channel Medium Access Control Schemes with ALOHA Reservation. *IEEE Transactions on Wireless Communications, 5*(8), 2143–2152. doi:10.1109/TWC.2006.1687730

Harris, A. F. III, Khanna, V., Tuncay, G., Want, R., & Kravets, R. (2016). Bluetooth Low Energy in Dense IoT Environments. *IEEE Communications Magazine, 54*(12), 30–36. doi:10.1109/MCOM.2016.1600546CM

Haselsteiner, E., & Breitfuß, K. (2006). Security in Near Field Communication (NFC). In *Proceedings of the Workshop on RFID security.*

Hassan, M., & Patel, H. (2016, April). Criticality- and requirement-aware bus arbitration for multi-core mixed criticality systems. In *IEEE real-time and embedded technology and applications symposium* (pp. 1–11). RTAS. doi:10.1109/RTAS.2016.7461327

Hautala, L. (2016, October 24). *Why it was so easy to hack the cameras that took down the web.* Retrieved from https://www.cnet.com/how-to/ddos-iot-connected-devices-easily-hacked-internet-outage-webcam-dvr/

Hautier, R., Macchetti, M., & Perrine, J. (2012). *Patent No. 2720167 A1.* European union.

Hawkings, R., Habli, I., Kelly, T., & Mc Dermid, J. (2013). *Assurance cases and prescriptive software safety certification: a comparative study.*

Heemels, W. P., & van de Wouw, N. (2010). Stability and Stabilization of Networked Control Systems. In A. Bemporad, W. P. Heemels, & M. Johansson (Eds.), *Networked Control Systems* (pp. 203–253). Berlin, Heidelberg: Springer-Verlag. doi:10.1007/978-0-85729-033-5_7

Heemels, W., Teel, A., van de Wouw, N., & Nesic, D. (2010, August). Networked control systems with communication constraints: Tradeoffs between transmission intervals, delays and performance. *IEEE Transactions on Automatic Control*, 55(8), 1781–1796. doi:10.1109/TAC.2010.2042352

Heinz, B., Heyszl, J., & Stumpf, F. (2014, Dec). Side-channel analysis of a high-throughput AES peripheral with countermeasures. In *Proceedings of the 2014 14th international symposium on Integrated circuits (ISIC)* (p. 25-29).

Hendricks, J., & Van Doorn, L. (2004). Secure Bootstrap Is Not Enough: Shoring up the Trusted Computing Base. In *Proceedings of the 11th workshop on ACM SIGOPS European workshop*. doi:10.1145/1133572.1133600

Hentunen, D., & Tikkanen, A. (2014). *Havex Hunts For ICS/SCADA Systems*. F-Secure.

Henzinger, T. A., Minea, M., & Prabhu, V. (2001). Assume-Guarantee Reasoning for Hierarchical Hybrid Systems. In *Proceedings of the 4th International Workshop on Hybrid Systems: Computation and Control (HSCC 2001)* (pp. 275–290). Rome: Springer.

Herber, C., Richter, A., Rauchfuss, H., & Herkersdorf, A. (2014, September). Spatial and temporal isolation of virtual CAN controllers. *SIGBED Rev.*, 11(2), 19–26. doi:10.1145/2668138.2668141

Hespanha, J., Naghshtabrizi, P., & Xu, Y. (2007, January 1). A survey of recent results in networked control systems. *Proceedings of the IEEE*, 95(1), 138–162. doi:10.1109/JPROC.2006.887288

Hetel, L., Daffouz, J., & Iung, C. (2008). Analysis and control of LTI and switched systems in digital loops via an event-based modelling. *International Journal of Control*, 81(7), 1125–1138. doi:10.1080/00207170701670442

Hinchey, M., & Sterritt, R. (2006). Self-Managing Software. *Computer*, 39(2), 107–109. doi:10.1109/MC.2006.69

Hoban, C.F., & Zisman, S.B. (1937). Visualizing the Curriculum.

Hoeller, A., Spitzer, B., Rauter, T., Iber, J., & Kreiner, C. (2016). *Diverse Compiling for Software-Based Recovery of Permanent Faults in COTS Processors. In 2016 46th annual ieee/ifip international conference on dependable systems and networks workshop (dsn-w)* (pp. 143–148). IEEE; doi:10.1109/DSN-W.2016.34

Höfig, K., Armbruster, M., & Schmid, R. (2014). A vehicle control platform as safety element out of context. HiPEAC Computing Systems Week. Barcelona.

Höftberger, O., & Obermaisser, R. (2013). Ontology-based Runtime Reconfiguration of Distributed Embedded Real-Time Systems. In *Proceedings of the 16th IEEE International Symposium on Object/Component/Service-Oriented Real-Time Distributed Computing (ISORC 2013)*. Paderborn: IEEE. doi:10.1109/ISORC.2013.6913205

Höftberger, O., & Obermaisser, R. (2013, June). Ontology-based runtime reconfiguration of distributed embedded real-time systems. In *Proceedings of the 2013 IEEE 16th International Symposium on Object/Component/Service-Oriented Real-Time Distributed Computing (ISORC)*.

Höller, A., Iber, J., Rauter, T., & Kreiner, C. (2016). Poster: Towards a Secure, Resilient, and Distributed Infrastructure for Hydropower Plant Unit Control. In *Adjunct Proceedings of the 13th International Conference on Embedded Wireless Systems and Networks (EWSN) [Poster]*.

Höller, A., Druml, N., Kreiner, C., Steger, C., & Felicijan, T. (2014). Hardware/Software Co-Design of Elliptic-Curve Cryptography for Resource-Constraint Applications. In *Proceedings of the 51st Annual Design Automation Conference.* ACM. doi:10.1145/2593069.2593148

Horne, B., Matheson, L., Sheehan, C., & Tarjan, R. E. (2001). Dynamic Self-Checking Techniques for Improved Tamper Resistance. In *Proceedings of the ACM Workshop on Digital Rights Management,* (pp. 141-159).

Horta, E. L., Lockwood, J. W., Taylor, D. E., & Parlour, D. (2002). Dynamic hardware plugins in an FPGA with partial run-time reconfiguration. In *Proceedings of the Design Automation Conference* (pp. 343-348). IEEE.

Howser, G., & McMillin, B. (2013). A multiple security domain model of a drive-by-wire system. In *Proceedings of the 2013 IEEE 37th Annual Computer Software and Applications Conference (COMPSAC)* (pp. 369-374). Kyoto: IEEE. doi:10.1109/COMPSAC.2013.62

Hoyningen-Huene, M., & Baldinger, M. (2010). Tractor-Implement-Automation and its application to a tractor-loader wagon combination. In *Proceedings of the 2nd International Conference on Machine Control & Guidance.* University of Bonn, Germany.

Huang, Y., Li, H., Campbell, K. A., & Han, Z. (2011). Defending False Data Injection Attack on Smart Grid Network Using Adaptive CUSUM Test. In *Proceedings of the 2011 45th Annual Conference on Information Sciences and Systems (CISS)* (pp. 1-6).

Hui, J., & Thubert, P. (2011). *Compression format for IPv6 datagrams over IEEE 802.15. 4-based networks.* IETF.

Hund, R., Willems, C., & Holz, T. (2013). Practical timing side channel attacks against kernel space aslr. In Proceedings of the 2013 IEEE symposium on Security and privacy (pp. 191–205). doi:10.1109/SP.2013.23

Hurley, C. (2003). *The worldwide wardrive: The myths, the misconceptions, the truth, the future.* Defcon.

Hutter, M., & Toegl, R. (2010). A Trusted Platform Module for Near Field Communication. In *Proceedings of the 2010 Fifth International Conference on Systems and Networks Communications* (pp. 136-141). doi:10.1109/ICSNC.2010.27

Hu, W., Tan, H., Corke, P., Shih, W. C., & Jha, S. (2010). Toward Trusted Wireless Sensor Networks. *ACM Transactions on Sensor Networks,* 7(1).

IBM. (2017). *Rational Doors.* Retrieved from http://www-03.ibm.com/software/products/de/ratidoor

ICS-CERT. (2016). *Cyber-Attack Against Ukrainian Critical Infrastructure.*

IEC 61499. (2015). Retrieved from http://www.iec61499.de/

IEC TR 62380 - Reliability data handbook - Universal model for reliability prediction of electronic components. (2005).

IEC. (1995). *Application and implementation of IEC 61131-3.*

IEEE. (20. 11 2016). *Official timeline of 802.11 development.* Retrieved from http://grouper.ieee.org/groups/802/11/Reports/802.11_Timelines.htm

İnci, M. S., Gulmezoglu, B., Eisenbarth, T., & Sunar, B. (2016). Co-location detection on the cloud. In F.-X. Standaert & E. Oswald (Eds.), *Constructive side-channel analysis and secure design: 7th international workshop* (pp. 19–34). Cham: Springer International Publishing. doi:10.1007/978-3-319-43283-0_2

İnci, M. S., Gulmezoglu, B., Irazoqui, G., Eisenbarth, T., & Sunar, B. (2015). *Seriously, get off my cloud! cross-vm rsa key recovery in a public cloud* (Tech. Rep.). Cryptology ePrint Archive. Report 2015/898. Retrieved from http://eprint.iacr.org

İnci, M. S., Irazoqui, G., Eisenbarth, T., & Sunar, B. (2016, December). Efficient adversarial network discovery using logical channels on Microsoft Azure. In *Proceedings of the Annual computer security applications conference,* Los Angeles, CA, US.

Initiative, S. (2015). *SOQRATES Initiative.* Retrieved 31. March 2016 from http://www.soqrates.de

Intel Corporation. (2017). *Intel Hyper-Threading Technology.* Retrieved from https://www-ssl.intel.com/content/www/us/en/architecture-and-technology/hyper-threading/hyper-threading-technology.html

International Electrotechnical Commission. (2006). *IEC 60812 - Analysis techniques for system reliability - Procedure for failure mode and effects analysis (FMEA).* Retrieved from https://webstore.iec.ch/preview/info_iec60812%7Bed2.0%7Den_d.pdf

International Electrotechnical Commission. (2011). *ISO/IEC 15026-2: Systems and Software Engineering – Systems and Software Assurance – Part 2: Assurance case.*

International Electrotechnical Commission. (2015). *IEC EN 62741 – Guide to the Demonstration of Dependability Requirements –.*

International Organization for Standardization - ISO. (2009). *IEC 61508 Functional safety of electrical/ electronic / programmable electronic safety-related systems.*

Irazoqui, G., Eisenbarth, T., & Sunar, B. (2015a). *Cross processor cache attacks.* Cryptology ePrint Archive Report 2015/1155. Retrieved from http://eprint.iacr.org/

Irazoqui, G., Eisenbarth, T., & Sunar, B. (2015c). Systematic reverse engineering of cache slice selection in intel processors. In Proceedings of the 2015 Euromicro conference on Digital system design (pp. 629–636). doi:10.1109/DSD.2015.56

Irazoqui, G., Eisenbarth, T., & Sunar, B. (2015b). *SSA: A shared cache attack that works across cores and defies VM sandboxing–and its application to AES. In Proceedings of the 2015 IEEE symposium on security and privacy* (pp. 591–604).

Irazoqui, G., İnci, M. S., Eisenbarth, T., & Sunar, B. (2014). Wait a minute! a fast, cross-vm attack on aes. In *Proceedings of the International workshop on recent advances in intrusion detection* (pp. 299–319). doi:10.1007/978-3-319-11379-1_15

Irazoqui, G., İnci, M. S., Eisenbarth, T., & Sunar, B. (2015). Lucky 13 strikes back. In *Proceedings of the 10th acm symposium on information, computer and communications security* (pp. 85–96).

Isakovic, H., & Grosu, R. (2016). A heterogeneous time-triggered architecture on a hybrid system-on-a-chip platform. In *Proceedings of the 25th International Symposium on Industrial Electronics (ISIE),* Santa Clara (pp. 244-253). IEEE. doi:10.1109/ISIE.2016.7744897

Isakovic, H., & Wasicek, A. (2013). Secure channels in an integrated MPSoC architecture. In *Proceedings of the 39th Annual Conference of the IEEE Industrial Electronics Society,* Vienna (pp. 4488-4493). IEEE. doi:10.1109/IECON.2013.6699858

ISO 10202-1. (1991). Financial transaction cards -- Security architecture of financial transaction systems using integrated circuit cards -- Part 1: Card life cycle. International Organization for Standardization.

ISO 18000-3. (2010). Information technology — Radio frequency identification for item management — Part 3: Parameters for air interface communications at 13,56 MHz. International Organization for Standardization.

ISO 26262 Road vehicles Functional Safety Part 1-10. (2011). ISO - International Organization for Standardization.

ISO. (2009). *IEC 61508 Functional safety of electrical/ electronic / programmable electronic safety-related systems.*

ISO. (2011). Functional Safety ISO26262 - Part 4: Product development at the system level. *2011*, 1-35.

ISO. (2011). *ISO 13053 Quantitative methods in process improvement – Six Sigma – Part 1–2.*

ISO. (2011). ISO 26262 Road vehicles Functional Safety Part 1-10. ISO - International Organization for Standardization.

ISO. (2011). *Road vehicles - Functional safety.* Geneva, Switzerland: ISO.

ISO. (2012). *ISO/IEC 17024:2012 Conformity assessment - General requirements for bodies operating certification of persons.* ISO.

ISO/IEC. (2015). *ISO/IEC 33000 series.*

ISO26262. (2011). *Road vehicles-functional safety-Part 5: Product development at the hardware level.*

ITSG. (2015). *Gesetz zur Erhöhung der Sicherheit informationstechnischer Systeme.* IT-Sicherheitsgesetz.

Iturbe, M. (2016). On the Feasibility of Distinguishing Between Process Disturbances and Intrusions in Process Control Systems using Multivariate Statistical Process Control. In Dependable systems and networks workshop. doi:10.1109/DSN-W.2016.32

Jacobs, M. (2013). Improving the precision of approximations in WCET analysis for multi-core processors. In *Proceedings of the 7th junior researcher workshop on real-time computing* (pp. 1–4).

Jaeger, T., Sailer, R., & Shankar, U. (2006). Policy-Reduced Integrity Measurement Architecture. In *Symposium on access control models and technologies.*

Jakub Stolfa, S. S. (2016). Automotive Quality Universities - AQUA Alliance Extension to Higher Education. In *EuroSPI 2016 Proceedings: 23rd European Conference on Systems, Software and Services Process Improvement* (pp. 176-187). Springer.

Jang, J. S., Kong, S., Kim, M., Kim, D., & Kang, B. B. (2015). SeCReT: Secure channel between rich execution environment and trusted execution environment. In NDSS.

Jelasity, M., Babaoglu, O., Laddaga, R., Nagpal, R., Zambonelli, F., & Sirer, E. … Smirnov, M. (2006). Interdisciplinary Research: Roles for Self-Organization. *IEEE Intelligent Systems, 21*(2), 50–58. doi:10.1109/MIS.2006.30

Jeon, C. J., Ji, M., Kim, J., Park, S., & Cho, Y. (2016). Design of positioning DB automatic update method using Google tango tablet for image based localization system. In *Proceedings of the Eighth International Conference on Ubiquitous and Future Networks (ICUFN)*, Vienna (pp. 644-646). doi:10.1109/ICUFN.2016.7537112

Jing, Q., Vasilakos, A. V., Wan, J., Lu, J., & Qiu, D. (2014). Security of the Internet of Things: Perspectives and challenges. *Wireless Networks, 20*(8), 2481–2501. doi:10.1007/s11276-014-0761-7

John, K. H., & Tiegelkamp, M. (2010). *IEC 61131-3: Programming Industrial Automation Systems.* Berlin, Heidelberg: Springer Berlin Heidelberg. doi:10.1007/978-3-642-12015-2

Johnson, T. T., Gannamaraju, R., & Fischmeister, S. (2015). A Survey of Electrical and Electronic (E/E) Notifications for Motor Vehicles. In *Proceedings of the 24th International Technical Conference on the Enhanced Safety of Vehicles (ESV)*, Gothenburg (pp. 1-15).

Johnson, T. T., Gannamaraju, R., & Fischmeister, S. (2015). A SURVEY OF ELECTRICAL AND ELECTRONIC (E/E) NOTIFICATIONS FOR MOTOR VEHICLES. *24th International Technical Conference on the Enhanced Safety of Vehicles (ESV)*, Gothenburg (pp. 1-15).

Jovicic, A. (2016). *Qualcomm Lumicast: A high accuracy indoor positioning system based on visible light communication*. Qualcomm Flarion Technologies.

Kaiser, B., Weber, R., Oertel, M., Böde, E., Nejad, B. M., & Zander, J. (2014). *Contract-Based Design of Embedded Systems Integrating Nominal Behavior and Safety. Complex Systems Informatics and Modeling Quarterly*.

Karlof, C., Sastry, N., & Wagner, D. (2004). TinySec: A Link Layer Security Architecture for Wireless Sensor Networks. In *Proceedings of the 2nd international conference on Embedded networked sensor systems* (pp. 162-175). doi:10.1145/1031495.1031515

Karlof, C., & Wagner, D. (2003). Secure routing in wireless sensor networks: Attacks and countermeasures. *Ad Hoc Networks*, *1*(2-3), 293–315. doi:10.1016/S1570-8705(03)00008-8

Kasinathan, P., Pastrone, C., Spirito, M. A., & Vinkovits, M. (2013). *Denial-of-Service detection in 6LoWPAN based Internet of Things. In WiMob* (pp. 600–607). doi:10.1109/WiMOB.2013.6673419

Kasper, M., Schindler, W., & Stöttinger, M. (2010, December). A stochastic method for security evaluation of cryptographic FPGA implementations. In Proceedings of the 2010 international conference on Field-programmable technology (pp. 146–153). IEEE. doi:10.1109/FPT.2010.5681772

Käsper, E., & Schwabe, P. (2009). Faster and timing-attack resistant aes-gcm. In C. Clavier & K. Gaj (Eds.), *Cryptographic hardware and embedded systems – CHES '09* (Vol. 5747, pp. 1–17). Springer Berlin Heidelberg. doi:10.1007/978-3-642-04138-9_1

Kelly, T., Bate, I., Mc Dermid, J., & Burns, A. (1997). Building a preliminary safety case: an example from aerospace. In *Proceedings of the Australian Workshop of Industrial Experience with Safety Critical Systems*, Sydney, Australia.

Kephart, J. O., & Chess, D. M. (2003). The Vision of Autonomic Computing. *IEEE Computer*, *36*(1), 41–50. doi:10.1109/MC.2003.1160055

Kernighan, B., & Ritchie, D. (1978). *The C Programming Language* (1st ed.). Prentice-Hall.

Khaitan, S. K., & McCalley, J. D. (2015, June). Design techniques and applications of cyberphysical systems: A survey. *IEEE Systems Journal*, *9*(2), 350–365. doi:10.1109/JSYST.2014.2322503

Khan, Z., Lehtomäki, J. J., Iellamo, S., Vuohtoniemi, R., Hossain, E., & Han, Z. (2017). IoT Connectivity in Radar Bands: A Shared Access Model Based on Spectrum Measurements. *IEEE Communications Magazine*, *55*(2), 88–96. doi:10.1109/MCOM.2017.1600444CM

Kim, K.-D., & Kumar, P. (2013, July 18). An Overview and Some Challenges in Cyber-Physical Systems. *Journal of the Indian Institute of Science: A Multidisciplinary Review Journal*, *93*(3), pp. 341-351.

Kim, T. T., & Poor, H. V. (2011). Strategic Protection Against Data Injection Attacks on Power Grids. *IEEE Transactions on Smart Grid*, *2*(2), 326–333. doi:10.1109/TSG.2011.2119336

Kim, Y., Daly, R., Kim, J., Fallin, C., Lee, J. H., Lee, D., & Mutlu, O. (2014). Flipping bits in memory without accessing them: An experimental study of dram disturbance errors. In *Proceeding of the 41st annual international symposium on computer architecture* (pp. 361–372). Piscataway, NJ, USA: IEEE Press. doi:10.1145/2678373.2665726

Kinney, S. L. (2006). *Trusted Platform Module Basics: Using TPM in Embedded Systems*. Newnes.

Kiss, I., Genge, B., & Haller, P. (2015). A Clustering-Based Approach to Detect Cyber Attacks in Process Control Systems. In *Proceedings of the 2015 IEEE 13th International Conference on Industrial Informatics (INDIN)* (pp. 142–148).

Kivity, A., Laor, D., Costa, G., Enberg, P., Har'El, N., Marti, D., & Zolotarov, V. (2014). OSv—optimizing the operating system for virtual machines. In *Proceedings of the USENIX annual technical conference (USENIX ATC)* (pp. 61–72).

Kleberger, P., Olovsson, T., & Jonsson, E. (2011, June). Security aspects of the in-vehicle network in the connected car. In Proceedings of the IEEE intelligent vehicles symposium (IV) (pp. 528–533). doi:10.1109/IVS.2011.5940525

Kocabaş, O., Savaş, E., & Großschädl, J. (2008, Dec). Enhancing an embedded processor core with a cryptographic unit for speed and security. In Proceedings of the international conference on Reconfigurable computing and fpgas RECON-FIG '08. (p. 409-414). doi:10.1109/ReConFig.2008.59

Kocher, P. (1996). Timing Attacks on Implementations of Diffie-Hellman, RSA, DSS, and Other Systems. In N. Koblitz (Ed.), *Proceedings of CRYPTO '96* (Vol. 1109, pp. 104–113). Springer-Verlag. doi:10.1007/3-540-68697-5_9

Kocher, P., Jaffe, J., & Jun, B. (1999). Differential Power Analysis. In M. J. Wiener (Ed.), *Proceedings of CRYPTO '99* (Vol. 1666, pp. 388–397). Springer-Verlag.

Kocher, P., Lee, R., McGraw, G., Raghunathan, A., & Moderator-Ravi, S. (2004). Security as a New Dimension in Embedded System Design. In *Proceedings of the 41st annual Design Automation Conference,*(pp. 753-760).

Kong, J., Acıiçmez, O., Seifert, J.-P., & Zhou, H. (2013, July). Architecting against software cache-based side-channel attacks. *IEEE Transactions on* Computers, *62*(7), 1276–1288.

Kong, J., John, J. K., Chung, E.-Y., Chung, S. W., & Hu, J. (2010). On the thermal attack in instruction caches. *IEEE Transactions on Dependable and Secure Computing, 7*(2), 217–223. doi:10.1109/TDSC.2009.16

Kopetz, H. (2011). *Real-Time Systems: Design Principles for Distributed Embedded Applications*. New York: Springer. doi:10.1007/978-1-4419-8237-7

Kopetz, H., Damm, A., Koza, C., Mulazzani, M., Schwabl, W., Senft, C., & Zainlinger, R. (1989). Distributed fault-tolerant real-time systems: The Mars approach. *IEEE Micro, 9*(1), 25–40. doi:10.1109/40.16792

Kopf, J., Cohen, M. F., & Lischinski, D. (2007). *Joint Bilateral Upsampling*. SIGGRAPH. doi:10.1145/1275808.1276497

Köppe, C. (2013). Towards a Pattern Language for Lecture Design: An inventory and categorization of existing lecture-relevant patterns. In Proceedings of the EuroPLoP 2013. ACM.

Köppe, C., & Rodin, R. (2013). Guided Exploration: an Inductive Minimalist Approach for Teaching Tool-related Concepts and Techniques. In *CSERC 13: Proceedings of the 3rd Computer Science Education Research Conference on Computer Science Education Research.* ACM.

Kornaros, G., Christoforakis, I., Tomoutzoglou, O., Bakoyiannis, D., Vazakopoulou, K., Grammatikakis, M., & Papagrigoriou, A. (2015, August). Hardware support for cost-effective system-level protection in multi-core SoCs. In Proceedings of the Euromicro conference on digital system design (pp. 41–48). doi:10.1109/DSD.2015.65

Kotaba, O., Nowotsch, J., Paulitsch, M., Petters, S. M., & Theiling, H. (2013). Muticore in real-time systems - temporal isolation challenges due to shared resources. In *Proceedings of the workshop on industry-driven approaches for cost-effective certification of safety-critical, mixed-criticality systems (WICERT).*

Kothmayr, T., Schmitt, C., Hu, W., Brünig, M., & Carle, G. (2012). A DTLS Based End-To-End Security Architecture for the Internet of Things with Two-Way Authentication. In *Proceedings of the 2012 IEEE 37th Conference on, Local Computer Networks Workshops (LCN Workshops)* (pp. 956-963).

Kothmayr, T., Schmitt, C., Hu, W., Brünig, M., & Carle, G. (2013). DTLS based security and two-way authentication for the Internet of Things. *Ad Hoc Networks*, *11*(8), 2710–2723. doi:10.1016/j.adhoc.2013.05.003

Krawczyk, H. (2001). The Order of Encryption and Authentication for Protecting Communications (or: How Secure Is SSL?). In *Proceedings of the Annual International Cryptology Conference* (pp. 310-331). doi:10.1007/3-540-44647-8_19

Krebs, B. (2016, October 21). *kresbonsecurity.com*. Retrieved January 4, 2017, from https://krebsonsecurity.com/2016/10/hacked-cameras-dvrs-powered-todays-massive-internet-outage/

Kreiner, C. (2014). Module matrix: a pattern for interdisciplinary industry training design. In *EuroPLoP 14: Proceedings of the 19th European Conference on Pattern Languages of Programs*. ACM. doi:10.1145/2721956.2721983

Kreiner, C. (2015). *Essential architectural views for dependable systems design*. 20th European Conference on Pattern Languages of Programs, EuroPLoP 2015.

Kreiner, C. (2015). Trident architectural views: a pattern for dependable systems design. *EuroPLoP '15 Proceedings of the 20th European Conference on Pattern Languages of Programs*. ACM.

Kreiner, C., Messnarz, R., Riel, A., Ekert, D., Michael Langgner, D. T., & Reiner, M. (2013). Automotive Knowledge Alliance AQUA – Integrating Automotive SPICE, Six Sigma, and Functional Safety. In *EuroSPI 2013: 20th European Conference Systems, Software and Services Process Improvement, Dundalk, Ireland*. Springer. doi:10.1007/978-3-642-39179-8_30

Krotofil, M., Larsen, J., & Gollmann, D. (2015). The Process Matters: Ensuring Data Veracity in Cyber-Physical Systems. In Proceedings of the ACM symposium on information, computer and communications security.

Kuyer, L., Whiteson, S., Bakker, B., & Vlassis, N. (2008). Multiagent Reinforcement Learning for Urban Traffic Control Using Coordination Graphs. In W. Daelemans, B. Goethals, & K. Morik (Eds.), *Machine Learning and Knowledge Discovery in Databases*, LNCS (Vol. 5211, pp. 656–671). Springer Berlin Heidelberg. doi:10.1007/978-3-540-87479-9_61

Kwon, C., Liu, W., & Hwang, I. (2014). Analysis and Design of Stealthy Cyber Attacks on Unmanned Aerial Systems. *Journal of Aerospace Information Systems*, *11*(8), 525–539. doi:10.2514/1.I010201

Kwon, H., Seo, H., Kim, S., & Lee, B. G. (2009). Generalized CSMA/CA for OFDMA Systems: Protocol Design, Throughput Analysis, and Implementation Issues. *IEEE Transactions on Wireless Communications*, *8*(8), 4176–4187. doi:10.1109/TWC.2009.080816

Laddaga, R. (2001). Active Software. In P. Robertson, H. Shrobe, & R. Laddaga (Eds.), *Self-adaptive software: First international workshop, IWSAS 2000* (pp. 11–26). Berlin, Heidelberg: Springer Berlin Heidelberg. doi:10.1007/3-540-44584-6_2

Langner, R. (2011). Stuxnet: Dissecting a Cyberwarfare Weapon. *IEEE Security & Privacy Magazine*, *9*(3), 49–51. doi:10.1109/MSP.2011.67

Langner, R. (2011). Stuxnet: Dissecting a Cyberwarfare Weapon. *IEEE Security \& Privacy*, *9*, 49-51.

Langner, R. (2011). *Stuxnet: Dissecting a Cyberwarfare Weapon. Security Privacy*. IEEE.

Lattner, A. D., Bogon, T., Lorion, Y., & Timm, I. J. (2010, April 12 - 15). A knowledge-based approach to automated simulation model adaptation. In S. Biaz (Ed.), *Proceedings of the 43rd Annual Simulation Symposium (ANSS'10), Spring Simulation Multi-Conference (SpringSim'10)*, Orlando, Florida, USA (pp. 200-207). doi:10.1145/1878537.1878697

Lauradoux, C. (2005). Collision attacks on processors with cache and countermeasures. In Weworc'05 (p. 76-85).

Le Malécot, E., & Inoue, D. (2014). The Carna Botnet Through the Lens of a Network Telescope. In *Foundations and Practice of Security* (pp. 426–441). Springer. doi:10.1007/978-3-319-05302-8_26

Lee, D. (2012, May). Flame: Massive cyber-attack discovered, researchers say. *BBC News*.

Lee, E. (2006). Cyber-physical systems - Are computing foundations adequate? *Paper presented at the NSF Workshop On Cyber-Physical Systems: Research Motivation, Techniques and Roadmap*, Austin, TX.

Lee, E. A. (2008). Cyber Physical Systems: Design Challenges. In *Proceedings of the 2008 11th IEEE International Symposium on Object and Component-Oriented Real-Time Distributed Computing (ISORC)* (pp. 363-369).

Lee, J.-S., Jeong, H., Park, J.-H., Kim, M., & Noh, B.-N. (2008). The Activity Analysis of Malicious HTTP-Based Botnets Using Degree of Periodic Repeatability. In *Proceedings of the International Conference on Security Technology SECTECH'08* (pp. 83-86).

Lee, R., & Chen, Y.-Y. (2010, June). Processor accelerator for AES. In *Proceedings of the 2010 IEEE 8th symposium on Application specific processors* (pp. 16-21). doi:10.1109/SASP.2010.5521153

Lee, S., Shih, M., Gera, P., Kim, T., Kim, H., & Peinado, M. (2016). Inferring fine-grained control flow inside SGX enclaves with branch shadowing. CoRR, abs/1611.06952

Lee, E. (2008). *Cyber physical systems: Design challenges. University of California at Berkeley, Electrical Engineering and Computer Sciences*. Berkeley: University of California at Berkeley.

Lee, R. M., Assante, M. J., & Conway, T. (2014). *German Steel Mill Cyber Attack* (pp. 1–15).

Lee, S., & Jung, S. (2012). Location awareness using Angle-of-arrival based circular-PD-array for visible light. In *Proceedings of the 18th Asia-Pacific Conference on Communications (APCC)*, Jeju Island (pp. 480–485).

Lennvall, T., Svensson, S., & Hekland, F. (2008). A Comparison of WirelessHART and ZigBee for Industrial Applications. In *Proceedings of the IEEE International Workshop on Factory Communication Systems* (pp. 85-88). doi:10.1109/WFCS.2008.4638746

Lepaja, S., & Bengi, K. (2001). A Random-Reservation Medium Access Protocol For Satellite Networks To Accommodate Real-Time Traffic. In *Proceedings of the IEEE Vehicular Technology Conference-Spring* (pp. 861–865). doi:10.1109/VETECS.2001.944501

Lepetit, V., Arth, C., Pirchheim, C., Ventura, J., & Schmalstieg, D. (2015). Instant Outdoor Localization and SLAM Initialization. In *Proceedings of the International Symposium on Mixed and Augmented Reality*.

Lesjak, C., Hein, D., Hofmann, M., Maritsch, M., Aldrian, A., Priller, P., . . . Pregartner, G. (2015). Securing Smart Maintenance Services: Hardware-Security and TLS for MQTT. In *Proceedings of the 2015 IEEE 13th International Conference on Industrial Informatics (INDIN)* (pp. 1243-1250).

Le, T.-H., Canovas, C., & Clédiere, J. (2008). An Overview of Side Channel Analysis Attacks. In *Proceedings of the 2008 ACM symposium on Information, computer and communications security* (pp. 33-43). doi:10.1145/1368310.1368319

Levinson, J. M. (2008). Map-Based Precision Vehicle Localization in Urban Environments. *Robotics: Science and Systems, III*, 121–128.

Lian, F.-L., Moyne, J., & Tilbury, D. (2001, February). Performance evaluation of control networks: Ethernet, ControlNet, and DeviceNet. *IEEE Control Systems, 21*(1), 66–83. doi:10.1109/37.898793

Liberzon, D. (2005). Switched systems. In *D. Hristu-Varsakelis, & W. S. Levine (Eds.), Handbook of networked and embedded control systems* (pp. 559–574). Boston: Birkhäuser. doi:10.1007/0-8176-4404-0_24

Lie, D., Thekkath, C., Mitchell, M., Lincoln, P., Boneh, D., Mitchell, J., & Horowitz, M. (2000). Architectural Support for Copy and Tamper Resistant Software. *ACM SIGPLAN Notices*, *35*(11), 168–177. doi:10.1145/356989.357005

Lilienthal, D. (2011). Top 4 Fun Boeing 787 Technical Facts. *NYC Aviation*. Retrieved from http://www.nycaviation.com/2011/09/fun-facts-revealed-at-boeings-787-technical-panel

Lipp, M., Gruss, D., Spreitzer, R., Maurice, C., & Mangard, S. (2016, August). Ar- mageddon: Cache attacks on mobile devices. In *Proceedings of the 25th USENIX security symposium (USENIX security 16)*. Austin, TX: USENIX Association.

Liserre, M., Sauter, T., & Hung, J. Y. (2010b). Future Energy Systems: Inegrating Renewable Energy into the Smart Power Grid Through Industrial Electronics. *IEEE Industrial Electronics Magazine*, (March), 18–37.

Liserre, M., Sauter, T., & Hung, J. (2010a). Future Energy Systems: Integrating Renewable Energy Sources into the Smart Power Grid Through Industrial Electronics. *IEEE Industrial Electronics Magazine*, *4*(1), 18–37. doi:10.1109/MIE.2010.935861

Liu, F., Yarom, Y., Ge, Q., Heiser, G., & Lee, R. B. (2015). Last-level cache side-channel attacks are practical. In IEEE symposium on security and privacy (pp. 605–622). doi:10.1109/SP.2015.43

Liu, K., Fridman, E., & Hetel, L. (2014). Networked control systems: A time-delay approach. In *Proceedings of the 2014 European Control Conference* (pp. 1434-1439). Strasbourg, France: IEEE.

Liu, M., Qiu, K., Che, F., Li, S., Hussain, B., Wu, L., & Yue, C. (2014). Towards indoor localization using visible light. In *Proceedings of the International Conference on Intelligent Robots and Systems (IROS)*, Chicago (pp. 143–148).

Liu, Y., Ning, P., & Reiter, M. K. (2009). False Data Injection Attacks Against State Estimation in Electric Power Grids. In *Proceedings of the Conference on Computer and Communications Security*, *14*(1), 1–33. doi:10.1145/1653662.1653666

Liu, K., Fridman, E., & Hetel, L. (2015). Networked control systems in the presence of scheduling protocols and communication delays. *SIAM Journal on Control and Optimization*, *53*(4), 1768–1788. doi:10.1137/140980570

Lloret, J., Canovas, A., Sendra, S., & Parra, L. (2015). A Smart Communication Architecture for Ambient Assisted Living. *IEEE Communications Magazine*, *53*(1), 26–33. doi:10.1109/MCOM.2015.7010512

Lo, C.-H., & Ansari, N. (2013). CONSUMER: A Novel Hybrid Intrusion Detection System for Distribution Networks in Smart Grid. *IEEE Transactions on Emerging Topics in Computing*, *1*(1), 33–44. doi:10.1109/TETC.2013.2274043

Lofberg, J. (2004). YALMIP: A Toolbox for modelling and optimization in MATLAB. In *Proceedings of the 2004 IEEE International Conference on Robotics and Automation (IEEE Cat. No.04CH37508)* (pp. 284-289). Taipei: IEEE. doi:10.1109/CACSD.2004.1393890

Longo, J., Mulder, E. D., Page, D., & Tunstall, M. (2015). *Soc it to em: electromagnetic side-channel attacks on a complex system-on-chip*. Cryptology ePrint Archive Report 2015/561. Retrieved from http://eprint.iacr.org

Lun, Y., D'Innocenzo, A., Malavolta, I., & Di Benedetto, M. (2016). Cyber-Physical Systems Security: a Systematic Mapping Study.

Lunttila, T., Lindholm, J., Pajukoski, K., Tiirola, E., & Toskala, A. (2007). EUTRAN Uplink Performance. In *Proceedings of the International Symposium on Wireless Pervasive Computing (ISWPC)*.

Lunze, J., & Grüne, L. (2014). Introduction to networked control systems. In J. Lunze (Ed.), *Control theory of digitally networked dynamic systems* (pp. 1–30). Switzerland: Springer International Publishing. doi:10.1007/978-3-319-01131-8_1

Lunze, J., & Lamnabhi-Lagarrigue, F. (2009). *Handbook of hybrid systems control: Theory, tools, applications*. New York: Cambridge University Press. doi:10.1017/CBO9780511807930

Macdonell, C., Ke, X., Gordon, A. W., & Lu, P. (2011). Low-latency, high-bandwidth use cases for nahanni/ivshmem. In Proceedings of the Kvm forum (Vol. 2011).

Macher, G., Armengaud, E., Brenner, E., & Kreiner, C. (2016). A Review of Threat Analysis and Risk Assessment Methods in the Automotive Context. In *Proceedings of the International Conference on Computer Safety, Reliability, and Security (SafeComp 2016)*. doi:10.1007/978-3-319-45477-1_11

Macher, G., Hoeller, A., Sporer, H., Armengaud, E., & Kreiner, C. (2015). A Comprehensive Safety, Security, and Serviceability Assessment Method. In *Proceedings of the 34th International Conference on Computer Safety, Reliability, and Security - SAFECOMP '15*, Delft, The Netherlands. doi:10.1007/978-3-319-24255-2_30

Macher, G., Hoeller, A., Sporer, H., Armengaud, E., & Kreiner, C. (2015). Service Deterioration Analysis (SDA): An Early Development Phase Reliability Analysis Method. In *Review at 45th Annual International Conference on Dependable Systems and Networks (DSN) - RADIANCE Workshop*.

Macher, G., Hoeller, A., Sporer, H., Armengaud, E., & Kreiner, C. (2015). Service Deterioration Analysis (SDA): An Early Development Phase Reliability Analysis Method. In *Review at 45th Annual International Conference on Dependable Systems and Networks (DSN) - RADIANCE Workshop*.

Macher, G., Sporer, H., Berlach, R., Armengaud, E., & Kreiner, C. (2015). SAHARA: A security-aware hazard and risk analysis method. In Design, Automation Test in Europe Conference Exhibition (DATE 2015) (pp. 621-624).

Macher, G., Sporer, H., Berlach, R., Armengaud, E., & Kreiner, C. (2015). SAHARA: A security-aware hazard and risk analysis method. In Design, Automation Test in Europe Conference Exhibition (DATE 2015), (pp. 621-624).

Macher, G., Sporer, H., Brenner, E., & Kreiner, C. (2016). Supporting Cyber-security based on Hardware-Software Interface Definition. In *Proceedings of the 23nd European Conference on Systems, Software and Services Process Improvement - EuroSPI '16*, Graz, Austria. doi:10.1007/978-3-319-44817-6_12

Macher, G., Stolz, M., Armengaud, E., & Kreiner, C. (2015). Filling the gap between automotive systems, safety, and software engineering. *Elektrotechnik und Informationstechnik, 132*, 142-148. doi:10.1007/s00502-015-0301-x

Macher, G., Hoeller, A., Sporer, H., Armengaud, E., & Kreiner, C. (2015). A combined safety-hazards and security-threat analysis method for automotive systems. In F. Koorneef & C. van Gulijk (Eds.), *SAFECOMP 2015 Workshops ASSURE, DECSoS, ISSE, ReSA4CI, and SASSUR, LNCS 9338* (pp. 237–250).

MacKenzie, C. M., Laskey, K., McCabe, F., Brown, P. F., Metz, R., & Hamilton, B. A. (2006). *OASIS standard*. Retrieved from https://www.oasis-open.org/standards/#soa-rmv1.0

Madnick, S. E., & Donovan, J. J. (1973). Application and Analysis of the Virtual Machine Approach to Information System Security and Isolation. In *Proceedings of the workshop on virtual computer systems* (pp. 210-224). doi:10.1145/800122.803961

MAENAD. (2014). *maenad.eu*. Retrieved 2017 from http://www.maenad.eu/

Magillem. (2017). Retrieved from http://www.magillem.com

Mahnke, W., Leitner, S.-H., & Damm, M. (2009). *OPC Unified Architecture*. Springer Science & Business Media. doi:10.1007/978-3-540-68899-0

Mainetti, L., Patrono, L., & Vilei, A. (2011). Evolution of wireless sensor networks towards the internet of things: A survey. In *Proc. of the International Conference on Software, Telecommunications and Computer Networks (SoftCOM)*, Split, Croatia.

Mangard, S., Oswald, E., & Popp, T. (2008). Power Analysis Attacks: Revealing the Secrets of Smart Cards. In Advances in information security. Springer.

Mangard, S., Oswald, E., & Popp, T. (2008). *Power Analysis Attacks: Revealing the Secrets of Smart Cards* (Vol. 31). Springer Science & Business Media.

Mannion, P., Duggan, J., & Howley, E. (2016). An Experimental Review of Reinforcement Learning Algorithms for Adaptive Traffic Signal Control. In T.L. McCluskey, A. Kotsialos, J.P. Müller et al. (Eds.), Autonomic Road Transport Support Systems (Autonomic Systems) (pp. 47-66). Birkhäuser Basel. doi:10.1007/978-3-319-25808-9_4

Manyika, J., Chui, M., Bisson, P., Woetzel, J., Dobbs, R., Bughin, J., & Aharon, D. (2015, June). *Unlocking the potential of the Internet of Things*. Retrieved from http://www.mckinsey.com/business-functions/digital-mckinsey/our-insights/the-internet-of-things-the-value-of-digitizing-the-physical-world

Mao, S., & Wolf, T. (2010, June). Hardware support for secure processing in embedded systems. *IEEE Transactions on Computers*, *59*(6), 847–854. doi:10.1109/TC.2010.32

Marinescu, R., Kaijser, H., Mikucionis, M., David, A., Seceleanu, C., & Henrik, L. (2014). Analyzing Idustrial Architectural Models by Simulation and Model-Checking. *Formal Techniques for Safety-Critical Systems*, *419*, 189–205. doi:10.1007/978-3-319-05416-2

Marinos, L., Belmonte, A., & Rekleitis, E. (2015). *Enisa Threat Landscape (Technical report)*. ENISA.

Markantonakis, K., Mayes, K., Sauveron, D., & Tunstall, M. (2010). Smart Cards. In H. Bidgoli (Ed.), Handbook of Technology Management (Vols. 2, pp. 248-264). Wiley.

Markit, I. H. S. (2014, August). *Smart Card Shipments to Rise by 2.1 Billion Units by 2019*. (IHS Markit Newsroom) Retrieved October 2016, from http://press.ihs.com/press-release/design-supply-chain-media/smart-card-shipments-rise-21-billion-units-2019

Martin, H., Krammer, M., Bramberger, R., & Armengaud, E. (2016). *Process-and Product-based Lines of Argument for Automotive Safety Cases*.

Masti, R. J., Rai, D., Ranganathan, A., Müller, C., Thiele, L., & Capkun, S. (2015). Thermal covert channels on multi-core platforms. In Proceedings of the 24th USENIX Security Symposium (USENIX Security 15) (pp. 865–880).

MathWorks. (2017). *Matlab Simulink*. Retrieved from https://de.mathworks.com/products/matlab.html

Mattern, F., & Floerkemeier, C. (2010). From the Internet of Computers to the Internet of Things. In *From active data management to event-based systems and more* (pp. 242–259). Springer. doi:10.1007/978-3-642-17226-7_15

Maurer, M., Gerdes, J. C., Lenz, B., & Winner, H. (2015). *Autonomes Fahren: Technische, rechtliche und gesellschaftliche Aspekte*. Springer Berlin Heidelberg. doi:10.1007/978-3-662-45854-9

Maurice, C., Le Scouarnec, N., Neumann, C., Heen, O., & Francillon, A. (2015). Reverse engineering intel last-level cache complex addressing using performance counters. In *Proceedings of the International workshop on recent advances in intrusion detection* (pp. 48–65). doi:10.1007/978-3-319-26362-5_3

Maurice, C., Neumann, C., Heen, O., & Francillon, A. (2015, July 9-10). C5: Cross-cores cache covert channel. In *Proceedings of DIMVA 2015, Detection of Intrusions and Malware, and Vulnerability Assessment*, Milano, Italy.

Mauro Biagi, S. P. (2015). LAST: A Framework to Localize, Access, Schedule, and Transmit in Indoor VLC Systems. *Journal of Lightwave Technology, 33*(9), 1872–1887. doi:10.1109/JLT.2015.2405674

McCluskey, T. L., Kotsialos, A., Müller, J. P., Klügl, F., Rana, O., & Schumann, R. (2016). *Autonomic Road Transport Support Systems. (Autonomic Systems)*. Birkhäuser Basel. doi:10.1007/978-3-319-25808-9

McFarland, M. C., Parker, A. C., & Camposano, R. (1990). The high-level synthesis of digital systems. In *Proceedings of the IEEE* (pp. 301-318). IEEE.

Mclvor, C., McLoone, M., & McCanny, J. V. (2003). Fast Montgomery Modular Multiplication and RSA Cryptographic Processor Architectures. In *Conference Record of the Thirty-Seventh Asilomar Conference on* Signals, Systems and Computers (Vol. 1, pp. 379-384).

Mellado, D., Fernandez-Medina, E., & Piattini, M. (2007). A common criteria based security requirements engineering process. *Computer Standards & Interfaces, 29*(2), 244–253. doi:10.1016/j.csi.2006.04.002

Mentor. (2017). Retrieved from https://www.mentor.com

Merriam-Webster. (2016). *Merriam-Webster Dictionary*. Von Merriam-Webster: https://www.merriam-webster.com/abgerufen

Messnarz, R. (2006). From process improvement to learning organisations. *SPIP Journal, 11*(3).

Messnarz, R., & Ekert, D. (2007). Assessment-based learning systems - learning from best projects. SPIP (Software Process: Improvement and Practice), 12(6).

Messnarz, R., Ekert, D., Reiner, M., & O'Suilleabhain, G. (2006). Human resources based improvement strategies - the learning factor. (Wiley, Ed.) SPIP (Software Process Improvement in Practice), 13(3).

Messnarz, R., Kreiner, C., & Riel, A. (2016, Sept.). Integrating Automotive SPICE, Functional Safety, and Cybersecurity Concepts: A Cybersecurity Layer Model. *Software Quality Professional, 18*(4).

Messnarz, R., Kreiner, C., Bachmann, O., Riel, A., Dussa-Zieger, K., Nevalainen, R., & Tichkiewitch, S. (2013, June 25-27). Implementing Functional Safety Standards - Experiences from the Trials about Required Knowledge and Competencies (SafEUr). In *EuroSPI 2013: 20th European Conference Systems, Software and Services Process Improvement*, Dundalk, Ireland (pp. 323-332). Springer. doi:10.1007/978-3-642-39179-8_29

Messnarz, R., Reiner, M., & Ekert, D. (2012). Europe wide industry certification using standard procedures based on ISO 17024. In *Technologies Applied to Electronics Teaching (TAEE)*. IEEE Computer Society. doi:10.1109/TAEE.2012.6235462

Michael Reiner, G. S. (2014). European Certification and Qualification. In EuroSPI 2014, Industrial Proceedings. Delta.

Microsoft Corporation. (2005). The stride threat model. Retrieved from http://msdn.microsoft.com/en-us/library/ee823878/%28v=cs.20/%29.aspx

Microsoft. (2016). *Microsoft Threat Modeling Tool*. Retrieved from https://www.microsoft.com/en-us/download/details.aspx?id=49168

Miller, C., & Valasek, C. (2013). Adventures in Automotive Networks and Control Units. In *Proceedings of the DEF CON 21 Hacking Conference*, Las Vegas, NV.

Miller, C., & Valasek, C. (2013). Adventures in Automotive Networks and Control Units. In *Proceedings of the DEF CON 21 Hacking Conference*, Las Vegas.

Miller, C., & Valasek, C. (2015). *Remote Exploitation of an Unaltered Passenger Vehicle*. Retrieved from http://illmatics.com/Remote%20Car%20Hacking.pdf

Miller, B., & Rowe, D. (2012). A survey SCADA of and critical infrastructure incidents. In *Proceedings of the 1st annual conference on research in information technology - riit '12* (p. 51). New York, New York, USA: ACM Press. doi:10.1145/2380790.2380805

Mishra, S., Shoukry, Y., Karamchandani, N., Diggavi, S., & Tabuada, P. (2015). Secure State Estimation: Optimal Guarantees Against Sensor Attacks in the Presence of Noise. In *Proceedings of the 2015 IEEE International Symposium on Information Theory (ISIT)* (pp. 2929-2933).

Mitchell, R., & Chen, I.-r. (2014). A Survey of Intrusion Detection Techniques for Cyber-Physical Systems. *ACM Computing Surveys (CSUR), 46*(4).

Mitchell, R., & Chen, I.-R. (2014). A Survey of Intrusion Detection Techniques for Cyber-Physical Systems. [CSUR]. *ACM Computing Surveys, 46*(4), 55. doi:10.1145/2542049

Modadugu, N., & Rescorla, E. (2004). *The Design and Implementation of Datagram TLS*. NDSS.

Moholkar, A. V. (2014, July). Security for cyber-physical systems. *International Journal of Computing and Technology, 1*(6).

Mollison, M. S., Erickson, J. P., Anderson, J. H., Baruah, S. K., & Scoredos, J. A. (2010, June). Mixed-criticality real-time scheduling for multicore systems. In *Proceedings of the 10th IEEE international conference on computer and information technology* (pp. 1864–1871). doi:10.1109/CIT.2010.320

Montagna, S., Viroli, M., Fernandez-Marquez, J. L., Serugendo, G. M., & Zambonelli, F. (2013). Injecting Self-Organisation into Pervasive Service Ecosystems. *Mobile Networks and Applications, 18*(3), 398–412. doi:10.1007/s11036-012-0411-1

Morin, B., Barais, O., Jezequel, J.-M., Fleury, F., & Arnor, S. (2009). *Models at Runtime to Support Dynamic Adaptation*. Los Alamitos: IEEE.

Mo, Y., Weerakkody, S., & Sinopoli, B. (2015). Physical Authentication of Control Systems: Designing Watermarked Control Inputs to Detect Counterfeit Sensor Outputs. *IEEE Control Systems, 35*(1), 93–109. doi:10.1109/MCS.2014.2364724

Muccini, H., Sharaf, M., & Weyns, D. (2016). Self-adaptation for Cyber-physical Systems: A Systematic Literature Review. In *Proceedings of the 11th international workshop on software engineering for adaptive and self-managing systems - seams '16* (pp. 75–81). New York, New York, USA: ACM Press. doi:10.1145/2897053.2897069

Müller, J. P., & Fischer, K. (2014). Application Impact of Multi-agent Systems and Technologies: A Survey. In *Agent-oriented software engineering* (pp. 27–53). Berlin, Heidelberg: Springer Berlin Heidelberg. doi:10.1007/978-3-642-54432-3_3

Müller-Schloer, C. (2004, September 8-10). Organic Computing: On the feasibility of controlled emergence. In *Proceedings of Second IEEE/ACM/IFIP International Conference on Hardware/Software Codesign and System Synthesis*, Stockholm, Sweden (pp 2-5). ACM Press. doi:10.1145/1016720.1016724

Murillo, L., Mura, M., & Prevostini, M. (2009). Semi-automated Hw/Sw Co-design for embedded systems: from MARTE models to SystemC simulators. In *Proceedings of the Forum on Specification & Design Languages (FDL)*.

Murillo, L. G., Mura, M., & Prevostini, M. (2010). *MDE Support for HW/SW Codesign: A UML-based Design Flow*. In *Advances in Design Methods from Modeling Languages for Embedded Systems and SoC's* (pp. 19–37).

Mushtaq, H., Al-Ars, Z., & Bertels, K. (2013, December). Accurate and efficient identification of worst-case execution time for multicore processors: A survey. In *Proceedings of the 8th IEEE design and test symposium* (pp. 1–6). doi:10.1109/IDT.2013.6727080

NASA. (2016). *Computers in Spaceflight: The NASA Experience*. Retrieved from http://history.nasa.gov/computers/contents.html

Nesic, D., & Teel, A. (2004a, October). Input-output stability properties of networked control systems. *IEEE Transactions on Automatic Control, 49*(10), 1650–1667. doi:10.1109/TAC.2004.835360

Nesic, D., & Teel, A. (2004b, September 11). Input-to-state stability of networked control systems. *Automatica, (40)*: 2121–2128.

Nest Labs. (2016). *Nest*. Retrieved 11 7, 2016, from https://nest.com

Neve, M., & Seifert, J.-P. (2007). Advances on access-driven cache attacks on aes. In E. Biham & A. Youssef (Eds.), *Selected areas in cryptography* (Vol. 4356, pp. 147–162). Springer Berlin Heidelberg. doi:10.1007/978-3-540-74462-7_11

Newcombe, R. A., Izadi, S., Hilliges, O., Molyneaux, D., Kim, D., Davison, A. J., & Fitzgibbon, A. et al. (2011). KinectFusion: Real-time 3D Reconstruction and Interaction Using a Moving Depth Camera. In *Proceedings of the 24th Annual ACM Symposium on User Interface Software and Technology*.

Nicholson, A., Webber, S., Dyer, S., Patel, T., & Janicke, H. (2012). SCADA security in the light of Cyber-Warfare. *Computers & Security, 31*, 418-436.

Nilsson, J. (1998). *Real-time control systems with delays* [Doctoral dissertation]. Lund university. Retrieved from http://lup.lub.lu.se/record/18692

Niruntasukrat, A., Issariyapat, C., Pongpaibool, P., Meesublak, K., Aiumsupucgul, P., & Panya, A. (2016). Authorization Mechanism for MQTT-based Internet of Things. In *Proceedings of the 2016 IEEE International Conference on Communications Workshops (ICC)* (pp. 290-295).

Nisan, N., Roughgarden, T., Tardos, É., & Vazirani, V. V. (2007). *Algorithmic Game Theory*. New York, NY, USA: Cambridge University Press. doi:10.1017/CBO9780511800481

NIST FIPS PUB 140-2. (2001). *Security Requirements for Cryptographic Modules*. National Institute of Standards and Technology Federal Information Processing Standards Publications 140-2.

NIST SP 800-57-1. (2016). *Recommendation for Key Management - Part 1: General*. National Institute of Standards and Technology Special Publication 800-57-1.

NIST. (1995). *An Introduction to Computer Security: The NIST Handbook*.

NIST. (2013). *Foundations for Innovation in Cyber-Physical Systems.*

Nof, S. Y. (1999). *Handbook of Industrial Robotics* (Vol. 1). John Wiley & Sons. doi:10.1002/9780470172506

Nowotsch, J., Paulitsch, M., Bühler, D., Theiling, H., Wegener, S., & Schmidt, M. (2014, July). Multi-core interference-sensitive WCET analysis leveraging runtime resource capacity enforcement. In *Proceedings of the 26th euromicro conference on real-time systems* (pp. 109–118). doi:10.1109/ECRTS.2014.20

Object Management Group (OMG). (2015). Retrieved from http://www.omg.org/

Object Management Group. (2015). *Structured Assurance Case Metamodel version 1.1.* Retrieved from http://www.omg.org/spec/SACM/1.1/

Object Management Group. (2016). Structured Assurance Case Metamodel (SACM), V2.0-Beta 1.

Office for Nuclear Regulation. (2013). *The purpose, scope, and content of safety cases, NS-TAST-GD-051 Revision 3.* Retrieved from http://www.onr.org.uk/operational/tech_asst_guides/ns-tast-gd-051.pdf

OICA. (2015). *Production Statistics for Motor Vehicels.* Retrieved from http://www.oica.net/category/production-statistics/2014-statistics/

Omg. (2015). OMG Systems Modeling Language (OMG SysML ™) v.1.4. *Source, 260.* Von http://www.omg.org/spec/SysML/1.2/PDF/

Oorschot, V., Somayaji, A., & Wurster, G. (2005). Hardware-Assisted Circumvention of Self-Hashing Software Tamper Resistance. *IEEE Transactions on Dependable and Secure Computing, 2*(2), 82–92. doi:10.1109/TDSC.2005.24

Open Virtual Platform. (2016). Retrieved from http://www.ovpworld.org

Oppliger, R. (1998). Security at the Internet Layer. *Computer, 31*(9), 43–47. doi:10.1109/2.708449

O'Regan, G. (2012). *A Brief History of Computing.* London: Springer Science & Business Media. doi:10.1007/978-1-4471-2359-0

Oreizy, P., Gorlick, M., Taylor, R., Heimhigner, D., Johnson, G., & Medvidovic, N. ... Wolf, A. (1999). An architecture-based approach to self-adaptive software. *IEEE Intelligent Systems, 14*(3), 54–62. doi:10.1109/5254.769885

Oren, Y., Kemerlis, V. P., Sethumadhavan, S., & Keromytis, A. D. (2015). The spy in the sandbox: Practical cache attacks in javascript and their implications. In *Proceedings of the 22nd ACM SIGSAC Conference on Computer and Communications Security* (pp. 1406–1418). doi:10.1145/2810103.2813708

Origin Consulting. (2011). GSN Community Standard Version 1.

Orland, K. (2016). Oculus working on wireless headset with "inside-out tracking". *ars Technica.* Retrieved from http://arstechnica.com/gaming/2016/10/oculus-working-on-wireless-headset-with-inside-out-tracking/

Osvik, D. A., Shamir, A., & Tromer, E. (2006). Cache attacks and countermeasures: the case of AES (extended version). In *Topics in cryptology - CT-RSA 2006, the cryptographers' track at the RSA conference 2006* (pp. 1–20). Springer-Verlag.

Ouyang, Y., Le, Z., Liu, D., Ford, J., & Makedon, F. (2008). Source Location Privacy against Laptop-Class Attacks in Sensor Networks. In *Proceedings of the 4th international conference on Security and privacy in communication networks* (p. 5). doi:10.1145/1460877.1460884

Ovren, H., Forssen, P.-E., & Törnqvist, D. (2013). Why Would I Want a Gyroscope on my RGB-D Sensor? In *Proceedings of the IEEE Workshop on Robot Vision (WORV)*. doi:10.1109/WORV.2013.6521916

Pa, Y. M., Suzuki, S., Yoshioka, K., Matsumoto, T., Kasama, T., & Rossow, C. (2015). IoTPOT: Analysing the Rise of IoT Compromises. In *Proceedings of the 9th USENIX Workshop on Offensive Technologies (WOOT 15)*.

Panel, S. G. I. (2010). *Guidelines for smart grid cyber security (tech. report No. 7628). Cyber Security Working Group.* NIST.

Paolino, M., Fanguede, J., Nikolaev, N., & Raho, D. (2016). Turning an open source project into a carrier grade vSwitch, for NFV: VOSYSwitch challenges & results. In *Proceedings of the 5th IEEE international conference on network infrastructure and digital content (NIDC)*.

Pardo-Castellote, G. (2003). OMG Data-Distribution Service: Architectural Overview. *Proceedings of the 23rd International Conference on Distributed Computing Systems Workshops* (pp. 200-206).

Pasqualetti, F., Dörfler, F., & Bullo, F. (2013). Attack Detection and Identification in Cyber-Physical Systems. *IEEE Transactions on Automatic Control*, *58*(11), 2715–2729. doi:10.1109/TAC.2013.2266831

Paxson, V. (1999). Bro: A System for Detecting Network Intruders in Real-Time. *Computer Networks*, *31*(23-24), 2435–2463. doi:10.1016/S1389-1286(99)00112-7

PCI Security Standards Council. (2016). *Data Security Standard - Requirements and Security Assessment Procedures.* Payment Card Industry Security Standards Council.

Pellizzoni, R., Meredith, P., Nam, M.-Y., Sun, M., Caccamo, M., & Sha, L. (2009). Handling mixed-criticality in SoC-based real-time embedded systems. In *Proceedings of the 7th ACM international conference on embedded software* (pp. 235–244). New York, NY: ACM. doi:10.1145/1629335.1629367

Percival, C. (2005). Cache missing for fun and profit. In Proc. of BSDCAN '05.

Pessl, P., Gruss, D., Maurice, C., Schwarz, M., & Mangard, S. (2016, August). Drama: Exploiting dram addressing for cross-cpu attacks. In Proceedings of the 25th USENIX Security Symposium (USENIX Security 16). Austin, TX: USENIX Association.

Plank, H., Holweg, G., Herndl, T., & Druml, N. (2016). *High performance Time-of-Flight and color sensor fusion with image-guided depth super resolution. In Design, Automation & Test in Europe Conference & Exhibition* (pp. 1213–1218). Dresden: DATE.

Plósz, S., Farshad, A., Tauber, M., Lesjak, C., Ruprechter, T., & Pereira, N. (2014). Security Vulnerabilities and Risks in Industrial Usage of Wireless Communication. In *Proceedings of the 2014 IEEE Emerging Technology and Factory Automation (ETFA)*, (pp. 1-8). doi:10.1109/ETFA.2014.7005129

Poddar, R., Datta, A., & Rebeiro, C. (2011). A cache trace attack on camellia. In M. Joye, D. Mukhopadhyay, & M. Tunstall (Eds.), *Security aspects in information technology* (pp. 144–156). Berlin, Heidelberg: Springer Berlin Heidelberg. doi:10.1007/978-3-642-24586-2_13

Potkonjak, M., Meguerdichian, S., & Wong, J. L. (2010, November). *Trusted sensors and remote sensing. In IEEE Sensors* (pp. 1104–1107).

Prehofer, C., Horst, O., Dodi, R., Geven, A., Kornaros, G., Montanari, E., & Paolino, M. (2016). Towards trusted apps platforms for open CPS. In *Proceedings of the 3rd international workshop on emerging ideas and trends in engineering of cyber-physical systems (EITEC)* (pp. 23–28). doi:10.1109/EITEC.2016.7503692

Prehofer, C., Kornaros, G., & Paolino, M. (2015). TAPPS - trusted apps for open cyber-physical systems. In S.K. Katsikas & A.B. Sideridis (Eds.), E-*democracy – citizen rights in the world of the new computing paradigms* (pp. 213–216). Cham: Springer International Publishing.

Proudler, G. (2005). Concepts of Trusted Computing. In C. Mitchell (Ed.), *Trusted computing. Proudler2005.* doi:10.1049/PBPC006E_ch2

Quisquater, J. J., & Samyde, D. (2001). Electromagnetic analysis (ema): Measures and counter-measures for smart cards. In *Proceedings of the International Conference on Research in Smart Cards: Smart Card Programming and Security E-SMART '01* (pp. 200–210). London, UK: Springer-Verlag. doi:10.1007/3-540-45418-7_17

Raciti, M., & Nadjm-Tehrani, S. (2012). Embedded Cyber-Physical Anomaly Detection in Smart Meters. In *Proceedings of the International Workshop on Critical Information Infrastructures Security*, (pp. 34-45).

Rajkumar, R., Lee, I., Sha, L., & Stankovic, J. (2010). Cyber-physical systems: The next computing revolution. In *Proceedings of the 47th Design Automation Conference* (pp. 731-736). Anaheim, California: ACM.

Rankl, W., & Effing, W. (2010). *Smart Card Handbook* (4th ed.). Wiley. doi:10.1002/9780470660911

Rasche, A., & Polze, A. (2005). Dynamic reconfiguration of component-based real-time software. In *Proceedings of the 10th IEEE International Workshop on Object-Oriented Real-Time Dependable Systems (WORDS 2005)*, Sedona (pp. 347-354). doi:10.1109/WORDS.2005.31

Raschke, W., Massimiliano, Z., Baumgartner, P., Loinig, J., Steger, C., & Kreiner, C. (2014). *Supporting evolving security models for an agile security evaluation.* IEEE. doi:10.1109/ESPRE.2014.6890525

Ratasich, D., Höftberger, O., Isakovic, H., Shafique, M., & Grosu, R. (2017). A Self-Healing Framework for Building Resilient Cyber-Physical Systems. In *Proceedings of the 20th IEEE International Symposium on Object/Component/Service-Oriented Real-Time Distributed Computing Conference (ISORC 2017)*, Toronto.

Rathi, N., De, A., Naeimi, H., & Ghosh, S. (2016). Cache bypassing and checkpointing to circumvent data security attacks on sttram. CoRR, abs/1603.06227.

Rathi, N., Naeimi, H., & Ghosh, S. (2016). Side channel attacks on sttram and low-overhead countermeasures. CoRR, abs/1603.06675.

Rauter, T., Höller, A., Kajtazovic, N., & Kreiner, C. (2015). Privilege-Based Remote Attestation: Towards Integrity Assurance for Lightweight Clients. In *Proceedings of the Workshop on ioT privacy, trust, and security.* doi:10.1145/2732209.2732211

Rauter, T., Iber, J., Krisper, M., & Kreiner, C. (2017). Integration of Integrity Enforcing Technologies into Embedded Control Devices: Experiences and Evaluation. In *The 22nd IEEE pacific rim international symposium on dependable computing.*

Ravi, S., Raghunathan, A., & Chakradhar, S. (2004). Tamper Resistance Mechanisms for Secure Embedded Systems. In *Proceedings of the 17th International Conference on VLSI Design* (pp. 605-611).

Ravi, S., Raghunathan, A., Kocher, P., & Hattangady, S. (2004). Security in Embedded Systems: Design Challenges. *ACM Transactions on Embedded Computing Systems*, *3*(3), 461–491. doi:10.1145/1015047.1015049

Raza, S., Shafagh, H., Hewage, K., Hummen, R., & Voigt, T. (2013). Lithe: Lightweight Secure CoAP for the Internet of Things. *IEEE Sensors Journal, 13*(10), 3711–3720. doi:10.1109/JSEN.2013.2277656

Rebeiro, C., & Mukhopadhyay, D. (2011). Cryptanalysis of clefia using differential methods with cache trace patterns. In A. Kiayias (Ed.), *Topics in cryptology – CT-RSA 2011* (pp. 89–103). Springer Berlin Heidelberg. doi:10.1007/978-3-642-19074-2_7

Rebeiro, C., & Mukhopadhyay, D. (2015). *A formal analysis of prefetching in pro- filed cache-timing attacks on block ciphers*. Cryptology ePrint Archive, Report 2015/1191. Retrieved from http://eprint.iacr.org

Referat, B. f. (2013). *Zukunftsbild Industrie 4.0*. Bundesministerium fuer Bildung und Forschung Referat.

Rein, A., Rieke, R., Jäger, M., Kuntze, N., & Coppolino, L. (2015). Trust Establishment in Cooperating Cyber-Physical Systems. In Security of industrial control systems and cyber physical systems.

Richter, A., Herber, C., Rauchfuss, H., Wild, T., & Herkersdorf, A. (2014, February). Performance isolation exposure in virtualized platforms with PCI passthrough I/O sharing. In E. Maehle, K. Römer, W. Karl et al. (Eds.), *Architecture of computing systems – ARCS 2014* (pp. 171–182). Lübeck, Germany: Springer International Publishing.

Riel, A., Bachmann, V. O., Dussa-Zieger, K., Kreiner, C., Messnarz, R., Nevalainen, R., . . . Tichkiewitch, S. (2012, June 25-27). EU Project SafEUr – Competence Requirements for Functional Safety Managers. In *EruoSPI 2012: 19th European Conference Systems, Software and Services Process Improvement*, Vienna, Austria. Springer. doi:10.1007/978-3-642-31199-4_22

Riviere, L., Najm, Z., Rauzy, P., Danger, J.-L., Bringer, J., & Sauvage, L. (2015). High precision fault injections on the instruction cache of armv7-m architectures. In Hardware oriented security and trust (host), 2015 ieee international symposium on (pp. 62–67). doi:10.1109/HST.2015.7140238

Rizzo, L., & Lettieri, G. (2012). Vale, a switched Ethernet for virtual machines. In *Proceedings of the 8th international conference on emerging networking experiments and technologies* (pp. 61–72). doi:10.1145/2413176.2413185

Roberts, R. D. (2013). A MIMO protocol for camera communications (CamCom) using undersampled frequency shift ON-OFF keying (UFSOOK) In Proceedings of the Globecom Workshops (pp. 1052–1057). doi:10.1109/GLO-COMW.2013.6825131

Roberts, L. G. (1973). Dynamic Allocation of Satellite Capacity through Packet Reservation. In *Proceedings of the AFIPS Conference, National Computer Conference and Exposition* (Vol. 42, pp. 711-716). doi:10.1145/1499586.1499753

Rodin, R. (2012). Meta Patterns for Developing a Minimalist Training Manual. In *Proceedings of the 19th Conference on Pattern Languages of Programs PLoP 2012*. ACM.

Roesch, M. (1999). Snort: Lightweight Intrusion Detection for Networks. In *Proceedings of LISA '99: 13th Systems Administration Conference* (pp. 229–238).

Roman, R., Najera, P., & Lopez, J. (2011). Securing the Internet of Things. *Computer, 44*(9), 51–58. doi:10.1109/MC.2011.291

ROS. (2017, 03 17). *Open Source Robotics Foundation*. Retrieved from Robot Operating System: http://www.ros.org/ RTCA/DO-297.

Rosen, R. (1985). *Anticipatory Systems: Philosophical, Mathematical, and Methodological Foundations (IFSR International Series on Systems Science and Engineering)*. Pergamon Press.

Ross, D. T. (1978). Origins of the APT language for automatically programmed tools. In R. L. Wexelblat (Ed.), *In History of programming languages I* (pp. 279–338). New York: ACM. doi:10.1145/960118.808374

Roughgarden, T. (2007). Routing games. In *N. Nisan, T. Roughgarden, É. Tardos et al. (Eds.), Algorithmic Game Theory* (pp. 461–486). New York, NY: Cambridge University Press. doi:10.1017/CBO9780511800481.020

Roughgarden, T., & Tardos, É. (2002). How bad is selfish routing? *Journal of the ACM, 49*(2), 236–259. doi:10.1145/506147.506153

Ruhland, A., Prehofer, C., & Horst, O. (2016, December). embSFI: An approach for software fault isolation in embedded systems. In M. Völp, P. Esteves-Verissimo, A. Casimiro, & R. Pellizzoni (Eds.), *Proceedings of the 1st workshop on security and dependability of critical embedded real-time systems*, Porto, Portugal (pp. 6–11). Retrieved from https://certs2016.uni.lu/Media/certs2016.uni.lu/Files/CERTS-2016-Ruhland-embSFI

Ruiz, A., Juez, G., Schleiss, P., & Weiss, G. (2015). *A safe generic adaptation mechanism for smart cars. In Proceedings of the 2015 IEEE 26th International Symposium on Software Reliability Engineering (ISSRE)* (pp. 161–171). ISSRE. doi:10.1109/ISSRE.2015.7381810

Rushby, J. (2008). Runtime certification. In *Proceedings of the Eighth Workshop on Runtime Certification,* Budapest, Hungary (pp. 21-35). Springer-Verlag. doi:10.1007/978-3-540-89247-2_2

Rushby, J. (2009). A safety-case approach for certifying adaptive systems. In *Proceedings of the AIAA Infotech @ Aerospace Conference.*

Rushby, J. (1994). Critical System Properties:Survey and Taxonomy. *Reliability Engineering & System Safety, 43*(2), 189–219. doi:10.1016/0951-8320(94)90065-5

Russell, R. (2008). virtio: Towards a de-facto standard for virtual I/O devices. *Operating Systems Review, 42*(5), 95–103. doi:10.1145/1400097.1400108

Saab, S., Rohatgi, P., & Hampel, C. (2016). *Side-channel protections for cryptographic instruction set extensions.* Cryptology ePrint Archive, Report 2016/700. Retrieved from http://eprint.iacr.org

Sadeghi, A., & Stüble, C. (2004). Property-based Attestation for Computing Platforms: Caring About Properties, not Mechanisms. *Proceedings of the 2004 Workshop on New Security Paradigms* (pp. 67–77).

SAE Vehicle Electrical System Security Committee. (2016). *SAE J3061- Cybersecurity Guidebook for Cyber-Physical Automotive Systems.* SAE - Society of Automotive Engineers.

SAFE Project. (2016). Retrieved from http://www.safe-project.eu/

SafeCer. (2017, 03 17). *Safety Certification of Software-Intensive Systems with Reusable Components.* Retrieved from http://www.safecer.eu/

Sailer, R., Zhang, X., Jaeger, T., & van Doorn, L. (2004). Design and Implementation of a TCG-based Integrity Measurement Architecture.

Saint-Andre, P., Smith, K., Tronçon, R., & Troncon, R. (2009). *XMPP: The Definitive Guide.* O'Reilly Media, Inc.

Saint-Andre, P. (2011). *Extensible Messaging and Presence Protocol (XMPP): Core.* IETF. doi:10.17487/rfc6122

Salehie, M., & Tahvildari, L. (2009). Self-adaptive software: Landscape and research challenges. *ACM Transactions on Autonomous and Adaptive Systems, 4*(2), 1–42. doi:10.1145/1516533.1516538

Saltzer, J. H., & Schroeder, M. D. (1975). The Protection of Information in Computer Systems. *Proceedings of the IEEE, 63*(9), 1278–1308. doi:10.1109/PROC.1975.9939

Samad, T., & Annaswamy, A. (2011). *The impact of control technology: Overview, success stories and research challenges.* IEEE Control Systems Society.

Sanchez-Reillo, R., Sanchez-Avila, C., Lopez-Ongil, C., & Entrena-Arrontes, L. (2002). Improving Security in Information Technology using Cryptographic Hardware Modules. In *Proceedings of the International Carnahan Conference on Security Technology* (pp. 120-123). IEEE. doi:10.1109/CCST.2002.1049236

Sanfelice, R. G. (2015). Analysis and design of cyber-physical systems: A hybrid control systems approach. In D. B. Rawat, J. Rodrigues, & I. Stojmenovic (Eds.), Cyber-physical systems: From theory to practice (pp. 3-33). Boca Reton: CRC Press. doi:10.1201/b19290-3

Sangiovanni-Vincentelli, A., Damm, W., & Passerone, R. (2012). Taming Dr. Frankenstein: Contract-Based Design for Cyber-Physical Systems. *European Journal of Control, 18*(3), 217-238.

Sarkar, P. G., & Fitzgerald, S. (2013). Attacks on SSL: A Comprehensive Study of Beast, Crime, Time, Breach, Lucky 13 & RC4 Biases.

Scahill, J. (2015, February 25). What Gemalto doesn't know what it doesn't know. The Intercept. Retrieved from https://theintercept.com/2015/02/25/gemalto-doesnt-know-doesnt-know/

Schaefer, M., Vokřínek, J., Pinotti, D., & Tango, F. (2016). Multi-Agent Traffic Simulation for Development and Validation of Autonomic Car-to-Car Systems. In T.L. McCluskey, A. Kotsialos, J.P. Müller et al. (Eds.), Autonomic Road Transport Support Systems. (Autonomic Systems) (pp. 165-180). Birkhäuser Basel. doi:10.1007/978-3-319-25808-9_10

Scharstein, D., R. S. (2003). High-accuracy stereo depth maps using structured light. In *Proc. IEEE Computer Society Conference on Computer Vision and Pattern Recognition* (pp. 1–195-1–202). doi:10.1109/CVPR.2003.1211354

Schindler, W., Lemke, K., & Paar, C. (2005). A Stochastic Model for Differential Side Channel Cryptanalysis. In J. Rao & B. Sunar (Eds.), *Cryptographic hardware and embedded systems – ches 2005* (Vol. 3659, pp. 30–46). Springer Berlin Heidelberg. doi:10.1007/11545262_3

Schmittner, C., Gruber, T., Puschner, P., & Schoitsch, E. (2014). Security application of failure mode and effect analysis (FMEA). In *Proceedings of the International Conference on Computer Safety, Reliability, and Seucirty (SafeComp 2014).* doi:10.1007/978-3-319-10506-2_21

Schneider, D., & Trapp, M. (2013). Conditional Safety Certification of Open Adaptive Systems. *ACM Trans. Auton. Adapt. Syst., 8*(2), 8.

Schneier, B. (1999). Attack Trees. *Dr. Dobb's Journal of Software Tools for the Professional Programmer.*

Schumann, R. (2016). Performance Maintenance of ARTS Systems. In T.L. McCluskey, A. Kotsialos, J.P. Müller et al. (Eds.), Autonomic Road Transport Support Systems. (Autonomic Systems) (pp. 181-196). Birkhäuser Basel. doi:10.1007/978-3-319-25808-9_11

Schunter, M. (2016). Intel software guard extensions: Introduction and open research challenges. In *Proceedings of the 2016 ACM workshop on software protection.* New York, NY: ACM. doi:10.1145/2995306.2995307

Schuster, T., Meyer, R., Buchty, R., Fossati, L., & Berekovic, M. (2014). SoCRocket - A virtual platform for the European Space Agency's SoC development. In *Proceedings of the 9th International Symposium on Reconfigurable and Communication-Centric Systems-on-Chip (ReCoSoC)*, Montpellier (pp. 1-7). IEEE. doi:10.1109/ReCoSoC.2014.6860690

Seaborn, M. (2015). *Exploiting the dram rowhammer bug to gain kernel privileges* (Tech. Rep.). Google Project Zero. Retrieved from https://googleprojectzero.blogspot.de/2015/03/exploiting-dram-rowhammer-bug-to-gain.html

Selić, B., & Gérard, S. (2014). *Modeling and analysis of real-time and embedded systems with UML and MARTE.* doi:10.1016/B978-0-12-416619-6.00008-0

Semasinghe, P., Maghsudi, S., & Hossain, E. (2017). Game Theoretic Mechanisms for Resource Management in Massive Wireless IoT Systems. *IEEE Communications Magazine, 55*(2), 121–127. doi:10.1109/MCOM.2017.1600568CM

Seo-Hyun, J., Jin-Hee, C., Yangjae, J., Sachoun, P., & Tae-Man, H. (2011). Automotive hardware development according to ISO 26262. In *Proceedings of the 13th International Conference on Advanced Communication Technology (ICACT2011)* (pp. 588-592).

Seuschek, H., De Santis, F., & Guillen, O. M. (2017). Side-channel Leakage Aware Instruction Scheduling. In *Proceedings of the fourth workshop on cryptography and security in computing systems* (pp. 7–12). New York, NY: ACM. doi:10.1145/3031836.3031838

Sha, L., Gopalakrishnan, S., Liu, X., & Wang, Q. (2009). Cyber-physical systems: A new frontier. In J. J. Tsai, & P. S. Yu (Eds.), Machine Learning in Cyber Trust (pp. 3-13). Springer US. doi:10.1007/978-0-387-88735-7_1

Sha, L. (2009, September). Resilient mixed-criticality systems. *Crosstalk, 22*(9-10), 9–14.

Shelby, Z., Hartke, K., & Bormann, C. (2014). *The Constrained Application Protocol (CoAP). Tech. rep.* IETF.

Shen, Y. L. (2015). Dense visual-inertial odometry for tracking of aggressive motions. In *Proceedings of the IEEE International Conference on Robotics and Biomimetics (ROBIO)*.

Shen, D., & Li, V. O. K. (2002). Stabilized Multi-Channel ALOHA for Wireless OFDM Networks. In *Proceedings of the IEEE Global Communications Conference (GLOBECOM 2002)* (pp. 701–705). doi:10.1109/GLOCOM.2002.1188169

Shi, J., Wan, J., Yan, H., & Suo, H. (2011). A survey of cyber-physical systems. In *Proceedings of the 2011 International Conference on Wireless Communications and Signal Processing (WCSP)*, Nanjing, China (pp. 1-6). IEEE.

Shostack, A. (2008). *Experiences threat modeling at Microsoft.* Dept. of Computing, Lancaster University UK, Modeling Security Workshop.

Shostack, A. (2014). *Threat modeling: Designing for security.* Wiley & Sons.

Siemens. (2004). *SN 29500-1 Expected values, general.*

Singh, M., Rajan, M. A., Shivraj, V. L., & Balamuralidhar, P. (2015). Secure MQTT for Internet of Things (IoT). In *Proceedings of the 2015 Fifth International Conference on Communication Systems and Network Technologies (CSNT)* (pp. 746-751).

Sinnhofer, A. D., Raschke, W., Steger, C., & Kreiner, C. (2015). Evaluation paradigm selection according to Common Criteria for an incremental product development.

Sinnhofer, A. D., Raschke, W., Steger, C., & Kreiner, C. (2015). *Patterns for Common Criteria Certification.* ACM. doi:10.1145/2855321.2855355

Sinnhofer, A., Oppermann, F., Potzmader, K., Orthacker, C., Steger, C., & Kreiner, C. (2016). Patterns to Establish a Secure Communication Channel. In *Proceedings of the 21st European Conference on Pattern Languages of Programs* (pp. 13:1-13:21). doi:10.1145/3011784.3011797

Skogestad, S., & Postlethwaite, I. (2007). Multivariable feedback control (2. ed.). West Sussex, England: Jon Wiley & Sons Ltd.

Smith, S. W., & Weingart, S. (1999). Building a high-performance, programmable secure coprocessor. *Computer Networks*, *31*(8), 831–860. doi:10.1016/S1389-1286(98)00019-X

Somani, G., Gaur, M. S., & Sanghi, D. (2015). DDoS/EDoS attack in Cloud: Affecting everyone out there! In *Proceedings of the 8th International Conference on Security of Information and Networks* (pp. 169-176). doi:10.1145/2799979.2800005

Sommer, M., Tomforde, S., & Hähner, J. (2016). An Organic Computing Approach to Resilient Traffic Management. In T.L. McCluskey, A. Kotsialos, J.P. Müller et al. (Eds.), Autonomic Road Transport Support Systems (Autonomic Systems) (pp. 113-130). Birkhäuser Basel. doi:10.1007/978-3-319-25808-9_7

Soqrates Initiative. (2015). *SOQRATES Initiative*. Retrieved 31. March 2016 from http://www.soqrates.de

SPIRIT. (2013). IEEE SA - 1685-2009 - IEEE Standard for IP-XACT, Standard Structure for Packaging, Integrating, and Reusing IP within Tool Flows. Retrieved from http://standards.ieee.org/findstds/standard/1685-2009.html

Sporer, H., Macher, G., Armengaud, E., & Kreiner, C. (2015). Incorporation of Model-Based System and Software Development Environments. *Proceedings of the 41st Euromicro Conference on Software Engineering and Advanced Applications, SEAA 2015* (pp. 177-180). doi:10.1109/SEAA.2015.65

Sporer, H., Macher, G., Kreiner, C., & Brenner, E. (2016). Resilient Interface Design for Safety-Critical Embedded Automotive Software. In *Proceedings of the Sixth International Conference on Computer Science and Information Technology, Academy & Industry Research Collaboration Center (AIRCC)*. doi:10.5121/csit.2016.60117

Stackelberg, H. (1952). *The Theory of the Market Economy*. Oxford University Press.

Standaert, F.-X., Malkin, T. G., & Yung, M. (2009). A Unified Framework for the Analysis of Side-Channel Key Recovery Attacks. In *Proceedings of the Annual International Conference on the Theory and Applications of Cryptographic Techniques* (pp. 443-461). doi:10.1007/978-3-642-01001-9_26

Standard, O. A. (2014). *MQTT Version 3.1*. OASIS.

Stankovic, J. A. (2014). Research Directions for the Internet of Things. *IEEE Internet of Things Journal*, *1*(1), 3–9. doi:10.1109/JIOT.2014.2312291

Steinbrücker, F., Sturm, J., & Cremers, D. (2011). Real-time visual odometry from dense RGB-D images. In *Proceedings of the 2011 IEEE International Conference on Computer Vision Workshops (ICCV Workshops)*, Barcelona. doi:10.1109/ICCVW.2011.6130321

Stoilov, T., & Stoilova, K. (2016). A Self-Optimization Traffic Model by Multilevel Formalism. In T.L. McCluskey, A. Kotsialos, J.P. Müller et al. (Eds.), Autonomic Road Transport Support Systems (Autonomic Systems) (pp. 87-112). Birkhäuser Basel. doi:10.1007/978-3-319-25808-9_6

Stouffer, K., Falco, J., & Scarfone, K. (2015). Guide to Industrial Control Systems (ICS) Security. Nist Special Publication, 800(82).

Strasser, M., & Stamer, H. (2008). A Software-Based Trusted Platform Module Emulator. In *Proceedings of the International Conference on Trusted Computing* (pp. 33-47).

Studer, R., Benjamins, R. V., & Fensel, D. (1998). Knowledge engineering: Principles and methods. *Data & Knowledge Engineering, 25*(1-2), 161–197. doi:10.1016/S0169-023X(97)00056-6

Sturm, J. (1999). Using SeDuMi 1.02, a MATLAB toolbox for optimization over symmetric cones. *Optimization methods and software, 11*(1-4), 625-653.

Sun, Y., Han, Z., & Liu, K. J. R. (2008, February). Defense of trust management vulnerabilities in distributed networks. *IEEE Communications Magazine, 46*(2), 112–119. doi:10.1109/MCOM.2008.4473092

Symantec. (2017). *Internet Security Threat Report 2017*. Retrieved from https://resource.elq.symantec.com/LP=3980?cid=70138000001BjppAAC&mc=202671&ot=wp&tt=sw&inid=symc_threat-report_regular_to_leadgen_form_LP-3980_ISTR22-report-main

Szijj, A., Buttyan, L., & Szalay, Z. (2015). *Hacking cars in the style of Stuxnet*. Retrieved from http://www.hit.bme.hu/~buttyan/publications/carhacking-Hacktivity-2015.pdf

Tabbara, M., & Nesic, D. (2008, June). Input-Output Stability of Networked Control Systems with Stochastic Protocols and Channels. *IEEE Transactions on Automatic Control, 53*(5), 1160–1175. doi:10.1109/TAC.2008.923691

Takai, I., Ito, S., Yasutomi, K., Kagawa, K., Andoh, M., & Kawahito, S. (2013). LED and CMOS image sensor based optical wireless communication system for automotive applications. *IEEE Photonics Journal, 5*(5), 6801418. doi:10.1109/JPHOT.2013.2277881

Tasaka, S., Hayashi, K., & Ishibashi, Y. (1995). Integrated Video and Data Transmission in the TDD ALOHA-Reservation Wireless LAN. In *Proceedings of the IEEE International Conference on Communications (ICC 1995)* (pp. 1387–1393). doi:10.1109/ICC.1995.524431

TCG. (2016). Trusted Computing Group. Retrieved January 1, 2016, from https://www.trustedcomputinggroup.org/

Teixeira, A., Sandberg, H., & Johansson, K. H. (2010). Networked control systems under cyber attacks with applications to power networks. In *Proceedings of the 2010 American Control Conference* (pp. 3690-3696). Marriott Waterfront, Baltimore, MD, USA: IEEE. doi:10.1109/ACC.2010.5530638

Thalheimer, W. (2006). *People remember 10%, 20%...Oh Really?* Retrieved from http://www.willatworklearning.com/2006/05/people_remember.html

The Common Criteria Recognition Agreement Members. (2014). *Common Criteria for Information Technology Security Evaluation.*

The MITRE Corporation. (2016). *Common vulnerabilities and exposures. the standard for information security vulnerability names.* Retrieved 05.12.2016 from https://cve.mitre.org/cgi-bin/cvekey.cgi?keyword=Android

The SPICE User Group. (2015). *Automotive SPICE Process Assessment / Reference Model V3.0.*

The UML Profile for MARTE: Modeling and Analysis of Real-Time and Embedded Systems. (2015). Retrieved from http://www.omgmarte.org/

The World Bank Group. (2016). *Mobile cellular subscriptions (per 100 people).* Retrieved from http://data.worldbank.org/indicator/IT.CEL.SETS.P2?end=2003&start=1984&view=chart

Thomopoulos, S. (1988). Simple and Versatile Decentralized Control for Slotted ALOHA, Reservation ALOHA, and Local Area Networks. *IEEE Transactions on Communications*, *36*(6), 662–674. doi:10.1109/26.2786

Tidwell, T., Larson, R., Fitch, K., & Hale, J. (2001). *Modeling Internet Attacks*. Retrieved from http://citeseerx.ist.psu.edu/viewdoc/download?doi=10.1.1.108.9040&rep=rep1&type=pdf

Tillich, S., & Großschädl, J. (2006). Instruction set extensions for efficient aes implementation on 32-bit processors. In L. Goubin & M. Matsui (Eds.), *Cryptographic hardware and embedded systems - ches 2006* (Vol. 4249, pp. 270–284). Springer Berlin Heidelberg. doi:10.1007/11894063_22

Tiri, K., Hwang, D., Hodjat, A., Lai, B., Yang, S., Schaumont, P., & Verbauwhede, I. (2005). A Side-Channel Leakage Free Coprocessor IC in 0.18 μm CMOS for Embedded AES-based Cryptographic and Biometric Processing. In *Proceedings of the 42nd Design Automation Conference* (pp. 222-227).

Tobias, M. H. (2005). *Robust 3D Measurement with PMD Sensors*. Zürich: Range Imaging Day.

Tolic, D., & Hirche, S. (2016, April). *Stabilizing transmission intervals for nonlinear delayed networked control systems [Extended Version]*. Retrieved December 5, 2016, from http://adsabs.harvard.edu/abs/2016arXiv160404421T

Törnqvist, H. O. (2013). Why would i want a gyroscope on my RGB-D sensor? In *Proceedings of the 2013 IEEE Workshop on Robot Vision (WORV)*.

Trimberger, S. (2012). *Field-Programmable Gate Array Technology*. Springer, US.

Trusted Computing Group. (2006). TPM Main Specification Level 2 Version 1.2.

Trusted Computing Group. (2007). *TCG Specification Architecture Overview* (pp. 1–24). No. August.

Tuyls, P., Schrijen, G.-J., Škorić, B., Van Geloven, J., Verhaegh, N., & Wolters, R. (2006). Read-Proof Hardware from Protective Coatings. In *Proceedings of the International Workshop on Cryptographic Hardware and Embedded Systems* (pp. 369-383).

UBM tech. (2013). *Embedded Market Survey*. UBM.

Udd, R., Asplund, M., Nadjm-Tehrani, S., Kazemtabrizi, M., & Ekstedt, M. (2016). Exploiting Bro for Intrusion Detection in a SCADA System. In *Proceedings of the Cyber-Physical System Security Workshop* (pp. 44–51). doi:10.1145/2899015.2899028

Uhrmacher, A. M., & Weyns, D. (2010). *Multi-Agent systems: Simulation and applications*. CRC Press.

Uhsadel, L., Georges, A., & Verbauwhede, I. (2008). Exploiting hardware performance counters. In Proceedings of the 5th workshop on Fault diagnosis and tolerance in cryptography FDTC'08. (pp. 59–67). doi:10.1109/FDTC.2008.19

UK Ministry of Defence. (1997). *Defence Standard 00-55, Requirements for safety related software in defence equipment*.

UK Ministry of Defence. (1997). *Defence Standard 00-55, Requirements for safety related software in defence equipment*.

Ukil, A., Bandyopadhyay, S., Bhattacharyya, A., Pal, A., & Bose, T. (2014). Lightweight security scheme for IoT applications using CoAP. *International Journal of Pervasive Computing and Communications*, *10*(4), 372–392. doi:10.1108/IJPCC-01-2014-0002

United States. Dept. of Defense. (1988). *Electronic Reliability Design Handbook*.

Unterluggauer, T., & Mangard, S. (2016). Exploiting the physical disparity: Side-channel attacks on memory encryption. In F.X. Standaert & E. Oswald (Eds.), *Constructive side-channel analysis and secure design* (pp. 3–18). Cham: Springer International Publishing.

Urbina, D. I., Giraldo, J., Cardenas, A. A., Tippenhauer, N. O., Valente, J., & Faisal, M. … Sandberg, H. (2016). Limiting the Impact of Stealthy Attacks on Industrial Control Systems. In *Proceedings of the 23rd aCM conference on computer and communications security*.

Urbina, D. I., Giraldo, J. A., Cardenas, A. A., Tippenhauer, N. O., Valente, J., Faisal, M., & Sandberg, H. et al. (2016). Limiting the Impact of Stealthy Attacks on Industrial Control Systems. In *Proceedings of the 2016 ACM SIGSAC Conference on Computer and Communications Security* (pp. 1092-1105). doi:10.1145/2976749.2978388

US Census Bureau. (02 2010). *Computer and Internet Use in the United States: 1984 to 2009*. Retrieved from http://www.census.gov/data/tables/time-series/demo/computer-internet/computer-use-1984-2009.html

van de Wouw, N., Naghshtabrizi, P., Cloosterman, M., & Hespanha, J. (2009). Tracking control for sampled-data systems with uncertain time-varying sampling intervals and delays. *International Journal on Robust Nonlinear Control, 20*(4), 387–411.

van de Wouw, N., Naghshtabrizi, P., Cloosterman, M., & Hespanha, J. (2010). Tracking control for sampled-data systems with uncertain sampling intervals and delays. *International Journal Robust and Nonlinear Control, 20*(4), 387–411.

van de Wouw, N., Nesic, D., & Heemels, W. (2012, March 30). A discrete-time framework for stability analysis of nonlinear networked control systems. *Automatica, 48*(6), 1144–1153. doi:10.1016/j.automatica.2012.03.005

van der Veen, V., Fratantonio, Y., Lindorfer, M., Gruss, D., Maurice, C., Vigna, G., & Giuffrida, C. (2016). Drammer: Deterministic rowhammer attacks on mobile platforms. In *Proceedings of the 2016 ACM SIGSAC conference on computer and communications security* (pp. 1675–1689). New York, NY, USA: ACM. doi:10.1145/2976749.2978406

Varadarajan, V., Zhang, Y., Ristenpart, T., & Swift, M. (2015, August). A placement vulnerability study in multi-tenant public clouds. In Proceedings of the 24th USENIX Security Symposium (USENIX Security 15) (pp. 913–928). Washington, D.C.: USENIX Association.

Varga, L. Z. (2016b, August 29-September 2). How Good is Predictive Routing in the Online Version of the Braess Paradox? In *Proceedings of 22nd European Conference on Artificial Intelligence (ECAI 2016)*, The Hague, The Netherlands, *FIAA* (Vol. 285, pp. 1696-1697).

Varga, L. Z. (2014, May 5-6). Online Routing Games and the Benefit of Online Data. In *Proceedings of Eighth International Workshop on Agents in Traffic and Transportation, at 13th Int. Conf. on Autonomous Agents and Multiagent Systems (AAMAS 2014)*, Paris, France (pp. 88-95).

Varga, L. Z. (2015). On Intention-Propagation-Based Prediction in Autonomously Self-adapting Navigation. *Scalable Computing: Practice and Experience, 16*(3), 221–232.

Varga, L. Z. (2016a, July 18-22). Benefit of Online Real-time Data in the Braess Paradox with Anticipatory Routing. In *Proceedings of 2016 IEEE International Conference on Autonomic Computing*, Würzburg, Germany (pp. 245-250). doi:10.1109/ICAC.2016.68

Varga, L. Z. (in press). Equilibrium with Predictive Routing in the Online Version of the Braess Paradox. *IET Software*.

Vasudevan, A., Owusu, E., Zhou, Z., Newsome, J., & McCune, J. M. (2012). Trustworthy Execution on Mobile Devices: What Security Properties Can My Mobile Platform Give Me? In *Proceedings of the International Conference on Trust and Trustworthy Computing* (pp. 159-178). Springer Berlin Heidelberg. doi:10.1007/978-3-642-30921-2_10

Vedaldi, A., & Soatto, S. (2008). Localizing objects with smart dictionaries.

Verein zur Weiterentwicklung des V-Modell XT e. V. (2015). *V-Modell XT, 2.0.* Retrieved from www.v-modell-xt.de

Verification Academy. (2012). *Coverage Cookbook.* Retrieved from https://verificationacademy.com/cookbook/coverage

Vieira, M. A. M., Coelho, C. N. Jr, da Silva, D. C. Jr, & da Mata, J. M. (2003). Survey on Wireless Sensor Network Devices. In *Proceedings of the IEEE Conference on Emerging Technologies and Factory Automation* (Vol. 1, pp. 537-544). doi:10.1109/ETFA.2003.1247753

Vinoski, S. (1993). *Distributed Object Computing with Corba 1.0 Introduction.*

Vinoski, S. (2006). Advanced Message Queuing Protocol. *IEEE Internet Computing, 10*(6).

Vuković, O., & Dán, G. (2014). Security of Fully Distributed Power System State Estimation: Detection and Mitigation of Data Integrity Attacks. *IEEE Journal on Selected Areas in Communications, 32*(7), 1500–1508. doi:10.1109/JSAC.2014.2332106

Wahle, J., Bazzan, A. L. C., Klügl, F., & Schreckenberg, M. (2000). Decision dynamics in a traffic scenario. *Physica A: Statistical Mechanics and its Applications, 287*(3-4), 669-681.

Wallgren, L., Raza, S., & Voigt, T. (2013). Routing Attacks and Countermeasures in the RPL-based Internet of Things. *International Journal of Distributed Sensor Networks, 9*(8), 794326. doi:10.1155/2013/794326

Walsh, G. C., & Ye, H. (2001, February). Scheduling of networked control systems. *IEEE Control Systems, 21*(1), 57–65. doi:10.1109/37.898792

Walsh, G., Ye, H., & Bushnell, L. (2002, May). Stability analysis of networked control systems. *IEEE Transactions on Control Systems Technology, 10*(3), 438–446. doi:10.1109/87.998034

Wang, Q., Khurana, H., Huang, Y., & Nahrstedt, K. (2009, April). Time valid one-time signature for time-critical multicast data authentication. In IEEE INFOCOM (pp. 1233–1241). doi:10.1109/INFCOM.2009.5062037

Wang, D., Minn, H., & Al-Dhahir, N. (2009). A Distributed Opportunistic Access Scheme and its Application to OFDMA Systems. *IEEE Transactions on Communications, 57*(3), 738–746. doi:10.1109/TCOMM.2009.03.070084

Wan, J., Zhang, D., Zhao, S., Yang, L. T., & Lloret, J. (2014, August). Context-aware vehicular cyber-physical systems with cloud support: Architecture, challenges, and solutions. *IEEE Communications Magazine, 52*(8), 106–113. doi:10.1109/MCOM.2014.6871677

Wardrop, J. G. (1952). Some theoretical aspects of road traffic research. *Proceedings of the Institution of Civil Engineers, Part II, 1*(36), pp. 352-378. doi:10.1680/ipeds.1952.11362

Warg, F., Vedder, B., Skoglund, M., & Soderberg, A. (2014). SafetyADD: A Tool for Safety-Contract Based Design. In *Proceedings of the IEEE International Symposium on Software Reliability Engineering Workshops WoSoCer Workshop.* Naples, Italy.

Wasicek, A., Höftberger, O., Elshuber, M., Isakovic, H., & Fleck, A. (2014). Virtual CAN Lines in an Integrated MPSoC Architecture. In *Proceedings of the 17th International Symposium on Object/Component/Service-Oriented Real-Time Distributed Computing,* Reno (S. 158-165). IEEE. doi:10.1109/ISORC.2014.34

Waze. (2016). Retrieved November 28, 2016, from http://www.waze.com

Weaver, V. M., Terpstra, D., & Moore, S. (2013). Non-determinism and overcount on modern hardware performance counter implementations. In Proceedings of the 2013 IEEE international symposium on Performance analysis of systems and software (ISPASS) (pp. 215–224). doi:10.1109/ISPASS.2013.6557172

Weimerskirch, A. (2014). V2V communication security: A privacy preserving design for 300 million vehicles. In *Proceedings of the workshop on cryptographic hardware and embedded systems (CHES)*, Busan, Korea.

Weingart, S. H. (2000). Physical Security Devices for Computer Subsystems: A Survey of Attacks and Defenses. Advanced Message Queuing Protocol*International Workshop on Cryptographic Hardware and Embedded Systems* (pp. 302-317). doi:10.1007/3-540-44499-8_24

Weiser, M. (1991). The Computer for the 21st Century. *Scientific American, 265*(3), 94–104. doi:10.1038/scientificamerican0991-94

Weissnegger, R., Pistauer, M., Kreiner, C., Römer, K., & Steger, C. (2015). A novel method to speed-up the evaluation of cyber-physical systems (ISO 26262). In *Proceedings of the 2015 12th International Workshop on Intelligent Solutions in Embedded Systems (WISES)* (pp. 109-114).

Weissnegger, R., Pistauer, M., Kreiner, C., Schuß, M., Römer, K., & Steger, C. (2016, July 25-27). Automatic Testbench Generation for Simulation-based Verification of Safety-critical Systems in UML. In A. Ahrens, & C. Benavente-Peces (Eds.), *Proceedings of the 6th International Joint Conference on Pervasive and Embedded Computing and Communication Systems*, Lisbon, Portugal (pp. 70-75). SciTePress. doi:10.5220/0005997700700075

Weissnegger, R., Schuß, M., Schachner, M., Pistauer, M., Römer, K., & Steger, C. (2016). A Novel Simulation-based Verification Pattern for Parallel Executions in the Cloud. In *Proceedings of the 21st European Conference on Pattern Languages of Programs Proceedings.* doi:10.1145/3011784.3011806

Weissnegger, R., Kreiner, C., Pistauer, M., Römer, K., & Steger, C. (2015). A Novel Design Method for Automotive Safety-Critical Systems based on UML/MARTE. In *Proceedings of the 2015 Forum on specification {\&} Design Languages*, Barcelona (pp. 177-184).

Weissnegger, R., Schuß, M., Kreiner, C., Pistauer, M., Kay, R., & Steger, C. (2016). *Bringing UML / MARTE to life: Simulation-based Verification of Safety-Critical Systems. In Proceedings of the 2016 Forum on Specification and Design Languages.* FDL.

Weissnegger, R., Schuß, M., Kreiner, C., Pistauer, M., Römer, K., & Steger, C. (2016). Seamless Integrated Simulation in Design and Verification Flow for Safety-Critical Systems. In A. Skavhaug, J. Guiochet, E. Schoitsch, & F. Bitsch (Eds.), *Computer Safety, Reliability, and Security: SAFECOMP 2016 Workshops, ASSURE, DECSoS, SASSUR, and TIPS, Trondheim, Norway, September 20, 2016, Proceedings* (pp. 359–370). Cham: Springer International Publishing; doi:10.1007/978-3-319-45480-1_29

Weyns, D., Schmerl, B., Grassi, V., Malek, S., Mirandola, R., & Prehofer, C. ... Göschka, K. M. (2013). On Patterns for Decentralized Control in Self-Adaptive Systems. In *Software engineering for self-adaptive systems ii* (pp. 76–107). doi:10.1007/978-3-642-35813-5_4

Whitman, M. E., & Mattord, H. J. (2011). *Principles of Information Security*. Cengage Learning.

Whitnall, C., Oswald, E., & Mather, L. (2011). An Exploration of the Kolmogorov-Smirnov Test as a Competitor to Mutual Information Analysis. In E. Prouff (Ed.), *Smart card research and advanced applications* (Vol. 7079, pp. 234–251). Springer Berlin Heidelberg. doi:10.1007/978-3-642-27257-8_15

Whittle, J., Sawyer, P., Bencomo, N., Cheng, B. H., & Bruel, J.-M. (2009). Relax: Incorporating uncertainty into the specification of self-adaptive systems. In *Proceedings of the 17th IEEE International Requirements Engineering Conference* (pp. 79-88). Atlanta: IEEE. doi:10.1109/RE.2009.36

Wiener, N. (1961). *Cybernetics Or Control and Communication in the Animal and the Machine*. MIT Press. doi:10.1037/13140-000

Wikimedia Commons. (2014). OODA loop. Retrieved from https://commons.wikimedia.org/wiki/File:OODA.Boyd.svg

Wikitude. (2016). Wikitude GmbH. Retrieved 12 05, 2016, from http://www.wikitude.com/

Winner, H. H. (2015). *Handbuch Fahrer- assistenzsysteme*.

Winter, J. (2008). Trusted Computing Building Blocks for Embedded Linux-based ARM TrustZone Platforms. In *Proceedings of the 3rd ACM workshop on Scalable trusted computing* (pp. 21-30). doi:10.1145/1456455.1456460

Wirth, N. (1971). The programming language pascal. *Acta Informatica*, *1*(1), 35–63. doi:10.1007/BF00264291

Woo, S., Jo, H. J., & Lee, H. L. (2015). A Practical Wireless Attack on the Connected Car and Security Protocol for In-Vehicle CAN. *IEEE Transactions on Intelligent Transportation Systems*, *16*(2).

Woodman, O. J. (2007). An introduction to inertial navigation.

Work group EGAS. (2015). *Standardized E-Gas Monitoring Concept for Gasoline and Diesel Engine Control Units, Version 6.0*.

Wurster, G., van Oorschot and Paul, C., & Somayaji, A. (2005). A generic attack on checksumming-based software tamper resistance. In *Proceedings of the 2005 IEEE Symposium on Security and Privacy (S\&P'05)*, (pp. 127-138). doi:10.1109/SP.2005.2

Xiao, Y., Zhang, X., Zhang, Y., & Teodorescu, R. (2016, August). One bit flips, one cloud flops: Cross-vm row hammer attacks and privilege escalation. In Proceedings of the 25th USENIX Security Symposium (USENIX Security 16) (pp. 19–35). Austin, TX: USENIX Association.

Xiao, Y., Zhang, Y., Gibson, J. H., & Xie, G. G. (2009). Performance Analysis of p-persistent Aloha for Multi-hop Underwater Acoustic Sensor Networks. In *Proceedings of the International Conference on Embedded Software and Systems* (pp. 305–311). doi:10.1109/ICESS.2009.61

Xu, W., Zhang, X., & Hu, H. (2012). Remote Attestation with Domain-Based Integrity Model and Policy Analysis. In *Dependable and Secure Computing* (pp. 429–442).

Xu, Z., Wang, H., & Wu, Z. (2015). A measurement study on co-residence threat inside the cloud. In Proceedings of the 24th USENIX Security Symposium (USENIX Security 15) (pp. 929–944). Washington, D.C.: USENIX Association.

Xue, M., Wang, W., & Roy, S. (2014). Security Concepts for the Dynamics of Autonomous Vehicle Networks. *Automatica*, *50*(3), 852–857. doi:10.1016/j.automatica.2013.12.001

Yaacoub, E., & Kadri, A. (2015). LTE Radio Resource Management for Real-Time Smart Meter Reading in the Smart Grid. *Proceedings of the IEEE ICC '15.*

Yaacoub, E., Kadri, A., & Abu-Dayya, A. (2011). An OFDMA Communication Protocol for Wireless Sensor Networks used for Leakage Detection in Underground Water Infrastructures. In *Proceedings of the IEEE International Wireless Communications and Mobile Computing Conference (IWCMC 2011).* doi:10.1109/IWCMC.2011.5982823

Yang, T. C. (2006, July 4). Networked control system: A brief survey. *IEEE Proceedings- Control Theory and Applications, 153*(4), 403-412.

Yarom, Y., & Falkner, K. (2014). Flush+ reload: a high resolution, low noise, l3 cache side-channel attack. In *Proceedings of the 23rd USENIX Security Symposium (USENIX Security 14)* (pp.719–732).

Yarom, Y., Ge, Q., Liu, F., Lee, R. B., & Heiser, G. (2015). *Mapping the intel last-level cache* (Tech. Rep.). IACR Cryptology ePrint Archive, Report 2015/905. Retrieved from http://eprint.iacr.org

Yarom, Y., Genkin, D., & Heninger, N. (2016). Cachebleed: A timing attack on openssl constant time rsa. In *Proceedings of the International conference on cryptographic hardware and embedded systems* (pp. 346–367). doi:10.1007/978-3-662-53140-2_17

Yuan, W., Howard, R., Dana, K., Raskar, R., Ashok, A., Gruteser, M., & Man-dayam, N. (2014). Phase messaging method for time-of-flight cameras. In *Proceedings of the Conference on Computational Photography (ICCP).*

Yu, J., & Zhao, J. (2012). *Segmentation of depth image using graph cut. In Fuzzy Systems and Knowledge Discovery* (pp. 1934–1938). FSKD.

Yumei, Z., & Yu, S. (2009). Analysis of Channel-aware Multichannel ALOHA in OFDMA Wireless Networks. *Information and Communications Technologies, 3*(2), 56–61.

Yung-chang, C., Li-ren, H., Hsing-chuang, L., Chih-jen, Y., & Ching-te, C. (2014). Assessing Automotive Functional Safety Microprocessor with ISO 26262 Hardware Requirements. In *Technical Papers of 2014 International Symposium on VLSI Design, Automation and Test* (pp. 3-6).

Zankl, A., Heyszl, J., & Sigl, G. (2017). Automated detection of instruction cache leaks in modular exponentiation software. In K. Lemke-Rust & M. Tunstall (Eds.), *Smart card research and advanced applications* (pp. 228–244). Cham: Springer International Publishing. doi:10.1007/978-3-319-54669-8_14

Zankl, A., Miller, K., Heyszl, J., & Sigl, G. (2016). Towards efficient evaluation of a time-driven cache attack on modern processors. In I. Askoxylakis, S. Ioannidis, S. Katsikas et al. (Eds.), *Computer security – esorics 2016* (pp. 3–19). Cham: Springer International Publishing. doi:10.1007/978-3-319-45741-3_1

Zhang, L., Gao, H., & Kaynak, O. (2013, February). Network-induced constraints in networked control systems - A survey. *IEEE Transactions on industrial informatics, 9*(1), 403-416.

Zhang, N., Sun, K., Shands, D., Lou, W., & Hou, Y. T. (2016). *Truspy: Cache side- channel information leakage from the secure world on arm devices.* Cryptology ePrint Archive, Report 2016/980. Retrieved from http://eprint.iacr.org

Zhang, T., Zhang, Y., & Lee, R. B. (2016). Memory dos attacks in multi-tenant clouds: Severity and mitigation. CoRR, abs/1603.03404

Zhang, N., Vojcic, B., Souryal, M. R., & Larsson, E. G. (2006). Exploiting Multiuser Diversity in Reservation Random Access. *IEEE Transactions on Wireless Communications, 5*(9), 2548–2554. doi:10.1109/TWC.2006.1687778

Zhang, W., Branicky, M. S., & Phillips, S. M. (2001, February). Stability of networked control systems. *IEEE Control Systems Magazine, 21*(1), 84–99. doi:10.1109/37.898794

Zhang, X., van Doorn, L., Jaeger, T., Perez, R., & Sailer, R. (2002). Secure Coprocessor-based Intrusion Detection. In *Proceedings of the 10th workshop on ACM SIGOPS European workshop* (pp. 239-242). doi:10.1145/1133373.1133423

Zhang, Y., Juels, A., Reiter, M. K., & Ristenpart, T. (2012). Cross-vm side channels and their use to extract private keys. In *Proceedings of the 2012 acm conference on computer and communications security* (pp. 305–316). doi:10.1145/2382196.2382230

Zhang, Y., Juels, A., Reiter, M. K., & Ristenpart, T. (2014). Cross-tenant side-channel attacks in paas clouds. In *Proceedings of the 2014 acm sigsac conference on com- puter and communications security* (pp. 990–1003). doi:10.1145/2660267.2660356

Zhou, Z., Gligor, V. D., Newsome, J., & McCune, J. M. (2012). Building Verifiable Trusted Path on Commodity x86 Computers. In *Proceedings of the 2012 IEEE Symposium on Security and Privacy* (pp. 616-630). doi:10.1109/SP.2012.42

Zhu, J., Wang, L., Yang, R., Davis, J. E., & Pan, Z. (2011). Reliability fusion of time-of-flight depth and stereo geometry for high quality depth maps. *IEEE Transactions on Pattern Analysis and Machine Intelligence, 33*(7), 1400–1414. PMID:20820074

Zhu, Q., & Basar, T. (2015). Game-Theoretic Methods for Robustness, Security, and Resilience of Cyberphysical Control Systems: Games-in-Games Principle for Optimal Cross-Layer Resilient Control Systems. *IEEE Control Systems, 35*(1), 46–65. doi:10.1109/MCS.2014.2364710

Zimmer, B., Bürklen, S., Knoop, M. I., Höfflinger, J., & Trapp, M. (2011). Vertical Safety Interfaces - Improving the Efficiency of Modular Certification. In Proceedings of the SAFECOMP 2011 (pp. 29–42). Naples: Springer.

Zimmer, C., Bhat, B., Mueller, F., & Mohan, S. (2015). Intrusion detection for CPS real-time controllers. In S. K. Khaitan, J. D. McCalley, & C. C. Liu (Eds.), *Cyber physical systems approach to smart electric power grid* (pp. 329–358). Berlin, Heidelberg: Springer.

Zonouz, S., Rrushi, J., & McLaughlin, S. (2014). Detecting Industrial Control Malware using Automated PLC Code Analytics. *IEEE Security and Privacy, 12*(6), 40–47. doi:10.1109/MSP.2014.113

Zorzi, M., Gluhak, A., Lange, S., & Bassi, A. (2010). From Today's Internet of Things to a Future Internet of Things: A Wireless-and Mobility-Related View. *IEEE Wireless Communications, 17*(6), 44–51. doi:10.1109/MWC.2010.5675777

Zuehlke, D. (2010). SmartFactory - Towards a factory-of-things. *Annual Reviews in Control, 34*(1), 129–138. doi:10.1016/j.arcontrol.2010.02.008

About the Contributors

Norbert Druml was born 1980 in Klagenfurt/Austria. After being self-employed for ten years in the field of embedded systems development, he received a Master's degree in Telematics and a doctoral degree in Electrical Engineering both from Graz University of Technology in Austria. In 2014, he joined Infineon Technologies Austria AG, where he has been leading several industrial research projects (in the fields of embedded systems, sensors, and security) and where he has been working as a concept engineer for the next generation sensor chips. His research interests include hardware/software co-design, secured embedded systems, and automotive sensing technology.

Armin Krieg received his Bachelor and Master's degree in Telematics from Graz University of Technology in 2007 and 2008, focusing on microelectronics and system-on-chip design. From 2010 to 2012 he worked in the POWER-MODES research project at the Institute for Technical Informatics at Graz University of Technology in collaboration with Infineon Technologies Austria AG and Austria Card GmbH. He received his doctoral degree in Electrical Engineering from the Graz University of Technology in 2013. From 2014 to 2015 he was involved in the specification of authentication devices for the Chipcard and Security department in the design center Graz of Infineon Technologies Austria AG. Currently, Armin is part of the top-level digital verification team for RF transceivers of the DMCE GmbH (owned by Intel). His research interests incorporate fault emulation as well as fault detection and recovery under the consideration of the device's power consumption.

Andrea Höller received her Master Degree in Information and Computer Engineering from Graz University of Technology, focusing on System-on-Chip Design and Information Security in the year 2013. From 2013 to 2016 she has conducted research on dependability for cyber-physical systems at the Institute for Technical Informatics (ITI) working in the HyUNIFY project in close collaboration with Andritz Hydro GmbH. In 2016, she earned her PhD degree at Graz University of Technology with a thesis on software-based fault-tolerance for resilient embedded systems. In the course of her research she first-authored 15 and co-authored more than 30 publications about dependability and security in the domain of cyber-physical systems. In September 2016, she joined the Contactless Innovation group of Infineon Technologies Austria AG at the Development Center Graz as a System and Digital Design Engineer. Currently she is working on the future of secured authentication and encryption for cyber-physical systems and the internet of things.

* * *

Tiago Amorim received his Master degree in Software Engineering from the Technical University of Kaiserslautern, Germany, and Blekinge Institute of Technology, Sweden, in 2013. In 2014 he was hired as Research Assistant by the Embedded Systems Engineering Department at Fraunhofer Institute of Experimental Software Engineering. Currently he works with research of safety and security for safety of cyber-physical systems for the Embedded Systems Quality Assurance Department at the same institute.

Eric Armengaud received his MSc. from ESIEE Paris, in 2002, the PhD. degree from the TU Vienna, in 2008 and the MBA degree from IBSA, in 2016. He has more than 15 years of experience in automotive embedded systems in different positions. He is currently project manager R&D within the AVL PTE business unit. Eric Armengaud is author and co-author of more than 70 peer reviewed publications and patents, and is guest lecturer at the University of Applied Sciences FH Joanneum.

Martin Benedikt received his MSc in Telematics in 2008 and his Ph.D. degree in Control Engineering from Graz University of Technology in 2013. After several years acting as scientific employee he is leading the group "Co-Simulation & Software" at the VIRTUAL VEHICLE Research Center Graz. Furthermore, he is product manager for the co-simulation platform ICOS. His main research interests include control system design, system modeling and holistic system simulation. Besides leading of several national projects he is actively participating within FP7, H2020 as well as coordinating ITEA3 European research projects.

Eugen Brenner is Associate Professor since 1996 at the Institute of Technical Informatics of the Graz University of Technology. He completed his master in Electrical Engineering 1983 in Graz. His PhD in Control Theory was finished 1987 also in Graz, dealing with optimal control in systems with limited actuating variables. He currently is head of the Study Commission and Dean of Studies for Information and Computer Engineering. Eugen Brenner's primary research interests developed from FPGA-based hardware extension to parallel systems, real-time systems and process control systems. The most recent focus targeting embedded systems is on modelling, software-development, systems engineering and systems security, including agile programming methods and smart service engineering.

Marcello Coppola is advanced architecture & innovation technical Director at STmicroelectronics. He has more than 20 years of industry experience with an extended network within the research community. He is a technology innovator, with the ability to accurately predict technology trends and solution requirements and is involved in different European research projects His research interests include hardware and software technologies for IoT, Cyber-Physical Systems, Automotive, Consumer and HPC with particular emphasis to system architecture, network-on-chip, security and low level software. He has co-authored more than 50 scientific publications and books and holds 25 patents. He was serving under different roles numerous top international conferences and workshops. He is member of the advisor board of IEEE computing now magazine and a senior member of the IEEE. He has graduated in Computer Science from the University of Pisa, Italy in 1992.

Mario Driussi is Senior Scientific Employee at Virtual Vehicle in Graz (Austria). He works in the Department E/E & Software on topics around embedded devices for the automotive domain, in particular at the thematic operating systems, middleware and SoA for safety critical systems.

Radu Grosu is a full Professor, and the Head of the Institute of Computer Engineering, at the Faculty of Informatics, of the Vienna University of Technology. Grosu is also the Head of the Cyber-Physical-Systems Group within the Institute of Computer- Engineering, and a Research Professor at the Department of Computer Science, of the State University of New York at Stony Brook, USA. The research interests of Radu Grosu include the modeling, the analysis and the control of cyber- physical systems and of biological systems. The applications focus of Radu Grosu includes distributed automotive and avionic systems, IoT, autonomous mobility, green operating systems, mobile ad-hoc networks, cardiac and neural networks, and genetic regulatory networks. Radu Grosu is the recipient of the National Science Foundation Career Award, the State University of New York Research Foundation Promising Inventor Award, the Association for Computing Machinery Service Award, and is an elected member of the International Federation for Information Processing, Working Group 2.2. Before receiving his appointment at the Vienna University of Technology, Radu Grosu was an Associate Professor in the Department of Computer Science, of the State University of New York at Stony Brook, where he co- directed the Concurrent-Systems Laboratory and co-founded the Systems-Biology Laboratory. Radu Grosu earned his doctorate (Dr.rer.nat.) in Computer Science from the Faculty of Informatics of the Technical University München, Germany. He was subsequently a Research Associate in the Department of Computer and Information Science, of the University of Pennsylvania, an Assistant, and an Associate Professor in the Department of Computer Science, of the State University of New York at Stony Brook, USA.

Stephanie Grubmüller is Researcher at Virtual Vehicle Research Center in Graz. She received her Master's degree in Telematics from Graz University of Technology in 2014. Her main research areas are model predictive control, distributed and networked control systems in automotive systems.

Berk Gulmezoglu was born in Turkey in 1990. He received the B.S. and M.S. degrees in Electrical and Electronics Engineering from Bilkent University, Ankara, Turkey, in 2012 and 2014, respectively. He is currently pursuing the Ph.D. degree at the Worcester Polytechnic Institute, Worcester, MA, USA. His research interests are detection and estimation, signal processing, UWB systems, cryptography, and side-channel attacks.

Sarah Haas received her Dipl.-Ing. degrees (M.Sc.) in Information and Computer Engineering as well as in Computer Science from Graz University of Technology, both in 2016. The focus in her studies was in Security, Embedded Systems and Sensor Networks, Machine Learning and Big Data Analysis, and Robotics. Since 2016, she has been a Ph.D. student in Information and Computer Engineering at Infineon Technologies Austria AG. Her research interests include security (in particular authentication mechanisms) of industrial robots.

Gerald Holweg was born in Graz, Austria, in 1960. He took his Masters degree (DI) in Electronic Engineering at the Graz University of Technology in 1983 and started his professional career as ASIC design engineer at AMI-Austria in October 1984, specialising in the areas of process parameter extraction, critical analogue ASIC design, mixed analogue/digital design, chip layout optimisation and the design of telecom circuits. In June 1987 he joined start-up company MIKRON-Austria as project manager for RFID ASICS and Subsystems and assumed Section Management of an RFID design group in 1991. From 1993 he was responsible for the definition and development of worldwide first Chip & Coil Contactless Smart Card (MIFARE®). In 1995, he took the position of Development Manager for the product line Contactless Smart Cards at MIKRON, which joined PHILIPS in June 1995. In February 1998 he started working as Director of Development for Chip Card and Security IC's at start-up Design Centre SIEMENS Entwicklungszentrum für Mikroelektronik in Graz, which changed to INFINEON Technologies Development Centre in 1999. Since 2003 he is responsible for Predevelopment Programs and Industrial Research Projects.

Oliver Horst is a staff researcher in the trusted applications research group at fortiss in Munich. Before this, he was a research engineer jointly at the Fraunhofer ESK and University of Augsburg for four years. There, he concentrated on future automotive software architectures, with a particular emphasis on virtualization techniques and electromobility. He attended the diploma program "Kerninformatik" at the TU Dortmund, which he completed in 2009. During his studies he focused on computer architecture, embedded systems and simulation. In his diploma thesis, he researched ways to reuse existing motor control software on new hardware platforms without recompilation at the corporate research department of Robert Bosch GmbH near Stuttgart. In his time as a student, he was working as part time software developer for various companies. Today, Mr. Horst is concerned with dependable software architectures and communication algorithms for cyber-physical systems, with special emphasis on multi-core platforms and mixed-criticality environments.

Johannes Iber is a PhD student at the Graz University of Technology. He works in the Industrial Informatics group, part of the Institute of Technical Informatics, under the supervision of Christian Kreiner. His research interests are model-driven engineering and self-adaptive software systems.

Gorka Irazoqui completed his Bachelor and Masters in Telecommunications engineer in Tecnun Universidad de Navarra. He holds a PhD from Worcester Polytechnic Institute in side-channel attacks in the cloud. He currently works in Nagravision/Kudelski security as a security engineer.

Haris Isakovic is a research assistant at Institute for Computer Engineering on Vienna University of Technology, working in the group of Professor Radu Grosu. His research topics include Hardware Architectures, Security, Real-Time Systems, and Operating Systems. Haris received a Master's degree in 2011, from Vienna University of Technology, and he is currently PhD candidate. He is involved in several European research initiatives: ACROSS, MultiPARTES, EMC2. He is working in areas of hardware architectures for safety critical and mixed-criticality applications, security mechanisms for MPSoC architectures and time-triggered communication, middleware services for partitioned operating systems.

Nora Koch graduated in Computer Science at the University of Buenos Aires, and received her PhD degree in Computer Science from the Ludwig-Maximilians-Universität (LMU) of Munich. She was a research assistant at the LMU for over 20 years and at fortiss GmbH, An-Institut Technische Universität München from October 2015 until March 2017. Nora has been involved in several FP5 to FP7 and H2020 European projects, and worked also as a consultant in the industrial area at F.A.S.T. Applied Software Technology, Cirquent and NTT DATA GmbH. She is the founder of the Web Engineering Group at the LMU, responsible for the development of the UWE methodology. Her main research interests focus on methods for the development of web applications, customization, security, and model-driven engineering. Further information — including her list of more than 130 publications — can be found at http://www. pst.informatik.uni-muenchen.de/people/former-members/koch.html.

George Kornaros is currently an Assistant Professor with the Technological Educational Institute of Crete, Dept. of Informatics Engineering, where he leads the Intelligent Systems and Computer Architecture Group. He was a System Architect of a few single-chip network processor designs for industry. His current research interests include multicore architectures, high-speed communication architectures, embedded and reconfigurable systems, and both full- and semi-custom IC design. He is involved in various European research projects, and currently serves on, or has served on various conferences and journals with different roles. He has published more than 50 technical articles, he is the holder of two patents, and has edited the book entitled MultiCore Embedded Systems (CRC Press, Taylor & Francis) in 2010. He received the Diploma degree in Computer Engineering from the University of Patras, Greece, in 1992. Prof. Kornaros is a member of the Technical Chamber of Greece.

Martin Krammer received his M.Sc. degree in Telecommunications and Informatics from Graz University of Technology, Austria, in 2010. He joined the Virtual Vehicle Research Center in 2009. Among his main research topics are embedded systems, systems engineering, as well as automotive functional safety and reliability engineering. He also contributes to the development of advanced co-simulation methodologies, applied in automotive engineering. This includes model based approaches for configuration and interface definitions as well as software development.

Christian Kreiner leads the Industrial Informatics competence group at Graz University of Technology, Institute of Technical Informatics. Research topics are architecture and quality engineering methods for industrial networked embedded systems, and process management systems - with special focus on functional safety and security. This includes flexible platform architectures, middleware, model-based techniques in engineering and at run-time, domain specific languages, and integrated development tool chains. Christian Kreiner is an intacs certified Automotive SPICE assessor, coordinator and trainer of ECQA job roles Automotive Sector Skills Alliance AQUA (ECQA Automotive Quality Skill integrated) and Functional Safety Manager. Christian Kreiner also has a long history in automated logistics systems as company co-founder, software and product line architect, and R&D head in industry.

Zhendong Ma is an information security and privacy expert at Austrian Institute of Technology. His research focuses on security of safety-critical cyber-physical systems (CPS) in multiple domains such as automotive, production and transport. His activities cover safety & security co-engineering, securing embedded systems and IoT devices, and Industrial Automation and Control System (IACS) security. He is leading and involved in national, EU and industry R&D projects. He holds a doctorate degree from Ulm University, Germany, while working on privacy and security of vehicular communication systems. He is a Certified Information Systems Security Professional (CISSP) and Global Industrial Cyber Security Professional (GICSP), and serves as an expert in IEC TC65.

Georg Macher received a MSc. degree in Telematics and worked as software development engineer on prototype vehicles at AVL List GmbH. In 2015 he received his PhD in Electronics at Institute of Technical Informatics at Graz University of Technology and joined the R&D department of AVL's powertrain engineering branch. He is active in the field of project management, system and software engineering and a member of the Soqrates working group focusing on automotive safety and& security.

Helmut Martin received his master degree in electrical engineering from Graz University of Technology in 2004. After his studies he has been working in the automotive industry in the software development and as functional safety engineer/manager for automotive system development for six years. By 2011, he started as researcher and project coordinator at the Virtual Vehicle Research Center and worked in the ARTEMIS EU Projects p/nSafeCer and VeTeSS and EMC2. His main research topics are the functional safety engineering for the automotive domain according ISO 26262 and model-based embedded systems engineering. Today, he investigates in the projects EMC2 and further on in AMASS on safety and security argumentation. In 2012, Mr. Martin founded the Functional Safety Community (FuSaCom), which address Functional Safety topics for different domains. In regular workshops, on different safety-related topics, the experience exchange between industry and research is fostered.

Richard Messnarz received his doctorate degree at Graz University of Technology. He is an Automotive SPICE and ISO 15504 principal assessor, and for the last 26 years he has been acting as a consultant and trainer for companies such as ZF Friedrichshafen AG, Robert BOSCH Automotive Steering, Robert BOSCH Automotive Electronics, MAGNA, HELLA, Continental Automotive, AVL, RENESAS, AUDI/VW, KTM Motorsport, T-Systems, and more. Messnarz focuses on system architecture, functional (safety) design, requirements management and safety (ISO 26262), and quality (ISO 15504) standards. He is an ECQA certified functional safety manager and ECQA certified trainer. He is teaching automotoive quality at the University of Applied Sciences, FH Joanneum, Graz. Messnarz manages EU initiatives to deal with innovation, international standards, and safety (www.eurospi.net), and he is the moderator of the German initiative SoQrates, where experiences and best practices for traceability, requirement management, system and software design, system test, and safety standards are exchanged. He is vice president of the European Certification and Qualification Association (ECQA), and chair of EuroSPI (www.eurospi.net).

Felix Jonathan Oppermann received his Master's degree in Computer Science from University of Oldenburg (Germany) in 2007. He obtained his PhD from Graz University of Technology in 2016 based on a thesis on programming and configuration of wireless sensor networks. Currently, he is working as a systems engineer for trust provisioning at NXP Semiconductors Austria GmbH. His research interests include wireless sensor networks, the Internet of Things, and security aspects of networked and embedded systems.

Clemens Orthacker, born 1980 in Graz, Austria. Studies Telematics at Graz University of Technology, with focus on IT security and Computer Vision. One year studies at IFSIC (Institut de Formation Supérieur en Information er Communication) at Université de Rennes 1, France. Employment as software developer at XiCrypt technologies. In 2006 Graduation to Dipl.-Ing. from Graz University of Technology. In 2006, employment as junior researcher at IAIK (Institut für Angewandte Informationsverarbeitung und Kommunikation) at Graz University of Technology with focus on e-Government. Technology evaluation for public bodies at A-SIT (Secure Information Technology Center - Austria). Various publications, e.g. Qualified Mobile Server Signature, SEC 2010. Since 2011 employment at NXP Semiconductors Austria. Since 2013 group lead Trust Provisioning at NXP Semiconductors. Various publications and patents pending.

Markus Pistauer (CEO, Member IEEE) holds a Master degree in Electrical and Electronic Engineering (1991) and a Ph.D. degree in Electronic and Control Engineering (1995), both from Graz University of Technology, Austria. From 1995 to 1999 he worked at Siemens AG (Semiconductor Division, now Infineon Technologies) and also as Professor at University of Applied Sciences, Carinthia. He has founded CISC Semiconductor in 1999 where he acts as CEO and in 2012 CISC Semiconductor Corp. in Mountain View, CA, USA. He is author and co-author of more than 70 papers published and holds several patents in the area of embedded systems.

Hannes Plank received his master's degree in Computer Engineering at the Graz University of Technology. He is employed as a PHD student at Infineon Technology Austria AG. His research is dedicated to the optical communication abilities of Time-of-Flight depth sensing systems. His interests include the Internet-of-Things, augmented reality, computational photography and embedded systems.

Christian Prehofer is research manager at fortiss GmbH, Munich, Germany, and affiliated with the TU München as a lecturer and with the Chang'an University as an adjunct professor. Christian Prehofer obtained his PhD at the Technical University of Munich in 1995, where he also received the habilitation degree in 2000. From 1998 to 2001 he was a system architect and group leader at Siemens in the area of communication systems. Since 2002, he has established a research group with a focus on self-organized systems at DoCoMo Euro Labs. From 2006 to 2009 he held positions as distinguished research leader and director in the area of Internet services at Nokia in Finland. Following this, he acted as chief researcher at Fraunhofer and as professor at the LMU München. His research interests are connected vehicle architecture and services, open platforms for integrated mobility solutions, Internet-applications as well as software technology and architecture for mobile and embedded systems. Since 2013, he is leading a research group at fortiss GmbH in Munich on Trusted Applications for Cyber-physcial Systems. He has more than 150 research publications and holds more than 30 patents.

Denise Ratasich received the B.S. degree and the M.S. degree in computer engineering from the Vienna University of Technology, Vienna, Austria, in 2011 and 2014, respectively. In 2014, she joined the Department of Computer Engineering, Vienna University of Technology, as a teaching and research assistant, and PhD student. Her current research interests include robotics, autonomous systems, sensor fusion, monitoring and reconfiguration in cyber-physical systems.

Tobias Rauter is a PhD student at the Graz University of Technology. He works in the Industrial Informatics group, part of the Institute of Technical Informatics, under the supervision of Christian Kreiner. His research interests are security and embedded systems.

Alvise Rigo is a software engineer and Linux kernel developer. Since June 2013 he is member of Virtual Open Systems, joining various European projects as virtualization expert. In July 2013 he has obtained a Master degree in computer engineering from the University of Padua, discussing the development experience of a computer vision application. His professional and research activities, focused mainly on hardware emulation and virtualization, allowed him to mature an in-depth knowledge of various Open Source projects, QEMU and its internals especially: concepts like MMU emulation, binary code generation and code translation are all part of his technical background. He experienced low level programming for ARM embedded systems, that introduced him to the ARM architecture, its components and hardware extensions. He counts various contributions to Open Source mailing lists, especially to Qemu-devel, where he constantly contributes proposing fixes and improvements.

Kay Römer is professor at and director of the Institute for Technical Informatics at Graz University of Technology, Austria. Before he held positions of Professor at the University of Lübeck in Germany, and senior researcher at ETH Zürich in Switzerland. Prof. Römer obtained his Doctorate in computer science from ETH Zürich in 2005 with a thesis on wireless sensor networks. His research interests encompass wireless networking, fundamental services, operating systems, programming models, dependability, and deployment methodology of networked embedded systems, in particular Internet of Things, Cyber-Physical Systems, and sensor networks.

Alejandra Ruiz is Research Engineer in the System Assurance group at TECNALIA since 2007. She currently leads the area of Modular Assurance and Certification of Safety-critical Systems, with particular focus on automotive, aerospace, railway and medical devices industries. She is the main contributor in these areas for European projects such as AMASS (Architecture-driven, Multi-concern and Seamless Assurance and Certification of Cyber-Physical Systems) EMC2 (Embedded Multi-Core systems for Mixed Criticality applications in dynamic and changeable real-time environments), RECOMP (Reduced Certification Costs for Trusted Multicore Platforms), OPENCOSS (Open Platform for EvolutioNary Certification of Safety-critical Systems) SafeAdapt (Safe Adaptive Software for Fully Electric Vehicles). She holds a Telecommunications Engineer degree, a Master degree in Advanced Artificial Intelligence and a PhD in telecommunications and computer science.

Martin Schachner is a Computer Science student at Graz University of Technology, Austria. In 2016 he graduated his bachelor with distinction and is currently working towards his master degree in the field of pervasive computing and computational intelligence. Since 2015 he is involved in European projects as a project assistant at the Institute for Technical Informatics (ITI). His work involves the research on new development methodologies for safety critical systems.

Christoph Schmittner received his M.Sc. in System and Software Engineering at the University of Applied Sciences Regensburg in 2013. His main research area is safety and security co-engineering. He works on safety, security analysis and co-analysis methods, connected and safety critical / fault & intrusion tolerant system architectures, functional safety and cybersecurity standards and inter-dependence of safety and security in critical systems. He works in multiple European and Austrian projects on safety&security co-analysis, co-design and co-assurance. He is member of the Austrian mirror committees for ISO/TC 22 Road vehicles and IEC TC 56 Dependability and designated Austrian expert in corresponding international standardisation groups (IEC 61508 and ISO 26262), member of the cybersecurity and safety tasks group for the development of edition 2 of ISO26262, member of TC65/WG20 "Industrial-process measurement, control and automation– Framework to bridge the requirements for safety and security", TC65/AHG2 "Reliability of Automation Devices and Systems" and TC65/AHG3 "Smart Manufacturing Framework and System Architecture".

Daniel Schneider received his Dipl.Inf. degree (M.Sc.) from TU Kaiserslautern in 2004. Afterwards he became an employee of the Fraunhofer Institute of Experimental Software Engineering (IESE) in Kaiserslautern. During his time at IESE, he assumed different roles (research scientist, project manager, senior engineer, program manager) and received his Ph.D. from TU Kaiserslautern. Since 2014 he is the head of the department "Embedded Systems Quality Assurance" (ESQ). Daniel Schneider was and is member and manager of numerous publicly as well as industry funded research projects. He is author and co-author of over 40 conference, journal and magazine publications, many of which focusing on engineering safety critical open adaptive systems.

Hermann Seuschek is a doctoral candidate in electrical engineering at the Chair of Security in Information Technology, Technical University of Munich (TUM), Germany. He graduated with a Dipl.-Ing. (equivalent to master) degree from TUM in 2005. Before he joined his current position, he worked for several years for Siemens Corporate Technology in the field of applied cryptography and embedded systems security. His research interests include secure hardware/software co-design of embedded systems with a focus on architecture, development tools, and side-channel analysis.

Andreas Sinnhofer received his MS in Electrical Engineering from Graz University of Technology in 2014. Between 2014 and 2017 he was working as a PhD Student at Graz University of Technology at the Institute of Technical Informatics in a cooperation project with NXP Semiconductors. Since end of 2016 he is working as a Software Architect at NXP Semiconductors. His research interests are Software Product Lines and Model based Development for secure systems.

Christian Steger received the Dipl.-Ing. degree (M.Sc.) in 1990, and the Dr. techn. degree (Ph.D.) in electrical engineering from Graz University of Technology, Austria, in 1995, respectively. He graduated from the Export, International Management and Marketing course at Karl-Franzens-University of Graz in June 1993 and completed the Entrepreneurship Development Program at MIT Sloan School of Management in Boston in 2010. He is strategy board member of the Virtual Vehicle Competence Center (ViF, COMET K2) in Graz, Austria. From 1989 to 1991 he was software trainer and consultant at SPC Computer Training GmbH., Vienna. Since 1992 he has been Assistant Professor at the Institute of Technical Informatics, Graz University of Technology were he heads the HW/SW codesign group at the Institute for Technical Informatics. Christian Steger was a substitute professor at the University of Saarland (Chair "Reactice system") from October 2010 to February 2011. Christian Steger was project leader of the BMVIT (FIT-IT) funded projects POWER-CARD, LOWSOM, SIMBA, HyPerSec, DAVID and scientific leader in POWERHOUSE, CoCoon, META[:SEC:], and SmartLX, ASIDS (FFG Competence Headquarter Program). His research interests include embedded systems, HW/SW codesign, HW/SW coverfication, SoC, power awareness, smart cards, and multi-DSPs. Christian Steger published more than 300 scientific papers as author and co-author. He is member of the IEEE and member of the OVE (Austrian Electrotechnical Association).

Josef Steinbaeck received the MSc. degree in Information and Computer Engineering from Graz University of Technology, Austria in 2016. His master's thesis with the topic 'Integration of a Time-of-Flight 3D Camera into a Mobile Sensing Platform' was carried out in cooperation with Infineon Technologies Austria AG. He is currently a PhD. student working at Infineon Technologies in Graz with the focus on automotive environmental perception sensors.

Georg Stettinger received the BSc and MSc degrees in electrical engineering from Graz University of Technology, Graz, Austria, in 2009 and 2011, respectively and the Ph.D. degree in information technology from Alpen-Adria University of Klagenfurt, Klagenfurt, Austria in 2015. He is currently a researcher at the VIRTUAL VEHICLE Research Center in the Electrics/Electronics and Software Area, Graz, Austria. His research interests are in the fields of system identification, state estimation, real-time simulation and automotive control systems.

Thomas Ulz received his Dipl.-Ing. degrees (M.Sc.) in Information and Computer Engineering as well as in Computer Science from Graz University of Technology, both in 2016. The focus in his studies was in Security, Embedded Systems and Sensor Networks, Control Systems, Machine Learning, and Robotics. Since 2016, he has been a Ph.D. student in Information and Computer Engineering at the Institute of Technical Informatics at Graz University of Technology in collaboration with Infineon Technologies Austria AG. His research interests include the security and trustworthiness of industrial Internet of Things devices.

Laszlo Zsolt Varga is habilitated docent at the Faculty of Informatics of ELTE University. He started research work in the eighties at KFKI (Budapest) in the field of parallel computing. He was visiting researcher in the early nineties at CERN (Geneva) and at the Department of Electronic Engineering at Queen Mary & Westfield College (University of London) where his research focused on basic and applied research into the development of multi-agent systems. Later he headed a unit at MTA SZTAKI (Budapest) researching and developing distributed internet applications. His current research interests include exploitation of real-time data in decentralized adaptive systems, like connected cars or internet of things. Further information: http://people.inf.elte.hu/lzvarga/.

Daniel Watzenig was born in Austria. He received his Master degree in electrical engineering and the doctoral degree in technical science from Graz University of Technology, Graz, Austria, in 2002 and 2006, respectively. He is currently Divisional Director of the Automotive Electronics and Embedded Control Department of the Virtual Vehicle Research Center in Graz. In addition, he is Associate Professor at the Institute of Electrical Measurement and Measurement Signal Processing, Graz University of Technology, Austria, since 2009. He is author or co-author of over 150 peer-reviewed papers, book chapters, patents, and articles. His research interests focus on sensor fusion and signal processing, sensors and control systems for automated driving, uncertainty estimation, and robust optimization methods. In 2005 he was a visiting researcher at the University of Auckland, New Zealand, working on multi-sensor arrays and statistical signal processing. In 2011 he was visiting researcher and guest lecturer at the Federal University of Rio de Janeiro. He is IEEE Senior Member of the IEEE Control Systems, Signal Processing, and Instrumentation & Measurement Societies. Furthermore, he is Vice President and member of the steering board of the EU ARTEMIS Industry Association. He is the Austrian representative (appointed by the Austrian Federal Ministry BMVIT) of Electrified, Connected, and Automated Vehicles within the International Energy Agency (IEA). Since 2016 he is Chair of the European Automotive Research Partners Association (EARPA) Task Force on Virtual Development and Validation.

Ralph Weissnegger received his Bachelor's and Master's degree in Telematics (Information and Computer Engineering) from Graz University of Technology, Austria, in 2013. Since 2014 he is with the Institute of Technical Informatics at Graz University of Technology where he is working towards his Ph.D. in Electrical Engineering. His research interests include design and verification of HW/SW codesigns, especially safety-critical systems. His Ph.D. is done in tight cooperation with CISC Semiconductor GmbH.

Ernest Wozniak is a Research Scientist at fortiss (group of Trusted Applications) in Munich. Obtained his master degree in 2010 from the AGH University of Science and Technology in Cracow, Poland, faculty of Computer Science. After completing his studies, he has worked for one year as Software Developer. Next, he obtained PhD degree from the University of Paris-Sud in 2014 based on his dissertation entitled "Model-based Synthesis of Distributed Real-time Automotive Applications". His PhD was developed in cooperation with the CEA LIST Institute, France. During his PhD program he participated in the exchange program with the McGill University, Canada where he worked on the optimization of the deployment of the real-time automotive systems. After that, he has worked for 2 years as a Systems Engineer at the DELPHI which is a Tier1 automotive supplier. From there he transferred to fortiss, to focus on the aspects related to the software and system architecture of the Cyber Physical Systems, in particular, development aspects (toolchain, model-based design, code generation), security (especially for the open platforms) and machine learning.

Elias Yaacoub received the B.E. degree in Electrical Engineering from the Lebanese University in 2002, the M.E. degree in Computer and Communications Engineering from the American University of Beirut (AUB) in 2005, and the PhD degree in Electrical and Computer Engineering from AUB in 2010. He worked as a Research Assistant in the American University of Beirut from 2004 to 2005, and in the Munich University of Technology in Spring 2005. From 2005 to 2007, he worked as a Telecommunications Engineer with Dar Al-Handasah, Shair and Partners. From November 2010 till December 2014, he worked as a Research Scientist / R&D Expert at the Qatar Mobility Innovations Center (QMIC). Afterwards, he joined Strategic Decisions Group (SDG) where he worked as a Consultant till February 2016. He is currently an Associate Professor at the Arab Open University (AOU). His research interests include Wireless Communications, Resource Allocation in Wireless Networks, Intercell Interference Mitigation Techniques, Antenna Theory, Sensor Networks, and Bioinformatics.

Andreas Zankl is a research fellow at the Fraunhofer Institute for Applied and Integrated Security (AISEC) in Munich, where he studies side-channel attacks in the microarchitecture of embedded processors. Previously, he completed his Master's degree at Graz University of Technology and worked on security evaluations of RFID-based systems at NXP Semiconductors Austria and Nanyang Technological University in Singapore.

Index

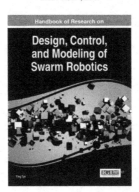

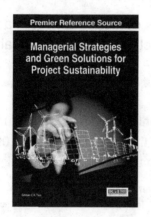

Printed in the United States
By Bookmasters